September 4–7, 2017
Valletta, Malta

I0054687

Association for Computing Machinery

Advancing Computing as a Science & Profession

DocEng'17

Proceedings of the 2017 ACM Symposium on
Document Engineering

Sponsored by:
ACM SIGWEB

In co-operation with:
ACM SIGDOC

Supported by:
HP, Adobe, FXPal, Conventions Malta, Ministry for Finance, Heritage Malta, & University of Malta

Association for
Computing Machinery

Advancing Computing as a Science & Profession

The Association for Computing Machinery
2 Penn Plaza, Suite 701
New York, New York 10121-0701

ISBN: 978-1-4503-4689-4 (Digital)

ISBN: 978-1-4503-5611-4 (Print)

Additional copies may be ordered prepaid from:

ACM Order Department
PO Box 30777
New York, NY 10087-0777, USA

Phone: 1-800-342-6626 (USA and Canada)
+1-212-626-0500 (Global)
Fax: +1-212-944-1318
E-mail: acmhelp@acm.org
Hours of Operation: 8:30 am – 4:30 pm ET

Printed in the USA

Welcome from the Symposium and PC Chairs

It is with honour and pleasure that we welcome you in Valletta for the 17th ACM Symposium on Document Engineering. DocEng 2017 is being organised by the University of Malta's Department of Systems and Control Engineering on the 4-7th September 2017. The symposium brings together experts in all areas of document engineering from both academia and industry, with the intention of presenting and discussing the most recent advances in the field of Document Engineering.

Building on the experiences of previous years, the DocEng symposium program consists of one day of tutorials followed by three days of paper presentations. The program offers three half-day tutorials on Historic Document Processing, Document Engineering Issues in Malware Analysis and User Evaluation in the Document Engineering Field. DocEng2017 also keeps alive the tradition of the Birds of a Feather discussion group which will be led by Charles Nicholas. Of course, the highlight of the symposium will be the keynote talks

- Sketched Visual Narratives for Image and Video Search by John Collomosse from the University of Surrey
- The Notarial Archives, Valletta: Starting from Zero by Theresa Zammit Lupi from the Valletta Notarial Archives.

DocEng received a total of 71 papers; 36 of these papers were submitted in April as full papers, with a further 35 papers being submitted in June as short papers and application notes. All papers were reviewed by at least three Program Committee members and based on these recommendations, the symposium accepted 13 (36%) papers as full papers, 13 (37%) as short papers with an oral presentation and a further 10 as poster presentations.

This year, DocEng participated in the Review Quality Collector, an initiative for improving the quality of scientific peer review whereby reviewers were invited to grade their co-reviewers on aspects related to helpfulness to authors, timeliness and helpfulness for decision. Reviewers were given a receipt for their work for the symposium and the five top-ranked reviewers will be recognised during the symposium.

The symposium continues in its support for student researchers who will be the future generation of researchers in document engineering. To this extent, DocEng2017 offers students the opportunity to select a student mentor during the conference. The mentors, senior and experienced researchers will be able to discuss the student research, providing advice, feedback and constructive criticism. With the support of ACM SIGWEB, students are given travel grants to help them participate in the symposium.

We would like to take the opportunity to thank ACM SIGWEB, HP, Adobe, FXPAL, The Malta Ministry for Finance, Conventions Malta and Heritage Malta for their generous support. The organisation of the symposium would not have been possible without the help and advice of the

Steering Committee, Tamir Hassan and TU Wien CVL team who provided support whenever this was needed as well as Michael Piotrowski who helped setup the DocEng webpages. The symposium and its proceedings are the product of the combined efforts of many people, including Stefania Cristina, the Program Co-Chair and Website manager; Carl Azzopardi the Local Chair; Sonja Schimmler the Tutorials Chair; Ethan Munson, our liaison with SIGWEB; Charles Nicholas who leads the Birds of a Feather discussions; Lucienne May Bugeja and her team at the University of Malta's Conferences Unit, Diana Brantuas and April Mosqus from ACM as well as Lisa Tolles and her colleagues at Sheridan Communications who gave the support necessary to prepare these proceedings.

The success of the symposium is owed to the authors who will be presenting their work in the symposium as well as the members of the Program Committee who made the time and effort to provide thorough reviews and who then participated in final selection discussions.

A final note of thanks is owed to Steven Simske, the chair of the Steering Committee for his prompt, constant support, encouragement and advice.

We hope that the Symposium will provide an engaging environment for participants to share ideas with researchers and practitioners from around the world. We also hope that these proceedings present a snapshot of the research work to date, providing an impact not only to current researchers but also archivable material for years to come.

We wish you a pleasant and fruitful stay in Malta,

Kenneth Camilleri
DocEng 2017 General Chair
University of Malta, Malta

Alexandra Bonnici
DocEng 2017 Program Chair
University of Malta, Malta

Table of Contents

Tutorials
Session Chair: Sonja Schimmler *(Universität der Bundeswehr München)*

Keynote I
Session Chair: Kenneth P. Camilleri *(University of Malta)*

Generation, Manipulation and Presentation
Session Chair: Tamir Hassan *(HP Labs)*

Collections, Systems and Management
Session Chair: Peter R. King *(University of Manitoba)*

User Interactions
Session Chair: Kim Marriott *(Monash University)*

Keynote II
Session Chair: Stefania Cristina *(University of Malta)*

Demonstrations and Poster Presentations of Short Papers

Document Analysis: Classification and Similarity
Session Chair: Frank Tompa *(University of Waterloo)*

Document Analysis: Content Analysis
Session Chair: David F. Brailsford *(University of Nottingham)*

Document Analysis & Visual Document Analysis
Session Chair: Steven J. Simske *(HP Labs)*

Multimedia and Mobile Documents
Session Chair: Ethan V. Munson *(University of Wisconsin-Milwaukee)*

DocEng 2017 Symposium Organization

General Chair:	Kenneth Camilleri *(University of Malta, Malta)*
Program Chair:	Alexandra Bonnici *(University of Malta, Malta)*
Program Co-Chair:	Stefania Cristina *(University of Malta, Malta)*
Workshop and Tutorials Chair:	Sonja Schimmler *(Universität der Bundeswehr München, Germany)*
BOF Chair:	Charles Nicholas *(University of Maryland, Baltimore County, USA)*
Local Chair:	Carl Azzopardi *(University of Malta, Malta)*
Steering Committee Chair:	Steven Simske *(HP Labs, Fort Collins, CO, USA)*
Steering Committee:	David Brailsford *(University of Nottingham, United Kingdom)*
	Dick Bulterman *(CWI, Netherlands)*
	Matthew Hardy *(Adobe Systems, San Jose, USA)*
	Tamir Hassan *(HP Labs, Vienna, Austria)*
	Peter King *(University of Manitoba, Canada)*
	Cerstin Mahlow *(University of Bern, Switzerland)*
	Kim Marriott *(Monash University, Australia)*
	Ethan Munson *(University of Wisconsin-Milwaukee, USA)*
	Charles Nicholas *(University of Maryland, Baltimore County, USA)*
	Sonja Schimmler *(Universität der Bundeswehr, Munich, Germany)*
	Jean-Yves Vion-Dury *(Xerox Research Centre Europe, France)*
	Tony Wiley *(OpenText, San Mateo, CA, USA)*
Program Committee:	Charlie Abela *(University of Malta, Malta)*
	Apostolos Antonacopoulos *(University of Salford, United Kingdom)*
	Vlad Atanasiu *(University of Fribourg, France)*
	George Azzopardi *(University of Malta, Malta)*
	Steven R. Bagley *(University of Nottingham, United Kingdom)*
	Helen Balinsky *(HP Labs United Kingdom)*
	Jean-Luc Bloechle *(Sugarcube IT / University of Fribourg, Switzerland)*
	Alexandra Bonnici *(University of Malta, Malta)*
	Uwe M. Borghoff *(Universität der Bundeswehr, Munich, Germany)*
	David F. Brailsford *(University of Nottingham, United Kingdom)*
	Anne Brüggemann-Klein *(Technische Universität München, Germany)*
	Michael Burch *(VISUS, University of Stuttgart, Germany)*
	Kenneth Camilleri *(University of Malta, Malta)*
	Pablo Cesar *(CWI: Centrum Wiskunde and Informatica, Netherlands)*
	Michael L. Collard *(The University of Akron, USA)*
	Niranjan Damera-Venkata, *(HP Labs, USA)*
	Angelo Di Iorio *(University of Bologna, Italy)*
	Markus Diem *(Computer Vision Lab, TU Wien, Austria)*
	Alexiei Dingli *(University of Malta, Malta)*
	Stefano Ferilli *(Universita' di Bari, Italy)*
	Stefan Fiel *(Computer Vision Lab, TU Wien, Austria)*

DocEng 2017 Sponsor & Supporters

Sponsor: sig web

In co-operation with: SIGDOC
Special Interest Group for Design of Communication

Supporters:

hp

Adobe ®

FX PAL
PALO ALTO LABORATORY

CONVENTIONS malta

MINISTRY FOR FINANCE

H Heritage Malta

UNIVERSITY OF MALTA
L-Università ta' Malta

Historical Document Processing

Basilis Gatos
Computational Intelligence Laboratory
Institute of Informatics and Telecom., NCSR "Demokritos"
15310 Athens, Greece
bgat@iit.demokritos.gr

Georgios Louloudis
Computational Intelligence Laboratory
Institute of Informatics and Telecom., NCSR "Demokritos"
15310 Athens, Greece
louloud@iit.demokritos.gr

Nikolaos Stamatopoulos
Computational Intelligence Laboratory
Institute of Informatics and Telecom., NCSR "Demokritos"
15310 Athens, Greece
nstam@iit.demokritos.gr

Giorgos Sfikas
Computational Intelligence Laboratory
Institute of Informatics and Telecom., NCSR "Demokritos"
15310 Athens, Greece
sfikas@iit.demokritos.gr

ABSTRACT

This tutorial focuses on recent advances and ongoing developments for historical document processing. It includes the main challenges involved, the different tasks that have to be implemented as well as practices and technologies that currently exist in the literature. The focus is given on the most promising techniques, related projects as well as on existing datasets and competitions that can be proved useful to historical document processing research.

CCS CONCEPTS

• **Applied computing** → **Document management and text processing; Document capture; Document analysis;**

KEYWORDS

Historical Documents, Preprocessing, Segmentation, Recognition, Keyword Spotting

1 INTRODUCTION

In the last decade, historical manuscript collections can be considered as an important source of original information in order to provide access to historical data and develop cultural documentation over the years. The main tasks that have to be implemented in the historical document image recognition pipeline, include preprocessing for image enhancement and binarization, segmentation for the detection of main page elements, of text lines and words and, finally, recognition or keyword spotting.

1.1 Format of the Tutorial

This tutorial[1] for historical document processing includes several presentations and demos and is presented by Dr. B. Gatos[2].

2 PREPROCESSING

2.1 Image Enhancement

The conservation and readability of historical documents is often compromised by several types of degradations which not only reduce the legibility of the historical documents but also affect the performance of subsequent processing such as document layout analysis and handwritten text recognition; therefore a preprocessing procedure becomes essential. One of the most common degradation is the bleed-through effect and for this reason several enhancement techniques which focus on this type of effect have been reported in the literature. Bleed-through is caused by seeping of ink from the reserve side or it appears when the paper in not complete opaque (show-through). Consequently, text information from the back interferes with the text in the front page and the use of binarization techniques is often not effective since the intensities of the reserve side can be very close to those of the foreground text. The enhancement techniques which cope with bleed-through effect can be divided into two categories according to the presence (or not) of the verso document image: (i) non-blind techniques in which both sides of the document image are available and (ii) blind techniques which process a single-side document image.

[1] This work was supported by the European Union's H2020 Programme under grant agreement no. 674943 (project READ).

[2] Basilis G. Gatos was born in Athens, Greece. He received his Electrical Engineering Diploma and his Ph.D. degree, both from the Electrical and Computer Engineering Department of Democritus University of Thrace, Xanthi, Greece. His Ph.D. thesis is on Optical Character Recognition Techniques. He is currently working as a Researcher at the Institute of Informatics and Telecommunications of the National Center for Scientific Research "Demokritos", Athens, Greece. His main research interests are in Image Processing and Document Image Analysis, OCR and Pattern Recognition. He has more than 150 publications in journals and international conference proceedings and has participated in several research programs funded by the European community. He is a member of the Technical Chamber of Greece, of the Editorial Board of the International Journal on Document Analysis and Recognition (IJDAR) and program committee member of several international Conferences and Workshops (e.g. ICDAR, ICFHR, DAS, International Workshop on Historical Document Imaging and Processing). He was co-organiser of ICFHR 2014 (Crete, Greece) and of DAS 2016 (Santorini, Greece).

2.2 Binarization

Document image binarization refers to the conversion of a color or grayscale image into a binary image. The main goal is not only to enhance the readability of the image but also to separate the useful textual content from the background by categorizing all the pixels as text or non-text without missing any useful information. Document image binarization techniques are usually classified in two main categories, namely global and local thresholding. Global thresholding methods use a single threshold value for the entire image, while local thresholding methods detect a local (adaptive) threshold value for each pixel. Global techniques are capable of extracting the document text efficiently in the case that there is a good separation between the foreground and the background. Several historical binarization methods have incorporated background subtraction in order to cope with several degradations.

3 SEGMENTATION

3.1 Layout Analysis

Layout analysis refers to the process of identifying as well as categorizing the regions of interest (e.g. text blocks, ruler lines, marginalia, figures, tables, drawings) which exist on a document image. A reading system requires the detection of main page elements as well as the discrimination of text zones from non-textual ones in order to facilitate the recognition procedure. Historical documents do not have strict layout rules and thus, a layout analysis method needs to be invariant to layout inconsistencies, irregularities in script and writing style, skew, fluctuating text lines, and variable shapes of decorative entities. Layout analysis methods reported in the literature can be classified into two distinct categories, namely bottom-up and top-down approaches. Bottom-up methods start from small entities of the document image (e.g. pixels, connected components). These entities are grouped into larger homogeneous areas leading to the creation of the final regions of interest. On the contrary, top-down methods start from the document image and repeatedly split it into smaller areas according to specific rules which, finally, correspond to distinct regions of interest. An alternative taxonomy can be defined based on the existence of training data. Supervised methods assume the existence of an already annotated dataset serving as the training part used to train an algorithm for distinguishing the regions of interest. Methods that do not make use of any prior knowledge and thus no training is involved, are said to belong to the category of unsupervised methods.

3.2 Text line Segmentation

Text line segmentation which is the process of defining the region of every text line on a document image constitutes one of the most important stages of the historical handwritten text recognition pipeline. Results of poor quality produced by this stage seriously affect the accuracy of the handwritten text recognition procedure. Several challenges exist on historical documents which should be addressed by a text line segmentation method. These challenges include (a) the difference in the skew angle between lines on the page or even along the same text line, (b) overlapping and touching text lines, (c) additions above the text line and (d) deleted text. Text line segmentation methods are said to fall broadly into four categories: (i) Projection-based methods, (ii) Smearing methods, (iii) Grouping methods and (iv) Hough transform based methods.

3.3 Word Segmentation

Word segmentation refers to the process of defining the word regions of a text line. Since nowadays most handwriting recognition methods assume text lines as input, the word segmentation process is usually necessary only for segmentation-based query by example keyword spotting methods. There are several challenges that need to be addressed by a word segmentation method. These include the skew along a text line, the existence of slant angle among characters as well as punctuation marks which tend to reduce the inter word distance and the non-uniform spacing of words. Algorithms dealing with word segmentation in the literature are based primarily on the analysis of the geometric relationship between adjacent components.

4 HANDWRITTEN TEXT RECOGNITION

Handwritten Text Recognition (HTR) becomes a challenging problem especially when dealing with historical documents. Major difficulties that appear concern (i) several degradations in the image quality, (ii) the large varieties in writing styles, language models, spelling rules and dictionaries, (iii) the use of abbreviations and special symbols as well as (iv) the limited amount of existing transcribed data that can be used for training. Based on the input that is provided to the recognition engine, we can distinguish the historical HTR methods to holistic and segmentation-based. Holistic methods do not segment the image into characters but use as input the text line or the word image. On the other hand, segmentation-based approaches rely on segmentation into smaller entities which may correspond to characters or character parts. Holistic methods include Multidirectional Long Short-Term Memory Neural Network techniques while more traditional modelling approaches are based on Hidden Markov optical character and N-gram language models. Segmentation-based approaches for historical document recognition examine the topology of the segmented entities or use dense SIFT features and involve a classifier based on a decision tree, nearest neighbor distance maps or a convolutional neural network.

5 KEYWORD SPOTTING

In cases where optical recognition is deemed to be very difficult or expected to give poor results, word spotting or keyword spotting has been proposed to substitute full text recognition. In word spotting the user queries the document database for a given word, and the spotting system is expected to return to the user a number of possible locations of the query in the original document.

Document Engineering Issues in Malware Analysis

Charles Nicholas
University of Maryland, Baltimore County
Baltimore, Maryland 21250
nicholas@umbc.edu

ABSTRACT

We present an overview of the field of malware analysis with emphasis on issues related to document engineering. We will introduce the field with a discussion of the types of malware, including executable binaries, malicious PDFs, polymorphic malware, ransomware, and exploit kits. We will conclude with our view of important research questions in the field. This is an updated version of last year's tutorial, with more information about web-based malware and malware targeting the Android market.

CCS CONCEPTS

• **Security and privacy** → **Malware and its mitigation**; • **Applied computing** → *Document management and text processing*;

1 INTRODUCTION

Malware analysis has become an important field within the general area of cybersecurity. Skilled malware analysts are in high demand, and they are employed in cybersecurity firms, financial institutions, intelligence and law enforcement agencies, and other large organizations.

For many years, most malware was written for the Windows OS and the x86 architecture. Windows is still an important malware target, since so many PCs run it, but in recent years the amount of malware targeted to the mobile telephone, especially the Android, has grown enormously. Although it focuses on Windows XP, we have found that Sikorski's "Practical Malware Analysis" [1] is still the best single resource for this area.

2 TOOLS AND TECHNIQUES

In the tutorial we will present an overview of the field of malware analysis, with emphasis on topics we believe to be of special interest to the Document Engineering community. Teaching materials for Android malware are starting to become available, but for our purposes we will focus on the Windows environment, since that platform is more likely to be more familiar to more people.

Malware on the Windows platform is often, but by no means always, found in executable binaries. Malware can be examined in static form, e.g. by inspection of the PE header and the system call import table. Windows provides tools for such activity, and many third party tools do so as well. IDA is a powerful disassembler, which allows the analyst to examine a suspect binary in a variety of forms, including raw assembly code and call graphs. Basic IDA functionality can be augmented with plug-ins written in C or Python.

Malware can also be studied in dynamic form, that is, by running it and seeing what happens. OllyDbg is one of several powerful debuggers available for the Windows platform, which has gained a following among malware analysts. Dynamic analysis is usually done from the safe confines of a virtual machine, running under the auspices of VMWare, for example.

Some collections of malware specimens are available to researchers, and these will be used as examples as appropriate. Alas, there is no shortage of malware to be studied, since malware production is easily automated. Collecting malware specimens for analysis is an important sub-area, and anti-virus companies for example devote much effort to this.

As time permits, we will discuss recent and ongoing work in malware analysis-in-the-large, which (to us) refers to finding patterns and trends in collections of malware. Malware specimens can be subjected to cluster analysis, based on static and dynamic characteristics. Malware attribution is and will remain a difficult problem, for reasons which we will explain.

3 AUDIENCE PARTICIPATION

Tutorial participants are welcome to bring their own laptops. We recommend installing a virtual machine platform such as VMWare or Virtual Box, with virtual machines running Windows and Linux. Participants that have IDA Pro (the free version 5.0) and OllyDbg installed, as well as Microsoft's System Tools suite, may be able to run some examples with us. However, participants that choose to leave their laptops at home will be at no disadvantage.

Charles Nicholas is a professor of computer science at UMBC. He has been involved in the Document Engineering field for many years, and has recently turned his attention to the problems of malware analysis in the large. His recent work has considered questions related to storing, searching, and finding patterns in large collections of malware. He has taught a combined graduate-undergraduate course in malware analysis at UMBC for several years.

REFERENCES

[1] Michael Sikorski and Andrew Honig. 2012. *Practical Malware Analysis*. no starch press.

Understanding the User: User Studies and User Evaluation for Document Engineering

Kim Marriott
Faculty of IT
Monash University
Caulfield, Australia
kim.marriott@monash.edu

Steven Simske
HP Labs
3390 E. Harmony Road, M/S 66
Fort Collins, CO 80528
steven.simske@hp.com

Margaret Sturgill
HP Labs
3390 E. Harmony Road, M/S 66
Fort Collins, CO 80528
margaret.sturgill@hp.com

Document engineering is all about building systems and tools that allow people to work with documents and document collections. A key aspect is the usefulness and usability of these tools. In this tutorial, we will look at the many different kinds of user studies and user evaluations that can be used to inform the design and improve utility and usability of document engineering applications. The tutorial will be based on actual studies and will also give participants a chance to explore how they might use these techniques in their research or system development. In the first part of the tutorial we will look at:

1. Controlled experiments (lab studies). These have been adopted from research methods in the psychological sciences and are widely used to answer questions (usually very focused) of the form "if I vary X how does that affect Y?" For instance, how do different layouts affect reading speed and comprehension?

2. Questionnaires, in-depth interview, focus groups and field studies. These provide more open-ended information and draw on techniques from anthropology/ethnography. For instance, do academics read research electronically or on paper and why/when do they choose each?

3. Participative design. Participative design, user-centered design and co-design includes the user in the whole development process. One case study is for the presentation of accessible eBooks.

4. User data collection and analysis. What kinds of user data can you collect, e.g. instrumented collection, eye tracking, and how do you analyze it.

Item (4.) segues neatly to the second part of the tutorial, in which we consider data analytics in more depth. How can data analytics be applied to User Evaluation in the Document Engineering Field? This is a two-direction relationship:

A. Data science to understand how users evaluate document sets (multiple versions, related documents, search results, other corpora). This includes functional measurements, user errors, tie to UI design, etc.

B. Data science to understand how to evaluate users based on their interaction with the document set (user analytics), including time to task completion, robustness to frustration, ability to complete task, etc.

In (A.) we use analytics to discern what types of workflows and user-document interactions to enable. In (B.) we use analytics to classify different types of users, in hopes of feeding this back to affect the design and architecture (structure and flow) of the user interface(s).

The goal of the 'data analytics' portion of the tutorial will be to introduce the audience to classification and evaluation approaches, and from these discuss how to build more robust systems for user study and evaluation. As output from this tutorial/workshop, we wish to help to identify research challenges and experiments to be performed by the document engineering research community.

DocEng '17, September 04-07, 2017, Valletta, Malta
© 2017 Copyright is held by the owner/author(s).
ACM ISBN 978-1-4503-4689-4/17/09.
http://dx.doi.org/10.1145/3103010.3109452

The Notarial Archives, Valletta: Starting From Zero

Theresa Zammit Lupi
Notarial Archives
St Christopher Street
Valletta, Malta
tzammitlupi@gmail.com

ABSTRACT

The main objective of this paper is to talk about my work as a book and paper conservator in the light of the current rehabilitation project at the Notarial Archives in St Christopher Street, Valletta. With its six centuries of manuscript material spread over two kilometres of shelving, the state of preservation of the archives has presented numerous challenges over the last years. The EU funds granted in recent months are a crucial investment that will ensure the safeguarding of the collection, but putting one's house in order is not just about money. A number of other considerations such as careful planning, multidisciplinary collaboration, clever marketing, accessibility, team-building and creating a clear vision for the future have been some of the central factors that continue to contribute to the success of this project. A discussion on the general preservation and conservation strategies that are being undertaken for the project will also be given.

KEYWORDS

archives, book and paper conservation, preservation, multidisciplinary collaboration.

ACM Reference format:
Theresa Zammit Lupi. 2017. The Notarial Archives, Valletta: Starting From Zero. In *Proceedings of DocEng '17, Valletta, Malta, September 04-07, 2017,* 1 pages.
https://doi.org/10.1145/3103010.3103025

SHORT BIOGRAPHY

Theresa Zammit Lupi studied book and paper conservation in Florence and London. She obtained her Ph.D. in the conservation of illuminated manuscripts in 2009 from Camberwell College, University of Arts London. Theresa has worked as a conservator, lecturer and consultant in Malta, the UK, Italy, Switzerland and Egypt. In 2016 she was awarded a Katharine F. Pantzer Fellowship at Harvard University. She is currently Head of Conservation at the Notarial Archives in Valletta, Malta. Theresa is an accredited member of the Institute of Conservation UK. She is the author of "Cantate Domino - Early Choir Books for the Knights in Malta" as well as a number of academic papers in peer-reviewed journals.

DocEng '17, September 04-07, 2017, Valletta, Malta
© 2017 Copyright held by the owner/author(s).
ACM ISBN 978-1-4503-4689-4/17/09.
https://doi.org/10.1145/3103010.3103025

Linear Extended Annotation Graphs

Vincent Barrellon
Univ Lyon, INSA-Lyon, CNRS, LIRIS, UMR5205
Villeurbanne, France F-69621
firstname.lastname@insa-lyon.fr

Sylvie Calabretto
Univ Lyon, INSA-Lyon, CNRS, LIRIS, UMR5205
Villeurbanne, France F-69621
firstname.lastname@insa-lyon.fr

Pierre-Edouard Portier
Univ Lyon, INSA-Lyon, CNRS, LIRIS, UMR5205
Villeurbanne, France F-69621
firstname.lastname@insa-lyon.fr

Olivier Ferret
Univ Lyon, Lyon 2, CNRS, IHRIM, UMR5317
Lyon, France F-69365
firstname.lastname@univ-lyon2.fr

ABSTRACT

Multistructured (M-S) data models were introduced to allow the expression of multilevel, concurrent annotation. However, most models lack either a consistent or an efficient validation mechanism. In a former paper, we introduced extended Annotation Graphs (eAG), a cyclic-graph data model equipped with a novel schema mechanism that, by allowing validation "by construction", bypasses the typical algorithmic cost of traditional methods for the validation of graph-structured data. We introduce here LeAG, a markup syntax for eAG annotations over text data. LeAG takes the shape of a classic, inline markup model. A LeAG annotation can then be written, in a human-readable form, in any notepad application, and saved as a text file; the syntax is simple and familiar – yet LeAG proposes a natural syntax for multilayer annotation with (self-) overlap and links. From a theoretical point of view, LeAG inaugurates a hybrid markup paradigm. Syntactically speaking, it is a *full* inline model, since the tags are all inserted along the annotated resources; still, we evidence that representing independent elements' co-occurring in an inline manner requires to make the annotation rest upon a notion of reference value, that is typical of stand-off markup. To our knowledge, LeAG is the first inline markup syntax to properly conceptualize the notion of elements' accidental co-occurring, that is yet fundamental in multilevel annotation.

CCS CONCEPTS

•Applied computing → Annotation; •Information systems → *Data model extensions;* •Theory of computation → *Data structures design and analysis;*

KEYWORDS

Multistructured data; Markup models.

DocEng '17, September 04-07, 2017, Valletta, Malta
© 2017 Copyright held by the owner/author(s). Publication rights licensed to ACM.
978-1-4503-4689-4/17/09...$15.00
DOI: http://dx.doi.org/10.1145/3103010.3103011

1 INTRODUCTION

The emergence of Digital Humanities has led to the development of a great number of digital scholarly publishing projects. Most favour the well-known XML-TEI annotation language for transcription and critical enrichment. Indeed, the TEI provides the scholar with an extremely well-documented schema [10], broad enough to fit almost any kind of primary document, and benefits from the assets of XML languages: it is extensible, can be queried, validated and transformed easily. The XML-TEI thus appears as the go-to technology for the editing scholar today.

Yet, editorial criticisms [26] apart, the TEI-XML language suffers from strong formal limitations, inherent to the XML model. In practice, trees are known not to fit some quite common textual description patterns [10, 20, 23]. In particular, XML does not handle overlapping elements, which is an obstacle towards multi-level [34] annotation; additionally, inclusion being represented by nesting in XML (i.e. the location of an element within the scope of another one), there is no way to represent accidental nesting or co-location, that is, the fact two elements occurring at the same place might be independent (and not included one into the other). Inter-elements relations (other than *structural* relations) cannot be represented but by attribute equalities (exemplified by the ID/IDREF mechanism), notoriously hard to restrict by means of a schema [3, 31] and possibly hindering querying [14]. Propositions have been made to conform TEI-XML with more expressive data models [6, 8, 10]; while interesting, those propositions are not compliant with the classic XML tools (XSD, XSLT, etc.) [17].

Some alternative 'multistructured' data models have been proposed to overcome the expressive limitations of XML, by relying on more general directed acyclic graph formalisms than just trees [31], or even cyclic graphs [16] – while maintaining the possibility to validate the data. Yet, acyclic models, if they do allow multilayer annotation, exhibit the same weakness as XML regarding the representation (and hence, the validation) of non-structural relations between elements; cyclic data models, that rely upon RDF, do not benefit from an efficient validation mechanism yet [29, 30].

In a former paper [2], we introduced extended Annotation Graphs (eAG), a cyclic-graph data model experimenting the simulation relation [19] as a validation mechanism. An interesting aspect of simulation is, as we evidenced, that it can be guaranteed *by construction*, enabling to validate cyclic, multistructured data *on the fly*, just like when using grammar-based validators for XML.

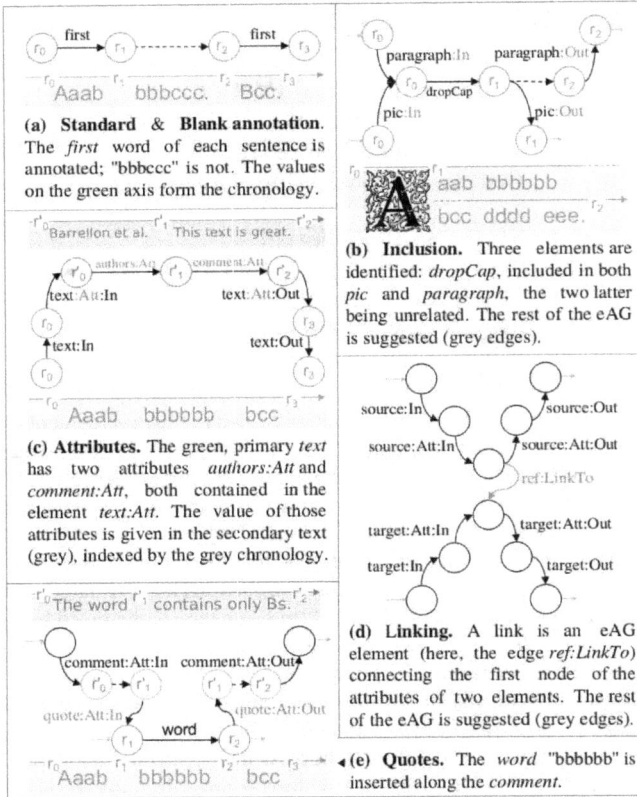

(a) Standard & Blank annotation. The *first* word of each sentence is annotated; "bbbccc" is not. The values on the green axis form the chronology.

(b) Inclusion. Three elements are identified: *dropCap*, included in both *pic* and *paragraph*, the two latter being unrelated. The rest of the eAG is suggested (grey edges).

(c) Attributes. The green, primary *text* has two attributes *authors:Att* and *comment:Att*, both contained in the element *text:Att*. The value of those attributes is given in the secondary text (grey), indexed by the grey chronology.

(d) Linking. A link is an eAG element (here, the edge *ref:LinkTo*) connecting the first node of the attributes of two elements. The rest of the eAG is suggested (grey edges).

◀ **(e) Quotes.** The *word* "bbbbbb" is inserted along the *comment*.

Figure 1: The eAG syntax in a nutshell.

We introduce here LeAG, a markup syntax for textual eAG annotations. LeAG takes the shape of a classic, inline markup model. Thus LeAG is an expressive, UI-independant annotation model: a LeAG document containing overlapping, multilayer annotation, can be written, in a human-readable form, in any notepad application. First, we provide the reader with a quick, example-based summary of the eAG data model. We then introduce the LeAG syntax based on the same examples, so as to make the translation between an eAG and a LeAG clear. We eventually elaborate how a LeAG document can be deterministically parsed into a corresponding eAG.

2 EXTENDED ANNOTATION GRAPHS

Extended Annotation Graphs (eAG) [2] is a schema-aware, stand-off markup model. Following [4], it is based upon the notion of **chronology**. A chronology is an ordered set of reference values that index the data to be annotated (e.g. inter-character positions for texts). An eAG is a rooted, single-leafed, directed and labelled graph whose nodes bear a reference value. Basically, a labelled edge connecting two nodes v_1 and v_2 is a tag put onto the portion of the data delimited by the reference values of v_1 and v_2. The edge and nodes together constitute an **element** – see Figure 1.a. The following notions refine this general principle.

Sequential annotation [Fig. 1.a] eAG enables to define not only elements, but also *sequences* of elements. An element B *directly* follows an element A iff the end of A and the start of B are one same node. eAG also enables to express *sparse* sequences : the gap between two consecutive elements is filled by a 'blank annotation'[1].

Inclusion [Fig. 1.b] It is possible to assess that a sequence S of elements is included in another element A (i.e. that A is constituted of the elements S), by encasing S between two edges $A:In$ and $A:Out$. An element can be included in more than one element. This property enables to express multitrees and goddags [28]. It is worth noting that a hierarchy of elements takes the shape of a path: we call them **hierarchical annotation path** (HAP). The spine of an eAG is an acyclic set of HAP sharing elements.

Attributes [Fig. 1.c] The attributes of an eAG element X are elements whose labels bear the suffix $:Att$, and that are included in a special element $X:Att$ itself included in X. The values of the attributes are not part of the initial, primary corpus: they belong to separate, secondary resources, indexed by a specific chronology.

Links [Fig. 1.d] Links are explicit relations between pairs of elements. In eAG, those relations are represented by special elements whose root belongs to the source element, and whose leaf belongs to the target element. The name of the linking element bears the suffix $:LinkTo$. A link can be structured (i.e. contain other elements) or be a single edge. eAG links may induce cycles; yet, they are handled by an SeAG schema just like any other element.

Quotes [Fig. 1.e] eAG introduced quoting elements to meet the need of scholars for inserting, inside a commentary, part of an exogenous, possibly annotated, resource [12]. A quoting element is an attribute whose content is a sequence of elements identified in the primary resources. Quotes necessarily result in cyclic graphs [2] (see p. 7); yet, they too are handled by SeAG schemas.

Apart from the expressive power of this syntax (illustrated below), the eAG model benefits from a **schema language** (SeAG) that manages multistructured, overlapping, cyclic annotation. SeAG validation relies upon the notion of rooted **simulation**[2] [2]. Intuitively, the existence of a simulation of an eAG I_S by a schema S implies that all the paths of I_S starting at its root have a corresponding path in S, whose label sequence is identical. Yet, as shown above, the syntactical structures of an eAG are made out of sequences of elements, i.e., of labelled paths. Thus, S is descriptive of I_S, because any sequence of elements in I_S must have a matching sequence in S. Conversely, S works like a schema: it simulates (validates) the graphs that contain solely sequences of elements it defines.

Figure 2 illustrates SeAG validation. The paths the schema S contains define the set of valid element sequences for the instances (e.g. [*Unit1 - Unit2 - Unit3*]). SeAG also makes use of epsilon edges, or blank annotations, to denote **optional** (e.g. *Unit3* can be bypassed by the ϵ_4 edge, resulting in [*Unit1 - Unit3*]) or **repeatable** elements (e.g. since ϵ_2 defines a cycle, any repetition of *6Letters* is valid).

Importantly, SeAG supports two kinds of multilayering annotation. First, two parallel paths of the schema can be instantiated, independently (i.e. without worrying about overlap), on the same resource (cf. I_a on Fig. 2). We call this **schema-based multilayering**. Second, *one* path of the schema can be instantiated *several times* on the same portion of the resources (cf. I_b, same fig.). This **simulation-based multilayering** allows the expression of self-overlapping elements, quite useful in linguistics, as illustrated below.

---

[1] Represented by dotted, 'epsilon edges' hereafter.

[2] *Node-typed* [2], rooted simulation actually; yet, node types can be omitted here.

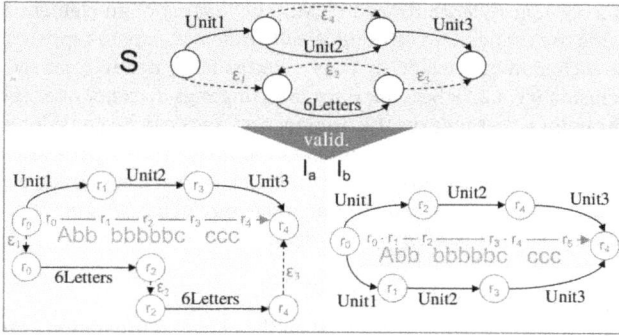

Figure 2: The schema S contains several parallel paths defining the valid element sequences. One element is optional (*Unit2*), one can be repeated (*6Letters*). The eAG I_a instantiates two different paths on the same text. I_b instantiates the same path of the schema *twice*.

3 A RUNNING EXAMPLE

A common linguistic annotation is the identification of anaphoric chains (AC). ACs are sequences of singular expressions so that if one of them refers to something, then they all do [9]. Consider the following text, adapted from *The Village of Ben Suc* by J. Schell:

> An ARVN officer asked a young prisoner questions, and when he failed to answer, beat him. An American observer who saw the beating that happened then reported that the officer "really worked him over". After the beating, the prisoner was forced to remain standing for hours.

One may identify, among others, the following ACs: [a young prisoner / he / him / him / the prisoner], [An American observer who saw the beating], [the beating that happened then / the beating]. Annotating the text in terms of ACs made out of *expressions* is not trivial in XML. Since ACs do not form neither a sequence nor a hierarchy, they cannot be represented as normal, spanning XML elements. The classic solution is to identify only the singular expressions in the text and then relate them together accordingly by their IDs in <linkgrp> elements [11]. That solution, apart from being hard to validate, does not represent the fact an AC is *composed of* expressions consistently with the XML syntax. Moreover, it does not extend to this example, which exhibits self-overlap [28][3].

In SeAG/eAG, annotating anaphoric chains is straightforward. Suppose we aim at identifying the ACs and their constitutive expressions, but also to qualify their relative weight, e.g. by reifying the relation 'this AC contains more expressions than that one'. The SeAG schema for that annotation is given on Figure 3. That schema defines an *Extract* element containing one, or several parallel, *ACs*, each containing one or more *Exp* elements; also, an *AC* may be the source of a *Longer:LinkTo* link targeting an *AC*. A corresponding eAG (restricted to the ACs relative to *the American observer* and *the beating*) is given on the same figure. Noteworthily, since eAG is a stand-off markup model, overlap is expressed naturally[4].

4 LINEAR EXTENDED ANNOTATION GRAPHS

Linear extended Annotation Graphs (LeAG) is an inline markup syntax for eAG. The purpose of LeAG is to enable the expression of eAG annotations by means of any notepad application, in a human-readable form. LeAG must therefore: 1) support unambiguous translation into the eAG syntax, and 2) enable to represent, by means of tags, multilayer, cyclic annotation.

The first part of this paragraph is a theoretical discussion about the hybrid nature of the LeAG markup, between the inline and stand-off paradigms, which will lead to the formulation of an equivalence relation for LeAG documents. We then introduce, step by step, the LeAG syntax: we gradually show how to represent the different bricks eAGs are made of in a markup manner: hierarchies, multitrees (and goddags), attributes, links and quotes. We then interrogate the correspondence between eAG and LeAG, in order to establish the parsability of LeAG into eAG.

4.1 Inline multilayer annotation

Multistructured models are meant to support the simultaneous expression of several annotation paradigms. For instance, one may want to annotate a text by identifying, independently, its *grammatical* (substantive, adjective, etc.) and its *semantic* (proposition, topic, etc.) structures. To achieve that goal, eAG makes a clear distinction between the representation of **inclusion**[5], which is a modelling relation that makes sense within one annotation paradigm, and **nesting** or **co-occurrence**[6], which is a fortuitous situation in which two independent elements occur at the same place. And indeed, the eAG syntax for inclusion is *explicit* (see Figure 1.b), while nesting *happens* when two elements X and Y are so that $ref(start(X)) \leq ref(start(Y))$ and $ref(end(Y)) \leq ref(end(X))$ – hence nesting is uniquely defined in terms of reference values.

Yet the notion of chronology is quite impacted by the shift from stand-off to inline markup. In eAG, in order to fit multimedia annotation, several chronologies can be defined, and each node is associated a value from one of those chronologies. In a text-only markup setting, a natural chronology is implied by the text itself: the set of inter-character positions. As a consequence, LeAG rests upon that single, natural chronology, that does not even need to be made explicit: tags are simply inserted, within the text stream to be annotated, at the position a corresponding node of an eAG would have made reference to. E.g., annotating the *substantive* in "Let us garlands bring." is done by inserting a pair of tags as follows: "Let us [Substantive}garlands{Substantive] bring."

Still, in spite of being considerably simplified compared to eAG, the notion of chronology is still *central* to LeAG, because it is absolutely necessary in order to represent co-occurrence or nesting. Consider the very elementary text stream ABC. A chronology for this text is: {$start() = before(A)$, $after(A) = before(B)$, $after(B) = before(C)$, $after(C) = end()$}. Identifying an element Ω between the positions $before(A)$ and $before(C)$ is done as follows: [Ω}AB{Ω]C. The text stream, since it has been added new characters (the ones that constitute the tags), has been altered by this operation.

---

[3]Cf. *An American observer who saw the beating* and *the beating that happened then*.
[4]Cf. the *Exp* elements ranging from r_1 to r_3 and r_2 to r_4 respectively.

[5]E.g. a *proposition* contains a *topic*.
[6]A word may happen to be both a *substantive* and the *topic* of a *proposition*: *topic* and *substantive* co-occur; *substantive* is nested in *proposition*;*topic* is included in *proposition*.

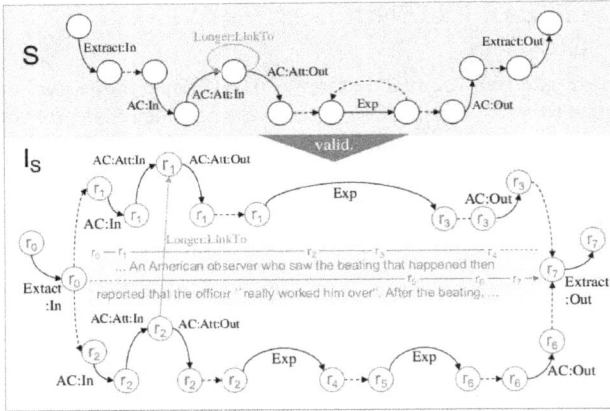

Figure 3: SeAG/eAG illustrating anaphoric chain annotation. An *Extract* contains overlapping AC, composed of overlapping *expressions*. The *Longer:LinkTo* link reifies a relation from the more to the less numerous AC.

Yet, interestingly, even in the annotated text stream, the original chronology is still operative to index a very particular text sub-stream, that is, the text stripped from the tags – i.e. the original stream. This may sound tautological; nonetheless, this remark is fundamental, since this bare text stream is the one an editor will consider when she wants to annotate the corpus independently from any previous annotation – that is, when proceeding to multilayer annotation. Indeed, if the editor wants to identify another element ω, ranging from $before(A)$ to $before(C)$, she may insert an opening tag at the position $before(A)$, and a closing tag at $before(C)$, without considering the other tags, resulting in[7] $A_1 = [\Omega]\{\omega\}AB\{\Omega\}\{\omega\]C$. One may also consider that, in the original text stream, $start() = before(A)$ – so the annotation $A_2 = [\omega][\Omega]AB\{\Omega\}\{\omega\}C$ (where $[\omega]$ is inserted at the position $start()$ this time) shall be considered equivalent to A_1. Similarly, since the two elements Ω and ω are independent, the order in which they are identified shall be indifferent: the two opening (closing, respectively) tags in A1 and A2 can be inverted, resulting in two more equivalent markups: $A_1' = [\omega][\Omega]AB\{\omega\}\{\Omega\}C$ and $A_2' = [\Omega][\omega]AB\{\omega\}\{\Omega\}C$.
Hence the following relation:

Equivalent LeAG. Let us call **trains of tags** the largest sets of tags, in a LeAG, that are not separated by a character from the original text. Two LeAG are **equivalent** iff they differ only by the order of the tags that belong to their respective trains of tags.

This notion of equivalence actually reflects the fact LeAG, though it is an inline markup syntax, rests upon a notion of chronology that is typical of stand-off markup models. Indeed, one way to interpret the above equivalence relation is by saying that in a LeAG, tags only *make reference* to the position they occupy in the original text stream. Surely, two tags making reference to the same position may be written in any order. Since, in practice, two such tags will not be separated by any character from the bare data and constitute a 'train of tags', it follows that in a train of tags, the order in which the tags are written is indifferent.

As a consequence, contrary to XML, the nesting of an element B inside the scope of an element A *cannot* be a means to represent the inclusion of B inside A. Thus a syntax is needed to represent inclusion (cf. 4.2.1). Second, since inserting tags does not alter the chronology that indexes the original text, tags can be considered not to take "any room" along that chronology. This suggests that inserting exogenous resources within the primary resources, e.g. structured comments, can be done *inside special tags that open and close at the same position in the original stream* (cf. 4.2.3).

4.2 The LeAG syntax

In the following paragraph, based on the above considerations, we gradually introduce the LeAG syntax. The content of the LeAG tags will be defined by means of formulae in which orange characters are constants and italics denotes variables. (Black) parenthesis are mathematical delimiters, not variables or constants. A **field** is either a variable or a formula enclosed in parenthesis. An optional field is followed by the character ?. A field that can be repeated is followed by +, one that is both optional and can be repeated is followed by *. Concatenation is implicit. Space characters are represented by underscores.

4.2.1 Mono-hierarchy of attribute-less elements. As stated above, some explicit syntax is needed to represent inclusion in a markup model that supports multilayer annotation. This paragraph presents how to express single-layered annotation. The next paragraph extends LeAG towards multilayered annotation.

Elementary spanning elements. An elementary spanning elements (ESE) is the syntactical structure dedicated to the labelling of a section of the primary resources, with the possibility to assess that the current element is included in other elements of the annotation. ESE are represented by a pair of opening and closing tags whose *substance* field has the same value, according to the following:

> $OTag := [\ substance \}$
> $CTag := \{\ substance \]$
> $substance := name\ fathers?\ (\ ,\ \_ID)?$
> $fathers := \_in\_ context$

Above, *name* is the name of the current element and works as a label on the primary resources enclosed by the pair of tags; *context* provides a designation of the elements that contain the current element[8]. The *ID* field will be discussed in the paragraph 4.2.4.

The **content of an element** is constituted of the tags themselves and the whole text (primary resources + tags) they span over.

Rule 4.2.1 The opening and the closing tags defining one ESE cannot belong to the same train of tags.

Back to the example. In order to identify *one* anaphoric chain in the extract of *The Village of Ben Suc*, it suffices to define three element names *Extract*, *AC* and *Exp* for the identification of the extract, the AC and its constituting expressions respectively, and to build the following pairs of opening/closing tags:

- [Extract} and {Extract] ;
- [AC in Extract} and {AC in Extract], assessing that an AC is included in an extract;
- [Exp in AC} and {Exp in AC], assessing that an expression is included in an AC.

---

[7]See paragraph 4.2.2 for the actual syntax for multilayer annotation.

[8]We will see that an element may have more than one father, thanks to the notion of grafts. See paragraph 4.2.2.

The following LeAG L_1 annotates the anaphoric chain regarding the young prisoner accordingly.

L_1 :[Extract}An ARVN officer asked [AC in Extract}[Exp in AC}a young prisoner{Exp in AC] several questions, and when [Exp in AC}he{Exp in AC] failed to answer, beat [Exp in AC}him{Exp in AC]. An American observer who saw the beating that happened then reported that the officer "really worked [Exp in AC}him{Exp in AC] over". After the beating, [Exp in AC}the prisoner{Exp in AC]{AC in Extract]was forced to remain standing for hours.{Extract]

4.2.2 Grafts: Multilayer annotation.

We now extend the above syntax to multilayer annotation. Multilayer annotation may occur in two distinct situations: first, the schema defines several annotation paradigms; second, one path of the schema is instantiated several times onto the same resources (Figure 2).

The challenge is to make sure that in any case, the tags of a multilayer LeAG shall be unambiguously associated with the layer(s) they are part of. When the set of the elements' names of two co-existing layers do not intersect, assessing to which layer a tag belongs is trivial. At the opposite, simulation-based multilayering, which is prone to self-overlap, will be problematic: in that case, two overlapping elements cannot be discriminated neither on the basis of their name nor by looking at the name of their fathers. Anaphoric chains annotation is a canonical example of such a setting.

For instance, in the excerpt of *The Village of Ben Suc*, consider the ACs relative to *the American observer* and *the beating* respectively. A naïve approach making use of the syntax for single-layered annotation would yield the following annotation – which is faulty:

[Extract}An ARVN officer [...] beat him. [AC in Extract}$_1$[Exp in AC}$_2$An American observer who saw [AC in Extract}$_3$[Exp in AC}$_4$the beating{Exp in AC}$_5${AC in Extract]$_6$ that happened then{Exp in AC]$_7$ reported that the officer "really worked him over". After [Exp in AC}$_8$the beating{Exp in AC}$_9${AC in Extract]$_{10}$, the prisoner was forced to remain standing for hours.{Extract]

Indeed, it is undecidable whether the *Exp* element starting at the tag 4 ends at tag 5 or 7. Moreover, there would be no way to ascertain to which *AC* an *Exp* ranging from tag 4 to tag 5 would belong to. An intuitive disambiguating solution – at least to the human eye – consists in colouring the tags belonging to distinct layers:

[Extract}An ARVN officer [...] beat him. [AC in Extract}$_1$[Exp in AC}$_2$An American observer who saw [AC in Extract}$_3$[Exp in AC}$_4$the beating{Exp in AC}$_5${AC in Extract]$_6$ that happened then{Exp in AC]$_7$ reported that the officer "really worked him over". After [Exp in AC}$_8$the beating{Exp in AC}$_9${AC in Extract]$_{10}$, the prisoner was forced to remain standing for hours.{Extract]

Now it is clear that the element starting at tag 2 ends at tag 5, overlapping with the element starting at tag 4 and ending at tag 7. Importantly, not only have we coloured differently the elements (2-5) and (4-7) in order to make their respective opening and closing tags match, but also have we given a common colour to the elements (3-10), (4-7) and (8-9), which indicates that the two expressions (4-7) and (8-9) belong to the same AC (3-10), for instance.

Grafts. The notion of *grafts* follows the above intuition. Grafts are coloured LeAGs that are anchored onto an existing LeAG. They express, either locally or at the scale of the whole document, some additional enrichment on top of the annotation that has, at a certain point in time, been done already.

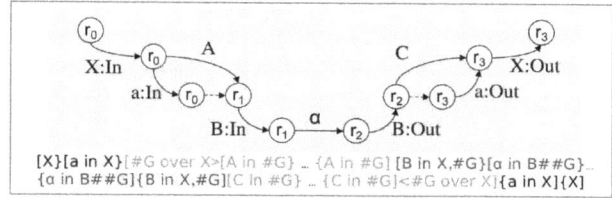

Figure 4: A LeAG and a matching eAG, where an element (B) has two fathers, one in the uncoloured hierarchy, and the other in a graft. The colours of B, namely #G and # (uncoloured), are repeated in the context of its son element α.

Consider the LeAG L_1 at the end of paragraph 4.2.1. L_1 identifies one AC and its constituting expressions (Exp), within an extract. A **graft** must be defined in order to identify, in *the same* extract, another AC, e.g. the AC regarding *the beating*, since this addition will result in a non-hierarchical LeAG. This is done as follows:

(1) The element of the existing annotation that will serve as the *context* of the graft is identified: Extract, here.

(2) A name of 'colour', *nameC*, is defined, in the form:
$$nameC := \# \, colour$$
where *colour* is a string that identifies the graft, e.g. "#Red".

(3) The range of the graft is specified by inserting, within the frame of the context element, a pair of colour tags:
$$Otag := [\; nameC \_over\_ context >$$
$$Ctag := < \; nameC \_over\_ context \;]$$
with the *nameC* and *context* fields as defined above. For instance, the span of the AC regarding "the beating" is the following:

[Extract} An American observer who saw [#Red over Extract>the beating that happened then reported that the officer "really worked [Exp in AC}him{Exp in AC] over". After the beating<#Red over Extract], [...] {Extract]

(4) Then *nameC* serves as a context for the top elements of the graft. Here, one AC element spans over the whole graft:

[Extract} [...] An American observer who saw [#Red over Extract>[AC in #Red}the beating that happened then reported that the officer "really worked [Exp in AC}him{Exp in AC] over". After the beating{AC in #Red]<#Red over Extract], [Exp in AC}the prisoner [...] {Extract]

(5) Elements included in the top elements of the graft are defined, their *context* field keeping record of the colour of the upper element. For instance, here, two Exp belong to the red AC:

[Extract}[...] An American observer who saw [#Red over Extract>[AC in #Red][Exp in AC#Red}the beating that happened then{Exp in AC#Red] reported that the officer "really worked [Exp in AC}him{Exp in AC] over". After [Exp in AC#Red}the beating{Exp in AC#Red]{AC in #Red]<#Red over Extract], [Exp in AC}the prisoner [...] {Extract]

Similarly, had one Exp element had any child, the context field of the tags defining that element would have been Exp#Red.

Based on that principle, the LeAG L_2 on Figure 5 identifies the three anaphoric chains regarding *the prisoner, the beating* and *the American observer* respectively – which is a case of simulation-based multilayer annotation with self-overlap.

```
L₁ :[Extract}An ARVN officer asked [Exp in AC}a young prisoner{Exp in
AC] questions, and when [Exp in AC}he{Exp in AC] failed to answer, beat
[Exp in AC}him{Exp in AC]. [#Blue over Extract>[AC in #Blue}[Exp
in AC#Blue}An American observer who saw [#Red over Extract>[AC
in #Red}[Exp in AC#Red}the beating<#Blue over Extract]{Exp in
AC#Blue}{AC in #Blue} that happened then{Exp in AC#Red} reported that
the officer "really worked [Exp in AC}him{Exp in AC] over". After [Exp in
AC#Red}the beating{Exp in AC#Red}{AC in #Red]<#Red over Extract],
[Exp in AC}the prisoner{Exp in AC}{AC in Extract]was forced to remain
standing for hours.{Extract]
```

Figure 5: Three-layered LeAG.

Complements. (1) Grafts are added on top of an existing annotation spanning over the whole document. Before the first graft is defined, the annotation has to be hierarchical[9]. Thus we can refer to this underlying hierarchical annotation as the **uncoloured hierarchy** of a LeAG. Tags of this hierarchy either have no explicit colour or, when they also belong to a coloured graft, the colour of that graft plus a 'blank' colour, # – see element α in Figure 4. (2) A graft may be defined either on the underlying hierarchy (Figure 4) or on an element from another graft. (3) An element may have several fathers, belonging to grafts or to the uncoloured hierarchy indifferently (cf. element B, Figure 4). (4) The span of the graft shall not necessarily equal the one of its context element (Figure 5).

4.2.3 Standard inserts: Attributes; structured comment. So far, we have seen how to label the primary resources by means of entangled hierarchies of elementary spanning elements. Still, editing is not only about labelling: sometimes, additional, structured information must be added on top of the labels. In XML, this kind of information constitutes elements' attributes; still, adding attributes to an element is like annotating the element itself, that is, for the editor, inserting secondary, structured data that does not bear on the primary resources but on the tags.

Similarly, providing the editor with means to express critical information, not by labelling the primary resources, but by inserting assertions is a useful feature. Introductions, comments and punctual notes, in their digital form, fall into that category of annotations. Attributes and punctual comments share the property of not being expressible with elementary spanning elements. In LeAG, both will be represented by means of **inserts**. An insert is similar to void elements in XML in that: (1) it is both opening and closing, which means, in the LeAG vocabulary, that inserts start and end at the same position; (2) it is self-contained, in the sense that the tag representing the insert is the insert's content.

Attribute insert: general syntax. The syntax of an attribute insert respects the following formula:

$$InsertA := [\; \texttt{Att\_of\_}\; context\; \_;\_\; LeAG\;]$$

where *context* is the coloured name of the element whose attributes are described in the insert, and *LeAG* is some structured data conform to the LeAG model, constituting the content of the attributes.

Attribute insert: example. So far, the passage of *The Village of Ben Suc* as a whole was simply labelled as an Extract. The following LeAG provides, as attributes of the Extract, the author's name, the title and the publication year of the novel:

```
[Extract}[Att of Extract ; [author}Jonathan Schell
{author][title}The Village of Ben Suc{title][year}1967
{year]]An ARVN officer, [...] for hours.{Extract]
```
The insert corresponds, in eAG, to a hierarchy of elements bearing the suffix :Att, included in the element Extract:

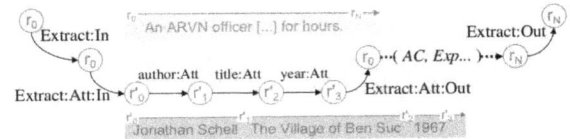

In the LeAG, there is no need neither to specify the :Att suffix for the elements defined inside the attribute insert, nor to indicate in the context field of the top elements among them, that they are included in the insert[10]. The same applies to comment inserts:

Comment inserts: general[11] syntax. The general syntax of a comment insert is the following:

$$InsertC := [\; name\; :\texttt{Att\_in\_}\; context\; (\;,\_\; ID)\; ?\; \_;\_\; LeAG\;]$$

where *name* is the name of the insert, *context* is the coloured name of the elements the insert is the son of and *LeAG* structured data conform to the LeAG model, constituting the content of the comment. The *ID* field will be discussed in the paragraph 4.2.4.

Comment insert: an example. The following LeAG incorporates a *comment* regarding the context of *The Village of Ben Suc*:

```
[Extract}An ARVN[Comment:Att in Extract ; [Att of Comment ;
[authorOfComment}Barrellon et al.{authorOfComment]]The
mention of the [acronym}ARVN{acronym] refers to the Vietnam
War.] officer asked [...] for hours.{Extract]
```
A comment being an element, it may possess attributes, as illustrated above (e.g. to specify the name of its authors).

Inserts in a train of tags. The case of inserts within a train of tags has to be discussed. Consider the LeAG [A}...{A][B in A ; *LeAG*][A}...{A]. In the absence of a schema, it is not possible to assess to which A element B belongs. If there is a schema that does not restrict the position of the element B either at the beginning or at the end of the element A, neither.

Second, consider [A}...[B in A ; L_1]{C in A ; L_2]...{A]. The LeAG itself is not ambiguous: it states that the inserts B and C occur at the same position. Yet, in the perspective of parsing the LeAG into an eAG (cf. paragraph 6), since in the corresponding eAG, two inserts will form a sequence, there is no indication in the LeAG about which insert will come first. The following conventional rule clarifies those situations:

Rule 4.2.3 When there is no schema or when the schema does not clarify the following situations, it shall be considered that (1) when an insert occurs in a train of tags where an opening and a closing tags identically match the context field of the insert, then the insert conventionally belongs to the *opening* element; (2) when two inserts with the same context field occur in the same train of tags, the alphabetical order between the tags considered as strings provides a conventional order between the inserts.

---

[9]This is not a tough constraint, since a single element spanning over the whole corpus is an elementary hierarchical annotation.

[10]*Id est*, there is no need to write [author in Att of Extract], for instance.

[11]A refinement of the following syntax will be proposed in the paragraph 4.2.4.

4.2.4 Links and Quoting elements.
The last aspect of eAGs that needs to be translated into LeAG is links or quotes. We have seen that in eAG, links and quotes are expressed harmoniously with the other elements (i.e. by means of nodes and edges) and, for that reason, can be properly *validated*. In particular, compared to XML where a link is but an ID/IDREF pair, in SeAG/eAG, the nature of the two elements connected by a link can inherently be restricted. Still, since links and quotes denote distant connections across the corpus that may result in cyclic annotations (i.e. along the text stream, the beginning of an element comes after its end), it is not possible to represent them by means of pairs of tags along the text stream. Thus, LeAG makes use of an additional feature: the ID field. ID fields work as an identifier of either the source or the end of a connection (link/quote), hence enabling to position the extreme *nodes* of such elements inside the LeAG, that is, to position the elements themselves. Yet, ID fields are not *tag* identifiers. Indeed, regardless of the parsing strategy adopted, there is no one-to-one correspondence between the *tags* of a LeAG and the *nodes* of an eAG expressing the same annotation, as evidenced below[12]:

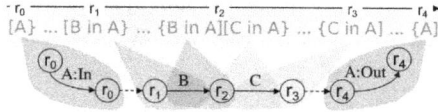

Indeed, because the element A contains other elements, the tag [A} translates into *two* nodes whose reference values point towards the position of [A} inside the document, connected by an edge A:In, while the tag [B} relates to *one* node only. Conversely, two tags may relate to the same node: since the element C starts where B ends, both {B] and [C} relate to the node that separates B and C.

Yet, a finer correspondence between the LeAG tags and a *subset* of the nodes of the corresponding eAG can be exploited for expressing links and quotes: (1) an opening tag positions (and hence, matches) the root of the corresponding element in the eAG; (2) a closing tag positions the leaf of the corresponding element in the eAG; (3) an insert positions both the root and the leaf of the corresponding element in the eAG. ID fields exploit that connection, as follows.

ID fields. Since opening and closing tags of ESE relate to either the root or the leaf of an element in the corresponding eAG, ESE ID fields contain a singleton value K. *A contrario*, an insert ID shall possibly designate the root and the leaf of the corresponding eAG element and thus contains a pair of values M and N:

$$ID := \text{ID}\_=\_K \text{ (singleton syntax)}$$
$$ID := \text{ID}\_=\_M\_->\_N \text{ (pair syntax)}$$

Basic example. Let us consider the following comment and a matching eAG (pink flags represent the node identifiers):

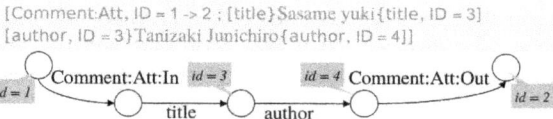

Noteworthily, the relation between ID values and root/leaves nodes is only *surjective*. Thus, the ID of the closing tag of an element and that of an element that immediately follows have to be the equal (e.g. {title, ID = 3] and [author, ID = 3}, above).

---
[12]Coloured shapes relate the eAG nodes/edges to the tags that set their position/label.

The syntax for links and quotes are based on that mechanism – plus some improvements on the insert syntax.

Quote elements. Quote elements enable to include an element identified in the primary resources within a comment. In eAG, quoting the ARVN acronym from the extract of *The Village of Ben Suc* within a comment can be done as follows:

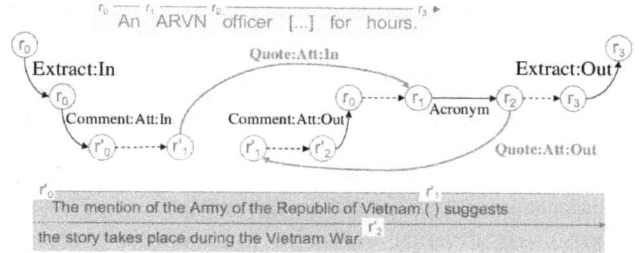

The two (orange) edges permit to *structurally include* the quoted element inside the comment element.

In LeAG, since the content of a comment has to be written inside the insert itself, quoting, inside the *LeAG* field of a comment, an element that has been identified elsewhere in the annotation cannot be done but by reference. Therefore, quoting elements appear as special comment inserts, whose *LeAG* field has been replaced by an ID field (with the pair syntax):

$$Quote := [\ name(\_in\_context)?(\ ,\_ID_1)?\ \_;\_ID_2\ ]$$
$$ID_i, i \in \{1,2\} := \text{ID}\_=\_M_i\_->\_N_i$$

The pair of values of the ID_2 field must then refer to some tag(s) somewhere else in the LeAG that delimit either an element or a sequence of elements.

Quote: example The LeAG representing the above eAG is:

```
[Extract}[Comment:Att in Extract ; The mention of the
Army of the Republic of Vietnam ([Quote ; ID = 1-> 2])
refers to the Vietnam War.]An [Acronym in Extract, ID =
1}ARVN{Acronym in Extract, ID = 2] officer [...] hours.{Extract]
```

This LeAG does correspond to the eAG above, since it states that the *Extract* contains a *Comment:Att*, made out of some not annotated text (which translates into an epsilon edge), followed by a *Quote* containing an annotation graph whose root and leaf have the identifiers '1' and '2' respectively; *Extract* further contains an *Acronym*, whose root and leaf identifiers are '1' and '2' respectively.

Links. An eAG link is an element whose root is a node from an element and whose leaf is a node from another element.

First, to represent such a graph in LeAG, we need to be able to identify a node *inside* any element. Consider the link in Figure 3. It connects the internal nodes of two *AC:Att* elements that contain nothing but those nodes. Yet, the *ID* fields of an insert with no *LeAG* field, suit to represent those *AC:Att* elements, only identifies the root and leaf of the matching element, not an internal node. To fill this gap, we define **void inserts**:

$$VoidInsert := [\ in\_context\ ,\_ID\ ]$$
$$ID := \text{ID}\_=\_N$$

Such an insert neither has a name nor a *LeAG* field, but it does have a context (the element it is included in) and an ID field. Placed immediately after an opening tag, e.g. [A}, a void insert [in A, ID = 1] enables to give the identifier '1' to a node that, in the corresponding eAG, is the node ending the *A:In* edge.

Second, we need a means to express that an element may start inside an element and end inside another one. For such a special element, we defined **link insert**:

Link := [*name* :LinkTo_in_ *context* ,_ *ID*(_;_ *LeAG*)?]
ID := ID_=_ *M* _->_ *N* OR ID_=_->_ *N*

The *LeAG* field defines the content of the link; if empty, the link is an edge. The leaf of the link, identified by the value of the variable *N* above, must be an internal node of some element, represented elsewhere by a void insert.

Link: example. Figure 3 illustrates how to annotate different, overlapping AC in an extract, and how links could reify an order relation between them. The following *LeAG* expresses the same annotation, extended to three ACs (*the prisoner, the beating, the American observer*) as in the eAG on Figure 3:

```
[Extract}An ARVN officer asked [AC in Extract}[AC:Att of
AC ; [Longer:LinkTo, ID = -> 2][Longer:LinkTo, ID
= -> 1]][Exp in AC}a young prisoner{Exp in AC] ques-
tions, and when [Exp in AC}he{Exp in AC] failed to answer,
beat [Exp in AC}him{Exp in AC]. [#Blue over Extract>[AC
in #Blue}[AC:Att of AC#Blue ; [in AC:Att#Blue, ID =
1]][Exp in AC#Blue}An American observer who saw [#Red over
Extract>[AC in #Red}[AC:Att of AC#Red ; [in AC:Att#Red,
ID = 2][Longer:LinkTo, ID = -> 1]][Exp in AC#Red}the
beating<#Blue over Extract]{Exp in AC#Blue]{AC in #Blue]
that happened then{Exp in AC#Red] reported that the officer "re-
ally worked [Exp in AC}him{Exp in AC] over". After [Exp
in AC#Red}the beating{Exp in AC#Red]{AC in #Red]<#Red
over Extract], [Exp in AC}the prisoner{Exp in AC]{AC in
Extract]was forced to remain standing for hours.{Extract]
```

4.3 Parsing LeAG

Let us consider that two eAG are **isomorphic** iff there is a bijective morphism ϕ between them so that a node and its image by ϕ share the same reference value.

LeAG is designed as a markup syntax for eAG. Ideally, there should have been a bijection between LeAGs and the classes of isomorphic eAGs. Yet, this is not the case: first, because two equivalent LeAG documents shall translate into the same eAG, and second, because several non-isomorphic eAGs could match a given LeAG – which is clearly problematic when considering parsing LeAG documents into eAG. For instance, the elementary LeAG [A}...{A][A}...{A] may reasonably translate into either of the following:

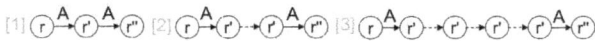

or any eAG made out of a sequence of two edges labelled *A* with the right reference values, separated by any number of epsilon edges. The problem is we cannot, in the absolute, prefer one eAG over the others, since all of them do represent the fact the LeAG document contains two *A* elements in a row – and also, and most importantly, because the different eAG *will not be validated against the same schemas*. Indeed, considering the three SeAGs below, the above eAG [1] is validated by the schema [S_1] only, [2] by both [S_2] and [S_3], and [3] by [S_3] only.

Choosing one solution against the others thus cannot be done but by considering a predefined schema. Hence parsing a LeAG means: given a SeAG, yielding a valid eAG that 'represents well' the LeAG – if such an eAG exists.

In the following, we discuss how to design a deterministic schema-aware LeAG parser. First, we propose to restrict SeAGs to non-ambiguous (N-A) ones [5], ambiguous schemas resulting in non-determinism. We then show that associating to the initial LeAG an eAG, validated by a N-A SeAG, containing the same sequences of elements, whose elements' span is the same, and whose inclusion relations are the same as in the LeAG, is deterministic in general – but not in some cases. We identify those cases and we show that there is a notion of a minimal eAG, that enables to deterministically single out one valid eAG among the others (up to isomorphism[13]).

Non-ambiguous SeAG. A SeAG is non-ambiguous (N-A) iff given any label sequence *w*, there is at most one path connecting the root of the SeAG to its leaf that, epsilon edges set apart, spells *w* [5]. Non N-A SeAG will result in non-deterministic parsing. See the following schema, that matches the LeAG [A}...{A][A}...{A] in two different ways – see graphs [1] and [2] below:

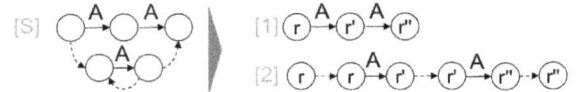

LeAG-eAG label sequences. First, we want to stress the fact the sequence of the tags in a LeAG implies the sequences of labels along the different paths the corresponding eAG is made out of, provided the eAG is so that each element of the LeAG has one and only one corresponding element in the eAG.

First let us consider hierarchical LeAGs. The rule 4.2.3 implies there is only one way to read the tags from a given train of tags, regardless of the order in which they are written: this ensures that each of the set of tags of the same colour, in a LeAG, defines one and only one hierarchy of elements. Since a given hierarchy of elements translates into one and only one sequence of labels (epsilon edges set apart) in the eAG model[14], a hierarchical LeAG can be associated only one label sequence in the eAG model – epsilon edges set apart. Now given grafts are hierarchies of elements that are included in a given element of the LeAG[15], and given links and quotes are also hierarchical structures whose connection with the rest of the eAG is determined by the identifier of their root and leaf, the previous discussion extends to LeAGs in general: the sequence of the labels along the paths of the eAG representing a graft, link, quote, is deterministically implied by the LeAG.

eAG equivalence. Two non-isomorphic eAGs are **equivalent** iff their elements form bijective pairs, so that: 1) the elements from each pair share the same name and 2) their previous, following and father and son elements, if they exist, form pairs, and 3) so that the reference values and identifiers at their root/leaf are identical.

Finding a valid eAG. Hierarchies form paths in an eAG. The label sequence of each hierarchical structure of an eAG matching a given LeAG is, as shown above, uniquely defined by the LeAG.

---

[13]The whole discussion that follows is 'up to isomorphism'.
[14]E.g. '*A* contains *X*' translates into the label sequence: [*X:In* / *A* / *X:Out*].
[15]We consider grafts are *included in* their context element, while an element might belong to both a graft and an outer element: it is always possible to change a graft sharing an element with its context into two grafts strictly included in this context.

Validating a LeAG L is then quite simple. If L is hierarchical, be ls the eAG label sequence corresponding to L. If there is a path in the schema whose label sequence, ϵ edges apart, spells out ls, the LeAG is valid and a valid corresponding eAG can be defined. If L contains one graft: be ls the eAG label sequence matching the uncoloured hierarchy within L, and l' the label sequence for the graft: L is valid if the schema contains a path that spells out ls and another path, inside the element in that path that matches the element in which there is a graft, that spells out l'. Recursively, this principle applies for grafts on grafts; it can be adapted for links and quotes.

Conveniently, in a N-A SeAG, two paths cannot spell the same label sequence, so if there is a path in a schema, say, that matches a hierarchical label sequence, then it is unique. Identically, if, in the context of an element, there is a path that matches the label sequence of a graft, it is also unique. If there are more than one valid eAG, then we know they still all correspond to the same paths in the schema. This means that some schemas are non-deterministic, i.e. that they validate several non-isomorphic, equivalent eAGs.

N-A Schemas validating several equivalent eAGs. We provide the following result: non deterministic N-A SeAGs are the SeAGs that contain a sequence of **at least two epsilon edges**.

A sequence of (two) epsilon edges may happen in two different patterns: the edges either form a cycle or not. The first, general problem with a sequence of two epsilon edges is, since epsilon edges are not represented in LeAG, that the reference values of the nodes of the sequence that do not work as the root or the leaf of an element are undetermined. For instance, the reference of the orange node in I'_{Sa} on Figure 6 can be given any value between r_1 and r_2. Hence, several eAGs, differing only by one reference value, can be associated to the left LeAG on that Figure.

Additionally, non-determinism may result in structurally different graphs. Cyclic sequences of two epsilon edges may result, in a valid, hierarchical eAG, in any even sequence of epsilon edges. Then, single-layered LeAG annotations, that translate into single-pathed eAGs, will be associated an infinity of equivalent, valid eAGs: see I_{Sa} in Figure 6. N-A schemas containing only linear sequences of two epsilon edges will, on the contrary, be deterministic for the parsing of hierarchical LeAGs, but not in case of simulation-based multilayering (Figure 6, right). Cyclic epsilon sequences will also be problematic in case of simulation-based multilayering.

One can check that the cases of non-determinism above necessitate a sequence of no less than two epsilon edges: the schemas that contain no or isolate epsilon edges are deterministic.

Minimal eAG. In order to make LeAG parsing with N-A schema deterministic, that is, to ensure that an equivalent class of LeAG documents be associated only isomorphic eAGs, we must single out one of the equivalent eAGs as a unique parsing solution.

Let $\mathcal{X}_S$ be an equivalent class of eAGs validated by the same schema S. For $G \in \mathcal{X}_S$, let us denote $|V_G|$ and $|E_G|$ the cardinal of its sets of nodes and edges respectively. We claim that, up to isomorphism, there is only one eAG $M \in \mathcal{X}_S$ that minimises both the values $size = |V_M| \times |E_M|$ and $Sref = \sum_{v \in V_M} ref(v)$. Then let M be the right representative of that eAG class for parsing under S.

LeAG parsability. For any class of LeAG documents, there is at most one minimal eAG validated by a given N-A SeAG schema, that preserves the LeAG elements, elements' span, identifiers and inclusion relations.

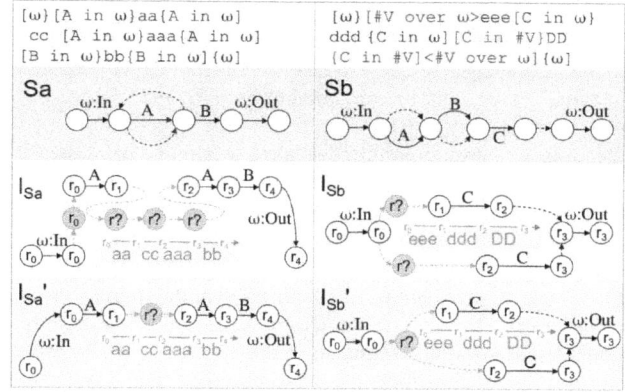

Figure 6: Parsing a LeAG (top, right and left) against a N-A SeAG schema (middle) may yield more than one equivalent eAG, either differing on reference values (r?) or by their structure (dotted orange epsilon edges).

5 RELATED WORK

Many schema-aware data models have been specifically proposed to overcome the limitations of XML by enabling, at the very least, the expression of not only one, but several hierarchies onto the same resources. Among the most notable such 'multistructured' data models, we may mention MulaX [13], XConcur [24], MSXD [7], Rabbit/Duck grammars [27]. Those are all built upon XML and make use of the same fundamental notions like elements, attributes, inclusion, etc. The general validation strategy for those models is to extract or isolate the different hierarchies of elements present in the documents, and validate each separately; they also investigate inter-hierarchy constraints.

LMNL [32] represents a more stripped-down vision of multilayer annotation. In many respects, LeAG borrows from LMNL. In LMNL, the user can identify *ranges* in a character stream and name them by means of pairs of opening and closing tags. Ranges themselves can be annotated by (meta)ranges, which inspired the attribute syntax in LeAG. Yet LMNL claims to be an *annotation* language solely, and not a *structuring* language: in particular, LMNL does not provide the user with means to represent inclusion or sibling relations. As we have seen in paragraph 4.1, indeed, inclusion is either represented by nesting, which limits the data model to trees, or by means of an explicit syntax; LMNL does not propose such syntax, and yet allows overlap and multilayering. By sweeping out the notion of inclusion, LMNL seemingly clears the paradox out; yet LMNL is not absolutely blind to the charms of hierarchies: it lies upon the notion of 'layers', that is, ranges that fully contain the ranges that start and end in their scope, which is reminiscent of XML hierarchies – but if such patterns cannot be interpreted in structural terms, can they be but fortuitous patterns? Still, because hierarchies are a classic and fundamental annotation structure [34], the LMNL model comes along with XML generators that can extract hierarchies from the data. Our point, on that matter, is that since hierarchies are so central, the best is to enable the editors to have direct control over their expression – which indeed demands additional syntax. Apart from those critical considerations, LMNL is an important annotation model, that goes beyond most others, in terms of expressivity; moreover, it benefits from a grammar-based validation language [31], able to embrace the multilayer documents as a whole, which can be compared only to RDF validators (or to the SeAG we propose [2]).

Indeed, several annotation models have originated from the RDF community. One may think of the pioneering RDFTef [33], the Open Annotation data model [22] or EARMARK [16]. The RDF data model, which imposes no restriction on the shape of the resulting graph, is very expressive; moreover, RDF annotation can be used as a complement to an existing TEI annotation [1], which is a way to ally the best of two worlds. One limitation though of RDF-based annotation languages is the current lack of a proper and computationally efficient validation mechanism. OWL is not natively suitable for validation [21, 25]; tweaks aiming at the expression of, say, integrity constraints, have been experimented, but results in huge execution time [30]. Nonetheless, RDF validation is a promising field of research, as illustrated by the ShEx [18] and SHACL [15] projects. Time complexity still seems to be quite high, but cutting it down is being investigated [29].

6 CONCLUSION

In this paper, we introduced LeAG, an inline markup syntax for extended Annotation Graphs. eAG is a *stand-off* annotation model, based upon a general, cyclic graph formalism: as one may expect, the model is thus highly expressive, fit to express multilayer annotation, but also distant connections across the annotation. The LeAG syntax illustrates that a similarly expressive *inline* markup model can be defined, at least for textual annotation. To achieve that goal, we defined a limited number of necessary syntactical structures (grafts and inserts). This way, the LeAG syntax is kept as simple as possible, while opening wide prospects in terms of editorial enrichments.

We also established the parsability of LeAG into eAG, that is, the fact a LeAG document translates into one corresponding eAG. This aspect of the LeAG syntax is crucial, since it indirectly provides the LeAG documents with a validation language, that is, SeAG, that comes as the validation mechanism for eAG. SeAG does not rely upon the notion of grammars, like most validation languages do, but on the simulation relation. From a technical point of view, simulation-based validation shines by enabling the validation of cyclic data, while keeping the algorithmic costs low. Moreover, as illustrated throughout this article, the ability of SeAG schemas to validate anaphoric chain annotations, which is a canonical linguistic annotation, also evidences the *editorial* relevance of that particular kind of validation for annotation purposes.

REFERENCES

[1] Gioele Barabucci, Angelo Di Iorio, Silvio Peroni, Francesco Poggi, and Fabio Vitali. 2013. Annotations with EARMARK in practice: a fairy tale. In *Proceedings of the 1st International Workshop on Collaborative Annotations in Shared Environment: metadata, vocabularies and techniques in the Digital Humanities*. ACM.

[2] Vincent Barrellon, Pierre-Edouard Portier, Sylvie Calabretto, and Olivier Ferret. 2016. Schema-aware Extended Annotation Graphs. In *Proceedings of the 2016 ACM symposium on Document engineering*. ACM, 45–54.

[3] Soběslav Benda, Jakub Klímek, and Martin Nečaský. 2013. Using schematron as schema language in conceptual modeling for XML. In *Proceedings of the Ninth Asia-Pacific Conference on Conceptual Modelling-Volume 143*. Australian Computer Society, Inc., 31–40.

[4] Steven Bird and Mark Liberman. 2001. A formal framework for linguistic annotation. *Speech communication* 33, 1 (2001), 23–60.

[5] Anne Brüggemann-Klein. 1993. Regular expressions into finite automata. *Theoretical Computer Science* 120, 2 (1993), 197–213.

[6] Gerrit Brüning, Katrin Henzel, and Dietmar Pravida. 2013. Multiple encoding in genetic editions: the case of" Faust". *Journal of the TEI* 4 (2013).

[7] Emmanuel Bruno and Elisabeth Murisasco. 2006. MSXD: a model and a schema for concurrent structures defined over the same textual data. In *Database and Expert Systems Applications*. Springer, 172–181.

[8] Hugh A Cayless. 2013. Rebooting TEI Pointers. *Journal of the Text Encoding Initiative* 6 (2013).

[9] Charles Chastain. 1975. Reference and Context. In *Language, Mind, and Knowledge*, Keith Gunderson (Ed.). Vol. 7. University of Minnesota Press, 194–231.

[10] TEI Consortium, Lou Burnard, Syd Bauman, and others. 2008. *TEI P5: Guidelines for electronic text encoding and interchange*. TEI Consortium.

[11] Dan Cristea, Nancy Ide, Laurent Romary, and others. 1998. Marking-up multiple views of a Text: Discourse and Reference. In *Proceedings of the First International Conference on Language Resources and Evaluation*.

[12] Paolo D'Iorio and Michele Barbera. 2011. Scholarsource: A digital infrastructure for the humanities. *Switching Codes. Thinking through New Technology in the Humanities and the Arts* (2011), 61–87.

[13] Mirco Hilbert, Andreas Witt, and Oliver Schonefeld. 2005. Making CONCUR work. In *Extreme Markup Languages*.

[14] HV Jagadish, Laks VS Lakshmanan, Monica Scannapieco, Divesh Srivastava, and Nuwee Wiwatwattana. 2004. Colorful XML: one hierarchy isn't enough. In *Proceedings of the 2004 ACM SIGMOD international conference on Management of data*. ACM, 251–262.

[15] Holger Knublauch and Arthur Ryman. 2015. Shapes Constraint Language (SHACL). *W3C First Public Working Draft* 8 (2015), W3C.

[16] Silvio Peroni. 2014. Markup beyond the trees. In *Semantic Web Technologies and Legal Scholarly Publishing*. Springer, 45–93.

[17] Pierre-Édouard et al Portier. 2012. Modeling, encoding and querying multi-structured documents. *Information Processing & Management* 48, 5 (2012), 931–955.

[18] Eric Prud'hommeaux, Jose Emilio Labra Gayo, and Harold Solbrig. 2014. Shape expressions: an RDF validation and transformation language. In *Proceedings of the 10th International Conference on Semantic Systems*. ACM, 32–40.

[19] Francesco Ranzato and Francesco Tapparo. 2010. An efficient simulation algorithm based on abstract interpretation. *Information and Computation* 208, 1 (2010), 1–22.

[20] Allen Renear, Elli Mylonas, and David Durand. 1996. Refining our notion of what text really is: The problem of overlapping hierarchies. *Research in humanities computing* 4 (1996), 263–80.

[21] Dave Reynolds, Carol Thompson, Jishnu Mukerji, and Derek Coleman. 2005. An assessment of RDF/OWL modelling. *Digital Media Systems Laboratory, HP Laboratories Bristol* 28 (2005).

[22] Robert et al. Sanderson. 2013. Open annotation data model. *W3C community draft* (2013).

[23] Desmond Schmidt. 2012. The role of markup in the digital humanities. *Historical Social Research/Historische Sozialforschung* (2012), 125–146.

[24] Oliver Schonefeld. 2007. XCONCUR and XCONCUR-CL: A constraint-based approach for the validation of concurrent markup. In *Data Structures for Linguistic Resources and Applications. Proceedings of the Biennial GLDV Conference*.

[25] Evren Sirin. 2010. Data validation with OWL integrity constraints. In *Web Reasoning and Rule Systems*. Springer, 18–22.

[26] C Michael Sperberg-McQueen. 1991. Text in the electronic age: Textual study and textual study and text encoding, with examples from medieval texts. *Literary and Linguistic Computing* 6, 1 (1991), 34–46.

[27] C Michael Sperberg-McQueen. 2006. Rabbit/duck grammars: a validation method for overlapping structures. In *Extreme Markup Languages*.

[28] C Michael Sperberg-McQueen and Claus Huitfeldt. 2000. Goddag: A data structure for overlapping hierarchies. In *Digital documents: Systems and principles*. Springer, 139–160.

[29] Slawek Staworko, Iovka Boneva, Jose E Labra Gayo, Samuel Hym, Eric G Prud'hommeaux, and Harold Solbrig. 2015. Complexity and Expressiveness of ShEx for RDF. In *LIPIcs-Leibniz International Proceedings in Informatics*, Vol. 31. Schloss Dagstuhl-Leibniz-Zentrum fuer Informatik.

[30] Jiao Tao, Evren Sirin, Jie Bao, and Deborah L McGuinness. 2010. Integrity Constraints in OWL. In *AAAI Conference on Artificial Intelligence*.

[31] Jeni Tennison. 2007. Creole: Validating overlapping markup. In *XTech*.

[32] Jeni Tennison and Wendell Piez. 2002. The Layered Markup and Annotation Language (LMNL).. In *Extreme Markup Languages*.

[33] Giovanni Tummarello, Christian Morbidoni, and Elena Pierazzo. 2005. Toward Textual Encoding Based on RDF. In *Proceedings of the 9th International Conference on Electronic Publishing*. IEEE.

[34] Andreas Witt. 2010. Different views on markup. *Text, Speech and Language Technology* (2010).

The Fábulas Model for Authoring Web-based Children's eBooks

Hedvan Fernandes Pinto
Federal University of Maranhão
São Luís, MA, Brazil
hedvan@laws.deinf.ufma.br

Carlos de Salles Soares Neto
Federal University of Maranhão
São Luís, Brazil
csalles@deinf.ufma.br

Sérgio Colcher
PUC-Rio
Rio de Janeiro, Brazil
colcher@inf.puc-rio.br

Roberto Gerson de Albuquerque Azevedo
PUC-Rio
Rio de Janeiro, Brazil
razevedo@inf.puc-rio.br

ABSTRACT

Nowadays, tablets and smartphones are commonly used by children for both entertainment and education purposes. In special, interactive multimedia eBooks running on those devices allow a richer experience when compared to traditional text-only books, being potentially more engaging and entertaining to readers. However, to explore the most exciting features in these environments, authors are currently left alone in the sense that there is no high level (less technical) support, and these features are usually accessible only through programming or some other technical skill. In this work, we aim at extracting the main features on enhanced children's eBooks and propose a model, named Fábulas—the Portuguese word for *fables*—that allows authors to create interactive multimedia children's eBooks declaratively. The model was conceived by taking, as a starting point, a systematic analysis of the common concepts, with the focus on identifying and categorizing recurring characteristics and pointing out functional and non-functional requirements that establish a strong orientation towards the set of desirable abstractions of an underlying model. Moreover, the paper presents a case study for the implementation of Fábulas on the Web, and discusses the authoring of a complete interactive story over it.

CCS CONCEPTS

• **Software and its engineering** → **Domain specific languages**; Model-driven software engineering; • **Applied computing** → *Hypertext / hypermedia creation*;

KEYWORDS

Interactive eBook; Multimedia Authoring; Conceptual Model

1 INTRODUCTION

With the advent of the Web and the popularization of portable electronic devices such as tablets and smartphones, electronic books (eBooks) have found a fertile environment to proliferate. Indeed,

DocEng'17, September 4-7, 2017, Valletta, Malta.
© 2017 ACM. 978-1-4503-4689-4/17/09...$15.00
DOI: http://dx.doi.org/10.1145/3103010.3103016

since the creation of the first eBook in 1971 by Michael Hart [15], eBooks have evolved to become not only a copy of printed books but also to include many new features available in the digital world, such as multimedia content and interactivity [4]. In particular, picture eBooks for children [30] extensively take advantage of those enhancement features to engage and entertain children on stories while serving as an educational platform as well.

Currently, to deploy enhanced eBooks for children, authors can use one of the format standards for eBooks, such as PDF [17], ePub [9], and Mobi [2], each one with their advantages and disadvantages. PDF, for instance, was created to provide a high-fidelity layout, similar to printed publications, whereas ePub and MOBI allow the adaptability of the layout for different screen sizes and devices. At some extent, those formats can also be supported in modern web browsers through plugins or using a polyfill approach [8] with HTML5/JavaScript. Another currently widely used approach for developing and delivering interactive eBooks is through software (or *apps*) in proprietary stores (e.g. Google Play and Apple Store) in which case they are sometimes called *book apps* [27, 30].

Some of the current eBooks formats can contain interactive elements. For instance, PDF supports hyperlinks and animation using videos or Flash (.SWF) [1]. Even so, it cannot fully support all the features required for elaborated interactive children's eBooks, such as audio recording and keeping control of complex object states during the story path. Other formats, such as ePub3 or native book apps, when taking advantage of imperative programming languages and low-level device APIs, can indeed support all the usual features on enhanced children's eBooks. However, for non-trivial features, such as animations and controlling object states during the story, these latter approaches do not provide high-level abstractions and require the authors to have technical skills.

Independently on how their final content is deployed, interactive children's eBooks usually share a common structure and use similar features. In this work, we aim at extracting those features and propose a model, named Fábulas—the Portuguese word for *fables*—, that allows authors to create interactive children's eBooks declaratively. Such a higher-level model can then be converted to one of the currently available eBook standard formats or can be directly interpreted by a Fábulas player. The Fábulas model is instantiated as an extension to HTML5 and interpreted in JavaScript, following a polyfill approach, which means it works seamlessly in current modern web browsers.

---

[1]https://helpx.adobe.com/indesign/using/dynamic-pdf-documents.html

The model discussed in this paper is part of the Fábulas project, which aims at providing an end-to-end platform for writers and educators to create and deliver interactive enhanced children's eBooks, and for children to consume those eBooks. Figure 1 schematically shows the Fábulas platform. The Fábulas platform permeates the three classical hypermedia environments: *authoring, storage, and exhibition*. Thus, it targets both authors and readers of children's eBooks. Authors interact with the authoring environment using graphical or textual authoring tools to create the eBooks. The eBooks are stored in a document format that conforms to the Fábulas model, and that can be published to the server. The reader uses the Fábulas player to search, read, and interact with the eBooks. This way, the Fábulas document model has to be easily handled by all of those three environments: authoring tools, distribution servers, and players.

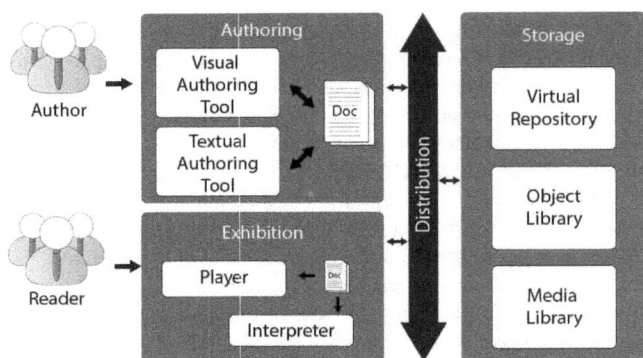

Figure 1: Overview of the Fábulas platform.

The remainder of the paper is mainly concerned with the requirements and the model used to create children's eBooks on the Fabulas platform. Section 2 discusses the main requirements for enhanced children's eBooks. Section 3 discusses the related work and compare them to the Fábulas model. Section 4 presents the Fábulas conceptual model. Section 5 details the implementation and usage of the Fábulas model, highlighting its main features through the development of a complete children's story. Finally, Section 6 brings our main conclusions and future work.

2 REQUIREMENTS FOR ENHANCED CHILDREN'S EBOOKS

To define the requirements of the Fábulas model, we have conducted a literature review on works trying to define similar requirements. Then, to validate and expand the literature review, we proceeded with a field study in which we analyzed current enhanced children's eBooks available on the Web and in popular application stores. From the literature review and the field study, we extracted the most common features on enhanced children's eBooks, and used them as the basis to the proposed model (detailed in Section 4).

From the literature review, more specifically from [6, 12, 14, 27, 30] we have extracted the following features:

- **Embedded media**, such as audio, video, and image, can be very helpful in engaging children on stories. Audio, for instance, can be used in different ways: additional effects

(e.g. synchronized with the presentation, or as a response to a user interaction), background music, narration, and voice recording [12]. In special, **audio narration (or read-aloud) feature** can be used to improve children's vocabulary and can increase comprehension of the story [14];

- **Narration overlays**, i.e., highlighting the text synchronized with the narration, can also be useful, mainly for children that are still learning to read;

- **Animations and in-page interactions**, when applied in the right way, can enrich the children's eBooks and help to capture the attention of children [26]. In special, **reactive animations** may be interesting to present visual cues as a response to user interaction;

- **Alternative story paths (or non-linear narrative)** allows children to feel empowered, and engage them by making their decisions important for the story progression. It also offers greater re-playability and stimulates exploration and curiosity;

- **Auto-play narrative** can be found in some types of children's eBooks and allow the automatic reproduction of the narrative (with or without audio narration);

- **Zoom** is another important feature, which offers children the possibility to take a closer look into details. It can be both **page zoom**, which allows children to see image details or interact with smaller enhanced elements, or **text-only zoom**, which allows increasing/decreasing the text size;

- **Single-page view** is preferred for interactive children's eBooks, whereas in other eBooks it is common to show two pages at a time;

- **Orientation rotation** of eBooks usually present two orientation options, landscape or portrait, and can respond to the position of the device or be fixed in the code.

In the field study, the eBooks were gathered from the Annenberg Learner [2] website and the book apps from Google Play [3] and Apple Store [4]. The criteria we used to select the eBooks in the field study were:

- it should be targeted for children in the age from 6- to 12-years-old;

- it should be an enhanced eBook, which means it should have interactivity, embedded media, or animation features;

- it should have at least 1000 downloads in the respective App stores;

- it should have some feature that was not found in the other selected children's eBooks.

Table 1 summarizes the features we have found in the analyzed eBooks. Those features are presented from the point of view of developers. And, they can be used as requirements to guide the development of authoring models and tools for interactive children's eBooks domain. Thus, this domain knowledge is used in the next section as guidelines governing the creation of the Fábulas conceptual model.

[2]https://www.learner.org/interactives/story/cinderella.html
[3]https://play.google.com/store/apps
[4]https://itunes.apple.com/

Table 1: Features found on the analyzed enhanced children's eBooks.

Features	Elements of a story (Cinderella) [5]	Tales with Gigi (Cinderella) [6]	Classic Fairy Tales (Cinderella) [7]	Livro mágico/Magic Book (O galinho Zé) [8]	The Jungle Book [9]	iStoryBooks (Seeing beyond the obvious) [10]	The Little Mermaid [11]	Alice for the iPad [12]
Narrative								
alternative story path				x				
multi-language support		x	x		x		x	
narration	x	x	x		x	x	x	
narration overlay						x	x	
auto-play	x	x	x			x	x	
zoom		x				x	x	x
Single page view	x	x	x		x	x		x
Orientation rotation*	l	l	l	l	l	p	l	p
Embedded media								
image	x	x	x	x	x	x	x	x
audio	x	x	x		x	x	x	x
text	x	x	x	x	x	x	x	x
video								
animation	x	x			x		x	x
Transitions								
page transitions		x	x		x	x	x	x
media transitions	x	x			x		x	x
Interaction forms								
click/touch/gestures	x	x	x	x	x	x	x	x
accelerometer								x
Widgets								
games	x	x	x				x	
quizzes	x							

* Orientation: p = portrait; l = landscape.

3 RELATED WORK

Since the 90's, there has been much effort on creating models and standards for interactive multimedia presentations [22]. Some of the most prominent technologies are SMIL [5], NCL [29], MPEG-4 XMT [18, 25], X3D [11], SVG [13], and HTML5 [8]. Nowadays, HTML5 is becoming the ubiquitous solution and is available in almost every device. The research and concepts developed by the other mentioned document models, however, are still useful for defining many types of interactive multimedia applications, and today most of them can be supported in modern web browsers through a polyfill approach. In such an approach, HTML5 can be extended and players for other multimedia languages can be implemented on top of the browser using JavaScript and APIs such as WebGL [20], WebSockets [16], etc. Current examples of those solutions are SMIL TimeSheets [7], Time Style Sheets [19], Web-NCL [24], and X3DOM [3]. In this paper, we follow a similar path by defining the Fábulas model and implementing it so that we can reuse the browser infrastructure and extend HTML5 with the concepts of our application domain.

One could argue that for our application domain, authors could directly use HTML5 (plus JavaScript) itself or one of the other document formats discussed above (plus some script language). Indeed, this is true, and most of the features needed by enhanced eBooks can be modeled in lower-level approaches using one of the above document models together with a scripting language. However, those document models are too general and the abstractions they provide are not always closely related to the concepts on interactive children's stories. Different from those general document formats for interactive multimedia presentations, our goal is the design of a minimal and restrictive model closely related to our application domain, i.e., interactive enhanced children's eBooks. (Meixner and Kosch, for instance, follow a similar path for the application domain of hypervideos [23].) After modeling the application using Fábulas, authors can then use a player that natively interpret the Fábulas specification or convert it to one of the lower level document model for multimedia presentations.

eBooks can be seen as a specialized class of interactive multimedia presentations. In its basic form, an eBook is only a sequence of pages, each page containing text and possibly fixed positioned figures. As aforementioned, more advanced eBooks, however, may also provide interactivity and non-linearity, embed other media types such as audio and video, and support animations, quizzes, games, etc. As previously mentioned, examples of eBook formats include PDF, MOBI, and ePub3.

PDF started as a binary format mainly for print fixed-layout documents, including only texts, fonts, and graphics. PDF, however, has evolved to support interactive elements such as annotation, form fields, audio, video, flash animation, and interactive 3D objects. This format is known as *Rich Media* or *Dynamic Media* PDF [17].

ePub is the open source standard for eBooks maintained by the *International Digital Publishing Forum* (IDPF)[13]. Different from PDF, the ePub 3.0 also support eBooks with flow layout, allowing that a page can be adapted to different devices and reading softwares. The current version of ePub, named ePub 3.0, is based on HTML5 and it allows to use multimedia objects (e.g. `<audio>` and `<video>`) features that were not supported in previous versions. The ePub 3.0 specification is divided in four main parts: *EPUB Publications*, *EPUB Content Documents*, *EPUB Open Container Format* e *EPUB Media Overlays*. From those, *Media Overlays* allows synchronizing the eBook text with additional audio. These features are based on the Daisy Talking books [10] standard, which was first created to support accessible books.

Some of the above eBook formats when extended with imperative languages—e.g., ePub3 is extended through JavaScript—can support the requirements of children's eBooks discussed in Section 2. However, we believe that for some recurrent structures on interactive children's eBooks—e.g., animation, in-page interactions, and reactive animations—there should be high-level declarative constructs, which are currently not present in those formats. The Fábulas model try to fill this gap by providing higher-level concepts that are close to the interactive enhanced children's eBook domain. The concepts proposed by the Fábulas model can be integrated in the general eBook formats above, or an interactive story specified in Fábulas can be converted to the lower-level eBook format standards. The next section details the Fábulas model.

4 FÁBULAS

Figure 2 presents the Fábulas conceptual model. The root concept of the Fábulas model is the *Fable*. A Fable represents a whole interactive story and is structured as one or more *Chapters*. Each *Chapter* may contain one or more *Pages*. Also, a *Fable* may contain no chapter, in which case it is composed only of *Pages*, or may be composed of a combination of both *Chapters* and *Pages*. Each *Page* of the story can be composed of different *media objects* and *agents*. The supported media objects are the conventional media objects found in HTML5, such as image, video, and audio. Also, as will be discussed in Section 5, the supported media types can be extended through a well-defined API. For instance, by default, the Fábulas model already supports an *animation* media object that is composed of a sequence of images that must be presented during a specific duration. An agent allows grouping multiple media object (and other agents) together with their behavior, as a reusable component.

The behavior of the media objects and the nonlinear narrative flow are defined through *Event-Condition-Action* (ECA) rules [21],

---

[13]http://idpf.org

i.e., each rule defines that when an event is detected, the system evaluates a condition, and if the condition is satisfied, the system execute the action(s). The *events* that can be used to trigger actions are the transitions on media objects or agent states, or user generated events, such as touching an object. The condition part may test if a property (a global, chapter, page, or agent property) is true. Finally, the supported actions may change the state of the presentation (e.g., changing the current page) or the state of media objects or agents.

The remainder of this section details the main concepts above, specifically: *media objects* and *agents*, and the supported *properties*, *events*, and *actions*.

4.1 Media objects and Agents

As previously mentioned, each *Page* may be composed of multiple media objects (e.g., text, images, video, etc.). Moreover, an important concept that differs Fábulas from related work is the *Agent* concept. In the Fábulas model, agents are a mechanism to encapsulate the media presentation objects and their associated behavior in the same object. Agents are inspired by the NCM (Nested Context Model) [28] event state machine. However, NCM has the same event state machine to control all medias. In Fábulas model, an agent can define its states and the transitions between them. The agent state machine is defined by a 5-tuple $SM = <S, B, s_0, \Sigma, \delta>$, where:

- S is a finite nonempty set of states
- B is the base composition
- s_0 is the initial state
- Σ is a set of events
- $\delta : S \times \Sigma \rightarrow S$ is the transition function

Each element of the 5-tuple has its corresponding tags in the Fábulas model. Table 2 shows the equivalence between the elements in the 5-tuple above and the elements in the Fábulas model.

Table 2: Equivalence between the agent state machine and the elements in the Fábulas model.

Agent SM	Fábulas model (example)	Description
S	`<state id="S">...</state>`	definition of a state, child of `<agent/>`
B	`<img src="..."/>`	media objects children of the agent
s_0	`<state id="s_0">...</state>`	first state defined in `<agent>`
Σ	`<on-touch>...</on-touch>`	events are children of an `<agent>` or `<state>`
$\delta : S \times \Sigma \rightarrow S$	`<changeto target="S"/>`	child of `<on-*/>`

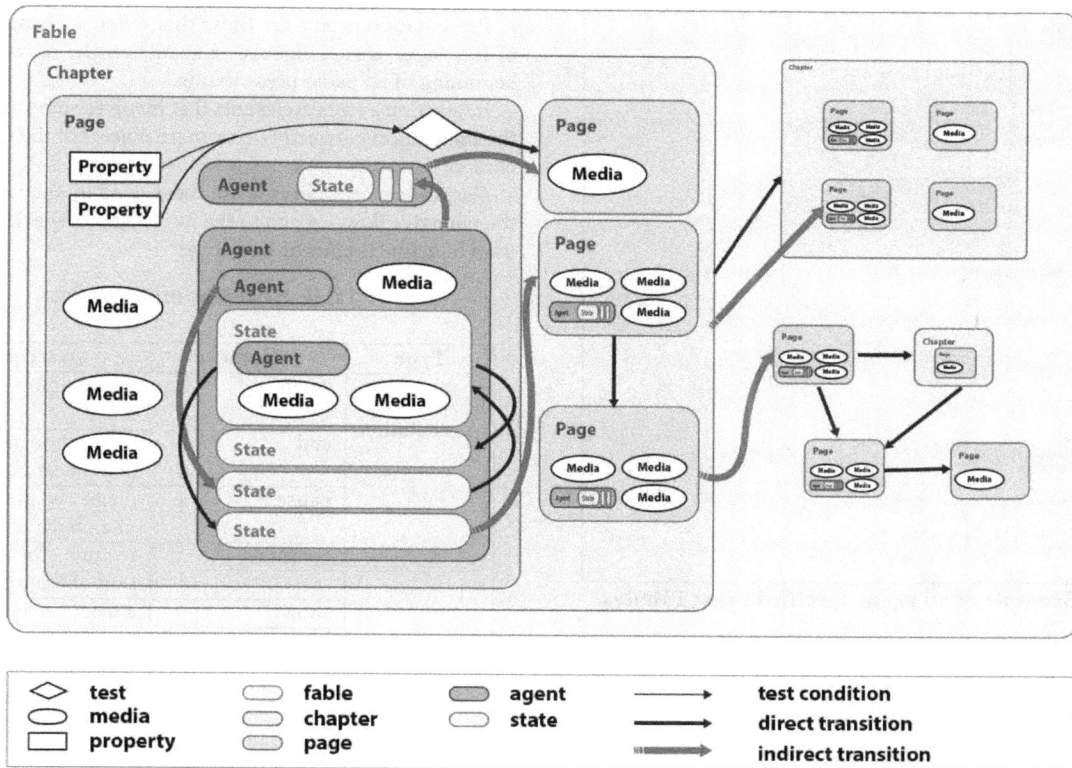

Figure 2: The Fábulas conceptual model for developing interactive children's eBook.

An agent state can group media objects and other agents and handle events emitted within its own composition or global events, e.g., user-generated events. The basic state of an agent is composed of the media objects defined as its direct descendent. At execution time, those elements are part of all the other presentation states. By default, the initial state of an agent is the first one defined by an `<agent>` element. The state of an agent can be transitioned by the *changeto* action, informing the next state.

Figure 3 shows an agent representing a "locked door" containing an internal "switch" agent, which, thanks to its self-contained definition, can be reused in different situations. Listing 1 shows a possible implementation of the agents in Figure 3. The "switch" agent (lines 2–13) and the event observation `<on-capture>` (lines 31–33) compose the basic state of the agent "door-with-lock". The "switch" agent contains two states "locked" and "unlocked". It starts in the "locked" state and, when clicked by the user, it goes to the "unlocked" state, and emits a custom event named "unlock" (lines 5–8). This custom event is emitted in the scope of the page in which

the agent is inserted. The initial state of the "doorwithlock" agent is named "locked-door" (lines 15–17) and is composed of one image only. When the event "unlock" is emitted this agent goes from the "locked-door" to the "unlocked" state (lines 18–23). When the user touches the agent in "locked-door" state, it goes to the "open" state (lines 24–29). And, if the user touches the agent in "open" state, the agent emits a *end_page* event (line 27) asking the system to go to the next page.

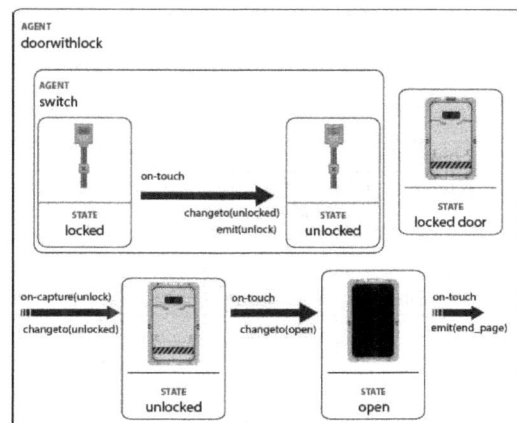

Figure 3: Agent example of a locked door.

[7] https://www.learner.org/interactives/story/cinderella.html
[8] https://play.google.com/store/apps/dev?id=6290881108498971005
[9] https://play.google.com/store/apps/details?id=es.cuentuvere.cuentosclasicos
[10] https://play.google.com/store/apps/details?id=br.com.fabricadesonhos.applivromagico
[11] https://play.google.com/store/apps/details?id=air.com.goodbeans.JungleBookStoryBook
[12] https://play.google.com/store/apps/details?id=com.infomarvel.istorybooks
[13] https://play.google.com/store/apps/details?id=com.storytoys.TheLittleMermaid.GooglePlay

23

```
1   <agent id="doorwithlock">
2     <agent id="switch">
3       <state id="locked">
4         <img src="switch-locked.png"/>
5         <on-touch>
6           <changeto target="unlocked"/>
7           <emit event="unlock" scope="page"/>
8         </on-touch>
9       </state>
10      <state id="unlocked">
11        <img src="switch-unlocked.png"/>
12      </state>
13    </agent>
14
15    <state id="locked-door">
16      <img src="locked-door.png"/>
17    </state>
18    <state id="unlocked">
19      <img src="locked-door.png"/>
20      <on-touch>
21        <changeto target="open"/>
22      </on-touch>
23    </state>
24    <state id="open">
25      <img src="open-door.png"/>
26      <on-touch>
27        <emit event="end_page"/>
28      </on-touch>
29    </state>
30
31    <on-capture event="unlock">
32      <changeto target="unlocked"/>
33    </on-capture>
34  </agent>
```

Listing 1: Example of an agent specified using Fábulas.

4.2 Properties

Pages, media objects, and agents may have a set of associated properties. The supported properties are sensitive to the object type. For instance, audio media objects have a volume property, which is not present in purely graphical media object, such as images. The properties are grouped into *system*, *object*, *physics*, and *user-defined* properties. System properties represent global features of the system, such as *lightLevel* and *soundLevel*. System properties can be inherited based on the scope of a composition, e.g., the *soundLevel* set for one page does not interfere with the volume set for other pages. Object properties directly define the presentation characteristics of the media objects or agents, e.g., width, height, transparency, etc.. Physics properties assign characteristics that can define the behavior of media objects when interacting with the enviroment; through pyshics properties, it is possible to simulate weigth, collision, and mobility for objects (see Table 3). Finally, the user-defined properties are custom-made properties defined by the author, and can be used as the author needs.

Table 3: List of the physics properties currently supported on Fábulas.

type	Name	Description
physics	solid	two *solid* media objects generate collision events when their borders touch
	heavy	add heavy mobility to the media object
	light	add light mobility to the media object
	draggable	user can drag the media object

4.3 Events

The default events supported by Fábulas (summarized on Table 4) can be divided into: *presentation* events, *interaction* events, and *narrative control* events.

Presentation events are those that reflect a change in the state of the pages, media objects, or agents on the narrative, e.g., the beginning of an audio presentation.

Interaction events are events that involves some user activity or the interaction between two or more objects of the narrative, e.g., click or gestures.

Narrative control events are those used by the user to control the narrative flow, e.g., go to the next page; in special, they can be used to define nonlinear narratives.

Table 4: Fábulas model events.

Type	Name	Description
presentation	begin	the begining of a media object
	end	the end or natural end of a media object
	pause	pause the presentation of a media object
	continue	resume the presentation of the media
	show	a media object is shown
	hide	a media object is hidden
interaction	touch*	user touches the media object or agent
	drag	user drags a media object or agent
	drop	user drops the media object or agent
	swipe**	user performs a swipe gesture on the screen
	tilt**	user performs a tilt on the device
	pinch**	user performs a pinch gesture on the screen
	collision***	collision between media objects
control	capture	capture custom events
	end_page	end of the presentation of the current page
	end_chapter	end of the presentation of the current chapter
	the_end	end of the history
	previous_page	user moved to previous page
	previous_chapter	user moved to the previous chapter

* equivalent to the mouse click
** depends on the device
*** needs the property solid

By default, a Fábulas player presents the pages in the order they appear in the story definition, which eases the development of linear narratives. By capturing narrative control events, it is possible to define additional navigation rules through the ECA paradigm. The default ordering of the pages, and the navigation rules allow authors to create alternative paths on the presentation flow, and to create more complex narratives. For instance, the `previous_page` event prescribes that the current page must be ended and the one that was being previously rendered must be presented again. The `previous_page` events works as a stack that saves the ordering in which the pages were visited, according to the followed narrative flow. In the first page the `previous_page` event has no effect.

4.4 Actions

Actions change the state of the objects in the narrative. Table 5 shows the actions supported by the Fábulas model.

Table 5: The actions supported by the Fábulas model.

Type	Name	Description
presentation	start	starts the presentation of a media object
	stop	finishes the presentation of a media object
	pause	pauses a media objects
	resume	resumes the presentation of a previously paused media object
	show	shows a media object
	hide	hides a media object
control	emit	emits a custom user event
	changeto	changes the *state* of an agent, a chapter, or a page
	set	changes the value of a property

The action `emit` fires an internal event to the execution machine. This event may be used as a trigger to other actions in other parts of the fable. The author can inform the scope for the propagation of the event, as one of the values: *fable*, *chapter*, or *page*. The *fable*, *chapter*, and *page* scopes, respectively, refers to all the elements in the fable, in the current chapter, or in the current page will be notified of the event. The agents, even those that are not currently active (such as agents in other pages, not presented yet) can be notified of events.

`Start` and `stop` actions can be used for all types of media. `Pause` and `resume` are actions usually applied to continuous media types, such as, video, audio, and animations. The `show` and `hide` actions are aimed mainly for graphic media object. The `hide` action, for instance, can hide temporal media objects such as videos, but it does not interrupt its execution. In the case of other media types, such as images, it presents the same result of the `start` and `stop` actions.

5 INTEGRATION OF FÁBULAS ON THE WEB

As aforementioned, the Fábulas model is currently integrated into the Web using a polyfill approach. The polyfill approach is especially useful for rapid prototyping because it relies on the multimedia execution machine of the browser, only extending what is needed, with the help of JavaScript libraries. In our implementation we use Angular.js [1]. Angular.js has an HTML compiler that allows the developer to define new syntax for default HTML5 elements or create new elements. Table 6 shows the elements we have created (or modified) for the implementation of the Fábulas model on HTML5.

Table 6: The elements of the Fábulas model.

Element	parent	attributes*
fable	-	id, src, width, height, bg-img, bg-sound, bg-sound-rep
chapter	fable	id, src, bg-img, bg-sound, bg-sound-rep, trans-in, trans-out
page	fable, chapter	id, src, bg-img, bg-sound, bg-sound-rep, trans-in, trans-out
property	fable, chapter, page	name, value
img**	page, div, agent, state	left, top, right, bottom, width, height
div**	page, div, agent, state	left, top, right, bottom, width, height
p**	page, div, agent, state	left, top, right, bottom, width, height
span**	page, p, div, agent, state	-
audio**	page, agent, state	-
video**	page, agent, state	left, top, right, bottom, width, height
animation	page, agent, state	id, left, top, right, bottom, width, height
agent	page, agent, state	id, left, top, right, bottom, width, height, draggable, heavy, light, solid
state	agent	id
on-(event)***	fable, chapter, page, agent	event****, target, test, delay
(action)***	on-(event)	event****, target, delay, value

* all elements contains the basics HTML attributes
** based on the HTML elements
*** event/action name
**** in case the capture event or emit action

In the Angular.js nomenclature, a *directive* is defined as a behavior that must be triggered when specific HTML constructs are found during the building process. These directives can be elements, attributes, class names, or comments.

As an example of defining a directive in Angular.js, let us take the source code on Listing 2 and Listing 3.

Listing 2 shows a code snippet containing a `<div>` element with the attributes *left*, *top*, *width*, and *height*, which are redefined by our implementation. Those attributes together with the *right* and *bottom* attributes (also redefined by our implementation) specify the position of a media object or agent.

Listing 3 shows the JavaScript code with the *left* attribute directive. (The other attributes directives are similar, so they are omitted here.) By defining that directive, when the page is loading, all the elements that have a *left* attribute will have the behavior described by the function of the *link* parameter (line 4). The type of the directive (element, attribute, class name, or comment) is constrained by the parameter *restrict* (line 3). In the example, the code affects any element that contain a *left* attribute. More complex combination can also be created using JavaScript functions, such as, "all the elements with tagname *x* that have an attribute *y*", and so on.

```
1   <div class="text" id="title" width="250" height="50" top="50"
        left="50">
2     The Little Knight
3   </div>
```

Listing 2: Example showing the usage of the attributes *left*, *top*, *width*, *height*.

```
1   fablePlayer.directive('left', ['$document', function(
        $document) {
2     return {
3       restrict: 'A',
4       link: function (scope, element, attr) {
5         element.css({
6           left: attr.left + 'px'
7         });
8       }
9     };
10  }]);
```

Listing 3: Definition of the Angular.js directive for the attribute *left*.

Our implementation takes advantage of the above-discussed mechanism provided by Angular.js to define all the elements and attributes of Table 6. This way, we can seamlessly integrate the Fábulas concepts into HTML5 webpages. From the authors viewpoint, they can use the Fábulas elements directly into HTML5 documents. To exemplify this integration, the next subsection discusses a concrete interactive story using web integrated Fábulas model.

5.1 Usage example

The interactive story discussed in this section, named "The Little Knight", is about a knight who, upon receiving the news of a friend with whom he had long lost contact, sets out on a journey to try to help him. Figure 4 shows the story flow of "The Little Knight", and the linear order in which the pages are defined in the story. The story unfolds in five pages. Four pages are part of the main story, and the last one is an alternative path. The main features contained in the story are images, audio, user interaction, navigation, and conditional tests.

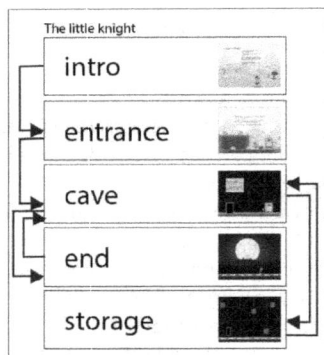

Figure 4: The story flow of "The Little Knight".

Listing 4 shows the source code of the required header and of the first page of the story, named "intro".

Since we use Angular.js, first, we need to import the library, the player code, and the default style for the application (lines 6–8). It is also needed to add the *ng-app* and *ng-controller* attributes on

the page to elements that will contain the <fable> element. In the example, they were placed in the <html> and <body>, respectively.

On the first page (lines 14–32) it is possible to note some of the Fábulas elements and attributes. For instance, the *bg-img* and *bg-sound* attributes on the <page> elements represent the background image and the ambient music for the page, respectively. For simple media types—such as text, image, audio, and video—the standard HTML tags are used. Moreover, all the elements can be stylized by CSS stylesheets, as in standard HTML5 pages. Besides simple media objects, this first page also defines an agent, the "board" agent (lines 17–24), which represents a board that, when touched by the user (<on-touch>, fires an event (<emit>) that ends the presentation of the current page and advances to the next ones (lines 20–22).

```
1   <!DOCTYPE html>
2   <html lang="en" ng-app="fablePlayer">
3     <head>
4       <meta charset="UTF-8">
5       <title>The little knight</title>
6       <script src="angular.min.js"></script>
7       <script src="fablePlayer.js"></script>
8       <link rel="stylesheet" href="fable-player.css">
9       <link rel="stylesheet" href="little_knight.css">
10    </head>
11    <body ng-controller="fablePlayerController">
12      <fable width="800" height="600">
13        <property name="hasantidote" value="false"></property>
14        <page id="intro" bg-img="BG.png" bg-sound="audio1.mp3">
15          <div class="text" id="title" width="250" height="50"
                top="50" left="50">O pequeno Cavaleiro</div>
16          <img src="char1.png" height="180" width="110"
                bottom="180" left="440"/>
17          <agent id="board" top="370" right="140" width="105"
                height="110">
18            <state>
19              <img src="board.png"/>
20              <on-touch>
21                <emit event="end_page"/>
22              </on-touch>
23            </state>
24          </agent>

26          <div width="200" height="300" top="100" left="300">
27            <p>Once upon a time there was a small knight who
                  received a letter from a friend.</p>
28            <p>He was very very very surprised, because this
                  friend was gone for years.</p>
29            <p>Except the news on the letter was not very good.
                  His friend had contracted a mysterious illness
                  and needed help to get the cure.</p>
30            <p>As fast as he could, he went to meet this
                  friend.</p>
31          </div>
32        </page>
33        ...
34      </fable>
35
36    </body>
37  </html>
```

Listing 4: Example of a story in an HTML page.

The second page, "entrance", is mainly composed of agents: one "board", one "door", one "bush with the key", three "bushes without a key" agents.

Listing 5 shows the part of code of the "entrance" page that contains the "board" agent. When this agent is touched by the user, it shows a warning with a tip about where he will find the key to open the door. Lines 3–6 show a simple animation of the board while it is in state (<state>) "swinging". When the board is in the "swinging" state and the user touches it (<on-touch>), it transitions to the "warning" state. After 3 seconds—due to the *delay* in the *changeto* action (line 9)—or when it is touched again (lines 17–18) it returns to "swinging" state.

Listing 6 shows the source code of the "bush with the key" agent and Figure 5 schematically shows its behavior, and how it interacts with the "door" agent. The main difference between the "bush with the key" agent, and the three others "bushes without a key" is the internal "key" agent (lines 11–19). When the "key" agent is touched, it emits the event "gotKey". The "gotKey" event is captured by the "door" agent.

```
1   ...
2   <page id="entrance">
3     <agent id="placa" top="510" right="230" height="50"
               width="50">
4       <state id="rebolando">
5         <animation dur="0.5" rep="indefined">
6           <img src="board1.png" height="50" width="50"/>
7           <img src="board2.png" height="50" width="50"/>
8         </animation>
9         <on-touch>
10          <changeto target="warning"/>
11          <changeto delay="3" target="animation"/>
12        </on-touch>
13      </state>
14      <state id="aviso">
15        <img src="board1.png" height="50" width="50"/>
16        <div class="warning">
17          The key is on the bushs.
18        </div>
19        <on-touch>
20          <changeto target="animation"/>
21        </on-touch>
22      </state>
23    </agent>
24    ...
25  </page>
26  ...
```

Listing 5: Code of the "board" agent, in the "entrance" page.

```
1   <page id="entrance">
2     ...
3     <agent id="bush" top="310" left="50">
4       <state id="closed">
5         <img src="bush.png" height="46" width="73"/>
6         <on-touch>
7           <changeto target="open"/>
8         </on-touch>
9       </state>
10      <state id="open">
11        <img src="openbush.png" height="50" width="50"/>
12        <agent id="key" top="0" left="10">
13          <state>
14            <img src="key.png" height="30" width="30"/>
15            <on-touch>
16              <emit event="gotkey" scope="page"/>
17              <stop target="key"/>
18            </on-touch>
19          </state>
20        </agent>
21      </state>
22    </agent>
23    ...
24  </page>
```

Listing 6: Source code of the bush that contains the key, in the "entrance" page.

Finally, still on the "entrance" page, Listing 7 shows the source code of the "door" agent. Lines 6–8 defines what happens when the event *on-capture* happens: the agent emits the "gotKey" event, and then transitions to the "unlocked" state. When the agent is in the "unlocked" state and it is touched (<on-touch>) the door emits the event end_page, that informs that the presentation of the current page must be finished and the next page must be shown.

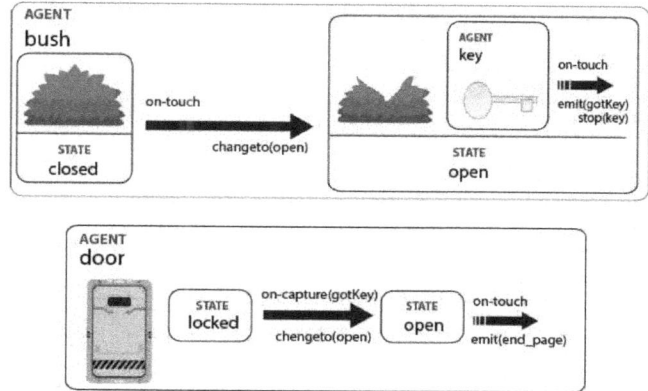

Figure 5: Agent "bush" and agent "key" interacting with agent "door".

```
1   ...
2   <page id="entrance">
3     ...
4     <agent id="door" bottom="50" right="100" height="150"
               width="100">
5       <img src="DoorLocked.png" height="150" width="100"/>
6       <state id="locked">
7         <on-capture event="gotkey">
8           <changeto target="open"/>
9         </on-capture>
10      </state>
11      <state id="open">
12        <on-touch test="hasKey">
13          <emit event="end_page"/>
14        </on-touch>
15      </state>
16    </agent>
17    ...
18  </page>
19  ...
```

Listing 7: Source code of the "door" agent, in the "entrance" page.

In the third page, named "cave", the reader can choose between two different paths on the story: the first one goes to the "storage" page; and, the second goes to the "end" page. Listing 8 shows the two agents, representing the two doors, that the reader can use them to choose his path. The "storage-path" event (line 7) is captured by the page (lines 37–39) that then changes to the "storage" page. The "endDoor" agent (lines 11–35) issues the event end_page (line 29) that closes the current page and goes to the next one in the sequence, i.e., the "end" page.

In the "storage" page—which source code is not shown here mainly for brevity, since, in principle, it uses similar contructs already disccussed—the reader can find the antidote for the friend of the knight in one of the three "boxes" agents. Those agents works very similarly to the "bushes with/without the/a key". When the user finds this antidote he changes the "hasAntidote" variable to *true*. In the "end" page, the "hasAntidote" variable is tested, and if its value is *true*, then, the friend of the knight will be cured, and the story ends; otherwise, the reader has to go back to look for the antidote on the "storage" page.

```
1   <page id="cave" bg-img="bg3.png">
2     ...
3     <agent id="storageDoor" bottom="30" left="100" height="150"
          width="100">
4       <state>
5         <img src="DoorOpen.png" height="150" width="100"/>
6         <on-touch>
7           <emit event="storage-path" scope="page"/>
8         </on-touch>
9       </state>
10    </agent>
11    <agent id="endDoor" bottom="30" right="100" height="150"
          width="100">
12      <img src="DoorLocked.png" height="150" width="100"/>
13      <agent id="switch">
14        <img src="button.png" left="-30" width="20" height="70"
            bottom="0"/>
15        <state id="locked">
16          <on-touch>
17            <emit event="unlock" scope="page"/>
18            <changeto target="unlocked"/>
19          </on-touch>
20        </state>
21        <state id="unlocked">
22        </state>
23      </agent>
24      <state id="locked">
25      </state>
26      <state id="open">
27        <img src="DoorOpen.png" height="150" width="100"/>
28        <on-touch>
29          <emit event="end_page"/>
30        </on-touch>
31      </state>
32      <on-capture event="unlock">
33        <changeto target="open"/>
34      </on-capture>
35    </agent>
36
37    <on-capture event="storage-path">
38      <changeto target="storage-path"/>
39    </on-capture>
40  </page>
```

Listing 8: Source code of the "cave" page.

6 CONCLUSION

In this work, we discussed the main requirements of interactive eBooks for children and we presented the Fábulas conceptual model for allowing authors to create them. The proposed conceptual model is instantiated in XML as an extension to HTML5 and following a polyfill approach, which allows a seamless integration with modern web browsers. Besides presenting the elements of the XML instantiation of Fábulas model, we also show a complete example that uses the main features of the model—in special, animation, object states control, and nonlinear narrative definition.

Although our current implementation, discussed in Section 5, is complete enough for supporting many types of enhanced interactive eBooks for children, it still does not fully support all the requirements discussed in Section 2 through high-level abstractions. Even though those requirements can be currently achieved by a lower-level approach using JavaScript, we also plan to provide abstractions for them in the future. In special, the following requirements will be the focus of extensions on the model: narration and narration overlay (e.g., using the media overlay from ePub3); multi-language support; complex animations; and, widgets.

Other future works include: the definition and formalization of guidelines and a complete process for authoring enhanced children's eBooks; and the integration of the concepts of the Fábulas model (e.g., the concept of agents) into the ePub3 document format. Finally, as previously mentioned, the model discussed in this paper is part of a bigger project that includes all the steps in the creation, distribution, and consumption of interactive eBooks for children. Thus, another future work, already initiated, is the development of an authoring tool based on the Fábulas model, which will allow authors to create and upload eBooks with a graphical authoring tool, easily reusing components developed by other authors.

REFERENCES

[1] Angularjs: Developer guide. https://docs.angularjs.org/guide. Accessed: 2017-04-10.
[2] Mobi. https://wiki.mobileread.com/wiki/MOBI. Accessed: 2017-04-10.
[3] J. Behr, P. Eschler, Y. Jung, and M. Zöllner. X3dom: A dom-based html5/x3d integration model. In *Proceedings of the 14th International Conference on 3D Web Technology*, Web3D '09, pages 127–135, New York, NY, USA, 2009. ACM.
[4] S. M. Benedetti. Ebook interativo: hipermídia no livro eletrônico. 2016.
[5] D. C. Bulterman and L. W. Rutledge. *SMIL 3.0: Flexible Multimedia for Web, Mobile Devices and Daisy Talking Books*. Springer Publishing Company, Incorporated, 2008.
[6] A. G. Bus, Z. K. Takacs, and C. A. Kegel. Affordances and limitations of electronic storybooks for young children's emergent literacy. *Developmental Review*, 35:79 – 97, 2015. Special Issue: Living in the "Net" Generation: Multitasking, Learning, and Development.
[7] F. Cazenave, V. Quint, and C. Roisin. Timesheets.js: When smil meets html5 and css3. In *Proceedings of the 11th ACM Symposium on Document Engineering*, DocEng '11, pages 43–52, New York, NY, USA, 2011. ACM.
[8] J. Choi, Y. Lee, and K. Kim. Html5 based interactive e-book reader. *International Journal of Software Engineering and Its Applications*, 8(2):67–74, 2014.
[9] G. Conboy, M. Garrish, M. Gylling, W. McCoy, M. Makoto, and D. Weck. EPUB 3.1 overview. Informational document, International Digital Publishing Forum (IDPF), Jan. 2017. http://www.idpf.org/epub3/latest/overview.
[10] D. Consortium et al. Daisy/niso standard. ansi/niso z39.86 specifications for the digital talking book, April 2012.
[11] L. Daly and D. Brutzman. X3d: Extensible 3d graphics standard [standards in a nutshell]. *IEEE Signal Processing Magazine*, 24(6):130–135, Nov 2007.
[12] K. M. Doty. Designing for interactive ebooks: an evaluation of effective interaction elements in children's ebooks, 2015.
[13] J. Ferraiolo, F. Jun, and D. Jackson. Scalable vector graphics (svg) 1.1 specification, w3c recommendation 14 january 2003. *URL: http://www.w3.org/TR/SVGll*, 2003.
[14] S. Grimshaw, N. Dungworth, C. McKnight, and A. Morris. Electronic books: Children's reading and comprehension. *British Journal of Educational Technology*, 38(4):583–599, 2007.
[15] M. Hart. *Project gutenberg*. Project Gutenberg, 1971.
[16] I. Hickson. The websocket api. *W3C Working Draft WD-websockets-20110929*, September, 2011.
[17] A. S. Incorporated. Pdf reference, sixth edition: Adobe portable document format version 1.7., November 2006.
[18] M. Kim, S. Wood, and L.-T. Cheok. Extensible mpeg-4 textual format (xmt). In *Proceedings of the 2000 ACM Workshops on Multimedia*, MULTIMEDIA '00, pages 71–74, New York, NY, USA, 2000. ACM.
[19] R. Laiola Guimarães, D. Bulterman, P. Cesar, and J. Jansen. Synchronizing web documents with style. In *Proceedings of the 20th Brazilian Symposium on Multimedia and the Web*, WebMedia '14, pages 151–158, New York, NY, USA, 2014. ACM.
[20] C. Marrin. Webgl specification. *Khronos WebGL Working Group*, 2011.
[21] D. McCarthy and U. Dayal. The architecture of an active database management system. *SIGMOD Rec.*, 18(2):215–224, June 1989.
[22] B. Meixner. Hypervideos and interactive multimedia presentations. *ACM Comput. Surv.*, 50(1):9:1–9:34, Mar. 2017.
[23] B. Meixner and H. Kosch. Interactive non-linear video: Definition and xml structure. In *Proceedings of the 2012 ACM Symposium on Document Engineering*, DocEng '12, pages 49–58, New York, NY, USA, 2012. ACM.
[24] E. L. Melo, C. C. Viel, C. A. C. Teixeira, A. C. Rondon, D. d. P. Silva, D. G. Rodrigues, and E. C. Silva. Webncl: A web-based presentation machine for multimedia documents. In *Proceedings of the 18th Brazilian Symposium on Multimedia and the Web*, WebMedia '12, pages 403–410, New York, NY, USA, 2012. ACM.
[25] F. C. Pereira and T. Ebrahimi. *The MPEG-4 book*. Prentice Hall Professional, 2002.
[26] E. Rhodes and G. Walsh. Recommendations for developing technologies that encourage reading practices among children in families with low-literate adults. pages 125–136, 2016.
[27] B. Sargeant. What is an ebook? what is a book app? and why should we care? an analysis of contemporary digital picture books. *Children's Literature in Education*, 46(4):454–466, 2015.
[28] L. F. G. Soares and R. F. Rodrigues. Nested context model 3.0: Part 1–ncm core. *Monografias em Ciência da Computação do Departamento de Informática, PUC-Rio*, (18/05), 2005.
[29] L. F. G. Soares and R. F. Rodrigues. Nested context language 3.0 part 8–ncl digital tv profiles. *Monografias em Ciência da Computação da PUC-Rio*, 1200(35):06, 2006.
[30] J. Yokota and W. H. Teale. Picture books and the digital world. *The Reading Teacher*, 67(8):577–585, 2014.

Effective Floating Strategies

Frank Mittelbach

LaTeX3 Project

Mainz, Germany

frank.mittelbach@latex-project.org

ABSTRACT

This paper presents an extension to the general framework for globally optimized pagination described in Mittelbach [7]. The extended algorithm supports automatic placement of floats as part of the optimization. It uses a flexible constraint model that allows for the implementation of typical typographic rules that can be weighted against each other to support different application scenarios.

By "flexible" we mean that the rules of typographic presentation of the content of a document element are not fixed—but neither are they completely arbitrary; also, some of these rules are absolute whereas others are in the form of preferences.

It is easy to see that without restrictions the float placement possibilities grow exponentially if the number of floats has a linear relation to the document size. It is therefore important to restrict the objective function used for optimization in a way that the algorithm does not have to evaluate all theoretically possible placements while still being guaranteed to find an optimal solution.

Different objective functions are being evaluated against typical typographic requirements in order to arrive at a system that is both rich in its expressiveness of modeling a large class of pagination applications and at the same time is capable of solving the optimization problem in acceptable time for realistic input data.

CCS CONCEPTS

• **Applied computing** → **Format and notation**; *Publishing*;

KEYWORDS

typesetting; macro-typography; pagination; page breaking; global optimization; automatic layout; adaptive layout

ACM Reference format:
Frank Mittelbach. 2017. Effective Floating Strategies. In *Proceedings of DocEng '17, Valletta, Malta, September 04–07, 2017,* 10 pages.
DOI: http://dx.doi.org/10.1145/3103010.3103015

1 INTRODUCTION

Pagination is the act of transforming a source document into a sequence of columns and pages. The main input is a stream of textual material that is typically read in sequential order, its arrangement into columns and pages therefore needs to preserve the sequential property.[1] In addition to the main textual input stream there may be one or more auxiliary input streams holding floats, i.e., elements such as figures and tables that are allowed a certain flexibility in placement with respect to the elements in the textual stream. The constraints posed against placement possibilities for elements in such streams vary depending on the target application; typical scenarios and their solutions are discussed in sections 3 and 4.

Automatically finding the optimal or at least a high quality solution to this problem is of high importance as each day endless hours are wasted by people attempting this task manually on countless documents. As of today, all available document production systems deploy greedy algorithms that decide the placement of objects when encountered and it is easy to prove that such an algorithms will produce inferior results in most cases. This means one either has to accept those results or undertake to correct them manually. Given that decisions about earlier parts of a document may well affect later parts, this is an inherently iterative process that is very labor intensive as anybody can confirm who had the *pleasure* to manual paginate a long document with a complicated float arrangement.

An algorithm that undertakes the task of automatic pagination has to transform the textual stream into a vertical galley, i.e., a sequence of unbreakable blocks (typically a line or several lines of text) separated by breakpoints where that galley can be split into columns and pages. In parallel it has to make decisions where to place the float stream elements on the pages (thereby reducing available column heights) in a way that best fulfills a number of (usually) conflicting constraints.

In Mittelbach [7] a framework for globally optimized pagination of a textual stream was presented in which the placement of floats was assumed to be externally predetermined. This paper now extends this framework by exploring necessary and sufficient requirements for optimizing float placement and text stream pagination together.

As the base framework used a dynamic programming methodology successfully, here we shall approach the extended problem using the same methodology and evaluate to what extent this methodology can be applied in real life applications. This naturally leads to a number of restrictions and assumptions we have to make in order to arrive at an algorithm that on one hand terminates in a reasonable time frame and on the other hand is rich enough to optimize a large class of interesting input documents.

A globally optimizing system is generally problematic since small changes in either the parameter values or the content of a document can have long-range changes which are difficult to predict. Such systems are, in this sense, non-robust and are therefore difficult to work with if they only provide full optimization according to some

---

[1] There are applications where this is not the case or not fully the case, e.g., in newspaper layout, where stories may be interrupted and "*continued on page X*", but in this paper we limit ourselves to formatting tasks where the sequential property is preserved.

global set of constraints.[2] As a mediation, an algorithm should offer the ability for local constraints that can freeze part of the pagination even if—according to its global rules— that part would become suboptimal this way.

The remainder of the paper is structured as follows: Section 2 gives a quick overview about related work. In section 3 we take a closer look at typical design criteria related to floats and their placement in documents. This section is based on unpublished work carried out by the author together with Chris Rowley in the early nineties. Section 4 discusses the implementation of these rules in the context of global optimization and the restrictions that have to be imposed in order to solve this task in polynomial time. The final section then provides some details on the algorithm as implemented in a prototype, followed by some concluding remarks.

2   RELATED WORK

Witten [9] gives a useful and concise overview about various research problems and solutions across the field of computer based typography. Beside other material it includes an interesting section on document pagination. Although by now more than thirty years old it covers a lot of ground that is still of interest. A fairly recent survey is presented by Hurst et al. [4].

In his PhD thesis Plass [8] developed a model for global optimization of the page make-up of documents containing floating elements. In his model, float placement decisions are made by evaluating a numerical "objective function" describing the "cost" of (individual) pages within a potential formatting of the document; then a placement is chosen which minimizes the sum of these cost over all pages of the document. As shown by Plass, the objective function used must be carefully chosen, otherwise the minimization problem can become NP-complete. The prototype implementation that he describes uses such a function with a limited number of customizable parameters.[3] In addition, some directions are given on how to extend this approach to cover a wider set of rules.

Since then a number of other researchers have worked on improved pagination algorithms, e.g., Wohlfeil [10] and Brüggemann-Klein et al. [2] addressed float placement using dynamic programming based on the Knuth/Plass algorithm with a restricted document model. Jacobs et al. [5] explored the use of layout templates that can be selected by an optimizing algorithm also based on Knuth/Plass to best fulfill a number of constraints. The system described there is similar in nature to the one described in this paper, but it seems to use a simplified text stream model when optimizing to counter-balance the complexity introduced through floats. As there is no further mention of the system in any later publication, it is not clear to what extent it was ever analyzed or got implemented. Finally, a very interesting approach is taken by Marriott et al. [6]. Their document model is based on horizontal scrolling, and is thus a very interesting alternative when globally optimizing online documents. For printed material that model is not really applicable and thus their findings aren't fully comparable.

3   FLOATS AND THEIR TYPOGRAPHIC RULES

In this section we briefly describe some reasonably straightforward examples of the type of flexibility which may be specified both for the placement of floats within the page structure of the document and also for the formatting of typical elements within a float.

3.1   Float types

There are two types of floats commonly referred to in typographical specs: figure and table floats. A figure-float typically contains, in addition to the figure itself: a caption (usually with a number for reference); in many cases a legend (some additional explanatory text); a source line (for photos or art work). A table-float also has both a caption and a legend; in addition it may well have footnotes to the table and a source line. Depending on the nature of the publication other types of floats (such as "programs", "examples", etc.), with their own typographic requirements, are possible.

An important aspect of float types is that they typically form independent input streams, i.e., floats from one stream are expected to appear in sequentially correct order in the output, but the order of objects from different streams is normally not restricted.[4]

Any system of practical importance needs to support at least two major types of such independent float streams. Despite this, in most parts of the paper we restrict the discussion to a single text and float stream to simplify the explanation and notation. The extensions to support additional float streams are straightforward—but it is important to note the resulting increase in the time complexity. Where necessary, we outline any special considerations.

3.2   Rules for float placement

The design rationale behind many of the rules for float placement is to produce layouts which enable the reader easily to find the float from the position of its first or main "call-out"[5] in the text whilst ensuring that the main text remains easy to locate and read without disruption. Many rules therefore control the placement of the float with respect to this call-out, as well as the order in which the floats appear.

More visually oriented rules, e.g., those specifying restrictions on the number of floats on a page, or the space occupied by them or by the remaining main text, capture the designer's desire to keep the main text as readable and uninterrupted as possible.

Rules such as the following are typical call-out constraints that need to be supported by algorithms implementing float placement:

- Floats will be placed in order of their first call-out. A possible alternative: The float placement is based on the main call-out, which may not necessarily be the first.

- A float will not appear in a column earlier than that on which its first call-out occurs. A more restrictive variation, that is sometimes asked for, is that a float must appear later than its call-out.

While the above examples show rules that allow sequential formatting (i.e., every object can be formatted when it is encountered),

---

[2]In today's TeX system, users are sometimes amazed (and dismayed) that deleting a word surprisingly results in a paragraph getting longer—messing up carefully handcrafted documents (including the float placement). This is a typical, albeit small scale problem of that nature, as TeX only optimizes paragraphs not the whole document.
[3]His function supports costs for the distance between call-out and float, distinguishing between forward and backward direction.

[4]For a pagination algorithm this means, unfortunately, a noticeable growth in time complexity per additional independent float stream.
[5]A place where the float is referred to.

a different variation of the second rule introduces a new type of complexity:

- A float can appear on the page before its first/main call-out, so long as it is still visible from this call-out position.

Moving a float in front of its call-out, as is allowed by this rule, typically involves reformatting of already typeset pages and thus, by possibly introducing a new page break, has the potential result of moving the call-out position itself to a later page. It is therefore difficult to implement when using a greedy algorithm. However, with a globally optimizing algorithm the full context has to be considered in any case, so that implementing rules of that nature is easily possible.

The examples so far restrict the float placement in just one direction, backwards away from the call-out. They could be augmented by a rule such as the following:

- All floats whose first call-out is in a particular subsection must be placed within that subsection. An even stronger variation would be that a float must be always visible from its call-out.

The problem with a rule like that, is that it may confine the placement too drastically so that it becomes impossible to typeset a document at all, while also obeying all other rules (i.e., those for floats and text placement). Therefore, such a rule usually requires additional rules that allow for the generation of pages with only floats in an emergency.

There are usually also many rules for the placement of floats onto the individual columns, pages, or page spreads and often these vary between different parts of the document. Examples are:

- There cannot be more than x floats on a single page.
- The top area of a column may receive a maximum of y floats, the bottom area of z floats.
- All the floats which appear on a page will be stacked vertically at the top of the page. One of the many possible alternatives would be that they can appear at the top or bottom (but not in both places);
- Floats can be horizontally placed if they are visually compatible (e.g., have identical heights). This kind of rule is also often requested for floats placed in adjacent columns.
- If more than $x\%$ of the space on a column is occupied by floats then no normal text will appear in that column.
- Every column must contain a minimum of $x\%$ of text.

The rules governing the visual attributes of the placement of floats can be far more complex than those which can be expressed by simple size dependencies like the ones above. For example, it is possible to formulate rules that try to visually balance the appearance of floats over a double spread. A good example of such a design is the layout of the journal *Scientific American*, in which floats are placed into a grid so as to satisfy certain visual considerations even if that means that they are not in the order of their call-outs.[6] Representing such type of rules as templated designs offers a good way to manage their complexity (cf. [5]).

What we can already see from the (sometimes conflicting) example rules above, is that placing of floats onto pages in relation

---

[6]Note that when using such rules, the floats are usually numbered according to the order in which they appear.

to paginated textual material depends a lot on the target application and can be quite varied. Thus any algorithm attempting to optimize document pagination needs to support a flexible and customizable constraint system in order to be applicable to a large set of documents.

3.3 Rules for the inner structure of floats

While for the discussion in this paper we are only marginally concerned with the detailed typographical rules that govern the inner structure of floats, it is important to note that due to such rules floats might be allowed to have a range of possible horizontal and vertical sizes. Such flexibility could be achieved by varying the formatting, e.g., by using different sized fonts (for a table) or by trimming and/or scaling (for a figure). If the float is composed of several objects, such as a caption and a legend, then the size and even the shape can also be varied by changing both the formatting of these elements and their relative placements within the float.

Sometimes the rules for placement and presentation are combined as in rules like the following:

- The first float to appear at the top of a page must not have its legend set at its side.

This is another type of rule which states that the formatting of other elements influences the layout and placement of the current object. While such rules very much complicate the use of greedy algorithms they do not pose additional issues for global optimization as they in fact limit the number of alternatives that the algorithm has to work through.

4 HANDLING FLOAT PLACEMENT RULES

Typographic rules such as those discussed in the previous section might require complex layout algorithms, not only due to the possibility of conflicting rules but also because formatting decisions can influence each other. In this section we will look at how and to what extent they can be implemented as part of a globally optimizing algorithm.

4.1 Initial definitions

4.1.1 The source document

With a few clearly marked as exceptions, we assume in this paper that our input document consists of a text stream $T = \{t_1, t_2, \ldots, t_n\}$ and a float stream $F = \{f_1, f_2, \ldots, f_\ell\}$. Each t_i is an unbreakable block of textual material that can vary in vertical size within some limits, i.e., it has a nominal height but can potentially shrink somewhat or grow taller. The text stream can be split between each block so that there are $n - 1$ breakpoints in the stream. The f_i are floats which are unbreakable and have fixed vertical sizes.

4.1.2 Paginations

A pagination of the input document onto k pages is then defined as the mapping $p : T \cup F \rightarrow \{1, 2, \ldots, k\}$ such that $p(t_i) \leq p(t_j)$ for $1 \leq i < j \leq n$ and $p(f_i) \leq p(f_j)$ for $1 \leq i < j \leq \ell$. In plain English this means that text and float elements are distributed across k pages and the elements in each stream retain their order in the output page sequence. In practice, the feasible paginations for a given document will lie in a small range given by $k_{\min} \leq k \leq k_{\max}$, i.e., usually a document can be paginated successfully into a different number of pages.

With $\mathcal{P}$ we denote the set of all possible paginations that can be constructed from the input document.

4.1.3 Objective functions

When we speak about finding an "optimal pagination" we mean that given a function $Q : \mathcal{P} \to \mathfrak{R}$ from the set $\mathcal{P}$ of possible paginations of the input document to the real numbers we seek an element $p_0 \in \mathcal{P}$ such that $Q(p_0) \leq Q(p)$ for all $p \in \mathcal{P}$. The function $Q(p)$ defines the "cost" when choosing pagination p and we try to find the pagination with least cost, of which there can be several. Q is therefore often called a cost-function or an objective function as it numerically encodes what is considered the quality of the solution. To do this in a meaningful way it needs to evaluate how well a particular pagination adheres to a given set of rules, weights the findings and arrives at a single number to make the quality of any two paginations comparable.

By using different objective functions it is in principle possible to specify a large variety of possible rules: both those that are absolute, i.e., preventing certain situations from arising, as well as those that mediate between conflicting goals.

4.1.4 The dynamic programming methodology

One requirement when applying the dynamic programming methodology [1, 3] to an optimization problem is that the problem can be divided into subproblems that overlap, i.e., that share common subsubproblems. The dynamic programming approach then solves each subsubproblem only once and saves the answer thereby avoiding recomputing that answer unnecessarily.

The pagination task is a problem of this nature if we consider as subproblems the questions: "How can one best paginate the text blocks $t_a, \ldots, t_b$ and the floats $f_c, \ldots, f_d$ into the page spreads $S_i, \ldots, S_j$?". We denote the resulting set of partial paginations that need to be compared to answer that question by

$$\mathcal{P}_{(S_i,\ldots,S_j)_{c,d}^{a,b}} \qquad (1)$$

with the convention that $b = a - 1$ means no text block is used and similarly $d = c - 1$ that no float is placed onto those spreads.

With this notation we can describe $\mathcal{P}$ as

$$\mathcal{P} = \bigcup_{k_{\min} \leq k \leq k_{\max}} \mathcal{P}_{(S_1,\ldots,S_k)_{1,\ell}^{1,n}}$$

and one of the many decompositions into subproblems would be, for example:

$$\mathcal{P}_{(S_1)_{1,c}^{1,a}} \times \mathcal{P}_{(S_2)_{c+1,c'}^{a+1,a'}} \times \mathcal{P}_{(S_3,\ldots,S_k)_{c'+1,\ell}^{a'+1,n}} \subset \mathcal{P}$$

It is clear that these subproblems overlap, e.g., , there are many that share the same set partitions for spreads $S_i, \ldots, S_j$ while being different for other spreads.

The other requirement needed to make dynamic programming applicable is that the problem exhibits what is called *optimal substructure*:

Definition 4.1. A problem exhibits *optimal substructure* (or obeys the *optimality principle)* if the optimal solution to the problem incorporates only optimal solutions to its subproblems, each of which can be solved independently.

This means that if p_{opt} is an optimal solution to the whole problem, then it is also an optimal solution when it is restricted to any of its subproblems:

$$p_{opt} \in \mathcal{P}_{(S_1)_{1,c}^{1,a}} \times \mathcal{P}_{(S_2)_{c+1,c'}^{a+1,a'}} \times \mathcal{P}_{(S_3)_{c'+1,c''}^{a'+1,a''}} \times \cdots \subset \mathcal{P}$$

For example, if restricted to $t_1, \ldots, t_{a'}$ and $f_1, \ldots, f_{c'}$, it must be an optimal solution for $\mathcal{P}_{(S_1,S_2)_{1,c'}^{1,a'}}$. Whether or not this is the case depends on the objective function being used. It must allow computing a value on the level of the subproblems and the results need to obey definition 4.1. Below we will see some examples where this is not the case.

4.2 The size of $\mathcal{P}$

Given an input document consisting of a text stream with n blocks (i.e., $n - 1$ possible breakpoints) and a single float stream with ℓ elements and assuming as the only constraint on floats is that the order of floats has to be preserved in the output, then by methods of elementary combinatorics the number of possible paginations into k pages is

$$\binom{k+\ell-1}{\ell}\binom{n-1}{k-1}$$

since we have to select ℓ pages (with repetitions allowed) to place the floats and need to select $k - 1$ out of the $n - 1$ breakpoints to split the galley across k pages.

If we further assume that the number of breakpoints and floats grow in proportion to the length of the document,[7] i.e., $n - 1 = n'(k-1)$ and $\ell = \ell'(k-1)$ then we get a lower bound on the number of paginations as follows:

$$\binom{k+\ell-1}{\ell}\binom{n-1}{k-1} \geq \left(\frac{k+\ell-1}{\ell}\right)^\ell \left(\frac{n-1}{k-1}\right)^{k-1} =$$

$$= \left(\frac{k+\ell'(k-1)-1}{\ell'(k-1)}\right)^{\ell'(k-1)} \left(\frac{n'(k-1)}{k-1}\right)^{k-1} = \left(\left(\frac{1+\ell'}{\ell'}\right)^{\ell'} n'\right)^{k-1}$$

Thus for any value of $n' > 1$ and $\ell' > 0$ this grows exponentially in k. As a typical column will contain between 20 and 50 breakpoints, the total number of theoretically possible paginations will get out of hand pretty fast. Of course, many of these paginations will be ridiculously bad or technically impossible (for example, due to space constraints on the pages), but without some testing we may not be able to rule them out beforehand.

4.3 How to make the problem tractable

Starting with this observation it is clear that we can only hope for a globally optimizing pagination algorithm to terminate in acceptable time, if it can find the optimal pagination without evaluating the objective function for each and every theoretically possible pagination.

For this the algorithm must be able to take into account some characteristics of the objective function being used. Otherwise all it can do is a brute-force approach, i.e., evaluating every possible pagination. This can be easily seen by the following simple adversary argument: Let's assume that there exists an algorithm that can find the minimum value v of an arbitrary objective function Q without

---

[7]To ease the calculations we define them to be a factor of the number of page breaks, i.e., $k - 1$.

evaluating it for all paginations and without making assumptions about Q and let p' be one of the paginations that is not evaluated by the algorithm. Then we can construct a new objective function Q' as follows:

$$Q'(p) = \begin{cases} v - 1 & \text{for } p = p' \\ Q(p) & \text{for all other paginations } p \end{cases}$$

Given the same input, the algorithm using this new function would still evaluate exactly the same paginations (as the assumption was that its behavior doesn't depend on the objective function). It will therefore find v as the minimum, as the pagination p' is not evaluated, even though the the correct value for the minimum is now $v - 1$.

4.4 Considering only the text stream

In the previous section we have seen that in order to succeed, there needs to be a way for the algorithm to discard or rather ignore many of the theoretically possible paginations without ever spending time on evaluating their "quality", since a brute-force evaluation means a time complexity with exponential growth.

What gets us a good deal towards this goal are the natural size restrictions in a pagination task, both for the input elements as well as for the output pages. While it is possible that in real documents elements from the text stream have a negative height, i.e., overprint each other, we expect that on the whole concatenating the elements will result in a growing vertical size. It is therefore not unreasonable to require the following restriction on the input document data: There exists a constant $c \geq 0$ such that

$$\sum_{i=j}^{k} height(t_i) > -c \quad \text{for all } 1 \leq j \leq k \leq n \tag{2}$$

This basically means that if there are elements with negative size they will happen only seldom, so that any "backtracking" that an algorithm needs to account for is limited to at most c.[8] With the restriction (2) we can immediately rule out many of the theoretically possible paginations in $\mathcal{P}$. If $p \in \mathcal{P}$ attempts to place the elements $t_j, \ldots, t_k$ onto one of the pages that can receive at most material of height H and if $\sum_{i=j}^{k} height(t_i) > H$, then we know that this particular pagination is impossible (as that page has overflowed). If furthermore $\sum_{i=j}^{k} height(t_i) > H + c$ we know that any pagination that tries to place $t_j, \ldots, t_k, t_{k+1}$ or further elements onto that particular page is impossible too, as, because of (2), the resulting total height of the material will always exceed H.

In the opposite direction it is reasonable to consider pages that are largely empty as unacceptable (though not technically impossible). Again this will weed out many paginations, i.e., those that consist of at least one page that contains too much unfilled space.

As shown in [7] the above restrictions, together with a suitable objective function, allow the implementation of a dynamic programming algorithm that solves the general pagination task in quadratic time given a predetermined float placement.

---

[8]In real-life documents c would be either zero or fairly small, e.g., the height of a typical text line or less.

4.5 Considering both text and float stream

With an argument similar to that for overfull pages produced from too many consecutive text stream elements, it is obvious that it is impossible to place more than a few floats onto a single page. This will therefore also rule out many of the theoretically possible paginations contained in $\mathcal{P}$.

However, in contrast to the text stream case this will, without further restrictive rules, still allow for exponentially many paginations that need to be considered. The reason is, ironically, the fact that there are typically only a few floats—that is, too few compared to the number of places that they can positioned to.

This can be seen with a simple counting argument: Assume we want to place ℓ floats onto k pages and only allow a maximum of one float per page (which requires $\ell \leq k$). Then through combinatorial rules we get a lower bound for the number of possible floats placements through

$$\binom{k}{\ell} \geq \left(\frac{k}{\ell}\right)^{\ell}$$

If we assume that ℓ is proportionally tied to k, then this grows exponentially in k as long as $\ell < k$. The same is true if we allow more floats per page, except that then the growth is even faster. The only exceptions are the degenerate cases (e.g., k with one float per page allowed, or $2k$ floats with two per page, etc.) as then there is only a single float placement solution, i.e., no variability whatsoever.

For this reason it is not realistic to approach the general pagination problem with floats by first looping through all possible float placements (exponential) and then for each finding the best pagination for the textual material (quadratic).

Instead we need to address text and float placement jointly and hope that with a suitable objective function that implements realistic typographic rules for text and floats, one can devise an algorithm that always completes in polynomial time. As we will prove in section 5.6 it is in fact possible to construct such an algorithm that shows a runtime complexity of $O(n^2 \ell)$ in the general case and $O(n\ell)$ if we assume a constant spread height.

4.6 Objective functions for float placement

Several of the rules discussed in section 3 involve the placement of floats in relation to their call-out. Thus, objective functions of practical importance that measure the quality of a pagination need to take account of both the placement of floats across the different (areas on) pages and for the distribution of the text stream material, as the latter determines where the call-outs will appear. This is another reason why it is usually not possible to approach the problem by first finding the best float placement and then simply fitting the text stream into the remaining space in the best possible manner.

Call-out-related rules come in two types: those that define some placement restriction in relation to the call-out, e.g., the float must be placed on or after the page of the call-out, and those that are based on the spatial relationship, e.g., the float should be preferably visible from the call-out or there should be less than three page turns necessary to reach the float from the call-out.

Both can be formulated as absolute rules, though typically that is only the case for the order relations, while spatial relationships are usually formulated as quality attributes, e.g., fewer page turns from call-out to float are considered "better".

4.6.1 Handling call-out/float distance constraints

Wohlfeil [10] considers the spatial relationship rules as the dominant rules and makes the following definition:

Definition 4.2. An objective function is called a natural measure iff increasing the page (page spread) difference between a float and its call-out leads to a worse pagination.

He then only considers objective functions that are natural measures according to that definition. While we agree that the spatial relationship is usually an integral ingredient for an objective function, other aspects of the the pagination, depending on the use case, may be of equal or higher importance. This aspect will have a weight so that it can be made of more or less importance in the objective function.

Plass [8] in his PhD showed that certain non-natural objective functions lead to NP-completeness of the problem, for example, a function that penalizes distances with an odd number of page turns and applies 0 otherwise—a truly odd function. Unfortunately, he was also able to show that the same is true, if one uses a function that takes the square of the page turns as its penalty—a function that is clearly natural in the above sense.

What these two objective functions have in common is that they both communicate information across long distances in the paginated document, in one case by oscillation and in the other case by growing at a rate that is not linear in the distance. It is therefore not possible to collapse different partial paginations in an algorithm and continue by considering only the best, as the "best" is not known until after the float placement for all call-outs already seen have been determined. In other words those functions do not exhibit the optimality principle from definition 4.1 as suboptimal partial paginations may lead to the optimal solution, eventually.

However, the previous argument does not apply if the objective function uses a cost formula that depends linearly on the distance. The unresolved cross-references (i.e., the call-outs for which we haven't yet seen a corresponding float) in a partial pagination are then no longer a problem. The exact position of a call-out in the partial pagination doesn't matter, as the cost for that is already accounted for as part of the cost of that partial pagination and any additional cost will be a linear addition depending only on the number of further page turns necessary to reach the float. So it is not surprising that Plass was able to show that with a simple linear objective function the pagination problem can be solved in polynomial time.

Using an objective function linear in page turns for the call-out constraints, as Plass and Wohlfeil did, models rules such as "a float should be visible from its call-out" or "a float should be placed close to its call-out" quite well, but a linear cost doesn't really do justice to the fact, that in the reader's perception the exact number of page turns is fairly unimportant if a float comes many pages after its call-out, while for the first page turns a degradation in quality is clearly felt. Yet a linear function always adds the same penalty for every additional page turn.

There are two ways to handle that better. First of all, we can define a maximum distance after which a partition is considered to be too bad be be taken into account at all. That fits with the human perception that a float should not appear a large number of pages after its call-out for no good reason.[9]

The problem with that approach is that a call-out may appear in different places in the solutions to different partial paginations so that this distance is only well-defined if we remember all involved partial paginations and treat them separately. A somewhat simpler approach is to keep track of the total number of unresolved cross-references, i.e., the total number of call-outs for which we haven't seen the corresponding floats. If this number then reaches a high-water mark we stop further evaluations and consider that particular partial solution unacceptable.

Of course, any pruning approach (i.e., dropping candidate solutions because of heuristics) has the danger that if we prune too much, we may miss out on the overall optimal solution in case an inferior earlier partial solution leads to a much better solution for later parts of the document.

The second possibility is that the objective function handles the first page turns in a special way and only then starts applying a linear cost formula. That can be done without violating the optimality principle, but it means that the algorithm has to work considerably harder, as it needs to keep track of more subproblems (before being able to decide which of them is better and which can be dropped).

4.6.2 Handling other call-out/float constraints

Rules that define a placement restriction based on the call-out position, e.g., "a float is not allowed in a column prior to that of its call-out", are usually formulated as absolute rules and thus simply limit the candidate paginations that the algorithm has to evaluate, but otherwise do not affect the dynamic programming approach.

However, they could be formulated as quality indicators in which case an objective function would need to account for the situation and charge an additional cost. As long as everything is confined a to local area (typically a single spread or even a single page) this will not change the problem status with respect to the optimality principle. For every rule of that type that is of practical importance that is fortunately the case. However, as we have learned through the example given by Plass,[10] one could construct rules for that space that would invalidate the optimal substructure criteria 4.1.

4.6.3 Specifications without call-out constraints

In a design without call-out/float constraints there are no natural incentives that favor a certain document region for each float (such as a low distance to a call-out position) and therefore the objective function implements only local aesthetic rules and rules for the text stream pagination (which are also essentially of a local nature), i.e., a chosen float placement now only affects the quality through a better or worse fit of the text blocks placed onto the page spreads.

Nevertheless, one can think of this as a special version of the case with call-out constraints, i.e., one in which all call-outs are at the very beginning of the document and the objective function adds a cost of zero for each necessary page turn. Thus, the same kind of objective function can be used, except that one can't do any

---

[9]Of course, there could be good reasons, e.g., if a single paragraph references twenty floats, then those floats will need to be positioned over several pages, simply for size reasons. Those boundary cases would need to be taken into account by an algorithm that prunes away unacceptable solutions.

[10]The rule that favors odd number of page turns over even number of page turns.

pruning due to the distance to the call-outs (as that distance is now irrelevant).

So while dynamic programming still works and the algorithm still completes in polynomial time, it will have to work much harder, as initially all placements are possible and need to be considered. Thus without some additional (possibly artificial) restrictions, a global optimizing algorithm will take a lot of time (and probably too much) even for smaller sized input documents.

A simple approach to reduce the complexity is to do the float positioning externally (as it is independent from the text stream partitioning) which is what the basic framework [7] already provides. However, this is clearly suboptimal as it misses out on the opportunities offered to achieve a better pagination of the text through small variations in the float placement.

A better alternative is to use artificial (invisible) call-outs within the document and a low or zero penalty charge for the distance from those call-outs. That way each float has an area of attraction in the paginated document and one can apply pruning techniques if it ventures too far away from the artificial call-out.

A different alternative is to make use of the fact that such designs typically want to see the floats placed "evenly" across the document. If that is the case it can be used to implement a pruning technique based on the fact that one knows roughly the average number of floats per spread for the whole document through

$$\frac{\ell}{k_{max}} \le av_{doc} \le \frac{\ell}{k_{min}}$$

and one can determine the average av_{sub} for each subproblem $\mathcal{P}(S_i,\dots,S_j)_{c,d}^{a,b}$ as that is simply

$$av_{sub} = \frac{d-c+1}{j-i+1}$$

With these values and two cut-off constants $0 < x < 1$ and $y > 1$ we can define subproblems as unacceptable if for them one of the following inequalities is true:

$$\frac{av_{doc}}{av_{sub}} < x \quad \text{for } av_{doc} < av_{sub} \text{ and } (j-i+1)\,av_{doc} > y \quad (3)$$

$$\frac{av_{sub}}{av_{doc}} < x \quad \text{for } av_{doc} > av_{sub} \text{ and } (j-i+1)\,av_{doc} > y \quad (4)$$

The second condition on (3) and (4) will ensure that we do not throw away subproblems with only a few spreads if there is a low float expectancy per spread.

A different, though related, approach is to support a number of templates for a spread, each requiring a specific number of floats being placed on that spread (no more, no less). Given that each spread can now hold a number of floats (that is restricted in both directions) it is easy for an algorithm to determine whether or not a partial pagination can ever become part of a complete pagination. Thus a lot of pruning can be achieved by throwing out partials with too many or too few floats.

Finally, instead of, or in addition to limiting the placement options by ignoring float placements that venture too far from the average distribution, as discussed above, one can also implement some evenness distribution measure, i.e., implement a cost for the variation in the frequency with which floats appear. If we do that then the objective function needs to be carefully constructed to

ensure the optimality principle still applies and the problem is not becoming NP-complete.

One way to achieve this is to use an objective function that charges a cost Δ based on the amount of change in number of floats from one spread to the next, i.e., if it stays the same the cost is zero and if it changes then the cost is calculated from the difference.

Such an objective function can be used with dynamic programming, i.e., it obeys the optimality principle if we slightly alter the specifications of the subproblems as follows: "How can one best paginate the text blocks $t_a,\dots,t_b$ and the floats $f_c,\dots,f_d$ into the page spreads $S_i,\dots,S_j$ if S_{i-1} contains x floats and the spread S_j contains y floats?" denoted as

$$\mathcal{P}(S_i,\dots,S_j)_{c,d}^{a,b}\Big|_y^x \quad (5)$$

For this S_0 (the artificial spread before the first spread) is assumed to contain a customizable number x_0 of floats. If we set $x_0 = 0$ then the algorithm will favor gradually increasing the number of floats and only later try to stay close to the average, while if we set it to $x_0 = \lfloor\frac{\ell}{k}\rfloor$ instead, the average will be favored throughout.

Clearly, compared to (1), the algorithm then has to work harder as there are more subproblems to evaluate. The overall complexity, however, will not change, as due to size limitations the total number of floats per spread is bounded by a constant c.

The optimal solution can then be calculated by

$$\min_{0 \le y < c}\left(\min_{p \in \mathcal{P}(S_1,\dots,S_k)_{1,\ell}^{1,n}|_y^{x_0}} \big(Q(p)\big) + \Delta(y - x_{last}) \right) \quad (6)$$

with x_{last} being another customizable value that indicates the number of floats to use on the last spread in order to avoid any extra cost there.

4.6.4 Handling other rules

In the previous section we have discussed a way to implement a cost for variations in the frequency with which floats appear. As this is essentially some information that involves data from arbitrary regions of the document, we must be careful to ensure that the resulting objective function can still be subjected to dynamic programming. We have therefore chosen to look only at the delta between two spreads, because this avoids the need to keep track of every float position.

But there are other rules that are inherently more local, e.g., involving only a single spread, and in that case an objective function can make arbitrarily complex calculations (based on that local input) to arrive at some additional costs for the situation, without ever getting into the danger of violating the optimality principle.

Some of these local rules are typically absolute in nature, e.g., "a maximum of four floats per spread is allowed" or "there can only be a single float in any of the bottom areas on a spread". In that case they simply limit the partial paginations that an algorithm has to work through. But, of course, if rules "favor" something that means there will be additional options to consider, for which an objective function could charge different costs.

It is also possible to support variations in the internal formatting of floats, e.g., rules such as "if two floats on a spread are similar in size, favor reformatting them to the same size and placing them both in the top area of opposite pages". As they only involve changes to and placement of elements on a single spread, an objective function supporting them will still obey the optimality principle.

Finally there are user/document specific constraints, e.g., "always/never place these two floats on a single spread ". Such constraints are typically absolute in nature, but again can also be easily implemented as preference rules, provided they involve only local formatting information.

5 THE EXTENDED ALGORITHM

The base algorithm for globally optimizing the pagination of a document not involving a float stream is described in [7, section 3]. In the current paper we therefore mainly discuss how to extend such an algorithm to handle float stream(s) in a flexible manner.[11]

5.1 The layout model

The layout of the target document is described by a sequence of spreads (opposing verso and recto pages that are visible at the same time by a reader) $S_1, S_2, \ldots, S_k$. These spreads are filled one after another by the algorithm until all source material is accounted for. If necessary, the last spread S_k is repeatedly applied, so that a given specification is valid for any amount of source material.

Each spread S_i defines a template layout consisting of:

- a number of text columns (whose sizes may differ)

and in the case with floats additionally

- a set of "named" areas that can receive floats; reception of a float will reduce (some of) the column sizes
- a set of constraints for the filling process.

A straight forward extension would be to support multiple templates per spread and have the algorithm try all of them (possibly with costs attached) as alternative paths during the optimization.

5.2 A recap of the base algorithm (simplified)

The main algorithmic idea is to construct the set of all possible paginations $\mathcal{P}$ gradually, i.e., by first using only a part of the input and building all ways to paginate that. Then taking more material and use it to extend the paginations already found thereby forming new partial paginations. In theory this process then continues until all input material is used and we have constructed the whole set $\mathcal{P}$. In practice, however, we remember the best partial solutions along the way and—by courtesy of the optimality principle—throw away those that are suboptimal as they cannot become part of the optimal solution.

To manage this, the algorithm maintains a data structure $A = \{t', t'', t''', \ldots\}$ of elements from the text stream that have been identified as being the best way to end some spread.[12] In the nomen-

clature of (1) an element t in that data structure ending spread S_i corresponds to the best answer for

$$\mathcal{P}_{(S_1,\ldots,S_i)_{1,0}^{1,t}}$$

Initially this data structure only contains a single element indicating the start of the document.

The main loop of the algorithm then loops sequentially through all elements of the text stream. For each element it evaluates if it is possible to build the next spread starting from any of the $t^* \in A$ and ending in the current t, i.e., it is attempting a solution for

$$\mathcal{P}_{(S_1,\ldots,S_{i+1})_{1,0}^{1,t}} \supseteq \mathcal{P}_{(S_1,\ldots,S_i)_{1,0}^{1,t^*}} \times \mathcal{P}_{(S_{i+1})_{1,0}^{successor(t^*),t}}$$

If this is possible[13] with at least one element from A then evaluating the objective function will tell which of them is the best and what the costs are. Then t will be added to A as a way to end S_{i+1} including the information that the best way to reach this point is through a particular t^*.

If the distance from some $t^* \in A$ to t gets too large, i.e., if there is too much material between the two, to be squeezed into a single spread, then t^* gets deactivated within A and will not be considered as a possible spread start any longer.

Eventually we will reach t_n (the end of the document) through this process. At this point we are able to answer which pagination $p \in \bigcup_k \mathcal{P}_{(S_1,\ldots,S_k)_{1,0}^{1,n}}$ has the smallest value with respect to the objective function Q. All we have to do now, is to move backwards through all the elements of A which we passed through to reach t_n.

5.3 Managing the float stream

Call-outs to floats are special elements in the text stream. As a preparatory step in the extended algorithm we build up a simple table listing information about all call-outs and basic information about the floats they refer to (such as distance from the start of the document, float type,[14] float column span, float height, and float sequence number).

As the text stream may contain paragraph variations, as explained in [7, section 3.4], a call-out can appear several times (with different document distance information) in the text stream. In that case we only record the minimum distance, the earliest point at which the call-out may show up.

This information can be used to estimate where in relation to the call-out a float can be placed (e.g., in the case of call-out/float order restrictions discussed in section 4.6.2) or to discard all paginations with a call-out/float distance that is way out of bounds.

5.4 Preparing for the next spread

At the point in the main loop where the text element t has been identified as the best way to end some spread S_i with floats up to and including f already placed, i.e., the best partial pagination in

$$\mathcal{P}_{(S_1,\ldots,S_i)_{1,f}^{1,t}}$$

the algorithm has to prepare for the collection of material for the next spread (which now also involves adding floats).

---

[11]In the discussion so far, we have always talked about combining a text stream with a single float stream, as this simplifies formulas and their discussion. Extending this to another float stream only adds an additional dimension and raises the time complexity accordingly, but is not otherwise introducing new issues. For this reason the discussion of the algorithm will also discuss adding only a single float stream; the actual prototype implementation supports several, though.

[12]We are glossing over details here as in reality the data structure maintains elements for ending every column along the way of building the full spreads. This is better in practice, as the objective function has a cost component per column. Thus we reduce the overall time complexity, if we subdivide the problem on column level.

Also associated with each $t^* \in A$ is the spread/column it ends and information about the next spread/column that is about to be build, i.e., t^* may appear several times in the data structure but starting different spreads/columns.

[13]Possible in this case means that white space "badness" of the resulting spread is below a defined threshold (columns are neither too empty nor overfull) and no other absolute rule is violated; see Mittelbach [7, sections 3.1 and 3.3] for details.

[14]If implementing more than one float stream.

For this it picks up the next spread S_{i+1} from the document layout model. This will have information about the column sizes on the spread, available areas for float placement and restrictions implementing absolute rules (such as the maximum number of floats allowed, etc.).

With this data and the data prepared in section 5.3 we can now make some educated guesses about how floats can be placed on this spread. For this the algorithm loops through all remaining unplaced floats and recursively builds up all possible float placements—only taking into account restrictions on the number of floats, area ordering, float/call-out relation constraints etc. Due to the fact that there are physical limits (e.g., size of the areas, number of floats allowed) and the fact that if a float can't be placed for some reason all further floats (from that stream) must be deferred too, this loop will in practice produce only a handful of different placement alternatives. This is also the place to implement pruning techniques related to the number of unplaced floats (i.e., floats for which we have earlier seen the call-out, but which have not yet been placed) or the distance from call-out to float (for which we can obtain some rough estimate through the call-out data from section 5.3). Any potential placement that exceeds the threshold for pruning will be disregarded.[15]

Each of these newly constructed placement guesses is a potential way forward to find extended partial paginations. With their help we can attempt to find answers for

$$\mathcal{P}_{(S_{i+1})\,\mathrm{successor}(f),f'}^{\mathrm{successor}(t),??} \qquad (7)$$

where f' is the last float placed onto the spread and ?? indicates that we haven't yet decided where in the text stream the spread will end (and there will most likely be several such places).

Now for each of the possible continuations from t to build the next spread we add one new element to A that records t and all relevant data from (7).

Some of these elements in A will be pretty short-lived, i.e., they may turn out to be impossible as starting points when the algorithm attempts to fill the spread with text blocks. After all, they have been conceived as conservative guesses about where call-outs will end up on the spread. Thus floats may get placed in positions that violate restrictions that can only be verified after adding the text blocks, e.g., a call-out may get pushed to a new column or out of the spread altogether, etc. The moment this becomes clear, we drop the element from A to avoid doing unnecessary work in the main loop of the algorithm.

5.5 Applying float rules

As discussed in section 4 some rules are of an absolute nature, i.e., they must be always obeyed, while others indicate a preference for one situation over the other. Such preference rules need to be implemented as part of the objective function.

Absolute rules can theoretically also be handled as part of an objective function definition by making the function return ∞ (or technically an extremely high value), but this is suboptimal for a number of reasons. First of all, returning any value at all means that there is something to compare and so this does not truly implement

---

an absolute rule, but rather one that we try to make only extremely unlikely to be chosen. Secondly, it is usually possible to test for such rules very early on without invoking any expensive bookkeeping or calculation steps only to throw that particular pagination away at a later stage. It is therefore best to have the algorithm make some quick tests at the earliest possible moment and throw away any partial pagination that violates one of these rules.

The algorithm therefore tests for most of the absolute rules involving float placement while recursively generating new potential float placements as outlined in section 5.4. Each violation found there will reduce the number of candidates that the algorithm has to work through in later step.

However, absolute rules that involve call-out/float relations cannot be decided at this point as we haven't yet filled the new spreads with textual material containing the call-outs. Thus, in that case one needs to defer the test to the point where the call-out in question is actually added to a spread and then check whether the float positioning violates any restriction.

5.6 Execution and complexity

Due to the choice of precomputing the set of candidate float placements along the way (and dropping them again if they appear to be wrong guesses) the overall algorithmic behavior is only marginally affected by including one or more float streams.

After tabulating some data for later use (as outlined in section 5.3), the extended algorithm starts with its main loop through all text stream elements. In contrast to the base algorithm the data structure A is however not just initialized with a single element denoting the start of the document. Instead the process explained in section 5.4 has already been used for the very first spread and thus A will start out with elements for all different float placement possibilities for the first spread.

The algorithm then proceeds as described in section 5.2 with the exception that each time we are about to add a new t to A we run the process from 5.4 and instead add elements for all distinct potential float placements.

Finally, when we reach the last text element we have to deal with any pagination that has unplaced floats, i.e., is an element of

$$\mathcal{P}_{(S_1,\ldots,S_k)\,1,\,x}^{1,\,n} \quad \text{with } x < \ell$$

We need to extend those (by adding one or more additional spreads) and charge some extra cost and then determine the optimal solution as the pagination with minimal costs.

In [7] we showed that the number of elements in A referring to different text blocks is bound by $O(n)$ or, if all spreads have the same height, by a constant. With floats involved each of them may now appear several times differing in the number of floats already placed which gives us a length growing in $O(n\ell)$ or $O(\ell)$, respectively. Thus, for any objective function that can be calculated in constant time, we have an overall complexity of $O(n^2\ell)$ or $O(n\ell)$ as the outer loop of the algorithm is of length n. With the same argument each additional independent float stream will add another factor of ℓ).

5.7 Details of the used objective functions

To ensure that the objective function used in the algorithm does not violate the optimality principle it is implemented as a linear

---

[15]Special care is needed not to drop all placements though, else there may be no way forward. Basically one should only mark a new placement as a candidate for pruning and make the final decision to drop or keep it only after having recursively generated all new possible placements.

function where we add "cost components" based on the next spread that we try to append to already existing partial paginations for the earlier spreads.

There are two places where this will happen: When we build the new float placement candidates in section 5.4 and add new elements to A, we can immediately add all those cost elements for that particular placement that depend only on how floats are placed onto that spread. For example, if there is an extra cost attached to putting at least one float into a bottom area (as opposed to putting floats only in top areas), then we add that cost at this point.

However, for any preference rule that depends on both float and text placement (or only on text placement) we have to wait until the spread gets filled, for example, if we allow floats before their call-out but penalize such a position, or if we allow widows and orphans in the text but penalize them. In such cases we know the cost only once we reach the end of the spread, i.e., when we try to build the spread from some $t^* \in A$ to the current point t.

5.8 Document content level constraints

Document level constraints are individual user directives used either to guide the algorithm towards a certain behavior or to more strongly force certain floats into specific positions.

Forced placements are done by requiring a certain float to appear on a precisely defined spread (or set of spreads). Any pagination with the float not on one of these spreads will be considered invalid and dropped. Additional granularity can be achieved by also requesting a placement only in certain named areas on those spreads. All remaining floats not listed in such a forcing rule will be placed by the algorithm according to its standard rule set.

These placement requests are, however, only honored if they do not conflict with any absolute rule from the standard set, e.g., it is not possible through user directives for a float to be placed before its call-out if that is forbidden by a general rule.

By using a small number of forcing rules and one or two explicit page breaks at strategic places in the text stream, it is possible to freeze a certain part of the pagination while other parts are still subject to globally optimized pagination.

Another common requirement is to enforce that groups of floats (typically two) always appear either on the same spread (so that they can be conveniently viewed simultaneously) or always appear on different spreads (for example, floats that contain questions and their answers). Such rules can easily be checked when building the set of possible float placements for the next spread, as discussed in section 5.4. If such a requirement is violated then the candidate float placement is simply dropped.

6 CONCLUSIONS

In [7] we presented a customizable framework and algorithms for globally optimizing the pagination of a text stream with reasonable speed. The limiting aspect of this work was that the float placements were predetermined and were thus independent of the pagination of the text. This earlier work also showed that the task of properly fitting a text stream into a fixed set of columns is often very difficult or even impossible to achieve without providing some extra degrees of freedom (e.g., by varying the column lengths, or reformatting paragraphs to a different number of lines).

We have here extended this framework to support float positioning as part of the optimization. In some sense the extra complexity introduced by the floats is a welcome addition to the pagination process, as it adds extra flexibility and this can be needed to be able to find "any" solution that fulfills basic typographic rules adequately.

However, while we have been able to show that it is possible to implement many typical typographic requirements concerning floats, the resulting complexity is of order $O(n^2 \ell^{(\# \text{ of float streams})})$ and that is starting to stretch the capabilities of todays computers—and thus the patience of users—at least for longer documents. Initial experiments (with just one float stream) are promising, but further tests with a larger corpus of typical documents and and at least two independent float streams are necessary to verify those findings. For example, "Through the Looking Glass" by Lewis Carroll, a typical novel-length book with 2561 breakpoints in its galley and 48 figures (resulting in roughly 49–51 pages when typeset in two columns), showed the following behavior on a MacBook Pro laptop:

- Standard LATEX 2 sec processing but no acceptable solution;
- Global optimization in 2–8 min with any parameter setting, as long as floats aren't allowed to be more than 5 page turns away from their call-outs (a reasonable cutoff point);
- Roughly 9 hours if the float/call-out distance is completely unrestricted, i.e., *all* float placements are considered.

If there are no call-out-related rules one could use the approaches discussed in section 4.6.3. These concepts are not yet incorporated into the framework and it will be interesting to see how well they are going to behave. This is not idle curiosity; there are very interesting applications that use only aesthetic rules. For example, think of placing advertisements or tasks like generating travel brochures, in which pictures are used more as fillers without a direct relation to the content. In such a context global optimization using such rules would allow for automated high-quality data base publishing.

REFERENCES

[1] Richard Bellman. 1957. *Dynamic Programming* (1 ed.). Princeton University Press, Princeton, NJ, USA.

[2] Anne Brüggemann-Klein, Rolf Klein, and Stefan Wohlfeil. 2003. Computer Science in Perspective. Springer-Verlag New York, Inc., New York, NY, USA, Chapter On the Pagination of Complex Documents, 49–68. http://dl.acm.org/citation.cfm?id=865449.865455

[3] Thomas H. Cormen, Charles E. Leiserson, Ronald L. Rivest, and Clifford Stein. 2009. *Introduction to Algorithms, Third Edition* (3rd ed.). The MIT Press.

[4] Nathan Hurst, Wilmot Li, and Kim Marriott. 2009. Review of Automatic Document Formatting. In *Proceedings of the 9th ACM Symposium on Document Engineering (DocEng '09)*. ACM, New York, NY, USA, 99–108. DOI: https://doi.org/10.1145/1600193.1600217

[5] Charles Jacobs, Wilmot Li, Evan Schrier, David Bargeron, and David Salesin. 2003. Adaptive grid-based document layout. Association for Computing Machinery, Inc. http://research.microsoft.com/apps/pubs/default.aspx?id=69470

[6] Kim Marriott, Peter Moulder, and Nathan Hurst. 2007. Automatic Float Placement in Multi-column Documents. In *Proceedings of the 2007 ACM Symposium on Document Engineering (DocEng '07)*. ACM, New York, NY, USA, 125–134. DOI: https://doi.org/10.1145/1284420.1284455

[7] Frank Mittelbach. 2016. A General Framework for Globally Optimized Pagination. In *Proceedings of the 2016 ACM Symposium on Document Engineering (DocEng '16)*. ACM, New York, NY, USA, 11–20. DOI: https://doi.org/10.1145/2960811.2960820

[8] Michael Frederick Plass. 1981. *Optimal Pagination Techniques for Automatic Typesetting Systems*. Ph.D. Dissertation. Stanford University, Department of Computer Science, Stanford, California 94305. Report No. STAN-CS-81-970.

[9] Ian H. Witten. 1985. Elements of computer typography. *International Journal of Man-Machine Studies* 23, 6 (Dec. 1985), 623–687. DOI: https://doi.org/10.1016/S0020-7373(85)80062-6

[10] Stefan Wohlfeil. 1998. *On the Pagination of Complex Book-Like Documents*. Ph.D. Dissertation. Fernuniversität Hagen, Hagen, Germany.

The Mitchell Library WordCloud: Beyond Boolean Search

Monika M. Schwarz
Monash University
monika.schwarz@monash.edu

Kim Marriott
Monash University
kim.marriott@monash.edu

Jon McCormack
Monash University
jon.mccormack@monash.edu

ABSTRACT

Libraries are increasingly offering on-line digital access to their collections. However, traditional search-based interfaces are restrictive and do not encourage the user to explore the collection in the same way that a physical collection does. We present the Mitchell WordCloud, a novel on-line interface to the David Scott Mitchell collection of the State Library of New South Wales. Based on interface design principles for explorative search, it presents the user with a word cloud derived from the collection and a list of titles. As the user drags words from the word cloud to tell the system what they like or dislike the title list is reordered. The surrounding interface elements – image bar, time line and Dewey bar – provide complementary insights into the collection. The traditional vector space model for measuring text similarity was extended to take account of user dislikes and to order words in the word cloud. User studies confirmed that the Mitchell WordCloud is easy to use and encourages exploration.

KEYWORDS

Library interface design, explorative search, word cloud, cosine similarity

1 INTRODUCTION

Libraries, like all cultural institutions, have an obligation to provide access to their collections. At the same time they have to protect and preserve their artefacts by restricting access to the more valuable parts of their collections. Fortunately, advances in web technologies and document recognition now make it possible for libraries to provide on-line digital access to their collections instead. As a result the on-line interface has now become the usual first access point to a library, one which allows users from all over the world to search and browse through a library collection without the need to physically enter the library.

However, an on-line interface creates new challenges. The on-line catalogue of a library with a traditional search-based interface can feel very restrictive. It is unable to illustrate the richness of a collection in the way physical books on the shelves do. The user cannot easily obtain an overview of a large collection or readily orient themselves in different thematic sections, nor can they physically browse shelves to make chance discoveries. We need to create on-line interfaces that move beyond search. Interfaces that allow the user to orient themselves within the whole collection while engaging them and encouraging them to explore the collection.

We present such an on-line interface that we have designed for the David Scott Mitchell collection of the State Library of New South Wales. The collection comprises nearly 40,000 items and is one of the richest collections of early Australian books and photographs. The library has started to digitise the collection and asked us to prototype an interface that could provide access to the collection when the digitisation is complete.

The prototype interface, which we call the Mitchell WordCloud for obvious reasons, is shown in Figure 1[1]. A central word cloud shows the most prominent words of the collection. Words from the cloud can be dragged into containers to make a positive or negative selection. The list to the right shows a ranked list of book titles based on the selection criteria and also offers preview word clouds for individual books and access to the digitised book. The image bar on top shows the images from the ranked list or an individual book. The time line at the bottom shows the publication years of the books while the coloured bar to the left reprises the Dewey classification system to provide orientation within a collection. All the elements of the application are manipulable and linked providing an engaging, responsive experience.

The main contributions of this paper are to

- Describe the novel interface of the Mitchell WordCloud and the design rationale. Importantly the interface makes full use of the digitised material, and not just the meta-data about the library collection.
- Describe a novel ranking technique and method for weighting terms in the word cloud that is based on the traditional vector space model but which also takes account of negative selections.
- Describe the results of a small user study evaluating the effectiveness of the interface. Overall feedback was very positive. One participant specifically commented on the value to library users saying that the *"WordCloud system could be really useful for some people. It's not as intimidating as a search box, you [...] have a starting point."* This was exactly our intent when designing the interface.

2 RELATED WORK

Interface design for cultural or document collections is a topic broadly investigated in information visualisation and related disciplines.

DocEng'17, September 4-7, 2017, Valletta, Malta

© 2017 Copyright held by the owner/author(s). Publication rights licensed to ACM.
978-1-4503-4689-4/17/09...$15.00
DOI: http://dx.doi.org/0.1145/3103010.3103017

---

[1] A running version of the Mitchell WordCloud is accessible at http://www.monalena.me/MitchellWordCloud

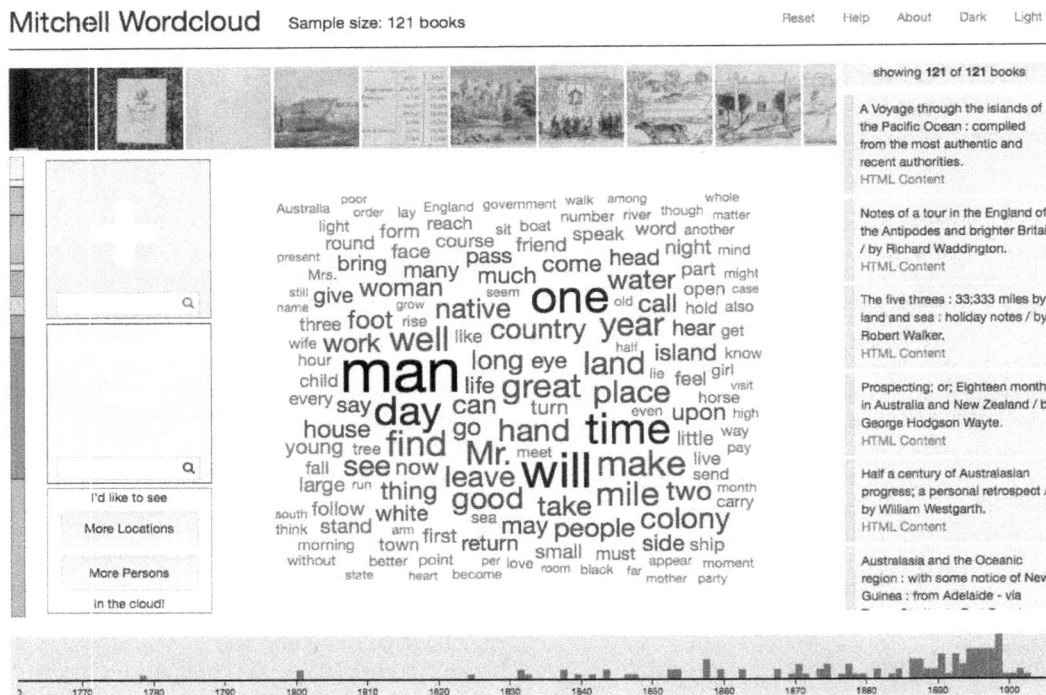

Figure 1: The Mitchell WordCloud

2.1 Visual Information Seeking

Some twenty years ago Shneiderman [21] gave the basic design rules for visual exploration in his **Information-Seeking Mantra**: "Overview first, zoom and filter, then details on demand." This has influenced many digital library interfaces and remains valid today. The concept of **previews and overviews** is also important [11]. While overviews enhance the overall understanding of a collection's organisation, previews of items in the collection enable the user to quickly judge whether the item is relevant to them. This approach ensures that the user can swiftly develop an understanding of the nature and scope of a collection.

Over the last decade a number of theories on alternative forms of information seeking have been developed. Marchionini [20] pointed out the difference between lookup search, which aims at mere fact retrieval or question answering, and **explorative search**, which 'blends searching and browsing' and is usually undertaken for learning (e.g. developing new knowledge) or investigative reasons (e.g. discovering gaps in existing knowledge). This was taken further by the introduction of the **information flaneur**, a theoretical construct that models the user seeking information on an urban flaneur in 19th century Paris who wanders the streets picking up impressions [7]. To please the 'curious, creative and critical' mindset of the information flaneur an information-seeking model needs to allow gradual shifts of horizontal exploration and vertical immersion. The design challenge for an interface incorporating

such shifts is to bring together high-level abstractions of an information space and detailed previews of the information resources while preserving orientation.

Other researchers have emphasised the significance of **serendipity** in search [1, 22]. Serendipity, the unexpected discovery of new knowledge by chance, happens in a physical library for example when noticing a book because of its striking cover. Design principles to support such serendipitous discoveries in digital data collections are the creation of multiple visual access points, highlighting of adjacencies, offering flexible pathways for exploration to encourage more open-ended searches and enticing curiosity and playful exploration.

In the broader context of cultural heritage collections such as archives, museums and libraries turning to digitisation, Whitelaw has called for more **generous interfaces**. He pointed out that traditional keyword search-based interfaces are inadequate access portals for such digital collections since users may lack the necessary background to formulate an appropriate query [26]. He also argues that, with the technical possibilities now in place, it is time to rethink traditional interfaces. It is time for generous interfaces, rich and browsable interfaces that convey the complexity and wealth of digital collections to the user [27]. Drawing from such different areas as information retrieval, information visualisation, human-computer interaction and digital humanities Whitelaw sums up the following principles for the creation of richer, more generous interfaces. These capture many of the points raised previously and provide a compelling summary of the design principles one should adhere to when creating an explorative interface for a library.

- **Overview**: With 'Show first, don't ask' Whitelaw states that an interface should not start off by requiring a query but instead offer rich information to the user to support their understanding of a collection (the need for an overview was first voiced by Shneiderman and has been stressed by many others since).
- **Detail or Preview of individual items**: A generous interface should provide samples of primary content that give contextual cues and invite exploration. This is similar to the previews proposed by Greene et al. [11]. The ideas of an overview and previews can also be compared with the need for horizontal exploration and vertical immersion as described in the information flaneur [7].
- **Movement or navigating relationships**: The structure of relationships within a collection (or its facets) has to be made evident to support the interpretability of a collection. Navigability of such relationships can be correlated to Marchionini's [20] interactive user interfaces but also to the gradual shifts postulated by the information flaneur.
- **Preserving orientation**: This aspect also reflects Shneiderman's opinions [21]. While exploring, users must be able to orientate themselves within the collection and backtrack their steps once the search has reached a dead end.
- Also, the **unfamiliarity** of the user with novel interfaces asks for a careful design that will not overwhelm or intimidate but instead entice the user to explore.

2.2 Explorative Interfaces

Enhancing the user's understanding of a library can be achieved by simply augmenting an existing search engine with a visualisation. This can be a treemap [5] or a network graph [2] like the WorldCat Identities Network[2].

A number of more holistic explorative interfaces have been developed in recent years. Some utilise a main visualisation panel with additional information and control provided in side panels. In **PivotSlice** [28] and **Refinery** [14] the main visualisation is a network graph. **BookFish**[3] shows only book covers, a sensible decision since this on-line browsing tool is aimed at children. In **BlendedShelf** a control panel can be used to show book selections in 3D on a virtual bookshelf [16].

The other approach is to provide multiple facets to sort and cluster a collection. In the context of a library collection these usually are aspects such as the author, the publication year, the keywords or, more serendipitously, the book cover colour or number of pages. Facets are usually represented by coordinated or linked views. **PivotPaths** arranges the facets of author, title and keywords in three vertical fields [9]. It focuses on relationships such as common keywords or co-authors, which are shown as edges linking the items. The **Bohemian Bookshelf** uses five appealingly designed visual features to model different facets of the collection for a table top display [22]. Each feature can be dragged to the middle to become enlarged and interactive. User studies of both these tools showed

that users were confused by their totally explorative nature and preferred to have an option for search as well. Similarly, **'Discover the Queenslander'** was designed using four different facets to encourage open-end searches [27]. The **Speculative W@nderverse** consists of four coordinated views and a toolbar for more traditional search and filter functions [13]. It can be seen as a picture book example of a generous interface, offering a rich overview and previews as well as highlighting relationships in a way that does not overwhelm the user.

2.3 Interfaces for Text Analysis Tools

The applications described above visualise meta-data: either extracted from a library catalogue (title, author, publication year) or created manually. But digitisation now makes it possible to extract information from the texts themselves to provide new and possibly more meaningful data (e.g. keywords or sections). A number of visualisations have been developed to show the results of text mining or topic modelling. They differ in whether they show an individual document or a document collection [17].

The most famous and now omnipresent text visualisation is the word cloud [24] which summarises a text as a group of words whose sizes indicate the frequency of that term. Tools that attempt to show more complex relationships between words are **Phrase Nets** [25], **Word Tree** [23] and **parallel tag clouds** [6] while **WordWanderer** uses a cloud to explore word co-occurrences in texts [8].

Making sense of large document collections with the help of visualisations has received some attention in the last few years. Most of these visualisations use a node-link structure. **WordBridge** binds tag clouds to the nodes and edges of a network graph to show the relationships between entities in a text corpus [15]. **FacetAtlas** uses multifaceted entity extraction, similarity measurement and index building to extract an entity-relational data model from raw text [4]. Representations of a document corpus based on topic modelling are usually visualised in a network [12, 18]. Another approach is to create different access points through different views as done in **JigSaw** [10] or **Serendip** [1]. The CorpusViewer of Serendip uses a matrix representation of titles and topics of a collection surrounded by control and preview panels. But Serendip also offers the possibility to explore texts and topics by ranks in other views.

These approaches to represent document collections based on text mining or topic modelling techniques result in rather complex visualisations. They demand some knowledge of the collection to navigate through them and may be daunting to the inexperienced user. Rather than encouraging exploration by the general public these interfaces are better suited to researchers or scholars for making sense of a large corpus or for deeper textual analysis. On the other hand the tools presented in Subsection 2.2 do have that playfulness but they show only the collection meta-data and do not exploit the leverage from the much richer information that is available from digitised texts.

Our aim when designing the Mitchell WordCloud was to bridge this gap. To build a library exploration tool that takes advantage of both meta-data and digitised texts but which is easy to understand and which encourages and entices the general public to explore the collection. A tool based on the design principles of Subsection 2.1.

---

[2]http://experimental.worldcat.org/idnetwork/
[3]http://www.bookfish.net.au

3 THE MITCHELL WORDCLOUD

3.1 The Data

We now describe the Mitchell WordCloud in detail. We start with the underlying data, which is taken from two sources.

Meta-data came from the official library search engine of the NSW State Library, from which we extracted the title, author, publication year, Dewey number and a unique 'bibUtil' number of about 27,000 titles.

The other data source was 135 digitized books from the history and geography section of the DSM collection. Due to poor OCR (optical character recognition) results, all German, some French and also two English books were discarded, leaving 121 books.

The digitized books came in folders containing an XML file of every page bound together by a navigation file and marked up according to the ALTO standard for OCR. The Stanford CoreNLP tool[4] was used for some simple natural language processing. After lemmatisation, named entity recognition (NER) was used to recognise compound words as well as names of persons, organisations and locations. Stop-words were excluded using http://www.ranks.nl/stopwords. Finally the term frequency, inverted document frequency and NER type for each term of each book were stored in a term-document-matrix. The digitized books also contained a large number of images. It was possible to extract everything tagged as an 'illustration' from the books. This included all elements that were recognised as non-textual during OCR and could be tables, signatures and hand-written notes, drawings, photographs, book spines or tables of content. About 2400 'illustrations' were extracted in total and cropped to size. Then they were stored in a folder according to the book they belonged to as both original and thumbnail images.

The collected data (metadata, term-document matrix and image folders) was stored in an SQLite database.

3.2 Architecture

The basic architecture of the system is a client-server structure with the page layout implemented using HTML5 and CSS3 and the visualisation logic using JavaScript. Most of the DOM-manipulating parts were written in D3 [3]. A python script uses the Flask framework[5] to connect browser and server side and contains the information retrieval logic which connects to the database.

3.3 The Interface Design

The interface design incorporates **multiple coordinated views**. Conceptually, the layout consists of a main panel containing the word cloud (fig. 2) and surrounding elements. To its left is the control panel with two selection containers to drag words into and two buttons. To the right and on the top of the application are the descriptive elements, the title list and image bar. Both elements describe individual items of the collection either by their titles and authors or by the images extracted from the books. At the bottom of the application and to the left are the time line and Dewey bar, orientation elements that give structure to the collection. These elements also have the potential to solve certain scalability issues

---

[4]http://stanfordnlp.github.io/CoreNLP/
[5]http://flask.pocoo.org

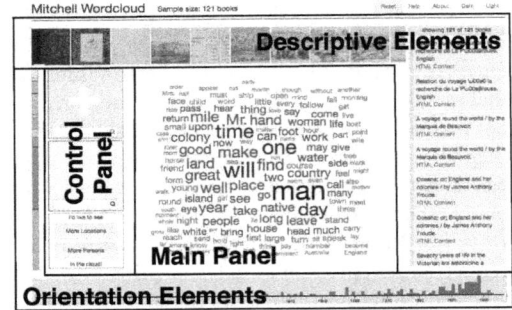

Figure 2: Interface layout

once the interface has to accommodate more books. The Dewey bar in particular can be redesigned to scale down into subsections. The application has a heading giving its name and number of the sampled books and links to reset the system, a 'help' feature explaining the functionality of the individual features and an 'about' page explaining the overall functionality and the background of the application.

The main panel doubles as display of the word cloud one can choose words from, and a preview to display enlarged versions of the images in the image bar. Just as the images individual titles can be selected and the main panel then displays a word cloud from that specific book, which, in turn, can again be used to choose words from. This supports the ongoing explorative nature of the design.

The **manipulation** of the application mainly works via the control panel. There are two **selection containers** into which the user can drag words. The green container stands for a positive and the red container for a negative selection. The buttons underneath the containers provoke a different weighing of the words in the cloud which will favour names of locations or persons. Interaction with these controls, e.g. dragging a word into or out of one container or pressing the buttons will trigger immediate changes to the word cloud and updates in the surrounding views.

While the time line and Dewey bar are mostly aimed at orientating the user within the collection they also offer ways to narrow down the book selection. The time line allows users to select a subset of the date range, restricting the selection of books to that range. The Dewey bar represents the different sections of the collection as bars stacked on top of each other, their height indicating the number of books in each section. It allows choosing sections based on subject classification. The application was designed in a responsive way where every manipulation triggers an immediate reaction in all parts of the visualisation.

The **colour scheme** for the interface is purposefully unobtrusive. The word cloud, title list and time line are displayed in greys. To signal the meaning of the containers the colours green and red seemed inevitable and they were consequently used in the title list to support the overall look of the interface. The Dewey bar reflects the NSW State Library's colour scheme for Dewey classification.

The **word cloud** is the heart of the application. It serves the double purpose of supplying the user with possible keywords and representing the books being explored. Initially it gives an impression of the whole collection; after selections have been made it

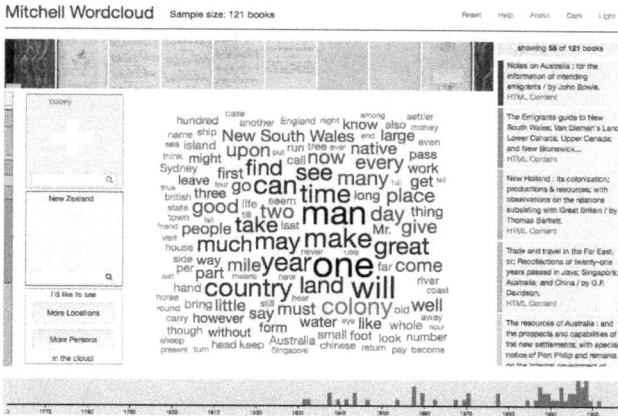

Figure 3: Example exploration step 1

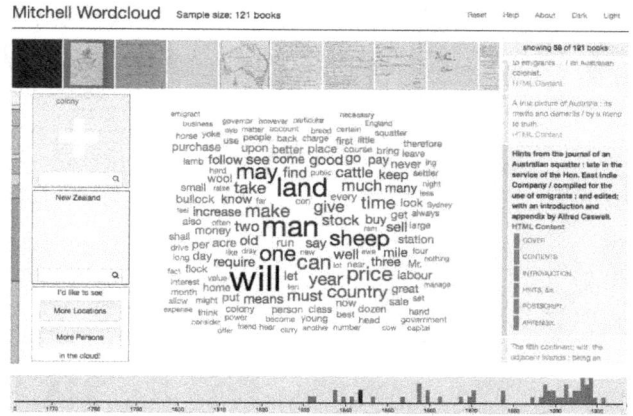

Figure 4: Example exploration step 2

reflects the reduced set of books; finally it can represent individual books. The word cloud was created using an algorithm written by Jason Davies[6], which chooses a maximum of 150 words from a selection and draws them on the screen in a spiral. It begins drawing at the centre with the most prominent and therefore largest words but fills the gaps with smaller words. It was modified to support easy selection of words so as to allow the user to drag words into the selection containers. Whenever the user makes such a selection a new cloud narrowed down by this selection is calculated and displayed. Every choice triggers a reordered cloud, however minimal the resulting changes are.

3.4 Application Logic

Once the user has chosen a word, be it positive or negative, a query is sent to the term-document-matrix stored in the database and a ranked list of corresponding books is determined. Based on that list a new set of the top 150 words for the word cloud is computed. The database is also queried for a list of titles, publication years and image numbers, then all of this information is sent back to the front-end to update the user interface.

Thus the application needs a way to retrieve a list of books that matches the selected terms. Initially we tried Boolean retrieval but this had the disadvantage that the list of books returned is not ranked and that books that "nearly" match the search will not be retrieved.

We therefore decided to use the vector space model for text retrieval [19]. Let D be the books in the collection, T the set of terms in the books and Q^+ and Q^- the set of positive and negative terms in the query, respectively. We first weighted the terms using as follows. The weight for term t and document d is

$$w(t, d) = tf(d, t) \cdot idf(t)$$

where the **term frequency**, $tf(d, t)$, is the number of times t occurs in d and the **inverted document frequency** is calculated as $idf(t) = \log \frac{|D|}{df(t)}$ where $df(t)$ is the number of books in which t

---

[6]https://github.com/jasondavies/d3-cloud

occurs. Note these are both pre-calculated and stored in the term-document-matrix.

We can compute a **relevance score** for each book based on the query terms:

$$rel(d) = \frac{\sum_{t \in Q^+} w(t, d) - \sum_{t \in Q^-} w(t, d)}{\sqrt{\sum_{t \in T} w(t, d)^2} \cdot \sqrt{|Q^+| + |Q^-|}}$$

This ranges between -1 and 1 and is the well-known cosine similarity extended to handle negative selections. The books are ranked based on this score.

The initial word cloud is computed by using total term frequency $\sum_{d \in D} tf(d, t)$. When the system is loaded or reset the 150 most frequent words of the collection stored in the term-document-matrix are given to the word cloud algorithm. The words in the matrix already exclude stop-words as well as single letters and numbers. It contains 136,638 individual words in total. Many words occur only once in the corpus and around 70% of words are mentioned less than 5 times.

The cloud currently contains some spelled out numbers like 'one'. In future these numbers should be included in the stop-word list. It might also be worth considering filtering out verbs like 'will' and 'can' based on their context in a sentence since they do not necessarily convey much meaning. Despite these weaknesses and the need to improve the word selection in future we feel the words determined by frequency still give a good first impression of the collection.

Initially the application also used term frequency to calculate the word cloud after a selection was made. But with a selection query the book list is ranked and we felt this should also be considered in the cloud. In the current application the term frequencies for each book are therefore multiplied with the relevance of the book,

$$\sum_{d \in D} rel(d) \cdot tf(d, t)$$

Combining term frequency with the relevance creates more tailored clouds, providing better incentives for the user to explore the collection.

43

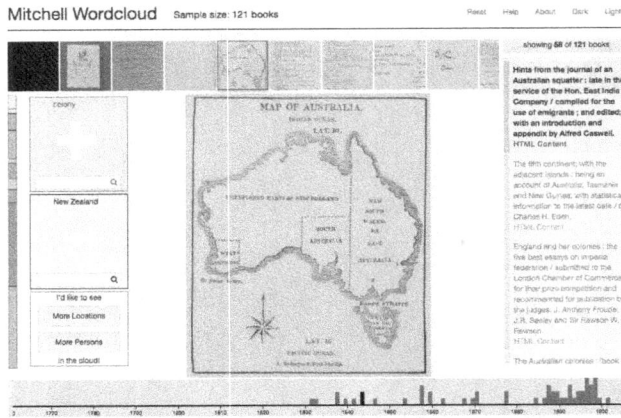

Figure 5: Example exploration step 3

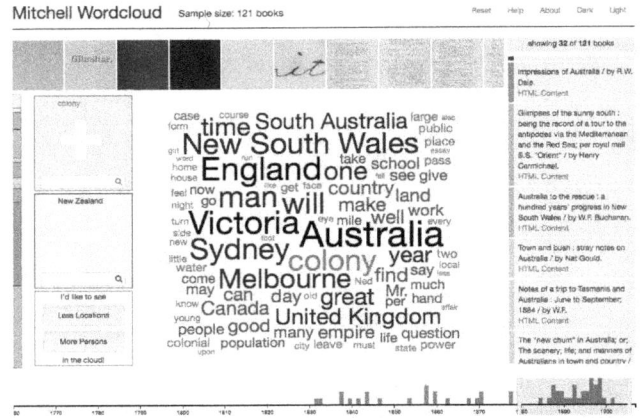

Figure 6: Example exploration step 4

3.5 Example Exploration

To illustrate how the application can be used and how all elements work together an example exploration will be described next. A similar exploration was also used in the user studies covered in Section 4 to familiarise the participants with the functionality of the application (single-step tasks). The user – let's call her Ann – is interested in early colonial literature. She starts her exploration by selecting the word 'colony' which she drags into the green container. This triggers a new word cloud from which, since she is more interested in Australia, Ann drags the word 'New Zealand' into the red container. This narrows the title list down to 58 books (fig. 3). Ann now scrolls through the title list until she finds a book with the title 'Hints from the journal of an Australian squatter'. She clicks on it to have a look at the word cloud of that book and also expands the table of contents in the title list. The book cloud contains a lot of words related to livestock farming like 'sheep', 'stock', 'land', 'price' and 'cattle' (fig. 4). Ann also scrolls through the images in the image bar until she discovers a map, which she clicks on to see an enlarged version in the middle of the screen (fig. 5). It is a political map of Australia where states like Victoria or Queensland are still missing. Tasmania is called 'van Diemen's Land' and the biggest part of the land is described as 'unexplored parts of New Holland'. Ann checks the publication date in the time line and sees that this is a book from the middle of the 1840s, a few years before states like Victoria were established. She decides to look at a younger selection of books next and chooses the timespan between 1880 and 1910 on the time line. The word cloud of the 32 books now remaining in the selection shows a shifted focus. The agricultural aspect has gone, words like 'city', 'coast' and 'island' show up instead. Together with the titles the words give away that this younger selection contains more travel than immigration literature. She presses the 'More Locations' button to see which locations are named in these books. And sure enough, the state 'Victoria' is now showing in the cloud (fig. 6). After checking the individual clouds of the first two strong matches she decides to borrow 'Glimpses of the sunny South' by Henry Carmichael from the library since it seems to have a strong focus on Victoria and Melbourne.

4 EVALUATION

We evaluated the Mitchell WordCloud in three different ways. The first was a theoretical critique, the second a small user study with students, while the third was an informal presentation to selected professional staff at the State Library of NSW. It has to be mentioned that the last two steps were performed with an older version of the Mitchell WordCloud (fig. 7). The current interface is the result of the feedback collected on both occasions.

4.1 Visual Information Seeking Critique

Our first method of evaluation was to critique the Mitchell Word-Cloud with respect to the visual information seeking guidelines that we presented in Section 2.1.

- **Overview:** The Mitchell WordCloud presents an information-rich interface without the need for an initial query. It offers the user incentives in the form of words in the central cloud which are derived directly from the texts themselves. By doing so it is able to help create an immediate idea of what the collection contains. It enables the overall understanding of the collection.

- **Detail or Previews:** The interface also provides visual cues in the form of primary content samples. The images in the image bar arouse interest and invite deeper exploration. Correspondingly, the title list and the book word clouds available through it also serve as previews of the primary content. The interface therefore offers opportunities for deeper exploration of parts of the collection.

- **Movement or navigating relationships:** The users are in full control of the application. They can narrow down the selection by choosing words, favour locations, set a time span or choose a Dewey section. To make clear that the resulting word cloud corresponds with their choices the transition to the new cloud is implemented not as a simple replacement but rather as a movement, a gentle reordering of the cloud. These gradual shifts help not to confuse the user.

- **Preserving orientation**: Orientation within the collection is offered through the Dewey bar and the time line. Both features make it possible to see the collection and the selections a user makes in context. This sense of orientation is missing in a traditional search interface. In addition both features offer the possibility to narrow the selection down to highlight specific aspects of the collection.
- **User unfamiliarity**: The Mitchell WordCloud is a novel interface that an average user is unfamiliar with. It was therefore designed to be pleasing to the eye and inviting, and care was taken to make every reaction intuitively understandable and logical.

It can therefore be said that the Mitchell WordCloud follows the major design principles recommended for the design of an explorative (or 'generous') interface.

Additionally, in order to create appropriate access points to a collection it is absolutely necessary to be familiar with the text corpus. If this is not possible then the help of experts in that domain is advisable. It is also necessary to design the interface using an iterative approach. Constant critical testing and re-assessment during the design of this interface has lead to numerous small changes and incremental improvements. It appears difficult to create a truly user-friendly interface with any other approach.

4.2 User Study

A user study in the form of semi-structured interviews was conducted to assess how usable and how engaging users would find the Mitchell WordCloud.

Participants. Eight participants were recruited from the student body of the Monash IT faculty. They were all in their twenties, two of them were female and seven described themselves as very experienced with computers. None of the participants were familiar with the David Scott Mitchell collection but three of them were familiar with similar collections.

Materials and Design. In the interviews, taking 40-60 minutes each, every participant was first given a short description of the interface and its elements. Subsequently the interview followed three stages. First the participants had to go through a set of simple one-step tasks as described in the example exploration in Section 3.5 and then perform a multi-step task. In the second stage the participants had time to freely explore the collection while thinking out loud. During the observation of this activity certain exploration strategies could be identified. In the final stage the participants were asked the following questions about their experience:

(1) During your exploration, did you find books that you found interesting?
Answer: yes/no
(2) If the answer is no, why not?
Answer: free
(3) If the answer is yes, which one(s) and what made you interested in them?
Answer: free
(4) Would you like to be able to use a tool like this in a library (table top) or on a library website? Why?
Answer: yes/no and free

(5) Which features in the application do you like best? Why?
Answer: free
(6) Which features do you like the least? Why?
Answer: free
(7) How easy or difficult did you find it to use the application? Why?
Answer: Likert scale (very difficult - somewhat difficult - neutral - not very difficult - not at all difficult) and free
(8) Did the application at any point show a behaviour you did not expect or understand?
Answer: free
(9) Have you used any similar or related tools to the one in this study previously? If yes, which one?
Answer: yes/no and free
(10) How familiar with the David Scott Mitchell collection were you before participating in this study?
Answer: Likert scale (very familiar - somewhat familiar - neutral - not very familiar - not at all familiar)
(11) How familiar are you with similar library collections to the one used in this study?
Answer: Likert scale (very familiar - somewhat familiar - neutral - not very familiar - not at all familiar)
(12) How experienced are you with using computers?
Answer: Likert scale (very experienced - somewhat experienced - neutral - not very experienced - not at all experienced)
(13) Any other comments or reflections on using the tool to explore the library collection?
Answer: free

Results. To judge the **usability** of the application the performance of the participants in the single-step tasks and their answers on the interview questions 5 to 8 were evaluated. Performing the single-step tasks in the first stage went quite smoothly with most of the participants showing little difficulty in using the interface.

When asked to rank the usability of the application the overall reaction to the prototype was quite positive. All participants graded the tool as not very or not at all difficult to use, describing it as *'easy to understand'*, *'intuitive'* and *'user friendly'*. The features participants found most convincing were the time line and the image bar, although half the participants also liked the containers, especially mentioning how intuitive the colours and symbols were. One person remarked positively on the combination of using a search function and the possibility to select words from the cloud as well, confirming the need to provide both options. The least convincing feature was the Dewey bar with one participant stating that it might be too technical for users unfamiliar with the Dewey Decimal system. Besides this some people were confused about the reaction of the application when positively selecting more than one word. Based on more words the cosine similarity algorithm includes more books (with a stronger ranking). In a search engine like Google this actually does not matter too much since people rarely check the results beyond the first page. But in the Mitchell interface some participants expected the selection to narrow down when choosing more words. Cutting the book list off at a dynamic threshold based on their cosine similarity score might address this problem.

The user studies also helped to identify some less intuitive features of the application which subsequently were improved. One participant compared the clouds after dragging the words 'man' and 'woman' into opposite containers and tasks like this can be performed quicker now with a search box in both containers. Regarding the image bar, one participant suggested adding a highlight on the thumbnail of a currently enlarged image so it could be found again when scrolling through the image bar. Most participants did not find out by themselves that the time line can be used to narrow down to a certain time span but quite enjoyed using it once told. Although aesthetically less pleasing, a box with handles around the time line is now used to make this more obvious. All in all no feature stood out as being clearly not accepted by a larger group.

To find out if the application **engages** as an explorative interface the observations during the multi-step task, the free exploration and the answers of the participants to the questions 1 to 4 were analysed. In the multi-step task the application was used like a search tool. The task was to find the photograph of a woman sitting in a rickshaw. Although all of the participants eventually found the picture, long search times and some necessity to give hints still proved that the application is not really apt for a complex search task.

In the exploration stage it was possible to observe different strategies that the participants used to explore the collection with some of them sticking to the same strategy throughout and others switching after a while (tab. 1). The first strategy was to use the tool like a search interface by typing terms of interest into the search box and then checking on the results before typing in the next term. This can be seen as the rather traditional look-up approach, although participants might extend some look-up searches with more explorative steps like scrolling through the image bar. The second strategy was the time line approach. Like a caterpillar crawling along a stick participants made small selections on the time line starting with the earliest books and then slowly worked their way through to the younger sections, sometimes jumping back and forth to compare clouds. For each selection they consulted the word cloud and title list but mostly made use of the image bar to view the tables and illustrations it offered for each timespan. The third strategy was rather a holistic approach. Here the participants jumped from feature to feature typing or dragging words into the containers, limiting the timespan, then scrolling through the book titles and finally looking at the images before starting the next round. The last two strategies can be seen as truly explorative approaches.

Tab. 2 shows the average exploration times for all exploration strategies. The time-line and holistic strategies took rather longer than the average exploration time but the search-box strategy only slightly less. More significant seems the fact that participants who stuck to one approach engaged with the tool much longer than those who switched strategies. Judging from the observed engagement with the collection this seems to indicate that participants with one strategy, no matter if rather traditional or more explorative, found the tool engaging while participants who switched might have struggled a bit to do so.

The answers to the interview questions seem to confirm that the tool is engaging. After skimming through early maps, ship logs or caricatures on Australian life all of the participants could name a book they wanted to know more about. Half of them mentioned

Search-box Approach	Time-line Approach	Holistic Approach	Total Time in minutes
x	-	-	8
x	-	-	10
x	-	-	14
x	x	-	5
-	x	-	20
-	x	x	5
-	x	x	13
-	-	x	20

Table 1: Exploration Strategies

	Time in minutes	SD
all explorations	11.8	5.6
search-box	10.6	4.5
time-line & holistic	14.5	6.2
one approach	14.4	5.0
approach switch	7.7	3.8

Table 2: Average Exploration Time

a personal interest or a research focus on a topic, the other half said that the images in the image bar had aroused their interest, one of them calling it a *'teaser effect'*. When asked if they would like to use a tool like this in a library or on a library website seven of them affirmed and one denied by reason of not being a regular library user. When prompted why they would like to use such an application participants said that it *'offers a quick look at a collection'*, that it was *'a completely new way of exploring content'* or that it simply was *'fun'*. One participant liked to have the *'images at your fingertips'*.

On the whole the participant's **feedback** about the system was quite positive. One participant stressed the value for library users:

> *"That word cloud system could be really useful for some people. It's not as intimidating as a search box, you kind of have a starting point. If someone does not have much experience with the library system goes in and wants to learn about just in general colonial Australia or travel literature they might not know which words to use to get the best results. And it could be quite daunting to think of words to use. If you have a word cloud, however, it's giving you the words to use. But I still think having a search box is important because there are some words that aren't in the word cloud that you would like to use."*

This is, in a nutshell, the reason we created the Mitchell WordCloud! The same participant also recognised the possibility to understand not just a single document but also a collection:

> *"There's two kinds of explorations you could do. One would be exploration to find what would be the best text, and then exploration to understand the corpus as a whole."*

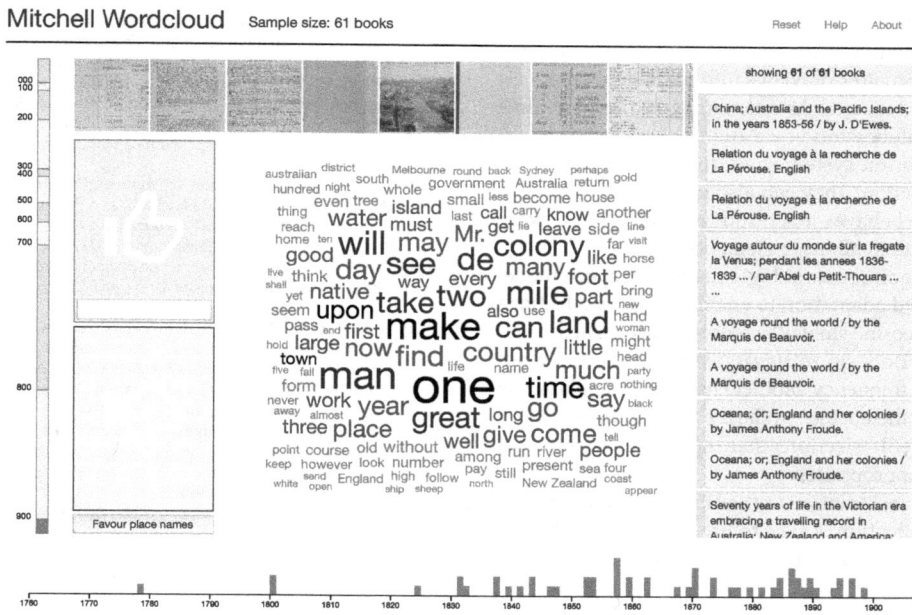

Figure 7: Old Mitchell WordCloud interface

With this in mind some participants started to think of other uses. A participant with an archival background said:

> *"This could be used for museum collections and library collections. ... I just keep thinking of everything we could use it for at work. ... That's really unique compared to what current systems provide."*

In summary, the user study confirmed both that the tool in general is easy to use and also works as an engaging explorative interface.

4.3 NSW State Library Staff

The interface was also demonstrated to three staff members of the NSW State Library in an informal presentation. The feedback in this presentation was similar to the results of the user studies. The image bar was perceived as the most positive feature as it makes the richness of the 19th century visual archive very apparent. The time line was judged to give interesting temporal information while the Dewey bar might be less interesting to library users.

A number of suggestions were made in this meeting and as a result more changes were implemented to the Mitchell WordCloud. To test the system with a larger size of books the original sample size of 61 books was increased with 60 books from the literature and rhetoric section. While incorporating the new books the stop-word list used thus far was replaced with a more extensive one since the original word cloud was criticised to contain too many meaningless words. Following a suggestion from the experts the titles in the title list now also contain links to HTML versions of the books and can be expanded to display a table of contents. One of the suggestions for improvement coincided with a result from the user studies: instead of displaying the images randomly in the bar the specialists preferred them in the order of the books in the title list. The Dewey bar is now designed to match the colour scheme the library uses in other projects[7] and displays genre information when moused over. The original option to show more place names in the word cloud was extended to distinguish between names of locations and/or persons. A few minor optical adjustments include plus/minus signs instead of thumbs up/thumbs down in the containers as well as small shifts in the layout to give the image bar more space.

The presentation proved how valuable feedback from the domain experts is for the creation of a novel interface for a cultural collection.

5 CONCLUSION

Restricted physical access to books and a shift in user behaviour to rather access libraries on-line call for new library interfaces that allow the explorative discovery of a collection. We have described the Mitchell WordCloud, an explorative interface for the David Scott Mitchell Collection. This is a novel application in as far as it combines the design principles developed for interface design for explorative search of cultural collections with the approach to integrate information extracted from the texts themselves to create new incentives in an interface. This involved multiple data pre-processing steps including extraction of the meta-data from the library search engine, lemmatisation and named entity recognition of the digitised books as well as extraction of illustrations from the digitised books.

A word cloud proved to be a powerful way to visually display the information derived from the texts. The interface therefore features the word cloud with the most prominent words in the center. Users interact with the cloud by dragging words into the containers to the left of the cloud. The descriptive elements of the interface, the

---

[7] http://dxlab.sl.nsw.gov.au/dx-lab-fellows-diary-2/

title list and the image bar, display the resulting selection. The title list displays the titles and the image bar the images of the selected books. Both features also offer previews into individual books via a book cloud or enlarged images. As orientating elements the time line modelled on the publication years and the Dewey bar based on the library classification system show the book selections in the context of the collection. They can also be used to restrict the selection. The interface behaves in a responsive way where every action triggers an update in all other elements.

As the underlying book retrieval logic the vector space model with a specially designed adaptation to enable negative selections in the form of negative cosine similarity scores showed a behaviour that was preferable to Boolean retrieval. While the initial word cloud is formed by term frequency another customized combination of term frequency and the cosine similarity score produces word clouds for the subsequent selections that represent the resulting book lists much more appropriately.

User studies and the presentation to the NSW State Library staff confirmed that the application is easy to use and successful as an explorative tool. The studies also provided valuable feedback for interface improvements.

It is necessary to use modern technology to open cultural collections like the David Scott Mitchell Collection to a wider public. We believe the Mitchell WordCloud does so in an inviting, playful and enjoyable way.

ACKNOWLEDGMENTS

We would like to thank all graduate students who participated in the user studies. We also thank Richard Neville, Kate Curr and Paula Bray from the NSW State Library for their collaboration. Special thanks go to Ross Gibson from the University of Canberra for his valuable contributions to this project.

REFERENCES

[1] Eric Alexander, Joe Kohlmann, Robin Valenza, Michael Witmore, and Michael Gleicher. 2014. Serendip: Topic model-driven visual exploration of text corpora. In *Visual Analytics Science and Technology (VAST), 2014 IEEE Conference on*. IEEE, 173–182.

[2] Miriam Allalouf, Dalia Mendelsson, and Evgeniy Mishustin. 2014. VISFACET: Facet Visualization Module for Modern Library Catalogues. In *Proceedings of the First Workshop on Knowledge Maps and Information Retrieval (CEUR workshop proceedings)*, Peter Mutschke, Philipp Mayr, and Andrea Scharnhorst (Eds.), Vol. 1311. London, UK, 61–69.

[3] Michael Bostock, Vadim Ogievetsky, and Jeffrey Heer. 2011. D³ data-driven documents. *Visualization and Computer Graphics, IEEE Transactions on* 17, 12 (2011), 2301–2309.

[4] Nan Cao, Jimeng Sun, Yu-Ru Lin, David Gotz, Shixia Liu, and Huamin Qu. 2010. Facetatlas: Multifaceted visualization for rich text corpora. *Visualization and Computer Graphics, IEEE Transactions on* 16, 6 (2010), 1172–1181.

[5] Edward C Clarkson, Krishna Desai, and James D Foley. 2009. Resultmaps: Visualization for search interfaces. *Visualization and Computer Graphics, IEEE Transactions on* 15, 6 (2009), 1057–1064.

[6] Christopher Collins, Fernanda B Viegas, and Martin Wattenberg. 2009. Parallel tag clouds to explore and analyze faceted text corpora. In *Visual Analytics Science and Technology, 2009. VAST 2009. IEEE Symposium on*. IEEE, 91–98.

[7] Marian Dörk, Sheelagh Carpendale, and Carey Williamson. 2011. The information flaneur: a fresh look at information seeking. In *Proceedings of the SIGCHI Conference on Human Factors in Computing Systems (CHI '11)*. ACM, 1215–1224. https://doi.org/10.1145/1978942.1979124

[8] Marian Dörk and Dawn Knight. 2015. WordWanderer: a navigational approach to text visualisation. *Corpora* 10, 1 (2015), 83–94.

[9] Marian Dörk, Nathalie Henry Riche, Gonzalo Ramos, and Susan Dumais. 2012. PivotPaths: Strolling through faceted information spaces. *Visualization and Computer Graphics, IEEE Transactions on* 18, 12 (2012), 2709–2718.

[10] Carsten Görg, Zhicheng Liu, Jaeyeon Kihm, Jaegul Choo, Haesun Park, and John Stasko. 2013. Combining computational analyses and interactive visualization for document exploration and sensemaking in jigsaw. *Visualization and Computer Graphics, IEEE Transactions on* 19, 10 (2013), 1646–1663.

[11] Stephan Greene, Gary Marchionini, Catherine Plaisant, and Ben Shneiderman. 2000. Previews and overviews in digital libraries: Designing surrogates to support visual information seeking. *Journal of the American Society for Information Science* 51, 4 (2000), 380–393.

[12] Brynjar Gretarsson, John O'Donovan, Svetlin Bostandjiev, Tobias Höllerer, Arthur Asuncion, David Newman, and Padhraic Smyth. 2012. Topicnets: Visual analysis of large text corpora with topic modeling. *ACM Transactions on Intelligent Systems and Technology (TIST)* 3, 2 (2012), 23.

[13] Uta Hinrichs, Stefania Forlini, and Bridget Moynihan. 2016. Speculative Practices: Utilizing InfoVis to Explore Untapped Literary Collections. *IEEE Trans. Vis. Comput. Graph.* 22 (2016), 429–438.

[14] S. Kairam, N. H. Riche, S. Drucker, R. Fernandez, and J. Heer. 2015. Refinery: Visual Exploration of Large, Heterogeneous Networks Through Associative Browsing. In *Proceedings of the 2015 Eurographics Conference on Visualization (EuroVis '15)*. Eurographics Association, Aire-la-Ville, Switzerland, Switzerland, 301–310. https://doi.org/10.1111/cgf.12642

[15] KyungTae Kim, Sungahn Ko, Niklas Elmqvist, and David S Ebert. 2011. Word-Bridge: Using composite tag clouds in node-link diagrams for visualizing content and relations in text corpora. In *System Sciences (HICSS), 2011 44th Hawaii International Conference on*. IEEE, 1–8.

[16] Eike Kleiner, Roman Rädle, and Harald Reiterer. 2013. Blended shelf: reality-based presentation and exploration of library collections. (2013), 577–582 pages. https://doi.org/10.1145/2468356.2468458

[17] Shixia Liu, Weiwei Cui, Yingcai Wu, and Mengchen Liu. 2014. A survey on information visualization: recent advances and challenges. *The Visual Computer* 30, 12 (2014), 1373–1393.

[18] Arun S Maiya and Robert M Rolfe. 2014. Topic similarity networks: Visual analytics for large document sets. In *Big Data (Big Data), 2014 IEEE International Conference on*. IEEE, 364–372.

[19] Christopher Manning, Prabhakar Raghavan, and Hinrich Schütze. 2008. *Introduction to Information Retrieval*. Cambridge University Press.

[20] Gary Marchionini. 2006. Exploratory search: from finding to understanding. *Commun. ACM* 49, 4 (2006), 41–46.

[21] Ben Shneiderman. 1996. The eyes have it: A task by data type taxonomy for information visualizations. In *Visual Languages, 1996. Proceedings., IEEE Symposium on*. IEEE, 336–343.

[22] Alice Thudt, Uta Hinrichs, and Sheelagh Carpendale. 2012. The Bohemian Bookshelf: Supporting Serendipitous Book Discoveries Through Information Visualization. In *Proceedings of the SIGCHI Conference on Human Factors in Computing Systems (CHI '12)*. ACM, New York, NY, USA, 1461–1470. https://doi.org/10.1145/2207676.2208607

[23] Frank Van Ham, Martin Wattenberg, and Fernanda B Viégas. 2009. Mapping text with phrase nets. *Visualization and Computer Graphics, IEEE Transactions on* 15, 6 (2009), 1169–1176.

[24] Fernanda B Viegas, Martin Wattenberg, and Jonathan Feinberg. 2009. Participatory visualization with Wordle. *Visualization and Computer Graphics, IEEE Transactions on* 15, 6 (2009), 1137–1144.

[25] Martin Wattenberg and Fernanda B Viégas. 2008. The word tree, an interactive visual concordance. *Visualization and Computer Graphics, IEEE Transactions on* 14, 6 (2008), 1221–1228.

[26] Mitchell Whitelaw. 2012. Towards generous interfaces for archival collections. *Comma* 2012, 2 (2012), 123–132.

[27] Mitchell Whitelaw. 2015. Generous Interfaces for Digital Cultural Collections. *Digital Humanities Quarterly* 9, 1 (2015). http://www.digitalhumanities.org/dhq/vol/9/1/000205/000205.html

[28] Jian Zhao, Christopher M Collins, Fanny Chevalier, and Ranjith Balakrishnan. 2013. Interactive exploration of implicit and explicit relations in faceted datasets. *Visualization and Computer Graphics, IEEE Transactions on* 19, 12 (2013), 2080–2089.

Small-Term Distribution for Disk-Based Search

Andrew Kane
University of Waterloo
Waterloo, Ontario, Canada
arkane@uwaterloo.ca

Frank Wm. Tompa
University of Waterloo
Waterloo, Ontario, Canada
fwtompa@uwaterloo.ca

ABSTRACT

A disk-based search system distributes a large index across multiple disks on one or more machines, where documents are typically assigned to disks at random in order to achieve load balancing. However, random distribution degrades clustering, which is required for efficient index compression. Using the GOV2 dataset, we demonstrate the effect of various ordering techniques on index compression, and then quantify the effect of various document distribution approaches on compression and load balancing.

We explore runtime performance by simulating a disk-based search system for a scaled-out 10xGOV2 index over ten disks using two standard approaches, document and term distribution, as well as a hybrid approach: small-term distribution. We find that small-term distribution has the best performance, especially in the presence of list caching, and argue that this rarely discussed distribution approach can improve disk-based search performance for many real-world installations.

CCS CONCEPTS

• **Information systems → Search engine indexing; Distributed retrieval;**

KEYWORDS

Index compression, Distributed search engines, Information retrieval, Index partitioning, Query performance, Run-time efficiency

1 INTRODUCTION

As document collection size increases, search engines can be scaled to provide good query performance by distributing their indexes across many disks. Clearly, any load imbalances in the system can degrade the performance of the distributed index.

There are also complications that occur within the index itself. A search index contains one postings list for each term in the dataset. These lists indicate the documents that contain the associated term and the number of times it occurs, using document identifiers and frequencies, respectively. The lists are typically ordered by document identifier to allow delta compression and merging of lists during query execution. Search queries simply find the postings

lists associated with the query terms, merge the lists, rank the documents, and display the highest ranked results [8, §4.1]. Reordering the documents (or renumbering the identifiers) gives significant list compression and query execution benefits that could degrade when distributing the index.

The two main approaches to distributing postings lists are *document distribution* (so-called "local" index organization), where all the postings for a document occur on the same disk, and *term distribution* (or "global" index organization), where all the postings for a term occur on the same disk. The former allows postings lists to be combined locally and provides well-balanced load during query execution, whereas the latter requires merging distributed lists but fewer disk seeks during query execution. Furthermore, document distribution allows linear scale-out to extremely large index sizes because each query returns only the top-k results which are small, meaning that network usage is low. On the other hand, term distribution cannot be used with large indexes, because the list sizes get larger as the system is scaled-out, thus eventually violating query latency requirements. Depending on the implementation, the volume of network traffic may also be a problem for term distribution, since postings lists need to be sent across the network and combined when answering a multi-term query.

In this paper, we examine both these approaches as well as the *small-term distribution* hybrid approach (first described in a patent application without any performance evaluation [13]; no patent has yet been awarded) that uses document distribution for large terms (i.e., terms with postings lists larger than a cutoff value), giving local merging of list and load balancing for the expensive portions of the query, and term distribution for small terms, giving fewer disk seeks. The three approaches to distributing postings lists are depicted in Figure 1. Notice that when the cutoff is 0, small-term distribution degenerates to document distribution, and when the cutoff is larger than the largest postings list size, it degenerates to full term distribution.

Rather than running experiments while varying the number of machines, processors, and disks, we compare the three distribution approaches under various system configurations using a new analysis technique. We first assume that loading the postings lists from disk dominates the query execution cost, then examine CPU and network costs. With this in mind, we track the disk transfer sizes and the number of seeks required to run actual queries based on the encoding sizes of the postings lists (corresponding to the query terms) for our chosen dataset. In this way we are using an actual workload to determine approximate disk execution costs.

Furthermore, we account for load imbalances by grouping queries into batches. The individual disk costs are summed over the queries in each batch, then the maximum cost over all the disks is used as the execution cost of the batch. Essentially, this batch level latency captures load imbalances without needing to examine actual query

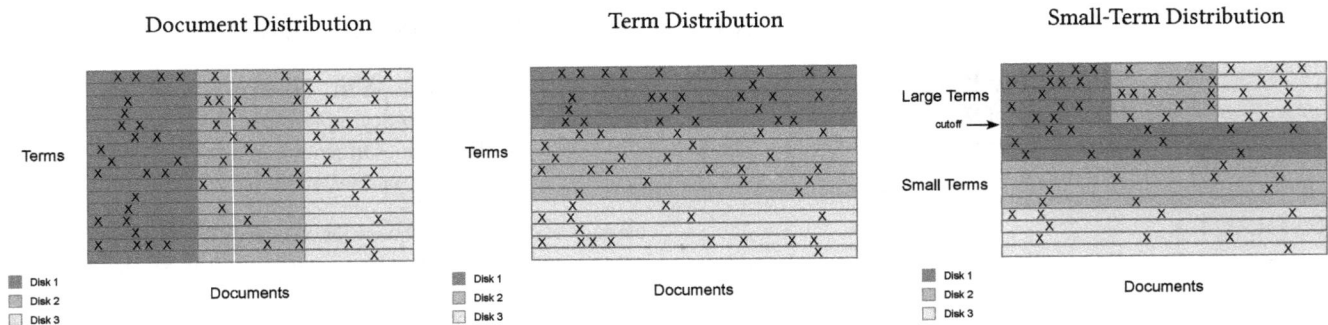

Figure 1: Distribution approaches applied to an index depicted as a matrix (adapted from [8], Fig 14.1), where rows are term postings lists and columns are documents. Each 'X' is a payload containing enough information to execute a query.

interaction and query latency. We divide this cost by the batch size and calculate the average over the workload to give *query takt times* (QTT) (i.e., the inverse of query throughput) that can be meaningfully compared across configurations.

Examining execution time results under varying batch sizes will give a strong indication of system performance. In order to examine potential problems with query latency, we also present the *99th-percentile query latency* (L@99%) for the distribution approaches. Presenting QTT and L@99% performance on the same graph quickly captures the system's performance characteristics for fast comparison.

As well as introducing our approach to analyzing performance, this paper includes the following contributions:

- We show how clustering within basic and combined orderings can improve index compression (Section 3).
- We show that document distribution produces a tradeoff between index balancing and clustering (Section 3).
- We show that small-term distribution of a search index across multiple disks (Section 4) is faster than document or term distribution, as demonstrated using a simple cost model (Section 5):
  - for a standard configuration (Section 7),
  - over a broad range of parameter values (Section 8),
  - especially when using caching (Section 9).

We believe that our novel method for comparing index distribution approaches using simple analysis to estimate latency and batched throughput can be adapted to other investigations. This work is thefi rst to present performance results for small-term distribution, an approach that deserves more attention in the literature.

2 RELATED WORK

Query Execution. List intersection has been studied extensively and is considered a fundamental building block for search engines. This process is usually executed as a conjunction of lists (i.e., a conjunctive AND query), which can be implemented using a simple merge algorithm when the lists are all sorted by document identifier. Multiple lists can be intersected using document-at-a-time or term-at-a-time processing [28]; the former requires little temporary space, while the latter causes intermediate lists to shrink, so they are often processed from smallest to largest.

When list intersection is generalized to include ranking information (i.e., adding frequency information to postings lists), queries

can use many other types of execution to improve runtime, since only the top-k results need to be returned.

Two common approaches for limiting list processing costs are max-score [28] and WAND [7], which require document-at-a-time processing. Another approach orders each list independently by frequency [3], which prevents simple merging of lists and thus requires combining lists in memory, but full lists may not need to be processed if sufficiently good results are already found (early query termination). Such optimizations, however, have little affect on the disk accesses involved in query execution, which is the bottleneck for most disk-based search systems. While list caching may make these optimizations more relevant to the systems we discuss here, considering how such optimizations interact with list distribution is left for future work.

Compression and Reordering. There are many encoding techniques that can be used with list intersection that are both fast and compact. For this study we use the OptPFD [30] approach, but others such as PForDelta (PFD) [32], Simple-9 [2], Simple-16 [31], or partitioned Elias-Fano codes [21] could have been used instead. It is common to include skips, as we do, to jump over unused portions of the lists. Some list intersection approaches prevent ranking information, such as occurrence frequency, from being included inside the encoding structure (e.g., bitvectors [9, 12]), thus limiting their usability, but producing large gains in both space and runtime. Other approaches can easily include such information immediately inside the encoding or in parallel on the block encoding level.

Reordering documents (i.e., renumbering internal document identifiers) can improve both space and runtime. One common technique reorders by URL [24] as we do for this study, but other techniques reorder at random or by clustering [6, 23], document size [8, §6.3.7], or global rank [14].

Distribution. Distributing search indexes across multiple disks or machines is a standard problem, so detailed descriptions can be found in most search engine textbooks [8, §14.1]. In this paper, we assume a single static index per disk (i.e., read optimized), rather than a dynamic index requiring merging of sub-indexes or in-place updates. We also assume a dedicated set of disks and machines, rather than a dynamic peer-to-peer approach. As stated in the introduction, postings lists are typically distributed by choosing which disk to hold either all postings for a given document or all postings for a given term.

The placement of documents when using document distribution can use any document ordering, but most cause load imbalances that limit system performance. As a result, random document distribution is typically used.

Term distribution can be improved in many ways, such as pipelining query processing [20] or duplicating lists [19], resulting in reduced network traffic and better load balancing. These benefits may have drawbacks, since they require term-at-a-time query processing between partitions and they determine the order in which lists are processed. Despite the improvements over the basic implementation, the term distribution approach still has problems producing consistently acceptable query latencies for large systems, though it can improve query throughput compared to document distribution.

Existing hybrid distribution techniques split postings lists into chunks of a certain size [29] (similar to RAID) or into a specified number of chunks [1] (capped by the partition count). These hybrid systems improve load balancing compared to term distribution and may save disk seeks; however, local list merging is not possible, resulting in an increase in network transfer of lists or the use of accumulators. Another hybrid approach starts as with document distribution of frequency ordered lists that are transferred to rankers in pieces, then converts lists to be term distributed during query execution [16]. Hybrid techniques have also been applied in the context of phrase-based indexes [22].

Earlier work recommended using document distribution across machines, then striping large lists on the disks within each machine [26]. This is similar to running document distribution across machines and small-term distribution within machines. However, using small-term distribution across machines can produce more efficient disk access at the expense of some additional network transfers. Follow-on work searching over abstracts recommended term distribution for systems with small postings lists, assuming a fast network is used [27].

In general, document distribution is used for large search systems, because it can scale-out linearly and balance load, while using little network traffic.

Caching. The two main levels of caching in search engines are result caching and list caching, both of which are highly effective because of significant repetition and temporal locality of queries [17]. As a result, many static, dynamic, and hybrid approaches have been explored [5, 15, 17]. Static approaches perform well, so we examine only static list caching in this paper, noting that adding result caching may not help for the low repetition query workload used in our experiments.

3 REORDERING DOCUMENTS

Search engines are normally thought to be 'embarrassingly parallel', because an index can easily be split into subindexes (or partitions) that are run in parallel using the document distribution approach. This process is complicated by the fact that the resultant system may not be as efficient as expected in terms of space and runtime.

For disk-based systems, where index size is critical to performance, the assignment of internal identifiers to documents (i.e., document ordering) will affect the index size and query runtime, and it is desirable to maintain the benefits of these orderings even after an index is split into partitions. Such orderings cause queries

to process at varying rates across the document identifier domain; therefore, load balancing of partitions becomes a concern when maintaining the document ordering. We examine this imbalance in index distribution, but leave complications from document updates and additions for future work.

Documents can be reordered (i.e., the internal document identifiers are reassigned using new numbers) to improve the compression of the encoded postings lists. Clearly, placing documents close to each other if they share terms (i.e., the typical tight clustering approach) will give lower document identifier differences (deltas) in the postings lists, which are then easier to compress. Placing large documents close together in the document identifier range (i.e., skewed clustering) can also reduce document identifier deltas and improve compression. Another approach places documents with many large frequencies together to improve overall compression of frequencies. These reordering techniques, however, do not change the list length and skips portions of the encoded postings list.

Throughout this paper, we use the TREC GOV2 corpus[1], indexed without stemming to extract document postings. The corpus size is 426GB in 25.2 million documents, generating 9 billion document postings for 49 million terms.

For our experiments, we encode postings lists as follows: The length of the list is stored using variable byte encoding. If the length is larger than 256, we encode an array of skips indicating the location and docID delta needed to skip over each chunk of 128 entries in the subsequent list. Each chunk encodes the docIDs using OptPFD (deltas minus one) and frequencies using OptPFD (without deltas, meaning values minus one).

$$encode(list) = length + skips + (docIDs + freqs)^+_{128} \quad (1)$$

We start by examining the effect of document ordering on index size without index distribution. Previous work has shown that ordering the GOV2 dataset by URL gives compression benefits equivalent to the best tight clustering techniques [24]. URL ordering has been shown to produce indexes that are approximately 50% of a randomly ordered index size [30]. (Other random orderings were equivalent, so only a single random ordering is presented here.) Our results achieve this amount of improvement for the document identifier portion of the encoding, but the entire encoding with URL ordering is 59% of the random ordering size, as shown in Table 1. Ordering instead by the number of unique terms found in each document (terms-in-document or td) to exploit skewed clustering does improve compression, but not as much as URL ordering. The original ordering maintained in the dataset is only slightly better than our random ordering.

Table 1: Encoding size (bits/posting) of basic orderings.

	length	skips	docIDs	freqs	total
rand	0.04	0.49	7.30	3.18	11.01
orig	0.04	0.49	6.84	3.04	10.40
td	0.04	0.49	5.35	2.63	8.51
url	0.04	0.49	3.66	2.34	6.53

Reordering techniques such as terms-in-document or URL ordering have tight and skewed clustering characteristics that can

---
[1]http://ir.dcs.gla.ac.uk/test_collections/gov2-summary.htm

produce significant benefits. Clearly, these techniques should be used broadly in real world search systems.

Combined. Skewed clustering can be combined with tight clustering byfi rst grouping based on skewed clustering and then ordering within each group using the tight clustering order. Following this method, wefi rst group the documents using terms-in-document (td) order so that each group contains similar numbers of postings, then order within each group by URL ordering. Our previous work showed that using four groups gave the best improvement in compression for postings lists without frequencies [12]. Applying this combined ordering (td4url) to our postings lists gives an index that is 4% smaller than URL ordering, as shown in Table 2.

In a similar manner, we attempt to skew the frequency values by grouping documents using their maximum frequency (mf) or their number of 'big' frequencies (bf), meaning frequencies larger than four. The resultant combined orderings (mf4url and bf4url) have not been previously explored in the literature. These orderings produce better compression than URL ordering, but are not as good as the previous combined ordering using terms-in-document. In particular, the size breakdown shown in Table 2 indicates a slight improvement for encoding the frequencies, but a degradation for encoding the document identifiers.

Table 2: Encoding size (bits/posting) of compound orderings.

	length	skips	docIDs	freqs	total
url	0.04	0.49	3.66	2.34	6.53
td4url	0.04	0.49	3.46	2.29	6.28
mf4url	0.04	0.49	3.55	2.28	6.37
bf4url	0.04	0.49	3.50	2.28	6.31

Since the improvements from these combined orderings are small, we ignore them for the remainder of this paper.

Distribution. When randomly distributing documents to partitions and ordering within each partition by URL, the amount of tight clustering in the entire index is reduced. Concatenating the document identifiers for the partitions and encoding with the resultant ordering gives an approximation of this reduction. Using this concatenated ordering, wefi nd that the encoding size degrades as the number of partitions increases, as shown in Figure 2. When using ten partitions, the resultant concatenated ordering (rand10url) is almost 12% larger than the unpartitioned URL ordering.

Non-random distribution techniques can be used to improve the tight clustering of documents within partitions, but this could cause load balancing problems. We measure imbalance as the relative difference of the maximum number of documents in a partition to the average number of documents per partition.

$$imbalance(P) = \frac{\max_{p \in P}(|p|)}{\text{avg}_{p \in P}(|p|)} - 1 \qquad (2)$$

where P is the set of partitions.

An existing approach splits the index by URL host name and sends each document to the partition that 'owns' its host name (IH-URL [10]). Maintaining this ownership mapping can be expensive, unless it uses a simple hash function. Applying this host-hashing technique to our dataset using ten partitions, the resulting ordering (host10url) has similar compression to URL ordering, but the partitions are very imbalanced, as shown in Table 3. Clearly, most of

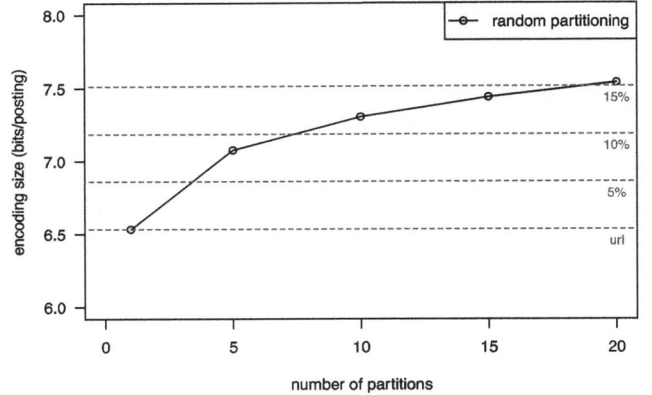

Figure 2: Encoding size when using random partitioning and URL ordering within partitions.

the tight clustering occurs within URL hosts, but hosts containing a large number of documents produce imbalance across partitions.

If we hash the documents using the host name and directories in the URL (hostdirs10url), the compression degrades and the imbalance is still large. If instead we hash on the host name, but spread each across a subset of the machines, then we can tune the compression vs. imbalance tradeoff. Indeed, hashing on the host name concatenated with one offi ve hashed values based on the remainder of the URL (host5mod10url) gives such a compression-imbalance tradeoff. Unfortunately, the imbalance rate is still larger than the compression improvement rate. Additional balancing may be achieved by ensuring that each host name is spread acrossfi ve distinct machines rather than relying on a hashed concatenation that will often repeat machines. We leave further exploration of this new *hash-modulo* technique for future work.

Table 3: Encoding size (bits/posting) and imbalance (%) when distributing over ten partitions.

	encoding size	imbalance (%)
url	6.53	0.0
rand10url	7.30	0.1
host10url	6.54	47.8
hostdirs10url	6.84	23.3
host5mod10url	7.00	8.4

We consider only URL ordering for the remainder of this paper and assume that document distribution causes negligible slowdowns that can be ignored. Note that small-term distribution has the same balancing and clustering problems as document distribution, so the relative performance of the two are directly comparable in subsequent results.

4 SMALL-TERM DISTRIBUTION

The *small-term distribution* hybrid method [13] uses term distribution for small postings lists and document distribution for large ones, with a tuneable *cutoff* threshold τ that determines which lists are large and which are small based on their encoding size, as shown in Figure 1. This approach is intended to save disk seek costs while maintaining good load balancing for a disk based search system. The definition encompasses document distribution, when $\tau = 0$, and term distribution, when τ exceeds the largest encoded list size. However, our analysis has found these extremes to be sub-optimal. After examining several cutoff thresholds, our analysis identifies how the best cutoff points perform for various configurations of index size and disk performance.

In order to process queries using small-term distribution, small lists are combined following the procedures for term distribution. Next the results are partitioned with respect to the documents assigned to each disk, and partitions are sent over the network to the corresponding machines accessing those disks. The query is then processed in parallel on these machines, and the top-k results are merged by a broker to form the final query results. If there are no large lists, then results can be returned directly from the term distribution portion, and if there are no small terms, then queries can be processed according to the procedures for document distribution. There are many optimizations designed for term distribution (Section 2) that can also be applied to the small-term distribution approach.

Small-term distribution has two major advantages over term distribution. First, small-term distribution can reduce network transfer, since large lists are never transferred over the network. Second, the portions of queries using large lists are both read from disk and executed in parallel, giving much better query latency and improved load balancing.

When comparing to document distribution, small-term distribution reduces the disk seek costs, which can be significant for small lists, and indeed, small indexes. The small-term distribution approach will also significantly reduce the dictionary sizes on each disk, since most terms are small, and are thus only stored on one disk rather than on many disks. For ranking systems, the single disk location for small lists makes per-term collection-wide information (e.g., inverse document frequency) more space frugal and easier to maintain. In fact, large term statistics using local disk information may be sufficiently accurate that collection-wide information would only need to be stored for the small (term-distributed) terms.

There are some drawbacks to the small-term distribution approach, beyond some added complexity in query processing. The initial indexing of a dataset is more complicated and data additions or updates are now harder. In many search systems, however, indexing and update mechanisms are less critical than search performance and are often run as offline processes. Systems handling updates and merges will have more fragmented lists that incur additional seek costs during loading and may thus benefit more from small-term distribution. An additional drawback is that a single point of failure may prevent responses for some queries, namely those relying on a small term found only on the inaccessible disk, as well as losing a portion of the query results for many remaining queries, namely those documents assigned to that same disk. (Failure in being able to respond to some queries is even more prominent with term distribution.) However, this failure type can be avoided through index replication, as is done for many systems employing term or document distribution.

The small-term distribution approach is unlikely to improve the performance of configurations where the indexes on each disk are very large, because the disk costs will be dominated by the time to transfer the data from disk. However, such configurations will not produce good query latency and may not be usable for *any* distribution approach.

5 SIMULATED EXECUTION MODEL

We calculate our performance numbers using a simple simulation of a static list intersection search system using a real query workload spread over a distributed index with postings list sizes based on a real dataset.

There are various potential bottlenecks that could limit the runtime performance of queries in a distributed, disk-based search engine. The most time-consuming functions are loading postings lists from disk, transferring lists across the network, and combining lists to calculate query results. For the purposes of our simulation, we start by assuming that loading lists from disk is the main bottleneck and thus model the distributed search system using disk read time only.

Our disk model comprises two values, the seek time (ms) and the disk transfer rate (MB/s), which are assumed to be constants. More precisely, the time to read a postings list (ms) is calculated as:

$$diskcost(list) = seek + 1000 \times |encode(list)| / transfer \qquad (3)$$

where $|encode(list)|$ is the size of the encoded list (Eq. 1) being read (in MB).

Postings lists are read in the order that they are required to answer queries, and we assume that there is no sharing of list reads between queries (i.e., no dynamic caching of terms shared among queries). Each list is read sequentially in its entirety into memory for processing, ignoring truncation optimizations[2], in order to reduce the disk cost by minimizing the number of seeks. In addition, all stop words and nonce words are preserved and no stemming is used, thus some lists may be large and there are many lists.

For simplicity, we assume that our entire measured dataset can reside on a single disk, and we simulate document distribution as a scale-out to multiple disks, each with its own processor to handle queries requiring data from that disk. Thus, the scale-out factor δ determines how many "copies" of the measured dataset are in a configuration, each representing a new set of documents. The scale-out factor also determines the number of disks.

The term and small-term distribution methods could assign a term's postings list in its entirety to exactly one disk and thus save seek costs over the document distribution approach. Unfortunately, these assignments could produce a load imbalance when queries access too much data from a single disk.

In order to capture load imbalance and parallel query execution, we deal with queries in a *batch* processing mode, as follows: We assume that each disk can start processing the next query in a batch as soon as it finishes the previous one, but that it must wait for all queries in a batch to complete before starting the next batch. As a result, the runtime of the batch is the time required by the slowest disk for that batch:

$$runtime(batch) = \max_{d \in disk} \sum_{q \in batch} \sum_{list \in q} diskcost_d(list) \qquad (4)$$

If the load is perfectly balanced across all disks, the total runtime for a query set is independent of the batch size. However, by varying

---

[2]Note, skipping does not help significantly at the disk read level.

the batch size, we can explore how load imbalances affect the system at different time scales. We can observe the effect of static load imbalance for the system by running the entire query set as a single batch. Alternatively, we can find the cumulative query latency for the query set by using a batch size of one, which is equivalent to running the queries sequentially. Using a small batch size allows for query concurrency while limiting the effect of load imbalance on query latency.

To compare results for varying batch sizes, we use *query takt time* (QTT), which is the average time between query completions (i.e., the inverse of query throughput). For a perfectly balanced system, QTT is the total disk cost per disk divided by the number of queries. In general, QTT can be calculated as the total batch runtime divided by the number of queries in the query set.

$$QTT(queryset) = \frac{\sum_{batch \in queryset} runtime(batch)}{\sum_{batch \in queryset} |batch|} \quad (5)$$

Our main metric of comparison is QTT using a small batch size, since it is indicative of the expected performance of the distributed system without allowing large interactions of queries that could degrade query latencies. For context in our initial experiments, we also provide QTT using a batch size of one (i.e., query latency under low load or when running sequentially) and a batch size large enough to include the entire query set (i.e., average work per query if there are no sustained load imbalances).

Our secondary metric of comparison is the 99th-percentile query latency (L@99%) using sequential processing (i.e., a batch size of one). This indicates the approximate query latency of the slow queries, which can be compared to the quality of service (QoS) guarantees required for the system. Based on experiments that measure the ability of a user to perceive delays, these QoS guarantees are often set to be in the range of 200ms/query.

6 ANALYSIS PARAMETERS

Using our encoding of postings lists (Section 3) with URL ordering and ignoring static costs like dictionary size, our GOV2 index is 6.88GB. Although the largest encoded list is 17.5MB, there are only 8435 lists over 100KB and just 2025 of those are over 500KB. (Note that these sizes are multiplied by the scale-out factor δ in subsequent graphs.) The rarity of large dense lists was previously observed by Moffat and Culpepper when using bitvectors to encode lists [18].

Our workload is a random sample of 10,000 queries[3] from the 100,000 TREC terabyte track efficiency task queries, with the remainder forming a training set. Like the corpus, the queries are tokenized, giving an average of 4.2 terms per query. When applied to the GOV2 dataset, the average number of postings in all lists used by a query is 15.9 million and these can be encoded in 10.9MB.

Our standard configuration analysis assumes disks can sustain a 220MB/s transfer rate and have an 8ms seek time. This performance aligns with published numbers for fast desktop drives from Seagate (6TB model ST6000DM001 has 220MB/s transfer and <8.5ms typical seeks for reads); many desktop drives are slower, even within the same model family (ST4000DM000 has 180MB/s transfer and <12ms typical seeks for reads). Subsequent analysis explores various seek times while keeping the same disk transfer rate.

---

[3]We repeated our tests using a random sample of 50,000 queries with identical results.

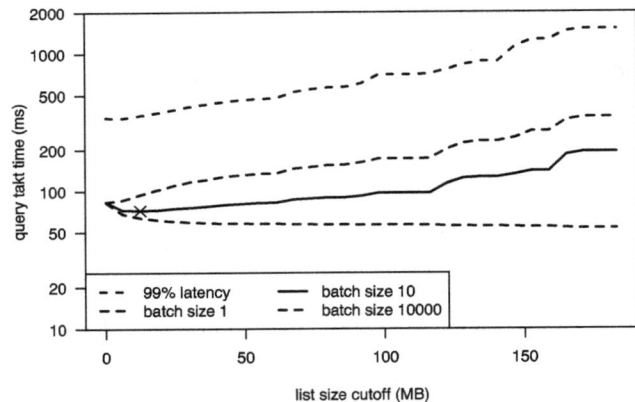

Figure 3: Performance for 10xGOV2 as a function of small-term cutoff threshold τ ($\tau = 0$ is equivalent to document distribution, $\tau \geqslant 175$ is equivalent to term distribution).

We interpret system performance using batches of queries, with the initial analysis using batches of size 10, but we also explore various batch sizes to see how this affects performance. In addition, we examine L@99% performance of the system to determine how our changes affect the performance of slow queries that may violate quality of service guarantees.

When distributing terms' postings lists to disks, they are assigned by taking the term identifier modulo the number of disks (i.e., round-robin based on lexicographic term ordering). Any terms not so distributed are assigned to the disks using document distribution.

We explore various parameter settings for batch size, seek time, and scale-out (i.e., increased disk counts hosting a proportional number of copies of GOV2, giving a scale-out factor represented by δ). Our analysis approach is, thus, to explore the simulated execution of a query set over a scaled-out version of the GOV2 dataset. Note that per-disk index size is limited by QoS guarantees for query latency.

7 STANDARD CONFIGURATION

In order to explore the detailed performance of the distribution approaches, we start with a prototypical configuration, then in Section 8 explore other configurations using various parameter settings.

We selected our *standard configuration* for initial analysis to be our GOV2 index with a scale-out factor of $\delta = 10$, denoted 10xGOV2. Our standard configuration, therefore, has an overall index size of 68.8GB and contains 252 million documents. Compared to a real index of 252 million documents, our standard configuration has better load balancing for document distributed lists and fewer small lists, but this should not significantly affect performance.

Figure 3 depicts the performance of document distribution (leftmost point), term distribution (rightmost point), and small-term distribution (all points in the middle) for the 10xGOV2 configuration. The graph includes four lines: the topmost (first) line captures L@99%; the second line represents batch size 1, which reflects the average single query latency under low load or when run sequentially; the third line represents batch size 10, which is our main measure of comparison; and the fourth line represents batch size 10000, which reflects the full workload QTT of the disk with the highest load. Note that we consider 29 small-term distribution cutoff values that are evenly spaced between document distribution at cutoff zero and term distribution at cutoff threshold $\tau = \delta \cdot 17.5 = 175$MB.

We can verify some of the numbers from Figure 3 using the query statistics presented earlier. The leftmost point for the QTT metric is the document distribution performance where all ten disks contain a copy of the GOV2 index. Therefore, on average per query, each disk performs 4.2 seeks (one per query term) plus a transfer of 10.9MB, thus requiring $4.2 * 8 + 10.9/0.220 = 33.6 + 49.5 = 83$ ms. This calculation also indicates that much of the time is due to seeks (i.e., $33.6/83 = 40\%$) when using document distribution for this configuration.

Similarly, the rightmost point for the batch size 10000 metric is the term distribution performance with almost ideal load balancing. With perfect load balancing, disk performance would be 4.2 seeks (one per query term) plus a transfer of 109MB all divided over the ten disks (i.e., $(4.2 * 8 + 109/0.220) * 0.1 = 53$ ms). This value is indeed what we calculated in our simulation, which validates the simulation and that our method of term assignment to disks produces good load balancing if amortized over a large number of queries. Following the rules of our simulation, this ideal load balancing value for term distribution is also the best possible QTT for any distribution approach when applied to the 10xGOV2 configuration.

The shapes of the curves in Figure 3 give some understanding of the three different distribution approaches. The leftmost point represents document distribution, which has the same performance for all batch sizes, since it is perfectly balanced in our simulation and very well balanced in general usage. The rightmost point reflects term distribution, which requires a lower amount of disk time overall, as shown by the line for batch size 10000, but quickly deteriorates from bad load balancing, as shown by the other batch size lines. The points between those endpoints represent the performance of small-term distribution using various cutoff thresholds: with small cutoff thresholds, small-term distribution has good load balancing, but this degrades as the cutoff threshold increases, as indicated by the increasing distance between the lines for batch size 1 and 10000.

In general, the line for batch size 10000 reflects the average work per query, but its values are determined by the disk that has to do the most work, so it would expose any sustained load imbalances in the system. This average work line decreases as the cutoff τ increases, since more lists use term distribution and therefore save the costs of some seeks.

Examining the performance of our 10xGOV2 index in Figure 3, we find that the term distribution approach has an average sequential query latency that violates QoS guarantees (i.e., rightmost point of second line) and has significant L@99% degradation (i.e., rightmost point of top line) making it unusable in a real system, even though performance with the other batch sizes is acceptable. Our main batch size 10 measure indicates that document distribution (leftmost point) is much faster than term distribution (rightmost point) agreeing with previous work showing that document distribution is generally superior.

The small-term distribution, however, performs better than either document or term distribution over a wide range of cutoff thresholds, namely $\tau \in [5.8, 58.3]$ MB. The best small-term configuration that we tested (marked with an X) occurs at $\tau = 11.6$MB, where the QTT for batch size 10 is 72ms compared to 83ms for document distribution, giving a 15% speedup. At this cutoff point, only 759 lists are above the cutoff, meaning that almost all the 49 million unique terms are spread across the ten disks reducing the dictionary sizes on each disk to 4.9 million terms. L@99% for small-term distribution degrades as τ increases, but the best small-term configuration also occurs at a point with little degradation.

Now we can verify our assumptions that the network and CPU costs are not performance bottlenecks for the best small-term configuration. The lists below the best cutoff point (i.e., the small term lists) represent only 0.86MB/query/disk, so if they were entirely transferred over the network at the 72ms/query processing rate, doubling for sending and receiving, that would take 0.19Gbits/s/disk. At this network transfer rate, two disks on each machine could be supported using a 1Gbit/s network card (i.e., 5 machines with 2 disks each is a reasonable deployment)[4].

The CPU speeds to execute a query in memory are much faster than the QTT for the standard configuration. When combined, these observations suggest that the small-term distribution approach is usable for this configuration and, indeed, is faster than either document or term distribution.

8 EXPLORING PARAMETERS

In Section 7 we examined how the choice of cutoff size τ for small-term distribution affects QTT and L@99%. In this section, we confirm the robustness of the performance improvements from using small-term distribution. In particular, we explore how query batch size β, disk seek time σ, and the size of the index (represented by the scale-out factor δ) affect performance.

Our standard configuration analysis uses the performance of the distribution methods for batch size 10, where this size was chosen to combine the effects of concurrency and load balance into one measure. The performance for batch sizes from 1 to 20 is presented in Figure 4, which includes our "standard" result (for batch size 10) marked with an X. In this and all other graphs in this section, the plot for small-term distribution reflects the best (i.e., lowest) QTT for the given combination of parameter settings when used together with one of our 29 potential cutoff thresholds. For the 10xGOV2 index, small-term distribution outperforms document distribution, even for small batch sizes except 1. Full term distribution performance, however, is inferior to both document and small-term performance for all batch sizes considered.

Both the term and small-term distribution approaches save disk seek costs over document distribution, and our standard configuration fixes the seek cost at 8ms. The QTT incurred for disk seek times from 0ms to 20ms is presented in Figure 5, which includes our standard 8ms seek cost marked with an X. The term distribution approach is slower than document distribution for all the seek times considered. Small-term distribution, however, outperforms document distribution, even for small seek times[5].

---

[4]Note, 1/5 of each list is used locally, so only 4/5 of each list must be transferred here.
[5]Note, small-term distribution appears to be slower than, instead of equal to, document distribution at $\sigma = 0$ms because of our limited choice of cutoff points.

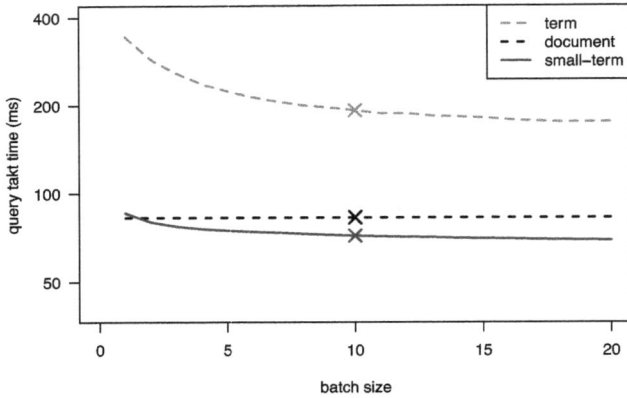

Figure 4: Effect of batch size β on performance of distribution methods for $\sigma = 8$, $\delta = 10$, and best choices of cutoff.

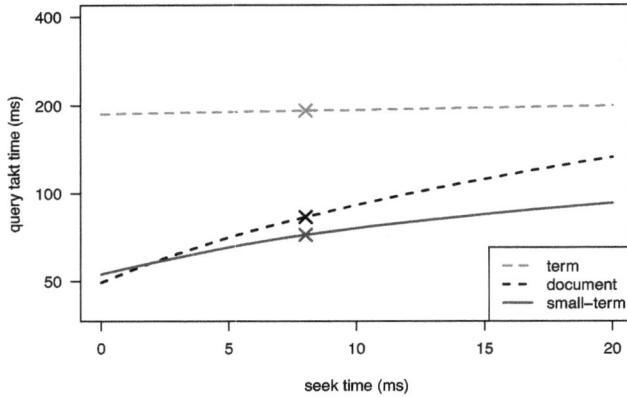

Figure 5: Effect of seek time σ on performance of distribution methods for $\beta = 10$, $\delta = 10$, and best choices of cutoff.

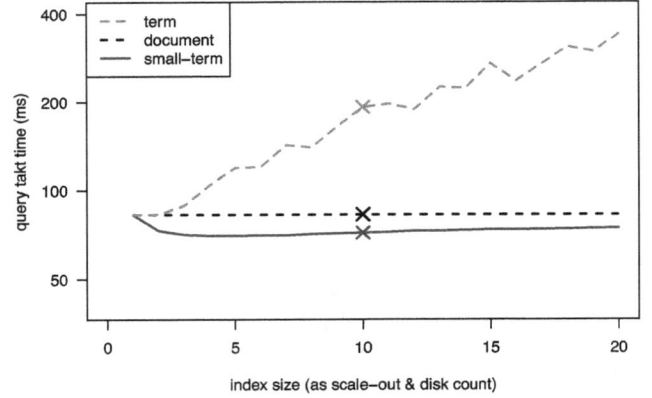

Figure 6: Effect of index size δ on performance of distribution methods for $\beta = 10$, $\sigma = 8$, and best choices of cutoff.

Based on these experiments, we conclude that small-term distribution outperforms both document and term distribution for a large range of batch sizes, seek times, and index sizes. When extremely large systems are required, however, out-of-the-box small-term distribution will necessarily suffer because even the "small" lists will become unacceptably large. In these circumstances, additional performance improvements could be realized by implementing small-term distribution in a hierarchical manner or by using document distribution over large partitions (first described in terms of *banks* of machines [13]), each implemented using small-term distribution. For example, the best small-term configuration in Figure 6 at disk count $\delta = 4$ can be scaled-out using document distribution over sub-collections of size 4xGOV2. Host distribution over small-term distribution could be used to alleviate the compression degradation of random partitioning, while still having reasonable balancing (similar to the hash-modulo approach from Section 3). Further exploration of these techniques is left for future work.

9 STATIC LIST CACHING

The pure disk-based search approach we have been examining is bottlenecked on disk access times, but real systems have some or all of the index in memory. This could simply be automatic via the operating system file cache or be designed into the search system itself. Many approaches to selecting the index portions to cache have been explored in the literature, but much of the benefit from caching can be realized with a simple static list cache, which picks the lists to cache based on a training set of queries. We consider a static list cache that contains all or none of the lists for a particular term across the entire system. Additional gains could be realized by caching partial lists, but we leave this for future work.

We use a cost-aware approach to pick the lists to cache; we order them by the disk cost from our model (Eq. 3) divided by the encoding size, where the list usage statistics come from the 90,000 query training set. This mimics the practice of using very large query logs to choose which lists to cache for ongoing query processing. We pick the best performance from three choices: selecting lists after ordering by the costs of document, term, or small-term (cutoff=1MB) distribution over the training set.

Our standard configuration is ten times the size of GOV2 distributed over ten disks (i.e., using a scale-out factor of $\delta = 10$). The QTT for configurations using scale-out factors between 1 and 20 are presented in Figure 6, which includes our standard scale-out factor of 10 marked with an X. As expected, all the distributions perform identically for the base case scale-out factor of $\delta = 1$, thus further validating our simulation code. The document distribution approach has a linear scale-out as expected, although balancing and clustering issues (Section 3) would cause this to slope upwards in a real system. Term distribution performs better than document distribution for small scale-out factors, but quickly degrades as the scale-out factor increases. Furthermore, term distribution is somewhat unstable as the scale-out factor increases, because we are doing modulo distribution of lists: commonly used lists may sometimes be placed on the same disk causing noticeable load imbalance, though term placement techniques may help [11]. Small-term distribution, however, outperforms document and term distribution for all the scale-out factors $\delta > 1$ considered, and it does not exhibit the anomalies resulting from load imbalance.

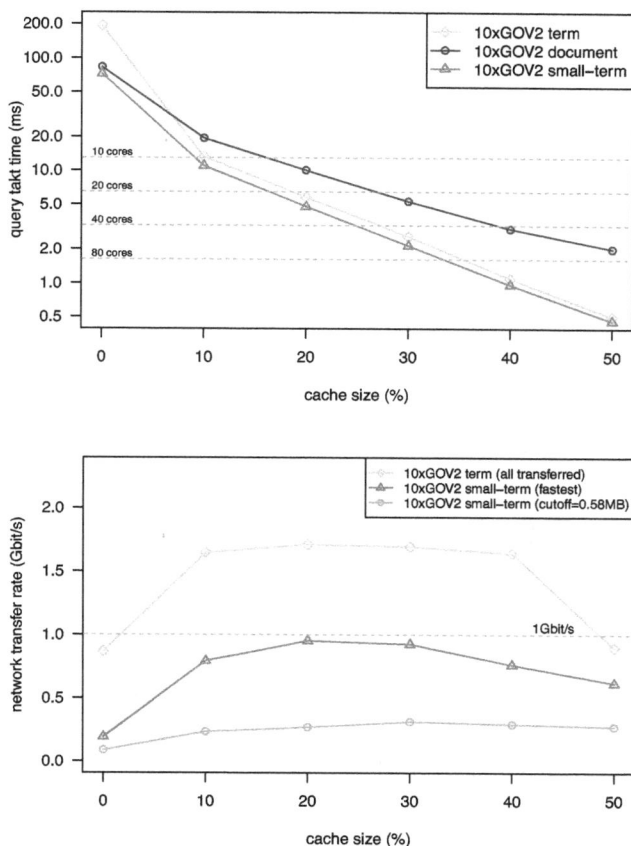

Figure 7: Effect of static list cache size on performance (top) and the amount of small term data per disk that must be transferred across the network (bottom) for 10xGOV2.

Even small amounts of caching can quickly improve the performance of a search system. With this improved performance, our previous choice of a batch size of 10 would require the system to be balanced over an extremely small time window. In order to alleviate this restriction, we increase the batch size proportional to the performance of document distribution, meaning the batch size becomes the average number of queries that can run in a specific amount of time. We pick the batch size to be the number of average length queries that can fit in 1 second, rounded to the nearest integer. Using this calculation our cache sizes of {0%, 10%, 20%, 30%, 40%, 50%} give batch sizes of {12, 52, 99, 187, 330, 497} respectively.

When caching is used, both term and small-term distribution are much faster than document distribution, as shown in Figure 7 (top). Even with a cache of just 10% of the index, small-term distribution has a 1.77x speedup which increases to a 4.4x speedup with 50% cache. Note that these numbers already account for disk read imbalances by using our batching calculations. Although when using list caching and our adjusted batch size, the performance of term distribution and small-term distribution are similar, small-term distribution does much better than term distribution for the slow queries. Even with 10% cache the small-term L@99% performance

using the fastest cutoff is well below 200ms at 121ms, while term distribution is still at 327ms and does not drop below 200ms until 30% cache. In this sense, small-term distribution is much more usable than term distribution, while maintaining many of the benefits of term distribution.

Small-term distribution does require more network transfer than document distribution; when using the fastest small-term cutoff value for 10xGOV2, the network transfer rate of the small terms, including both sending and receiving, could saturate a 1Gbit/s network when using caching, as shown in Figure 7 (bottom)[6]. However, using the smallest cutoff value of 0.58MB, this network transfer rate drops significantly (and is more stable) with only a small degradation in query performance.

On the other hand, when all the lists are transferred, the network costs of term distribution can become significant, as also shown in Figure 7 (bottom). The network transfer rate for term distribution can be reduced by processing queries on the machine containing the most data for that query or by using pipelining to transfer only truncated intermediate results. Even if the network transfer rate is not a bottleneck for system performance, term distribution may have imbalances in the distribution of query processing work (i.e., CPU costs).

Modern systems can often place the full search index in memory, even for relatively large datasets. The memory based performance is much faster in terms of both throughput and latency, but it can still violate quality of service guarantees in some cases. For comparison, we include an estimate of performance numbers for an in-memory search system. The SIGIR 2015 workshop on reproducibility, inexplicability, and generalizability of results (RIGOR) [4] executed queries on several search systems using Amazon EC2 hardware for the GOV2 dataset with the best system having an average query runtime of 26ms. However, this performance did not include reordering by URL which should allow queries to run in half the time, so we assume a single CPU core can process GOV2 queries in 13ms. The same performance is possible for our 10xGOV2 configuration if the scale-out "copies" can be run in parallel on 10 separate CPU cores. This processing mode is possible for document distribution and for small-term distribution (since the slow queries will contain large lists). We assume linear CPU scaling, which gives us the dotted lines on Figure 7 (top). Thus when using term or small-term distribution, a 10% cache allows disk transfers to keep up with queries processed using 10 CPU cores and a 40% cache provides data faster than can be handled by a system using 80 CPU cores.

Term distribution, however, assumes a single global index which must be processed on a single core and could violate our expected 200ms quality of service guarantee. Other hybrid distribution approaches [1, 29] also use a global index design and simply try to spread the large lists across disks or to duplicate lists. As a result, they have the same single core processing problems as term distribution. This situation only gets worse with larger scale-out values, however, queries can be run in parallel using multiple threads on a single machine [25]. Even with threading, the CPU work involved in query processing could become a bottleneck from load imbalance (i.e., too many queries executed on one machine).

---

[6]Note, this rate includes local portions of lists that do not need to be transferred.

The ability to parallelize and balance query processing in the small-term distribution approach is a clear win over other hybrid distribution approaches.

10 CONCLUSIONS

In this paper we have demonstrated that distributing small postings lists (those for terms that appear in few documents) using term distribution and the remaining lists using document distribution outperforms both standard document distribution and standard term distribution. The improvement in performance when using *small-term distribution* is evident in the query throughput (measured as the *query takt time* (QTT) when queries are processed in small batches), with little effect on the 99th-*percentile latency* (L@99%) when queries are processed sequentially. Small-term distribution also has a clear advantage over other hybrid distribution approaches, because it can process queries in parallel without special threaded query execution, thus avoiding query degradation in scale-out situations.

For a 252 million document index over ten disks, we showed that small-term distribution produced a 15% speedup with respect to the standard document distribution approach and much higher speedups when using caching, up to 4.4x faster than document distribution for a 50% cache. We also showed that small-term distribution outperforms document and term distribution for a wide range of batch sizes, seek times, and index sizes. As such, the small-term distribution approach will improve disk-based search engine performance for many real world installations. For example, a search system with multiple partitions on RAID storage (giving low latency and fast restarts) would benefit from using small-term distribution, especially if the stripe size is larger than the small-term cutoff and the small-term lists do not cross stripe boundaries.

Our experimental method used a novel form of analysis, simulating the performance of a disk-bottlenecked search engine using batches with data obtained from GOV2, a real dataset with a real query workload. This method of analysis made it possible to explore a wide variety of system configurations without running numerous time-consuming conventional experiments, while maintaining the benefits of using real query and data characteristics.

Future Work. We plan to explore additional compression algorithms and document orderings (i.e., beyond OptPFD compression and URL ordering). Examining additional datasets and query workloads would also help explore the configuration space to determine the situations in which to use each of the term, document, and small-term distribution approaches.

Our analysis approach using small batches to combine latency and load balancing requirements could also be applied to other optimizations, such as document ordering and document placement. While we applied our analysis approach to simulated execution performance, it could also combine actual executions of partitions run independently, thus avoiding full distributed system runs.

ACKNOWLEDGMENTS

This research was supported by the University of Waterloo, by the Natural Sciences and Engineering Research Council of Canada, and by Mitacs.

REFERENCES

[1] Ahmad Abusukhon, Michael P. Oakes, Mohammad Talib, and Ayman M. Abdalla. 2008. Comparison between document-based, term-based and hybrid partitioning. In *ICADIWT*. 90–95.

[2] Vo Ngoc Anh and Alistair Moffat. 2005. Inverted index compression using word-aligned binary codes. *Information Retrieval* 8, 1 (2005), 151–166.

[3] Vo Ngoc Anh and Alistair Moffat. 2005. Simplified similarity scoring using term ranks. In *SIGIR*. 226–233.

[4] Jaime Arguello, Matt Crane, Fernando Diaz, Jimmy Lin, and Andrew Trotman. 2016. Report on the SIGIR 2015 workshop on reproducibility, inexplicability, and generalizability of results (RIGOR). In *ACM SIGIR Forum*, Vol. 49. 107–116.

[5] Ricardo Baeza-Yates, Aristides Gionis, Flavio P. Junqueira, Vanessa Murdock, Vassilis Plachouras, and Fabrizio Silvestri. 2008. Design trade-offs for search engine caching. *TWEB* 2, 4 (2008), 20:1–28.

[6] Dan Blandford and Guy Blelloch. 2002. Index compression through document reordering. In *DCC*. 342–351.

[7] Andrei Z. Broder, David Carmel, Michael Herscovici, Aya Soffer, and Jason Zien. 2003. Efficient query evaluation using a two-level retrieval process. In *CIKM*. 426–434.

[8] Stefan Büttcher, Charles Clarke, and Gordon V. Cormack. 2010. *Information retrieval: Implementing and evaluating search engines*. The MIT Press.

[9] J. Shane Culpepper and Alistair Moffat. 2010. Efficient set intersection for inverted indexing. *TOIS* 29, 1 (2010), 1:1–24.

[10] Moran Feldman, Ronny Lempel, Oren Somekh, and Kolman Vornovitsky. 2011. On the Impact of Random Index-Partitioning on Index Compression. *CoRR* abs/1107.5661 (2011), 1–9.

[11] Byeong-Soo Jeong and Edward Omiecinski. 1995. Inverted file partitioning schemes in multiple disk systems. *TPDS* 6, 2 (1995), 142–153.

[12] Andrew Kane and Frank Wm. Tompa. 2014. Skewed partial bitvectors for list intersection. In *SIGIR*. 263–272.

[13] Kevin Lang, Swee Lim, and Choongsoon Chang. 2008. Hybrid term and document-based indexing for search query resolution. (April 4 2008). US Patent App. 12/098,376.

[14] Xiaohui Long and Torsten Suel. 2003. Optimized query execution in large search engines with global page ordering. In *VLDB*. 129–140.

[15] Xiaohui Long and Torsten Suel. 2005. Three-level caching for efficient query processing in large web search engines. In *WWW*. 257–266.

[16] Mauricio Marin and Veronica Gil-Costa. 2007. High-performance distributed inverted files. In *CIKM*. 935–938.

[17] Evangelos P. Markatos. 2001. On caching search engine query results. *Computer Communications* 24, 2 (2001), 137–143.

[18] Alistair Moffat and J. Shane Culpepper. 2007. Hybrid bitvector index compression. In *Proc. of the 12th Australasian Document Computing Symposium*. 25–31.

[19] Alistair Moffat, William Webber, and Justin Zobel. 2006. Load balancing for term-distributed parallel retrieval. In *SIGIR*. 348–355.

[20] Alistair Moffat, William Webber, Justin Zobel, and Ricardo Baeza-Yates. 2007. A pipelined architecture for distributed text query evaluation. *Information Retrieval* 10, 3 (2007), 205–231.

[21] Giuseppe Ottaviano and Rossano Venturini. 2014. Partitioned Elias-Fano indexes. In *SIGIR*. 273–282.

[22] Knut Magne Risvik, Trishul Chilimbi, Henry Tan, Karthik Kalyanaraman, and Chris Anderson. 2013. Maguro, a system for indexing and searching over very large text collections. In *WSDM*. 727–736.

[23] Wann-Yun Shieh, Tien-Fu Chen, Jean Jyh-Jiun Shann, and Chung-Ping Chung. 2003. Inverted file compression through document identifier reassignment. *Information Processing & Management* 39, 1 (2003), 117–131.

[24] Fabrizio Silvestri. 2007. Sorting out the document identifier assignment problem. *Advances in Information Retrieval* (2007), 101–112.

[25] Shirish Tatikonda, B. Barla Cambazoglu, and Flavio P. Junqueira. 2011. Posting list intersection on multicore architectures. In *SIGIR*. 963–972.

[26] Anthony Tomasic and Hector Garcia-Molina. 1993. Query processing and inverted indices in shared-nothing text document information retrieval systems. *The VLDB Journal* 2, 3 (1993), 243–276.

[27] Anthony Tomasic and Hector Garcia-Molina. 1996. Performance issues in distributed shared-nothing information-retrieval systems. *Information Processing & Management* 32, 6 (1996), 647–665.

[28] Howard Turtle and James Flood. 1995. Query evaluation: strategies and optimizations. *Information Processing & Management* 31, 6 (1995), 831–850.

[29] Wensi Xi, Ohm Sornil, Ming Luo, and Edward A. Fox. 2002. Hybrid partition inverted files: Experimental validation. In *ECDL*. 422–431.

[30] Hao Yan, Shuai Ding, and Torsten Suel. 2009. Inverted index compression and query processing with optimized document ordering. In *WWW*. 401–410.

[31] Jiangong Zhang, Xiaohui Long, and Torsten Suel. 2008. Performance of compressed inverted list caching in search engines. In *WWW*. 387–396.

[32] Marcin Zukowski, Sandor Heman, Niels Nes, and Peter Boncz. 2006. Super-scalar RAM-CPU cache compression. In *ICDE*. 59:1–12.

Maintaining Integrity and Non-Repudiation in Secure Offline Documents

Ahmed Shatnawi
University of Wisconsin-Milwaukee
Department of EECS
Milwaukee, WI 53201-0784
shatnaw3@uwm.edu

Ethan V. Munson
University of Wisconsin-Milwaukee
Department of EECS
Milwaukee, WI 53201-0784
munson@uwm.edu

Cheng Thao
Concordia University, St. Paul
Department of Mathematics &
Computer Science
St. Paul, MN 55104-5494
cthao@csp.edu

ABSTRACT

Securing sensitive digital documents (such as health records, legal reports, government documents, and financial assets) is a critical and challenging task. Unreliable Internet connections, viruses, and compromised file storage systems impose a significant risk on such documents and can compromise their integrity especially when shared across domains while they are shared in offline fashion.

In this paper, we present a new framework for maintaining integrity in offline documents and provide a non-repudiation security feature without relying on a central repository of certificates. This framework has been implemented as a plug-in for the Microsoft Word application. It is portable because the plug-in is attached to the document itself and it is scalable because there are no fixed limits on the numbers of users who can collaborate in producing the document. Our framework provides integrity and non-repudiation guarantees for each change in the document's version history.

CCS CONCEPTS

•Security and privacy →Software security engineering;

KEYWORDS

Secure document engineering;Version control; XML document

1 INTRODUCTION

The research presented in this paper seeks to improve the collaborative development of documents and is motivated by several different concerns. First, recent events, such as the publication of private emails immediately before the 2017 French presidential runoff, have demonstrated that document security can be of profound importance. A particularly interesting feature of that event was that some of the published email messages were purported to have been altered or faked. Second, collaborative documents are often shared outside the controlled environment of a central repository or a highly engineered application that supports offline collaboration and/or natively supports version-aware documents. This may happen because sharing via email or flash drive is more

DocEng '17, September 4–7, 2017, Valletta, Malta.
© 2017 ACM. 978-1-4503-4689-4/17/09...$15.00
DOI: https://doi.org/10.1145/3103010.3121038

convenient to users. Or it may happen because Internet access is not sufficiently stable for users to rely on a system that requires a constant online connection. Finally, for many collaborative documents, the complete provenance (or version history) of the document content is important. This might be for establishing credit or blame for the content or for deducing possible motivations for the content.

Together, these concerns focus our interest on providing security in the form of *integrity* and *non-repudiation* of the content and the *provenance* of the content for *offline, collaborative* documents. Defining these key terms:

- A system that maintains *integrity* guarantees the accuracy of data during the whole document lifecycle.
- A system that maintains *non-repudiation* is able to provide a non-repudiable proof of actions the known users have made.
- The *provenance* of a collaborative document's content establishes which authors are responsible for which parts of the content. In practice, a document's provenance can be thought of as a version history.
- *Offline, collaborative* documents have multiple authors and are stored on users' personal storage devices, such as flash drives or personal computer drives, rather than being shared via a canonical copy on a centralized repository or cloud service.

In this paper, we introduce a new secure framework for XML-based documents that preserves data integrity and non-repudiation for the document's full version history. The framework supports offline sharing of documents among collaborating authors by using version-aware XML document technology [2, 14] to store version information inside the document itself. We use digital certificates to achieve integrity and non-repudiation for offline XML documents. Our proposed framework remedies the lack of integrity in offline documents and will also provide users with a mechanism to identify who made changes in the document and keep a secured record for each revision of the document that is signed by a legitimate user. Specifically, our proposed framework will answer the following questions:

(1) Has the shared file been modified?
(2) Are the modifications made by known users?
(3) What changes did the known users make to the document? Moreover, can we prove it?
(4) For each change made to the document, can we determine the author, the computer making the change, and the time at which the change was made with non-repudiable certainty?

We have chosen to develop our framework for MS Word because we have access to the code that provides version control discussed in [2] and because Word is so widely adopted and its documents are so often shared in an offline manner. Moreover, MS Word documents are stored in an XML format [1]. Word documents are meant to be a portable, non-centralized way to collaborate and share data. Our proposed framework is general and could be applied in any environment using an XML document representation, but MS Word provides a useful and practical test case for our ideas.

The remainder of this paper is organized into four sections. Section 2 presents our proposed framework design and implementation. Section 3 discusses feasibility and how we evaluated our proposed work. Section 4 discusses related research. Finally, section 5 wraps up our main ideas and points out the advantages of using our framework, some unresolved problems, and possible future work.

2 DESIGN AND IMPLEMENTATION

Our solution uses both Version-aware XML technology [2, 14] and Digital Signature [6]. Our key software component is an extension of Coakley et al.'s Version Aware Word Document plug-in [2] that adds our security features. The plug-in, implemented by Coakley et al. maintains a version history by saving document snapshots in a new sub-folder of the MS Word file (actually, a zipped folder) called "history" without taking into account securing the integrity of these snapshots and the document content. This sub-folder contains an index file called "revision-history.xml" that points to further sub-folders named with unique IDs. The plug-in is implemented in C#. We found, as did Coakley et al., that Word's plug-in API was challenging to work with.

Our extension modified Coakley et al.'s Version Aware Word Document plug-in to support both document integrity and non-repudiation, along with storing more end-users' information who collaborated on a document to be used for forensics (e.g., IP address, MAC address, etc.).

Figure 1 illustrates our framework, in which key entities are marked with numbers. The first time that an end user (denoted by 3) wants to start working with our system, that user must get access to our plug-in. We currently use an *application host* (1) to provide starter documents that have the plug-in embedded. The application host also acts as an intermediate certificate authority (CA) that is verified by a very well known root CA(e.g Verisign), to which the user can provide and confirm some identifying information (i.e. name, email address, cellphone number, etc.) in order to become a known user and receive a personal certificate that will be used to sign documents. In addition to the plug-in, the documents also contain the certificates of the root CA (4) and the intermediate CA (1), which were used in the chain validating the end user's certificate. The end users (3) are shown sharing the documents (2) that they are collaborating on, which they do using the standard Word application. The plug-in helps the authors by automatically signing the document each time it is committed. The authors can then share the document with the newly committed changes with their collaborators and the person who is in charge to generate the final version of the document; knowing that everyone can verify the document's integrity.

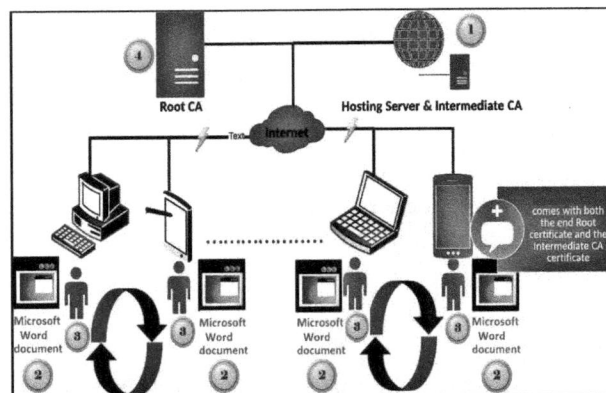

Figure 1: Initial setup to download the Word secure version-aware document along with obtaining the end user's certificate signed by the intermediate Certificate Authority (CA) over a secure channel. The curved arrows show that end users could share the files offline, and the lightning symbol represents a network connection present for the initial setup but not necessary reliable afterwards.

In this framework, the only times that end users must go online are when they first need to get a document containing the plug-in and whenever they need to obtain a new certificate. The former case could be a one-time only event, but the latter case might have to occur periodically since certificates can expire or be revoked.

After downloading the Word document, end users may modify and share the Word document offline or via online services. When a user commit changes to the document, the following integrity XML tags and data are added in the revision-history.xml file. These features will be embedded in the revision-history.xml as shown in Figure 2:

    (a) Version-aware data.
    (b) The current author's certificate.
    (c) A signed digest for the whole document along with the certificate ID that has been used for signing.
    (d) Other forensic information will be attached to the current revision to identify the user who made the revision.

Our framework then checks for both integrity and non-repudiation by using the information stored in the revision-history XML file inside the Word document as shown in Figure 2. Although our framework does not prevent illegal tampering by altering or injecting data in the Word document, it will detect any modifications made by unknown users in the Word file, even including style changes.

Our extended plug-in adds the capability to import the user's digital certificate, verify the user's certificate and verify the integrity of the document when loaded. When the user is done editing the document, the user has the ability to sign the document. Signatures are persistent and the document holds the signatures for every revision made. This is different from Word's own document signing feature, which removes all previous signatures when a new collaborator signs the document.

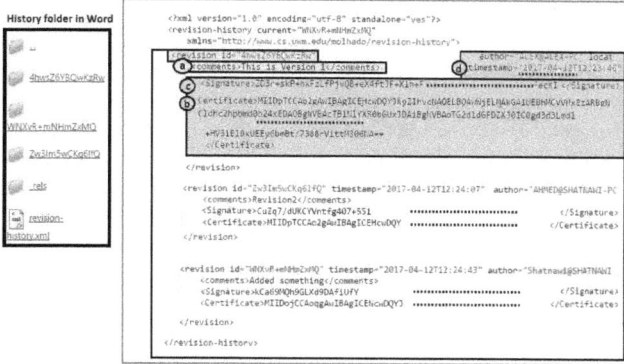

Figure 2: A sample Background Check Report word document signed by three different users. The lines of asterisks represents elided parts of the certificate and forensic data.

3 EVALUATION

In order to evaluate our framework, we performed a range of tests using a document that records a background check written with MS Word. We chose this particular document because it is a natural example of a document that might be passed among a series of collaborating authors performing different parts of an employee background check, in an environment where it is important to be sure that only known users are making changes. Our use case scenarios fall into two categories:

(1) Integrity based: Testing whether our framework preserves the integrity of documents and their revisions while shared among multiple users.

(2) Non-repudiation based: Testing whether our framework provides a non-repudiable evidence of which users made which changes.

We tested many scenarios, focusing on the questions we posed in the introduction and we verified that our proposed system is able to:

(1) Detect whether or not a shared file been modified.

(2) Determine whether each modification was made by a known user.

(3) What exact changes the known users made on top of a document along with a solid proof which user made which change.

(4) Determine the author, the computer making the change, and the time for each change made.

One interesting user case scenario we conducted involved a collaboration among four users: A, B, C, and D. If the four users used their valid certificates using our plugin, any other known users were able to see the exact changes made by the users, verify the integrity of their revisions, and see proof of what they changed in the document. However, let us suppose that when User D loads the document, the system says that the changes apparently made by C are not signed by a valid certificate. In this case, D knows that those changes are not trustworthy. At this point, D can either reject the document or D can try to validate the changes by a secondary pathway (e.g. directly contacting C for a new, valid document), or

D can reject the changes and work from the valid revision signed by B.

Other scenarios we tested involved a malicious attempt by an anonymous user to tamper with User A's file contents. Our framework detected such tampering attempts and notified the user who received the tampered file. Our framework also detects when a user has not relied on our plugin for editing.

Reverse engineering, such as re-saving a document without a signature and discerning the signature by subtraction has been considered in our proposed framework. Since each user will share his committed document with all the collaborators, any user can check whether any information has been subtracted from any signed document.

Reverse engineering, such as re-saving a document without a signature and discerning the signature by subtraction has been considered in our proposed framework. Since each user will share his committed document with all the collaborators, any user can check whether any information has been subtracted by comparing with other signed documents If a signature does not appear in a document, but appears in other documents, then the signature must have been removed from that document. We did not implement the feature to check for this type of problem automatically, but it could easily be done.

4 RELATED WORK AND DISCUSSION

Version-aware documents [14] provide a self-contained and portable XML document representation that includes a full version history in one XML file, including a simple signature mechanism to ensure integrity of the version data. Coakley *et al.*'s version-award Word documents [2] adapted this approach to the MS Word environment. The complex multi-file storage representation of MS Word forced a shift away from the signed reverse-delta representation to a collection of unsigned document snapshots. Our work enhances that of Coakley *et al.* by adding security features beyond those of the original system.

The preservation of data integrity while collaboratively editing XML-like documents online has been addressed by multiple researchers [7, 9, 12], but there is less research on offline XML documents. Liu *et al.* [8] discussed how to preserve XML document integrity by using concatenated hash functions, but they did not discuss how to validate the users' certificates.

The Automated Policy Enforcement eXchange (APEX) framework [13] is designed to ensure the enforcement of security policies as a document's content changes over time. It assumes that a document is constructed from a structured set of components and that many users may share the component while having various roles (e.g. owner, author, reviewer, reader). Components may have differing security settings and those settings may change over time as the document's content changes. A key innovation of APEX is the recognition that fixed security settings are not sufficient to prevent information leakage. For example, a document may not contain any classified or confidential data at the time of creation, so its security parameters might allow usage of exposure operations such as copying and sharing. But later on, confidential data could be added to the document and fixed security parameters would still allow exposure operations, leading to data leakage. APEX provides automated policies that adapt the security parameters to the evolving document. The APEX framework focuses on prevention of information leakage. In contrast, our proposed framework focuses more on detection of document integrity problems and on providing non-repudiable forensic information about changes made to the document. The two approaches are almost orthogonal and it is possible to conceive of merging the ideas.

Considerable research has been published on providing secure access control and updates in a distributed, cooperative environment for online tree-structured documents such as XML [3, 4]. One important issue is to know if shared files have been tampered with by a non-authorized third party. An adversary might try to provide false information or inject harmful scripts into files that will affect applications parsing the documents. While the negative effects of false information are fairly obvious, the risks from XML injection could be quite severe and could include consequences such as data destruction or denial of service via malicious queries. Our approach provides the same kind of guarantees for offline documents.

Perlman [11] discusses trust models, pointing out that since verifying digital certificates cannot be done without verifying the entire certificate chain, offline users must have a strategy for doing this. Offline users might rely on certificate stores in the browser or operating system to get the certificates that were used to sign end-users' and intermediate CA certificates. Perlman's discussion highlights a limitation of our work, which is that, over a long time, certificates in the version history may expire. We leave the resolution of this problem to future work.

Our framework makes sharing of Word documents offline possible without connecting to a centralized service, while preserving integrity and ensuring non-repudiation of all changes made to the document. It could also be useful for auditing the authorship chain of the document. Importantly, the framework stores all certificates necessary for document validation inside the document itself, making the document's validity provable at all times. Furthermore, validation is unlikely to require network access in order to reach key certificate authorities since our representation includes the authorities' own certificates.

MS Word itself provides a limited form of version control and also allows users to sign their documents. But Word does not provide a complete version history, so someone receiving a signed document knows only who last signed the document. Our approach provides an extensive document history with author signatures at each step of the version history.

5 CONCLUSION

In this paper, we have studied the problem of sharing sensitive offline Word documents. Our new proposed framework provides persistent integrity, detects tampering in any part of the document, and provides tools suitable for doing forensics when the validity of changes has been questioned.

Automatically signing the documents in a stealth mode without any human interaction can be provided in the future by checking if the document has been changed when the user tries to exit Word without committing the document.

Our framework could be applied to other applications where sharing files are likely to be conducted offline. While ensuring both integrity and non-repudiation is important, we would like to investigate and consider the applicability of our proposed framework for developing countries and remote geographical areas or to times of crises, such as geographical disasters where online services might be expensive or, at best, intermittent. An example of such a case is the distributed XML-based electronic health records system, developed for adoption in countries where both internet and electricity are limited and unreliable (e.g., SmartCare [5, 10]).

REFERENCES

[1] 2016. ISO. Information technology-Document description and processing languages- Office Open XML File Formats ISO/IEC 29500-1:2016. (2016).
[2] Stephen M Coakley, Jacob Mischka, and Cheng Thao. 2014. Version-Aware Word Documents. In *Proceedings of the 2nd International Workshop on (Document) Changes: modeling, detection, storage and visualization*. ACM, 2.
[3] Andreas Ekelhart, Stefan Fenz, Gernot Goluch, Markus Steinkellner, and Edgar Weippl. 2008. XML Security - A Comparative Literature Review. *J. Syst. Softw.* 81, 10 (Oct. 2008), 1715–1724.
[4] José Luis Fernández-Alemán, Inmaculada Carrión Señor, Pedro Ángel Oliver Lozoya, and Ambrosio Toval. 2013. Security and privacy in electronic health records: A systematic literature review. *Journal of biomedical informatics* 46, 3 (2013), 541–562.
[5] H Fusco, T Hubschman, V Mweeta, Benjamin H Chi, Jens Levy, Moses Sinkala, et al. 2005. Electronic patient tracking supports rapid expansion of HIV care and treatment in resource-constrained settings [Abstract MoPe11. 2C37]. In *3rd IAS Conference on HIV Pathogenesis and Treatment*.
[6] Shafi Goldwasser, Silvio Micali, and Ronald L. Rivest. 1988. A Digital Signature Scheme Secure Against Adaptive Chosen-message Attacks. *SIAM J. Comput.* 17, 2 (April 1988), 281–308.
[7] Yunhua Koglin, Giovanni Mella, Elisa Bertino, and Elena Ferrari. 2005. An update protocol for XML documents in distributed and cooperative systems. In *Distributed Computing Systems, 2005. ICDCS 2005. Proceedings. 25th IEEE International Conference on*. IEEE, 314–323.
[8] Baolong Liu, Joan Lu, and Jim Yip. 2009. XML Data Integrity Based on Concatenated Hash Function. *CoRR* abs/0906.3772 (2009).
[9] Gerome Miklau and Dan Suciu. 2005. Managing Integrity for Data Exchanged on the Web.. In *WebDB*. 13–18.
[10] Keith Mweebo. 2014. Security of electronic health records in a resource limited setting: The case of smart-care electronic health record in Zambia. (2014).
[11] Radia Perlman. 1999. An overview of PKI trust models. *Network, IEEE* 13, 6 (1999), 38–43.
[12] Jothy Rosenberg and David Remy. 2004. *Securing Web Services with WS-Security: Demystifying WS-Security, WS-Policy, SAML, XML Signature, and XML Encryption.* Pearson Higher Education.
[13] Steven J Simske and Helen Balinsky. 2010. APEX: automated policy enforcement eXchange. In *Proceedings of the 10th ACM symposium on Document engineering*. ACM, 139–142.
[14] Cheng Thao and Ethan V Munson. 2011. Version-aware XML documents. In *Proceedings of the 11th ACM symposium on Document engineering*. ACM, 97–100.

Distributing Text Mining tasks with *librAIry*

Carlos Badenes-Olmedo
cbadenes@fi.upm.es
Universidad Politécnica de Madrid
Ontology Engineering Group
Boadilla del Monte, Spain

José Luis Redondo-García
jlredondo@fi.upm.es
Universidad Politécnica de Madrid
Ontology Engineering Group
Boadilla del Monte, Spain

Oscar Corcho
ocorcho@fi.upm.es
Universidad Politécnica de Madrid
Ontology Engineering Group
Boadilla del Monte, Spain

ABSTRACT

We present *librAIry*, a novel architecture to store, process and analyze large collections of textual resources, integrating existing algorithms and tools into a common, distributed, high-performance workflow. Available text mining techniques can be incorporated as independent plug&play modules working in a collaborative manner into the framework. In the absence of a pre-defined flow, *librAIry* leverages on the aggregation of operations executed by different components in response to an emergent chain of events. Extensive use of Linked Data (LD) and Representational State Transfer (REST) principles are made to provide individually addressable resources from textual documents. We have described the architecture design and its implementation and tested its effectiveness in real-world scenarios such as collections of research papers, patents or ICT aids, with the objective of providing solutions for decision makers and experts in those domains. Major advantages of the framework and lessons-learned from these experiments are reported.

CCS CONCEPTS

•**Applied computing** → **Document management and text processing;** •**Computer systems organization** → *Architectures* ;

KEYWORDS

large-scale text analysis; NLP; scholarly data; text mining; data integration

1 INTRODUCTION

Given the huge amount of textual data about any domain that is daily being produced or captured in any imaginable domain, it becomes crucial to provide mechanisms for programmatically processing this raw data so we can make sense out of it: discarding all the noisy, non-relevant information and keeping only the data that can bring value for the involved agents (general consumers, experts, companies, investors...). While some specific tools already allow for advanced sense-making operations, others opt for composing a solution where different analysis techniques are integrated under a uniform data schema. However, this integration involves significant efforts on reconciling data sources, coordinating processing operations, and efficiently exploiting results from the execution of those techniques. There is the need for a more flexible paradigm where tools and algorithms for textual document analysis, from different programming languages and technologies, can operate independently and in a collaborative manner creating a common document oriented work-flow through their actions. In the context of the scientific publications, the personalized recommendation of research papers based on their content is a key novel feature for performing a smart selection of relevant resources over very big collections of scientific content. From the set of values and different attributes extracted from the papers and by generating advanced knowledge models about the information they contain we can bridge across the different relevant pieces of information and allow users to navigate them in a more efficient and powerful way. This knowledge about a specific document is frequently acquired by different techniques focused on revealing certain aspects of it, that are later combined to achieve one particular task. The architecture presented in this paper aims to ease the way different software modules work together and lays the foundation for efficiently process big volumes of textual documents in a distributed, decoupled manner.

2 RELATED WORK

The annotation of human-readable documents is a well-known problem in the Artificial Intelligence domain in general and Information Retrieval and Natural Language Processing fields in particular. There already exist a broad set of tools and frameworks able to analyze text for automatically producing such annotations, at very different levels of granularity: from minimal units such as terms and entities, to descriptors at the level of the entire collection such as topics or summaries. For example, StanfordNLP [7] framework allows to perform different operations such as PoS or Named Entity Recognition in various languages. Others like Mallet[1] or SparkLDA[2] perform topic modeling and clustering. The system we propose looks at the transversal problem of making those standalone tools coexisting under the same solution. Being able to effectively integrating them under a common ecosystem helps to seamlessly obtain different kind of annotations and boost the way those solutions can make sense of document collections.

Certain systems among the research and industrial communities have already integrated some of the annotation tools introduced

This work is supported by project Datos 4.0 with reference TIN2016-78011-C4-4-R, financed by the Spanish Ministry MINECO and co-financed by FEDER.
Author's addresses: C. Badenes-Olmedo and J.L. Redondo-García and O. Corcho , Ontology Engineering Group, Universidad Politécnica de Madrid.

DocEng '17, September 04–07, 2017, Valletta, Malta.
© 2017 ACM. 978-1-4503-4689-4/17/09...$15.00
DOI: https://doi.org/10.1145/3103010.3121040

---

[1]http://mallet.cs.umass.edu
[2]https://spark.apache.org/mllib/

above. For example, [2] works with records from the biomedical domain, where robustness and high precision are prioritized. Therefore they rely on techniques supported by GATE[3] framework, which widely supports hand-crafted, domain specific techniques such as rules or finite state transducers. On the other side of the spectrum we find [6], where the authors try to annotate text from a much noisier, sparser and error-prone medium: a tweet stream. Therefore they do not rely on any linguistic feature, due to the unpredictable way short social media post are written. We observe how each of those examples has very specific needs and leverages on certain annotation tools in order to accomplish the tasks it was originally created for. In both systems the involved components are highly coupled so they can not be easily extended to contemplate complementary annotation tools or alternative modules. On the contrary, *librAIry* advocates loosely interconnected components that make the architecture more reusable and expandable in other systems across domains.

One crucial problem regarding the re-usability and expansion possibilities of those systems and the tools they leverage on is the language they have been developed in. For example, Mallet uses Java, but others like spaCy [4] are python-based. To the best of our knowledge, there has not been any significant efforts on reconciling into a single architecture such heterogeneous set of tools, therefore minimizing the engineering effort and maximizing scalability of the system so it can be applied to very different domains and textual annotation tasks.

In addition, available annotation systems rely on certain storage solutions that are suited for some tasks but are less adequate others. For example [5] uses a relational database (MySQL[5]) to ensure reliability and speed in managing the indexed information. In [8], the authors leverage on Virtuoso triple-store to provide native graph operations over the data. But new requirements may be considered for those systems so different storage needs can come into play. For example, column oriented databases (Cassandra[6]) can help to better handle high-volume queries on specific data fields. Same goes with text oriented indexes such as ElasticSearch [7], which can provide customized text-based search operations over the available information. *librAIry* straightforward supports the coexistence of different storage solutions, so it can be agnostic to the kind of underlying storage modules implemented. Thanks to the distributed nature of the proposed architecture, different databases can be synchronized under the same common environment working together to store and deliver results in a more efficient manner.

3 LIBRAIRY

librAIry is a framework where different text mining tools, available in various languages and technologies, can operate in a distributed, high-performance and isolated manner creating a common workflow through their actions. Instead to work towards a pre-defined sequence of actions, synchronization across modules is achieved through the aggregation of the operations executed by them in response to an emergent chain of events. This raises both technical

[3]https://gate.ac.uk/
[4]https://spacy.io
[5]https://www.mysql.com/
[6]http://cassandra.apache.org
[7]https://www.elastic.co

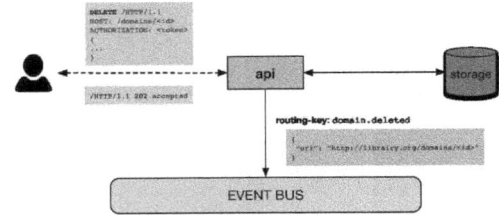

Figure 1: Domain deleted flow.

and functional challenges to coordinate multiple executions. From the technical point of view, isolated environments and communication mechanisms are provided so initially dissimilar tools can be executed with maximum guarantees. From the functional point of view, all executions are coordinated to reach a final result as aggregation of partial results derived from each execution.

3.1 Functional Features

The architecture is articulated around three main concepts: (1) the **resource** such as *document*, a *part* of a *document*, or a *domain*. (2) the **actions** performed over them: *create*, *update* or *delete* a resource. And (3) the new **state** that is reached by the resource after an action is performed, such as *created*, *updated* or *deleted*. An **event** is a message containing details about those three aspects, published on a shared event-bus available for all the modules deployed in the framework. This will, in turn, allow that any module can perform actions on one or more resources in response to a new state reached by a given resource. Actions executed in parallel from distributed environments.

3.1.1 Resources. Two main kinds of resources are considered: those derived from external sources such as (1) *documents* from textual files (e.g. a research paper), (2) *parts* from logical divisions of a *document* (e.g. rhetorical classes or sections), and (3) *domains* from sets of *documents* (e.g. a conference or journal), and those derived from processing the previous ones such as *annotations*.

To better illustrate this model, consider to explore the research papers published at the SIGGRAPH conference in 2016. First, every paper will be materialized as a new *document* containing the full-text. Immediately after, the *document* will be automatically associated to several *parts*, each of them grouping sentences by rhetorical class (e.g. approach, background, challenge, future work and outcome) and by section (e.g abstract, introduction). Finally, a new *domain* will be created grouping all these *documents*. Different analysis will be performed extending the initial set of resources with more annotations at several representational levels: at *document level*, full-text based annotations are provided such as named-entities, compounds and descriptive tags. At *relational level*, connection between resources are found (e.g. semantic similarity-based relationships). And finally, at *domain level* annotations such as tags and summaries are composed describing the corpus of *documents*.

3.1.2 Event-based Paradigm. An event illustrates a performed action, i.e. a resource and its new state. It follows the Representational State Transfer (REST)[4] paradigm, but taking into account

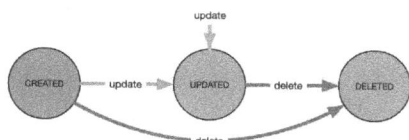

Figure 2: Resource states.

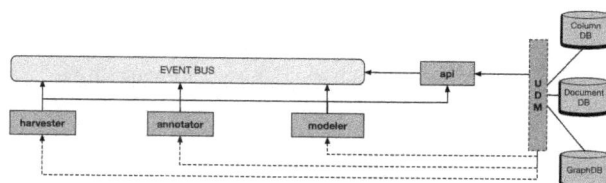

Figure 3: Modules.

the state reached after an action, i.e *created*, *deleted* or *updated*. Thus, an event contains the resource type and the new state reached by a specific resource.

3.1.3 Linked Data Principles . Data in *librAIry* is individually addressable and linkable [9] following the Linked Data principles defined by T. Berners-Lee [1]. Thus, resources (i.e. a *domain*, a *document*, a *part* or an *annotations*) have: (1) a URI as name, (2) a retrievable (or dereferenceable) HTTP URI so that it can be looked up, (3) a useful information provided by using standard notation (e.g. JavaScript Object Notation (JSON)) when it is looked up by URI, and (4) links to other URIs so that other resources can be discovered from it.

3.2 Framework Architecture

Following a publisher/subscriber approach, all the modules in the framework can publish and read events to notify and to be notified about the state of a resource. Therefore, the system flow is not unique and is not explicitly implemented, instead distributed and emergent flows can appear according to particular actions on resources.

3.2.1 Event-Bus. We use the Advanced Message Queuing Protocol (AMQP) as the messaging standard in *librAIry* to avoid any cross-platform problem and any dependency to the selected message broker. This protocol defines: *exchanges, queues, routing-keys* and *binding-keys* to communicate publishers and consumers.A message sent by a publisher to an exchange is tagged with a routing-key. Consumers matching that routing-key with the binding-key used to link the queue to that exchange will receive the message. In *librAIry* this key follows the structure: *resource.status.*Since a wildcard-based definition can be used to set the key, this paradigm allow modules both listening to individual type events (e.g. domains.createdfor new domains), or multiple type events (e.g. #.created for all new resources).

3.2.2 API. A HTTP-Rest Application Program Interface (API) was designed for interaction with end-users. Any external operation motivated by a user will be handled here. Some of them, usually those related to reading operations, will be completely managed by this module getting all the data from the internal storage. However, those operations implying a modification of the status of some resource (e.g. creation of a *document*), may be also performed by other modules listening for that type of event asynchronously. This module publishes to the following routing-keys: *domain.(created;updated;deleted), document.(created;updated;deleted), part.(created;updated;deleted),* and *annotation.(created;updated;deleted).*

3.2.3 Storage. Multiple types of data can be handled in this ecosystem. Inspired in the Data Access Object (DAO) pattern, we have created a Unified Data Manager (UDM) providing access to any type of data used in the system. Three types of databases have been considered:

- **column-oriented database**: Focused on unique identified and/or *structured data*. This storage allow us searching key elements across resources.
- **document-oriented database**: Focused on indexing raw text. This storage allow us to execute advanced search operations over all the information gathered about a textual resource.
- **graph database**: Focused on relations. This storage allow us exploring resources through the relationships between them.

3.2.4 Modules. The modules composing *librAIry* have been designed following the microservices architectural style. A module is a cohesive (i.e. it implements only functionalities strongly related to the concern that it is meant to model [3]) and independent process working on the framework with a specific purpose. This purpose is defined by both the routing-key and the binding-key associated to the events handled by the module.

These are the main types of modules identified in *librAIry*:

- **Harvester**: creates system resources such as *documents*, *parts* and *domains*, from local or remote located textual files.
  - Listening for: nothing
  - Publishing to: *document.(created), part.(created), domain.(created;updated)*
- **Annotator**: retrieves named-entities, compounds, lemmas and other annotations resulting of Natural Language Processing (NLP) task execution from *documents* and *parts*.
  - Listening for: *document.(created;updated), part.(created;updated)*
  - Publishing to: *annotation.(created;deleted)*
- **Modeler**: builds representational models from a given *domain*.
  - Listening for: *domain.(created;updated)*
  - Publishing to: *annotation.(created;deleted)*

4 EXPERIMENTS AND LESSONS-LEARNED

librAIry has been used in some real scenarios such as a research-paper repository for the European project DrInventor [8], a support to decision makers for analyzing patents and public aids for the

---
[8]http://drinventor.eu

ICT sector, and also as a book recommender for an online content platform. This has allowed us to identify some weak and strong points of the framework and iterate over the architecture to come with the described solution.

The following modules have been developed[9]: (1) a ***general-purpose harvester*** which retrieves text and meta-information from PDF files in local or remote file-system; (2) a ***research paper-oriented harvester*** focused on collecting and processing more specific textual files (e.g. scientific papers) creating both *documents* and *parts* inferred from the rhetorical classes of the paper; (3) a ***Stanford CoreNLP-based Annotator*** which discovers named-entities, compounds and lemmas from *documents* and *parts*; (4) a ***Topic Modeler*** based on Latent Dirichlet Allocation (LDA) which creates probabilistic topic models for each *domain* in the framework. They are annotated with the set of topics (i.e. ranked list of words) discovered from the corpus, and both *documents* and *parts* of that domain are also annotated by the vector of probabilities to belong to these topics. It uses the Spark implementation of the algorithm; and (5) a ***Word Embedding Modeler*** which creates a *word2vec* model from the *documents* contained in a *domain*.

Due to linear scalability and high performance features, Cassandra has been used to support the column-oriented storage functionality, Elasticsearch as document-oriented storage and Neo4j as graph-oriented storage.

All modules in *librAIry* have been packaged as Docker [10] containers and uploaded to Docker-Hub [11] to facilitate the installation of the system.

Maximizing information re-usability and minimize irrelevant data, becomes specially important when the system handles large collections of data (around million of documents). Fine-grained resource definitions have been key to achieve this, so modules execute actions only when really necessary. When a new *domain* is created, for instance, a new Topic Model is trained for that *domain* and is used to calculate the semantic similarity between the *documents* (and the *parts*) in that domain. If a new *document* (or *part*) is added to that *domain*, the model is trained again and the semantic similarities are re-calculated. However, this becomes unfeasible when the domain is frequently updated and it is composed by a large number of documents. One solution has been to define a new type of resource between domains and documents, models, that describes the representational state (e.g. topic model) of a collection of documents. Thus the model is only re-trained when a significant amount of *documents* are added to the sampling data set and not to the entire *domain*. This less transient model is used to calculate semantic similarities between the *document* collection (and *parts*) inside a *domain* in a more efficient way. Following this more precise execution of tasks, the routing-keys should include the URI of the implied resource into the definition, not only in the content of the message. It would allow modules listening to both the type of a resource or to a specific resource (or subsets, via regular expressions).

While the storage modules are always used to save/update/delete a resource, they are not always required from the end-user. The graph storage, for instance, makes sense when a path between two documents or parts is requested for a given *domain*. However, some *domains* are not intended to be explored by their linked resources. A more fine/grained definition of resources will allow graph-storage being only used when necessary.

On the other hand, distributed execution of NLP tasks (not only in threads, but also in machines) has proved to be especially useful to handle large collection of *documents*. It requires less processing time than a monolithic solution (e.g. CoreNLP application) and it also provides a dynamic load balancing between modules.

5 CONCLUSIONS AND FUTURE WORK

In *librAIry*, existing algorithms and tools coming from different technologies can work collaboratively to process and analyze large collections of textual resources which has been successful applied to some real scenarios [12].

A new model definition based on the previously mentioned principle of maximizing information re-usability and minimize irrelevant data is being studied to create a more fine-grained resource design. New domains, in the sense of particular vocabularies or specific textual formats, are also being analyzed to be included into the system via specific harvesters and/or more precise annotators. Moreover, a template-based mechanism oriented to facilitate the integration of new tools and techniques into the system is being built to make easier to develop new modules as well as increasing the available modules at Docker-Hub.

REFERENCES

[1] Christian Bizer, T Heath, and T Berners-Lee. 2009. Linked data-the story so far. *International journal on Semantic Web and Information Systems* 5, 3 (2009), 1–22. DOI:http://dx.doi.org/10.4018/jswis.2009081901
[2] Hamish Cunningham, Valentin Tablan, Angus Roberts, and Kalina Bontcheva. 2013. Getting More Out of Biomedical Documents with GATE's Full Lifecycle Open Source Text Analytics. *PLOS Computational Biology* (2013). DOI:http://dx.doi.org/10.1371/journal.pcbi.1002854
[3] Nicola Dragoni, Saverio Giallorenzo, Alberto Lluch Lafuente, Manuel Mazzara, Fabrizio Montesi, Ruslan Mustafin, and Larisa Safina. 2016. Microservices: yesterday, today, and tomorrow. *CoRR* abs/1606.0 (2016), 1–17. DOI:http://dx.doi.org/10.13140/RG.2.1.3257.4961
[4] Roy T Fielding and Richard N Taylor. 2002. Principled Design of the Modern Web Architecture. *ACM Transactions on Internet Technology* 2, 2 (2002), 407–416. DOI:http://dx.doi.org/10.1145/514183.514185
[5] Laura I Furlong, Holger Dach, Martin Hofmann-Apitius, and Ferran Sanz. 2008. OSIRISv1. 2: a named entity recognition system for sequence variants of genes in biomedical literature. *BMC bioinformatics* 9, 1 (2008), 84.
[6] Chenliang Li, Jianshu Weng, Qi He, Yuxia Yao, Anwitaman Datta, Aixin Sun, and Bu-Sung Lee. 2012. TwiNER: Named Entity Recognition in Targeted Twitter Stream. ACM, New York, NY, USA, 721–730. DOI:http://dx.doi.org/10.1145/2348283.2348380
[7] Christopher Manning, Mihai Surdeanu, John Bauer, Jenny Finkel, Steven Bethard, and David McClosky. 2014. The Stanford CoreNLP Natural Language Processing Toolkit. In *Proceedings of 52nd Annual Meeting of the Association for Computational Linguistics: System Demonstrations*. DOI:http://dx.doi.org/10.3115/v1/P14-5010
[8] Giuseppe Rizzo, Raphäel Troncy, Oscar Corcho, Anthony Jameson, Julien Plu, Juan Carlos Ballesteros Hermida, Ahmad Assaf, Catalin Barbu, Adrian Spirescu, Kai-Dominik Kuhn, and others. 2015. 3cixty@ Expo Milano 2015: Enabling Visitors to Explore a Smart City. (2015).
[9] S Turchi, L Ciofi, F Paganelli, F Pirri, and D Giuli. 2012. Designing EPCIS through Linked Data and REST principles. *Software, Telecommunications and Computer Networks ({SoftCOM}), 2012 20th International Conference on* (2012), 1–6.

---

[9] https://github.com/librairy
[10] https://www.docker.com
[11] https://hub.docker.com/u/librairy/

---

[12] http://drinventor.dia.fi.upm.es

MACE: A New Interface for Comparing and Editing of Multiple Alternative Documents for Generative Design

Loutfouz Zaman
University of Ontario Institute of Technology
Oshawa, Canada
loutfouz.zaman@uoit.ca

Wolfgang Stuerzlinger
Simon Fraser University
Vancouver, Canada
w.s@sfu.ca

Christian Neugebauer
University of Applied Sciences Bonn-Rhein-Sieg, Germany
christian@neugemail.de

ABSTRACT

We present a new interface for interactive comparisons of more than two alternative documents in the context of a generative design system that uses generative data-flow networks defined via directed acyclic graphs. To better show differences between such networks, we emphasize added, deleted, (un)changed nodes and edges. We emphasize differences in the output as well as parameters using highlighting and enable post-hoc merging of the state of a parameter across a selected set of alternatives. To minimize visual clutter, we introduce new difference visualizations for selected nodes and alternatives using additive and subtractive encodings, which improve readability and keep visual clutter low. We analyzed similarities in networks from a set of alternative designs produced by architecture students and found that the number of similarities outweighs the differences, which motivates use of subtractive encoding. We ran a user study to evaluate the two main proposed difference visualization encodings and found that they are equally effective.

CCS CONCEPTS

• **Human-centered computing** → **Graphical user interfaces**.

KEYWORDS

Alternatives; generative design; exploration; parallel editing; difference visualization.

ACM Reference format:

L. Zaman, W. Stuerzlinger, and C. Neugebauer. 2017. MACE: A New Interface for Comparing and Editing of Multiple Alternative Documents for Generative Design. In *Proceedings of DocEng '17, Valletta, Malta, September 04-07, 2017,* 10 pages.
https://doi.org/10.1145/3103010.3103013

1 INTRODUCTION

Parametric and generative design is a modern design technology in which a set of rules or an algorithm generates the output,

such as an image, sound, architectural model, or animation. In parametric design, typically only values are changed. Generative systems can produce much more varied output and uses either a set of rules, a data-flow program, or even an algorithm as the underlying generative model to ensure that the generated output matches the goals, as specified as part of the model. Current examples include *Max/MSP* (cycling74.com), *NodeBox* (nodebox.net), *Grasshopper 3D* (grasshopper3d.com) and *Houdini* (sidefx.com). With parametric and generative technologies, it is possible to explore a much larger number of viable design options compared to what is possible with manual operations. However, how users can compare alternatives in such a large space of design options has not been investigated in detail.

Since designers routinely generate dozens of alternatives based on a single idea [36], basic techniques for comparing them, such as juxtaposition, synchronized zooming and panning, and uniform layouts, are not enough. This is especially true of environments that employ data-flow languages. Designers may want to superimpose their newer creations over earlier ones to see how their newer versions deviate from the previous version. They may want to become immediately aware how the parameters of subjunctive nodes differ between alternatives, or even want to see the differences in the networks' structures.

In this paper, we present *MACE* (Multiple Alternatives – Comparison and Editing), a novel user interface that facilitates the comparison of multiple alternatives in generative design which also includes new mechanisms that facilitate interactive editing in a difference visualization mode. We implemented these techniques as an extension of *GEM-NI* [36]. See Figure 1.

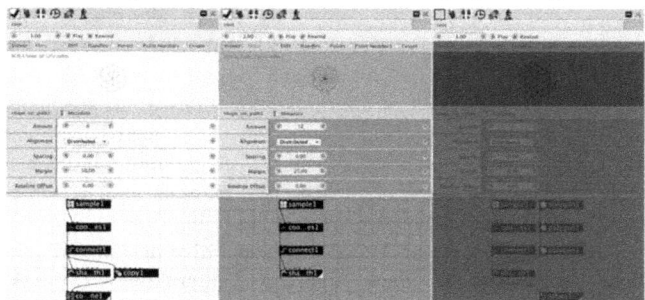

Figure 1. The "Flower of Life" worked example in *GEM-NI*.

GEM-NI [36] enables the user to quickly generate sets of alternative solutions through a multitude of techniques, edit them in parallel with undo capabilities, and supports merging of alternatives. Moreover, *GEM-NI* also provides GUI mechanisms to manage the set of alternatives. The work presented here extends *GEM-NI* with new difference visualization techniques and with techniques that enable editing in difference visualization mode.

To support such comparisons better, we implemented the following explicit difference visualization techniques:

- a new interactive difference visualization that simultaneously compares more than one DAG (directed acyclic graph) against a given reference;
- two types of encoding: subtractive and additive to show/hide common elements for better difference readability and scalability;
- two levels of abstraction for subtractive encoding: alternative and node-focused difference visualization for the selected alternative or node to give the user the control over visual clutter;
- visualizing differences in parameters with the ability to synchronize the parameter state.

2 RELATED WORK

2.1 Generative Design

Generative design enables designers to create endless design variations based on a model. This model can vary just in parameters, be expressed as varying networks of computational nodes and/or constraints, or even full algorithms across alternatives. By structuring design concepts as models, it is possible to explore a much larger number of viable design options compared to what is manually possible. Generative modeling is a fast method for exploring design possibilities and is used in various design fields such as art, architecture, and product design. Then, the central role of the designer involves continuously modifying the generative model based on the resultant outcomes. Through this the designer navigates the solutions space. A very simple approach is to just have the user repeatedly select attractive solutions to zero in on desirable options [24]. Better approaches give the user more control.

To compensate for the lack of adequate software features to support easy and efficient exploration of a design space, current designers rely on strategies, referred to as idioms of use [32]. Some common idioms for comparing design alternatives are opening different file "versions" in different windows, or using layers [31]. Yet, current computational design tools still do not support the comparison of alternative solutions in an adequate manner, nor do comparison modes permit interactive editing. Moreover, such adaptations sometimes create more problems than they solve, e.g., when the file naming and window management overhead becomes large.

The user interface of *MACE* aids generative design through easy comparison of more than two alternatives through enhanced difference visualizations and by permitting editing in the difference visualization mode.

2.2 Difference and History Visualization for Graphs

History visualization, versioning, differencing and version merging graphs, trees and node-link diagrams are all related to the area of dynamic graph drawing, which deals with the problem of visualizing data that evolves linearly over time. Most of the work cited below targets generic undirected graphs and trees. Yet, generative models use directed edges to represent the data flow. Almost all the approaches below reduce the problem to showing only *pair-wise differences* between graphs or trees.

A difference map is a graph that encodes all of the differences between the node and edge sets between two graphs [3]. Such maps produce fewer errors when determining the number of edges inserted or removed from a graph evolving over time and were also preferred [5]. *MACE* employs a new variant of a difference map, which excludes nodes and edges common to the compared graphs.

Animation can also be used to compare graphs, e.g., [6, 29, 35]. Zaman et al. [35] demonstrated that animation was beneficial for graphs with non-matching layouts. This is not applicable for *MACE*, as *GEM-NI* synchronizes node positions across alternatives. Animation is better suited for showing gradual transitions, i.e., successive graphs that represent an evolving change of a single data set [13]. In our application domain, we deal with situations well beyond the evolution of a single graph. The closest relevant work compares multiple graphs at the same time. It is important to highlight that in generative design non-linear creation and editing of alternatives is the norm. In other words, generative design typically is ill described by a linear time flow. Thus, time/history-based difference visualization techniques such as animation and small multiples are not directly applicable to the comparison of alternative designs. *MACE* employs new graph difference techniques to illustrate the changes between alternatives.

Graham et al. [12] surveyed multi-tree visualization. They distinguish five methods of comparing nodes in two trees: edge drawing, coloring, animation, matrix representation, and agglomeration. Gleicher et al.'s [11] work offered a taxonomy of visual designs for comparison, which groups designs into three basic categories. They identify that all visual designs are assembled from the building blocks of juxtaposition, superposition and explicit encodings. Alper et al. [1] evaluated two techniques for weighted graph comparison and found that matrix representations are more effective than node-link diagrams. As our work involves directed and unweighted graphs, such techniques are not applicable. Layering is commonly used in diagram differencing and merging, e.g., [8, 34, 35] and superimposes multiple graphs. Yet, it can only handle a very small number of graphs simultaneously. Thus, it is most useful for showing pair-wise differences.

Side-by-side views are a special case of graph difference visualization, which show only two versions. *DualNet* [27] visualizes sub-networks of node-link diagrams with side-by-side views. All work discussed below in this paragraph focuses only on trees, rather than graphs. Thus, most of these methods are not directly applicable to our context. *TreeJuxtaposer* [26] targets the comparison of large trees with side-by-side views. *TreeVersity* [15–17, 19] shows changes in topology and node values. The system uses glyphs that pre-attentively highlight changes and also highlights created and removed nodes.

TreeVersity2 [18, 19] enables the exploration of changes in trees over time. Guerra-Gomez et al. [19] identified and classified five types of tree comparisons. Except for the comparison of topological differences between two trees, none of the types of comparisons identified there apply to the DAGs used in *GEM-NI*. Instead of topological differences *MACE* identifies structural differences between two or more DAGs. Moreover, Guerra-Gomez et al.'s node types do not correspond to our context, as nodes in *GEM-NI* do not have categorical attributes, can contain data unsuitable for interpolation.

Another static visualization approach uses agglomeration. Graham and Kennedy [13] presented a DAG visualization to interact with a set of multiple classification trees to identify overlaps and differences between groups of trees and individual trees with up to six classifications. *Zoomology* [20] compares two classification datasets where two trees are merged into a single overview. Isenberg et al. [21] presented a new system that facilitates hierarchical data comparison in co-located collaborative environment using structural comparison through overlay. Their system dealt with up to six trees. *CandidTree* [22] merges two trees into one and visualizes location and sub-tree structure structural uncertainty. Yet, agglomeration is not applicable to (generative design) networks, as neither individual nodes nor sub-networks can be combined meaningfully into a hierarchy in DAGs.

Difference visualization is also used in software engineering, usually for UML diagrams. Förtsch et al. [9] presented a survey on solutions for differencing and merging of software diagrams and listed requirements for UML diagram versioning tools. Ohst et al. [28] introduced an approach that highlights common and specific parts of two diagrams. Zaman et al. [34] later demonstrated a system where graphs are displayed side-by-side with differences marked. Girschick [10] introduced a similar system, where eight colors were used to visualize eight different types of changes in class diagrams. A user survey for the Pounamu system [25] found positive feedback for their difference visualization, the support for incremental changes, merging, and the overall support for diagram-based design activities. Most of the approaches for UML diagram differencing are applicable to other forms of node-link diagrams and graphs. A single unified diagram for graph comparison was studied by Dadgari et al. [8]. They evaluated multiple graph differencing and merging techniques qualitatively and found that a translucent layer approach was preferred for simple pair-wise comparisons. A unified graph approach was also proposed by Andrews et al. [2]. A side-by-side approach for graph differencing was also investigated by Zaman et al. [35] in the *DARLS* system. *DARLS* displays two versions of a diagram side-by-side with differences marked, even if a node was moved.

Most directly related to our difference visualizations in *MACE* is Shireen et al.'s [30] conceptual prototype of a user interface for parallel work with design alternatives, which included a difference visualization. However, they only showed nodes that are common.

In summary, most previous work addresses the problem of showing pair-wise differences. Animation and small multiples were used for visual comparisons of more than two DAGs. Yet, this is only effective for content that has evolved linearly. None of these approaches can handle the visual comparison of a dozen or more different DAGs that have evolved non-linearly or in parallel.

3 MACE

Here, we present novel extensions of the original *GEM-NI* system [36]. to enable comparison of multiple alternatives.

The user can switch between the normal (viewing) mode, where typical interaction occurs for creating and editing alternatives, and the *"diff mode"*, where *differences* of all alternatives are displayed against a chosen *reference*. The user can use any alternative as the reference. To get into this mode, one alternative must be designated by the user as the reference through a GUI button, clicking on a menu button, or a key short cut. The other alternatives (further referred to as *compared alternatives*) are then compared to it. In diff mode, differences are visualized in all three views (output, parameter and network), as applicable. The *diff mode* is fully interactive. For visualizing differences between the networks, we use two different approaches: subtractive and additive encoding.

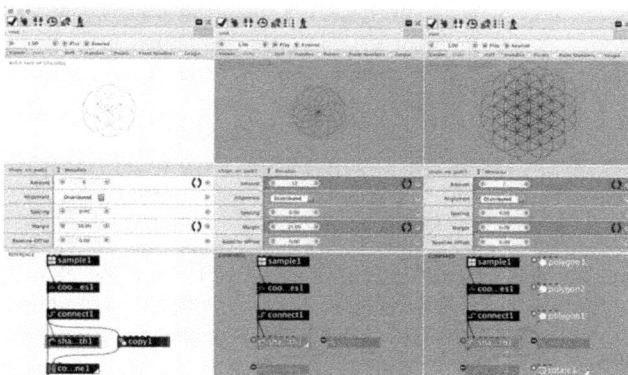

Figure 2. Difference visualizations of the "Flower of Life" example using additive layering.

3.1 Additive Layering

Additive layering is a direct adaptation of the layering technique from previous work [35] to multi-network comparisons. The word "layering" highlights the fact that this is a form of superposition. The word "additive" refers to additive encoding, which was identified by Gleicher et al. [11]. Figure 2 demonstrates this technique. The leftmost alternative was chosen as reference. The nodes SAMPLE1, COORDINATES1 and CONNECT1 are unchanged between the three alternatives. The differences start to appear with SHAPE_ON_PATH1, which is the next node in these networks. In the center and right alternatives, this node differs from the reference node in two parameters: Amount and Margin. These parameters are highlighted in red to indicate the difference in the parameter view. The state of a parameter can be synchronized between non-idle alternatives by clicking on the synch button in the parameter field. This is an extension of selective merging [36] to a lower level form of merging differences. A "≠" sign is displayed to the top left of the node to emphasize this further through an inequality metaphor. The node is also highlighted in red. Nodes COPY1 and COMBINE1 with the corresponding connectors are not present in both the center and right alternatives. This is shown using transparency. A "−" sign in the top left of these nodes, which emphasizes this further through a reduction/subtraction metaphor. New nodes POLIGON1 (2 and 3), ROTATE1 and new connectors, which don't exist in the reference, are highlighted in green. A "+" sign is displayed in the top left of the node to emphasize this through an addition metaphor. The word "reference" or "compared" appears in the top left corner of the network view of each alternative as an additional aid to distinguish between the reference and compared alternatives. Deleted connectors relative to the active compared alternative are also displayed in the reference using transparency. This works for both additive layering and subtractive layering described below. See an example in Figure 8, where four deleted connectors are shown in the reference network relative to the compared active network.

3.2 Subtractive Layering

Our design for subtractive layering is in part based on the subjunctive interface proposed (but not implemented) by Shireen et al. [30]. Unlike in additive layering, common unchanged nodes are not shown in compared alternatives (with one exception, discussed below). See the example in Figure 3. Only nodes with modified states are shown, which are either changed, deleted or new nodes. Connectors to and from unmodified nodes are instead shown on the nodes in the reference as dashed curves, which emphasizes that these connectors cross network boundaries. In addition, unmodified common nodes are highlighted in the reference in yellow. Drawing every single connector would add significant clutter. Due to that, and after trying different variations, we came up with a design that minimizes showing redundant connectors through a simple rule: we draw cross-network connectors only for nodes which cannot be connected to the other nodes within the compared alternative because these other nodes are hidden. E.g., in the center alternative in Figure 3 the COMBINE1 and SHAPE_ON_PATH1 nodes are both shown. Therefore, a connector between them is only drawn in the center alternative as a solid line, and not between COMBINE1 in the center alternative and SHAPE_ON_PATH1 in the reference.

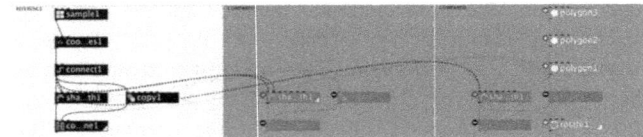

Figure 3. Difference visualizations of the "Flower of Life" example using subtractive layering.

3.2.1 Abstraction of Connectors. To reduce clutter further, we provide two additional mechanisms: alternative and node focused visualizations. In Figure 4a, the user selects the center alternative as active, which hides cross-network connectors to the right alternative. The user then selects SHAPE_ON_PATH1, which hides all the connectors which do not involve this node (Figure 4a).

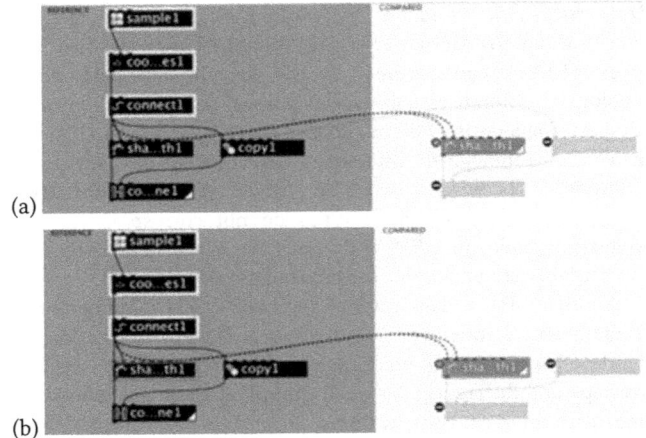

Figure 4. (a) alternative-focused visualization, (b) node-focused visualization.

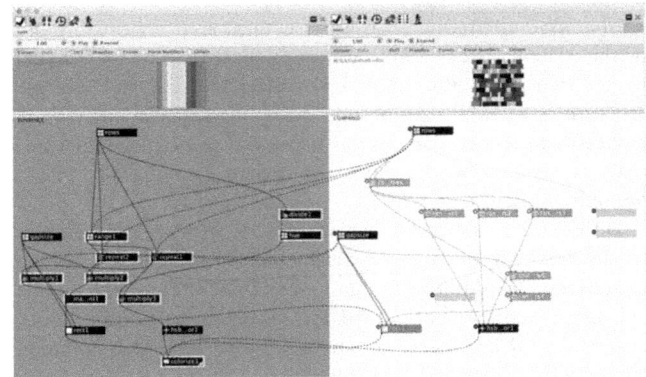

Figure 5. Showing differences in connectors between unchanged nodes.

3.2.2 Showing Differences in Connectors between Unchanged Nodes. We also implemented a technique to illustrate differences in node *connections* that involve one or more unchanged nodes. In this visualization, we reveal unchanged, common nodes that have one or more changed connections. Figure 5 shows an example, where nodes ROWS, GAPSIZE and HSB_COLOR1 are shown in the compared alternative (contrary to the rule of hiding common unchanged nodes in subtractive layering). This is done to highlight that in ROWS one outgoing connector was deleted and two new connectors were added, in GAPSIZE one outgoing connector was added, and in HSB_COLOR1 one incoming connector was deleted and three were added.

3.2.3 Design Motivation and the Research Hypothesis. We employ subtractive encoding—a complementary approach to the additive encoding identified by Gleicher et al. [11]. Subtractive encoding removes *common* nodes from the compared graphs. This technique reveals and/or highlights changed, unchanged, added and removed nodes in the compared network relative to the reference and could reduce visual clutter in the compared network. Thus, if there are no differences between a reference and compared network and there is nothing to show in the compared network, visual clutter is non-existent or minimal. On the other hand, if the overall number of changes is substantial, then the difference visualization might visually "overwhelm" the content. To characterize this, we propose using the relative percentage of nodes and edges shown in each difference visualization between two alternatives as an approximation to quantify relative difference, D_{rel}:

$$D_{rel} = \frac{n_{\neq} + n_{+} + n_{-} + e_{+} + e_{-}}{n_{ref} + e_{ref}}$$

Here, $n_{\neq}$ is the number of changed, n_{+}—the new and n_{-}—the deleted nodes in the compared network, n_{ref} is the total number of nodes in the reference, e_{ref} is the total number of connectors in the reference, e_{+}—the new and e_{-}—the deleted connectors in the compared network. If there are no changes, $D_{rel} = 0$. If the number of displayed nodes and edges in the compared view is equal to or exceeds the number of nodes in the reference, $D_{rel} \geq 1$.

For subtractive layering to be effective, the average D_{rel} of typical designs must be low. We believe that alternatives for a design problem will likely show substantial similarities due to the *shared goal*. Thus, we expect fewer differences among data-flow networks for alternatives compared to the number of similarities. To test this hypothesis we computed these numbers for the dataset of the second user study conducted on *GEM-NI* [33]. For the outcomes, we performed all pairwise comparisons of all alternatives to the first design. Averaging across all participants yields a low difference of $\mu_{D_{rel}} = .29$, $\sigma_{D_{rel}} = .22$, $N = 20$. Given that the average is substantially closer to zero than one, this suggests that showing differences instead of commonalities is an appropriate design choice for difference visualization across multiple alternatives.

3.2.4 Interactive Editing. We believe it would be trivial to describe how interactive editing works with additive layering. So, we will focus on the subtractive encoding instead. To enable interactive editing with subtractive layering we employ our "reveal-to-edit" feature. The interface mechanics we discuss here are in part based on the subjunctive interface proposed by Shireen et al. [30].

3.2.5 Worked Example. Consider the same design scenario as in the worked example of *GEM-NI* [36]. This time imagine Ann wants to recreate the three designs with subtractive layering enabled. She first creates the design on the left (Figure 1). She then creates a clone of the design (Figure 6a) and enables the diff mode by setting the left design as the reference (Figure 6b). Subtractive encoding hides all visualizations that are common between the original (left) and the clone (right). Therefore, the network view of the clone becomes empty. She then selects SHAPE_ON_PATH1, COPY1 and COMBINE1. By clicking anywhere in the network view of the clone and holding down a modifier, she then reveals these three nodes (Figure 6c). She then sandboxes the clone, changes two parameters of SHAPE_ON_PATH1 ("Amount" and "Margin") and deletes COPY1 and COMBINE1. This is how she arrives at the "Tube Torus" (Figure 6d). She then creates a clone of "Tube Torus" (Figure 7), sandboxes it and completes the final design as described in original worked example [36].

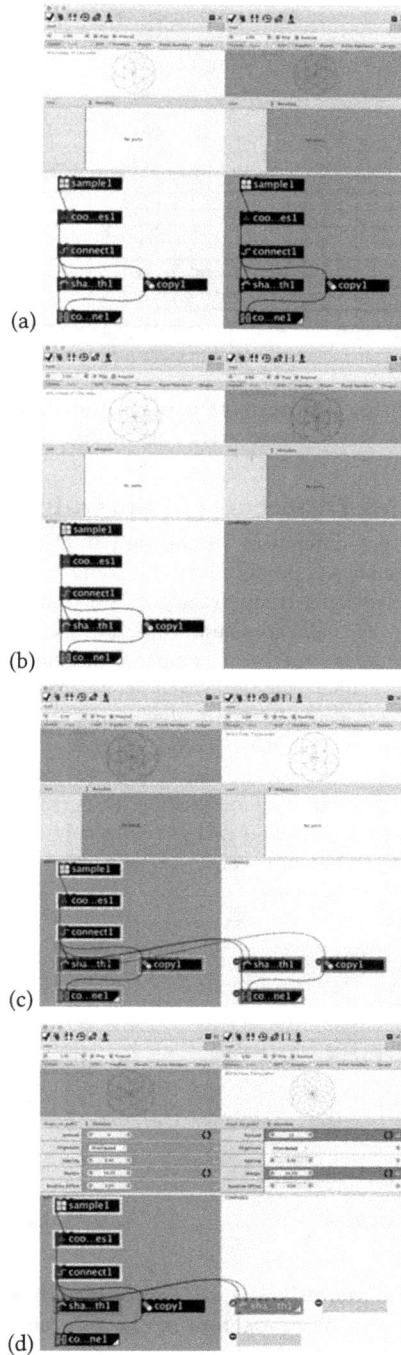

Figure 6. Editing alternatives using interactive difference visualization with subtractive encoding. (a) The original and a clone; (b) subtractive encoding; (c) SHAPE_ON_PATH1, COPY1 and COMBINE1 revealed in the clone for further editing; (d) "Amount" and "Margin" changed in SHAPE_ON_PATH1; COPY1 and COMBINE1 are deleted.

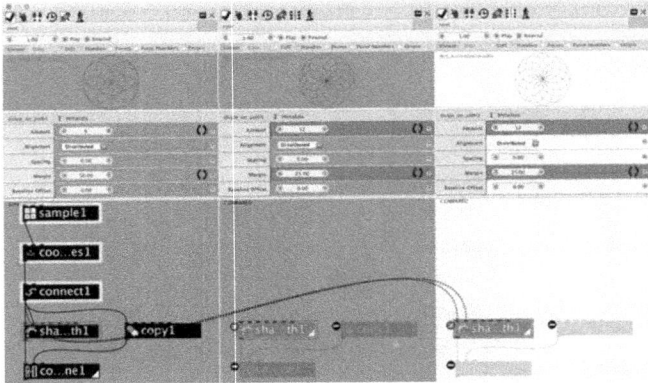

Figure 7. Editing alternatives using interactive difference visualization with subtractive encoding: cloning of a design.

3.3 Showing Differences in the Output View

To illustrate the differences in the output of the generative design, the geometry produced by the rendered node of the reference is displayed transparently in the output view in a bottom layer for all compared alternatives. This directly superimposes the geometry of compared alternatives over the reference to enable simple visual comparisons. Figure 8 demonstrates an example where the design in the compared view superimposes over the reference view. To deal with cases where this is visually too intrusive, we provide an option to disable this functionality by unchecking the corresponding "diff" checkbox. Figure 8 shows an example with subtractive layering, however, the technique works in combination with both subtractive and additive layering.

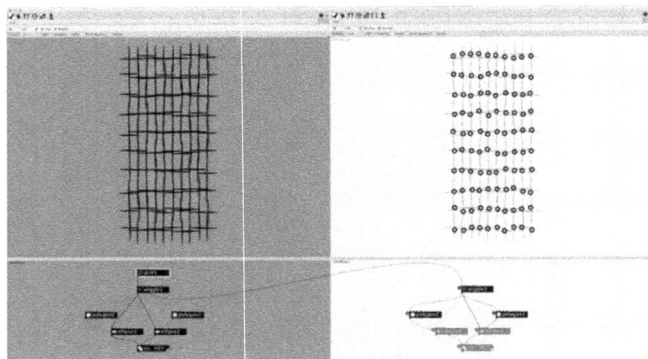

Figure 8. Demonstration of difference visualization in the output view and in connectors in the reference networks view.

4 USER STUDY

In our previous user studies we evaluated how *GEM-NI* supports creativity. In those studies participants engaged in creative tasks and ranked *GEM-NI* against an unenhanced version of *NodeBox* [33, 36] through a psychometric survey. Experts also ranked participants' designs in terms of quality [33]. In the work presented here, we ran an empirical user study to compare subtractive against additive layering for difference visualization

in *MACE*. The goal of the user study was to investigate the hypothesis that subtractive encoding is more effective for visualizing differences of data-flow networks of designs for a common design goal.

4.1 Participants

Twelve participants (one female) were recruited for the study. Participants were between 18 and 48 years old with an average (μ = 28.42) and had on average 17.75 years of experience using a desktop/laptop computer. Three were left handed, but all chose to use the mouse with their right hand for the experiment. Six participants indicated that they were regular users of data comparison and differencing tools such as the Track Changes feature in Microsoft *Word* and the Unix *diff* tool, three were familiar with these tools, but were not using them, two had used them in the past, and one never heard of the concept before. Three participants had experience using either data-flow programming or generative design tools. Ten participants used diagrams in their current line of work, two used them in the past.

4.2 Apparatus

The user study was conducted on a MacBook Pro laptop with a USB wheel mouse and a 27" external 2560×1440 display.

4.3 Experimental Design

Half of the participants evaluated the additive layering first, while the other half evaluated the subtractive layering first. We used a repeated measures design with one between factor (techniques order: subtractive layering first vs. additive layering first) and one within factor (differencing technique: subtractive layering vs. additive layering).

The dependent variables were trial completion time and the error rate (measured as the number of attempts).

4.4 Procedure

Participants were presented with 15 sets (tasks) of alternatives one after another in the fixed order. Previous work [35] had identified that the presentation order does not seem to affect the outcome of this type of experiment substantially. In each of these sets, the alternative highlighted in white was compared to the reference alternative, which for simplicity was always chosen to be the leftmost alternative in every set. All the alternatives starting from the second one were compared to the reference. The participants had to identify the changes for each of these comparisons.

Our procedure employed a hybrid approach based on the idea of using a dialog [4] for gathering responses. But unlike Archambault et al.'s work, in our user study the participants had to identify all changes in the networks until success or a timeout occurred, similar to other previous work [35]. Unlike that work [35], participants had to specify only the number of occurrences for each type of change, rather than explicitly selecting all changes. See Figure 9. After the participant successfully identified all the changes of each category (new nodes, new connectors, deleted nodes, deleted connectors and changed nodes), had entered their numbers in the dialog and clicked

"Validate", or after a timeout occurred, the next task was presented using the next alternative to the right. When the participant completed all the comparisons, the next set was then pre-loaded. Participants could use the mouse to select the numbers from the list menus, or to use the number and the <tab> key (for switching to the next field), whichever they felt more comfortable with. The combinations of the two input methods were also allowed. We also demonstrated how to zoom in and out, pan and reset the network view. This was necessary in tasks with many (5+) alternatives as they appeared too small for easy identification.

This procedure was repeated for both difference visualization techniques. For the subtractive technique, the dialog did not display the dashed connector image to avoid confusion. All the comparisons were made in the alternative-focused connector abstraction mode.

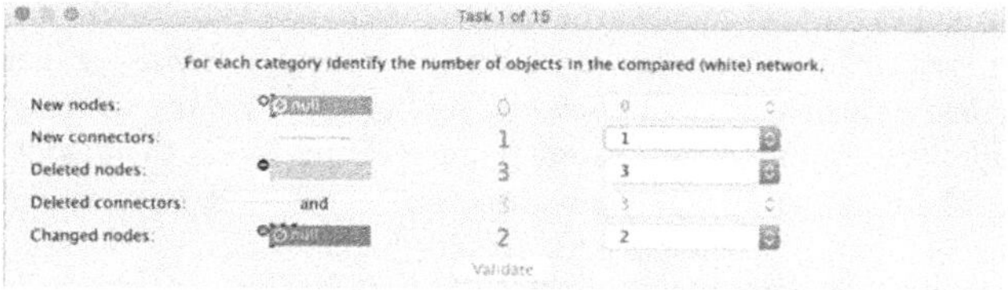

Figure 9. Task dialog state after an unsuccessful attempt.

4.5 Tasks

We picked 15 sets of generative designs with varying number of alternatives as tasks for this user study. The first set was the "Flower of Life" example with three alternatives (Figure 1), which was used as a practice set where each participant tested the two techniques during the initial exposure. The results obtained from this set were discarded. Sets 2-8 were picked from the dataset of second user study that we conducted on *GEM-NI* [33]. Sets 9-10 were created by a graduate student at Simon Fraser University. Sets 11-15 were picked from a generative design book [7].

Excluding the first two trials from the "Flower of Life" example that were discarded, a total of 38 comparisons with each technique remained. On average, each set contained 3.73 alternatives, with a maximum of 8 and minimum of 2. On average the number of nodes in the reference was 9.53, with 10.4 connectors. In the compared alternative, the average number of nodes was 10.49, with 11.12 connectors. On average the number of new nodes was 1.05, new connectors – 2.12, deleted nodes – 0.97, deleted connectors – 1.54, and changed nodes – 2.05.

4.6 Pilot Study

We recruited four participants for a pilot. This allowed us to fix the user interface issues and to improve the reliability of the collected data. Notably, we made changes to the dialog to prevent participants from re-submitting their response without making changes in all the fields where they made mistakes. We learned that it was essential to prevent participants from modifying responses which were entered correctly in previous attempts. Moreover, we identified that the task took a bit too long and was too challenging – networks where participants had to identify more than 20 new/changed/deleted nodes were

particularly frustrating regardless of the technique. Thus, we modified one of the networks by grouping nodes to reduce the number of visible changes. In two tasks, we could not sensibly cluster the nodes, and so we removed them. In the pilot we confirmed that a timeout of 2 minutes was appropriate, which also agrees with previous work [35]. One participant stated that grid lines were making the task too confusing because it was difficult to tell them apart from deleted connectors, and so we disabled them. With these changes, we then performed the main user study.

4.7 Results

4.7.1 Trial Completion Time. The main effect of technique was not significant, $F_{1,10} = 3.45$, $p > .05$. On average, additive layering took 28.5s and subtractive 26.2s. We did not observe a main ordering effect on time, $F_{1,10} = 1.03$, $p > .05$. However, the interaction between order and technique was significant, $F_{1,10} = 51.96$, $p < .0001$ (power = 0.99 at $\alpha = 0.05$). A Tukey-Kramer analysis on the interaction between order and technique revealed among others that when additive layering was evaluated first, additive layering was much slower (35.4 s) than subtractive layering when subtractive layering was evaluated first (28.5 s). See Figure 10.

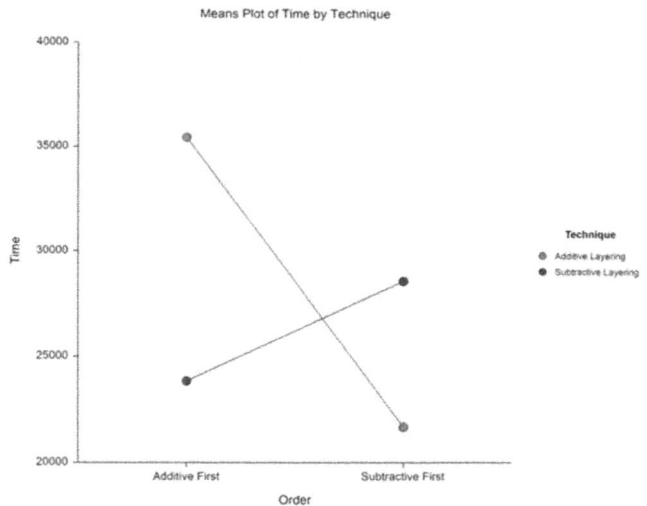

Figure 10. Interaction between order and technique.

4.7.2 Error Rate. The main effect of technique was not significant, $F_{1,10} = 2.25$, $p > .05$. On average, 0.143 errors were found with additive layering, 0.12 – with subtractive layering. The main ordering effect on time was not observed, $F_{1,10} = 0.65$, ns. The interaction between order and technique was significant, $F_{1,10} = 5.37$, $p < .05$ (power = 0.55 at $\alpha = 0.05$). However, a Tukey-Kramer analysis on the interaction between order and technique failed to reveal this difference.

4.7.3 Correlations with Difference. Using the proposed measure for the pairwise difference (Section 3.2.3) we found that the average difference of the set used in this study was $\mu_{D_{rel}} = . 59$, $\sigma_{D_{rel}} = 1.06$, $N = 44$. A correlation analysis revealed a very weak correlation between difference and trial completion time (0.2) and even lower value between difference and error rate (0.1). We then looked at the absolute difference, D_{abs}:

$$D_{abs} = n_{\neq} + n_{+} + n_{-} + e_{+} + e_{-}$$

We found that the correlation between D_{abs} and trial completion time was 0.69, and correlation between D_{abs} and error was rate 0.52.

4.8 Feedback from Participants

Participants were asked to rank each of the two differencing techniques on a Likert scale from 1 to 10 (10 being the best). The results are summarized in Figure 11. The rankings are consistent with our findings. 7 of 12 participants ranked the technique they did last higher than the technique they did first and three ranked them equally. Out of the two participants who ranked the first technique higher, one wrote in the freeform feedback that the subtractive layering technique was easier because he did it second, although he believes the additive technique is better. Two participants who ranked subtractive layering higher stated that they believe there is less clutter with this technique. One participant believed that additive layering is better because it appeared to him that there were fewer connectors to count. Another participant wished that one could toggle between the number of compared alternatives presented at a time and wished connectors also had labels like nodes. Yet another participant expressed that the only thing that appeared different to him was the presence of connectors across the networks in the subtractive layering. One participant left more informative feedback. He said that grey connectors are hard to see and that he would add a squiggle when they overlapped to tell them apart. He also stated that hovering on a node and animating its connectors would help and that having a legend telling how many there are for each node would be better.

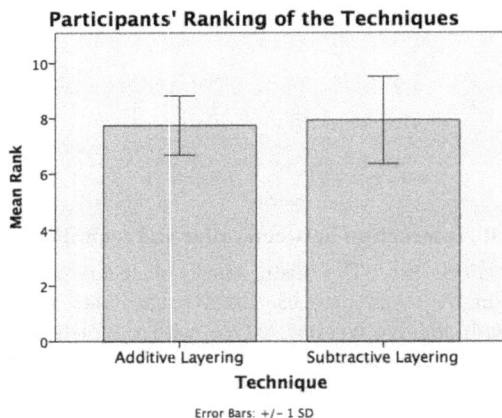

Figure 11. Participants' ranking of the differencing techniques. Error Bars: ±1 SD.

5 DISCUSSION

The problem of showing differences is important for generative design because designers typically create several alternatives based on a single idea, which they use as a reference. Designers also tend to work on multiple design alternatives concurrently [23]. Then management of these alternatives becomes an issue, which requires also the ability to visualize differences between alternatives. We presented a solution to difference visualization for alternative graphs: added, deleted, (un)changed nodes in both the reference and all compared graphs as well as added and deleted connections.

Pairwise difference visualization for directed graphs with nodes identifiable by name is not new, e.g., [35]. Comparing more than two such graphs of the evolution of a *single* data set can be done with animation and/or time slices, e.g., [29]. Yet, in generative design, where parallel and non-linear creation and editing of alternatives is the norm, we deal with situations well beyond the evolution of a single graph. Animation is therefore not applicable. Agglomeration is also not applicable because we are dealing with DAGs, not trees. Thus, we proposed using subtractive and additive encoding. Subtractive encoding is a new form of explicit encoding where members of the intersection are removed from the compared graph. This extends Gleicher et al.'s taxonomy work [11]. Subtractive layering extends a) the layering approach used in several instances of previous work, such as [2, 8, 35], by hiding unchanged nodes to reduce clutter and drawing connectors to the reference to enhance juxtaposition; b) side-by-side views [14, 26, 27] by going beyond pair-wise comparisons; c) existing work on subjunctive interfaces [30], *TreeVersity* [15–17, 19] and *TreeVersity2* [18, 19] to show a larger variety of difference visualizations. Both of our approaches also show difference visualizations of multiple group nodes. This supports scalability to generative networks with many nodes, where node grouping becomes a necessity as otherwise the graph becomes much too large for a single screen.

Subtractive encoding is as an extension to Shireen et al.'s [30] concept for parallel creation and editing of alternatives. In their prototype Shireen et al. included an option to create an empty design model. The user then selects a node in the original design and inserts it in the subjunctive graph at which point a new instance of the design is created for editing. In contrast, our interface requires that a user creates a clone (a branch from an earlier state) to start editing a new alternative. Subjunctive nodes are revealed as common nodes with the original. We did this to make the interface for editing in difference visualization mode transparent and minimally intrusive within *GEM-NI*. In contrast to Shireen et al.'s work [30], *GEM-NI* pushes changes always to all the non-idle alternatives. *GEM-NI* does not distinguish between the original or an alternative when pushing changes. Any design can change the role from the original to an alternative by pressing a GUI button. In Shireen et al.'s conceptual prototype [30] users can substitute or replace certain features of a design by creating new structures in the relevant subjunctive graphs, connecting them to the prototype, and removing the substituted nodes from the alternative. Our interface enhances this further by also displaying nodes and connectors that were removed from the original as we designed the interface to serve as a difference visualization interface as well. This way all the differences between the original and the alternatives can be visualized at once. To reduce visual clutter, Shireen et al.'s conceptual prototype [30] emphasizes nodes and connectors related to the currently selected alternative and de-emphasizes everything else. We implemented a variant of this in *MACE*. If the user sets the active document to any document other than the original, all the links connecting other alternatives to the original are removed, but when the user sets the original alternative as active then everything is shown. Furthermore, selecting the active node hides other connectors in that alternative. If needed, the user can disable difference visualizations in *GEM-NI* by disabling *MACE*. This effectively enables the user to focus on a single alternative, similar to the design of Shireen et al. subjunctive dependency graphs [30].

MACE also introduces "reveal-to-edit", a new way to interact with hidden, common nodes. The "dragging" solution proposed by Shireen et al. [30] is less user friendly and does not match standard GUI conventions.

Given that alternatives for a design problem will likely be similar due to the shared goal, we expect fewer differences among the data-flow networks of alternatives compared to the number of similarities. This assumption underlies the design of subtractive layering. We performed an analysis on the alternatives obtained through a user study to test this assumption. Using the introduced difference measure, based on measuring the visual similarity of the alternative networks, we computed a low degree of difference, which confirmed the appropriateness of the design choice of the technique. The correlation analysis between relative difference, trial completion time and error rate did not reveal a strong correlation. This is not too surprising. The following example clarifies this. The largest value for D_{rel} in the study set was 6. The corresponding pair is shown in Figure 12. Arguably, despite the large D_{rel}, identifying these differences should not be difficult since there are not that many nodes and edges in total. While this measure helped us to motivate our work, it's D_{abs} that relates to the actual task measures.

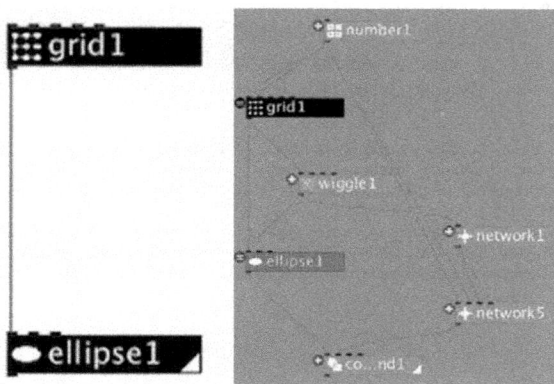

Figure 12. An example where $D_{rel} = 6$.

Our hypothesis was that subtractive layering improves the readability of our difference encoding by keeping visual clutter low because the designs share a common goal. Contrary to our intuition, the findings and participants' feedback reject this hypothesis. We showed that this is true for networks with an average number of 10 nodes and connectors. Still, these findings are not that surprising. Previous work [35] demonstrated that

there is no significant difference between difference visualization techniques for static diagrams and our results complement those findings. Although not significantly so, the layering technique in this previous work was found most efficient. Thus, in our current user study, we were essentially comparing subtractive layering to the best-known technique.

Nevertheless, the interaction between order and technique is an interesting finding. Additive layering seems initially far more challenging to learn than subtractive layering – when additive layering was presented first it took 24% time longer to complete the task. One possible explanation could be that the larger amount of node clutter with additive layering forced participants to check for changes in connections between unchanged nodes. We observed this issue during the user study on multiple occasions, yet did not have a mechanism in place to log this. Given this finding, subtractive encoding could be a better choice for difference visualizations for novice users.

Our evaluation has limitations. We do not account for situations when a participant falsely identifies a change of one type and fails to identify another change of the same type. Then, the total number of changes will add up to the correct number but the identified changes will be incorrect. Also, participants cannot be prevented from guessing the number of changes. Another issue is that the task also involves dealing with inputting the responses through the interface of the dialog, rather than purely identifying changes, which means that there is also a learning curve for the dialog, which may not relate to the rate at which participants identify the changes. We were not able to directly adopt the approach used in *DARLS* [35], due to the fact that in *NodeBox* connectors cannot be selected directly.

Finally, we believe that the ideas behind our difference visualizations generalize to other visual programming environments, including 3D modeling (e.g., *Grasshopper 3D*, *Houdini*). For other types of media, such as video or audio (e.g., *Max/MSP*), a different approach to illustrating differences may be necessary.

6 CONCLUSION AND FUTURE WORK

We presented a new interface for interactive difference visualizations for generative design alternatives. The new techniques enable comparison of more than two alternatives at a time and enable differencing for the output, parameter and network views. The techniques are interactive and enable creating and editing alternatives through cloning of the original design and using the "reveal-to-edit" feature. The interface also allows post-hoc merging of the state of a parameter across a set of alternatives. For the network view, we investigated two difference visualization approaches: subtractive and additive layering. We introduced new ways to emphasize added, deleted, (un)changed nodes, and connectors. Subtractive layering is based on the idea of subtractive encoding, which we hypothesized as being useful in data that has more similarities than the differences, such as the alternatives we are dealing with. We used a difference measure to confirm the appropriateness of the approach for at least one alternatives dataset produced by designers. We evaluated subtractive against additive layering in a repeated measures experiment to investigate the hypothesis. The results were not confirmatory, but our findings suggest that subtractive layering may be better suited for novice users.

In the future, we will investigate the scalability of our techniques for even larger numbers of alternatives and investigate other approaches to difference visualizations. In our work we only focused on the difference visualizations and not editing. Our future user studies will evaluate the editing technique in *MACE*. We are also considering a direct comparison with *DARLS*. Additionally, we will explore difference visualizations for visual programming environments in other domains.

ACKNOWLEDGMENTS

We gratefully acknowledge financial support from the NSERC Discovery program and the GRAND NCE. We would also like to thank Robert Woodbury, Maher Elkhaldi and Naghmi Shireen for their feedback on an early version of the difference visualizations in *MACE*.

REFERENCES

[1] Alper, B., Bach, B., Henry Riche, N., Isenberg, T. and Fekete, J.-D. 2013. Weighted Graph Comparison Techniques for Brain Connectivity Analysis. *Proceedings of the SIGCHI Conference on Human Factors in Computing Systems* (New York, NY, USA, 2013), 483–492.

[2] Andrews, K., Wohlfahrt, M. and Wurzinger, G. 2009. Visual Graph Comparison. *Information Visualisation, 2009 13th International Conference* (Jul. 2009), 62–67.

[3] Archambault, D. 2009. Structural differences between two graphs through hierarchies. *Graphics Interface 2009* (Kelowna, British Columbia, Canada, 2009), 87–94.

[4] Archambault, D., Purchase, H. and Pinaud, B. 2011. Animation, Small Multiples, and the Effect of Mental Map Preservation in Dynamic Graphs. *IEEE Transactions on Visualization and Computer Graphics*. 17, 4 (Apr. 2011), 539–552.

[5] Archambault, D., Purchase, H.C. and Pinaud, B. 2011. Difference Map Readability for Dynamic Graphs. *Graph Drawing*. U. Brandes and S. Cornelsen, eds. Springer Berlin Heidelberg. 50–61.

[6] Bach, B., Pietriga, E. and Fekete, J.-D. 2014. GraphDiaries: Animated Transitions and Temporal Navigation for Dynamic Networks. *IEEE Transactions on Visualization and Computer Graphics*. 20, 5 (May 2014), 740–754.

[7] Bohnacker, H. 2012. *Generative Design: Visualize, Program, and Create with Processing*. Princeton Architectural Press.

[8] Dadgari, D. and Stuerzlinger, W. 2010. Novel User Interfaces for Diagram Versioning and Differencing. *British HCI* (2010).

[9] Förtsch, S. and Westfechtel, B. 2007. Differencing and Merging of Software Diagrams - State of the Art and Challenges. *ICSOFT (SE)* (2007), 90–99.

[10] Girshick, M. 2006. *Difference Detection and Visualization in UML Class Diagrams*. TU Darmstadt.

[11] Gleicher, M., Albers, D., Walker, R., Jusufi, I., Hansen, C.D. and Roberts, J.C. 2011. Visual comparison for information visualization. *Information Visualization*. 10, 4 (Oct. 2011), 289–309.

[12] Graham, M. and Kennedy, J. 2010. A survey of multiple tree visualisation. *Information Visualization*. 9, 4 (Dec. 2010), 235–252.

[13] Graham, M. and Kennedy, J. 2007. Exploring multiple trees through DAG representations. *IEEE transactions on visualization and computer graphics*. 13, 6 (Dec. 2007), 1294–1301.

[14] Guerra Gómez, J.A. *Exploring Differences in Multivariate Datasets Using Hierarchies: An Interactive Information Visualization Approach*. University of Maryland.

[15] Guerra-Gómez, J.A., Buck-coleman, A., Pack, M.L., Plaisant, C. and Shneiderman, B. 2013. TreeVersity: Interactive Visualizations for Comparing Hierarchical Datasets. *Transportation Research Record (TRR), Journal of the Transportation Research Board (2013)*. (2013), 21.

[16] Guerra-Gómez, J.A., Buck-Coleman, A., Plaisant, C. and Shneiderman, B. 2011. TreeVersity: Comparing tree structures by topology and node's attributes differences. *2011 IEEE Conference on Visual Analytics Science and Technology (VAST)* (Oct. 2011), 275–276.

[17] Guerra-Gómez, J.A., Buck-coleman, A., Plaisant, C. and Shneiderman, B. 2012. TreeVersity: Visualizing Hierarchal Data for Value with Topology Changes. *Proceedings of the Digital Research Society 2012*. 2, (Jul. 2012), 640–653.

[18] Guerra-Gómez, J.A., Pack, M.L., Plaisant, C. and Shneiderman, B. 2013. Discovering temporal changes in hierarchical transportation data: Visual analytic & text reporting tools. *Transportation Research Part C: Emerging Technologies*. 51, (2013), 167–179.

[19] Guerra-Gómez, J.A., Pack, M.L., Plaisant, C. and Shneiderman, B. 2013. Visualizing Change over Time Using Dynamic Hierarchies: TreeVersity2 and the StemView. *IEEE Transactions on Visualization and Computer Graphics*. 19, 12 (2013), 2566–2575.

[20] Hong, J.Y., D'Andries, J., Richman, M. and Westfall, M. 2003. Zoomology: ComparingTwo Large Hierarchical Trees. *Poster at Compendium of InfoVis 2003*. (2003), 120–121.

[21] Isenberg, P. and Carpendale, S. 2007. Interactive Tree Comparison for Co-located Collaborative Information Visualization. *IEEE Transactions on Visualization and Computer Graphics*. 13, 6 (Nov. 2007), 1232–1239.

[22] Lee, B., Robertson, G.G., Czerwinski, M. and Parr, C.S. 2007. CandidTree: Visualizing Structural Uncertainty in Similar Hierarchies. *Human-Computer Interaction – INTERACT 2007*. C. Baranauskas, P. Palanque, J. Abascal, and S.D.J. Barbosa, eds. Springer Berlin Heidelberg. 250–263.

[23] Lunzer, A. and Hornbæk, K. 2008. Subjunctive Interfaces: Extending Applications to Support Parallel Setup, Viewing and Control of Alternative Scenarios. *ACM TOCHI*. 14, 4 (Jan. 2008), 17:1–17:44.

[24] Marks, J., Andalman, B., Beardsley, P.A., Freeman, W., Gibson, S., Hodgins, J., Kang, T., Mirtich, B., Pfister, H., Ruml, W., Ryall, K., Seims, J. and Shieber, S. 1997. Design galleries: a general approach to setting parameters for computer graphics and animation. *SIGGRAPH '97* (New York, NY, USA, 1997), 389–400.

[25] Mehra, A., Grundy, J. and Hosking, J. 2005. A generic approach to supporting diagram differencing and merging for collaborative design. *ASE 2005* (Long Beach, CA, USA, 2005), 204–213.

[26] Munzner, T., Guimbretière, F., Tasiran, S., Zhang, L. and Zhou, Y. 2003. TreeJuxtaposer: scalable tree comparison using Focus+Context with guaranteed visibility. *SIGGRAPH 2003*. 22, 3 (2003), 453–462.

[27] Namata, G.M., Staats, B., Getoor, L. and Shneiderman, B. 2007. A dual-view approach to interactive network visualization. *CIKM 2007* (Lisbon, Portugal, 2007), 939–942.

[28] Ohst, D., Welle, M. and Kelter, U. 2003. Differences between versions of UML diagrams. *ACM SIGSOFT Software Engineering Notes*. 28, 5 (Sep. 2003), 227–236.

[29] Rufiange, S. and McGuffin, M.J. 2013. DiffAni: Visualizing Dynamic Graphs with a Hybrid of Difference Maps and Animation. *IEEE Transactions on Visualization and Computer Graphics*. 19, 12 (Dec. 2013), 2556–2565.

[30] Shireen, N., Erhan, H., Botta, D. and Woodbury, R. 2012. Parallel development of parametric design models using subjunctive dependency graphs. *ACADIA 2012* (San Francisco, CA, USA, Oct. 2012), 57–66.

[31] Terry, M., Mynatt, E.D., Nakakoji, K. and Yamamoto, Y. 2004. Variation in element and action: supporting simultaneous development of alternative solutions. *CHI 2004* (New York, NY, USA, 2004), 711–718.

[32] Woodbury, R. 2010. *Elements of Parametric Design*. Routledge.

[33] Zaman, L. 2015. *User Interfaces and Difference Visualizations for Alternatives*. York University.

[34] Zaman, L., Kalra, A. and Stuerzlinger, W. 2011. DARLS: differencing and merging diagrams using dual view, animation, re-layout, layers and a storyboard. *CHI 2011 Extended Abstracts* (Vancouver, BC, Canada, 2011), 1657–1662.

[35] Zaman, L., Kalra, A. and Stuerzlinger, W. 2011. The effect of animation, dual view, difference layers, and relative re-layout in hierarchical diagram differencing. *Graphics Interface 2011* (St. John's, Newfoundland, Canada, 2011), 183–190.

[36] Zaman, L., Stuerzlinger, W., Neugebauer, C., Woodbury, R., Maher, E., Shireen, N. and Terry, M. 2015. GEM-NI: A System For Creating and Managing Alternatives In Generative Design. *CHI 2015* (Seoul, Korea, 2015).

Interactive Documents based on Discrete Trials

Alex F. Orlando, Isabela Zaine, Maria G. Pimentel,
Deisy G. De Souza, Cesar A. C. Teixeira
University of São Paulo - Federal University of São Carlos
São Carlos, SP-Brazil
alex_orlando,mgp,isazaine@usp.br--ddgs,cesar@ufscar.br

ABSTRACT

Interactive documents offer users alternatives for accessing the content available. In Education, researchers employ *Individualized Learning Programs* as interactive multimedia documents in order to teach students a variety of subjects. In order to author such interactive document, domain experts have to control features such as pace, duration, response-based criteria, and the hierarchy of learning units. We present how individualized learning programs can be modeled as interactive documents based on discrete trials and deterministic finite automata. We also report the main numbers associated with the use of a companion system deployed in real environments by domain specialists and learners.

CCS CONCEPTS

• **Applied computing** → **Hypertext / hypermedia creation**; *Education*; • **Information systems** → **Document structure**; *Information storage systems*;

KEYWORDS

Interactive multimedia, individualized learning program, automata.

1 INTRODUCTION

Interactive documents offer users non-linear alternatives for accessing content. Document engineering has contributed to the educational domain, for instance, with alternatives to support the authoring of interactive books by integrating contents from Wikipedia articles [1, 8]. In another effort, models and tools to support the authoring of graphics in eBooks to blind children [5].

For many educators, interactive documents should offer individualized content to students. Based on the principles of Behavior Analysis and Individualized Learning Programs, Keller created the *Personalized System of Instruction (PSI)* [7]. One strategy to facilitate learning using *Individualized Learning Programs (ILPs)* based on PSI is to structure them into discrete and consecutive trials (tests) [13].

Matching-To-Sample (MTS) is a procedure for teaching arbitrary relations using discrete trials and conditional discriminations. In each trial a sample stimulus and a set of comparison stimuli are presented. Stimuli range from visual (pictures and printed words), auditory (songs and dictated words), tactile (e.g. Braille) and even composites (e.g. video). The learner's task is to select the comparison defined as correct depending on the sample stimulus. Correct and incorrect responses produce differential feedback. *Individualized Learning Programs* as interactive multimedia documents based on MTS have been successful, for instance, in teaching reading to people with intellectual disabilities, autism spectrum disorders, and to students with typical development who find it difficult to learn in the classroom by conventional methods [3].

Toward authoring Individualized Learning Programs as interactive multimedia documents based on MTS, domain experts have to be aware, and to control, features such as pace, duration, response-based criteria, and the hierarchy of learning units. Giving the lack of models offered in the literature, as summarized in Section 2, in this paper we present our approach for modeling individualized learning programs as interactive multimedia documents based on discrete trials and deterministic finite automata.

In this paper Section 2 summarizes related work and Section 3 presents the modeling of individualized learning programs as interactive documents. Considering the system we built to allow the model to be used by domain specialists, Section 4 presents the main numbers associated with the system. Section 5 summarizes limitations and Section 6 presents our final remarks.

2 RELATED WORK

The *Computer-Aided Personalized System of Instruction* [11] offers learning units as study and test materials, so that each student is able to maintain his own study pace. Initially applied to university students, it aimed at teaching complex skills.

Web-Based Personalised System of Instruction is a pedagogical approach for the teaching of cognitive abilities to various groups using *Virtual Learning Environments* such as *Blackboard*. In particular, the extensive use of short video clips is proposed as specially suitable for learning math [12].

TECH8 is a modular and adaptive *Intelligent Tutoring System* which collects metadata and other variables for the learning process. The results of the evaluations indicate that materials properly created for *TECH8* are better than traditional teaching methods, but no better than individualized one-on-one, face-to-face teaching [4].

The demand for supporting individualized learning programs lead to the proposal of many patented methods and systems solutions (e.g., [2]) along with a large number of research contributions (e.g., [10]). Overall, these solutions employ machine learning-based approaches to select which content to present to the user considering students' performance and goals. This approach demands that the alternatives for content be previously authored and persisted a database. However, such automated approaches do not work well in cases in which specific minimal units have to be mastered. In this case, even though the units may be recombined to create alternatives [3], features such as the number of repetitions allowed for each trial, the time allowed for each trial and set of trials must be defined by the domain specialist, considering each learning goal in particular. Independently of the teaching domain, a model that allows such features involving discrete trials to be specified and supported in authoring and presentation engines have not been reported. Such model is the goal of our discussion hereafter.

3 INTERACTIVE DOCUMENTS BASED ON DISCRETE TRIALS

The representation presented in this section was modeled using a participatory design approach with specialists in Special Education and Psychology [9]. The modeling inherit their vocabulary.

3.1 Representation of Learning Units

A teaching program may have hundreds or thousands of discrete trials. Specialists, in the authoring process, group sequences of related trials into larger units called "blocks". A block is a learning unit that usually has more complex goals than the sequences of trials, such as teaching the symbolic relations between sets of stimuli, or training the student to be able to execute a subsequent block. Stimuli may be visual (e.g. pictures), auditory (e.g. utterances), tactile (e.g. Braille) or composites (e.g. video).

In some scenarios, the concept of "step" is also used, which refers to a group of blocks. A step represents a content unit that needs to be mastered by the learner, requiring the student to learn smaller units and pass some tests on that subject, before advancing to a new unit. During a learning session, a learner usually takes only one step. The word "step" is borrowed from the expression "one step at a time", which is one of the pillars of the PSI method. Finally, a "program" is comprised by a set of steps. In summary:

- a program has a set of steps,
- steps are sets of blocks, and
- blocks are sets of discrete trials.

Following the above hierarchy, programs are arranged in successively larger and more abstract sets, and all such units are bound by conditional and non-conditional flows. Additionally, units in all levels must have an entry point.

The hierarchy enables the definition of a script or plan of studies, thus allowing domain experts to control the order and pace at which the program will be applied. The hierarchy of learning units, in which users navigate according to rules and conditions specified by the domain specialist, behaves like a kind of reactive system.

Reactive systems can be modeled using finite automata, which are abstract machines that can be, at any given time, in one or more of a finite number of states (internal configurations). In an automaton, the "control" (current state) moves from state to state as a consequence of some external input. In *Deterministic Finite Automata (DFA)*, the control is exactly in one state at a time, unlike *Non-Deterministic Finite Automata (NFA)* in which the control can be in many states at once [6].

We settled on the DFA modeling for our approach since it is simple, has a concise graphical notation (state diagrams) and is relatively easy to comprehend by domain experts. Besides that, it

has a significant number of software implementations available, an eventual homegrown implementation would not be too complex to develop, and it has a vast associated literature and corpus of research. Other alternatives have been considered, such as flow charts, state charts, and Petri nets [14], but those were deemed too complex at the time for the problem the researchers had in hand and thus were discarded.

In our approach, a DFA models learning units as follows:

- Q: finite, non-empty set of learning units
- Σ: finite, non-empty set of evaluation criteria
- δ: transition function
- q_0: the initial learning unit inside a given program or higher-level unit
- F: set of final states, equal to the whole Q set.

The set Q represents the learning unit constituent of a more complex unit. For example, when representing a block of trials, its states would be the equivalent of occurrences (instances) of trials, in the same way that objects are instances of classes in Object-Oriented Programming and class-based programming languages. Similarly, steps are composed of occurrences of blocks, as well as programs are composed of occurrences of steps.

The input alphabet Σ refers to the evaluation criteria, which are satisfied by the performance of the learner. It can be stated that the input alphabet in the proposed model is the behavior (performance) of the learner, and that this behavior dictates the current state of the machine and its operation.

The state-transition function δ, defined by the expression $\delta : Q \times \Sigma \rightarrow Q$, summarizes to which state the abstract machine will move based on the current state (the learning unit being shown to the learner) and an input (the satisfaction of the criteria). A given unit can either originate or be the target of several transitions simultaneously. Since the model is based on a DFA and thus is deterministic, the domain expert must ensure that, given a source state and an input, there is only one transition that accepts them.

The initial state q_0 contained in Q is the first learning unit executed within a larger learning unit. The choice of q_0 must be made manually by the domain expert, and a larger unit should always have exactly one initial state.

Finally, the set of final (acceptable) states F is always the Q set itself, thus rendering the latter unnecessary. This design decision was made by the authors early in the project based on the assumption that the domain experts should design learning programs completely suited to learners' performance, leaving no room for unintended or unpredictable behavior. Another option considered early in the design phase was to have both final and non-final states just like in the classical DFA model, however there has been no agreement on what should happen once all input has been received and the current state was not an accepting state. Options included sending an e-mail to a proctor or putting the program on a "suspended" state (requiring manual intervention), but both were considered non scalable and inefficient.

In summary, in the model the learning units at all levels are interconnected by transitions that are traversed upon satisfaction of some criteria based on the behavior of the learner. Each complex unit (block, step or program) has an initial state, and all states are considered final, that is, the end of a unit is considered to be valid regardless of the last executed unit. Following this line of reasoning, programs must be arranged in successively larger and more abstract sets, and all such units must be bound by conditional and non-conditional transitions.

An overview of how an Individualized Learning Program is structured is given in Figure 1. In this example, the program (the top-level structure in the hierarchy) has a set of steps $S1$ and $S2$; $S2$ has a set of blocks $B1$ and $B2$; $B2$ has a set of trials $T1$ and $T2$. Figure 1d corresponds to trial $T2$ to be presented to a learner. Trial $T2$ has four stimuli: the word *tomato* and three images, including the one the user is expected to select.

3.2 Companion Implementation

The participatory design approach adopted for the definition of the model included the building of an associated software infrastructure called *GEIC (Computerized Individual Teaching Manager)* [9]. The model and the infrastructure, developed in several iterations, have evolved continuously to this day.

When using the system, a learner views an Individualized Learning Program as nothing more than an interactive book. By default, a learner is not warned of the beginning and end of blocks and steps: these abstractions deliberately do not exist for him. For a learner, however, there is a more important concept that must be discussed: the (learning) session.

In the context of Individualized Learning Programs, a session is a period of time in which structured interactive learning content is presented to the learner who, in turn, perform tasks associated with the content. A session may last from a few minutes to over an hour, and may contain from a few trials to hundreds of them. A teaching plan defines the interval between consecutive sessions, which can range from a few minutes to a few days. To finish an Individualized Learning Program the learner usually performs dozens of sessions.

The model allows the allocation of one or more steps per session. The software implementation must guarantee that, once a current session is finished by the learner, the next session of that learner points to the next step in the sequence (as planned by the domain expert). A learner's enrollment in a program is concluded when there are no more steps to be executed in that program.

At presentation level, in order for users to navigate through learning programs as interactive documents, the notation used in the system to run the programs in accordance with the model is as follows. The top-level structure is the *Session Execution* itself. It represents a whole executed learning session, which includes:

- An enrollment
- A student
- A program
- The tutor (if any) that supported the student
- A set of step executions

A given enrollment in an ILP can have many session executions. For *Step Execution*, the most important attributes are:

- An occurrence of a step
- A set of block executions

Similarly, a *Block Execution* attributes includes:

- An occurrence of a block
- A set of trial executions

A *Trial Execution* represents all the information stored from the moment a trial is presented to the student until the moment it finishes it and another trial take its place. Attributes include:

- An occurrence of a trial
- A set of interactions

While a trial is presented to a learner, he has a number of opportunities to give the correct answer. Each opportunities is called an *Interaction*. An interaction has attributes:

- Latency: the time taken by the learner to produce a response
- Result: if his answer is correct, incorrect, canceled etc.
- A set of selections (if any)

Only some variations of trials contain a list of selections. A *Selection* is the more fine-grained element in the session execution structure and it represents each action performed by the learner on each trial. Examples of selections include mouse clicks in a sample stimulus, each letter clicked in order to construct a full word, etc.

Summarizing, a session execution is a set of step executions, which are a set of block executions, composed by trial executions, which are finally composed of interactions and selections of the stimuli corresponding the the trial. In fact, this hierarchy fully describes the path taken by the student in the corresponding ILP, as well details of the student's performance in each trial.

4 HIGHLIGHTS FROM USE

Since its first release of GEIC in 2009 [9], many positive results have been achieved, e.g.:

- A total of 664 different domain specialists have used the system up to this date, with an increase of 10% occurred in the last two years.
- The domain specialists have authored a total of 465 distinct programs. Each teaching program may have from hundreds to thousands of discrete trials.
- The total number of different trials is 25576 and of different stimuli is 10844. Stimuli are reusable components.
- A total of 4546 different students have executed 89079 sessions over the years, from which 11275 in the last two years. These students were from 180 different schools and 58 different cities. Most programs are targeted at children with some types of learning difficulties, which explains the relatively small number of students.

In the context of programs designed to teach children with difficulties in reading, stimuli can be letters, symbols, words, sentences, as well as their corresponding images and utterances. This means that the set of stimuli includes, e.g, the picture for "tomato" and the other pictures shown in Figure 1, the audio with the pronunciation of 'tomato' and the other pictures, as well as separate recorded pronunciation and graphics for the letters 't', 'o', 'm' and 'a'. These and any of the other 10844 stimuli could be used (if permission granted) in any new trial being authored by a domain expert – including to form the word "tomato" associated, in a trial, with its picture and pronunciation. Figures 2 and 3 show real programs authored by domain specialists: the first with 11 states and the later with hundred of states. In both figures, each small rectangle corresponds to a Step (Fig. 1b) and it is further structured in Blocks (Fig. 1c) and Trials (Fig. 1d).

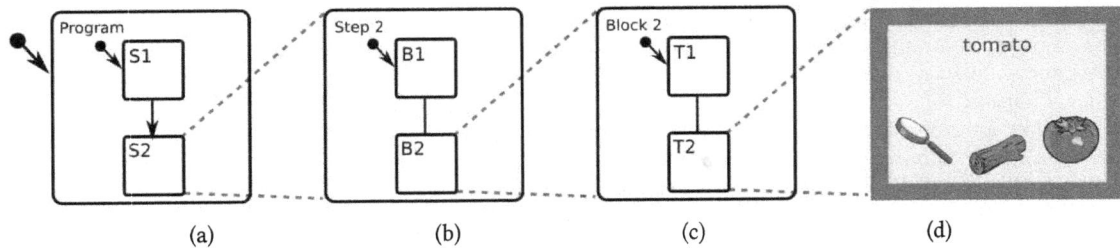

Figure 1: Abstract representation of an Individualized Learning Program. (a) Program contains Step *S*1 and Step *S*2; (b) Step *S*2 contains Block *B*1 and Block *B*2; (c) Block *B*2 has Trial *T*1 and Trial *T*2; (d) Trial *T*2 presented to a learner.

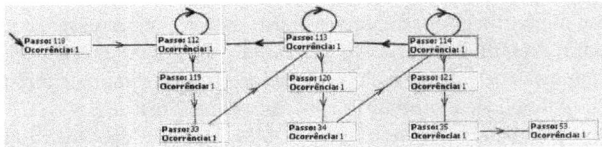

Figure 2: A small program created by a specialist. Each small rectangle corresponds to a Step (Fig. 1b) and it is further structured in Blocks (Fig. 1c)

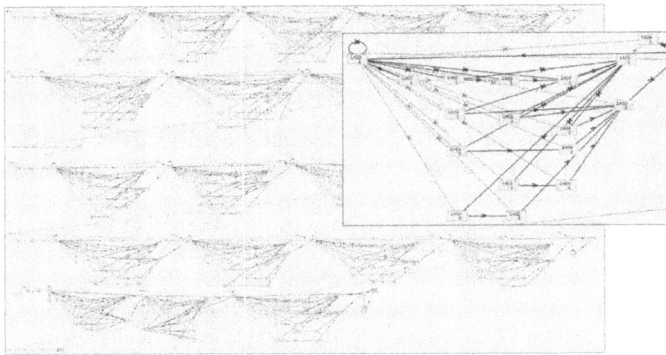

Figure 3: A large program created by a specialist (with detail)

5 LIMITATIONS

As the scale of the implementation increased, and as a direct consequence of the deficiencies of the existing representation, the difficulty in developing quality large ILPs become evident. Not infrequently, ILPs with programming errors were made available to students, which caused disruption and waste of resources for all parts involved. Recurring learning programming errors include unreachable learning units (no transition ever takes to them), unresolvable trials, steps with heterogeneous lengths (ranging from a few minutes to hours), and infinite loops (endless cyclic graphs).

In many programs an unnecessary explosion in the number of learning units (states). Often, programs have hundreds of unnecessary occurrences of steps, largely due to the lack of mechanisms that allow the reuse of trials and blocks, and also due to the lack of flexibility in the definition of transition criteria.

While some of these issues involve trade-offs (e.g., legibility *vs.* expressiveness), others demand providing better tools to specialists.

6 FINAL REMARKS

We presented how individualized learning programs can be modeled as interactive documents based on discrete trials and deterministic finite automata. We also highlighted features of an implementation that exemplifies how systems benefit from such modeling. We have also reported the actual number of users, both domain specialists and learners, and the numbers of programs currently in use.

Currently, we are investigating metadata vocabularies for the learning design domain, alternative representations for Individualized Learning Programs (graphical or textual), and the issue of unnecessary explosion in the number of learning units. We are also employing techniques from graph theory and algorithm analysis in order to verify the correctness and efficiency of interactive documents modeled using discrete trials.

ACKNOWLEDGMENTS

We thank the domain specialists who helped us to design our system. We thank FAPESP, CNPq and CAPES for financial support.

REFERENCES

[1] S. A. Battle and M. Bernius. Transquotation in ebooks. In *ACM DocEng '10*, pages 69–72, 2010.
[2] B. P. Bergeron. Instruction based on competency assessment and prediction, Jan. 10 2017. US Patent 9,542,853.
[3] D. G. de Souza, J. C. de Rose, T. C. Faleiros, R. Bortoloti, E. S. Hanna, and W. J. McIlvane. Teaching generative reading via recombination of minimal textual units: A legacy of verbal behavior to children in brazil. *IJP&PT*, 9(1):19, 2009.
[4] K. Dolenc and B. Aberšek. TECH8 intelligent and adaptive e-learning system: Integration into technology and science classrooms in lower secondary schools. *Computers & Education*, 82:354 – 365, 2015.
[5] C. Goncu and K. Marriott. Creating ebooks with accessible graphics content. In *ACM DocEng '15*, pages 89–92, 2015.
[6] J. E. Hopcroft, R. Motwani, and J. D. Ullman. *Introduction to automata theory, languages, and computation*. Pearson Education, 1979.
[7] F. S. Keller. Neglected rewards in the educational process. Jan. 1967.
[8] C. Liang, S. Wang, Z. Wu, K. Williams, B. Pursel, B. Brautigam, S. Saul, H. Williams, K. Bowen, and C. L. Giles. BBookX: An automatic book creation framework. In *ACM DocEng '15*, pages 121–124, 2015.
[9] A. F. Orlando. Computational infrastructure to manage individualized learning programs *(in Portuguese)*. Master's thesis, UFSCar, Brazil, 2009.
[10] R. Paiva, M. Ferreira, and M. Frade. Intelligent tutorial system based on personalized system of instruction to teach mathematical concepts. *JCAL*, 2017.
[11] J. J. Pear, G. J. Schnerch, K. M. Silva, L. Svenningsen, and J. Lambert. Web-based computer-aided personalized system of instruction. *New directions for teaching and learning*, 2011(128):85–94, 2011.
[12] A. Rae and P. Samuels. Web-based personalised system of instruction: An effective approach for diverse cohorts with virtual learning environments? *Computers & Education*, 57(4):2423 – 2431, 2011.
[13] T. Smith. Discrete trial training in the treatment of autism. *Focus on Autism and Other Developmental Disabilities*, 16(2):86–92, 2001.
[14] P. D. Stotts and R. Furuta. Petri-net-based hypertext: Document structure with browsing semantics. *ACM Transactions on Information Systems*, 7(1):3–29, 1989.

DocHandles: Linking Document Fragments in Messaging Apps

Laurent Denoue, Scott Carter, Jennifer Marlow, Matthew Cooper
FX Palo Alto Laboratory
Palo Alto, CA
{denoue,carter,marlow,cooper}@fxpal.com

ABSTRACT

In this paper, we describe DocHandles, a novel system that allows users to link to specific document parts in their chat applications. As users type a message, they can invoke the tool by referring to a specific part of a document, e.g., "@fig1 needs revision". By combining text parsing and document layout analysis, DocHandles can find and present all the figures "1" inside previously shared documents, allowing users to explicitly link to the relevant "document handle". Documents become first-class citizens inside the conversation stream where users can seamlessly integrate documents in their text-centric messaging application.

CCS CONCEPTS

• **Document preparation Multi/Mixed Media Creation** • **Computer Graphics** • **Image Manipulation** • **Image Processing**

KEYWORDS

Document capture; image processing; enterprise messaging; interactive documents

1 INTRODUCTION

Over the last few years, messaging applications such as Slack have been adopted by millions of users. With these new communication tools, users frequently share documents they are working on, either as links for example to Google Docs, or by directly attaching document files.

After a file is linked to or attached, users start discussing its contents: They give each other feedback about what needs to be changed, or refer to a specific table or figure that others should pay attention to, for example a link to a PDF paper that is relevant to their research. Unfortunately, making sense of what is referred

DocEng '17, September 4-7, 2017, Valletta, Malta
© 2017 Association for Computing Machinery.
ACM ISBN 978-1-4503-4689-4/17/09...$15.00
https://doi.org/10.1145/3103010.3121036

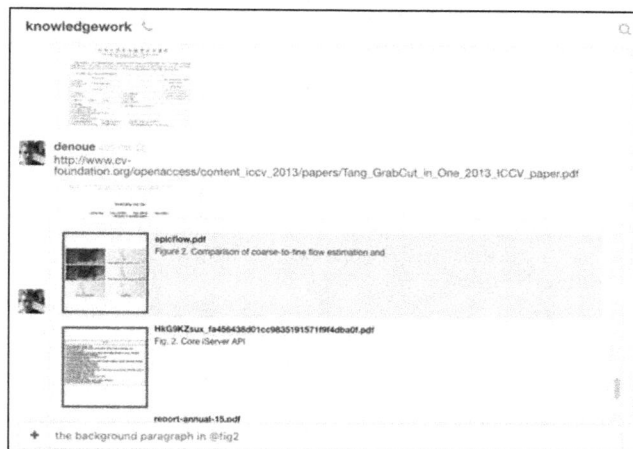

Figure 1: When the user types "@fig2", she is shown a list of figures extracted from recently shared documents; each suggestion corresponds to the "figure 2" in that document, along with the document filename or title and caption.

to can be cognitively expensive, and hinders the normal flow of messages. Misunderstanding can be further exacerbated for teams distributed across time zones who frequently read messages hours after they have been posted.

This work is inspired by behaviors that we observed in the chat logs of teams of knowledge workers using Slack to communicate and co-edit a variety of documents. We found that small groups often make edit documents such as research papers in Microsoft Word, or presentations in PowerPoint, and used natural language to guide their collaborators to specific parts of a document.

For example, we noted that people often added text comments after sharing links, documents or images. Comments included specific parts of the documents (e.g., "introduction section") or mentioned aspects of their structure (e.g., "slide 1"). People also spent a fair amount of time telling others where files are, what has been uploaded, commented on, or edited. Finally, different versions of the same file were uploaded with text describing what was done. People used numbered lists or references to page, figure, and slide numbers to clarify what they were referring to, especially if they occurred in between other messages.

While typing comments about the document into Slack may have been easy, there remained a disconnect between the discussion in Slack and the relevant parts of the document that needed attention. In other words, collaborators had to switch between the Slack conversation and the document itself in another program, or move the conversation into a document application with integrated chat.

Previous systems have attempted to augment chat spaces with recommended content [1] without directly linking to documents or their fragments. Other systems augment web clients with chat capabilities, but require manual selection of the appropriate fragment of the currently rendered page [2].

To better integrate chat-based conversations with documents, we describe the design and implementation of DocHandles where users can explicitly link specific parts of documents they are referencing. When a user types "@" in her message, the system matches the subsequent characters to determine the relevant document fragment. For example, in Figure 1, the user typed "@fig2" and the system immediately shows her a list of possible figures corresponding to "figure 2" in recently shared documents. The user simply clicks on a suggested figure to link it to her message. With this tool, recipients immediately understand more of the message intent and document context. They can see the figure by hovering over the link or access it within the original document page by clicking on it.

We describe below how the system analyses documents shared in the chat application, and recommends document fragments based on the user's message.

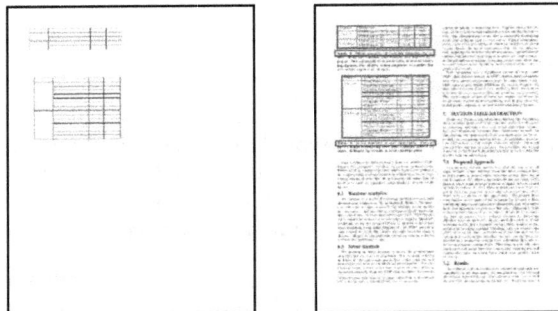

Figure 2. Left: the binary image without text rendered; right: the page with detected captions and tables.

2 SEMANTIC LAYOUT ANALYSIS

To link "@fig2" typed by a user to the actual figure 2 of a document, we developed a new document layout engine that finds images in documents and associates each with its nearby caption (if any). With the caption, the system matches the figure/table number with the message content.

To deal with various file formats used in enterprise chat messaging applications, documents are first converted to PDF. LibreOffice[1] is used to convert Microsoft Office documents such as Word and PowerPoint. Links to Google Docs are also quite common, so we export them as PDF by modifying the link to obtain their PDF versions (see [4]).

2.1 DOCUMENT IMAGE PROCESSING

Similar to the processing flow of PDFFigures2 [3], our document layout engine renders each document page image without text elements via a modified version of XPDF. A binary image is then obtained by thresholding the grayscale page image (we use 168 out of 255 gray values) and the bounding boxes of connected components are found. For each page, we also use XPDF to extract each word and its bounding box on that page.

For business documents seen in our Slack teams, this binary image clearly shows areas of the page where images, graphs or tables are present, see Figure 2. We now explain how the text and connected components of binary images are used to form the final document layout. Extracting graphical content from document images is an active area of research [3,6,7].

2.1 FINDING CAPTIONS

Word bounding boxes are grouped into text lines, and the following regular expression is used to find likely captions:

```
/^(graph|chart|figure|table|tab\.?|algorithm|alg\.?|fig\.?)\s*\d+\s*(\.|:|−)/
```

Each caption bounding box is retained and used later to associate it with its corresponding image. Figure 2, right, shows that the captions for each table were found. Note that for our purposes, we do not need to detect the complete caption, because the first line alone links users' messages to potential captions. Also, the first line is an informative cue for users in the interface showing suggestions (see Section 4).

2.1 DETECTION OF FIGURES

The boxes of connected components are recursively merged if they are close to each other, and are not separated by the bounding box of a caption, as found in the previous step. We use 10 pixels on document images rendered at 72 DPI to decide whether to group two boxes.

Graphs or flowcharts often contain text elements near graphical elements. Since the binary image was obtained without rendering text, the next step grows each region box to include nearby words, using the bounding boxes of text elements found previously.

2.2 FINDING TABLES

The previous step fails to detect tables that might contain horizontal lines that were too far from each other to be grouped. We further group those if they are vertically aligned, i.e., if their left and rightmost positions are equal within a 2-pixel threshold to accommodate binarization errors. Tables without rules could be detected using dedicated methods such as [6,7].

---

[1] https://www.libreoffice.org/

2.3 FINETUNING WITH CAPTIONS

For many images, the previous step fails to group distinct elements that appear together in one figure. For example, a figure might span the entire width of a document page, but the individual components are not all within the 10-pixel threshold used to group them in step 2.1. To address this issue, we observed that caption text usually spans the whole width of the corresponding figure. We thus use this box width as a heuristic to group figure elements that are above this caption box. The result is a better grouping of the actual figure elements that constitute one figure, as shown in Figure 3.

2.4 LINKING IMAGES TO CAPTIONS

Figure 3. Left: the binary image without text rendered; right: the page with detected caption and figure. Note that the initial boxes (orange) were merged to span the width of the nearby caption box.

After finding the bounding boxes of detected images, graphs and tables, the system then associates the captions with their corresponding figures. We use Euclidian distance to determine which caption should be linked to a given image.

The result of this step is a JSON file that contains the bounding boxes of likely figure areas along with their captions. This structure is used in the next step to match a user's message to specific content in documents. To detect whether a file is likely a presentation file (e.g., PowerPoint), we simply use the aspect ratio of the page dimensions. These results are filtered to generate the candidate lists for users to interactively review to create links.

3 TEXT MESSAGE PARSING AND MATCHING OF RELEVANT DOCUMENTS

To inform our implementation, we analyzed the message logs of three Slack teams over a period of four months and extracted the most frequent words people use when referring to document fragments in their messages, namely "page", "slide", "figure", "table" and "algorithm". Other words such as "paragraph" or "introduction" are also common, but we decided to focus our implementation efforts on the aforementioned keywords for now. People also often cite passages of documents in their messages, e.g., "please change XXX into YYY". We have not yet implemented this detection.

Users often abbreviate keywords, e.g., "fig" for "figure", "tab" instead of "table", "p" for "page" and "alg" for "algorithm". These variations are captured by two regular expressions that match the root of the keyword, followed by a number. For figures, tables and algorithms, we use the following expression:

```
/^(figure|table|tab\.?|algorithm|fig\.?)\s*(\d+)\s*(\.?|:?|-?)/gi
```

To detect mentions of a page or slide number, we use this second expression:

```
/^(page|slide|p|pg)\.?\s*(\d+)/gi
```

Given a user's message prefix (the text typed after the "@" sign), these two expressions thus yield null, or a couple {keyword, number}. If a match is found, the JSON file generated in the document analysis step (see Section 2) allows us to find the corresponding page, slide, or figure in each document that was shared in the conversation. If a slide keyword is detected, only documents classified as presentations are kept.

The list of matching document page regions is sorted by most recent document first, because our analysis of the Slack logs indicates that users are more likely to refer to a document when it was most recently shared in the conversation. We include only documents shared within the current channel.

4 INTEGRATION IN CHAT APPLICATIONS

To test our algorithms, we integrated them into our custom enterprise chat application called DocuChat and instantiated them as a Slack "bot".

4.1 INTEGRATION IN DOCUCHAT

We developed DocuChat, a custom web-based chat application like Slack, to quickly test new techniques for interacting with documents inside chat applications. Our web-based interface gives full access to users' actions, especially in our case keyboard events, providing in turn a more integrated user experience. All screenshots in this paper come from DocuChat.

In DocuChat, users can quickly pick or drag and drop documents from their desktop onto the web application. Similarly, if they link to a known document type in their message, DocuChat automatically follows the link, downloads the document, converts it to a PDF and previews it below the message. Clicking on the thumbnail shows users the document inside the browser window, avoiding unnecessary downloads and application switching. We use Mozilla's PDFJS to render PDF files inside the web browser. The layout analysis is performed on the server on each document, yielding a JSON file that contains all words as well as image positions and associated captions and stored in a database.

When the user types a "@", the system looks for characters that follow and tries to match this suffix against a caption, e.g., "fig1" will find the couple {"figure","1"} as explained in section 3.

The list of all figures appears in an overlay window, along with the document title and associated caption if found, as shown in Figure 1. Since chat applications are text-centric, we allow users to TAB or use arrow keys to pick a suggestion. They can also click with their mouse. Upon picking a suggestion, the system creates a hyperlink that encodes the document identifier along with the page number and image number on that page. For example, "@fig2" typed by the user is converted into "@fig2#390-4-5" if the figure was the 5th image on page 4 of document 390.

Figure 4. When a user clicks the link, the system shows them the document

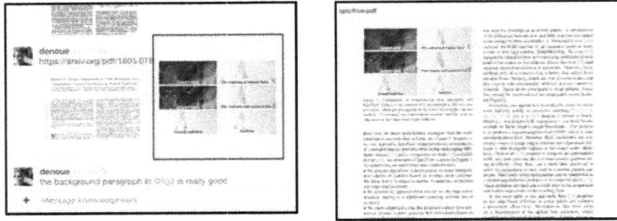

Figure 5. Left: clicking the DocHandle link in the chat message, shows the original document automatically scrolled to the area of interest (here "figure 2").

Because such hyperlinks would clutter the text box and perhaps even confuse users, the caption of the hyperlink only shows the original user's content, here "@fig2" only, as shown in Figure 4. When the message is posted, any user can hover over the link to view the corresponding region of interest (ROI) in the document image, as shown in Figure 5 left, inside the blue border.

Finally, if a user clicks on the hyperlink, they are shown the original document, scrolled to that exact location, see Figure 5 right. The interface supports a seamless transition between text-centric chat messages and the specific document-centric context of the conversations.

4.2 INTEGRATION IN SLACK

Slack's popularity stems in part from its rich set of APIs, allowing third-party services to write "bots". Once a bot is invited to a channel, it can receive all posted messages, including attachments. We wrote DocuBot, a Slack bot that users can invite to their channel. DocuBot indexes all attached documents posted on the channel, and looks for links to documents in messages. Like in DocuChat, each document is indexed by our document layout analysis system.

If a message is found to match a caption, the bot retrieves a list of suggestions (as in the case of DocuChat) and posts them as a Smart Slack Message that includes image thumbnails of the relevant document fragments. Only the user who typed that message sees this first message. She can ignore it, but she can also click on a button associated with one of the images to pick a suggestion. Upon receipt, the bot then posts the selected figure to the channel so that all users can see the explicit link between the previous message and the document fragment. Unlike DocuChat, this Slack bot does not have fine control over the previous message, but the integration is nonetheless important because DocHandles can be deployed and tested by many more teams that already use Slack.

5 CONCLUSIONS

We described DocHandles, a new technique that enriches text-based chat conversations about documents by allowing users to quickly link specific and relevant portions of documents inside their messages. Anecdotal evidence with a few users from our laboratory and friends shows that users like to create these DocHandles links because they effectively augment their messages while preserving the ease of text-centric communication in this medium. Additionally, users like to read messages that contain explicit mentions of document fragments because they reduce ambiguity and link conversations to relevant content.

Future work will focus on extending the layout analysis and matching functions presented in this paper. In particular, PowerPoint slides typically lack numbering of their figures. The algorithm will thus need to classify each detected image area as a type, e.g., table, figure, algorithm, graph, pie-chart. One method would be to use neural networks to classify detected images as shown in [5].

Finally, analysis of Slack message logs has shown that users copy verbatim some passages in documents. We can readily use the text extracted from the PDF documents to match those. But users will not necessarily type "@" before the text excerpt and the user interaction will need to change: the system could for example monitor the current message's contents and pro-actively insert an icon or hyperlink where it thinks that content relates to a document fragment, letting users quickly validate with a button press or TAB.

REFERENCES

[1] S. Loh, D. Lichtnow, A. Justin C. Kampff, J. de Oliveira. Recommendation of Complementary Material during Chat Discussions. Knowledge Management & E-Learning: An International Journal (KM&EL), Vol 2, No 4 (2010)

[2] Kifi. https://techcrunch.com/2016/07/12/google-acquires-deep-search-engine-kifi-to-enhance-its-spaces-group-chat-app/

[3] C. Clark and S. Divvala.. PDFFigures 2.0: Mining Figures from Research Papers. Proc. of ACM/IEEE-CS on Joint Conf. on Digital Libraries. ACM, 2016.

[4] Labnol https://www.labnol.org/internet/direct-links-for-google-drive/28356./

[5] Y. Rangoni, A. Belaid. Document Logical Structure Analysis Based on Perceptive Cycles. IAPR Workshop on Document Analysis Systems. Springer, 3872, , 2006.

[6] M Fan, DS Kim. Detecting Table Region in PDF Documents Using Distant Supervision. 2015, arXiv:1506.08891.

[7] L. Hao, L. Gao, X. Yi and Z. Tang, "A Table Detection Method for PDF Documents Based on Convolutional Neural Networks," IAPR Workshop on Document Analysis Systems (DAS), 2016

The RASH JavaScript Editor (RAJE)
A Wordprocessor for Writing Web-first Scholarly Articles

Gianmarco Spinaci
DASPLab, DISI, University of
Bologna, Bologna, Italy
gianmarco.spinaci@studio.unibo.it

Silvio Peroni
DASPLab, DISI, University of
Bologna, Bologna, Italy
silvio.peroni@unibo.it

Angelo Di Iorio
DASPLab, DISI, University of
Bologna, Bologna, Italy
angelo.diiorio@unibo.it

Francesco Poggi
DASPLab, DISI, University of
Bologna, Bologna, Italy
francesco.poggi5@unibo.it

Fabio Vitali
DASPLab, DISI, University of
Bologna, Bologna, Italy
fabio.vitali@unibo.it

ABSTRACT

The most used format for submitting and publishing papers in the academic domain is the Portable Document Format (PDF), since its possibility of being rendered in the same way independently from the device used for visualising it. However, the PDF format has some important issues as well, among which the lack of interactivity and the low degree of accessibility. In order to address these issues, recently some journals, conferences, and workshops have started to accept also HTML as Web-first submission/publication format. However, most of the people are not able to produce a well-formed HTML5 article from scratch, and they would, thus, need an appropriate interface, e.g. a word processor, for creating such HTML-compliant scholarly article.

To provide a solution to the aforementioned issue, in this paper we introduce the RASH JavaScript Editor (a.k.a. RAJE), which is a multi platform word processor for writing scholarly articles in HTML natively. RAJE allows authors to write research papers by means of a user-friendly interface hiding the complexities of HTML5. We also discuss the outcomes of a user study where we asked some researchers to write a scientific paper using RAJE.

RASH version: https://w3id.org/people/essepuntato/papers/raje-doceng2017.html

CCS CONCEPTS

• **Computers in other domains** → Personal computers and PC applications;

KEYWORDS

HTML-based scholarly articles, RAJE, RASH, RASH framework, Research Article in Simplified HTML, Web-first format, research communication

1 INTRODUCTION

Currently, the most used format for submitting and publishing scholarly articles is the Portable Document Format (PDF) [2]. One of the main strengths of this format is its hard formatting style that ensures to be read and visualised by any device in the same way. However, PDF has also important drawbacks, such as the lack of interactivity, the fact that its monolithic structure is not appropriate for sharing its content on the Web as a common web page, and its known difficulties regarding the accessibility of its content by people with disabilities [12]. Usually, in order to submit an article to a particular venue such as a journal or a conference, authors need to create a document that will be exported as PDF. Such document is usually written with a word processor (e.g. Microsoft Word or OpenOffice) or by means of appropriate markup languages such as LaTeX. While in the first case the rendering of the document (and, thus, of the final PDF to export) is what the word processor shows in the screen, LaTeX obliges its users to compile the document in order to understand how it will be rendered in PDF.

In the last years, the use of PDF as submission/publication format has been criticised by several people and movements (e.g. Linked Research[1]), and several discussions have raised the issue of using another (Web-first, accessible, and open) format for preparing and sharing scholarly works, i.e. HTML [1]. Following this idea, several conferences and journals have started to experiment the use of HTML as submission format. For instance the 15th[2] and the 16th International Semantic Web Conference[3], the 13th and the 14th Extended Semantic Web Conference, the 20th International

[1]https://linkedresearch.org/
[2]http://iswc2016.semanticweb.org/
[3]http://iswc2017.semanticweb.org/

Conference on Knowledge Management and Knowledge Engineering[4], the Poster and Demo session at 13th International Conference on Semantic Systems[5], and journals like Data Science[6] published by IOS Press, are among those that have started to adopt HTML.

One of the most used and appreciated formats[7] for creating HTML-based scholarly papers is the Research Articles in Simplified HTML (RASH)[8] [16]. RASH is a markup language that restricts the use of HTML elements to only 32 elements and enables one to include also RDF statements [8]. In addition, it uses the new Digital Publishing WAI-ARIA Module 1.0 [10] for specifying accessible structural semantics to the various document parts. While the framework that has been developed for RASH includes a lot of conversion tools from word processor formats (e.g. the Open Document Format used by Open Office and the Open XML format used by Microsoft Word), no native editor for facilitating the creation of Web-first RASH article has been proposed yet.

In this paper, we introduce the **RASH JavaScript Editor** (RAJE), a *What You See Is What You Get* (WYSIWYG) word processor for writing scholarly articles in HTML, according to the RASH format. In particular, RAJE allows authors to write research papers in HTML natively by means of a user-friendly interface, instead of writing raw markup with an IDE, a text editor or any external word processor. RAJE guarantees to its users the benefits of a word processor combined with the ones given by an HTML-based format, i.e. interactiveness, accessibility and easiness to be processed by machines. In addition, RAJE uses the GitHub API so as to allow authors to store their articles online, to keep track of changes by means of the GitHub services, and to share the articles with others. This paper has been written by using RAJE itself, and it was converted into the appropriate layout requested by the conference by means of the RASH Online Conversion Service (ROCS)[9] [9].

The rest of the paper is organised as follows. In Section 2 we describe some of the most important HTML-based editors, while in Section 3 we give some background about RASH and the existing tools in the RASH framework. In Section 4 we introduce RAJE, and we provide a high-level description and show some details about its implementation. In Section 5 we present the outcomes of a user testing session we have run by involving people in the Academia so as to understand the level of perceived usability of RAJE when used for writing a scholarly article. Finally, in Section 6 we conclude the paper sketching out some future developments.

2 RELATED WORKS

Several works have been developed for easing the creation of HTML-based scholarly papers. In this section, we introduce some of the most relevant ones, by discussing their main characteristics. All these editors are powerful and successfully used by the community. The reason why we decided to implement a new one is its strong connection with RASH. The tool, in fact, is not a plain HTML editor but it is customised to work on the RASH format. RASH is based on a peculiar pattern-based structure and RAJE helps authors to easily create and maintain that structure. Though, some features of the other editors were implemented or included in RAJE as well, as described in the following sections.

Authorea[10] is an online platform to write and edit scientific papers. Every article is an HTML document and Git repository simultaneously. The main goal for the development of Authorea was to fix collaborative problems that could come out during the creation of technical, scholarly and scientific writings[11], so as to allow authors to take advantages of using Git versioning system and keeping track of every single displayed change. In addition, every article is accessible from anywhere, by using any device connected to the Internet, and no TeX installation is required for producing the final PDF layout necessary for the submission. In addition, Authorea allows one to write mathematical notations, tables, plots and figures in each LaTeX and MathML[12].

Dokieli[13] [5] is a client-side editor for decentralised article publishing, annotations, and social interactions. Since Dokieli follows a pure decentralisation principle, authors can publish the paper where they prefer. In particular, Dokieli complies with the Solid protocol[14], based on the Linked Data Platform W3C standard [4] [3], so as to allows one to edit the HTML-based scholarly article in the browser and to save it directly to server storage.

Fidus Writer[15] is an open source WYSIWYG collaborative HTML-based word processor made for academics who need to use citations and formulas within papers. All the articles created with it can be exported in more ways: as a website, a paper, or an ebook. Independently from the particular export, the editor allows authors to focus on the content of the paper, while the final layout can be chosen once the content is finalised. FidusWriter supports LaTeX for adding footnotes and citations directly inside the documents and allows a real-time collaboration with other users.

TinyMCE[16] is a WYSIWYG HTML-based editor that can be instantiated within an existing HTML page. It is a huge project that involves more than 150 contributors with almost 6500 commits on Github[17]. Its include facilities for formatting, table insertion, image editing, customizable themes, and it is accessible for users with disabilities – in fact, it

---

[4] http://ekaw2016.cs.unibo.it
[5] https://2017.semantics.cc
[6] http://datasciencehub.net/
[7] https://github.com/essepuntato/rash/#venues-that-have-adopted-rash-as-submission-format
[8] https://github.com/essepuntato/rash
[9] http://dasplab.cs.unibo.it/rocs

[10] https://www.authorea.com/
[11] http://www.astrobetter.com/blog/2015/07/13/why-should-i-use-authorea-to-write-my-papers/
[12] https://www.authorea.com/users/3/articles/6055-how-is-authorea-different-from-google-docs/
[13] http://dokie.li/
[14] https://solid.mit.edu/
[15] https://www.fiduswriter.org/
[16] https://www.tinymce.com/
[17] https://github.com/tinymce/tinymce

follows WAI-ARIA guidelines [7] so as to make HTML documents compatible with screen readers such as JAWS and NVDA. It is already integrated with frameworks such as JQuery and Angular.js, or inside common content management systems such as Wordpress or Joomla.

3 BACKGROUND

In order to understand some design choices of RAJE, as well as some elements of the interface, we need to provide some background about RASH, the language on top of which the editor has been built.

3.1 Research Articles in Simplified HTML

The RASH format is a markup language that restricts the use of HTML elements to only 32 elements for writing academic research articles. It allows authors to add RDF statements [8] to the document by means of the element `script` with the attribute type set to "application/rdf+xml", "text/turtle" or to "application/ld+json". In addition, RASH strictly follows the Digital Publishing WAI-ARIA Module 1.0 [10] for expressing structural semantics on various markup elements used.

A RASH document begins as a simple (X)HTML5 document, by specifying the generic HTML DOCTYPE followed by the document element `html` with the usual namespace "http://www.w3.org/1999/xhtml" specified. The element `html` contains the element `head` for defining metada-ta of the document according to the DCTERMS and PRISM standards, and the element `body` for including the whole content of the document. On the one hand, the element `he- ad` of a RASH document must/should include some information about the paper, i.e., the paper title (element `title`), at least one author and other related information (i.e., affiliations, keywords, categories, by using the elements `meta` and `link`). On the other hand, the element `body` mainly contains textual elements (e.g., paragraphs, emphases, links, and quotations) for describing the content of the paper, and other structural elements (e.g., abstract, sections, references, and footnotes) used to organised the paper in appropriate blocks and to present specific complex structures (e.g., figures, formulas, and tables).

Note that RASH is one of the proposals for using HTML-based language in scientific articles. Other approaches exist and are valid works though. However, the discussion about RASH and its competitors is out of the scope of this work – more details can be found in [16], in which we also discussed how the internal structure of RASH. In particular, it is worth mentioning here the usage of structural patterns for describing markup documents within RASH, that heavily impacted on the design and behaviour of RAJE. The systematic use of these structural patterns is an added value in all stages of the documents' life-cycle: they can be guidelines for creating well-engineered documents and vocabularies, as well as helpers to manipulate structural components in documents.

3.2 The RASH Framework

RASH is accompanied by its Framework[18], which is a set of specifications and writing/conversion/extraction tools for writing articles in RASH. In particular the RASH Framework includes tools for checking the validity of RASH documents, visualising RASH documents on browsers with different layouts, for converting RASH documents into LaTeX and ODT/DOCX files into RASH, and for automatically annotate RASH elements with their actual (structural) semantics according to the Document Components Ontology (DoCO)[19] [6].

4 THE RASH JAVASCRIPT EDITOR

This section presents the main features of RAJE and some details about its implementation. It is split into three parts: we first present the basic functionalities, then we go deeper in the support for collaborative editing available in RAJE and finally, we provide some implementation details.

4.1 Editing articles in RAJE

RAJE is a stand-alone multi-platform software used to generate RASH documents. Its sources[20] and the related binary files[21] are available on GitHub a licensed according to the ISC License[22], as all the other tools included in the RASH Framework.

Before starting the development of the tool, we collected a series of desiderata and needs that such an editor should properly address. The requirements were identified by our research group and then shared with external researchers who helped us to extend and refine the list. Overall, about twenty people were involved, with different skills and positions, including PhD students, researchers and professors. Their background was also heterogeneous, with most people from computer science but also some experts in economics, social sciences, biology and humanities.

The full list of requirements is shown below:

- being totally compatible with RASH and HTML5;
- relying on the existing tools developed for visualising RASH documents, included in the RASH Framework;
- simplifying the writing of the document keeping things as natural as possible;
- not enabling the user to personalise the actual rendering of the document according to specific layouts – the focus must be on the content only;
- following the best practices already used in existing word processors such as Microsoft Word and Open Office for creating structures typical of scholarly articles (lists, tables, figures, references, etc.);
- allowing the creation of mathematical formulas by means of an appropriate interface, hiding the complexities of

---

[18]https://github.com/essepuntato/rash
[19]http://purl.org/spar/doco
[20]https://github.com/essepuntato/rash/tree/master/sources/raje
[21]https://github.com/essepuntato/rash/tree/master/tools/RAJE
[22]https://github.com/essepuntato/rash/blob/master/LICENSE

the language used for storing such formulas with Web-first formats, e.g. MathML;

- interacting with GitHub for easing the storing, sharing, and preservation of the articles.

In the following subsections, we provide a brief discussion about how the typical structures of a scholarly article can be created by means of RAJE.

4.1.1 Article metadata. The metadata of a RASH document are stored inside the `head` element by using `meta` or `link` elements. These metadata are rendered by the browser as shown in Fig. 1 and include the title (mandatory), the author list (mandatory), the ACM subject categories (optional), and the keywords (optional). RAJE permits to act on any of these metadata.

Every element in this metadata section can be easily edited by clicking on it − and the cursor will be placed where requested. The title is usually accompanied with a subtitle. To insert the subtitle, one can simply press `enter` at the end of the title. Once added, the subtitle can be filled up with text, and the author can proceed to the next editable element pressing `enter` again.

Any author listed has its own button set for adding a new author after it or for removing the selected one. It is possible to specify more affiliations for the same author by pressing the `enter` key once the cursor is placed in the affiliation area, just after the author's name. This action will add a new placeholder that can be edited by typing new text or removed by pressing `enter` again as shown in Fig. 2.

Categories and *keywords* can be also edited by clicking on the specific sections, and pressing the `enter` key allows one to add additional keywords/categories.

4.1.2 Mathematical formulas. From the version 0.6, RASH has started to support the use of different languages for writing mathematical expressions, which include MathML, LaTeX and AsciiMath[23]. All these formulas are actually rendered by means of the MathJax processor[24], while they will be stored in MathML in the final RASH source. This flexibility of using several formats allowed us to create an intuitive and easy-to-use environment in RAJE in which users write down formulas using only AsciiMath as input − since, from preliminary tests we run, AsciiMath seemed to be the language easier to learn, write and remember [11].

However, even if AsciiMath is the easier language for mathematical formulas that can be adopted in the contest of RASH documents, it could be difficult anyway to remember all the kinds of operation it allows one to specify. In order to address this issue, RAJE also includes several buttons (labelled "Operations", "Misc", "Relations", "Symbols", and "Formulas", as shown in Fig. 3) that allow one to select an operation among a list of instructions. The way all these buttons are presented to the user has been guided by considering the OpenOffice formula editor.

---

[23]http://asciimath.org/
[24]https://www.mathjax.org/

4.2 Collaborative editing in RAJE

Since we wanted to have a system that allows anyone to store and share the article on the Web, we implemented a module that allows authors to push the article on a GitHub repository by means of the GiyHub API. GitHub is a web-based version control repository that offers all of the distributed version control and source code management features of Git, and enables access control and several collaboration facilities (e.g. bug tracking, feature requests, task management). In this context, any article created by RAJE can be seen as a repository on GitHub.

The first time an author pushes the article on GitHub, a new repository is created with all the code (i.e. the main text content in HTML) and assets (CSSs, JavaScript files, etc.) needed for guaranteeing a correct visualisation of the article. The repository URL is created according to the schema `https://github.com/{author_username}/{repository_name}`, where `{author_username}` is replaced with the author's GitHub username, while the `{repository_name}` is the title of the article.

During the editing phase, if a user wants to store online the content of a document, he must be first logged in with its own Github account, which certifies its identity. Then the user has the option to save the document online, on Github servers. This action can be executed in two ways: the shortcut `ctrl`shift+s+ (`cmd`shift+s+ if OSX) or the button "push" under the dropdown with author's Github profile avatar on the top-right of the RAJE interface. A success message is shown once the commit finished successfully.

4.3 Technical overview

In this section, we introduce some details about the technical implementation of RAJE and the libraries we have reused for this purpose.

4.3.1 Editing the content. The whole set of elements allowed in RASH are added using the contenteditable attribute. When a RASH document is loaded and after the rendering process implemented in the RASH Framework, all sections are moved inside a new wrapper with the attribute contenteditable set to true. The contenteditable way grants a lot of useful commands (implemented by browsers in different ways) such as **undo**, **redo** and **insertHtml**. The insertHtml command is called with the execCommand function, passing as parameter the HTML string to be attached where the caret is set.

Everything is modified (text and structure) in the wrapper created at run time with contenteditable, is treated as a single undo level. Unfortunately, this will happens only using these commands, e.g. modifications using vanilla JavaScript or JQuery libraries are not undo levels. Browsers and in particular Chromium have not implemented yet some kind of APIs to access and modify the local undo buffer. In order to grant a better undo mechanism, it must be implemented from scratch again or using a helper external library.

RASH: Research Articles in Simplified HTML

Documentation - Version 0.6, December 28, 2016

Silvio Peroni silvio.peroni@unibo.it
Department of Computer Science and Engineering, University of Bologna, Bologna, Italy

ACM Subject Categories
Applied computing, Document management and text processing, Document preparation, Markup languages
Applied computing, Document management and text processing, Document preparation, Annotation

Keywords
format for scholarly papers HTML markup language Semantic Publishing

Figure 1: Header of a rendered **RASH** document as shown in **RAJE**.

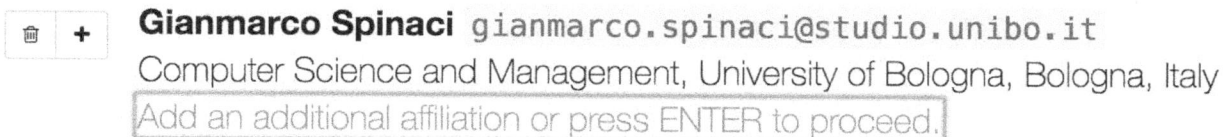

Gianmarco Spinaci gianmarco.spinaci@studio.unibo.it
Computer Science and Management, University of Bologna, Bologna, Italy
Add an additional affiliation or press ENTER to proceed.

Figure 2: Adding a new affiliation in **RAJE**.

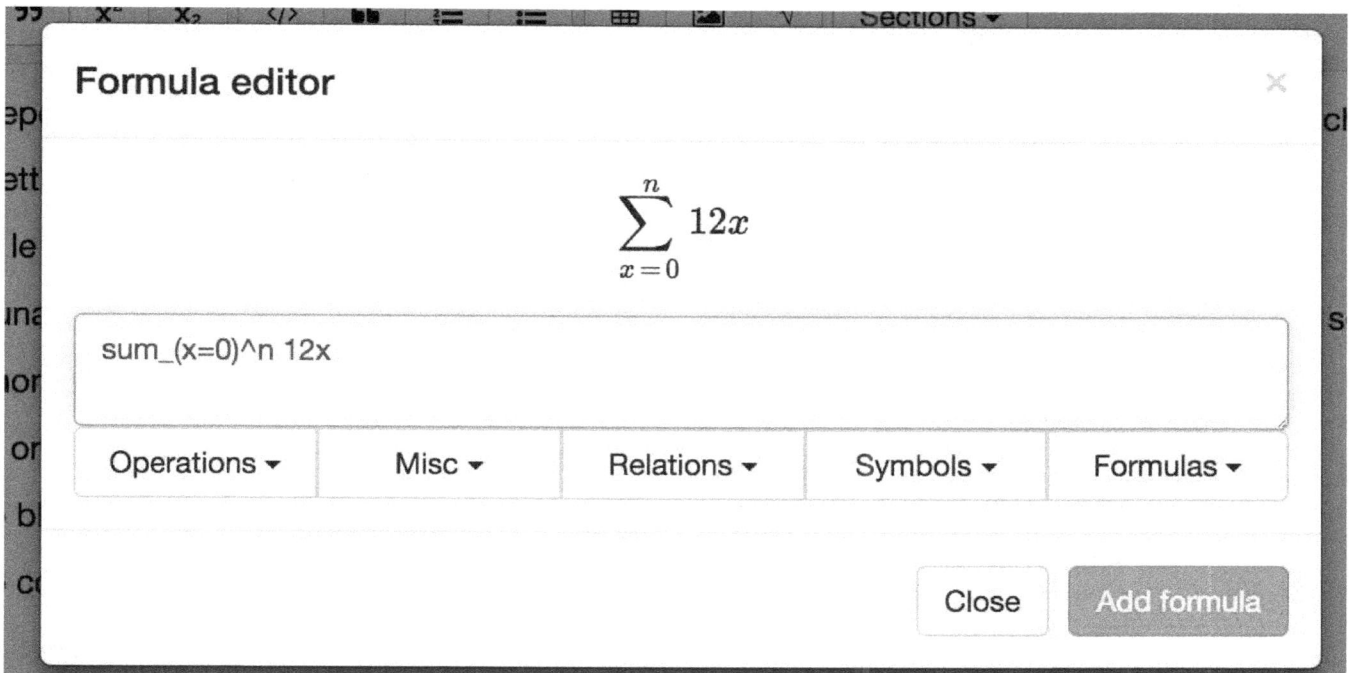

Formula editor

$$\sum_{x=0}^{n} 12x$$

sum_(x=0)^n 12x

| Operations ▾ | Misc ▾ | Relations ▾ | Symbols ▾ | Formulas ▾ |

Close   Add formula

Figure 3: The formula editor in **RAJE**.

4.3.2 Electron and other APIs. RAJE is based on Electron[25], which allows developers to generate multi-platform software using only web-based technologies: HTML, CSS,

---
[25]https://electron.atom.io/

and JavaScript. Electron is an Open Source framework created by Github developers, based on Node.js[26]. Practically speaking, Electron is a browser wrapper, since it uses Chromium to create multi-platform softwares. RAJE uses the File System APIs in Electron so as to execute create/read/update/delete (CRUD) operations on files. When an author wants to generate a new article, RAJE creates its directory and move inside the whole required assets bundle (which are CSS stylesheets and JavaScript scripts) using the functions defined in this API.

The communications between RAJE and GitHub via its APIs is implemented using a specific wrapper: Octonode[27]. Octonode is built on the Github API v3, and it grants a lot of actions on contents, users, and repositories available in GitHub. The Octonode library makes available different methods to authenticate with Github. RAJE has a mechanism for directly connecting to a GitHub account by authorising it to access its personal information, as shown in Fig. 4. This window will describe what kind of permissions RAJE needs: it can read all public information about the user (such as email, name, biography and so on) and about public repositories.

Once the authorisation is given, an access token is generated and used for the following requests to/from the GitHub repository. When the token is stored, all future requests (such as create a repository or push a commit) are instantly served because everything is saved inside a local variable of the user. When a new article is opened, a local folder is created with the document and all the needed assets. When authors want to push changes to a repository that does not exist yet, it is created automatically.

4.3.3 Core scripts. The splash window shown after opening RAJE is just an HTML file with its own JavaScript and CSS, which allows one to create a new document or to open an existing one. Once created/opened, the editor shows a skeleton of a RASH document (i.e. an HTML page) shown in Fig. 5, which is visualised according to the *rash.js* script. In addition, this HTML page also includes the *raje.js* script, for enabling users to edit the document by means of a toolbar and other useful elements.

Thus, *raje.js* implements the *editor behaviour* of RAJE and it is explicitly included in the HTML document produced by it. However, open the HTML document with a common browser will result in viewing it by means of the visualisation facilities made available by the RASH Framework as implemented in *rash.js*. All the RAJE project flow is totally based on the *raje.js* script, that has been developed by concatenating the following eight scripts (each with its own behaviour and purpose):

(1) init.js;
(2) caret.js;
(3) const.js;
(4) core.js;
(5) shortcuts.js;
(6) toolbar.js;
(7) derash.js;
(8) rendered.js.

Init.js is the initialization script, which initialises all the variables, it extends JQuery object adding additional functions, and it calls the `$(document).ready()` function to show the whole editor.

The second script, *caret.js*, provides some utility methods about the caret and its position within the content. It contains functions to check if the caret is inside an element, and to create a selection that wraps entirely the node where the caret is. All the methods here are based on Rangy[28], a cross-browser JavaScript range, and selection library.

The file *const.js* defines constant values that are used by the other scripts.

The fourth script, i.e. *raje.js*, implements a set of actions to add elements into the body (sections, cross references, inlines, etc.). These actions can use the browser content-editable APIs (e.g. to add undo/redo functionalities) or the method `document.execCommand('insertHTML')` for adding an HTML string to the caret.

All shortcuts used in the editor are defined in the *shortcuts.js* script. All of them are bound inside an init function called when the document is ready. The shortcuts are all implemented using Mousetrap[29], a simple library for handling keyboard shortcuts in JavaScript.

The entire graphic elements set is defined in the *toolbar.js* script. In particular, it adds the toolbar and all the modal windows used in RAJE (e.g. for creating formulas).

The document rendered in RAJE (or in any browser) is slightly different from the actual sources since *rash.js* applies some transformations so as to guarantee a correct visualisation of all the metadata and the content of the article in consideration. Thus, in order to recreate correctly the structure of the sources that must be stored, we have implemented the *derash.js* script. This script is used when a user asks to save the article, and it allows the creation of a well-indented HTML code compliant with RASH that will be stored in the file system.

Last but not least, the *rendered.js* script contains everything to handle communication from the document to other services, such as GitHub and the Electron File System APIs.

5 EVALUATION

In order to estimate the perceived usability of RAJE for writing scholarly articles, we have involved some people from the academic domain in a user testing session. All the material and the outcomes of the test are available at [18]. The test has been organised as a Discount Usability Test, which is a specific kind of test that involves a small group of people. Past studies [15] [14] have demonstrated that it is possible to find up to 80% of the main bugs involving only 5 people. In this section, we present the setting and the outcome of the evaluation we performed.

---

[26]https://nodejs.org
[27]https://github.com/pksunkara/octonode

[28]https://github.com/timdown/rangy
[29]https://craig.is/killing/mice

Authorize application

RAJE: RAsh Javascript Editor by @gspinaci would like permission to access your account

Review permissions

👤	**Personal user data** Full access	⌄
📕	**Repositories** Public only	⌄
📡	**Notifications** Read access	⌄

RAJE: RAsh Javascript Editor

No description

Visit application's website

ⓘ Learn more about OAuth

Figure 4: The modal for authorising RAJE to access to user's GitHub information.

The test gave us a lot of valuable indications, even if it was preliminary. In the near future, we plan to perform a full comparison between RAJE and other editors, as those listed in Section 2.

5.1 Settings

We asked 6 subjects to perform two unsupervised tasks. There were no administrators observing the subjects while they were undertaking these tasks. All the subjects were volunteers who responded to personal emails. In the first task, we asked the participants to reproduce the content of a PDF of a scholarly article[30] using RAJE. In the second task, we asked to the participants to push the article to GitHub by using the functionalities implemented in RAJE and to write down the URL of the repository created.

The test session was structured as follows. We first asked subjects to complete a short multiple-choice questionnaire about their background knowledge and skills in writing scholarly articles. In particular, we asked them to answer to seventeen assertions according to a five-point scale (strongly disagree, disagree, neutral, agree, strongly agree). These assertions were organised according to four different categories:

- Knowledge about document formats (DOC(X), ODT, etc.);

- Experience in using word processors and HTML-based editors;
- Expertise in writing scholarly articles;
- Adoption of control version systems.

Then, we asked participants to complete the aforementioned two tasks using RAJE **without having any prior knowledge** about the tool. Finally, we asked the participants to fill in two short questionnaires, one multiple choice, i.e. a System Usability Scale (SUS) questionnaire [17], and the other textual, to report their experience of using RAJE to complete these tasks.

5.2 Outcomes

All the six people involved (from Canada, Sweden, Germany, Italy, and England) has answered positively to our invitation. In particular, we received 6 full feedbacks about the usage of the current version of RAJE.

The usability score for RAJE was computed using the System Usability Scale (SUS) [17], a well-known questionnaire used for the perception of the usability of a system. It has the advantage of being technology independent (it has been tested on hardware, software, Web sites, etc.) and it is reliable even with a very small sample size. In addition to the main SUS scale, we also were interested in examining the sub-scales of pure Usability and pure Learnability of the

Placeholder title

Jon Doe jon.doe@example.com

Computer Science and management, University of Bologna, Bologna, Italy

ACM Subject Categories
Subject

Keywords
Keyword

Abstract

Write down a **fantastic** abstract right now!

1. Hello_world()

this.edit("right now!")

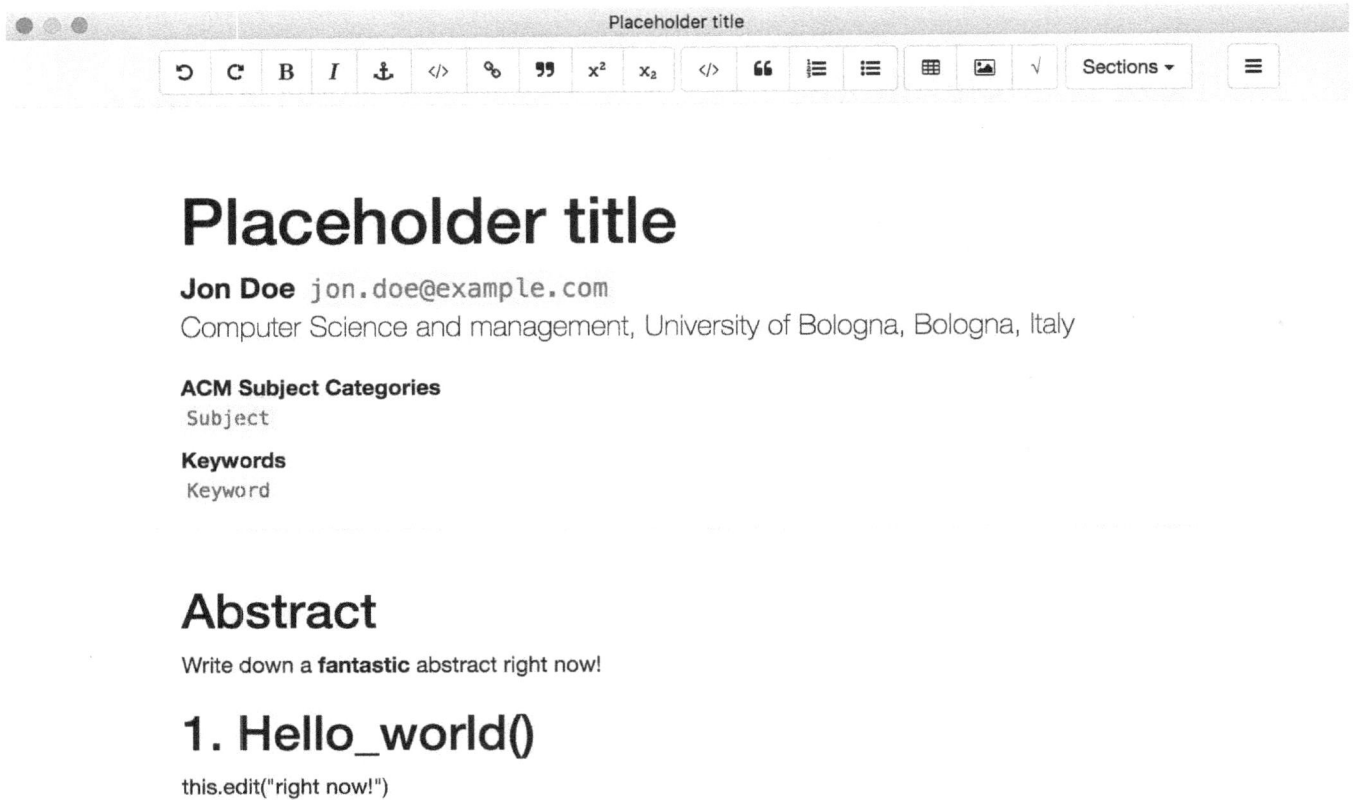

Figure 5: The skeleton presented by RAJE after the creation of a new article.

system, as proposed recently by Lewis and Sauro [13]. In the analysis of the SUS scores, we have noticed that one of the participants was a clear outlier since he experienced a misconfiguration of the system that prevented him from using RAJE correctly. Thus, for the SUS analysis, we decided not to consider the answers he provided, that were radically different from the other five participants indeed.

The mean SUS score for RAJE was 69 (in a 0 to 100 range), slightly surpassing the target score of 68 to demonstrate a good level of usability [17]. The mean values for the SUS sub-scales Usability and Learnability were 65.6 and 82.5 respectively. In addition, four sub-scores were calculated for each participant by considering the values of the answers given in the background questionnaire, according to the four categories introduced in the previous section (knowledge on document formats, experience in using word processors, expertise in writing articles, and adoption of control version systems). We compared these sub-scores with the SUS values and the other sub-scales using the Pearson's r, obtaining the results illustrated in Fig. 6 (where the dashed line is a linear regression).

We found a small negative correlation between all the experience sub-scores and the Learnability score, which seems to highlight that the more background knowledge one has the more the system is difficult to learn. Similarly, the expertise in writing articles seems to be negatively correlated with any SUS score obtained. However, each correlation measure appears to be not statistically significant and we would need to enrich our dataset to come to a more precise conclusion.

Table 1: Axial coding of the personal comments of the participants expressed in the final questionnaires.

Category	Positive	Negative
Interface	**9**	4
Text editor functionalities	8	**15**
Github integration and sharing	1	1
Publishing and output	0	2
Tool efficiency	6	1
Other integrations	0	1

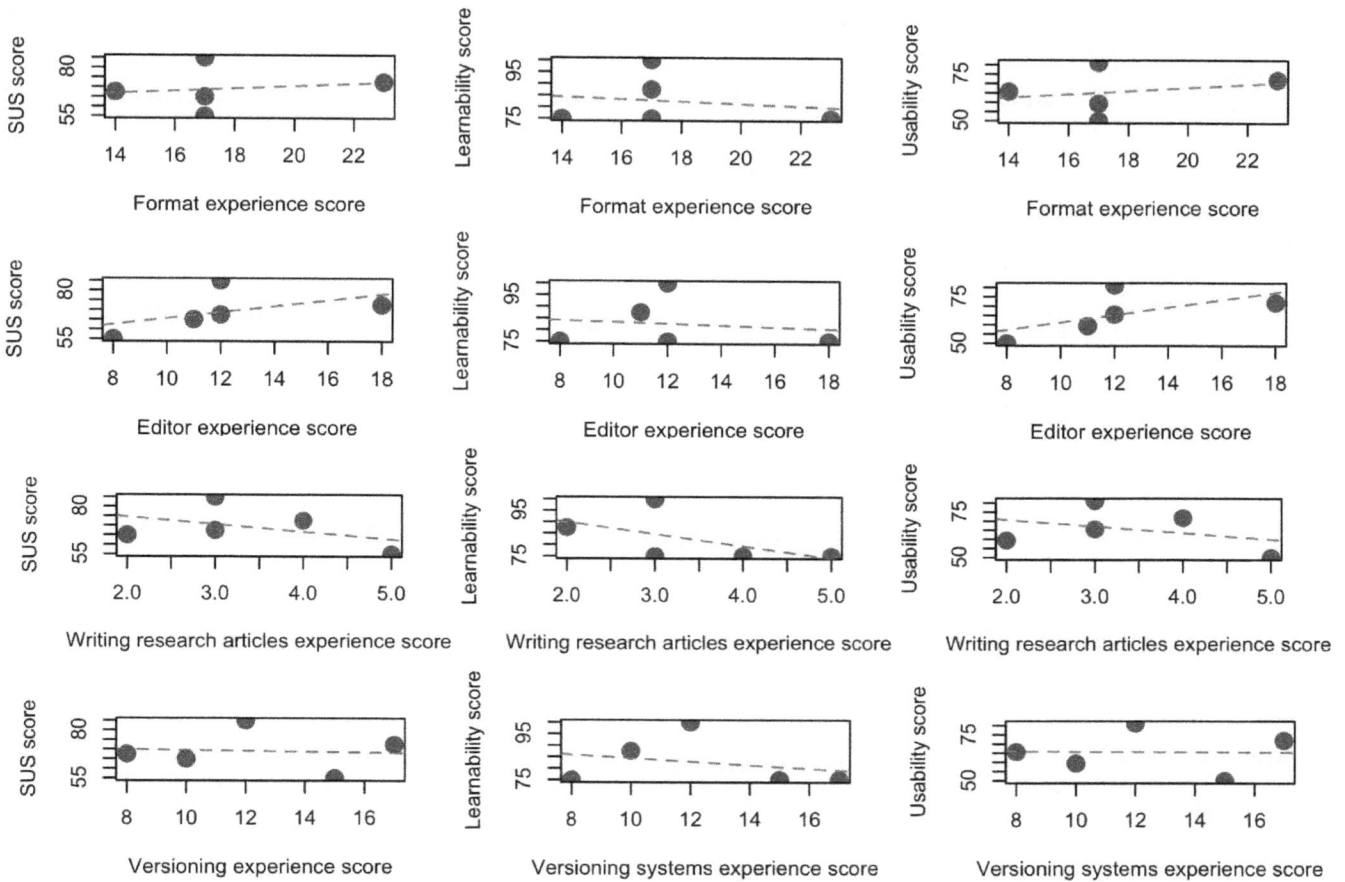

Figure 6: The comparisons between the SUS scores (and subscales) and all the four background scores.

Axial coding [19] of the personal comments expressed in the final questionnaires by all the six participants revealed a some widely perceived issues, as shown in Table 1. The most affected category concerns the functionalities made available by RAJE. In fact, some bugs were faced by testers, and in some cases those bugs denied the normal flow of tool. Basic keyboard shortcuts such as `ctrla+` to select the entire content of a single metadata or the `tab` key to navigate from a table cell to the next one was not implemented yet, and they have been perceived as important flows. The insertion of elements has shown some issues that prevented the participants to add some structures (such as tables, figures and formulas) were requested. Another important issue highlighted was the lack of a form for adding structured bibliographic references, e.g. by using the fields proper to BibTeX. On the other hand, the category about the interface provided by RAJE has been evaluated rather positively. In particular, the interface has been considered intuitive and minimal, and the toolbar icons have been easy to understand thanks to their familiarity with the existing word processors. Finally, all the participants praised the efficiency of the tool, since it allowed them to address the writing task very quickly.

6 CONCLUSION

In this paper we introduce the RASH JavaScript Editor (RAJE), a WYSIWYG word processor for writing scholarly articles in HTML by means of the RASH format. In particular RAJE allows authors to write research papers in HTML natively by means of a user-friendly interface, instead of writing raw markup with a IDE, text editors or external word processors. RAJE has been developed for enabling the use of an alternative format, i.e. HTML, to PDF, which has important drawbacks such as the lack of interactivity, the fact that its monolithic structure is not appropriate for sharing its content on the Web as a common webpage, and its known difficulties regarding the accessibility of its content by people with disabilities. RAJE has been used during an user testing session that involved six participants so as to understand its perceived usability. The outcomes of this evaluation are encouraging, and they also provided us with important feedback for improving the tool.

In the future, we plan to fix existing bugs and issues highlighted by the preliminary evaluation. The evaluation will be extended to a full comparison between RAJE and other editors, including usability tests with different classes of users and on articles of different disciplines and research areas.

We also plan to add new features to RAJE. In particular, one of these features would enable the use of annotations on the document by means of hypothes.is[31]. In addition, the implementation of mechanisms for allowing a better navigation of the document, e.g. via a table of content, could be quite useful for long texts, and we are currently experimenting on some approaches to propose in the current version of RAJE for addressing this aspect.

REFERENCES

[1] Aalbersberg I. PDF versus HTML — which do researchers prefer? (2013) https://www.elsevier.com/connect/pdf-versus-html-which-do-researchers-prefer (last visited April 10, 2017)

[2] Brady, E., Zhong, Y., Bigham, J.P. (2015). Creating accessible PDFs for conference proceedings. In Proceedings of the 12th Web for All Conference (W4A 2015): 34-37. ACM. DOI: https://doi.org/10.1145/2745555.2746665

[3] Capadisli, S., Guy, A. (2017). Linked Data Notifications. W3C Proposed Recommendation, 21 March 2017. https://www.w3.org/TR/ldn/

[4] Capadisli, S., Guy, A., Lange, C., Auer, S., Berners-Lee, T. (2017). Linked Data Notifications. To appear in the Proceedings of the 14th Extended Semantic Web Conference 2017. http://csarven.ca/linked-data-notifications

[5] Capadisli, S., Guy, A., Verborgh, R., Lange, C., Auer, S., Berners-Lee, T. (2017). Decentralised Authoring, Annotations and Notifications for a Read-Write-Web with dokieli. To appear in the Proceedings of the 17th International Conference on Web Engineering (ICWE 2017). Canonical URL: http://csarven.ca/dokieli-rww

[6] Constantin, A., Peroni, S., Pettifer, S., Shotton, D., Vitali, F. (2016). The Document Components Ontology (DoCO). In Semantic Web, 7 (2): 167-181. DOI: https://doi.org/10.3233/SW-150177

[7] Craig, J., Cooper, M. (2014). Accessible Rich Internet Applications (WAI-ARIA) 1.0. W3C Recommendation, 20 March 2014. https://www.w3.org/TR/wai-aria/

[8] Cyganiak, R., Wood, D., Lanthaler, M. (2014). RDF 1.1 Concepts and Abstract Syntax. W3C Recommendation, 25 February 2014. https://www.w3.org/TR/rdf11-concepts/

[9] Di Iorio, A., Gonzalez-Beltran, A., Osborne, F., Peroni, S., Poggi, F., Vitali, F. (2016). It ROCS! The RASH Online Conversion Service. In the Companion Volume of the Proceedings of the 25th International World Wide Web Conference (WWW 2016): 25-26. DOI: https://doi.org/10.1145/2872518.2889408

[10] Garrish, M., Siegman, T., Gylling, M., McCarron, S. (2016). Digital Publishing WAI-ARIA Module 1.0. W3C Candidate Recommendation, 15 December 2016. https://www.w3.org/TR/dpub-aria-1.0/

[11] Krautzberger P. (2014). ASCIIMathML to the rescue https://www.peterkrautzberger.org/0167/

[12] Lazar, J., Allen, A., Kleinman, J., Malarkey, C. (2007). What frustrates screen reader users on the web: A study of 100 blind users. International Journal of Human-Computer Interaction, 22 (3): 247-269. https://doi.org/10.1080/10447310709336964

[13] Lewis, J. R., Sauro, J. (2009). The Factor Structure of the System Usability Scale. In Proceedings of the 1st International Conference on Human Centered Design (HCD09). DOI: https://doi.org/10.1007/978-3-642-02806-9_12

[14] Nielsen J. Why You Only Need to Test with 5 Users (2000) https://www.nngroup.com/articles/why-you-only-need-to-test-with-5-users/ (last visited March 10, 2017)

[15] Nielsen, J. (2009). Discount Usability: 20 Years. https://www.nngroup.com/articles/discount-usability-20-years/ (last visited March 10, 2017)

[16] Peroni S., Osborne F., Di Iorio A., Nuzzolese A. G., Poggi F., Vitali F., Motta E. Research Articles in Simplified HTML: a Web-first format for HTML-based scholarly articles (2016). https://w3id.org/people/essepuntato/papers/rash-peerj2016.html (last visited April 10, 2017)

[17] Sauro, J. (2011). A Practical Guide to the System Usability Scale: Background, Benchmarks & Best Practices. ISBN: 978-1461062707

[18] Spinaci, G., Peroni, S. (2017). Outcomes of a user testing session involving six users in writing a scholarly article with RAJE. Figshare. DOI: https://doi.org/10.6084/m9.figshare.4836191

[19] Strauss, A. Corbin, J. (1998). Basics of Qualitative Research Techniques and Procedures for Developing Grounded Theory (2nd edition). Sage Publications: London. ISBN: 978-0803959408

---

[31] https://hypothes.is/

Sketched Visual Narratives for Image and Video Search

John Collomosse
University of Surrey
Guildford
Surrey, United Kingdom
j.collomosse@surrey.ac.uk

ABSTRACT

The internet is transforming into a visual medium; over 80% of the internet is forecast to be visual content by 2018, and most of this content will be consumed on mobile devices featuring a touch-screen as their primary interface. Gestural interaction, such as sketch, presents an intuitive way to interact with these devices. Imagine a Google image search in which you specify your query by sketching the desired image with your finger, rather than (or in addition to) describing it with text words. Sketch offers an orthogonal perspective on visual search - enabling concise specification of appearance (via sketch) in addition to semantics (via text). In this talk, John Collomosse will present a summary of his group's work on the use of free-hand sketches for the visual search and manipulation of images and video. He will begin by describing a scalable system for sketch based search of multi-million image databases, based upon their Gradient Field HOG (GF-HOG) descriptor. He will then describe how deep learning can be used to enhance performance of the retrieval. Imagine a product catalogue in which you sketched, say an engineering part, rather than using a text or serial numbers to find it? John will then describe how scalable search of video can be similarly achieved, through the depiction of sketched visual narratives that depict not only objects but also their motion (dynamics) as a constraint to find relevant video clips. The work presented in this talk has been supported by the EPSRC and AHRC between 2012-2016.

KEYWORDS

Gestural interaction, image search, multimedia, sketched visual narratives

ACM Reference format:
John Collomosse. 2017. Sketched Visual Narratives for Image and Video Search. In *Proceedings of DocEng '17, Valletta, Malta, September 04-07, 2017,* 1 pages.
https://doi.org/10.1145/3103010.3103024

SHORT BIOGRAPHY

Dr John Collomosse is a Senior Lecturer in the Centre for Vision Speech and Signal Processing (CVSSP) at the University of Surrey. John joined CVSSP in 2009, following 4 years lecturing at the University Bath where he also completed his PhD in Computer Vision and Graphics (2004). John has spent periods of time at IBM UK Labs, Vodafone R&D Munich, and HP Labs Bristol. John's research is cross-disciplinary, spanning Computer Vision, Computer Graphics and Artificial Intelligence, focusing on ways to add value and make sense of large, unstructured media collections - to visually search media collections, and present them in aesthetic and comprehensible ways. Recent projects spanning Vision and Graphics include: sketch based search of images/video; plagiarism detection in the arts; visual search of dance; structuring and presenting large visual media collections using artistic rendering; developing characters animation from 3D multi-view capture data. John holds 70 refereed publications, including oral presentations at ICCV, BMVC, and journal papers in IJCV, IEEE TVCG and TMM. He was general chair for NPAR 2010-11 (at SIGGRAPH), BMVC 2012, and CVMP 2014-15 and is an AE for C&G and Eurographics CGF.

Towards a Model and a Textual Representation for Location-based Games

Cristiane Ferreira
Federal University of Ceara
Fortaleza, Ceara, Brazil
cristianeferreira@great.ufc.br

Carlos Salles
Federal University of Maranhao
São Luís, Maranhao, Brazil
csalles@deinf.ufma.br

Luis Santos
Federal University of Ceara
Fortaleza, Ceara, Brazil
luissantos@great.ufc.br

Fernando Trinta
Federal University of Ceara
Fortaleza, Ceara, Brazil
fernandotrinta@great.ufc.br

Windson Viana
Federal University of Ceara
Fortaleza, Ceara, Brazil
windson@great.ufc.br

ABSTRACT

Location-Based Mobile Games (LBMGs) are a subclass of pervasive games that make use of location technologies to consider the players' geographic position in the game rules and mechanics. This research presents LEGaL, a language to model and represent the structure and multimedia contents (e.g., video, audio, 3D objects, etc.) of LBMGs. LEGaL is an extension of NCL (Nested Context Language) that allows the modelling and representation of mission-based games by supporting spatial and temporal relationships between game elements.

KEYWORDS

Location-based games, NCL, Game Modeling, Multimedia Document

ACM Reference format:
Cristiane Ferreira, Carlos Salles, Luis Santos, Fernando Trinta, and Windson Viana. 2017. Towards a Model and a Textual Representation for Location-based Games. In *Proceedings of DocEng'17, September 4–7, 2017, Valletta, Malta.,* 4 pages.
DOI: https://doi.org/10.1145/3103010.3121035

1 INTRODUCTION

The development of mobile technology has broadened the digital platforms on which digital games can run. Its peculiar characteristics (e.g., embedded sensors, communication capacity, and omnipresence) enabled the popularisation of pervasive games. In fact, before the digital era, traditional games were designed and played in the physical world, relying on real-world properties such as objects, physical space, etc. [5]. Pervasive games, sometimes called Alternative Reality Games, are capable of mixing these two genres by integrating virtual and real environments using mobile and ubiquitous technologies [3]. These games use smartphones' sensors to infer player's context (e.g., location, nearby objects) and introduce this knowledge in the gameplay. This research focuses on modelling a popular sub-type of Pervasive Games called Location-Based Mobile Games (LBMGs). LBMGs use the players' location to update the game state during runtime. As a consequence, players have to move in the real world to progress and reach goals in the game. Pokémon GO is a notorious LBMG [4].

The development process of a LBMG is a multidisciplinary project involving distinct professionals, such as artists, interface and sound designers, and also mobile developers. A successful game project requires a clear communication among team components, specially regarding its game design. Some digital game modelling approaches use UML (Unified Modeling Language) for this task [8]. Other research goes further and proposes DSLs (Domain-Specific Languages) [2] [1] for game modelling and representation. Despite these examples (some of them applied to pervasive games), there is no well-defined model for representing LBMGs. Some LBMG authoring tools use their proper notations for the visual representation of game workflow, its mechanics, and related multimedia objects. However, there is no uniformity between these representations. The absence of an explicit model for LBMGs (i.e., the game structure and its media) impairs their understanding by the professionals involved in the development of these games. Besides, the same issue can happen to users and developers of LBMGs authoring tools. This problem hinders the evolution of authoring tools and a possible integration with other platforms since a standard, or even an open representation, is not available for developers.

Therefore, this research aims at designing a declarative language for the description of LBMGs inspired by the multimedia language NCL (Nested Context Language). Our goal is to inherit NCL concepts that guarantee the representation of both temporal and spatial aspects of these games. Being NCL compliant, we aim at using the existing NCL tools for editing, interpreting, and testing the new language, while still keeping NCL compatibility. The proposed language is called LEGaL (Location-based mobile Game Language). It allows intuitive and explicit modelling LBMGs mechanics and rules. It includes the media used in each mechanic of such games (e.g., animations, 3D objects), with support for temporal aspects, as well as spatial relations of these multimedia documents.

2 LEGAL

LEGaL (Location-based mobilE Games Language) is an extension of the NCL multimedia language that includes specific elements to

Table 1: LEGaL Media types.

Type/subtype	File format	Type/subtype	File format
text/plain	txt	image/png	png
image/jpeg	jpg, jpeg	audio/mp3	mp3
video/mpeg	mpeg, mpg	video/3gpp	3gp
text/plain	obj, mtl	application/gml+xml	gml

Table 2: Node properties.

Property	Values	Description
mandatory	true/false	Defines whether a mission is mandatory
occurrence	Positive integer	Sets how many times the mission can be performed
visibility	true/false	Indicates if a mission can be executed
requirements	List of values	Stores a list of required missions

Table 3: Values of parameters defining players' actions.

Value	Description	Value	Description
0	Run a media	1	Catch a media
2	Create a media	3	Drop a media

support the design of LBMGs. The proposed language allows the description of rules and mechanics of LBMGs. Moreover, LEGaL specifies the modelling of game missions in a textual document. This modelling includes the game structure, its components, and specifications about the media used in game mechanics. LEGaL inherits the structure and entities from NCL.

We used NCL as the basis for the design of the LEGaL structure and components due to its ability for describing interactions between users and media. Also, NCL supports basic content such as images, videos, texts, etc. Furthermore, NCL allows media synchronisation, ordering of media execution, and the use of conditional triggers. This last feature enables the definition of actions to be executed as responses to certain conditions. LEGaL allows the game designer to separate how the game is structured of its execution and its visual interface. In this way, LEGaL is a standard format for exchange the game specification among multiple tools. So, in theory, with LEGaL, a game designer may create an LBMG in a particular tool, and run it in another environment that interprets and executes its LEGaL representation. Moreover, LEGaL is the first step to enable syntactic and semantic analysis of the game model, which can be extended for model checking it.

2.1 Language Conception

LEGaL is a declarative language. It is based on the NCM entity concept and has an XML representation. The layout of LEGaL components resembles an NCL document structure. A LEGaL document can be translated into a directed nested graph, where nodes and edges are used to describe LBMGs concepts. The resulting graph of this model represents missions that a user must accomplish in an LBMG. The graph also includes missions composition (media with which the player interacts), and the relationships between the missions and media files. It introduces the game flow, from its inception to its accomplishment. LEGaL graphs use two types of nodes: **context nodes** (composites nodes), and **media nodes**. The former represents nesting of nodes in the graph. The edges of the graph represent the relationships between the nodes, i.e., the game flow. In LEGaL, ordering and time synchronisms between nodes are defined by the connectors and links.

Relationships between composite nodes, as well as simple nodes, are constructed by causal relationships, in which a condition must be satisfied for an action to be performed. Relationships are multi-point. They contain one or more source points, which will trigger an action, and one or more target points, which will be affected by the action. In LEGaL, points in a relationship may describe game missions or media that players must interact with. For mission nodes, relationships reflect the correct order that missions must be accomplished. In other words, some missions may be marked as prerequisites to other missions, defining the game flow.

2.2 Mission Properties and Game Score

We add some properties to the context node for representing mission information. For instance, the number of times a mission can be played, which missions are required to be played before playing the others, etc. Table 2 contains four of these properties and its possible values. Listing 1 illustrates a context node defined using the new properties.

```
1   <context id="mission3">
2       <port id="port" component="mdAudio"/>
3       <property name="mandatory" value="true"/>
4       <property name="occurrence" value="unbounded"/>
5       <property name="visibility" value="true"/>
6       <property name="requirements" value="mission1 mission2"/>
7       <media id="location" type="application/gml+xml" scr="media/
        location.gml"/>
8       <media id="mdAudio" type="audio/mp3" src="media/audio.mp3"/>
9   </context>
```

Listing 1: Context node with additional properties.

There are four types of actions supported by LEGaL: execute, create, collect, and drop media. The execute action consists of exhibiting one or more media, such as playing an audio or video, displaying a text or visualising a 3D object. The create action allows players to produce game media, like images and videos. Additionally, drop media action enables players to place a media in a determined location and collect action allow players to collect media placed in a specific location. The action parameter was created to store the desired action when defining a media. The parameter receives an integer value between 0 and 3 representing the corresponding action. Table 3 presents each value.

2.3 Spatial Representation

In the proposed language, a media node indicates game missions' location. The node type is application/gml+xml and consists of a GML (Geography Markup Language) with ".gml" extension. GML is an XML extension developed to express geographic features. The extension uses points, lines, polygons and geometric shapes defined by Cartesian coordinates and associated to spatial reference systems. LEGaL uses GML to specify activation areas for a game mission, thus being able to describe a polygon representing a mission's location. Listing 2 illustrates a media node representing a mission location.

```
1  <media id="location" type="application/gml+xml" scr="media/location.
      gml"/>
```

Listing 2: Mission Location.

The location of players and missions' activation areas is key to gameplay of LBMG. In this work, an activation area is a planar region defined bi-dimensional coordinates. These areas can be defined as regular or irregular polygons, and circles. Spatial relation between activation areas is the foundation to the RCC (*Region Connection Calculus*). RCC is a vital model to define topological relations in bi-dimensional space. The model defines eight basic relations between two areas: *disconnected, externally connected, equal, partially overlapping, tangential proper part, tangential proper part inverse, non-tangential proper part, non-tangential proper part inverse* [7].

We added a set of events to LEGaL to handle relations between space and players' actions. As a result, the following events can be linked to media nodes: onEntering, onLeaving, and onStaying. onEntering is triggered when a player enters the activation area of a mission. Conversely, onLeaving is launched when a player exits an activation area. Finally, onStaying is triggered if a player remains inside an activation area during a determined time. Listings 3 and 4 show examples of connectors and links, respectively. In this case, a media is executed when a player enters an activation area.

```
1  <casualConnector xconnector="onEnteringStart">
2      <simpleCondition role="onEntering"/>
3      <simpleAction role="start"/>
4  </casualConnector>
```

Listing 3: Connector using the onEntering event.

```
1  <link xconnector="onEnteringStart">
2      <bind role="onEntering" component="location"/>
3      <bind role="start" component="audio"/>
4  </link>
```

Listing 4: Relation using the onEntering event.

2.4 XML Representation

LEGal textual representation is an XML document. The block structure defines grouping of language components. As in an ordinary NCL application, the document must have a definition header (<ncl>), a program header (<head>), a program body (<body>), and the closing of the document (</ncl>). Elements <head> and <body> must be declared as children of the <ncl> element. NCL language tokens are used in the definition of the LEGaL document to describe the game's components and behaviour.

First, the game developer must specify the GML document, which contains geolocation points related to the missions. Then, he should define descriptors, which detail how the game media will execute. After this step, connectors and links are identified, and then the media must be specified. Next step is to set the ports for the flow composition of the game missions. Listing 5 exemplifies the basic document structure that LEGaL uses to specify an LBMG.

```
1  <?xml version="1.0" encoding="ISO-8859-1"?>
2  <ncl id="" xmlns="http://www.ncl.org.br/NCL3.0/EDTVProfile">
3      <head>
```

```
4      <descriptorBase ... > <!-- descriptors --> </descriptorBase>
5      <connectorBase ... > <!-- connectors --> </connectorBase>
6      </head>
7      <body>
8          <port ... /> <!-- initial ports -->
9          <context ... > <!-- missions -->
10             <port ... />
11             <media ... > ... </media> <!-- media objects -->
12             ... <!-- relationships between media --> ...
13         </context>
14         ... <!-- relationships between missions --> ...
15     </body>
16 </ncl>
```

Listing 5: Basic code structure of LEGaL.

2.5 LEGaL Parser

We have provided support for using LEGaL to LAGARTO (*LocAtion-based Games AuthoRing TOol*) [6] by integrating the LEGaL parser into the tool. We have developed a *parser* of the LEGaL and added it to LAGARTO tool. This tool allows the visual modeling of LBMGs, once it generates a representation of games in a relational database using the Hybernate framework. The tool also includes a mobile application that runs LBMGs and connects with the LAGARTO's Game Server, which, in turn, accesses Hibernate. We then discard the visual part of the tool. We created a new way to generate games in the LAGARTO database. We used a LEGaL document, the associated media, and a GML document as input. Figure 1 illustrates the new tool configuration. We developed the LEGaL parser in Java that receives as input the game model (a ".ncl" file) and the media files described in that document. It parses the XML document and generates mechanics and associations that define the game in the LAGARTO's Game Server by inserting objects with the Hibernate framework. This process produces a LBMG ready to be executed by the LAGARTO Scout mobile application. We used this process to regenerate the AudioRio game. Once the textual description of the game was specified, the parser took 1599 milliseconds to generate the Hibernate instances and to transfer the media associated with this game.

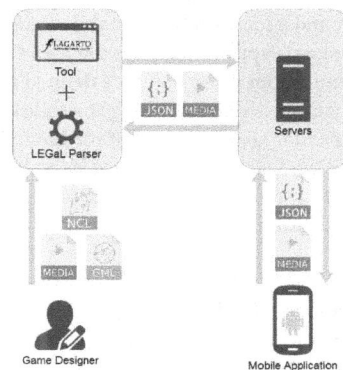

Figure 1: LEGaL Parser integration.

3 PROOF OF CONCEPT

We have implemented a proof of concept (PoC) that includes the second game pattern, *Follow-the-Path*, in which a player must follow a pre-established route for playing. This PoC deals with the modeling and rewriting of the game AudioRio[1]. This cultural game was developed earlier without the use of LEGaL. We chose this game because of its small size and the access to its multimedia documents. These characteristics allowed us to rewrite AudioRio in a textual representation with LEGaL, without using any visual modeling tool. The game consists of an audio-guided tour by Points of Interest where there is a river (the Pajeú) covered, in the center of a metropolis at South America. In the game, the player must visit these points. He will listen to an informative audio each time he enters the region of the points defined by the game designer. Figure 2 illustrates the main screen of the game.

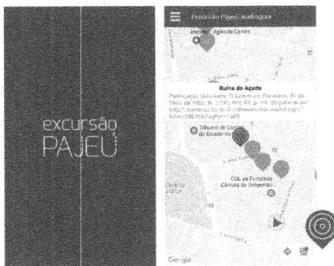

Figure 2: AudioRio for Android.

Each game mission of is a geo-located map point. The user's avatar and the mission point have a radius of action. Thus, the user must be at a minimum distance from each point for hearing its relative audio. When within this area (a circular region) the sound is automatically played. The information considered for point activation are latitude, longitude, and pre-defined radius. At AudioRio, there is no mandatory order for visiting points in the game. This way, the user chooses where to start the tour and which points to visit first. The game finishes when the user visits all the predefined location points.

AudioRio consists of 18 missions. Each mission is composed of two media: a text and a location file, and the relationship between them. The mobile game application uses the TTS (Text-to-Speech) feature to play audio from these text files defined in each mission. We rewrote the game with LEGaL using the following elements[2]: **(i) Context nodes** that are composed of media nodes; **(ii) Media nodes** containing the location and the media to be executed; **(iii) The input ports** that define by which nodes the game can start; and **(iv) The communication ports** of the nodes that define the game flow.

All media in the game must be in a directory specified in the LEGaL XML document. Listing 6 shows an excerpt of the game, which models one of the AudioRio's missions. In the modelling, the mission is identified by msWaterReservoir and the port that allows access to the mission content is pWaterReservoir. LEGaL allows game developers to define ports that indicate the first node

---

[1] www.excursaopajeu.com
[2] https://goo.gl/uAVaGT

---

to be executed (i.e., by which mission the player should start the game). For instance, in the AudioRio model, the port pEntrance1 leads to the execution of the msWaterReservoir mission. In this game, the player can start on any mission and the missions do not have an order of accomplishment. Thus, for the modelling of AudioRio, we declared a start port for each mission node.

```
1   <!-- game start port -->
2   <port id="pEntrance1" component="msWaterReservoir" interface="
        pWaterReservoir"/>
3
4   <context id="msWaterReservoir">
5       <port id="pWaterReservoir" component="locWaterReservoir"/>
6       <property name="mandatory" value="true"/>
7       <property name="occurrence" value="unbounded"/>
8       <property name="visibility" value="true"/>
9
10      <media id="locWaterReservoir" type="application/gml+xml" scr="
            media/waterReservoir.gml"/>
11      <media id="mdText1" type="text/plain" scr="media/text1.txt"/>
12
13      <link xconnector="onEnteringStart">
14          <bind role="onEntering" component="locWaterReservoir"/>
15          <bind role="start" component="mdText1"/>
16      </link>
17  </context>
```

Listing 6: AudioRio Mission described with LEGaL.

4 FINAL CONSIDERATIONS

The absence of an explicit model of an LBMG impairs its understanding by the professionals involved in its creation. In this paper, we presented the first effort to modelling and represent this kind of game. We proposed a language (based on NCL) that allows the intuitive and precise representation of the mechanics and rules of an LBMG. LEGaL includes the media used in the mechanics of these games with support for temporal and spatial aspects. Our goal is also to provide a canonical model to be used by LBMG authoring tools. With the structure and media of LBMG represented as NCL document, game developers would in the future take benefit from tools that edit, test, and check NCL documents. As future work, we want to support model checking mechanisms to avoid possible inconsistencies in the game modelling or the mechanics and rules created by the game's author.

REFERENCES

[1] Ely Fernando do Prado and Daniel Lucrédio. 2015. A Flexible Model-Driven Game Development Approach. In *Components, Architectures and Reuse Software (SBCARS), 2015 IX Brazilian Symposium on*. IEEE, 130–139.
[2] Victor Guana, Eleni Stroulia, and Vina Nguyen. 2015. Building a game engine: A tale of modern model-driven engineering. In *Proceedings of the Fourth International Workshop on Games and Software Engineering*. IEEE Press, 15–21.
[3] Guo Hong. 2015. *Concepts and Modelling Techniques for Pervasive and Social Games*. Ph.D. Dissertation. Norwegian University of Science and Technology.
[4] N Labs. 2016. Pokémon Go. (2016). http://www.pokemongo.com
[5] Carsten Magerkurth, Adrian David Cheok, Regan L Mandryk, and Trond Nilsen. 2005. Pervasive games: bringing computer entertainment back to the real world. *Computers in Entertainment (CIE)* 3, 3 (2005), 4–4.
[6] Luís Fernando Maia, Carleandro Nolêto, Messias Lima, Cristiane Ferreira, Cláudia Marinho, Windson Viana, and Fernando Trinta. 2017. LAGARTO: A LocAtion based Games AuthoRing {TOol} enhanced with augmented reality features. *Entertainment Computing* (2017), –. http://www.sciencedirect.com/science/article/pii/S1875952117300502
[7] David A Randell, Zhan Cui, and Anthony G Cohn. 1992. A spatial logic based on regions and connection. *KR* 92 (1992), 165–176.
[8] Emanuel Montero Reyno and José Á. Carsí Cubel. 2008. Model Driven Game Development: 2D Platform Game Prototyping.. In *GAMEON*, Vicente J. Botti, Antonio Barella, and Carlos Carrascosa (Eds.). EUROSIS, Vaencia,Spain, 5–7.

SketchTab3d: A Hybrid Sketch Library using Tablets and Immersive 3D Environments

Charlotte Boddien, Jill Heitmann, Florian Hermuth, Dawid Lokiec, Carlos Tan,
Laura Wölbeling, Thomas Jung, Johann Habakuk Israel
Hochschule für Technik und Wirtschaft Berlin
12459 Berlin, Germany
israel@htw-berlin.de

ABSTRACT

This paper proposes a 2d sketching tool and an immersive 3d sketch library as an approach to easily create and access documents (i.e. sketches). The sketch library allows users to store, arrange and assemble their own sketches and others' in theoretically unlimited space. A user can get an idea about the general activities of all users since the sketch library is updated whenever changes are made.

The system provides 2d and 3d means to access the sketch library. Whereas the 2d interfaces offers a standard dash board, the 3d environment provides unrestricted spatial access to the sketch library. Furthermore, a 2d sketching interfaces is provided in order to create sketch-based documents. Possible application areas are in the fields of engineering, design, public displays, shared knowledge applications, and art. The system was evaluated among eight participants regarding its pragmatic and hedonic qualities as well as searching performance. The results suggest that the users appreciate the particular combination of 2d and 3d technologies in SketchTab3d and requested for improvement in the 3d interaction technique. No significant differences were found in the search performance, however the physical demand during searching was perceived significantly higher in the 3d condition than in the 2d condition.

CCS CONCEPTS

• **Human-centered computing~Interaction techniques** •
Human-centered computing~Interactive systems and tools

KEYWORDS

Sketching; 3d user interfaces; 3dui; sketch-based interaction and modelling; collaboration; virtual reality; mixed reality.

1 INTRODUCTION

Sketching has been an essential practice in all creative and artistic processes through externalization, reflection and self-communication [12]. The role of sketching has been investigated particularly in engineering and design. A large body of work provides empirical support for the utility of conventional handwriting sketching in these domains (e.g. [10,13]), despite the ongoing digitization. Primary advantages of sketches discussed here are quick creation, low cost, disposability, variety, clear vocabulary, minimal detail, and their nature of a proposal [1]. Typically, pen and paper sketches are created during the first stages of product development or design processes. In later stages, a few designs are selected and remodelled with computer modelling software [9].

Some existing research investigated the effects of collaborative sketching by means of multi-sensory interfaces. Among others, Chen et al. [2] developed a systems that allowed two users to access and collaboratively sketch onto a table-top system, employing Wii-controllers as pens and an HTML5 canvas as drawing board. However, despite the relevance of sketches during creative development processes, interaction techniques to store, access, and manipulate them have been insufficiently studied. In particular, 3d libraries for 2d sketches were not introduced so far.

The aim of this paper is twofold. It introduces a novel interaction approach, which provides hybrid 2d and 3d access to the same documents (i.e. sketches). Furthermore, it offers 2d interaction techniques to create sketch-based documents. With regard to the usage of immersive 3d-environments as a medium to display and create sketches, the system has similarities with previous work such as to the popular Google Tilt Brush [4] and early systems by Keefe [8].

In the following sections, we describe the 2d and 3d components of the system.

2 THE SKETCHTAB3D SYSTEM

SketchTab3d consists of a 2d and a 3d part. The 2d part allows for creating and managing 2d sketches. It has a web-based interface which uses HTML canvases as drawing areas and provides a dashboard which shows thumbnail images and the names of existing sketches. The 3d part such as the 3d library, allows to store, arrange and assemble 2d sketches in three-dimensional space. It employs a CAVE, an immersive 3d environment, to display the sketches free floating in space. SketchTab3d combines the advantages of drawing on a flat surface with the expressiveness and capabilities of 3d environments. The integration of 2d and 3d environments should overcome drawbacks of previous immersive sketching systems which omitted (passive) haptic and were inappropriate to create refined illustration (cf. [8]). The system also includes typical features of existing immersive sketching systems [4,7,11] such as moving and arranging sketches in three-dimensional space. After a sketch is created and placed in the three-dimensional space, regardless of user's physical presence, the sketch is constantly being updated every time the user modifies it using the tablet interface. As the tablet interface uses web-technologies, the modification on existing sketches can be done f anywhere. Such changes can be observed in real time within the 3d library, which serves as a universal access point to a constantly evolving set of sketches. The frequency of changes in all sketches gives an ambient and poetic impression of the current activities of the collaborating users. Within the 3d library, users can freely navigate and place sketches at any position. Consequently, spatial structures of sketches can be gradually developed by reflecting logical considerations and/or artistic thoughts.

2.1 The tablet-based 2D tool

The 2d part of the system offers a dashboard and the possibilities to create, modify and delete sketches. The functionality is similar to existing mobile sketching applications (e.g. Notability, Mind Objects etc.). It was implemented using web technologies (see below) and runs on every HTML5 enabled browser.

After a user logs into the system, he or she is redirected to the dashboard, which shows the names, creation dates and thumbnails of all sketches of this particular user (Figure 1). The user has several options, such as entering the CAVE mode (see below), adding a new sketch (plus icon), editing an existing sketch or login out.

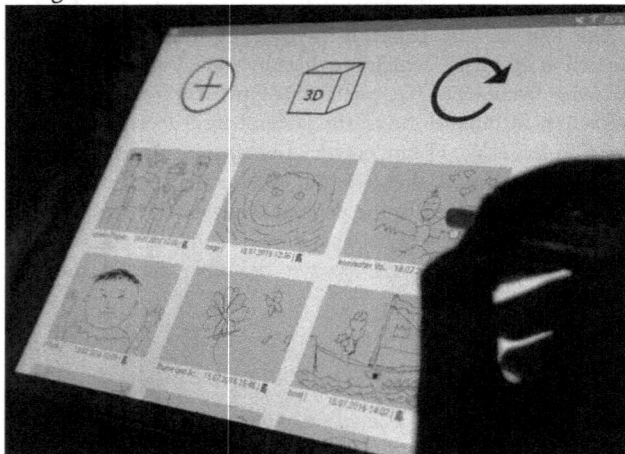

Figure 1. Dashboard of the tablet-based sketching tool.

If the user chooses to add a sketch, he or she has to enter a name for it. The user can also click onto a preview image of an existing sketch to view and edit it. In both cases, the sketch view which contains the sketching panel and a couple of icons is opened (Figure 2). Users can immediately start sketching - using either a mouse, a stylus or fingers.

2.2 Backend and system architecture

The 2d and 3d components of SketchTab3d use the identical database (currently PostgreSQL). Within the database, sketches, polylines, vertices and owners are defined. The last modification date is saved per polyline and a 3d position in world coordinates is saved per sketch describing its position in the 3d library within the CAVE. The backend of the system was written using Ruby on Rails. It communicates with the 2d frontend through a REST-based API, which uses JSON as data format. The communication with the CAVE occurs over a UDP socket. Status codes are exchanged to describe user commands (e.g. load a sketch from the 3d library into the sketchpad), the latest 3d positions of sketches, or error codes. For compatibility and performance reasons, the 3d component loads the sketch data directly from the database, bypassing the Ruby on Rails interface.

Figure 2. Sketch view of the tablet-based tool.

2.3 The 3d sketch library

The CAVE application serves two purposes: To render sketches in the virtual 3d space and to offer the user ways to interact with the sketches. When a user enters the 3d library, he or she can see all sketches which were previously placed (Figure 3). Sketches remain in their positions even after a re-start of the system, as their positions are saved in the database.

The 3d sketch library was written in C#, using the game engine Unity. It runs in a CAVE [3], an immersive environment consisting of four walls using back-projection and active shutter technology. The user tracking is realised by two Kinect cameras. A Wii remote controller is used to interact with the application (e.g. to navigate, select etc). Tracking data is exchanged via the VRPN protocol. The following 3d interaction techniques are available:

Dropping: The user can drop sketches into the 3d library by selecting the sketch from the dashboard (or creating a new one) and then clicking a "pick/drop" button in the 2d interface. This prompts the 3d library to load the sketch from the database and makes it appear at the current position of the tablet. Then the user is able to reposition by moving through the virtual space and holding the device toward the desired direction – the sketch will move accordingly. To drop the sketch at its current position, the user presses the button again.

Moving: In a similar way, sketches can be selected from the virtual scene by pointing the device towards them. Once a sketch is selected, it can be repositioned by picking up and dropping down again using the same button as before.

Loading: A selected sketch can also be loaded from the scene onto the device by pressing the "load" button. This prompts the 3d library to send the ID of the selected sketch to the web application, which then opens the sketch for editing.

Whenever a sketch is edited, regardless of the user 's presence in the CAVE, its representation in the 3d library is updated in real time. To realize this, the 3d library application saves a timestamp for every sketch when it is loaded into the scene. When the timestamp in the database is updated, the 3d library reloads and draws the lines of the sketch, while leaving its position unchanged.

3 EVALUATION

3.1 Participants and Methods

To investigate the effects of the 3d sketch library on the user performance, the workload as well as onto the pragmatic and hedonic qualities of the SketchTab3d system, we conducted a user study among eight computer science students and professionals (mean age 31.9 yr., *SD*=6.0). We employed the 7-point scale AttrakDiff questionnaire [6]. This questionnaire transcends standard usability questionnaires by measuring not only the user-perceived usability in terms of pragmatic functional quality (PQ) but also attributes of interactive products, namely stimulation by the product (HQ-S) and identification with the product (HQ-I) as well as the product's attraction (ATT). The 100-point scale NASA-TLX [5] was used to measure the workload, and the execution time and error rate to measure the user performance. Dependent t-tests were conducted to investigate the significant difference between the means of two sample groups.

Figure 3. The 3d sketch library.

3.2 Tasks

Participants were asked to perform two tasks. In the first task, they had to familiarize themselves with the 2d interface by sketching an outer space scenario. Then they were asked to place the sketch at any desired position in the 3d environment, using the tablet-based interaction techniques mentioned above (the Wii controller was not employed). The AttrakDiff questionnaire had to be answered after the first subtask with respect to the 2d interface and after the second task with respect to the overall system.

For the second tasks, five sketches were displayed in the sketching tool, accessible through thumbnail images in the dashboard, and in the 3d library, the sketches were arranged circularly around the centre of the CAVE. In both conditions, the participants had to search and count particular patterns, namely a crossed circle (symbol 1) and a star (symbol 2). The order and the contents of the sketches were the same in both conditions. The sequence of the conditions and the search tasks were permutated. Time measurement began when the participants faced the stimulus and stopped when they called the number of found symbols. The error rate was calculated based on the difference of the real number of symbols and the number mentioned by the participant.

3.3 Results

Regarding the first task, all AttrakDiff subscales except ATTR showed significant differences (Figure 4). The pragmatic quality of the 2d condition (M_{PQ2d}=5.27, SD_{PQ2d}=1.66) was ranked higher than for the condition including the 3d environment (M_{PQ3d}=4.32, SD_{PQ3d}=1.69, $t(7)$=2.557, p=0,038). The hedonic quality was ranked higher for the overall system (M_{HQ3d}=5.13, SD_{HQ3d}=0.63) than for the 2d condition (M_{HQ2d}=4.03, SD_{HQ2d}=0.61, $t(7)$=-5,660, p=0,001).

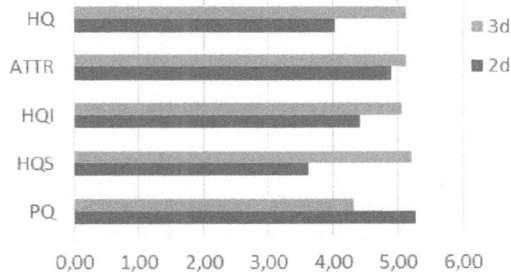

Figure 4. Results of the AttrakDiff for task one.

The means of the NASA-TLX showed no significant differences between the 2d and 3d search condition (M_{TLX2d}=23.04, SD_{TLX2d}=14.99, M_{TLX3d}=27.60, SD_{TLX3d}=10.79), neither did any of the subscales (Figure 5) except physical demand, which was lower in the 2d (M_{PD2d}=4.41, SD_{PD2d}=1.76) than in the 3d condition (M_{PD3d}=15.99, SD_{PD3d}=5.36, $t(7)$=-2,506, p=0,041).

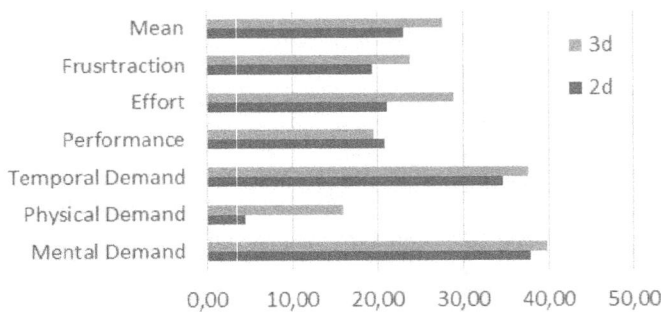

Figure 5. Results of the NASA-TLX for task two.

The results for the searching task are listed in Figure 6. T-tests for independent groups revealed no statistical differences for both symbols neither in the search time (M_{S12d}=18.4s, SD_{S12d}=3.3s, M_{S13d}=23.2d, SD_{S13d}=5.0s, M_{S22d}=30.1s, $SD_{S2,2d}$=26.6s, M_{S23d}=12.7s, $SD_{S2,3d}$=4.8s) nor in the error rates (M_{S12d}=7.9%, SD_{S12d}=5.5%, M_{S13d}=8.6%, SD_{S13d}=5.2%, $M_{S2,2d}$=11.2%, $SD_{S2,2d}$=12.8%, M_{S23d}=4.2%, $SD_{S2,3d}$=3.6%). During the search task, one participant opened the sketches in the 2d condition, all others viewed only the thumbnail images in the dashboard.

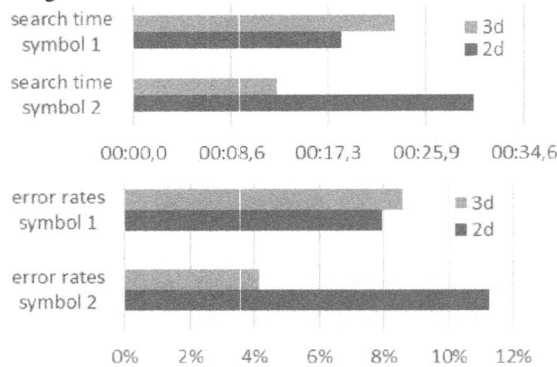

Figure 6. Search times and error rates for task two.

4 DISCUSSION

The intention of the first task was to investigate, whether the additional 3d sketch library adds pragmatic or hedonic qualities to the overall system. The results are contradictory. While the users rate that the pragmatic quality drops when the 3d sketch library is added, they find the overall system more desirable when it is included. We speculate that the low accuracy of the tracking contributed to the low PQ-ratings and improvements in the tracking could also improve PQ. However, users might have seen no real benefits from the 3d extension and perceived only a general stimulation by the immersive 3d library.

With respect to the second task, the 3d condition is regarded particularly less efficient than the 2d condition in the NASA-TLX subscales for physical demand and (mental and physical) effort. However, the results of the subscales for mental demand and overall performance are nearly equal. This suggests that the strategies to solve the task were similar, yet they involved more

physical effort in the 3d case. Participants obviously could not perceive any benefits from the 3d visualization. This might be due to the task being too easy. Only one participant opened the detailed sketch view during the 2d condition, the others solved it by using thumbnail images in the dashboard. A challenging search task which involves a spatial memory by including more sketches and sophisticated spatial arrangements in the 3d task could reveal different results.

5 CONCLUSION

We proposed a system consisting of a web-based 2d sketching tool and a sketch library within an immersive 3d-environment to discuss new possibilities to create, store, arrange and collaborate by means of sketches.

We investigated advantages of this particular combination of 2d and 3d technologies and the mixed results were found. As the participants regarded the pragmatic qualities of the overall system lower and the physical effort of the 3d environment higher than the 2d tool, the system could be regarded unsuccessful. On the other hand, the results also suggest that participants found the overall system desirable. We interpret the latter as a promising result and will therefore continue our research in the following directions: improve the tracking stability in the 3d environment, enhance the 2d sketching functionalities, test functions for cooperation, investigate setups with more spread sketches, and evaluate the system in public space.

References

1. William Buxton. 2007. *Sketching User Experiences: Getting the Design Right and the Right Design*. Morgan Kaufmann Publishers, San Francisco.
2. Rui Chen, Po-Jui (Ray) Chen, Rui Feng, Yilin (Elaine) Liu, Andy Wu, and Ali Mazalek. 2013. SciSketch. *Proceedings of the 8th International Conference on Tangible, Embedded and Embodied Interaction - TEI '14*, ACM Press, 247–250.
3. C Cruz-Neira, D J Sandin, T A DeFanti, Kenyon R.V., and J C Hart. 1992. The CAVE: audio visual experience automatic virtual environment. *Communications of the ACM* 35, 6: 64–72.
4. Google. 2016. Tilt Brush. Retrieved July 11, 2016 from https://www.tiltbrush.com/
5. S G Hart and L E Staveland. 1988. Development of NASA-TLX (Task Load Index): Results of empirical and theoretical research. In *In Human mental workload*, P A Hancock and N Meshkati (eds.). North-Holland, Amsterdam, 139–183.
6. Marc Hassenzahl. 2004. The Interplay of Beauty, Goodness and Usability in Interactive Products. *Human-Computer Interaction* 19: 319–349.
7. Daniel F Keefe, Daniel Acevedo Feliz, Tomer Moscovich, David H Laidlaw, and Joseph LaViola. 2001. CavePainting: A Fully Immersive 3D Artistic Medium and Interactive Experience. *ACM Symposium on Interactive 3D Graphics (SI3D'01)*, ACM Press, 85–93.
8. Daniel F Keefe, Robert C Zeleznik, and David H Laidlaw. 2007. Drawing On Air: Input Techniques for Controlled 3D Line Illustration. *IEEE Transactions of Visualization and Computer Graphics (TVCG)* 13, 5: 1067–1080.
9. Luke Olsen, Faramarz F. Samavati, Mario Costa Sousa, and Joaquim A. Jorge. 2009. Sketch-based modeling: A survey. *Computers & Graphics* 33, 1: 85–103. http://doi.org/10.1016/j.cag.2008.09.013
10. Pierre Sachse. 2002. *Idea materialis: Entwurfsdenken und Darstellungshandeln. Über die allmähliche Verfertigung der Gedanken beim Skizzieren und Modellieren*. Logos Verlag, Berlin.
11. Steven Schkolne. 2006. Making Digital Shapes by Hand. *Interactive Shape Editing, ACM SIGGRAPH Courses 2006*, ACM Press, 84–93.
12. Donald A Schön. 1983. *The Reflective Practitioner. How professionals think in action*. Basic Books, New York.
13. B Tversky. 2003. Sketching for Design and Design of Sketches. In *Human Behaviour in Design*, U Lindemann (ed.). Springer-Verlag, Berlin, 79–86.

A Tool for Mixing XML Annotations

Bertrand Gaiffe

Atilf–CNRS and University of Lorraine

Nancy, France

ABSTRACT

XML documents, in particular critical editions are usually very heavily annotated. They usually represent abbreviations, variant readings, edition operations etc. Among such documents, only a part of the character contents of the file is the actual edition of the text. Very often, one wants to run automatic tools on this "simple" text and thereafter re-embed the result into the original file. The tool we present here is dedicated to this embedding of annotations. In order to achieve this, the tool sets the problem as an ambiguous input and parses that ambiguous input by the grammar of the XML language. It then proposes those solutions that are syntactically correct. In case there are none, the input is modified and reparsed until at least one solution is found.

The tool is available at https://github.com/bgaiffe/XMLMixer.

CCS CONCEPTS

• **Software and its engineering** → **Extensible Markup Language (XML)**; • **Information systems** → *Data encoding and canonicalization*; • **Theory of computation** → *Parsing*;

KEYWORDS

XML, multiple hierarchies, parsing

1 INTRODUCTION

When working on XML documents, in particular when using XML to produce complex editions, one faces very heavily encoded documents. For instance, we may have:

```
<app>
  <lem>n'enp<ex>re</ex>sist</lem>
  <rdg wit="#P">n'e<ex>m</ex>preist</rdg>
  <rdg wit="#J">n'emprenist</rdg>
  <rdg wit="#H">n'emp<ex>re</ex>sist</rdg>
</app>
```

meaning that the form *n'enp<ex>re</ex>sist* (in the edition) appears as *n'e<ex>m</ex>preist* in manuscript P, as *n'emprenist* in manuscript J and as *n'emp<ex>re</ex>sist* in manuscript H. Moreover, in *n'enp<ex>re</ex>sist*, the *'re'* part of the word is abbreviated (this is what <ex> means).

Suppose now that you have a list of terms that should appear in a glossary ; among the forms is "enpresist", then, doing it by hand, you would produce (tagging <w> the words in the glossary):

Publication rights licensed to ACM. ACM acknowledges that this contribution was authored or co-authored by an employee, contractor or affiliate of a national government. As such, the Government retains a nonexclusive, royalty-free right to publish or reproduce this article, or to allow others to do so, for Government purposes only.

DocEng'17, September 4–7, 2017, Valletta, Malta

© 2017 Copyright held by the owner/author(s). Publication rights licensed to Association for Computing Machinery.

ACM ISBN 978-1-4503-4689-4/17/09...$15.00

https://doi.org/10.1145/3103010.3121028

```
<app>
  <lem>n'<w corresp="EMPRENDRE1">enp<ex>re</ex>sist</w>
    </lem>
  <rdg wit="#P">n'e<ex>m</ex>preist</rdg>
  <rdg wit="#J">n'emprenist</rdg>
  <rdg wit="#H">n'emp<ex>re</ex>sist</rdg>
</app>
```

(the <w> has to be entierely into the <lem> because it is shorter).

What we want to do, however, is doing that automatically; it should be as simple as running a script that from a document in which you have *"n'enpresist"* would produce

"n'<w corresp="EMPRENDRE1">enpresist</w>"

and then re-embed this annotation into the original document.

In order to do that, the steps are:

(1) extract the text of the edition and the extra ornaments (notes), so that you can re-embed the notes latter. In our case, your document becomes:

```
<app xml:id="someId"><lem>n'enp<ex>re</ex>sist
</lem></app>
```

(2) extract the text of the document and produce an auxiliary file that will enable you to re-embed the tagging. The auxilliary file will look like[1]:

```
0   11   <app xml:id=''someId''><lem>
5   7    <ex>
```

which means "app and lem", in this order, enclose the characters from 0 to 11, "ex" encloses the characters from 5 to 7.

(3) produce your new tagging ; to keep the explanation short it will be:

```
2   11   <w corresp="EMPRENDRE1">
```

(4) re-embed all but the notes:

```
<app xml:id="someId"><lem>n'<w
corresp="EMPRENDRE1">enp<ex>re</ex>sist</w>
</lem></app>
```

(5) and finally, put the extra readings (the ornaments) back in order to get the complete result.

Steps 1, 2 and 5 are easily produced by XSL stylesheets. Step 3 is what the user produces, be it automatic or not. The mixing tool we describe in the remaining of the paper takes care of step 4. The tool takes two arguments: a XML file and a companion file and embeds the annotations from the companion file into the XML file.

In the remaining of the paper, we describe the problem (section 2) and we propose a two steps approach: first produce a Direct Acyclic Graph (DAG) that enumerates possible documents and a

---

[1]This auxiliary file is inspired by the companion files Eric de la Clergerie designed for is project "Passage'[6], the numbers are index of characters in the text.

second parse that DAG in order to keep well formed XML documents only. Section 3 describe the production of the DAG and section 4 is dedicated to parsing. In section 5, we propose a solution when no well formed document is found in the DAG. The last sections give some details about the implementation and conclude.

2 FORMULATION OF THE PROBLEM

In our example, the constraints are summarized in table 1. In table 1, text positions are related to the text ("n'enpresist") as follows: $_0n_1'_2e_3n_4p_5r_6e_7s_8i_9s_{10}t_{11}$. Therefore, the 5th character (p) is betweens text positions 4 and 5. Table 1 then specifies that <app> has to appear at position 0 as well as <lem>. The constraint at the second line of the table specifies that <app> has to be before <lem>.

texte pos.	symbols	constraints
0	<app>	
0	<lem>	app < lem
2	<w>	
5	<ex>	
7	</ex>	
11	</app>	
11	</lem>	</lem> < </app>
11	</w>	

Table 1

The constraints of table 1 may as well be represented by a direct acyclic graph (DAG) that enumerates all possible documents that verify the constraints.

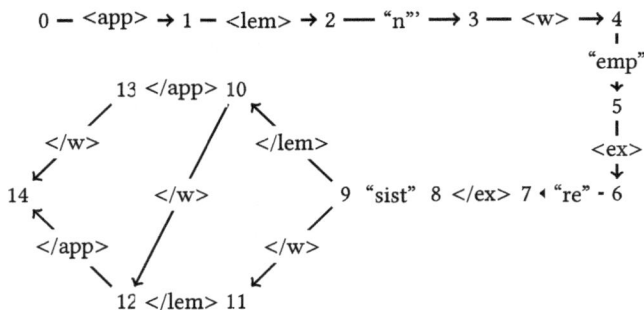

Figure 1

The DAG, between state 9 and state 14 represents all total orders compatible with the contraint that </lem> is before </app> (this is the three last lines of table 1).

The DAG is a compact representation of documents. On this particular example, three documents are represented, that correspond to possible paths trough the DAG. The three documents are:

```
<app><lem>n'<w>enp<ex>re</ex>sist</lem></app></w>
<app><lem>n'<w>enp<ex>re</ex>sist</lem></w></app>
<app><lem>n'<w>enp<ex>re</ex>sist</w></lem></app>
```

However, only the third of these documents is a well-formed XML document. If we parse the DAG with the grammar of the XML language, only one of the three documents it represents remains, that is:

```
<app><lem>n'<w>enp<ex>re</ex>sist</w></lem></app>
```

In order to build the tool proposed in the introduction, we thus need to be able to produce such DAGs as the one of figure 1. We also to need a parser that parses such DAGs by the grammar of the XML language. This will be described in sections 3 an 4. It may happen however that no document from the DAG is a well formed XML document. This happens when the constraints lead to such situations as <a>...<b> ...</a>. We then have a parsing failure and we have to repair the DAG. We then get something like: <a>...<b> next="#next"> ...</b></a><b xml:id="next">... This is the subject of section 5.

3 PRODUCING THE DAG

Producing the DAG boils down to get all total orderings from a partial order. As the worst case complexity of the parsing is a function of the number of nodes of the graph, we have to minimize the number of states.

The algorithm proceeds by levels[2]. For each node already produced it is associated the set of elements that remain to be sorted. If such a subset is already associated to a node, we reuse it. From a node, we build outgoing edges labeled by all minimal elements. In our previous example, this cooresponds to the graph of figure 2[3].

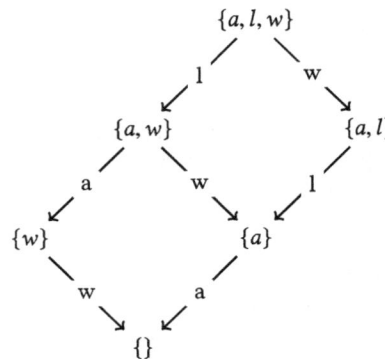

Figure 2

Two remarks here:
- we simplify the order constraints so that relations that may be deduced by transitivity are removed (this simplifies the computation of the smallest elements at each node);
- the general shape of the DAG representing the whole file is a string (around the text nodes) with lattices at some points.

Somehow, the DAG looks like the diagram in Figure 3.

The linear sections are made of text nodes (no textNode may appear in a non linear section) and non ambiguous tags. The parser will run left to right and step in parsing will be on textnodes.

---

[2]Levels are the cardinality of the subset yet to be totally ordered.
[3](l, w, a) are abbreviations for </lem>, </app> and </w>

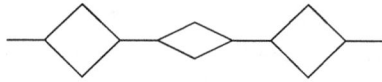

Figure 3

4 PARSING

The parser implemented is an unoptimised Earley parser[3]. The only requirement is that we need a parser that admits ambiguity in parsing (typically a chart parser). We parse the input by the following grammar of the XML language (see Figure 4)[4].

```
Document -> Prolog Element LMisc
Document -> Prolog Element
Document -> Element LMisc
Document -> Element
LMisc -> Misc
LMisc -> Misc LMisc
Misc -> Comment
Misc -> PI
Misc -> S
Element -> "Stag" Content "Etag"
Element -> "Stag" "Etag"
Content -> SContent
Content -> Content SContent
SContent -> "TxtNode"
SContent -> Element
SContent -> "Comment"
SContent -> "PI"
Prolog -> LMisc
Element -> Stag(autoclose)
```

Figure 4: XML Grammar

Our terminals have parameters: tag names and attributes for "Stag", textual contents for "TxtNode", etc. They ressemble SAX events (and actually the serialization of the results is done through 'Streaming Api for XML' (StAX). However, we presuppose that our documents are well-formed except for tag crossings. We therefore do not care about characters authorized or not in XML, about attributes not being repeated etc. Our grammar is thus a real simplification of the grammar for the XML language.

The result of the parsing is a grammar (the grammar of the intersection language between the XML grammar and our DAG input [1]). This grammar's non terminals are non terminals from the original grammar together with indexes (states of the DAG) corresponding to the part of the DAG covered by the analysis.

In practice, each use of the reduction rule in the earley parser produces a rule in the grammar that expresses the results [4, 5][5]

On our example, the result (part of the result because we only have an XML fragment) would be (indexes are these of figure 1):

From this result grammar, we extract a result (there may be more than one) when the parsing is successfull. It may happen

---

[4] Among the differences with a full grammar of the XML languages, we do not consider CDATA.
[5] The grammar is cleaned at the end of the parsing: all un-reachable rules are removed.

```
Element_0_14 ::= Stag("app")_0_1 Content_1_12
                 Etag("app")_12_14
Content_1_12 ::= SContent_1_12
SContent_1_12 ::= Element_1_12
Element_1_12 ::= Stag("lem")_1_2 Content_2_11
                 Etag("lem")_11_12
Content_2_11 ::= Content_2_3 SContent3_11
Content_2_3  ::= SContent_2_3
SContent_2_3 ::= TxtNode("n'")_2_3
SContent_3_11 ::= Stag("w")_3_4 Content_4_9
                  Etag("w")_9_11
....
```

however that no path in the DAG leads to a parsing. In such a case, we modify the DAG as described in the next section.

5 ERROR CORRECTION

The only kind of syntactic error we want to correct are these that correspond to elements that cross. Namely, this corresponds to such situations as: <a>..<b>...</a>. In such a case, we want to produce a correction like:

<a>...<b next=#repair>...</b></a><bxml:id="repair">...

That is, we close the tag that needs to be closed and we reopen it later. In order to do so, when the parser fails we need to choose what error to correct (even when the parsing is succesfull, there are a lot of parsing paths that fail). The next step, once the error to correct is choosen is of course to actually correct it.

5.1 Choosing the error to corect

When the parsing fails, this means that no parsing item is produced that scans the text. Errors are failed scans, that is items of the form [i,j, $\alpha \rightarrow \beta \bullet Etag("a")\gamma$] with Etag("a") a closing node whereas we find at state j another closing node Etag("b"). This is illustrated by the following situation:

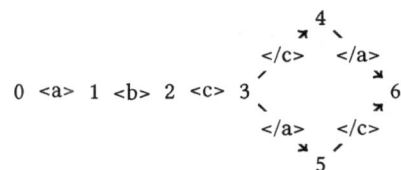

Figure 5

The analysis fails with two items that fail scanning into the sub-DAG after state 3. Namely:

[2, 3, Element ::= Stag("c") Content $\bullet$ Etag("c")] fails in state 3 because it scans Etag("a") and

[1, 4, Element :: Stag("b") Content $\bullet$ Etag("b")] fails in state 4 because it scans Etag("a").

The correction chosen is the second one because it happens in state 4 which is at level 1 in the sub-DAG whereas the first happens at level 0 in the sub-DAG.

5.2 Doing the correction

At states such as 3 in the previous example (see Figure 5), we keep the ordering chains, that is the ordering constraints, that were used to compute the sub-DAG (in this particular case, we have only `</c>` and `</a>` which means, these two elements and no order constraint). We must add [`</b>`, `<b>`], [`</b>`, `</a>`] and [`</a>`, `<b>`]: we close *b* before we reopen it, and we have to close *b* before we close *a* and we reopen *b* after we close *a*. The sub-DAG computed with these new elements and constraints replaces the sub-DAG between state 3 and state 6 in Figure 5. Figure 6 illustrates the result (x and /x are respective abbreviations for `<x>` and `</x>`).

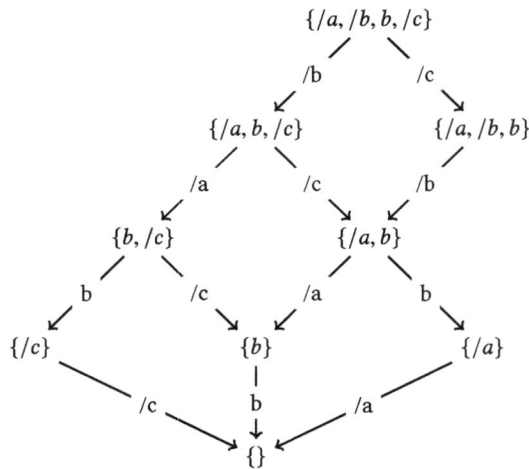

Figure 6

With this new sub-DAG, the parsing succeeds on the path /c, /b, /a, b. In the general case, a sole correction may not suffice ; we thus perform corection until a parse is found.

6 SOME DETAILS ABOUT THE IMPLEMENTATION

Classes that represent the OpenElementNodes and CloseElementNodes contains non only a QName, a Namespace and attributes, but they also contain an ID in case the openElement and the closeElement come from the companion file[6]. The idea is that a closeElement node that comes from the companion file cannot close an openElement node coming from the XML file, and, more generally that in a companion file such as:

```
15    25    <a>
18    37    <a>
```

the solution $_{15}$`<a>`....$_{18}$`<a>`....$_{25}$`</a>`....$_{37}$`<a/>` is not an admitted one. The one admitted is:

$_{15}$`<a next='#repair1'>`.......$_{18}$`</a><a><a xml:id='repair1'>` ...$_{25}$`</a>`....$_{37}$`</a>`.

---

[6]The parameters of the program are a XML file and a companion file with the intent that the annotations from the companion file are integrated into the XML file.

7 CONCLUSION AND PERSPECTIVES

We described a tool for inserting annotations into an XML file. This tool is developped in Java and takes as arguments: an XML file and a companion file that specifies the points in the PCDATA at which XML elements have to be inserted. The tool aims at avoiding unnessessary opening and closing of tags. This gives more readable files that are also much easier to process with such tools as XSLT. In order to insert these annotations in the most readable manner, the tool parses a DAG describing all the XML documents that respect the contraints and a parser selects those that are compatible with the grammar of the XML language[2]; at the end of the process, one of the possible solutions is given. Eventually, some XML elements are split in order to get a weel formed solution..

Three important improvements are possible:

- the result of the program is one among some possible solutions; a context free grammar enumerates the results, but we could take a schema as a parameter and filter the possible solutions through this schema.
- the program may be used to combine annotations from two versions of an XML file, or to state it another way, two XML files on the same textual contents. A probably usefull tool would align textual contents so that the two XML files may differ sligthly (for instance on whitespaces).
- the memory footprint of the program is quite hight (on big XML files, it is necessary to increase the Java machine's memory). As we have ambiguous parsing, the worst case in terms of memory used is in the square of the number of states of the DAG ; however, a huge lot could be spared by optimizing the parser.

REFERENCES

[1] Y Bar-Hillel, M. Perles, and E. Shamir. 1961. On formal properties of simple phrase structure grammars. *Zeitschrift fur Phonetik Sprachwissenschaft und Kommunikationforshung* 14, 3 (1961), 143–172.

[2] Marc Dymetman. 2004. Chart-parsing techniques and the prediction of valid editing moves in structured document authoring. In *Proceedings of the 2004 ACM Symposium on Document Engineering*. Milwaukee, Wisconsin, USA.

[3] Jay Earley. 1970. An efficient context-free parsing algorithm. *Communication of the ACM* 13, 2 (1970).

[4] Dirk Grune and Ceriel J.H. Jacobs. 2008. *Parsing techniques, a practical guide* (2nd edition ed.). Springer.

[5] Bernard Lang and Sylvie Billot. 1989. The Structure of Shared Forests in Ambiguous Parsing. In *Proceedings of the ACL*, Vol. 27. Vancouver, BC, Canada, 143–151.

[6] Eric Villemonte de la Clergerie, Christelle Ayache, Gaël de Chalendar, Gil Francopoulo, Claire Gardent, and Patrick Paroubek. 2008. Large scale production of syntactic annotations for French. In *First International Workshop on "Automated Syntactic Annotations for Interoperable Language Resources"*. Hong-Kong.

Authenticity in a Digital Era: Still a Document Process

The Case of Laboratory Notebooks

Lorraine Tosi
Université de Technologie de Troyes, CNRS, ICD,
Tech-CICO
lorraine.tosi@utt.fr

Aurélien Bénel
Université de Technologie de Troyes, CNRS, ICD,
Tech-CICO
aurelien.benel@utt.fr

ABSTRACT

Asymmetric cryptography brings the ability for anyone on earth to check the signature of a digital object (Diffie & Hellman, 1976 [15]). From that perspective, trusted timestamping of a digital object provides very strong evidence of its author or inventor and integrity (Haber, 1991 [5]). 26 years later, one might have expected that trusted timestamping would have long ago replaced traditional paper laboratory notebooks, which has not happened yet. In this paper, we argue that the reason is that authenticity is a document process: while trusted timestamping remains a necessary part of the process, a digital object must be involved in a sociotechnical process in order to become a document. We first point out the gap, intractable with paper, between the strict administrative workflow required to create strong evidence, and the fluidity of collaborative authoring needed for creativity. This gap is relevant to laboratory notebooks, as they are commonly used by inventors to attest that they discovered elements at a specific time, in a specific context. Then we explain the design and implementation of our software system, according to document theory (Buckland, 1997 [3]), in order to reinvent the whole process to minimize the administrative burden, while preserving its well-known and valuable properties.

CCS CONCEPTS

• **Security and privacy** → **Usability in security and privacy**; • **Applied computing** → **Document management**; *Annotation*; *Document metadata*; • **Human-centered computing** → *HCI design and evaluation methods*; *Collaborative and social computing*; • **Software and its engineering** → *Designing software*;

KEYWORDS

Document systems and workflows; Security and privacy; User Experience; Collaborative authoring and editing; Digital archiving.

1 INTRODUCTION

In contrast to our predecessors, who wanted to help users of paperbound laboratory notebooks go digital, our objective is to provide the good properties of a paperbound laboratory notebook to people.

DocEng'17, September 4–7, 2017, Valletta, Malta.
© 2017 Copyright held by the owner/author(s). Publication rights licensed to ACM.
978-1-4503-4689-4/17/09...$15.00
DOI: https://doi.org/10.1145/3103010.3121034

We aim the vast number of innovators that never used one because of paperbound laboratory notebook's awkwardness, or because all of their research outputs were already digital. Good properties of paperbound laboratory notebook, which computer files usually do not have, are what makes them acceptable in an intellectual property (IP) trial. We will begin with an analysis and state of the art, to understand stakeholders and actions about laboratory notebooks document process. Our system, combining a wide set of analysis and evaluation tasks, is designed to circumvent a 'blind spot' we found in the state of the art. We will then explain the design of our software. We also will present hypotheses derived from 'document theory' [3] and their concrete manifestations in the design of our software. These several paradigms match creativity, collaborative authoring and editing features, in innovators documents workflows. We will finally give context feedbacks from our different types of field interventions.

2 ANALYSIS AND CONTRIBUTION

2.1 Related work

The state of the art about laboratory notebooks dematerialization projects is interdisciplinary (communities as Computer-Supported Cooperative Work, CHI...). Concerning the projects method, researchers usually began with interviews and observations of paper laboratory notebooks use. One of the most interesting findings was the coexistence of a wide range of notebooks: from the most personal, to the most collective, from creative free-form, to 'disciplined' ones, used for archival and legal uses [11]. Whereas contributors are reluctant to duplicate elements solely to share them [7], duplication often occurs with a useful form of rewriting for new recipients [11].

A commercial software postpones the problem. As stated in a quite extensive review [10], the vast majority of electronic laboratory notebooks were designed as a digitalization of the already-existing notebooks in laboratories where one can find many technicians or students, and where the main use of the notebooks is to ensure and control the quality of experiments.

2.2 Contribution

An actual laboratory notebook, designed for intellectual property, is a specific matter. Focusing on invention requires to embrace all of its steps, particularly those that do not occur next to the lab bench and those that are rarely logged in the existing notebooks [6]. Paradoxically, most of these steps already leave digital traces that hold legal value (e.g., e-mails, slides, notes, diagrams, photographs, programs, and data). It is only by preserving existing document formats, user-defined structures, and *ad hoc* workflows that we can provide a solution that is better suited as intellectual property.

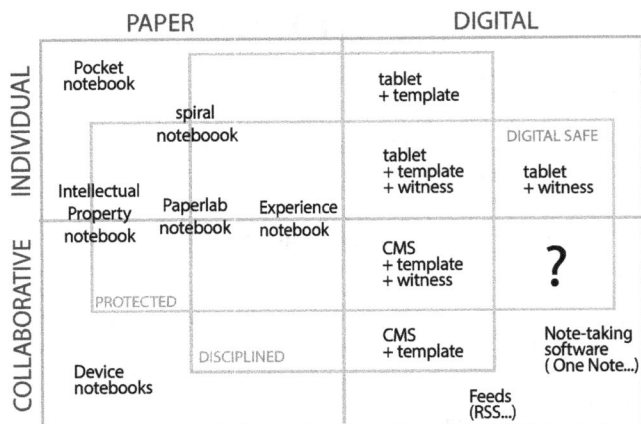

Figure 1: State of the art of laboratory notebooks artifacts (four sets Carroll diagram). It is hard to find a system allowing a digital protected document process that is still collaborative.

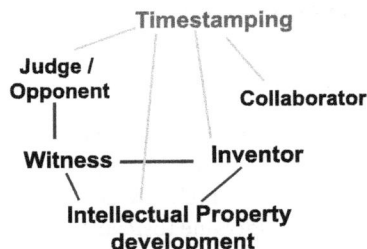

Figure 2: Timestamp transforms trust issues between stakeholder, so the user focuses on documents

Interestingly, there is still a missing intersection in the state of the art [11] for a digital, collective, protected but 'undisciplined' laboratory notebook (see Figure 1). The creative process enabled by fluidity is also what prohibits the resulting innovation from being protected, as safe as a vault.

3 DESIGN AND IMPLEMENTATION OF LEX4LAB

During our study of document nature, we could learn much from libraries and archives theorists. Among researchers in information sciences and information technologies, there has been a renewed interest in *documents* as a richer alternative to *information* and *data*, even attempting to apply definitions stated in the 1950s to digital documents [2, 3]. We adopted these paradigms designing our electronic laboratory notebook Lex4Lab from 2013 to 2017.

3.1 Everything can become a document

Our software Lex4Lab has been designed and implemented using Agile project management. Following the 'release early, release often' principle, features have been regularly delivered since April 2013 and until very recently.

A mere description of our system could be that it turns the laptop of every inventor into a laboratory notebook with a legal value. Transforming any computer file into a non self-reliant document, particularly to "substantiate the inventor's claims of having the ideas on or before a given date" is no longer truly a technical problem [5]; a computer protocol can be used to request a time-stamping authority (compliant to technical and organizational requirements) to generate a timestamp token that results from the cryptographic signature of the current time and the hash of the file. As with well-known paper methods (such as regularly time-stamped notebooks, letters mailed to oneself and left unopened, or deposit at a public notary), this protocol can be used to ensure that neither the content

nor the timestamp can be altered by anyone but the time-stamping authority [5].

Surprisingly, although such timestamping formats, protocols [1] and organizational requirements [9] have been defined, implemented and massively deployed for a long time, they have been used mainly to timestamp digital signatures (to prevent algorithms obsolescence). These standards have not been used as frequently to timestamp more general data or documents. Digital signature is often considered as the only way to seal documents. However, digital signature is an organizational nightmare for some people's everyday use. Trust issues rely on several organizational matters that change according to context and countries. Our system shifts trust issues between each stakeholder by trust towards a third-party providing timestamping technology (see Figure 2).

What we did was to fetch these timestamping techniques in the digital desktop environment of our users:

- on any digital file, the system context menu provides timestamping related actions (see Figure 3),
- a special folder icon on the desktop provides a complete list of timestamped documents,
- from the context menu or the special folder, the timestamped documents can be checked in a visible and pedagogic manner [14].

Actually, timestamping initially acts as a type of witness (see Figure 4). This 'third party' allows each revision of a document to become a material item in any dispute. Timestamp provides proof that "this document was in this particular state at this particular time". Trusted timestamping is a warranty here. Trusted timestamping shows its advantage when used in collaboration, acting as a warranty seal; each time users share documents and data through this system, documents are timestamped. Document integrity and authenticity become verifiable. The timestamping activity can indicate the state of an idea or experiment in property intellectual legal disputes. It can also show when an invention has grown (increase of the timestamp number). Therefore, human witnesses will sign a record of invention (or statement) to strengthen the invention.

Files from Lex4Lab could be acknowledged as a electronic written proof in litigation, according to French law. A French lawyer will soon write a legal opinion about Lex4Lab according to European regulation eIDAS.

110

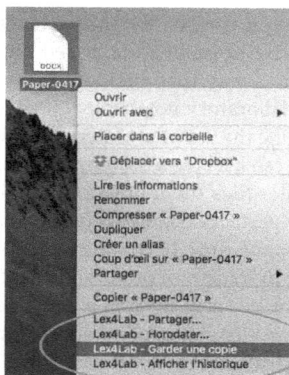

Figure 3: "One click" feature: from a working draft to the electronic laboratory notebook

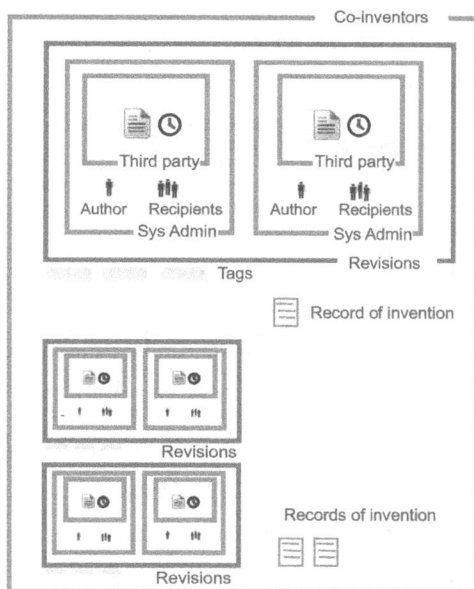

Figure 4: Document process in Lex4Lab matches collaborative authoring and editing at any stage. Timestamping initially acts as a type of witness

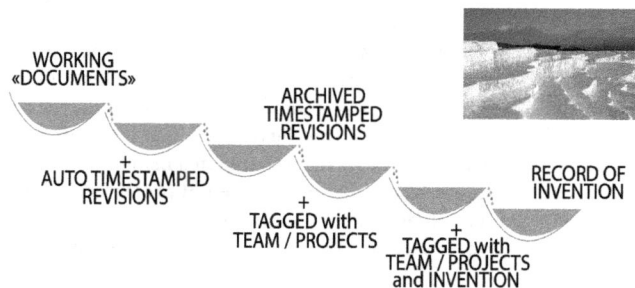

Figure 5: "Settling ponds" as a metaphor for 'documentarisation' of the most valuable working drafts

3.2 Becoming a document is a process

A document is a proof, and everything can be transformed into a document (including an antelope![2]), provided that it has been 'appraised', has been given an identifier and a location among a 'corpus', and has been described such that it can be referenced by other documents, accessed and preserved [2, 3]. Similar to its preservation, a document's description should also be considered a process; although *standardized attributes* (date, producers, and recipients) should be provided early in the process to make manipulation easier, *heuristic attributes* (such as tags) can be provided gradually to help interpret these documents [2, 16]. As a matter of fact, considering becoming a document as a process is not very different from the 'Three ages theory' in archival studies [8]. Y. Pérotin used an other metaphor: the archival process is similar to a sequence of settling ponds [4]. We can apply this metaphor to laboratory notebook system (see Figure 5). In each pond, only a few documents will arise, according to their administrative use or their historical value. Then a few documents will flow into the next pond: the most valuable documents according to IP.

The real challenge is not to create a document that would be perfect at first but to *documentarise* [16] important documents step-by-step, as their value becomes more evident, to obtain an increasingly better proof (see Figure 5). In too many document management systems, the mandatory description tasks needed at document creation are such a burden that users often prefer typing false data. So we definitely needed to fit every discipline and every user's operating system and file management, letting the user choose what type of file he wants to integrate in the laboratory notebook. The user remains free to create, to organize and to send his documents in the manner he previously used to. Features are continuous timestamping of personal drafts (timestamp ASAP), tracked in each revision (or not), archiving of revisions of interest. An invention could arise later from these revisions, and be recorded using an efficient tagging feature. On any digital file, the system context menu provides timestamping-related actions. A special folder icon on the desktop provides a complete list of timestamped documents. Timestamped documents can be checked in a visual and pedagogic way [14].

3.3 A document is a shared reference

Any document should be a shared reference that supporters and critics can access to check its content and authenticity. We believe that we cannot separate laboratory notebook and collaboration. A user should not need to duplicate his work only to contribute to a shared notebook. The user can maintain its own organization in work files, regardless of how the contributors will use the documents. Our software allows the sharing of a document directly from personal files and the tracking of modifications. From teamwork to personal work, our architecture makes co-writing easy because a document's round-trip is no longer a problem. Remaining context and linking information are embedded in all functions. We were able to provide a one-click way to send the documents (see Figure 3), and these documents are received by mail as an invitation link, which is similar to well-known cloud folders. The key difference is that documents are timestamped in all exchanges, while sharing a document means that this current revision is significant. Timestamping allows documents to be shared in a manner that contrasts to simple emails where documents are not protected. When it is time to claim an invention, the author can actually request a contributor to join as a co-author or co-inventor via a record of invention.

3.4 Testing

From 2012 to 2017, several studies were led in university such as semi-directive interviews (spring 2012, November 2015) and workshops. There were led with researchers, research engineers, and PhD students. Interviewees had a few unpleasant experiences with intellectual property management, but with no real evidence at hand, they gave up defending their rights at the time, and provided elements to help us design a software that would solve similar issues. Since 2013, in the early releases, while the software was difficult to install, and had a very limited functional scope, its core features was completely usable. Indeed, we got far more concerned by bugs when they started to have impact on our own data, and by ergonomic glitches when we began to use the software on a regular basis.

In March 2015, once the installer and the auto-updater was implemented, we organized two workshops. The workshops took place in the real settings of two sessions with six target users [13]. While conducting the workshops, users who never heard of cryptographic matters eventually wondered about trusted timestamping.

We can check a project member's document history from April 2013 to May 2016 (only with real documents), both in a qualitative and a quantitative way. This user would rather have a specic document type: presentations (Keynote and Powerpoint). The user explains that a meeting, a conference or a lecture are when you take intellectual property risks, mainly towards external actors: companies, offices, colleagues, researchers from other universities.

A long-term user study was effectively led from November 2015 to 2017 in a French university to test our software across the entire life span of a project. Thirteen 'power users' of this university who met IP matters in their work are using the system, while we get continuous feedbacks. After many security tunings (for LDAP, HTTPS, reverse proxy, backups...), we finally obtained an official server for the university in April 2016.

Therefore we can begin to answer the question "are the most sensitive documents with respect to intellectual property considerations also the most shared and the most described documents in the software Lex4Lab?". Even if our electronic laboratory notebook was not used in litigation, the user cannot know what could later be used in IP trials. The user can only rely on the fact that one of his documents, shared, tagged reviewed in collaboration between project actors, will really help in litigation.

4 CONCLUSION AND PERSPECTIVES

Instead of digitizing laboratory notebooks, we provided the good properties of paperbound laboratory notebooks to innovators that have not used them previously. We showed how to bring cryptographic timestamping to innovators, based on hypotheses from document theory, in a way that distinguishes our software from existing electronic laboratory notebooks.

Instead of enforcing the use of predetermined forms or templates, because everything can become a document, we provide timestamping for any computer files the innovator chooses to use. Instead of aiming to create perfect documents (with all metadata and signatures) in one step, because becoming a document is a process, we make it possible to transform proto-documents into full-fledged documents over time in a step-by-step process. Instead of thinking about our software as a 'digital safe', because a document is a shared reference, the main feature of our software is that it allows users to share documents, enabling both co-writing and traceability.

Our software is now installed in a university setting and is published by a software editor. We want project teams to tell us their stories about their use of Lex4Lab, using self-confrontation [12], based on their document histories. We hope our software will help innovators to better protect their own intellectual property, using timestamping as a witness, whatever the document process.

REFERENCES

[1] C Adams, P Cain, D Pinkas, and R Zuccherato. 2001. Internet X. 509 Public Key Infrastructure Time-Stamp Protocol (TSP). (2001).
[2] Suzanne Briet, Ronald E. Day, Laurent Martinet, and Hermina G. B Anghelescu. 2006. *What is documentation?: English translation of the classic French text.* Scarecrow Press, Lanham, Md. http://ella.slis.indiana.edu/~roday/briet.htm
[3] Michael K. Buckland. 1997. What Is a 'Document'? *JASIS* 48, 9 (1997), 804–809.
[4] Marcel Caya. 2004. La théorie des trois âges en archivistique. En avons-nous toujours besoin?. In *ELEC, Conférence de l'Ecole des chartes*, Vol. 2.
[5] Stuart Haber and W. Scott Stornetta. 1991. How to Time-Stamp a Digital Document. *J. Cryptology* 3, 2 (1991), 99–111.
[6] Catherine Letondal, Aurélien Tabard, and Wendy E Mackay. 2009. *Quand tu l'as écrit, tu l'as lu !* Rapport de recherche 1526. Laboratoire de Recherche en Informatique (LRI). https://www.lri.fr/~bibli/Rapports-internes/2009/RR1526.pdf
[7] Gerard Oleksik, Natasa Milic-Frayling, and Rachel Jones. 2014. Study of electronic lab notebook design and practices that emerged in a collaborative scientific environment. In *Computer Supported Cooperative Work, CSCW '14, Baltimore, MD, USA, February 15-19, 2014.* ACM, 120–133. DOI:https://doi.org/10.1145/2531602.2531709
[8] Yves Pérotin. 1966. Administration and the 'Three Ages' of Archives. *The American Archivist* 29, 3 (1966), 363–369.
[9] D PINKAS, N POPE, and J ROSS. 2003. *Policy Requirements for Time-Stamping Authorities (TSAs).* Request for comments (informational) 3628. IETF. http://www.ietf.org/rfc/rfc3628.txt
[10] Michael Rubacha, Anil K Rattan, and Stephen C Hosselet. 2011. A review of electronic laboratory notebooks available in the market today. *Journal of the Association for Laboratory Automation* 16, 1 (2011), 90–98.
[11] Aurélien Tabard, Wendy E. Mackay, and Evelyn Eastmond. 2008. From individual to collaborative: the evolution of prism, a hybrid laboratory notebook. In *Proceedings of the 2008 ACM Conference on Computer Supported Cooperative Work, CSCW 2008, San Diego, CA, USA, November 8-12, 2008,* Bo Begole and David W. McDonald (Eds.). ACM, 569–578.
[12] Jacques Theureau. 2010. Les entretiens d'autoconfrontation et de remise en situation par les traces matérielles et le programme de recherche 'cours d'action'. *Revue d'anthropologie des connaissances* 4, 2 (2010), 287–322.
[13] Lorraine Tosi, Aurélien Bénel, and Francois Devoret. 2015. Améliorer l'expérience utilisateur pour encourager la confiance entre collaborateurs. In *IHM'15, Toulouse, France, octobre 2015.* https://publications.icd.utt.fr/7551d4be492436d69cf9f41af42cead7
[14] Lorraine Tosi, Aurélien Bénel, and Karine Lan. 2015. Digital signature services for users - Improving user experience to support trust among work partners. In *Symposium on Usable Privacy and Security, SOUPS'15, Ottawa, Canada, July 22-24, 2015.* https://publications.icd.utt.fr/70957022f8b5c3842fd93698e009b29d
[15] Diffie Whitfield and Hellman Martin E. 1976. New Directions in Cryptography. In *IEEE Transactions On Information Theory, Vol. It-22, No. 6.*
[16] Manuel Zacklad. 2006. Documentarisation processes in Documents for Action (DofA): the status of annotations and associated cooperation technologies. *Computer Supported Cooperative Work (CSCW)* 15, 2-3 (2006), 205–228.

Fast Binarization with Chebyshev Inequality

Ka-Hou Chan
MPI-QMUL Information Systems
Research Centre
Macao Polytechnic Institute
Macao, China
chankahou@ipm.edu.mo

Sio-Kei Im
MPI-QMUL Information Systems
Research Centre
Macao Polytechnic Institute
Macao, China
marcusim@ipm.edu.mo

Wei Ke
Macao Polytechnic Institute
Macao, China
wke@ipm.edu.mo

ABSTRACT

In order to enhance the binarization result of degraded document images with smudged and bleed-through background, we present a fast binarization technique that applies the Chebyshev theory in the image preprocessing. We introduce the Chebyshev filter which uses the Chebyshev inequality in the segmentation of objects and background. Our result shows that the Chebyshev filter is not only effective, but also simple, robust and easy to implement. Because of its simplicity, our method is sufficiently efficient to process live image sequences in real-time. We have implemented and compared with the Document Image Binarization Contest datasets (H-DIBCO 2014) for testing and evaluation. The experimental outcomes have demonstrated that this method achieved good result in this literature.

CCS CONCEPTS

•Applied computing →*Document capture;*

KEYWORDS

Chebyshev Inequality; Thresholding; Handwritten Document; Segmentation; Binarization

1 INTRODUCTION

For the current binarization algorithms, there are always some differences between the segmentation result and the human recognition. Often, for a particular method, some texts are gained and some others are lost when processing an obscure document image. It is well-known that image binarization methods on established benchmarks across different metrics, those optimal results of the binarization algorithms still have subjectivity, such as the need of parameter configurations in various algorithms. Meanwhile, there are large bodies of document image binarization methods that have been proposed.

For the local thresholding, an adaptive binarization algorithm based on local mean and standard deviation is proposed in [9]. Later, [13] proposes the standard deviation of the dynamic range in [9] that can reduce the noise issues in the non-target area. They have the advantage to detect the text but also introduce a lot of

DocEng '17, September 4–7, 2017, Valletta, Malta.
© 2017 ACM. 978-1-4503-4689-4/17/09...$15.00
DOI: https://doi.org/10.1145/3103010.3121033

background noise. Under extremely dark or bright illumination, changing the threshold to decrease the background noise also decreases the text detection rate. Moreover, the bleed degradation is observed in historical documents through a variety of image outputs. Many authors look forward to finding algorithms that are able to deal with a variety of issues in the formation of degraded images, but degradation still remains an unsolved problem in document image binarization, due to document thresholding errors. Some methods have incorporated the background estimation and normalization steps with the local contrast computation to improve binarization results.

2 RELATED WORK

For the various reasons of degradation, current techniques have good results only for certain types of degradation [8]. Then [1] proposes to set the threshold as a midrange value, which is the mean of the minimum and maximum gray-scale values in the local kernel. However, if the contrast is below a certain threshold then those neighbors are considered to consist of only one class of pixels, either the object or the background, depending on the midrange value. [14] proposes to detect the text edge by using the Otsu [11] method, and uses a local thresholding formula which gives better results than those of [7]. [4] proposes a binarization method by the combination of four methodologies: local contrast analysis, contrast expansion, threshold selection and noise removal. The method performs well for documents filled with text objects, but issues a lot of noise in document images with only a few characters. In [5], the method performs inpainting [2] by using the foreground of the method in [13] that can be filled in using local statistics, such as mean and deviation, as the inpainting mask, and introduces the Gaussian model for the binarization thresholding.

Inspired by the justifications of these methods, we introduce in this paper a novel thresholding scheme by using the Chebyshev inequality. This method does not require any prior information about the contrast of the text in an image. It is most suitable for filtering those document images with low contrast and dense noise. The processing time of this one-pass filter is in $O\left(k^2\right)$ for each pixel, where k is size in pixel of the adaptive local kernel. Since k is independent to the size of an image, the filter is thus sufficiently efficient to process live image sequences. We demonstrate that our method gives superior results in terms of performance and quality, compared with the existing binarization methods listed in [10]. This method can be used to binarize degraded document images in gray-scale with aging background and various kinds of ink in real-time.

3 METHODOLOGY

In this paper, we presents a new algorithm for binarizing text document images with back-to-front (bleeding or show-through) interference. The major idea behind the paper is to use a non-linear filter (applying Chebyshev) as a pre-processing optimization step before any other binarization process. In an image, the gray-values of any pixel and its neighbors can be grouped as set of sample data for statistical analysis. These samples may have a completely arbitrary distribution initially, except for the mean and variance. We know nothing else about the pixels and want to find the part of data samples of our interest. Commonly, the probability of a pixel being a part of the text is often less than that of being a part of the background. Thus, the concept of our proposed method is to use the probability in the binarization process for segmentation results.

3.1 Chebyshev Inequality

Similar to other techniques, we also find the mean and variance as local adaptive attributes. However, we do not use them for binarization directly because the condition for thresholding is weak and dispersed. In order to integrate and compute a bound on the fraction of the distribution more accurately once we have the mean and variance, we employ the Chebyshev inequality [6] to obtain the upper bound in Eq. 1,

$$P\left(|x - \mu| \geq \lambda\right) \leq \frac{\sigma^2}{\lambda^2}, \tag{1}$$

for any $\lambda > 0$, where x is a random pixel of samples with finite mean μ and variance σ^2. This inequality gives us a way to handle the extreme situation in which the only things we know about the samples, or the probability distribution, are the mean and the standard deviation (σ). It implies that in any probability distribution, almost all values are close to the mean, and the chance of a value being outside that range is no more than $\frac{\sigma^2}{\lambda^2}$. As the most general form of the two-sided Chebyshev inequality, it places a bound on how much the distribution can be concentrated far away from the mean. However, this inequality generally gives a poor upper bound because this bound gets increasingly weaker as λ goes up. Thus, we adopt another variant called the one-sided Chebyshev inequality [6] in Eq. 2,

$$P\left(x - \mu \geq \lambda\right) \leq P_{max} \equiv \frac{\sigma^2}{\sigma^2 + \lambda^2}. \tag{2}$$

The advantage of Eq. 2 is that it provides a stronger upper bound $P_{max} \in [0, 1]$. Since the distribution may be arbitrary, this justification can therefore be applied under a variety of very general situations to obtain significant results. Let $t = \lambda + \mu$ and x a random variable drawn from a distribution with mean μ and variance σ^2. Then, for $x \geq t$, Eq. 2 can be rewritten to

$$P\left(x \geq t\right) \leq P_{max}\left(t\right) \equiv \frac{\sigma^2}{\sigma^2 + (t - \mu)^2}. \tag{3}$$

Suppose we randomly select a pixel as t from an image with its local adaptive mean μ and variance σ^2, it can be said that within t and its neighbors the ratio of the pixels with gray-values equal to or greater than t is no more than $P_{max}\left(t\right)$. Even for a document image with low contrast, since it is just a comparison of the numerical values without considering the contrast ratio, the bound can thus provide a good approximation of the amount of interested pixels within a given sample.

3.2 Chebyshev Filter

It is worth noting that the two-sided Chebyshev inequality tells about the absolute difference. It can only find out the probability of a sample x with an absolute difference from μ greater than λ, but cannot tell the probability of either $x > \mu$ or $x < \mu$. In contrast, the one-sided Chebyshev Inequality can clearly tell us the probability of a sample that is greater than t in a local region. Thereby, we can use the gray-scale value of the current pixel as t in Eq. 3 to evaluate the condition of its neighbors and have the result in range $[0, 1]$. According to above discussion, we can make use of this to find out the percentage of data that are clustered around the mean. Furthermore, the right hand side of Eq. 3 can be scaled up to the range of gray-scale values, for example $0 - 255$, as a filter result, and thus can be used in the following filter for segmentation of text objects and background.

To take into consideration of the noise attribute of low featured images, although this method works reasonably well for the smooth area so far, it may not handle the document images with cluttered and confused noise properly. This is because a bright pixel is often considered as an object where the denominator in Eq. 3 is bigger but the numerator is smaller, so the proposed technique is more dependent on the local image smoothness. In most practical studies, the noise variance is unknown and varies spatially. It is well known that the noise variance of a local area can be estimated by the local variance of a flat area. Based on this idea, an adaptive algorithm is devised to estimate the local noise to improve the above Chebyshev filter. Theoretically, after the local $P_{max}\left(t\right)$ associated with each pixel in a small range is computed, the polarization of the probability in this range is a good estimate of the noise variance. Thus, we introduce a small adjustment, called the pixel redundancy, as an improvement to the Chebyshev filter. Since the major processing is to calculate the local mean and variance for the probability of each pixel, the Chebyshev filter results can then be de-noised by increasing the pixel redundancy (r), which can further tighten the upper bound of the Chebyshev inequality in Eq. 3.

PROOF. For $r \in \mathbb{R}$ and $r \geq 0$, we have,

$$\frac{\sigma^2}{\sigma^2 + (t - \mu)^2} \geq \frac{\sigma^2}{\sigma^2 + (t + r - \mu)^2}.$$

Refer to Eq. 3, we obtain,

$$P_{max}\left(x \geq t\right) \geq P_{max}\left(x \geq t + r\right).$$

□

Therefore, we can further tighten the upper bound by the following modified version of Eq. 3,

$$P_{max}\left(t, r\right) \equiv \frac{\sigma^2}{\sigma^2 + (t + r - \mu)^2}. \tag{4}$$

Notice that, t and r are symmetrical in Eq. 4, we have the partial differential equation about t and r as follows,

$$\frac{\partial P_{max}}{\partial t} = \frac{\partial P_{max}}{\partial r} = -\frac{2\sigma^2 (t + r - \mu)}{\left[\sigma^2 + (t + r - \mu)^2\right]^2}. \tag{5}$$

We can tell from the equations, as r increases, the objects and background will become darker. The darkening speed is getting slower and slower. This means darkening of the dark objects in the source image, which become light objects in the filter result, is faster than that of the light background, which becomes dark after the filtering. Because the noise pixels can often be bounded in the redundant condition ($r \geq \mu - t$), so the noise in background can be calmed down by increasing r. This can well capture intensity variations and thus produce good results.

4 IMPLEMENTATION

We now give the implementation of the Chebyshev filter for binarization in detail. The computation of the filter is based on the local mean μ and the variance σ^2 of all the pixels in the local range of a gray-scale image. Let I be the original gray-scale images with pixel range $[0, 255]$, and we regard the dark as foreground and the light as background. In statistical terms, the result of the filtering is to recover the current expectations M_1 and M_2 (refer to the equations below) over the filtered region, let X be a discrete random variable taking values x_i with probabilities $P(x_i)$, then the expected values are defined as follows,

$$M_1 = E(X) = \sum_i x_i \cdot P(x_i)$$

$$M_2 = E\left(X^2\right) = \sum_i x_i^2 \cdot P(x_i).$$

From the above, we compute the mean μ and the variance σ^2,

$$\mu = E(X) = M_1$$

$$\sigma^2 = E\left(X^2\right) - E(X)^2 = M_2 - M_1^2 \qquad (6)$$

The variance can be interpreted as a quantitative measure of the width of a distribution. As a result, it should place a bound on how much of the distribution can be concentrated far away from the mean. Thus, the result O that corresponds to the Chebyshev filtered image is produced by Alg. 1, referencing the Open Source Computer Vision (OpenCV 3.1.0) standard library [3].

4.1 Performance and Quality Analysis

In Alg. 1, this filter moves a square window of size k over the image to obtain the statistics term by multiple traversals of the k^2 pixels, so the time complexity is $O\left(k^2\right)$ for each pixel. The filter also requires additional memory space for storing the mean (M) and the variance (S) per pixel. Here, a high-precision array is used to take into account of the fractional parts for the Chebyshev inequality. Further, we segment the object pixel candidates by using the MEAN (of neighborhood area) adaptive thresholding method. It is worth mentioning that the redundancy r in Eq. 4 offsets the gray-scale value of each pixel, we therefore must cancel these offsets before the segmentation. We do this by subtracting the redundancy r from the pixels of the kernel k through the invocation of the *adaptiveThreshold* method.

As shown in Fig. 1, the majority of large size background can be determined in the Chebyshev filter, only a small part of uncertain background and foreground is taken into account for the threshold determination. After the Chebyshev filter operation, the image

---

Algorithm 1: ChebyshevFilter(I, O, k, r).

Data: I: Mat // Original input image
Data: k: int // Local kernel range
Data: r: float // Redundancy offset
Result: O: Mat // Output binarization image

1 **begin**
2   Mat G; // Convert I to gray-scaled image G
3   cv::cvtColor(I,G,CV_BGR2GRAY);
4   /*   */
   /* Ensure dark objects on light background   */
   /*   */
5   Mat M; // Obtain the mean of I within range k
6   cv::blur(G, M, k);
7   Mat S; // Obtain the mean of squares of I
8   cv::blur(G^2, S, k);
9   /*   */
   /* Calculate the variance by using Eq. 6   */
10   Mat $V \leftarrow S - M^2$;
11   /*   */
   /* Calculate the Chebyshev result by Eq. 4   */
12   Mat $C \leftarrow \dfrac{V}{V + (G + r - M)^2} \times 255$;
13   /*   */
   /* Using the MEAN adaptive thresholding method   */
14   Mat O;
15   cv::adaptiveThreshold(C, O, $\cdots$, k, r);
16 **end**

---

contrast computed in the objects is obviously larger than that computed in the background. Hence, the ratio between the total number of pixels that correspond to components of small heights and the number of those components is expected to be very low, and only the undetermined region is considered in obtaining the threshold, so the region of the segmentation of objects is reduced.

5 EVALUATION

To measure the quality and processing time required by each method, we used only one image (*H07*) from the testing in H-DIBCO 2014. The computer used was a PC with Intel(R) Xeon(R) processor (4 real cores) at 2.00GHz and 8.0GB of Ram memory. Our experiments are implemented by OpenCV 3.1.0 in C++ and run in 64-bit environment. For each encountered measure, we compare our method for the detailed performance with the practices of the contests in H-DIBCO 2014 [10], together with the widely used binarization techniques of Otsu [11] and Sauvola [13]. In Tab. 1, the processing times come from [10], while the evaluation result is re-calculated by the H-DIBCO 2016 Evaluation Tool [12].

As we can see from the table, our method is among the upper half, and the binarization quality is as good as those of the methods P02 and P05. However, the processing times of the better three methods are significantly slower than ours. This is largely because of the simplicity of the Chebyshev filter. As shown in Fig. 1, it is worth mentioning that our method is able to roughly segment the stained region on the left side of the original image, while the then winner of the contest completely erased the region as noise in the

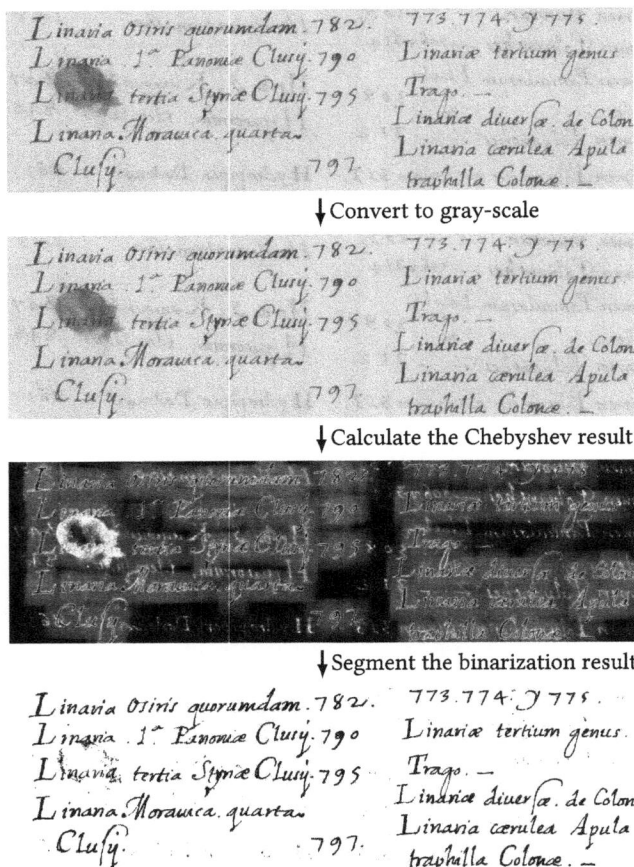

↓ Convert to gray-scale

↓ Calculate the Chebyshev result

↓ Segment the binarization result

Figure 1: Filter-out such noise in aging background on hand-written image (*H07*) of H-DIBCO 2014 contests, processed by Alg. 1.

Table 1: Detailed evaluation for out method and presented papers in H-DIBCO 2014.

Rank	Proposed Method	FM (%)	pseudo-FM (%)	PSNR	DRD	Time (sec)
1	P06	96.01	96.97	21.56	0.95	17.43
2	P02	95.63	96.73	21.19	1.06	7.23
3	P05	92.61	94.93	18.91	1.90	16.20
Our Method		91.33	96.50	18.32	2.23	<0.30
4	P04	89.44	89.75	17.03	3.54	14.84
5	P01	88.66	88.23	16.61	3.91	21.19
6	P03b	79.68	86.94	14.53	6.53	4.65
7	P07	78.24	86.68	14.33	6.71	0.30
8	P03a	72.05	85.29	13.69	7.24	4.61
	Otsu [11]	84.19	86.90	15.29	5.90	–
	Sauvola [13]	90.02	95.41	17.68	2.74	–

background. We can conclude that our method has the balance of performance and quality.

6 CONCLUSION

The idea of our proposed technique is to make use of the probability information of text strokes. We first implement a Chebyshev filter over local ranges to effectively estimate the properties of a document image. However, a direct application of the Chebyshev inequality as in Eq. 3 instead emphasizes the noise with low contrast. Therefore, we introduce the pixel redundancy to improve the filter results. With this optimization, the noise in the background can be reduced significantly. At the same time, the upper bound of the Chebyshev inequality is also tightened, this reduces the region of the segmentation of objects. Following the Chebyshev filtering, the result image in gray-scale is segmented by the MEAN adaptive thresholding method to produce the binary image. In particular, our method has been evaluated agained the methods presented in H-DIBCO 2014. It has produced binary images with the quality comparable to that of the methods among the best. Plus, our method is robust and effective, especially suitable for filtering-out such noise in aging background and images of degraded kinds of ink.

ACKNOWLEDGEMENT

This work was supported by the Macao Science and Technology Development Fund through Project 138/2016/A3.

REFERENCES

[1] John Bernsen. 1986. Dynamic thresholding of grey-level images. In *International conference on pattern recognition*, Vol. 2. 1251–1255.
[2] Marcelo Bertalmio, Guillermo Sapiro, Vincent Caselles, and Coloma Ballester. 2000. Image inpainting. In *Proceedings of the 27th annual conference on Computer graphics and interactive techniques*. ACM Press/Addison-Wesley Publishing Co., 417–424.
[3] Gary Bradski and Adrian Kaehler. 2008. *Learning OpenCV: Computer vision with the OpenCV library*. O'Reilly Media, Inc.
[4] Basilios Gatos, Ioannis Pratikakis, and Stavros J Perantonis. 2008. Improved document image binarization by using a combination of multiple binarization techniques and adapted edge information. In *ICPR 2008. 19th International Conference on Pattern Recognition, 2008*. IEEE, 1–4.
[5] Rachid Hedjam, Reza Farrahi Moghaddam, and Mohamed Cheriet. 2011. A spatially adaptive statistical method for the binarization of historical manuscripts and degraded document images. *Pattern Recognition* 44, 9 (2011), 2184–2196.
[6] Wassily Hoeffding. 1963. Probability inequalities for sums of bounded random variables. *Journal of the American statistical association* 58, 301 (1963), 13–30.
[7] Shijian Lu, Bolan Su, and Chew Lim Tan. 2010. Document image binarization using background estimation and stroke edges. *International Journal on Document Analysis and Recognition (IJDAR)* 13, 4 (2010), 303–314.
[8] Rafael G Mesquita, Carlos AB Mello, and LHEV Almeida. 2014. A new thresholding algorithm for document images based on the perception of objects by distance. *Integrated Computer-Aided Engineering* 21, 2 (2014), 133–146.
[9] Wayne Niblack. 1985. *An introduction to digital image processing*. Strandberg Publishing Company.
[10] Konstantinos Ntirogiannis, Basilis Gatos, and Ioannis Pratikakis. 2014. Icfhr2014 competition on handwritten document image binarization (h-dibco 2014). In *2014 14th International Conference on Frontiers in Handwriting Recognition (ICFHR)*. IEEE, 809–813.
[11] Nobuyuki Otsu. 1979. A threshold selection method from gray-level histograms. *IEEE Transactions on systems, man, and cybernetics* 9, 1 (1979), 62–66.
[12] Ioannis Pratikakis, Konstantinos Zagoris, George Barlas, and Basilis Gatos. 2016. ICFHR2016 Handwritten Document Image Binarization Contest (H-DIBCO 2016). In *2016 15th International Conference on Frontiers in Handwriting Recognition (ICFHR)*. IEEE, 619–623.
[13] Jaakko Sauvola and Matti Pietikäinen. 2000. Adaptive document image binarization. *Pattern recognition* 33, 2 (2000), 225–236.
[14] Marcel Van Herk. 1992. A fast algorithm for local minimum and maximum filters on rectangular and octagonal kernels. *Pattern Recognition Letters* 13, 7 (1992), 517–521.

Post-Processing OCR Text using Web-Scale Corpora

Jie Mei[†], Aminul Islam[‡], Abidalrahman Moh'd[†], Yajing Wu[†], Evangelos Milios[†]

[†]Faculty of Computer Science, Dalhousie University
{jmei,amohd,yajing,eem}@cs.dal.ca
[‡]School of Computing and Informatics, University of Louisiana at Lafayette
aminul@louisiana.edu

ABSTRACT

We introduce a (semi-)automatic OCR post-processing system that utilizes web-scale linguistic corpora in providing high-quality correction. This paper is a comprehensive system overview with the focus on the computational procedures, applied linguistic analysis, and processing optimization.

CCS CONCEPTS

• **Applied computing** → **Document analysis**; • **Information systems** → *Data analytics*; • **Computing methodologies** → *Natural language processing*;

KEYWORDS

OCR Error Correction; OCR Post-Processing; Statistical Learning

1 INTRODUCTION

There are massive amounts of data – including magazines, books, and scientific articles – stored and transmitted in the digital image formats, such as Portable Document Format (PDF) or Joint Picture Group (JPG). To extract the textual information for using in a data mining pipeline, optical character recognition (OCR) engines have been developed for converting image data into machine-readable text. However, the accuracy of the OCR-generated text can be affected by many factors, such as algorithmic defects (e.g., segmentation, classification inaccuracy), limited hardware conditions (e.g., poor scanning equipment), and complex content status (e.g., a mixture of text fonts, complicated page layout) [10]. Although OCR engines include linguistic analysis in character recognition and segmentation [12], such analysis is limited and blind to the overall recognition performance.

In this paper, we overview our OCR post-processing system, which is an integrated correction engine that consumes OCR-generated text and produces its correction. The computational procedure can be conducted in a fully automatic manner, where optional interactive candidate selection can be integrated to further optimize the correction output. Utilizing web-scale linguistic corpora, our system conducts an elaborate candidate generation and a comprehensive linguistic analysis for correcting each error, and thus able to suggests high-quality candidate corrections that are orthographically similar to the error, consistent with the topic, and coherent to the context. We also optimize the processing flow for efficiently applying this model to real-world usage.

2 RELATED WORKS

OCR post-processing systems can be categorized as manual, semi-automatic, and automatic according to the degree of automation. A manual system that builts a full-text search tool to retrieve all occurrences of original images given a text query is introduced in [11]. It relies fully on the user to validate and correct OCR errors.

A number of studies view the post-processing of OCR output as the initial step in the error correction pipeline and involve continuous human intervention afterwards [13, 14]. These models are designed to reduce the human effort of manually correcting errors. Integration of dictionaries and heuristics to correct as many OCR errors as possible before giving the text to human correctors is performed in [13]. Further work records the previous human corrections to update the underlying Bayesian model for automatic correction [14].

One of the most recently proposed automatic systems, [4], made use of three *n*-gram statistical features extracted from three million documents to train a linear regressor for candidate ranking. Correction candidates suggested by this model are not restricted to those found in OCR outputs. However, existing methods make use of solely *n*-gram frequencies without knowing the characteristics of OCR errors and are, thus, biased to select common words from the *n*-gram corpus.

A different direction of research uses an ensemble approach on the outputs of multiple OCR engines for the same input image and selects the best recognition for each word as the final output [5, 7–9]. Combining complementary recognition results from different OCR engines is claimed to lead to a better output [5]. The overall error rate is demonstrated to decrease with additional OCR engines involved, regardless of the performance of each added model in [9]. The application of both OCR recognition votes and lexical features to train a Conditional Random Field model and evaluate the test set in a different domain is proposed in [8]. While such models have proved useful, they select words only among OCR model recognitions and are blind to other candidate words. Besides, they require the presence of the original OCR input and effort of multiple OCR processing.

DocEng'17, September 4–7, 2017, Valletta, Malta.
© 2017 ACM. 978-1-4503-4689-4/17/09...$15.00
DOI: http://dx.doi.org/10.1145/3103010.3121032

3 SYSTEM OVERVIEW

The post-processing workflow of our system, shown in Fig. 1, follows the conventional error correction steps: *error word detection*, *candidate correction generation* for the detected errors, and *candidate ranking* [6].

Our system applies web-scale linguistic corpora, including a word *n*-gram corpus and lexicons. A lexicon is a word list, which is interchangeable with "dictionary" in the literature. A word *n*-gram corpus is a collection of *n*-grams (i.e. *n* consecutive words in the text) with occurrence frequency in a document set, where some notable examples are Google Book *n*-gram [1] or Google Web 1T 5-gram corpus [2].

3.1 Computational Procedure

Text Preprocessing. To achieve a fully automatic text correction system, we integrate a text preprocessing step before error detection to handle potential formatting issues.

Word Segmentation. Words are segmented using Google *n*-gram tokenization[3], and over-segmented fragments are merged using heuristics. Unlike other correction models that split words by whitespace [6], we apply Google *n*-gram tokenization to generate more meaningful words, with rules that segment punctuations into separate tokens, disambiguate quotations, split hyphenated words, and separate contractions such as *she'll* into *she* and *'ll*. OCR error may contain mis-recognized punctuation, for example *<family → famil}^>*, in which a word is split into multiple tokens. Using heuristic rules designed for general noise texts, we automatically disambiguate such erroneous word fragments and merge them into one unit to detect.

Error Detection. Words and corresponding context *n*-grams are statistically analyzed for error word identification. A word is detected as an error if it fulfills one of the following two conditions: (1) its unigram frequency is less than a threshold, or (2) there is no context *n*-gram, with frequency in the corpus that exceeds another predefined threshold. According to Zipf's law [15], the word length correlates to the word frequency. We thus set up a unigram threshold that increases with the length of the detected word.

Candidate Generation. The candidate corrections for each error are merged from two types of generation algorithms: *reverse Levenshtein distance search* and *word n-gram context search*. Both algorithms search for candidates in the unigram corpus, where the former one selects candidates that are orthographically similar to the error word and the latter one prefers candidates that are coherent with the local context. When searching for candidates in word *n*-gram corpus, we also retrieve the corresponding statistics for use by subsequent contextual analysis in order to avoid repeated search in the large corpus.

Linguistic Analysis. Different measures are applied to quantitatively analyze the linguistic features for each generated candidate. For each candidate, the analysis results from different measures are collected. The candidate set that is considered in the subsequent

[1] https://books.google.com/ngrams
[2] https://catalog.ldc.upenn.edu/ldc2006t13
[3] https://catalog.ldc.upenn.edu/docs/LDC2006T13/readme.txt

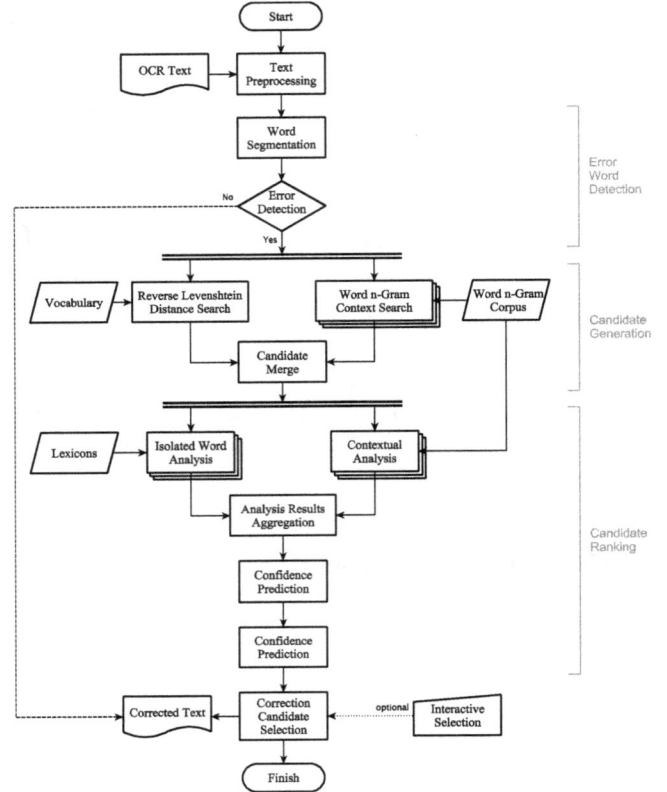

Figure 1: Process flowchart of the proposed OCR post-processing system.

steps is the union of the top-ranked candidates in each linguistic analysis.

Confidence Prediction. The confidence of each candidate being a valid correction is predicted by a supervised regressor given the candidate analysis result, which is used to rank among all candidates of an error.

Candidate Selection. The top-ranked correction candidates are automatically selected to substitute the error words in the text. In addition, an interactive candidate selection can be optionally adopted to optimize the selection among a ranked candidate list.

3.2 Linguistic Analysis

A list of the applied linguistic features is given in Table 1. According to the required textual information, we categorize the applied linguistic analysis in two types: (1) *isolated-word analysis* that uses the error word for candidate evaluation, and (2) *contextual analysis* that considers the context words. Besides, these two analysis types utilize different corpora, as shown in Fig. 1.

Edit Distance. Edit distance is a fundamental technique in quantifying the difference between two strings and is widely used for approximate string matching. We apply the unit-cost Levenshtein distance value to evaluate candidates.

Table 1: System applied linguistic features.

Analysis Type	Linguistic Feature
Isolated-word Analysis	Levenshtein distance
	Lexical similarity
	Language Popularity
	lexicon existence
Contextual Analysis	Exact context coherence
	Relaxed context coherence

Lexical Similarity. While edit distance measures the differences between two words, it is blind to the similarity in two character sequences. Thus, we apply a lexical similarity measure, [3], which considers the common subsequences between two given strings.

Language popularity. We consider the adequacy of the suggested candidates to avoid selecting the uncommon words, which are measured by the candidate word frequency in a corpus.

Lexicon existence. We want highly ranked candidates to be semantically consistent with the text topic. The evaluation score for each topic is a boolean value that indicates the existence of the candidate in the according lexicon. With this type of feature, the model is able to estimate the topics of the training data and distinct the semantically related candidates in ranking.

Exact Context Coherent. An appropriate correction candidate should be coherent with the context where the error occurs. Using statistics from a web-scale 5-gram corpus, we evaluate suggested candidates their syntactic coherence with local context in text.

Relaxed Context Coherent. Consider there are limited candidates that can be suggested from the exact 5-gram context containing rare words, we relax the 5-gram matching condition by allowing mismatched word.

3.3 Processing Optimization

It is computationally intensive to adopt the proposed feature-based statistical approach to OCR Error correction. To leverage linguistic analysis in candidate ranking, the analytic result of each linguistic feature is computed for all generated candidates. While relaxing the generation criteria (i.e. increase the distance threshold in reversed Levenshtein distance or the number of relaxed words in context search) increases the probability of including the correction in the generated candidates, the number of candidates increases drastically and thus requiring more computation in analyzing their linguistic features. It is especially problematic when using web-scale corpora.

To facilitate parallel computing with MapReduce, we define analyzing batch as a series of analyzing jobs for the same linguistic feature of multiple words. In addition, we apply optimization strategies in processing multiple words within batch: For isolated-word analysis, we distinguish unique words in the analyzing batch before computation to avoid re-computation for error words with the same string representation. For contextual analysis, we first collect and distinguish unique 5-grams contexts from error words in batch. Consider 5-gram records in the corpus are ordered lexicographically, we cluster contexts according to their leading words and

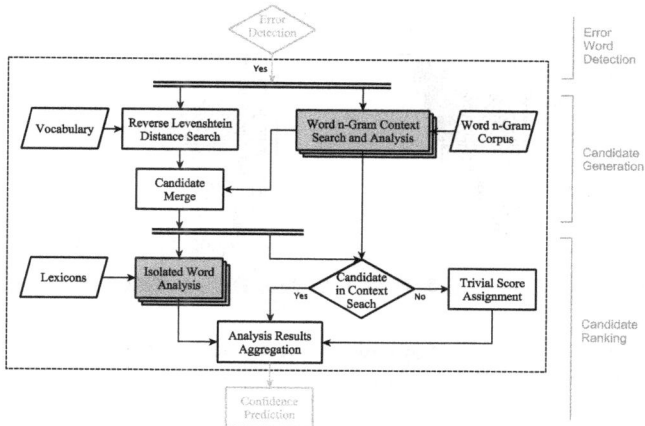

Figure 2: Process flowchart of the computational reduced candidate generation and linguistic analysis. Gray blocks are able to be processed in batch mode.

search each cluster in a bounded corpus region containing records with the same leading words.

To further reduce expensive search operations in a web-scale 5-gram corpus, we modify the processing workflow of candidate generation and linguistics analysis to reduce computation as illustrated in Fig. 2. Since contextual analysis leverages frequency statistics in 5-gram corpus, a candidate receives nontrivial analytics score from a context feature only if it is generated from the 5-gram corpus and frequency statistics used for analyzing such candidate can be retrieved during search. Thus, we compute contextual features for candidates that are generated from the same feature and assign trivial contextual analytics scores for the rest candidates.

4 EVALUATION

We evaluate the system on an OCR text generated by Tesseract[4] from a book titled "Birds of Great Britain and Ireland, Vol. 2" [1]. This dataset contains listed OCR-generated errors along with the ground truth and OCR text for benchmark testing.[5] We investigate the following questions:

- How capable is each linguistic evaluation of distinguishing the intended correction within the top suggestions? How differently does each linguistic contribute to the candidate generation?

- How much can feature-based prediction optimize an automatic candidate selection?

4.1 Applied Linguistic Corpora

We use Google Web 1T 5-gram corpus, containing word 1-gram (unigram) to 5-gram, which is generated from approximately 1 trillion word tokens that extracted from publicly accessible web pages. Words recorded in the unigram corpus are used as the system vocabulary.

We use three lexicons: (1) *Wikipedia entities* extracted from page titles in Wikipedia, (2) *domain-specific glossaries* containing rare

---

[4]https://github.com/tesseract-ocr/tesseract
[5]https://github.com/jmei91/MiBio-OCR-dataset

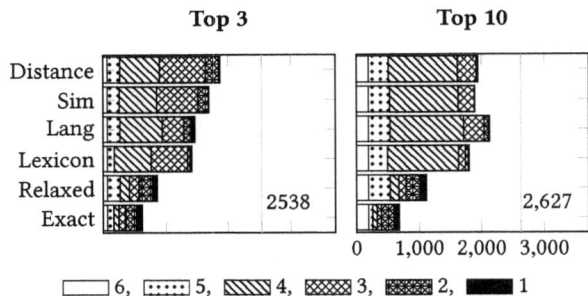

Figure 3: The coverage and distinctiveness of the linguistic features in locating the ground truth corrections.

terms in different domains, and (2) a *biodiversity terminology list* to fit the topic of the evaluation data.

4.2 Candidate Suggestion Evaluation

We evaluate the contribution of different linguistic evaluations on candidates generation. Given the top 10 candidates from each linguistic evaluation, Fig. 3 shows the number of intended corrections located by each evaluation. The distinctiveness levels of the discovered corrections are represented in colors, where the darker bar indicates the corresponding portion of candidates that are top-ranked in fewer features and vice versa. It shows that the lexical analysis using edit distance is the most effective way of identifying the intended correction, given the fact that a large portion of OCR errors are orthographically similar to their correction. The correction coverage can be further improved with other evaluation measures involved, where some corrections are uniquely suggested from word popularity analysis and contextual analysis. While the top candidates suggested from contextual analysis have limited correction coverage, they are able to find corrections that are uncommon and orthographically dissimilar, and thus important for improving the overall correction coverage.

We compare candidate generation with Aspell version 0.60.7. Aspell is an open-source error correction software preinstalled in Linux distributions. Although Aspell contains a comprehensive dictionary, it suggests candidates only within a limited Damerau-Levenshtein distance and thus only a small fraction of corrections, which are orthographically similar to the errors, are able to be find.

4.3 Candidate Ranking Evaluation

Our system in average generates more than 42,000 candidates for each error, given distance threshold 3 in reverse Levenshtein search and one mismatching word in n-gram context search. The intended corrections should be ranked close to the top. We evaluate the prediction accuracy given a ranked candidate list. Experimentally, we apply an AdaBoost.R2 [2] regressor on top of decision trees with the linear loss function. Table 2 shows that there are 61.05% of the OCR error can be corrected in a fully automatic manner. Involving user interaction for selection among top 10 candidates, the system accuracy can be improved to 76.62%, which is significantly higher than the accuracy from interactive mode supported by Aspell.

Table 2: Candidate ranking performance evaluation.

System	Proposed System				Aspell
P@n	1	3	5	10	
Precision	0.6105	0.7145	0.7378	0.7662	0.2583
Δ		+0.1040	+0.0233	+0.0284	

5 CONCLUSION

We have introduced an OCR post-processing system for automatically correcting OCR-generated errors in the text. Web-scale corpora are applied to candidate generation and linguistic analysis for each feature. By integrating different linguistic analysis results in a regression process, our system is able to select and rank high-quality candidates. Evaluated on an OCR-generated natural history book, our system can correct 61.5% of the errors in a fully automatic manner and 76.62% by interactive selection from among the top 10 candidates.

REFERENCES

[1] Arthur G. Butler, William Frohawk, Frederick, and H. GrÃŭnvold. 1907. *Birds of Great Britain and Ireland. by Arthur G. Butler*. Vol. 2. Hull; Brumby & Clarke. 341 pages. http://www.biodiversitylibrary.org/item/35947#page/13/mode/1up

[2] Yoav Freund and Robert E Schapire. 1997. A Decision-Theoretic Generalization of On-Line Learning and an Application to Boosting. *J. Comput. Syst. Sci.* 55, 1 (08 1997), 119–139. https://doi.org/10.1006/jcss.1997.1504

[3] Aminul Islam and Diana Inkpen. 2009. Real-word Spelling Correction Using Google Web 1Tn-gram Data Set. In *Proceedings of the 18th ACM Conference on Information and Knowledge Management (CIKM '09)*. ACM, New York, NY, USA, 1689–1692. https://doi.org/10.1145/1645953.1646205

[4] I. Kissos and N. Dershowitz. 2016. OCR Error Correction Using Character Correction and Feature-Based Word Classification. In *2016 12th IAPR Workshop on Document Analysis Systems (DAS)*. 198–203. https://doi.org/10.1109/DAS.2016.44

[5] Shmuel T Klein, M Ben-Nissan, and M Kopel. 2002. A voting system for automatic OCR correction. (August 2002).

[6] Karen Kukich. 1992. Techniques for Automatically Correcting Words in Text. *ACM Comput. Surv.* 24, 4 (12 1992), 377–439. https://doi.org/10.1145/146370.146380

[7] William B. Lund and Eric K. Ringger. 2009. Improving Optical Character Recognition Through Efficient Multiple System Alignment. In *Proceedings of the 9th ACM/IEEE-CS Joint Conference on Digital Libraries (JCDL '09)*. ACM, New York, NY, USA, 231–240. https://doi.org/10.1145/1555400.1555437

[8] William B. Lund, Eric K. Ringger, and Daniel D. Walker. 2013. How well does multiple OCR error correction generalize?. In *Proc. SPIE*, Vol. 9021. 90210A–90210A–13. https://doi.org/10.1117/12.2042502

[9] W. B. Lund, D. D. Walker, and E. K. Ringger. 2011. Progressive Alignment and Discriminative Error Correction for Multiple OCR Engines. In *2011 International Conference on Document Analysis and Recognition*. 764–768. https://doi.org/10.1109/ICDAR.2011.303

[10] Jie Mei, Aminul Islam, Yajing Wu, Abidalrahman Moh'd, and Evangelos E. Milios. 2016. Statistical Learning for OCR Text Correction. *CoRR* abs/1611.06950 (2016). http://arxiv.org/abs/1611.06950

[11] GÃijnter MÃijhlberger, Johannes Zelger, and David Sagmeister. 2014. User-driven Correction of OCR Errors: Combining Crowdsourcing and Information Retrieval Technology. In *Proceedings of the First International Conference on Digital Access to Textual Cultural Heritage (DATeCH '14)*. ACM, New York, NY, USA, 53–56. https://doi.org/10.1145/2595188.2595212

[12] Ray Smith. 2007. An Overview of the Tesseract OCR Engine. In *Ninth International Conference on Document Analysis and Recognition (ICDAR 2007)*, Vol. 2. 629–633. https://doi.org/10.1109/ICDAR.2007.4376991

[13] Kazem Taghva, Julie Borsack, and Allen Condit. 1994. Expert system for automatically correcting OCR output. *Proc. SPIE* 2181, 270–278. https://doi.org/10.1117/12.171114

[14] Kazem Taghva and Eric Stofsky. 2001. OCRSpell: an interactive spelling correction system for OCR errors in text. *International Journal on Document Analysis and Recognition* 3, 3 (2001), 125–137. https://doi.org/10.1007/PL00013558

[15] George Kingsley Zipf. 1935. The psycho-biology of language. (1935).

qqmbr and indentml: Extensible Mathematical Publishing for Web and Paper

Ilya V. Schurov

National Research University Higher School of Economics

Myasnitskaya, 20, 301k

Moscow, Russia 101000

ilya@schurov.com

ABSTRACT

We present qqmbr, novel publishing system aimed at preparation of high-quality mathematical publications. One source can be converted to a single interactive webpage, multi-page website or PDF (via LaTeX). The markup language behind qqmbr entitled indentml is designed to be both human-readable and machine-readable (easily parsable). It is possible to extend basic qqmbr markup with custom tags that enrich its semantics and build plugins and applications that query qqmbr documents, extract information from them and process it in an arbitrary way without much effort.

CCS CONCEPTS

• **Information systems** → *Document structure*; • **Software and its engineering** → *Markup languages*; • **Human-centered computing** → *Collaborative and social computing systems and tools*;

KEYWORDS

markup languages, XML, LaTeX

1 INTRODUCTION

Today in 2017 most of mathematical papers and books are still prepared in LaTeX and published either in print form or as PDF files available via the Internet. For example, the best-known service of mathematical e-prints arXiv.org hosts PostScript and PDF versions of submitted papers as well as their LaTeX sources. It looks like the obvious anachronism to stick with a format aimed at the paper at the age of web technologies that provide much richer media. In our opinion, this situation is due to lack of technologies that allow easy preparing mathematical content suitable for web-publication.

The first problem here is mathematical equations typesetting in the Web. We have to mention MathML as a language that aimed to deal with it. However, MathML code is too verbose, and it is practically impossible to type MathML manually, so one has to use some other tools to produce MathML code. Also, browser support of MathML is still not so good.

A more successful approach here is presented by JavaScript libraries MathJax and KaTeX [1, 2] that process HTML document on the client side, look for LaTeX-formatted formulas inside and typeset them using MathML, HTML+CSS or SVG. They work pretty well. However, MathJax and KaTeX deal only with individual equations and cannot convert the whole paper or book to a webpage.

One way to overcome this issue is to create a full-featured converter from LaTeX documents to HTML. There are several efforts on developing such a converter (LaTeX2HTML, TtH, TeX4ht and others), but they all are only partially successful. The problem is that TeX markup is very rich and customizable, so it is hard to parse it with anything different from TeX itself.

A promising tool in this field is plasTeX [14] which is written in Python and tries to parse (some subset of) LaTeX to programmatically-accessible DOM that can be rendered to other formats (currently, HTML is supported). This approach is similar to the presented in this paper. The main disadvantage comparing to our approach is the complexity of LaTeX markup that leads to possible parsing bugs (one can find some of them on GitHub issue page of the project). We also propose less verbose markup that makes it easier to type and read the source code of documents, especially useful to embed complex data structures into the source (see e.g. quizzes example below).

Another approach is to adopt different markup language for mathematical writings while keeping formulas in LaTeX markup. The best-known attempts use Markdown or similar markup languages and extend it to provide LaTeX-like features: references, bibliography, environments and so on. [3–5, 8]. The problem here is a limited extensibility of Markdown-like markups: it was designed to be simple and human-readable as much as possible and is not very naturally extensible. It is possible to include custom blocks or invent new syntax to add new features, but the resulting syntax most likely will be not as elegant and concise as LaTeX's. Also parsing and post-processing of Markdown requires much effort that limits the possibility of developing new extensions.

The third approach is to use some subset of HTML or another XML-like language that can be easily parsed and converted to HTML with CSS styling [6, 7]. Such languages are easily extensible (as the name suggests) but rather verbose. Verbosity makes them unsuitable for manual writing by human beings.

We present here a novel approach that takes the best from all the worlds. First we present a new markup meta-language called *indentml* [10] that is similar to XML from a logical point of view, extensible and easily parsable but much less verbose. The main feature of *indentml* is an extensive usage of indents to mark the beginning and ending of a block (tag content), just like it is done in Python (and YAML). Then we construct *indentml dialect* called *qqmath* which is based on *indentml* and used to prepare scientific papers and books. This language looks very similar to LaTeX. Finally, we describe publishing platform *qqmbr* [13] that allows one to convert qqmath source to an interactive website. All the software we are presenting is free and open source, available under MIT license.

2 METALANGUAGE INDENTML

Loosly speaking, *indentml* is indent-based XML without attributes.

2.1 Document model

From a logical point of view, document in *indentml* is a representation of a tree which internal nodes are tags and leaves are tags or strings. Specifically, every tag's content is ordered list of strings and tags. This makes *indentml* XML-compatible from logical point of view.

To define *indentml dialect* one have to specify set of allowed tags.

Parsing is a translation from *indentml* dialect markup to internal tree representation. When a document is parsed, one can process this tree with any appropriate programming tools. Specifically, one can use one of the possible *formatters* to convert the internal representation to some new format. For the sake of the paper, parsed document will be represented as attribute-free XML.

2.2 Markup rationale

Now let us discuss the markup itself. We begin with some rationale behind our design decisions.

Analysing the structure of a typical document in LaTeX (like scientific paper), one can see that it mainly consists of two types of elements: large block of text (for example, environments like {theorem}) and inline syntax (for example, emphasized text with \emph{...} or internal references with \ref{...}. Inline syntax have to allow command to accept several arguments, like in \href{<url>}{<description>}. (We are not interested in the syntax that represents mathematical equations itself as we are going to use Mathjax to typeset them.)

The usual way to create a block is to specify its beginning and ending by some markers. In LaTeX this is usually done with \begin{...}-\end{...} commands, in XML opening and closing tags are used, in a programming language like C opening and closing curve brackets are used and so on. Blocks can be nested, and it is often a style recommendation to visually emphasize them with the increased indent. In Python, an indent is the only way to specify the block. This approach makes the code more clear and concise: one doesn't have to write any command to close the block. A similar approach is used for example in YAML. We found it is very convenient and decided to use indents as the way to declare a block.

We also need some kind of inline syntax as well that we mostly borrow from LaTeX, but tweak a little bit to fit our tree model.

Two types of tags exist in markup: block tags and inline tags. They are equivalent in the resulting tree. However, sets of allowed block tags and inline tags can be different in the definition of dialect.

2.3 Block tags

Block tags are typed at the beginning of the line, possibly after several spaces that mark *indent of a tag*. Block tag starts with *tag beginning character* (by default it is backslash \) and ends with the whitespace or newline character. All the lines below the block tag which indent is greater than tag's indent are appended to the tag. The tag is closed on dedent. E.g.

```
\tag
    Hello
    \othertag
        I'm indentml
    How are you?
I'm fine
```

will be translated into the following XML tree:

```
<_root><tag>Hello
<othertag>I'm indentml
</othertag>How are you?
</tag>I'm fine</_root>
```

The *rest of a line* where block tag begins will be attached to that tag either, but it is handled a bit differently if it contains other valid block tags or a *separator character* (by default it is pipe |). Every block tag begins a new line. For example:

```
\image \src http://example.com \width 100%
    Some image
```

Is equivalent to

```
\image
    \src
        http://example.com
    \width
        100%
    Some image
```

This syntax allows to add subtags in a compact way and use them as a replacement for attributes.

If *separator character* presented, the line is splitted by this character and every part is attached to its own _item tag. For example:

```
\a http://example.com | some example
```

Is translated to

```
\a
    \_item
        http://example.com
    \_item
        some example
```

This allows one to create short lists easily.

2.4 Inline tags

Inline tags are started with tag beginning character and ended by bracket: { or [. Type of a bracket affects the processing. *Tag content* is everything between its opening bracket and the corresponding closing bracket. It can spread over several lines — in this case, all physical lines are joined into one logical line (i.e. all linebreaks are treated as if there were escaped).

The content of the inline tag with square brackets is processed just like the first line of a block tag.

For example:

```
Take a look
at \a[example\href http://example.com], okay?
```

Is equivalent to

```
Take a look
at
\a example \href http://example.com
, okay?
```

One can use pipe to separate "arguments" of a tag, so the following short syntax is possible:

```
Look at \a[example|http://example.com].
```

In this case the formatter should use the content of the corresponding _item pseudo-tags added by the parser.

The content of inline tag with curve brackets is attached to the corresponding tag as is, without any special processing.

3 QQMATH AND QQMBR

3.1 qqmath

qqmath is LaTeX-like *indentml*-based language used to write mathematical documents and aimed at web representation as the main target. Its features include:

- Basic text structure
  - several levels of headers,
  - theorem-like environments (theorem, lemma, etc.),
  - enumerated and itemized lists,
  - inline emphatization.
- References by labels for environments, sections, and equations.
- Several environments for display formulas (equation, align).
- Quizzes.
- Programmatically generated images embedding (using matplotlib and plotly).

Example source code:

```
\h1 Exponent of complex number \label s:ex
\theorem \label thm:1
    Let $x$ be a real number. Then
    \equation \label eq:main
        e^{ix} = \cos x+i\sin x.
\proof
    Let us recall series for exponent,
    sine and cosine and compare them
    with \ref{eq:main}.
```

See Fig. 1 for rendered output.

Consider also the following example of *quiz* element. It demonstrates the extensibility of the markup: one can naturally embed arbitrary structured information into the document in XML-style manner, see Fig. 2 for rendered output.

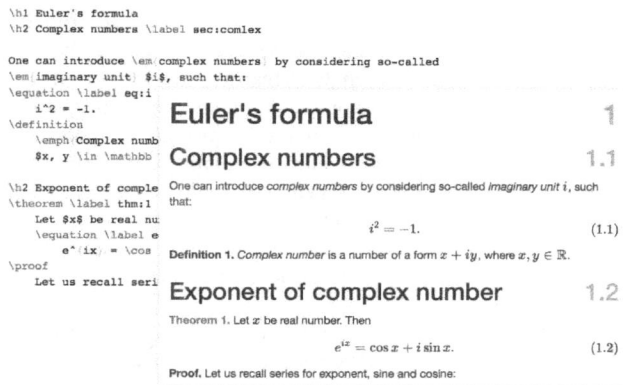

Figure 1: Screenshot of *mathbook* source code and rendered HTML page.

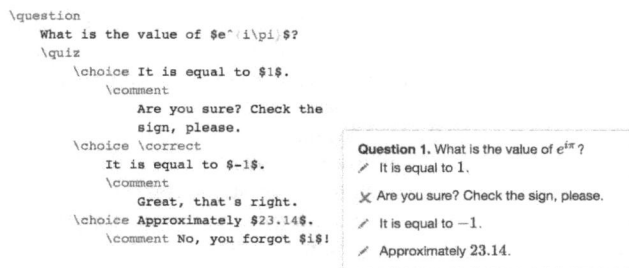

Figure 2: quiz source code and output: comments are shown after a click on a particular answer.

```
\question
    What is the value of $e^{i\pi}$?
    \quiz
        \choice It is equal to $1$.
            \comment
                Are you sure? Check the
                sign, please.
        \choice \correct
            It is equal to $-1$.
            \comment
                Great, that's right.
        \choice Approximately $23.14$.
            \comment No, you forgot $i$!
```

3.2 qqmbr

qqmbr is a publishing platform that converts *qqmath* source to a website. All the formulas are processed with MathJax either on client-side or on server-side. In the latter case, MathJax is run using Node.js (with Mathjax-node package) as a post-processing step.

It is possible to convert every chapter (level-1 section) of the source to its own webpage. Cross-chapter references are treated correctly. All elements that are internally-referenceable (sections, theorems and so on) with labels are also externally-referenceable with permanent URLs: *qqmbr* convert label to HTML id property of the corresponding element and provide appropriate anchors.

Also, some specific web-enabled features are supported. For example, when a user hovers pointer on a reference to an equation, small pop-up window with this equation appears. This allows one to save time on clicking and scrolling back-and-forth to recall the equation. Also, a similar feature is enabled for definitions of special terms, that can be especially useful for textbooks.

Quizzes are displayed with hidden answers. The reader has to click on the option in a quiz to check if this answer is correct or not.

The author can embed pictures that are drawn with Python code using libraries `matplotlib` and `Plotly`. In the latter case, the resulting images can be interactive — for example, rotatable 3D-images are supported. The source code that draws the pictures can be shown, collapsed by default or hidden.

4 APPLICATIONS

We consider *indentml* as a general-purpose metalanguage (like XML, JSON or YAML) that can be used in various settings beyond scientific publishing. As an example, we used it to create a website that compares Python and JavaScript syntax [12].

The author prepared a book in Differential Equations with *qqmbr* exclusively [9]. It consists now of 14 chapters, the overall size of the sources is about 300K characters. It uses all the features of *qqmbr* mentioned above. Every chapter is hosted as a separate static HTML page, automatically generated from the *qqmath* sources.

The sources are hosted on GitHub and the readers can suggest fixes using GitHub's pull request system. The author's students fixed typos in this way without any prior knowledge of *qqmath* syntax.

Also see [11] for interactive demonstration of *qqmath* features.

5 FURTHER DEVELOPMENT

5.1 indentml meet XML

Currently one has to write Python code to process *indentml* as the parser is written in Python. An alternative is to convert *indentml* to a proper XML and then use any XML-aware tool (i.e. XSLT) for validations and transformations. Basic XML formatter (i.e. converter from *indentml* to XML) is implemented already. However, lack of attributes in *indentml* can make it harder to process the resulting attribute-free XML with usual tools. The possible approach here is to develop more sophisticated XML formatters that can use the schema of a particular dialect and produce more convenient XML files. For example, in *qqmath* dialect we can specify that tag \equation has attribute \label and then convert

```
\equation \label eq:2
    x^2 + y^2
```

into the following XML:

```
<equation label="eq:2">
    x^2 + y^2
</equation>
```

5.2 Extension of qqmbr

Many things can be done by extending *qqmbr*. One can introduce custom tags with custom semantics, then write some code that uses new tags, for example, to draw some widgets on the rendered webpage. This can be done by extending existing *qqmbr* code in Python.

Also, a user can query the document programmatically. For example, one can introduce tags for problems and their solutions. Then by default, all the solutions can be hidden from the reader. The author can write a very simple program that extracts all the problems with their solutions from the document and prepare new document from them that can be given to the teacher.

Due to ease of parsing it is easy to write formatters that use output formats different from HTML. Currently, a formatter that produces LaTeX output is under development.

6 CONCLUSION

We presented *qqmbr* — *indentml*-based publishing system that fills the gap between LaTeX, Markdown, and XML in scientific publishing. It benefits from clean, concise and easily parsable syntax that resembles both LaTeX and XML. The features include basic mathematical formatting capabilities as well as some unique options that were made available by extensive use of modern web technologies.

All the software presented is free and open source (MIT licensed). It is written in Python (with some elements of JavaScript) and easily extensible.

ACKNOWLEDGMENTS

The author is grateful to the anonymous referees for valuable comments and references.

REFERENCES

[1] Davide Cervone, Volker Sorge, Christian Lawson-Perfect, and Peter Krautzberger. *MathJax: A Javascript Library for Rendering Mathematics*. http://http://mathjax.org.
[2] Emily Eisenberg and Ben Alpert. *KaTeX: The fastest math typesetting library for the web*. https://khan.github.io/KaTeX/.
[3] Hans Petter Langtangen. *doconce: Lightweight markup language*. http://hplgit.github.io/doconce/doc/web/index.html.
[4] Daan Leijen. 2016. Rendering Mathematics for the Web Using Madoko. In *Proceedings of the 2016 ACM Symposium on Document Engineering (DocEng '16)*. ACM, New York, NY, USA, 111–114. https://doi.org/10.1145/2960811.2967168
[5] Tim T.Y. Lin. *ScholarlyMarkdown Project*. http://scholarlymarkdown.com.
[6] Thomas Park. *PubCSS: Formatting Academic Publications in HTML and CSS*. http://thomaspark.co/2015/01/pubcss-formatting-academic-publications-in-html-css/.
[7] Silvio Peroni, Francesco Osborne, Angelo Di Iorio, Andrea Giovanni Nuzzolese, Francesco Poggi, Fabio Vitali, and Enrico Motta. *Research Articles in Simplified HTML: a Web-first format for HTML-based scholarly articles*. https://w3id.org/people/essepuntato/papers/rash-peerj2016.html.
[8] RStudio Inc. *R Markdown*. RStudio Inc. http://rmarkdown.rstudio.com.
[9] Ilya V. Schurov. *Differential equations*. http://math-info.hse.ru/odebook/.
[10] Ilya V. Schurov. *indentml: indent-based general-purpose tree-like language*. https://github.com/ischurov/indentml.
[11] Ilya V. Schurov. *Live qqmath example*. http://math-info.hse.ru/qqmathpreview/.
[12] Ilya V. Schurov. *Python v. JS*. https://github.com/ischurov/pythonvjs.
[13] Ilya V. Schurov. *qqmbr: mathematical layout for web and paper*. https://github.com/ischurov/qqmbr.
[14] Kevin D. Smith. *plasTeX — A Python Framework for Processing LaTeX Documents*. http://tiarno.github.io/plastex/.

The Common Fold: Utilizing the Four-Fold to Dewarp Printed Documents from a Single Image

Sagnik Das, Gaurav Mishra, Akshay Sudharshana, Roy Shilkrot
Stony Brook University, New York, USA
{sadas,gamishra,ayedageresud,roys}@cs.stonybrook.edu

ABSTRACT

Handheld cameras are currently the device of choice for performing document digitization, due to their convenience, ubiquity and high performance at low cost. Software methods process a captured image, to rectify distortions and reconstruct the original document. Existing methods struggle to reconstruct a flattened version given a single image of a document distorted by folding. We propose a novel non-parametric page dewarping approach from a single image based on deep learning to identify creases due to folds on the paper. Our method then performs a 2D boundary method based on polynomial regression, and a Coons patch, to get a flattened reconstruction. We found our method improves OCR word accuracy by more than 2.5 times when compared to the original distorted image.

CCS CONCEPTS

•Computing methodologies → Reconstruction; •Applied computing → Document scanning;

KEYWORDS

Folded Document Dewarping, Document Reconstruction, Document Image Processing

1 INTRODUCTION

Digitization of documents has become a common task nowadays to make printed documents electronically accessible. Traditionally this was done using flatbed scanners. With the proliferation of hand-held devices equipped with high-resolution cameras, scanning is now performed in far less structured environments and settings. In many cases paper documents are scanned after being folded or warped, exhibiting non-uniform geometric deformation that renders digitization challenging and severely cripples OCR performance. These non-uniform complex deformations comprise of distortion from the camera's optics and skewing due to non-orthogonal camera axis to the plane. The prime goal in dewarping folded scanned documents from handheld cameras is therefore to estimate the 3D shape of the warped paper and flatten it without adding more noise or distortion. This requires using more hardware or complex computation, for example structured light [20], multiple

views of the document [29] or estimating shape from shading [8]. Imposing a parametric model requires manual tuning of the parameters and restrictive assumptions on the input, while capitalizing on features of the input to make single-image dewarping possible.

In this paper, we propose a non-parametric deep learning based page dewarping approach utilizing the common half fold: two folds in half, horizontally then vertically or vice versa. Our novel technique addresses the document dewarping problem using a convolutional neural network (CNN) combined with piecewise polynomial regression. CNNs are extremely powerful and recently have been successful in solving difficult computer vision problems. We first treat the problem as a semantic segmentation task and use fully CNN [17] to learn the visual appearance of folding (i.e. creases). Learning is performed on a large synthetic yet realistic image dataset created using the Blender [1] ray-tracing engine. Given the creases, we divide the paper to four quadrants, and fit piecewise polynomials along the edges to approximate their shape. Finally it is flattened by mapping each point to a corresponding quadrilateral employing a Coons-patch[7].

The contributions of our work are: (i) a novel CNN-based folded paper segmentation technique utilizing a large synthetic dataset, (ii) a rectification method utilizing Coons-patch and piecewise polynomial regression. In the following section we present a literature survey on the topic of document image dewarping. The rest of the paper discusses the details of our proposed method, its preliminary results and its evaluation.

2 RELATED WORK

Many existing approaches address digital rectification of folded, deformed and curved documents, mostly in systems that require automatic OCR capability. Dewarping is majorly approached in four ways: (i) Shape from Shading (SfS), (ii) shape from boundary, (iii) shape from 3D reconstruction and (iv) shape from text lines. See Table 1 for a concise compilation of the related methods.

Shape from Shading. Initially proposed by Wada et al. [27], this method performs photometric reconstruction of the surface utilizing the variable shade it receives from a directional light source. Courteille et al. [8], Zhang et al. [30] extended [27] with virtual flattening using digital cameras instead of scanners.

Shape from boundary. This method involves finding and using the edges of the paper to estimate its deformation, assuming evident folding, no self-occlusions and the paper can be well segmented from the background. Brown et al. [5] proposed a single-image reconstruction method, not unlike our proposed method, that uses the boundary to cope with page-curl and harsh folding while rectifying with a Coons-patch.

Shape from text lines. This method approaches reconstruction by assuming the document mostly contains distinguishable printed characters arranged in lines, and then fitting parametric curves to

DocEng '17, September 4–7, 2017, Valletta, Malta.
© 2017 Copyright held by the owner/author(s). Publication rights licensed to ACM.
978-1-4503-4689-4/17/09...$15.00
DOI: https://doi.org/10.1145/3103010.3121030

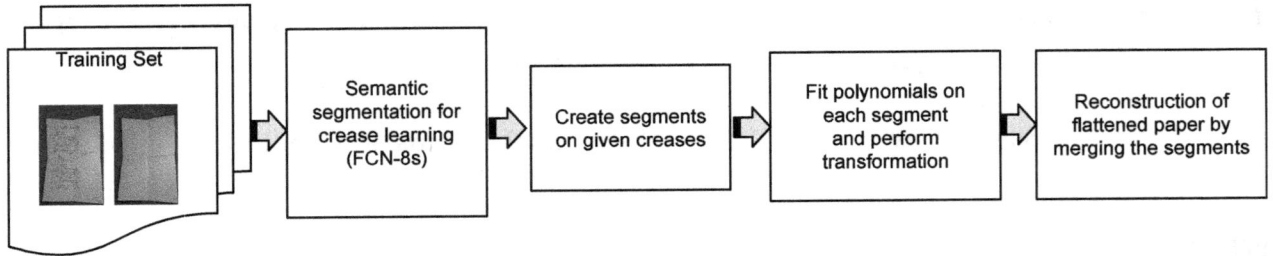

Figure 1: Proposed methodology pipeline

Table 1: Recent works on warped paper rectification, their reconstruction method ("Method"), type of fold they address ("Fold") and the rectification method ("Rect.").

Work	Year	Method	Fold	Rect.
Wada et al. [27]	1997	SfS	Curl	Mesh
Courteille et al. [8]	2007	SfS	Curl	Mesh
Zhang et al. [30], [23], [32]	2009	SfS	Curl	Mesh
Brown and Tsoi [5]	2006	Boundary	Any	Coons
He et al. [12]	2013	Boundary	Curl	
Cao et al. [6]	2003	Cylinder	Curl	Direct
Ezaki et al. [10]	2005	Line-fit	Curl	Spline
Ulges et al. [26]	2005	Line-fit	Curl	Local
Lu et al. [18]	2006	Line-fit	Curl	Local
Fu et al. [11]	2007	Line-fit	Curl	Spline
Stamatopoulos et al. [22]	2011	Line-fit	Curl	Spline
Tian et al. [24]	2011	Line-fit	Curl	Mesh
Meng et al. [19]	2012	Line-fit	Curl	Mesh
Liu et al. [16]	2015	Line-fit	Curl	Spline
Kim et al. [14]	2015	Line-fit	Curl	
Yamashita et al. [28]	2004	Multiview	Any	Mesh
Tsoi and Brown [25]	2007	Multiview	Any	Mesh
Koo et al. [15]	2009	Multiview	Curl	
You et al. [29]	2017	Multiview	Any	Mesh
Pilu [21]	2001	S-L	Curl	Mesh
Brown et al. [3], [4], [2]	2005	S-L	Any	Mesh
Zhang et al. [31]	2008	S-L	Any	Mesh
Meng et al. [20]	2014	S-L	Curl	Spline

them. The methods differ in the way they rectify, some utilize the fitted splines to transform to a regular grid [10, 11, 16, 22], while others flatten the local rectangle of the warped word [18, 26] or re-projecting a fitted mesh to a flat quad [19, 24].

Shape from 3D reconstruction. To handle arbitrarily warped documents several works employed specialized hardware or multiple views of the paper to obtain a photometric 3D model, and then apply a flattening mechanism. Before the advent of consumer-grade range cameras, researchers used visible-light projector-camera systems [3, 4, 21, 31] or a specialized laser-plane [20] to create a structured light (S-L) reconstruction. Recently more interest is given to 3D reconstruction from multiple images by way of triangulation, since taking more images with a mobile device is simple and highly available [15, 25, 28, 29]

3 DEWARPING SYSTEM DESCRIPTION

Our proposed dewarping mechanism utilizes the parameters of a structured deformation of the document – a standard way of

folding. It has no dependencies on any calibrated hardware as in [4, 31] or the content of the document as in [16]. Moreover, in contrast to some recent methods of multiview 3D reconstruction [25, 29], our method works on a single image input, which makes it highly appealing to use with handheld devices. Our method relies on crease detection using a CNN and dividing the paper into smaller segments, which we assume are relatively flat and therefore can be flattened with a boundary method. Finally, we stitch all the parts together using image matching and blending to achieve the final output. Although in this work we make the assumption that the paper is folded in a specific way (double half fold), our pipeline is generic and can handle other arbitrary folding with little change to the algorithm.

3.1 Dataset Creation

We have created a synthetic realistic dataset using Blender [1], of more than 12,000 ground-truth labeled images. Utilizing Blender's python scripting environment we randomize the parameters of a 3D model of a double half folded paper. We used ray-tracing to render the model with different lighting and camera angles to generate our training and test images. Since all the geometry is within our control, we are able to create a precise ground-truth image where the crease is labeled red (upcrease) and green (downcrease). A sample image pair is shown in fig. 2 (a) and (b). Later we convert ground-truth images to class label matrix to train the CNN.

3.2 Semantic segmentation for learning creases

In order to perform learning on the parameters of folding (i.e. creases) we formulate the problem as a semantic segmentation task, where non-crease pixels and crease pixels belong to different class. We fine-tune the [17] network, pre-trained on PASCAL VOC 2011 [9] FCN-8s, using our own dataset. As a preprocessing step we performed local contrast normalization (LCN) [13] to our training images. Sample output from our fine-tuned CNN is shown in fig. 2. In cases where the detected creases are not continuous our post-processing step using probabilistic Hough transform and 2D line geometry recovers a full crease. An illustrative example of our algorithm is shown in fig. 2.

3.3 Polynomial fitting on segment boundaries

After segmentation we take the crease output and divide the page into four different segments, assuming a double half fold. First, we find the boundary of the entire page by thresholding, then using the crease labeling we find the boundary of the four quadrants. We sample sparse 2D coordinates on each quadrant boundary $L = \{(x_0, y_0), \cdots, (x_n, y_n)\}$ and fit a polynomial curve c along these points, s.t. the mean square error: $\frac{1}{n} \sum_i (y_i - c(x_i))^2$ is minimal.

(a) Test image (b) Groundtruth of image (c) Detected crease (d) Imfused with groundtruth

(e) Groundtruth of image (f) Detected Crease (g) Postprocessed by Houghline transform (h) Imfused with groundtruth

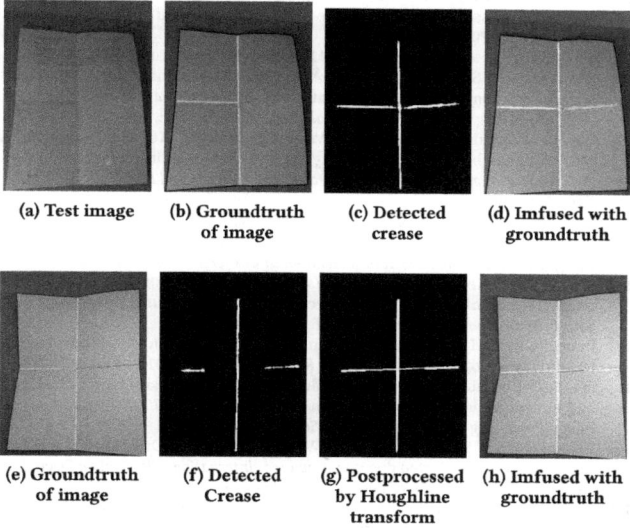

Figure 2: Creases detected by the CNN and post-processing using Hough transform and 2D line geometry

We found that regularized cubic polynomials were enough to show an acceptable fit. Given four polynomials $C = \{c_0, c_1, c_2, c_3\}$ we can find the four corner points by intersection. Then, using each polynomial's parametric equation $p_i(t) = (x(t), y(t))$ we formulate a Coon's patch [7] over all the polynomials for that segment. For an illustration of the Coons patch see fig. 3 (a).

In fig. 3 $c(u, 0)$, $c(u, 1)$, $c(0, v)$, $c(1, v)$ corresponds to the curves c_0, c_1, c_2, c_3 respectively. We map each pixel in the Coons patch to a pixel in a quadrilateral R by computing the two parameters u and v of the Coons patch: $(u, v) = (i/H, j/W)$, where H and W is the height and width of R, (i, j) is location of an interior pixel in R. Given u and v we can find out a pixel coordinate on the patch (source pixel) $C(u, v)$ by Eq. 1 which is then mapped into the known target pixel, $R(i, j)$:

$$
c(u,v) = \begin{bmatrix} (1-u) \\ u \end{bmatrix}^t \begin{bmatrix} c(0,v) \\ c(1,v) \end{bmatrix} + \begin{bmatrix} c(u,0) \\ c(u,1) \end{bmatrix}^t \begin{bmatrix} (1-v) \\ v \end{bmatrix}
$$
$$
- \begin{bmatrix} (1-u) \\ u \end{bmatrix}^t \begin{bmatrix} c(0,0) & c(0,1) \\ c(1,0) & c(1,1) \end{bmatrix} \begin{bmatrix} (1-v) \\ v \end{bmatrix} \tag{1}
$$

3.4 Merging and reconstruction

All four quadrants are merged to get the final reconstructed image after post-processing on the output. Our merging algorithm involves two major steps: (i) finding the best matching seam between segments and (ii) blending the segments using the seam match. This task is challenging since it is highly susceptible to artifacts caused by small misalignment, and thus prone to limitations. After merging,the reconstructed image has non-uniform luminance in the four quadrants. We apply the method in [25] to create a uniformly lit image. Output for these steps is illustrated in fig. 4.

4 RESULTS

Figure 4 shows examples of the final reconstruction output of our system. We performed OCR analysis using pytesserect (v0.1.7) library on the outputs. We used 20 document-images of 1200×1600

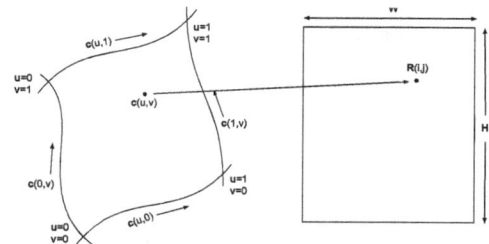

(a) Representation of Coons Patch. $c(u, v)$ represents an interior point, where $0 \le u, v \le 1$. $R(i, j)$ is an interior pixel in the mapped quadrilateral

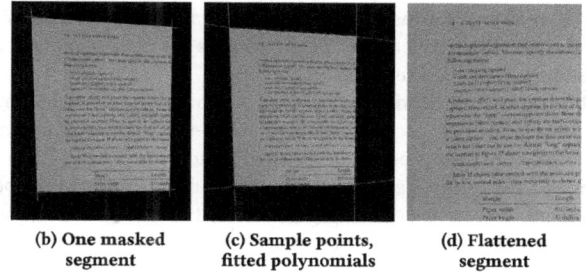

(b) One masked segment (c) Sample points, fitted polynomials (d) Flattened segment

Figure 3: Coons patch rectification.

resolution from a synthetic test set, containing a total of 3260 words. We have chosen low-resolution images to emulate camera characteristics of hand-held devices. Baseline OCR accuracy is obtained on original document images before folding. To evaluate the effectiveness of our rectification mechanism We have compared our results with original non-dewarped image and with perspective rectified image (manually done using GIMP2). Results are summarized in Table 2. See additional results in the supplementary material.

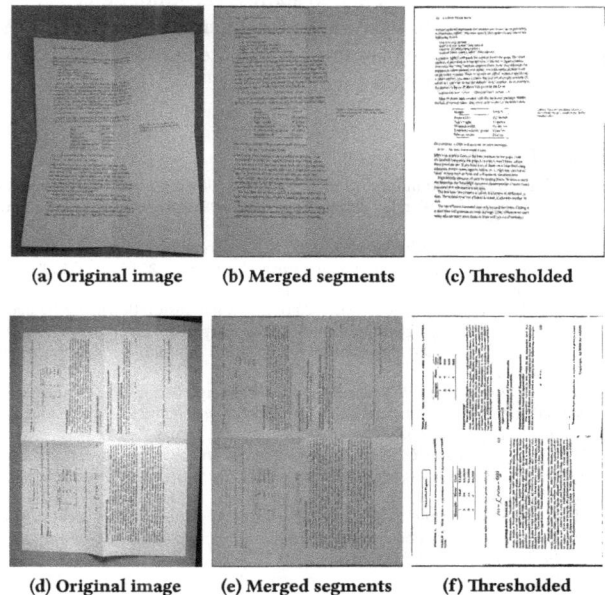

(a) Original image (b) Merged segments (c) Thresholded

(d) Original image (e) Merged segments (f) Thresholded

Figure 4: Output of Merging and Reconstruction, (a-c): Synthetic test image and (d-f): Real test image result

Table 2: OCR performance comparison of our method

Method	% Words Correct
Our method	56.44% ±14%
Perspective rectification	33.89% ±20%
No rectification	20.08% ±9%
Baseline	69.94% ±15%

5 LIMITATIONS

We identified several limiting factors of our current method:

Half-fold assumption: In this work, we focused on the half-fold rather than generalized foldings. However crease detection is scalable given a large training set and image merging is straightforward.

Crease detection: Our synthetic training set does not generalize over all real-world situations, and relies on shading variation. We found cases when one or two of the creases are not recognized at all leading to a failed reconstruction.

2D boundary method: This method is suboptimal for achieving adequate geometric rectification and under-utilizes the geometric similarity constraints between adjacent quadrants.

Segment merging: Template matching fails in finding a proper alignment in presence of non-rigid deformation. Other techniques from the image stitching domain may perform better.

6 CONCLUSION

We presented an approach to document reconstruction from a single image of a double half-folded page. Most existing methods either make different assumptions about the paper, use specialized hardware or take multiple images as input. Our approach uses a CNN and a 2D boundary reconstruction method, which is capable of running on a mobile device. We have shown that OCR performance increases significantly when compared with the original warped document.

In the future we would like to address the limitations listed in section 5 and generalize the model for different kinds of folds. As mentioned, we are also planning to evaluate our method's performance while running it on a mobile device.

REFERENCES

[1] Blender Online Community. Mon 10/24/2016. *Blender - a 3D modelling and rendering package.* Blender Foundation, Blender Institute, Amsterdam. http://www.blender.org

[2] Michael S Brown and Charles J Pisula. 2005. Conformal deskewing of non-planar documents. In *Computer Vision and Pattern Recognition, 2005. CVPR 2005. IEEE Computer Society Conference on*, Vol. 1. IEEE, 998–1004.

[3] Michael S Brown and W Brent Seales. 2001. Document restoration using 3D shape: a general deskewing algorithm for arbitrarily warped documents. In *Computer Vision, 2001. ICCV 2001. Proceedings. Eighth IEEE International Conference on*, Vol. 2. IEEE, 367–374.

[4] Michael S Brown and W Brent Seales. 2004. Image restoration of arbitrarily warped documents. *IEEE Transactions on pattern analysis and machine intelligence* 26, 10 (2004), 1295–1306.

[5] Michael S Brown and Y-C Tsoi. 2006. Geometric and shading correction for images of printed materials using boundary. *IEEE Transactions on Image Processing* 15, 6 (2006), 1544–1554.

[6] Huaigu Cao, Xiaoqing Ding, and Changsong Liu. 2003. A cylindrical surface model to rectify the bound document image. In *Computer Vision, 2003. Proceedings. Ninth IEEE International Conference on*. IEEE, 228–233.

[7] Steven A Coons. 1967. *Surfaces for computer-aided design of space forms.* Technical Report. DTIC Document.

[8] Frédéric Courteille, Alain Crouzil, Jean-Denis Durou, and Pierre Gurdjos. 2007. Shape from shading for the digitization of curved documents. *Machine Vision and Applications* 18, 5 (2007), 301–316.

[9] M. Everingham, L. Van Gool, C. K. I. Williams, J. Winn, and A. Zisserman. The PASCAL Visual Object Classes Challenge 2011 (VOC2011) Results. http://www.pascal-network.org/challenges/VOC/voc2011/workshop/index.html. (????).

[10] Hironori Ezaki, Seiichi Uchida, Akira Asano, and Hiroaki Sakoe. 2005. Dewarping of document image by global optimization. In *Document Analysis and Recognition, 2005. Proceedings. Eighth International Conference on*. IEEE, 302–306.

[11] Bin Fu, Minghui Wu, Rongfeng Li, Wenxin Li, Zhuoqun Xu, and Chunxu Yang. 2007. A model-based book dewarping method using text line detection. In *Proc. 2nd Int. Workshop on Camera Based Document Analysis and Recognition, Curitiba, Barazil.* 63–70.

[12] Yuan He, Pan Pan, Shufu Xie, Jun Sun, and Satoshi Naoi. 2013. A book dewarping system by boundary-based 3D surface reconstruction. In *Document Analysis and Recognition (ICDAR), 2013 12th International Conference on*. IEEE, 403–407.

[13] Kevin Jarrett, Koray Kavukcuoglu, Yann LeCun, et al. 2009. What is the best multi-stage architecture for object recognition?. In *Computer Vision, 2009 IEEE 12th International Conference on*. IEEE, 2146–2153.

[14] Beom Su Kim, Hyung Il Koo, and Nam Ik Cho. 2015. Document dewarping via text-line based optimization. *Pattern Recognition* 48, 11 (2015), 3600–3614.

[15] Hyung Il Koo, Jinho Kim, and Nam Ik Cho. 2009. Composition of a dewarped and enhanced document image from two view images. *IEEE Transactions on Image Processing* 18, 7 (2009), 1551–1562.

[16] Changsong Liu, Yu Zhang, Baokang Wang, and Xiaoqing Ding. 2015. Restoring camera-captured distorted document images. *International Journal on Document Analysis and Recognition (IJDAR)* 18, 2 (2015), 111–124.

[17] Jonathan Long, Evan Shelhamer, and Trevor Darrell. 2015. Fully convolutional networks for semantic segmentation. In *Proceedings of the IEEE Conference on Computer Vision and Pattern Recognition*. 3431–3440.

[18] Shijian Lu, Ben M Chen, and Chi Chung Ko. 2006. A partition approach for the restoration of camera images of planar and curled document. *Image and Vision Computing* 24, 8 (2006), 837–848.

[19] Gaofeng Meng, Chunhong Pan, Shiming Xiang, and Jiangyong Duan. 2012. Metric rectification of curved document images. *IEEE transactions on pattern analysis and machine intelligence* 34, 4 (2012), 707–722.

[20] Gaofeng Meng, Ying Wang, Shenquan Qu, Shiming Xiang, and Chunhong Pan. 2014. Active flattening of curved document images via two structured beams. In *Proceedings of the IEEE Conference on Computer Vision and Pattern Recognition*. 3890–3897.

[21] Maurizio Pilu. 2001. Undoing page curl distortion using applicable surfaces. In *Image Processing, 2001. Proceedings. 2001 International Conference on*, Vol. 1. IEEE, 237–240.

[22] Nikolaos Stamatopoulos, Basilis Gatos, Ioannis Pratikakis, and Stavros J Perantonis. 2011. Goal-oriented rectification of camera-based document images. *IEEE Transactions on Image Processing* 20, 4 (2011), 910–920.

[23] Chew Lim Tan, Li Zhang, Zheng Zhang, and Tao Xia. 2006. Restoring warped document images through 3d shape modeling. *IEEE Transactions on Pattern Analysis and Machine Intelligence* 28, 2 (2006), 195–208.

[24] Yuandong Tian and Srinivasa G Narasimhan. 2011. Rectification and 3D reconstruction of curved document images. In *Computer Vision and Pattern Recognition (CVPR), 2011 IEEE Conference on*. IEEE, 377–384.

[25] Yau-Chat Tsoi and Michael S Brown. 2007. Multi-view document rectification using boundary. In *Computer Vision and Pattern Recognition, 2007. CVPR'07. IEEE Conference on*. IEEE, 1–8.

[26] Adrian Ulges, Christoph H Lampert, and Thomas M Breuel. 2005. Document image dewarping using robust estimation of curled text lines. In *Document Analysis and Recognition, 2005. Proceedings. Eighth International Conference on*. IEEE, 1001–1005.

[27] Toshikazu Wada, Hiroyuki Ukida, and Takashi Matsuyama. 1997. Shape from Shading with Interreflections Under a Proximal Light Source: Distortion-Free Copying of an Unfolded Book. *Int. J. Comput. Vision* 24, 2 (Sept. 1997), 125–135. https://doi.org/10.1023/A:1007906904009

[28] Atsushi Yamashita, Atsushi Kawarago, Toru Kaneko, and Kenjiro T Miura. 2004. Shape reconstruction and image restoration for non-flat surfaces of documents with a stereo vision system. In *Pattern Recognition, 2004. ICPR 2004. Proceedings of the 17th International Conference on*, Vol. 1. IEEE, 482–485.

[29] Shaodi You, Yasuyuki Matsushita, Sudipta Sinha, Yusuke Bou, and Katsushi Ikeuchi. 2017. Multiview Rectification of Folded Documents. *IEEE Transactions on Pattern Analysis and Machine Intelligence* (2017).

[30] Li Zhang, Andy M Yip, Michael S Brown, and Chew Lim Tan. 2009. A unified framework for document restoration using inpainting and shape-from-shading. *Pattern Recognition* 42, 11 (2009), 2961–2978.

[31] Li Zhang, Yu Zhang, and Chew Tan. 2008. An improved physically-based method for geometric restoration of distorted document images. *IEEE Transactions on Pattern Analysis and Machine Intelligence* 30, 4 (2008), 728–734.

[32] Zheng Zhang, CL Lim, and Liying Fan. 2004. Estimation of 3D shape of warped document surface for image restoration. In *Pattern Recognition, 2004. ICPR 2004. Proceedings of the 17th International Conference on*, Vol. 1. IEEE, 486–489.

Improving Version-Aware Word Documents

Alexandre Azevedo Filho
University of Wisconsin-Milwaukee
Department of EECS
Milwaukee, WI 53201-0784
valenca2@uwm.edu

Ethan V. Munson
University of Wisconsin-Milwaukee
Department of EECS
Milwaukee, WI 53201-0784
munson@uwm.edu

Cheng Thao
Concordia University, St. Paul
Department of Mathematics &
Computer Science
St. Paul, MN 55104-5494
cthao@csp.edu

ABSTRACT

Coakley *et al.* described how they developed Version Aware Word Documents, which is an enhanced document representation that includes a detailed version history that is self-contained and portable. However, they were not able to adopt the unique-ID-based techniques that have been shown to support efficient merging and differencing algorithms.

This application note describes how it is possible to adapt existing features of MS Word's OOXML representation to provide a system of unique element IDs suitable for those algorithms. This requires taking over Word's Revision Save ID (RSID) system and also defining procedures for specifying ID values for elements that do not support the RSID mechanism. Important limitations remain but appear surmountable.

CCS CONCEPTS

•**Software and its engineering** →**Software configuration management and version control systems;**

1 INTRODUCTION

Collaborative writing is commonly used in organizations. The process of creating a document by multiple people can be challenging when working with complex and detailed documents. A version control system provides a set of methods that allow groups to achieve an organized and productive collaboration. Two of its main functions are to allow users to maintain a history of changes to the document and to merge changes made in parallel by different authors.

Sophisticated Version Control Systems (VCSs) usually require access to a central repository to store and manipulate version data. Experience has shown that such VCSs often require a technical user base. In contrast, the user base for office documents is typically non-technical and finds it difficult to work with a repository. Thus, developing a sophisticated offline VCS is a necessary task.

Thao and Munson showed that high quality merging is possible when unique element IDs are stored inside XML documents [7]. In order to support their approach, we are introducing a novel way to preserve IDs in Word documents. This allows us to provide a

DocEng '17, September 4–7, 2017, Valletta, Malta.
© 2017 ACM. 978-1-4503-4689-4/17/09…$$15.00
DOI: https://doi.org/10.1145/3103010.3121027

sophisticated versioning solution for Word documents that relies only on standard Open Office XML attributes and elements.

2 BACKGROUND

This research is a continuation of a line of research on versioning of office documents. Thao and Munson [7] initially presented an efficient three-way merging algorithm for XML documents that relies on the document elements having unique IDs. Later, they described the Version-Aware XML Document format [8], which stores the full version history of the document in a preamble of the document file and also relies on the unique ID approach for version differencing and merging. Version Aware documents can be stored offline, outside a repository, while maintaining the same kind of versioning history and supporting the same operations.

It is reasonable to ask whether one can expect XML-based applications to maintain unique IDs on their document elements. Pandey and Munson [6] addressed this question by showing that the LibreOffice Writer application could be modified to support unique IDs with only small changes to the application source code. Coakley *et al.* [4] tried to bring the version-aware approach to MS Word documents by implementing a version-aware plug-in. However, they were unable find a way to use the unique ID approach and instead adopted matching techniques similar to those of Lindholm's 3dm system [5]. Furthermore, they had to store their versioning information in separate XML files within the larger zip file used by MS Word. The problem with matching techniques is that they are slower and less correct than the unique ID approach.

MS Word itself supports version control through two main features. "Track Changes" keeps a detailed history of changes made to the document, even if made by multiple users. A user trying to create a final version of the document can choose to accept or reject each of the changes. The "Compare" feature is used when authors have been making changes in parallel to the same document. It allows the differences in the two parallel versions to be compared and also supports merging of the two versions. A key limitation of MS Word is that it does not maintain a full version history graph. Instead, it only has the notion of an original accepted version and of a current version produced by the users' changes.

In this application note, we extend the work of Coakley *et al.* to provide better Version Aware Word Documents. We propose a structure where we add unique IDs to Microsoft Word XML documents relying only on XML elements and attributes provided by the Microsoft Word architecture and its Office Open XML file format (OOXML) [3]. This allows our system to use the XML differencing and merging algorithms of Thao and Munson [7], which have better performance than Coakley's matching techniques. Also, our version history information can be embedded directly in the document

```
<w:p w:rsidR="0011569B" w:rsidRDefault="0011569B" w:rsidP="00
    E200CD">
    <w:pPr>
        <w:pStyle w:val="TableContents"/>
        <w:snapToGrid w:val="0"/>
        +<w:rPr>
    </w:pPr>
    <w:r>
        +<w:rPr>
        <w:t>Brazil</w:t>
    </w:r>
</w:p>
```

Figure 1: XML listing for a paragraph structure

```
<w:p w:rsidR="7E80B124" w:rsidP="00E200CD" w:rsidRDefault="0011569
    B">
    <w:pPr>
        <w:pStyle w:val="TableContents"/>
        <w:snapToGrid w:val="0"/>
        +<w:rPr>
    </w:pPr>
    <w:r w:rsidRPr="6CA63AA1">
        +<w:rPr>
        <w:t>Brazil</w:t>
    </w:r>
</w:p>
```

Figure 2: XML listing for a paragraph in our application

content file (document.xml), which has the potential to simplify document security measures.

OOXML [2] specifies the format of MS Office files, such as the "docx" files of MS Word. A docx file is actually a zipped folder containing files and further subfolders. One of the most important of those files is "document.xml" which specifies the document structure and its textual content. Non-text content is generally stored in other files or subfolders and linked to document.xml by an indirect reference scheme.

In the next two sections of this application note, we describe how we successfully attach unique IDs to the important paragraph and table structures of OOXML. The following section describes the challenges we face with images because of details of the indirect referencing system. The final section is our conclusion.

3 PARAGRAPHS

The paragraph is the main block-level content element in an OOXML word processing document. In OOXML terms, *block-level* means a unit of content that starts on a new line. The paragraph element is used to represent many document elements that other document formats (e.g. HTML) represent with distinct elements, such as lists, list items, quotations, etc. Each paragraph element ¡w:p¿ can contain a single paragraph properties element ¡w:pPr¿ and one or more run ¡w:r¿ elements. A run element generally defines a non-block area of text that shares a common set of formatting properties, though it can also contain non-text elements like images, drawings and special characters. MS Word uses run elements to represent many types of inline formatting features for which other formats have distinct elements. Each run element contains a single run properties element ¡w:rPr¿ and may contain a single content element, which is most commonly text ¡w:t¿ [2]. The OOXML code for a simple paragraph is shown in Figure 1.

RSID (Revision Save ID) attributes are important for our application. RSIDs attributes were introduced in 2003 to allow applications to merge two versions of the same document that have been edited in parallel [1]. Each time a document is opened, edited, and saved, a random RSID value is generated for the editing session and certain changed elements (mostly the block elements, such as paragraphs) are marked with this session RSID. The ID values are 32-bit unsigned hexadecimal integers. Thus, RSIDs allow you to see what was done in a single session and most documents have multiple elements with the same RSID value. There are multiple RSID attributes and, as far as we can tell, their differences are not well-documented. Figure 1's paragraph element shows three such attributes: w:rsidR,

w:rsidRDefault, and w:rsidP. We use the w:rsidR attribute, because our study of MS Word's behavior leads us to believe that this is the primary RSID attribute.

The Version Aware Document approach works best if each versioned element has a unique ID within the document. In fact, the differencing and merging algorithms do not pay attention to element type and use only the IDs. So, we take two steps to support those algorithms. First, we "hijack" the RSID system in order to record partial UIDs on certain elements. Second, we develop a process for defining *versioning IDs* (VIDs) for all elements, based on the explicitly recorded RSIDs. It is the VIDs that are used in the merging algorithm, while only the RSIDs appear in the document.xml file.

We modify the document.xml file by giving each paragraph ¡w:p¿ element a unique rsidR value. So, even if a set of edits were made in the same session, each edited paragraph will have a distinct RSID. (Obviously, this will defeat the MS Word "combine documents" feature.) Furthermore, we use another RSID attribute, "w:rsidRPr" to give each run ¡w:r¿ element a unique RSID value. This allows us to distinguish the multiple runs in a paragraph from each other. Figure 2 shows the XML for the content shown in Figure 1 after we modify it so that the paragraphs have distinct w:rsidR values and the run has gained a w:rsidRPr value.

A VID is a unique ID for all elements within a paragraph, including elements like paragraph properties ¡w:pPr¿ and text ¡w:t¿. The value of a VID is a 64-bit unsigned hexadecimal integer. For elements that have an explicit RSID attribute value (either w:p or w:r), the VID is the RSID value concatenated with #00000000. All other elements in a paragraph will be children of an element with an RSID value. The VID for these elements will be the RSID value of the parent concatenated with the cryptographic hash of the element's name (as a 32-bit unsigned hexadecimal integer). This rather odd tactic works because all elements that appear in the paragraph structure, other than the run ¡w:r¿ element, can only appear a single time within their parents.

4 TABLES

Tables are also a widely used feature of word processing documents and they presented challenges for defining IDs that required us to be creative. The main components of a Table, showed in Figure 3, are the tags: table ¡w:tbl¿, table row ¡w:tr¿, table cell ¡w:tc¿ and their respective properties plus the table grid ¡w:tblGrid¿. In general, a table contains one or more rows, each of which contains one or more cells. In general, cells contain only a series of (possibly empty)

```
<w:tbl>
    <w:tblPr>
        <w:tblW w:w="0" w:type="auto"/>
        <w:tblInd w:w="-8" w:type="dxa"/>
        <w:tblLayout w:type="fixed"/>
        +<w:tblCellMar>
        <w:tblLook w:noVBand="0" w:noHBand="0" w:lastColumn="0" w:
            firstColumn="0" w:lastRow="0" w:firstRow="0" w:val="
            0000"/>
    </w:tblPr>
    <w:tblGrid>
        <w:gridCol w:w="3600"/>
        <w:gridCol w:w="3634"/>
    </w:tblGrid>
    <w:tr w:rsidTr="00E200CD" w:rsidR="0011569B">
        <w:tc>
            <w:tcPr>
                <w:tcW w:w="3600" w:type="dxa"/>
                +<w:tcBorders>
                <w:shd w:val="clear" w:color="auto" w:fill="auto"/
                    >
            </w:tcPr>
            +<w:p w:rsidR="0011569B" w:rsidP="00E200CD" w:
                rsidRDefault="0011569B">
        </w:tc>
        <w:tc>
            +<w:tcPr>
            +<w:p w:rsidR="0011569B" w:rsidP="00E200CD" w:
                rsidRDefault="0011569B">
        </w:tc>
    </w:tr>
    +<w:tr w:rsidTr="00E200CD" w:rsidR="0011569B">
    +<w:tr w:rsidTr="00E200CD" w:rsidR="0011569B">
</w:tbl>
```

Figure 3: XML Listing for table. This table has 3 rows, but the listing has only expanded the first

```
<w:tbl>
    <w:tblPr>
        <w:tblCaption w:val="ID:F6AB2FBF"/>
        <w:tblW w:w="0" w:type="auto"/>
        <w:tblInd w:w="-8" w:type="dxa"/>
        <w:tblLayout w:type="fixed"/>
        +<w:tblCellMar>
        <w:tblLook w:noVBand="0" w:noHBand="0" w:lastColumn="0" w:
            firstColumn="0" w:lastRow="0" w:firstRow="0" w:val="
            0000"/>
    </w:tblPr>
    <w:tblGrid>
        <w:gridCol w:w="3600"/>
        <w:gridCol w:w="3634"/>
    </w:tblGrid>
    <w:tr w:rsidTr="00E200CD" w:rsidR="00E200CD">
        <w:tc>
            <w:tcPr>
                <w:tcW w:w="3600" w:type="dxa"/>
                +<w:tcBorders>
                <w:shd w:val="clear" w:color="auto" w:fill="auto"/
                    >
            </w:tcPr>
            +<w:p w:rsidR="7E80B124" w:rsidP="00E200CD" w:
                rsidRDefault="0011569B">
        </w:tc>
        <w:tc>
            +<w:tcPr>
            +<w:p w:rsidR="41DF3A23" w:rsidP="00E200CD" w:
                rsidRDefault="0011569B">
        </w:tc>
    </w:tr>
    +<w:tr w:rsidTr="00E200CD" w:rsidR="85AA33DD">
    +<w:tr w:rsidTr="00E200CD" w:rsidR="C2409107">
</w:tbl>
```

Figure 4: XML Listing for table in our application. This table has 3 rows, but the listing has only expanded the first

paragraphs, but while it is rare, the table structure can be recursive with a cell element holding another table in addition to one or more paragraphs.

The way we assign IDs in the table XML structure is the following:

- To identify the Table element ¡w:tbl¿, we place an ID in the value attribute of the table caption element ¡w:tblCaption¿, which is one of the table's property elements. This is necessary because is not possible to add an RSID attribute to to the table tag. Adding a table caption element does not cause any visible changes because the caption is only accessible via a table properties dialogue. (Of course, a user could alter the ID we create through the table properties dialog and undermine our technique.) The ID in the table caption is expanded into a VID by concatenating it with zero (#00000000).

- All the remaining table property tags appear only once within the table. So, as we did for the paragraph properties elements, each one receives a VID by concatenation of the ID in the table caption and the hash of the property's element name.

- Table grid ¡w:tblGrid¿ is the only place that an individual tag, for example ¡w:gridCol¿, can appear more than one time. To solve this issue we keep a list of the children tags of table grid.

- Table rows do support the w:rsidR attribute, so we use it as we did for runs within paragraphs. The VID for the row is the RSID value concatenated with zero.

- Unfortunately, table cells also do not support the RSID attribute, but we need to compute a unique VID for each cell. However, we noted that every table cell contains a paragraph, even though the paragraph might be empty. So, we create a VID for each cell by computing the hash of w:tc element name and concatenating it with the RSID of the cell's first paragraph.

- For the table column property elements, the VID is the concatenation of the RSID from the cell's first paragraph with the hash of the property's element name.

5 EXTERNAL OBJECTS

One challenge that we still face involves external objects that are stored outside the main XML document file. External objects are non-textual media (images, video, animation) that Word includes as external references. As was mentioned in the introduction, MS Word docx files are actually zipped folders containing files and further subfolders. Figure 5 illustrates the structure of a docx file. For the current discussion, there are three important elements of the zipped structure, all of which are in the "word" folder:

- The "document.xml" file is the main XML content file and essentially stores the structure and textual content of the document. External media elements, such as images, are specified in document.xml using abstract reference values, like "rId3" and "rId7".

- The "media" subfolder holds media elements like images that are included by indirect reference in the document.xml file.

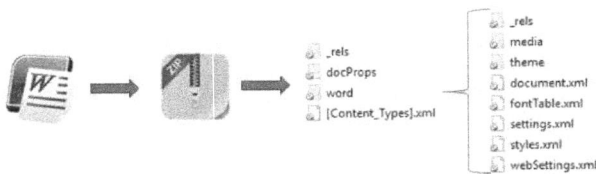

Figure 5: Word document as ZIP file

- The _rels/document.xml.rels file encode the relationships between the abstract reference values and the names of files in the media folder.

Our current implementation focuses entirely on the document.xml file and ignores the media folder. Some of our future work will be to extend our processing to include these media elements, as well as the styles.xml file, which encodes named styles and is also outside our application's current scope.

6 IMPLEMENTATION STATUS

We have implemented an MS Word plug-in that supports the ID features for paragraphs and tables described in Sections 3 and 4. We have tested the implementation sufficiently to be confident that the IDs are persistent through a load-edit-save cycle. That is, if an element has an associated RSID value at load time, the value will be found on that element in the saved file in these circumstances:

- The element was not changed during editing;
- The element's internal content was changed;
- The element was cut and then pasted in a new location;

If the entire element is deleted, then the ID will disappear from the file. Based on these guarantees, our plug-in is able to perform three-way merges of document versions on separate branches of the version tree, using the efficient algorithm described by Thao and Munson [7].

7 CONCLUSION

We have been able to provide improved Version Aware Word Documents by extending the work of Coakley *et al.* [4]. By developing strategies to define Versioning IDs for all document elements, we have made it possible to use the XML differencing and merging algorithms developed by Thao and Munson [7]. This required identifying OOXML structures, the RSID attributes, that we could take over in order to record partial IDs on important elements. Then, to create fully usable VIDs, we defined rules by which they could be reliably created, based on the RSID values recorded in the XML file. We can be confident that these changes improve on the original work because the ID-based three-way merging algorithms are faster and more accurate than the matching-based approach used by Coakley *et al.*.

We showed that is possible to create a structure where we can rely only on the XML elements in the Microsoft Word XML architecture. Thus, other solutions can use the same idea to rely only on the Word XML document instead of trying to embed extra XML files in the docx structure. We also note that the entire effort would be simplified if Word (and other similar applications) would provide an attribute on all elements that could be used as a unique ID.

REFERENCES

[1] [n. d.]. Microsoft Office Word 2003 documentation. https://msdn.microsoft.com/en-us/library/ee364478(v=office.11).aspx. ([n. d.]). Accessed: 2017-05-27.
[2] [n. d.]. Office Open XML. http://officeopenxml.com/. ([n. d.]). Accessed: 2017-05-26.
[3] 2016. ISO. Information technology-Document description and processing languages- Office Open XML File Formats ISO/IEC 29500-1:2016. (2016).
[4] Stephen M Coakley, Jacob Mischka, and Cheng Thao. 2014. Version-Aware Word Documents. In *Proceedings of the 2nd International Workshop on (Document) Changes: modeling, detection, storage and visualization.* ACM, 2.
[5] Tancred Lindholm. 2004. A three-way merge for XML documents. In *Proceedings of the 2004 ACM symposium on Document engineering.* ACM, 1–10.
[6] Meenu Pandey and Ethan V Munson. 2013. Version aware LibreOffice documents. In *Proceedings of the 2013 ACM symposium on Document engineering.* ACM, 57–60.
[7] Cheng Thao and Ethan V Munson. 2010. Using versioned tree data structure, change detection and node identity for three-way XML merging. In *Proceedings of the 10th ACM symposium on Document engineering.* ACM, 77–86.
[8] Cheng Thao and Ethan V Munson. 2011. Version-aware XML documents. In *Proceedings of the 11th ACM symposium on Document engineering.* ACM, 97–100.

Classification of MathML Expressions Using Multilayer Perceptron

Yuma Nagao
University of Tsukuba
Tsukuba, Ibaraki, Japan
ynagao@klis.tsukuba.ac.jp

Nobutaka Suzuki
University of Tsukuba
Tsukuba, Ibaraki, Japan
nsuzuki@slis.tsukuba.ac.jp

ABSTRACT

MathML consists of two sets of elements: Presentation Markup and Content Markup. The former is more widely used to display math expressions in Web pages, while the latter is more suited to the calculation of math expressions. In this paper, we consider classifying math expressions in Presentation Markup. In general, a math expression in Presentation Markup cannot be uniquely converted into the corresponding expression in Content Markup. If the class of a given math expression can be identified automatically, such conversions can be done more appropriately. Moreover, identifying the class of a given math expression is useful for text-to-speech of math expression. In this paper, we propose a method for classifying math expressions in Presentation Markup by using a kind of deep learning; multilayer perceptron. Experimental results show that our method classifies math expressions with high accuracy.

CCS CONCEPTS

• **Computing methodologies → Supervised learning by classification;** • **Software and its engineering →** *Extensible Markup Language (XML);*

KEYWORDS

MathML, classification, multilayer perceptron

ACM Reference format:
Yuma Nagao and Nobutaka Suzuki. 2017. Classification of MathML Expressions Using Multilayer Perceptron. In *Proceedings of DocEng '17, Valletta, Malta, September 04-07, 2017,* 4 pages.
https://doi.org/.1145/3103010.3121026

1 INTRODUCTION

MathML (Mathematical Markup Language) is a standard markup language for describing math expressions. MathML consists of two set of elements: Presentation Markup and Content Markup. The former describes layout structures of

math expressions, and is widely used to display math expressions in Web pages. On the other hand, the latter describes semantic meanings of math expressions, and is suited to automatic calculation of math expressions. One of the challenging problem related to Presentation MathML is classification, i.e., given a MathML expression e, identify the class (e.g., hypergeometric function, bessel-type function, etc.) that e belongs to. If we can identify the class of a given Presentation MathML expression automatically, it is helpful for various applications, e.g., Presentation to Content MathML conversion, text-to-speech, and so on.

In this paper, we propose a classification method for Presentation MathML expressions. Our method classifies MathML expressions by using multilayer perceptron, which is a kind of deep learning model having a simple structure. The difficulty in taking such an approach is that the size of MathML expressions are arbitrary, while multilayer perceptron requires input of fixed length. Thus, it is impossible to input MathML expressions to multilayer perceptron directly. To address this problem, our method converts a Presentation MathML expression into a fixed length vector, which is based on binary branch vector [8]. We train a multilayer perceotron by using such vectors and classify MathML expressions by the multilayer perceptron. Experimental results show that our method classifies math expressions with high accuracy.

Related Works

Kim et al. [1] propose a classification method for MathML expressions. They extract features from math expressions and classify them by using support vector machine (SVM). They use labels of nodes and contiguous sequence of leaf nodes as a feature, in which parent-child relationships of tree structures are not considered. A drawback of SVM is that SVM requires proper features which must be extracted and selected according to characteristics of data manually. On the other hand, deep learning (e.g., multilayer perceptron) can extract features automatically from input data.

There are some researches on semantic enrichment from math expressions [3, 4, 6]. [6] extracts semantic meaning of math identifiers from math expressions and texts surrounding the expressions. [3] proposes a method for specifying a meaning of math identifiers. The method uses classes of math expressions as a feature. On the other hand, we estimate the classes of math expressions without using texts surrounding the expressions. [4] proposes a method for classifying math documents.

2 VECTOR REPRESENTATION OF MATHML EXPRESSIONS

MathML expressions are represented as trees of various sizes. On the other hand, most classification algorithm (e.g., multilayer perceptron, SVM, etc.) requires input of fixed length. Therefore, we must convert MathML expressions to vectors of fixed length.

In this section, we give a procedure for converting MathML expression to vector of fixed length. This vector is a slight but essential extension of binary branch vector [8]. We describe this extension in Sec. 2.2.

2.1 Binary Branch and Binary Branch Vector

An *unranked labeled ordered tree* is denoted $T = (N, E, Root(T))$, where N is the set of nodes, E is the set of edges and $Root(T)$ is the root node of T. By $(u, v) \in E$ we mean an edge from parent node u to child node v.

A *full binary tree* (*binary tree* for short) is denoted $B(T) = (N, E_l, E_r, Root(T))$, where E_l and E_r are the sets of left edges and right edges in $B(T)$, respectively. If v is the first child of u, then we write $\langle u, v \rangle_l \in E_l$. Similarly, if v' is the second child of u, then we write $\langle u, v \rangle_r \in E_r$.

MathML expressions are represented as unranked labeled ordered trees, in which the number of child elements is not restricted. We convert them to full binary trees whose nodes have either zero or two children. A binary tree $B(T)$ is obtained from an unranked labeled ordered tree T as follows. Initially, $B(T)$ consists of the same set of nodes as T and no edges.

(1) For each node u in T, do the following.
   (a) Let $v_1, v_2, ..., v_n$ be the children of u. Add an edge (v_{i-1}, v_i) to $B(T)$ for every $2 \leq i \leq n$.
   (b) Add an edge (u, v_1) to $B(T)$.
(2) Insert empty node ϵ so that all internal nodes in $B(T)$ have exactly two child nodes.

A *binary branch* is a one level subtree of a binary tree. This consists of root node, left child and right child. Formally, binary branch $BiB(u)$ is defined as $BiB(u) = (N_u, E_{u_l}, E_{u_r}, Root(T_u))$, where

- $N_u = \{u, u_1, u_2\}(u \in N; u_i \in N \bigcup\{\epsilon\}, i = 1, 2)$,
- $E_{u_l} = \{\langle u, u_1 \rangle_l\}$,
- $E_{u_r} = \{\langle u, u_2 \rangle_r\}$,
- $Root(T_u) = u$.

A *binary branch vector* $BRV(T)$ of a tree T is defined as $BRV(T) = (b_1, b_2, ..., b_{|\Gamma|})$, where Γ is an ordered set of binary branches in a dataset, $|\Gamma|$ is the size of Γ and b_i represents the number of occurrences of the ith binary branch in $B(T)$. We show an example in Fig. 1. In the dataset, there are two binary trees $B(T_1)$ and $B(T_2)$ converted from MathML expressions T_1 and T_2. Each cell in the right table represents the number of occurrences of a binary branch. For example, binary branch (math, mn, ϵ) occurs once in $B(T_1)$ and $B(T_2)$. Therefore, the two columns of the table represent binary branch vectors corresponding to $B(T_1)$

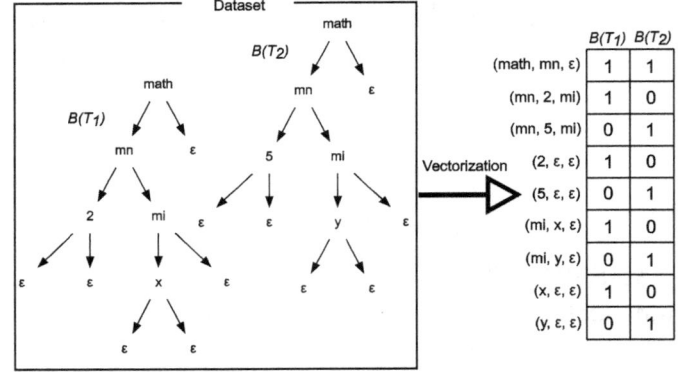

Figure 1: Converting MathML expressions to binary branch vectors

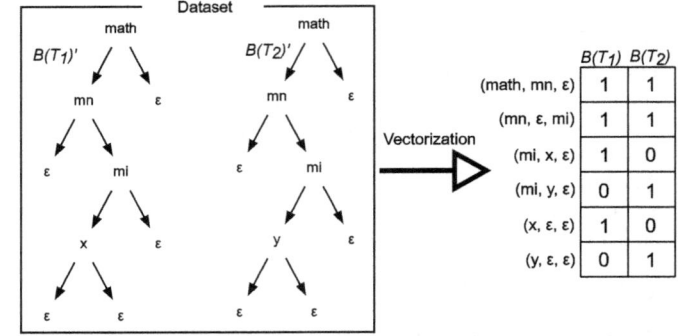

Figure 2: Dimensionality reduction by converting text of mn element to empty node ϵ

and $B(T_2)$, respectively. That is, $BBV(T_1) = (1, 1, ..., 0)$ and $BBV(T_2) = (1, 0, ..., 1)$.

2.2 Dimensionality Reduction

Each element of a binary branch vector is the number of occurrences of a binary branch in a dataset. Therefore, as the dataset becomes larger, the size of Γ increases accordingly. In particular, the number of binary branches tends to considerably grow when MathML expressions have substructures which are similar but have different numeric values. However, such "non-structural" differences may reduce the accuracy of classification. This is because similar MathML expressions tend to contain similar substructures that have different numeric values, therefore MathML expressions that should be classified into the same class may wrongly be classified into different classes due to substructures that are similar but different numeric values. Thus, we reduce the sizes of binary branch vectors by erasing the text of **mn** elements. In Presentation MathML, **mn** elements represent numeric numbers. We give an example of dimensionality reduction. Consider the binary trees in Fig. 1. We replace the texts of **mn** elements (2 and 5) with ϵ. As the result, binary branches rooted by mn elements are converted to the same binary branches and we obtain two binary trees $B(T_1)'$ and $B(T_2)'$ in Fig. 2. In comparison with binary branch vectors in Fig. 1, the binary branch vectors in Fig. 2 are of smaller length.

3 CLASSIFICATION OF MATHML EXPRESSIONS

Our method classifies binary branch vectors converted from MathML expressions by a multilayer perceptron. In this section, we give an overview of multilayer perceptron and the construction of our model.

3.1 Multilayer Perceptron

A multilayer perceptron is composed of an input layer, any number of hidden layers and an output layer. Each layer consists of units which receive multiple inputs and calculate an output (see Fig. 3). The net input $u_j^{(l+1)}$ of jth unit in $l+1$th layer is

$$u_j^{(l+1)} = \sum_i w_{ji}^{(l)} z_i^{(l)} + b_j^{(l+1)},$$

where $w_{ji}^{(l)}$ is a weight, $b_j^{(l+1)}$ is a bias and $z_i^{(l)}$ is the output of $u_i^{(l)}$. Here, the output z_i of u_i is given as $z_i = f(u_i)$, where f is an activation function. ReLU is a popular activation function for multilayer perceptron defined as follows.

$$f(u) = \max(0, u).$$

For multi-class classification, softmax function

$$z_k = \frac{\exp(u_k)}{\sum_i \exp(u_i)}$$

is generally used for output layer. The output z_k of softmax represents the probability that a given input belongs to class C_k. Weights and biases are updated in order to minimize the error between outputs and correct answers of training data. In the case of multi-class classification, the cross entropy error function

$$E = -\sum_k t_k \log z_k$$

is generally used, where z_k is an output and t_k is kth element of a correct answer. SDG and Adam are known as typical optimizers to minimize the error (details are omitted).

3.2 Our Model

Our model consists of an input layer, two hidden layers and an output layer. The number of units in the input layer is same as the size of binary branch vectors. Each hidden layers has 512 units and activated by ReLU. The output layer has the same number of units as MathML classes and activate by softmax. We use Adam as the optimizer to minimize the cross entropy error. We also tried other models (e.g., one with three or more hidden layers) but found no noticeable improvement.

4 EXPERIMENTS

In this section, we present our experimental results.

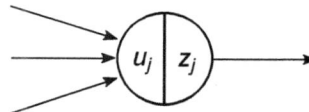

Figure 3: Construction of a unit

4.1 Dataset

In our experiments, we use the following two datasets.

4.1.1 The wolfram function site. We collected HTML files exhaustively and extracted MathML expressions from the wolfram function site [5]. We obtained 307,676 MathML expressions and 14 classes. We used 70% of them for training data and used 30 % for test data.

4.1.2 MREC (Mathematical REtrieval Collection). MREC [2] is a dataset of scientific papers in arxiv.org translated to XML. The math expressions in the papers are written in Presentation MathML. MREC is composed of MREC2011.3 and MREC2011.4. The expressions in the latter have embedded semantic meanings and the former expressions do not. Since our method does not use specified semantic meaning of expression, we used the former for the experiment.

MREC contains too short expressions (e.g., x, Δ, etc.) for which classification is meaningless. Therefore, we removed MathML expressions which do not have mi elements or less than two elements except math and mrow elements from the dataset. Note that a math element is the root node of a MathML expression and that mrow elements influence neither display nor meaning of an MathML expression.

The MREC dataset has originally 34 classes. We chose 20 classes that have more than 100,000 expressions, and carefully examined the classes. As the result, we find that some classes have parent-child relationships or are very similar to each other, and that these classes should be merged into the same class. Therefore, we merge such classes and obtain the following 12 classes. For example, class 5 consists of hep-ex, hep-lat and hep-th, which are original classes of MREC.

   (1) astro-ph
   (2) cs
   (3) cond-mat
   (4) gr-qc
   (5) hep-ex, hep-lat, hep-th
   (6) alg-geom, dg-ga, math, q-alg
   (7) math-ph
   (8) chao-dyn, nlin, solv-int
   (9) nucl-ex, nucl-th
  (10) physics
  (11) q-bio
  (12) quant-ph

We extracted 100,000 MathML expressions from each of the 12 classes. We used 70% of them for training data and used 30 % for test data.

Table 1: Accuracy for the wolfram function site

Method	Accuracy
Our method	**99.35**
SVM [1]	99.03

Table 2: Accuracy for MREC

Method	Accuracy
Our method	**83.54**
SVM [1]	28.16

4.2 Experimantal Results

We compare our method and the SVM-based method proposed by Kim et al. [1]. They define five features: labels of nodes (Tag), texts of mo elements which represent operators (Operator), texts of mi elements which represent identifiers (Identifier), bigram of plain text in expressions (String Bigram) and bigram of identifier and operator (I&O). To classify MathML expressions, they compared several combinations of the features as the inputs of SVM with liner kernel. In their experimental results, the combination of Tag, Operator, String Bigram and I&O shows the highest accuracy. However, the expressions in our datasets contain few plain texts that can be used as the String Bigram feature. Therefore, we use Tag, Operator, Identifier and I&O, which marked the second highest accuracy in their experiment. We adjust a penalty parameter C of SVM ($C = 2^{-10}, 2^{-9}, ..., 2^{10}$) because the value of C is not specified in their paper.

Tables 1 and 2 show the results. Table 1 shows the accuracies of the two methods in the wolfram function site. The result shows that both of methods achieve high accuracy. Further, our method slightly outperforms the SVM-based method ($C = 2^8$). The reason why such high accuracies are obtained is that the dataset is "clean", that is, it has well-formed structures (e.g., order of variables, operators, etc.) and unified notations of identifiers.

Table 2 shows the accuracies of the two methods for MREC. Our method (83.54%) outperforms the SVM-based method ($28.16\%, C = 2^0$). Both of the accuracies are lower than those of the wolfram function site. This is because the expressions of MREC are much less "clean" than these of the wolfram function site. For example, in the expressions of MREC the notation of identifiers are not unified, because the expressions are written by various authors. The result means that our method is much robust and effective to less "clean" expressions than the SVM-based method.

Finally, let us consider the sizes of input vectors. Here, we denote binary branch vector before dimensionality reduction as *BBV with mn* and binary branch vector after dimensionality reduction as *BBV without mn*. For the wolfram function site, the sizes of BBVs without mn are 2,184 and BBVs with mn are 558,777. This means that similar substructures

which have different numeric values frequently appear in the dataset. The size of BBVs with mn are smaller than the sizes of feature vectors for the SVM-based method (8,113). For MREC, the sizes of BBVs without mn are 39,833 and BBVs with mn are 72,019. Since the sizes of feature vectors for the SVM-based method are 91,146, our vectors are smaller. Thus, by using our method, we can obtain better classification results with smaller input vectors.

5 CONCLUSIONS

In this paper, we proposed a method for classifying MathML expressions based on multilayer perceptron. Experimental results showed that our method can classify MathML expressions with higher accuracy than the SVM-based method and we succeeded in reducing the size of binary branch vectors by our dimensionality reduction processing.

As a future work, it is necessary to compare dimensionality-reduced binary branch vectors with their original vectors to see the effectiveness of dimensionality reduction. Furthermore, we need to consider comparing our model with more complex models (e.g., Tree-LSTM[7]). We also have to tune hyperparameters (number of units and layers, etc.) of our model. It is not clear whether the hyperparameters used in our experiment are optimum or not. Due to tuning of hyperparameters, we may expect to higher accuracies.

REFERENCES

[1] Shinil Kim, Seon Yang, and Youngjoong Ko. 2012. Classifying Mathematical Expressions Written in MathML. *IEICE Transactions on Information and Systems* E95.D, 10 (2012), 2560–2563.

[2] Martin Líška, Petr Sojka, Michal Růžička, and Petr Mravec. 2011. Web Interface and Collection for Mathematical Retrieval: WebMIaS and MREC. In *Towards a Digital Mathematics Library.*, Petr Sojka and Thierry Bouche (Eds.). Masaryk University, Bertinoro, Italy, 77–84.

[3] Minh-Quoc Nghiem, Giovanni Yoko Kristianto, and Akiko Aizawa. 2013. Using MathML Parallel Markup Corpora for Semantic Enrichment of Mathematical Expressions. *IEICE Transactions on Information and Systems* E96.D, 8 (2013), 1707–1715.

[4] Tam T. Nguyen, Kuiyu Chang, and Siu Cheung Hui. 2012. Adaptive Two-view Online Learning for Math Topic Classification. In *Proceedings of the 2012 European Conference on Machine Learning and Knowledge Discovery in Databases - Volume Part I (ECML PKDD'12)*. Springer-Verlag, Berlin, Heidelberg, 794–809.

[5] Wolfram Research. 2017. The Wolfram Function Site. (2017). Retrieved May 25, 2017 from http://functions.wolfram.com/

[6] Moritz Schubotz, Alexey Grigorev, Marcus Leich, Howard S. Cohl, Norman Meuschke, Bela Gipp, Abdou S. Youssef, and Volker Markl. 2016. Semantification of Identifiers in Mathematics for Better Math Information Retrieval. In *Proceedings of the 39th International ACM SIGIR Conference on Research and Development in Information Retrieval (SIGIR '16)*. ACM, New York, NY, USA, 135–144.

[7] Kai Sheng Tai, Richard Socher, and Christopher D. Manning. 2015. Improved Semantic Representations From Tree-Structured Long Short-Term Memory Networks. *CoRR* abs/1503.00075 (2015).

[8] Rui Yang, Panos Kalnis, and Anthony K. H. Tung. 2005. Similarity Evaluation on Tree-structured Data. In *Proceedings of the 2005 ACM SIGMOD International Conference on Management of Data (SIGMOD '05)*. ACM, New York, NY, USA, 754–765.

Learning before Learning: Reversing Validation and Training

Steven Simske
HP Labs
3390 E. Harmony Road, M/S 66
Fort Collins, CO 80528 USA
steven.simske@hp.com

Marie Vans
HP Labs
3390 E. Harmony Road, M/S 66
Fort Collins, CO 80528 USA
marie.vans@hp.com

ABSTRACT

In the world of ground truthing—that is, the collection of highly valuable labeled training and validation data—there is a tendency to follow the path of first training on a set of data, then validating the data, and then testing the data. However, in many cases the labeled training data is of non-uniform quality, and thus of non-uniform value for assessing the accuracy and other performance indicators for analytics algorithms, systems and processes. This means that one or more of the so-labeled classes is likely a mixture of two or more clusters or sub-classes. These data may inhibit our ability to assess the classifier to use for deployment. We argue that one must learn about the labeled data before the labeled data can be used for downstream machine learning; that is, we reverse the validation and training steps in building the classifier. This "learning before learning" is assessed using a CNN corpus (cnn.com) which was hand-labeled as comprising 12 classes. We show how the suspect classes are identified using the initial validation, and how training after validation occurs. We then apply this process to the CNN corpus and show that it consists of 9 high-quality classes and three mixed-quality classes. The effects of this validation-training approach is then shown and discussed.

CCS CONCEPTS

• **Applied Computing** → **Document management and text processing**; • **Computing methodologies** → **Machine learning**, machine learning approaches

KEYWORDS

Ensemble methods, validation, training, classification, TF*IDF

ACM Reference Format:
Steven Simske and Marie Vans. 2017. Learning before Learning: Reversing Validation and Training. In Proceedings of DocEng '17, Valletta, Malta, September 04-07, 2017, 4 pages.
https://doi.org/10.1145/3103010.3121044

1 INTRODUCTION

In the world of analytics, algorithms and intelligent systems are usually rated based on their accuracy on test data. However, suppose you gave a history test to the world's top mathematicians, and whoever performed best on the Napoleonic Wars would be awarded the Fields Medal. Obviously, we can see that the wrong set of testing data was used. In the world of big data, it is not always this easy to discern what test data to use for validation—and which to ignore. Using k-fold cross validation, for example, may introduce redundancy or correlation within the data set, so that a condition known as over-training occurs. With large labelled data sets, certain events may occur with low frequency, resulting in class imbalance. We can address the former by keeping the training and validation sets separate from the test set. We address the latter by pruning the training and test sets so that they are uniform in size. But, what if, even after these approaches, certain data have significantly different clustering and/or classification behavior from the rest of the data? Surely, some amount of difference is acceptable. However, in some cases, the classes (irrespective of their labels) are simply of too poor quality to use in the validation process; that is, in relatively assessing which deployment classifier to employ [1]. What is needed is a fair, automated, and efficient way of eliminating suspect classes from the validation set (and re-introducing them, of course, in the training set) so that we can more reasonably assess the relative accuracies of deployment classifiers. This is particularly valuable when an ensemble of simple classifiers are to be used: we use a (majority) subset of the training data for validation of the deployment classifier **before** proceeding with training and testing: we employ validation→training→testing rather than the usual training→validation→testing. The "pre-validation" does not affect training, it simply determines what ensemble of simple classifiers will be used for the actual training.

2 METHODS AND MATERIALS

Term frequency times inverse document frequency, or TF*IDF [2,3], is commonly used in information retrieval and classification tasks [4,5,6]. We have previously defined a total of 112 TF*IDF methods for use as ensemble classifiers of text: 14 inverse document frequency methods for each of 8 term document frequency methods. These were computed for a set of CNN articles, which were assigned to 12 classes. Within each class, articles were assigned to two equally-sized groups: one for training and one for testing. To avoid class imbalance, we were able to have 98 files per class: 49 for the validation and training steps and 49 for testing. To build a measure, we multiply one of the TF measures by one of the IDF equations, providing an ensemble of 112 simple classifiers.

A validation or training experiment consists of preprocessing each document and creating a stream of tokens composed of individual words using the sharpNLP [7] C# open source project. The stream is then converted into a bag of words consisting of all non-stop words in each file. Once the TF*IDF measures are generated for each word in the file, we can create a master list of words for all the files in a given class. We create this master list by summing all the TF*IDF values for each word and dividing this sum by the number of files in which the word is found (normalization). This gives us a single TF*IDF measure for each word found in a class which we can then use for classifying articles from the test set of documents.

During testing, we first determine the TF*IDF measure values for all the words in a document. We then compare them with the normalized values for that word in each of the classes using the dot product of the TF*IDF value for the word in the test file with that of the normalized TF*IDF value for the word in each training class. The class that produces the highest dot product value sum with the file is then assigned as the class for that document. This procedure is used for all the test files in each class for each of the 112 TF*IDF measures.

A TF*IDF measure will classify a file or document set as one of 12 CNN-provided classes (Business, Health, Justice, Living, Opinion, Politics, Showbiz, Sport, Tech, Travel, US, World). The confusion matrix is constructed by creating a two-dimensional matrix in which the rows represent the "true" or "actual" class, while the columns represent the class assigned by the classification algorithm described above. To determine the accuracy of the TF*IDF measure, we divide the sum of values in the diagonal of the confusion matrix by the total number of files in all test files for all classes:

$$Accuracy = \frac{\sum(a_{1,1} \dots a_{n,n})}{\sum_{i=1}^{nClasses} nfiles} \quad (1)$$

We then sort the TF*IDF measures by accuracy from highest to lowest accuracy and set a minimum accuracy to identify a subset of the 112 TF*IDF measures that best classify the files. We found that no single TF*IDF could classify all the documents with high accuracy [8]. We did achieve relatively high accuracy "validation" classifiers by combining the individual TF*IDF measures.

We define a new figure of merit metric to address the elimination of "suspect classes" during validation (that is, before training). The CNN corpus [9] consists of news texts extracted from the CNN website (www.cnn.com). This test corpus has high quality writing in English, reporting on 12 general interest classes as described above. The set we used consisted of 1176 documents assigned equally to 12 classes (98 document per class). The news articles obtained from the CNN website were carefully chosen in order to contain only text; thus, news articles with figures, videos, tables and other multi-media elements were discarded. Sentence segmentation was performed by the Stanford CoreNLP [10]. Stop

words [11] were removed although this had little effect on classification since TF*IDF methods were used. Word stemming [12] converts each word into its root form, removing its prefix and suffix. After this stage, the text is structured in XML and included in the XML file that corresponds to the news article.

We used the 112 simple TF*IDF classifiers and weighted combinations of them ("boosting") for the weak and ensemble classification [13]. On training data, the poorest performing classes are consistently Travel, Living, Opinion, US, and Tech, in that order. We next used the top TF*IDF classifiers in weighted voting [14]. The best classification results were generally obtained with 6 TF*IDF weak classifiers in combination. We devised a metric, the "Figure of Merit", to automatically determine when to stop removing classes from the validation set, defined in Equation 2.

$$FigureOfMerit = \frac{\%error\_reduction}{\%error\_remaining/(df)} \quad (2)$$

The numerator is the amount of overall error reduced by removing the most suspect class. The denominator is the error remaining divided by the degrees of freedom (df) of the number of classes being compared, which is the (number of classes)-1. The denominator is the expected value of error reduction if all of the classes are equally useful. So, if the Figure of Merit is greater than unity, we have reason to believe the current "suspect" class should indeed be removed from the validation set (though of course re-introduced for the subsequent training set).

We also wished to provide novel, quantitative methods for providing sensitivity analysis on the confusion matrix during validation. Imbalance in the confusion matrix during validation was determined using confusion matrix entropy [14]:

$$e_1 = \frac{-\sum_i \sum_j \left[\left(\frac{c_{ij}}{c_{ij}+c_{ji}} \right) * \ln\left(\frac{c_{ij}}{c_{ij}+c_{ji}} \right) \right]}{N(N-1)}$$

$$e_2 = \frac{-\sum_i \sum_j \left[\left(\frac{c_{ji}}{c_{ij}+c_{ji}} \right) * \ln\left(\frac{c_{ji}}{c_{ij}+c_{ji}} \right) \right]}{N(N-1)} \text{ and } e = e_1 + e_2 \quad (3)$$

Because many of the elements in the confusion matrix are 0 (the matrix is sparsely populated), we also introduced two new metrics to describe non-uniformity in the confusion matrix. These new metrics, taken together, should provide as much rigor as confusion matrix entropy, and have the additional advantage of being appropriate for sparse matrices. The first metric is the Relative Absolute Transposition Difference (RATD) which is given by:

$$RATD = \frac{\sum_{i=1}^{N} \sum_{j=i+1}^{N} |c_{ij} - c_{ji}|}{\sum_{i=1}^{N} \sum_{j=1, j \neq i}^{N} c_{ij}} \quad (4)$$

Where c_{ij} =confusion matrix element at position (i,j). This value gives a meaningful measure of how much variability is contained in erroneously assigning two classes with respect to each other. Higher values for RATD imply greater imbalance in classes, referred to as "attractor" and "repeller" classes [14]. The RATD is further modified to have logarithmic behavior using:

$$RATD = -ln\left(\frac{\sum_{i=1}^{N}\sum_{j=i+1}^{N}|c_{ij}-c_{ji}|}{\sum_{i=1}^{N}\sum_{j=1,j\neq i}^{N}c_{ij}}\right) \quad (5)$$

The second new metric helps describe the overall variability in the confusion matrix, irrespective of the existence of attractor and/or repeller classes. The Mean Difference of Off-Diagonal Expected Values of elements, or MDODEV, is given by:

$$MDODEV = \frac{\sum_{i=1,i\neq j}^{N}\sum_{j=i+1}^{N}|c_{ij}-\mu|}{\sum_{i=1}^{N}\sum_{j=1,j\neq i}^{N}c_{ij}} \quad (6)$$

This value uses the confusion matrix expected value, **μ**:

$$\mu = \frac{\sum_{i=1,i\neq j}^{N}\sum_{j=i+1}^{N}c_{ij}}{N(N-1)} \quad (7)$$

3 RESULTS

On test data, after training on all 12 classes, the accuracy of the best performing individual TF*IDF is 0.4473 while the accuracy of the worst performing individual TF*IDF is 0.1650. After this full-class-set training, we next performed training on 11, 10, 9, 8 and 7 classes after removing Travel, Living, Opinion, US and Tech classes, respectively and cumulatively. Removing these classes was used to validate the ground truth data. The best and worst performing individual TF*IDF measures were, in each case, similar to those with all 12 classes. Obviously, removing a class with poor accuracy should increase the overall classification accuracy, but more importantly, we established that the Figure of Merit is above unity for the removal of the first three suspect classes, then drops well below unity (Table 1).

Table 1: Figure of Merit for sequential removal of five most suspect classes. "Peak Accuracy" is for the combination of the 12 highest accuracy simple classifiers.

Removed Classes	Classes Removed	Peak Accuracy	Figure of Merit
0	[None]	0.655	N/A
1	Travel	0.688	1.06
2	Travel, Living	0.727	1.29
3	Travel, Living, Opinion	0.773	1.62
4	Travel, Living, Opinion, US	0.791	0.60
5	Travel, Living, Opinion, US, Tech	0.808	0.53

Table 2 presents the measurements of RATD and MDODEV. These measures are much higher, as expected, for the confusion matrices corresponding to poor classification accuracy—the so-

called (worst) examples. The higher values for RATD confirm the higher variability in comparing transposed values for poor classifiers. Similarly, the higher MDODEV values confirm the higher variability in confusion matrix mis-assignment for poor classifiers. However, for the purposes of this paper, we are primarily concerned with how the elimination of the poor quality classes affects RATD and MDEDOV for good classifiers. Thus, we wish to mainly compare RATD and MDEDOV for 12 (best) and 9 (best) classes. Here, RATD decreases by 46.3% and MDEDOV decreases by 26.0%, indicating that removing the classes results in more entropic intra-class behavior.

Table 2: RATD (Eq. 5) and MDODEV (Eq. 6) for the best and worst TF*IDF classifiers with all 12 classes and the 9 classes remaining after pruning with the Figure of Merit (Eq. 1).

Number of Classes and (best/worst)	RATD (Equation 7)	MDODEV (Equation 8)
12 (best)	1.0832	0.9819
12 (worst)	3.5579	1.6366
9 (best)	0.5814	0.7267
9 (worst)	3.2016	1.5569

We performed training and validation using all 12 classes or the "best" 9 classes. Each approach selected TF*IDF measures providing 100% accuracy on the 588 documents in the training set. For training on 12 classes, there were 10 such TF*IDF measures, named {TFIDF-12}; for training on 9 classes, there were 19 such TF*IDF measures, named {TFIDF-9} (a superset of {TFIDF-12}).

4 DISCUSSION AND CONCLUSIONS

This paper proposes a new ordering for validation, training and testing in classification. The approach is not about optimizing the classification accuracy, performance or robustness per se. Rather, it is about ensuring that the data used to later optimize the classification is not misdirecting or even contradicting that purpose. Suppose that a subset of classes used in the training data have much higher variability than the rest of the classes, which are the majority of the classes. These classes may make it difficult to assess how well the later-evaluated deployment classifiers will work on the other classes of data, but how do we decide which classes of ground truth are likely better to remove than keep? We propose that the Figure of Merit and the histogram, RATD and MDODEV analytics give us a set of tools for deciding how to optimize an ensemble classifier on a reduced set of ground truth.

Because of the 100% success on the training data, we achieved identical accuracy improvement for both {TFIDF-12} and {TFIDF-9} on the test data. However, the minimum expected degrees of freedom for the 112 TF*IDF measures is the number of IDF-1 + the number of TF-1; that is, 14-1+8-1 = 20. This implies that the 19 members of {TFIDF-9} almost certainly cover the TF*IDF space better than the 10 members of {TFIDF-12}. Moreover, the odds of {TFIDF-9} being a superset of {TFIDF-12} is given by the following ratio of combinations (102!19!/9!112!):

$$p(superset) = \binom{102}{9} / \binom{112}{19} = 1.767 \times 10^{-14} \quad (8)$$

With this very small probability of the extra 9 TFIDF values in {TFIDF-9} being chosen by chance over those in {TFIDF-12}, we may conclude that some additional insight into optimizing the ensemble classifier has been gained by the approach herein.

The improved deployment accuracy justifies leaving out the three classes (Living, Opinion and Travel) from the training set per the Figure of Merit, RATD and MDODEV. If we analyze the original confusion matrix (data not shown), we find that these three classes have a combined 6.1% accuracy, compared to the 57.6% accuracy for the other nine classes. These three classes distribute their errors similarly to the distribution of errors of the other classes; that is, sending most of their errors to the classes with highest recall (the so-called "attractor classes" [14]); that is, to Business, Justice, Showbiz and World. The classes removed in the validation phase have both low recall and (relatively) high precision, meaning they are "repeller" classes and so distribute their error across other classes. Combined, these three classes have only three false positive assignments compared to 222 false positive assignments for the other nine classes: attracting false positives at 1/25 the rate of the other classes. These three classes act as an independent set of ground truth from the other nine classes. This means that subsequent evaluation of deployed ensemble classifiers determines how well the classifiers handle two relatively independent ground truth sets, and not a continuum of ground truth. This may not preclude a deployment classifier from performing well on this more complex data set, but it does pose a different "pattern" of classification challenge, which in itself is of value to determine using the methods shown herein. Table 2 provides another window on the improved cohesiveness of the nine classes after removing the Living, Opinion and Travel classes from the training set. The measurements RATD and MDEDOV decrease by 46.3% and 26.0%, respectively, for the best initial classifier after reducing the number of classes. The values of RATD and MDEDOV do not change for the worst of the initial classifiers after validation, which emphasizes the assertion that the 9 classes are a different type of class set from the 12 classes— not simply a reduction in the number of classes.

Training the deployment classifiers on a more cohesive ground truth set (9 classes) constitutes a **different ensemble configuration** from training the deployment classifiers on the original set of 12 classes. A different deployment classifier is recommended for these two cases (i.e. an ensemble of 19 rather than 10 simple classifiers). At minimum, the 12-set deployment classifier likely must better handle discontinuous data sets than they do continuous data sets. This may be disadvantageous when, after deployment, the amount of data to be handled is generally much greater than the training data and as such is likely to require a more robust classifier that can handle largely overlapping classes. The "learning before learning" approach (validation before training) and its direct measurement through the Figure of Merit supports what was observed for the confusion matrix, the RATD, and MDEDOV. We believe we ended up with a differently behaving 9-class training set than the original 12-class training set. Three suspect classes were culled from the training set, and the Figure of Merit sharply increased until the last of these was removed, then sharply dropped below unity. Discontinuities such as these are generally rare, and outlines a means of determining when ground truth data contains discontinuities. Much remains to be established both theoretically and empirically, but the data presented herein support the hypothesis that both validation-before-training classification accuracy and analytics of the validation-before-training confusion matrix can be used to provide a set of ground truthing data that may lead to enhanced ensemble classifier sets. Finally, the approach can be viewed as a specialized form of dimensionality reduction of the training set where the primary classes are pruned rather than using principal component analysis (PCA) or related methods. In previous work [1], noisy training data is removed from all labelled classes, rather than considering labelled classes as units to be inappropriate for training purposes. Future work will focus on comparing and contrasting these approaches.

ACKNOWLEDGMENTS

The CNN corpus [9] was produced thanks to Professor Rafael Lins of the Universidade de Pernambuco and his team.

REFERENCES

[1] H. Malik and V.S. Bhardwaj, Automatic training data cleaning for text classification, Data Mining Workshops (ICDMW), 2011 IEEE 11th International Conference on Pp. 442-449.
[2] Gerard Salton and Christopher Buckley, Term-Weighting Approaches in Automatic Text Retrieval, Information Processing and Management 24.5 (1988): 513-23.
[3] Stephen Robertson, Understanding inverse document frequency: on theoretical arguments for IDF, Journal of documentation 60.5 (2004): 503-520.
[4] K.L Kwok, Experiments with a component theory of probabilistic informational retrieval based on single terms as document components. ACM Transactions on Information Systems, 8(4). (1990), Pp. 363-386.
[5] J. Ramos, Using tf-idf to determine word relevance in document queries, Proceedings of the first instructional conference on machine learning (2003).
[6] S. Karbasi, and M Boughanem, Effective level of term frequency impact on large-scale retrieval performance: by top-term ranking method, Proceedings of the 1st international conference on Scalable information systems, ACM (2006), pp. 37.
[7] CodePlex. 2013. SharpNLP – open source natural language processing tools. Retrieved from https://sharpnlp.codeplex.com/#.
[8] A. M. Vans and S. J. Simske, Identifying top performing TF*IDF classifiers using the CNN corpus. Submitted for publication to the Journal of Imaging Science and Technology (JIST), September, 2016.
[9] R. D. Lins, S. J. Simske, L. S. Cabral, G. F. P. Silva, R. J. Lima, R. F. Mello e L. Favaro, "A multi-tool scheme for summarizing textual documents," 11th IADIS International Conference WWW/INTERNET, Madrid, Spain, 2012.
[10] Stanford CoreNLP: http://nlp.stanford.edu/software/corenlp.shtml.
[11] C. Silva and B. Ribeiro, "The importance of stop word removal on recall values in text categorization." IJCNN, volume (3) , 2003.
[12] W. Frakes and R. Baeza-Yates, "Information Retrieval: Data Structures and Algorithms". Prentice Hall. 1992
[13] M. Vans and S. Simske, "Summarization and Classification of CNN.com Articles using the TF*IDF Family of Metrics." Archiving 2016, April 2016, pp.21-23.
[14] S. Simske, "Meta-Algorithmics: Patterns for Robust, Low-Cost, High-Quality Systems", Singapore, IEEE Press and Wiley, 2013.

Detecting In-line Mathematical Expressions
in Scientific Documents

Kenichi Iwatsuki
The University of Tokyo
7-3-1 Hongo
Bunkyo-ku, Tokyo 113-8656, Japan
iwatsuki@nii.ac.jp

Takeshi Sagara
InfoProto Co., Ltd.
1-15-2 Ochiai
Tama-shi, Tokyo 206-0033, Japan
sagara@info-proto.com

Tadayoshi Hara
InfoProto Co., Ltd.
1-15-2 Ochiai
Tama-shi, Tokyo 206-0033, Japan
harasan.g@gmail.com

Akiko Aizawa
National Institute of Informatics
2-1-2 Hitotsubashi
Chiyoda-ku, Tokyo 101-8430, Japan
aizawa@nii.ac.jp

ABSTRACT

One of the issues in extracting natural language sentences from PDF documents is the identification of non-textual elements in a sentence. In this paper, we report our preliminary results on the identification of in-line mathematical expressions. We first construct a manually annotated corpus and apply conditional random field (CRF) for the math-zone identification using both layout features, such as font types, and linguistic features, such as context n-grams, obtained from PDF documents. Although our method is naive and uses a small amount of annotated training data, our method achieved an 88.95% F-measure compared with 22.81% for existing math OCR software.

KEYWORDS

PDF structure analysis; mathematical formula recognition; in-line mathematical expression detection; math IR; scientific paper mining

1 INTRODUCTION

Recent advances in natural language processing (NLP) techniques have enabled researchers to automatically extract and use scientific knowledge from scientific publications [6, 11]. However, these techniques require "natural language sentences" that can be analyzed by standard NLP tools, such as dependency parsers or named entity extractors. Extracting natural language sentences from PDF documents is quite laborious and time-consuming and thus causes a serious delay in the development of semantic analysis.

In the past, the automatic extraction of metadata has been the main motivator in PDF structure analysis [10, 13]. Several works also exist that target the identification of the section structures of

DocEng'17, September 4–7, 2017, Valletta, Malta
© 2017 Association for Computing Machinery.
ACM ISBN 978-1-4503-4689-4/17/09...$15.00
https://doi.org/10.1145/3103010.3121041

scientific papers [3, 12], and extraction of figures and tables [2]. However, the quality of the extracted sentences, in terms of NLP, has not been sufficiently considered in previous studies.

One of the critical issues in extracting natural language sentences from PDF documents is the identification of non-textual elements in a sentence. In this paper, we postulate that identifying *in-line* mathematical expressions is specifically important. In-line mathematical expressions include complex mathematical structures, such as "$\sum$" or "$\int$", in addition to symbols or variables that accompany their explicit natural language definitions, such as "where w is a sequence of words" or "the probability distribution $p(W|c)$." Unexpectedly, our analysis showed that it is not a trivial task to distinguish in-line mathematical expressions from dictionary words that appear in italics. Identifying this notation is useful not only for reducing the errors of sentence parsing, but also enabling further scientific text mining because mathematical expressions often convey key concepts in scientific information dissemination.

Recently, deep-learning techniques have just created an opportunity for progress on mathematical OCR, which is the task of converting mathematical images into MathML [4], which is a standard XML representation of mathematical expressions[1]. Once such a technique is established, identifying in-line mathematical expressions becomes more critical. For example, the definitions of mathematical variables can effectively enhance the search of independent-line mathematical expressions [7]. However, to the best of our knowledge, there has never been a study that has focused on the detection of in-line mathematical expressions.

Based on this background, we report in this paper our preliminary results on the issue. In our method, we first construct a manually annotated corpus and apply conditional random fields (CRFs) for math-zone identification using both layout features such as font types, and linguistic features such as context n-grams, obtained from PDF documents. We investigate the effectiveness of the method by comparing the results with an existing math OCR tool (InftyReader[2] [5]). We also identify influential features by an ablation test to demonstrate that both types of features contribute to performance. Although our method is naive and uses only a

---

[1]https://www.w3.org/Math/
[2]http://www.inftyproject.org/en/

PDF document

```
15 B-Secti Introduction
16 B-Body This paper is an attempt to
17 I-Body indexing as a process of ge
18 I-Body clusters overlapping with e
19 I-Body ual clusters, referred to as
20 I-Body paper, contain multiple sub
21 I-Body ements, such as document
22 I-Body words, and other related to
23 I-Body ample, a cluster in Figure 1
24 I-Body documents written by a sp
25 I-Body authors related to a subjec
26 E-Body of terms'.
```

Figures and tables extraction
Line detection

Line type identification

Segmentation into blocks

```
<span class="word" id="w-2-0-1" data-bdr="0.15066,0.40337,0.27164,0.41683" data-ftype="2" data-space="space">Introduction</span>
<span class="word" id="w-2-1-0-0" data-bdr="0.11765,0.42448,0.15241,0.43684" data-ftype="4" data-space="bol">This</span>
<span class="word" id="w-2-1-0-1" data-bdr="0.15948,0.42448,0.20377,0.43684" data-ftype="4" data-space="space">paper</span>
<span class="word" id="w-2-1-0-2" data-bdr="0.21080,0.42448,0.22278,0.43684" data-ftype="4" data-space="space">is</span>
<span class="word" id="w-2-1-0-3" data-bdr="0.22975,0.42448,0.24857,0.43684" data-ftype="4" data-space="space">an</span>
<span class="word" id="w-2-1-0-4" data-bdr="0.25557,0.42448,0.31796,0.43684" data-ftype="4" data-space="space">attempt</span>
<span class="word" id="w-2-1-0-5" data-bdr="0.32518,0.42448,0.34103,0.43684" data-ftype="4" data-space="space">to</span>
<span class="word" id="w-2-1-0-6" data-bdr="0.34806,0.42448,0.40541,0.43684" data-ftype="4" data-space="space">provide</span>
<span class="word" id="w-2-1-0-7" data-bdr="0.41278,0.42448,0.42170,0.43684" data-ftype="4" data-space="space">a</span>
```

In-line math span detection

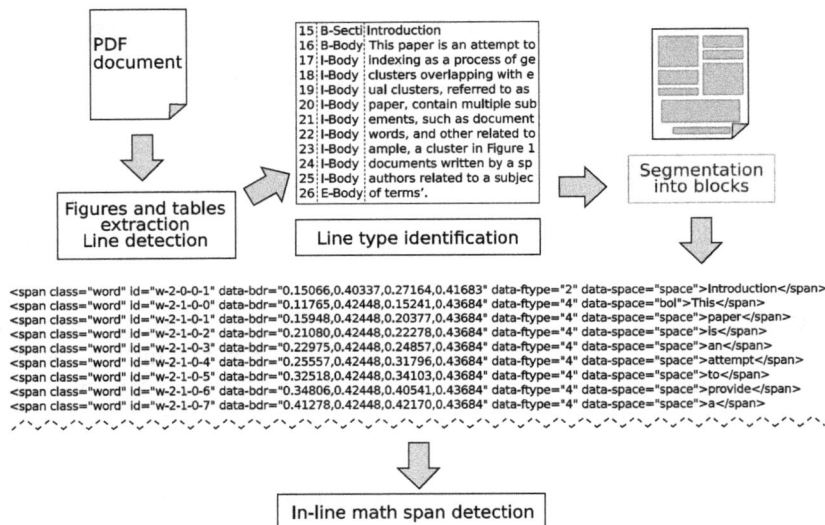

Figure 1: Preparing data for the in-line math span detection module.

small amount of annotated training data, the results are promising and we expect that our investigation will provide a strong basis for similar techniques.

2 RELATED WORK

2.1 PDF Structure Analysis of Scholarly Documents

Despite the worldwide movement toward XML publication by leading publishers, the majority of scientific papers are still published ing PDF format [11]. Since PDF is a layout-based format for printing, it is not easy to recognize the logical structure of a paper if only PDF files are available.

Existing tools to analyze PDF scientific articles have mostly applied machine learning techniques, such as support vector machines (SVMs) or CRF, to manage the ambiguity. Several state-of-the-art tools include CERMINE (SVM and CRF) [13], GROBID (CRF) [10], and OCR++(CRF) [12]. In a comparative study in 2015 [9] GROBID was reported to be the best performing system for metadata extraction. Then, CERMINE and OCR++ were reported to be improvements over GROBID.

Evaluation datasets has been created manually [12] based on the bibliographical meta-data that corresponds to PDF papers [9, 10] or semi-automatically constructed using the XML full-text version of papers [13].

2.2 Formula Identification

Non-textual objects in scientific papers include figures, tables, and pseudo-code. Among them, mathematical expressions that appear as in-line objects are difficult to recognize using standard layout analysis techniques.

Recently, Lin et al. [8] proposed a method for identifying a text line for independent-line mathematical formulae. Once the regions for mathematical expressions are identified, automatic formula identification methods can be applied to convert the math images to standard formats such as MathML. Deng et al. [4] applied constitutional and recurrent neural networks for the image-to-XML conversion of mathematical expressions and reported 75% accuracy on their dataset. InftyReader [5] can identify in-line math expressions. However, because only limited features are considered for the detection, it may not be sufficient to handle a wide range of mathematical expressions. In this paper, we use a more general framework based on sequential labeling.

3 METHOD

3.1 Data Preparation

First, we needed to determine where we should place our in-line math detection module within the workflow of PDF structure analysis. We assumed that in-line math detection was applied after segment identification and labeling, but before sentence splitting (Figure 1). Therefore, the input to the detection module was a sequence of space-separated tokens with their font types and the positions of the corresponding word bounding boxes. Linguistic features, such as POS tags and dependencies, were not considered in this study.

Considering the availability of manually annotated labels, we used our own in-house PDF analysis tool [1] for data preparation. In our workflow, all the text lines in the document were first extracted using poppler[3], ImageMagick[4], and pdffigures [5]. Using information about the positions of characters, the utility called pdfto-text included in poppler automatically integrated characters into words. Then, we manually categorized the text lines into 38 predefined classes including *title*, *author*, *section header*, *theorem*, and *figures*. Then, consecutive text lines with the same label were merged into a single block. The blocks that were labeled as *body* became the input to the in-line math detector.

---

[3]https://poppler.freedesktop.org/
[4]https://legacy.imagemagick.org/
[5]http://pdffigures.allenai.org/

It should be noted that, unlike up-to-date tools such as GROBID, our annotation explicitly labeled independent-line math formulae, which enabled us to exclude them from our dataset. We used manually annotated data only for the purpose of evaluation. Automatic segmentation was also possible, for which we obtained the accuracy 96.54% with CRF when we used 130 papers as training data. For this paper, we focused on born-digital PDF papers, not OCR-processed PDFs.

3.2 Construction of the Annotated Dataset

We selected 74 papers from ACL Anthology[6]. Each paper contained a minumum of one mathematical expression, a maximum of 699 mathematical expressions, and an average of 156 mathematical expressions. The average number of words per math span was 3.61. Of all the math spans, 11.3% consisted of only one letter, which usually denoted a variable and whose detection was useful for tasks such as the extraction of the explanation of each variant.

In our annotation, each maximal text region of the mathematical expression that satisfied the following policy was annotated as an "in-line mathematical expression." For further details, refer to the guidelines at https://github.com/Alab-NII/inlinemath.

(1) Annotate every minimal region that (structurally and semantically) satisfies the following conditions:

(1-a) the region can be recognized as playing the role of (structurally/semantically) composing a natural language sentence containing the region; and

(1-b) the region has a mathematically-closed (independent) structure.

(2) Cover any structures and notations specific to mathematics, which do not appear in the text of neutral domains.

3.3 CRF Features

To identify in-line mathematical expressions, we tagged every word using CRF[7]. We used three types of labels: beginning of math expression (B), inside math expression (I), and outside math expression (O). The size of the window around the current word was five words (two words to the left and two words to the right). For CRF features, we used the following:

- word (word)
- font (font of the word (font name and font size))
- length (length of the word)
- samew (whether the same word is contained in an independent formula) (T/F)
- samef (whether the same font is used in an independent formula) (T/F)
- samewf (samew and samef) (T/F)
- alpha (whether the word consists of only letters) (T/F)
- greek (whether the word contains a Greek letter) (T/F)
- math (whether the word contains a mathematical symbol) (T/F)
- single (whether the word is a single character) (T/F)
- mainfont (whether the font of the word is the same as the body text) (T/F)

---

[6]http://aclanthology.info/
[7]We used CRFsuite (http://www.chokkan.org/software/crfsuite/) in our implementation.

- block (label of the block containing the word)
- url (whether the word is a part of a URL (T/F)

4 EXPERIMENTS

4.1 Baseline and Performance Measures

As a baseline, we used the latest version of InftyReader[8] Ver.3.1.3.1. InftyReader [5] is currently the most commonly used OCR-based mathematical content recognition system. For preprocessing, InftyReader returns the positions and sizes of the rectangular regions of all mathematical expressions in a document. Based on the information, we identified the in-line mathematical expressions detected by InftyReader.

The performance was evaluated using precision, recall, and the F-measure calculated as follows: $Precision = \frac{a_i}{b_i}$, $Recall = \frac{a_i}{c_i}$, and $F\text{-}measure = \frac{2 \cdot Precision \cdot Recall}{Precision + Recall}$, where a_i denotes the number of words in paper i that are math expressions and tagged correctly, b_i denotes the number of words that are tagged as math expressions, and c_i denotes the actual number of words in the math expressions.

4.2 Performance

The precision, recall, and F-measure values for five-fold cross-validation are shown in Table 1. *Micro-average* denotes the case in which the score was calculated based on the word count. *Macro-average* denotes the average of the performance scores for each paper. As is shown in Table 1, InftyReader achieved a high recall but low precision, which indicates that it selected candidates with low confidence. By contrast, our CRF-based method performed reasonably for both precision and recall, which resulted in a substantial performance difference in terms of F-measure (22.81% vs. 88.95% for the micro-average, and 23.84% vs. 80.41% for the macro-average).

To determine which feature was important, an ablation test was conducted. The same experiments were conducted after removing one feature. If the removed feature was significant, the scores should have decreased a great deal. Table 2 shows the results of the ablation test. The word and mainfont features were the two most influential features, which demonstrates that both linguistic (e.g. word) and layout (e.g. font) features contributed to the identification task.

Table 1: Overall performance.

	Precision	Recall	F-measure
InftyReader (micro-avr.)	13.06%	89.98%	22.81%
Our method (micro-avr.)	94.93%	83.68%	88.95%
InftyReader (macro-avr.)	13.82%	86.74%	23.84%
Our method (macro-avr.)	86.54%	75.09%	80.41%

4.3 Error Analysis

We further analyzed the cause of the relatively low recall values. Our analysis demonstrated that the problematic math expressions could be categorized into the following three types: The first type is mathematical expressions infrequently used, such as V_{todo},

[8]http://www.sciaccess.net/en/InftyReader/

Table 2: Results of feature ablation test (micro average).

Removed feature	Precision	Recall	F-measure
word	88.77%	73.99%	80.71%
font	93.54%	77.21%	84.60%
length	92.67%	78.25%	84.85%
samew	92.02%	78.98%	85.00%
samef	92.69%	79.35%	85.50%
samewf	92.69%	79.36%	85.51%
alpha	93.09%	78.92%	85.42%
greek	92.42%	79.10%	85.24%
math	92.96%	79.13%	85.49%
single	92.71%	89.98%	85.59%
mainfont	92.67%	77.42%	84.36%
block	93.16%	77.36%	84.52%
url	92.81%	79.52%	85.65%

$RankPos_i$, and lp_{misc}, which are not typically contained in learning datasets. Since word features are significant, these expressions are unlikely to be classified as mathematical expressions. The second type is parentheses. There were some cases where the system recognized "(" as a math expression but not ")." The third type is variables in texts. We found many failure cases where variables were expressed using the same font as narrative text, such as "p", not "*p*." Since the font feature was weighted highly in our trained CRF, variables with body text fonts were unlikely to be correctly recognized.

4.4 Discussion

Table 3 shows the relationship between the number of papers used for training. It can be observed that the amount of performance improvement was only small compared with the data size. Table 4 shows the top 10 weighted features obtained using the CRFSuite default options. Our CRF relied more on individual words than general features and seemed to overfit the training set. A simple solution for this would be to increase the size of the training dataset. However, considering the annotation cost, a more realistic solution would be to use more elaborate feature engineering or introduce a neural network-based framework.

Table 3: Relationship between the number of learned papers and scores (micro-avr.).

# of learn data	37	59.2	72	73
# of test data	37	14.8	2	1
Precision	91.56%	94.93%	92.66%	92.54%
Recall	78.61%	83.68%	80.51%	80.75%
F-measure	84.60%	88.95%	86.16%	86.25%

5 CONCLUSION

We proposed a method to detect in-line mathematical expressions using CRF and achieved an 88.95% F-measure, even though the learning dataset was small. To the best of our knowledge, this is the first work that has focused on in-line math, and the score was far better than the existing math OCR tool. We found that words and

Table 4: Top-10 weighted features.

Feature (1-5)	Lbl.	Wght.	Feature (6-10)	L.	W.
word[0]=.	O	3.17	word[0]=M2	O	-2.04
word[0]=,	O	3.12	word[0]=M1	O	-1.95
word[0]=CW1	B	2.46	word[0]=M1	B	1.79
word[0]=CW2	B	2.25	word[0]=)	O	1.67
word[0]=M2	B	2.14	mainfont[0]=T	O	1.56

fonts were important for distinguishing math expressions from narrative text.

Detecting in-line mathematical expressions is important to exploit information from scholarly articles using NLP technologies. Note that narrative text and math expressions should be addressed in a different manner. For example, it matters whether "a" is a variable or an indefinite article. The proposed method also serves as a critical component in math information retrieval for scientific articles. For example, we can apply the description extraction developed in [7] to generate pairs such as {W, "*a sequence of words*"} and {A_{ji}, "*acoustic frames*"}.

The CRF-based implementation is simple and can be easily applied to a large scale scientific paper collection. We expect that the proposed method would be the baseline for in-line math detection and related areas.

ACKNOWLEDGMENTS

This work was supported by JST CREST Grant Number JP-MJCR1513, Japan.

REFERENCES

[1] Takeshi Abekawa and Akiko Aizawa. 2016. SideNoter: Scholarly Paper Browsing System based on PDF Restructuring and Text Annotation. In *COLING*. 136–140.
[2] Christopher Clark and Santosh Divvala. 2016. PDFFigures 2.0: Mining Figures from Research Papers. In *JCDL*. 143–152.
[3] Isaac G. Councill, C. Lee Giles, and Min-Yen Kan. 2008. ParsCit: an Open-source CRF Reference String Parsing Package. In *LREC*. 661–667.
[4] Yuntian Deng, Anssi Kanervisto, and Alexander M Rush. 2016. What You Get Is What You See: A Visual Markup Decompiler. *arXiv preprint arXiv:1609.04938* (2016).
[5] Yuko Eto and Masakazu Suzuki. 2001. Mathematical Formula Recognition Using Virtual Link Network. In *ICDAR*. 762–767.
[6] Halil Kilicoglu. 2017. Biomedical Text Mining for Research Rigor and Integrity: Tasks, Challenges, Directions. *Brief. Bioinform.* (2017).
[7] Giovanni Yoko Kristianto, Goran Topic, and Akiko Aizawa. 2017. Utilizing Dependency Relationships between Math Expressions in Math IR. *Inf. Retr. J.* 20, 2 (2017), 132–167.
[8] Xiaoyan Lin, Liangcai Gao, Zhi Tang, Josef Baker, Mohamed Alkalai, and Volker Sorge. 2013. A Text Line Detection Method for Mathematical Formula Recognition. In *ICDAR*. 339–343.
[9] Mario Lipinski, Kevin Yao, Corinna Breitinger, Joeran Beel, and Bela Gipp. 2013. Evaluation of Header Metadata Extraction Approaches and Tools for Scientific PDF Documents. In *JCDL*. 385–386.
[10] Patrice Lopez. 2009. GROBID: Combining Automatic Bibliographic Data Recognition and Term Extraction for Scholarship Publications. In *TPDL*. 473–474.
[11] Horacio Saggion and Francesco Ronzano. 2016. Natural Language Processing for Intelligent Access to Scientific Information. http://taln.upf.edu/pages/coling2016tutorial/COLING2016_T3_NLP_FOR_SCIENTIFIC_PUBLICATION_v7.pdf. In *COLING*. 9–13.
[12] Mayank Singh, Barnopriyo Barua, Priyank Palod, Manvi Garg, Sidhartha Satapathy, Samuel Bushi, Kumar Ayush, Krishna Sai Rohith, Tulasi Gamidi, Pawan Goyal, and Animesh Mukherjee. 2016. OCR++: A Robust Framework For Information Extraction from Scholarly Articles. In *COLING*. 3390–3400.
[13] Dominika Tkaczyk, Paweł Szostek, Mateusz Fedoryszak, Piotr Jan Dendek, and Łukasz Bolikowski. 2015. CERMINE: Automatic Extraction of Structured Metadata from Scientific Literature. *Int. J. Doc. Anal. Recognit.* 18, 4 (2015), 317–335.

High Performance Computational Framework for Phrase Relatedness

Zichu Ai
Dalhousie University
Zichu.Ai@dal.ca

Jie Mei
Dalhousie University
jmei@cs.dal.ca

Abidalrahman Moh'd
Dalhousie University
abidalrahman.mohd@dal.ca

Norbert Zeh
Dalhousie University
nzeh@cs.dal.ca

Meng He
Dalhousie University
mhe@cs.dal.ca

Evangelos Milios
Dalhousie University
eem@cs.dal.ca

ABSTRACT

TrWP is a text relatedness measure that computes semantic similarity between words and phrases utilizing aggregated statistics from the Google Web 1T 5-gram corpus. The phrase similarity computation in TrWP is costly in terms of both time and space, making the existing implementation of TrWP impractical for real-world usage. In this work, we present an in-memory computational framework for TrWP, which optimizes the corpus search using perfect hashing and minimizes the required memory cost using variable length encoding. Evaluated using the Google Web 1T 5-gram corpus, we demonstrate that the computational speed of our framework outperforms a file-based implementation by several orders of magnitude.

CCS CONCEPTS

• **Information systems** → *Structured text search*;

KEYWORDS

Semantic Text Similarity; Efficient Indexing; Searching; Compression

1 INTRODUCTION

Document relatedness is an important research topic in the field of Natural Language Processing (NLP) that is useful for many tasks, including plagiarism detection, document classification, and machine translation. As very large data collections, such as the Google Web 1T 5-gram corpus [3], become available, the performance of many text similarity algorithms has been enhanced because of the enrichment of semantic information, and Google Trigram Method (GTM) has been demonstrated to be one of the most effective algorithms [6]. *Text relatedness using word and phrase relatedness method (TrWP)* [8] improves GTM by recognizing that semantic units that capture related concepts may be represented by phrases composed of two or more words. Related phrases (of one or two words) are recognized by their occurrences in same contexts. The introduction

DocEng'17, September 4–7, 2017, Valletta, Malta.
© 2017 ACM. 978-1-4503-4689-4/17/09...$15.00
DOI: https://doi.org/10.1145/3103010.3121039

of phrase contexts increases the performance of text relatedness calculations using Person correlation as criteria but requires large data structures to manipulate and analyze those contexts, so storage space is a problem. A document similarity calculation may trigger hundreds of queries requesting for phrase similarities, so the query speed is also crucial. We may perform file indexing for the corpus and load only the potion of those corpus related to a query into memory during calculation to save memory, but the file I/O is slow. To support fast queries, it is imperative to store all data structures in memory, which we achieve by designing compact data structures to represent context information. Specifically, we use two ideas: First, we map unigrams and bigrams to unique indexes using the perfect hashing function. Second, we show that the context array now representing words by their associated integer indices can be compactly encoded using variable length encoding.

The resulting high-performance framework is more than 10,000 times faster than the file-based system for answering a phrase similarity query, and the construction process of all data structures cost approximately 4 hours.

2 TEXT RELATEDNESS USING WORD AND PHRASE RELATEDNESS

In this section, we review TrWP [8], an unsupervised text similarity algorithm using word n-gram statistics. TrWP extends GTM by including bigram-bigram and unigram-unigram similarities during text similarity calculation. These phrase similarities are calculated using *phrase context* as shown in 2.1.

2.1 Phrase Similarity Calculation

Phrase similarity is queried based on the calculation performed on phrase contexts generated from Google Web 1T n-gram corpus. The types of n-gram contexts we consider are shown in Table 1, where the grams in italic font constitute the phrases contexts while grams in normal font forming the target phrases.

Consider two n-grams, P_1 and P_2, whose relatedness is what we want to compute. First, we extract all contexts of each of P_1 and P_2 in the n-gram corpus. Second, we perform lexical pruning on the contexts, which removes contexts that satisfy certain conditions. One condition is related to the presence of stopwords in a context: *left contexts* with a stopword in the left-most position are removed, *right contexts* with a stopword in the right-most position are removed, and *left-right contexts* with stop words at both ends are also removed. Third, we detect identical contexts (in terms of words and context type) shared by P_1 and P_2. Fourth, we perform statistical

Table 1: Phrase context notations. This table shows three context types, based on the position of the target phrase in the *n*-gram

Context Category	Context Example
right context	bachelor *lives alone*
left-right context	*nice* bachelor *person*
left context	*very tall* bachelor
right context	large number *of files*
left-right context	*very* large number *generator*
left context	*multiply a* large number

pruning on these identical contexts: (1) For each context of P_1 and each context of P_2, we collect their frequencies; (2) Compile the frequencies of all identical contexts into two arrays, one for P_1 and one for P_2; () For each array, we compute the average frequency μ_{sr} and the standard deviation σ_{sr} of each array; (d) We remove all contexts whose frequency is outside the range of $\mu_{sr} \pm \sigma_{sr}$.

Given target phrases P_1 and P_2, we define an identical context of P_1 and P_2 as PCI and an original context (before detection of identical contexts) as PC. The relatedness score of two phrases P_1 and P_2 is computed using the following four steps:

1. For each identical context pair, we calculate the ratio (minimum / maximum) between them, and multiply it with the sum of their frequencies. Then we sum the results of all k statistically pruned identical context pairs, to obtain the relatedness strength RS, in Eq.1:

$$RS = \sum^{k} \left(\frac{min(C(PCI_1), C(PCI_2))}{max(C(PCI_1), C(PCI_2))} \cdot sum(C(PCI_1), C(PCI_2)) \right) \quad (1)$$

2. In this step we compute the cosine similarity between all the non-pruned (identical and non-identical) phrase contexts of P_1 and P_2 as:

$$cosSim(PC_1, PC_2) = \frac{PC_1 \cdot PC_2}{||PC_1|| \cdot ||PC_2||} \quad (2)$$

3. We combine the relatedness strength and cosine similarity generated from the context arrays, defined as RS_COS:

$$RS\_COS = RS(PCI_1, PCI_2) \cdot cosSim(PC_1, PC_2) \quad (3)$$

4. We define the normalized phrase relatedness as the NGD [4] normalization of RS_COS:

$$NGD(RS\_COS) = e^{\left\{ -2 \cdot \frac{max(\log C(P_1), \log C(P_2)) - \log(RS\_COS)}{\log N - min(\log C(P_1), \log C(P_2))} \right\}} \quad (4)$$

3 HIGH PERFORMANCE COMPUTATIONAL FRAMEWORK

Our objective is to ensure compact storage and fast retrieval of target phrases and phrase contexts in order to accelerate the calculation and make the algorithm practical for large text collections. We follow the two main ideas: First, we map each unigram and bigram to a unique integer *ID* using perfect hashing. This leads to both a more compact representation of phrases and manipulation of phrases. Secondly, to reduce the size of our data structures, we compress context arrays using delta coding and variable-length coding.

Mapping n-gram to Indexes. The first step, perfect hashing, involves mapping keys in string format,called S, to integer *ID*s for fast calculation and compact storage. Here we apply the *Hash, displace and compress* (CHD) algorithm[2][1] for the generation of a minimal perfect hash function, which ensures constant time for the retrieval of indexes. A minimal perfect hash function h for a set S of k keys ensures that each key in S maps to a unique integer *ID* in the range $[0, k-1]$. However, if we apply h to a key not in S, it also produces an integer in this range. To detect whether a given query key x is in fact in S, we store the elements in S in a string array A, storing element $y \in S$ at index in the array. Give a query key x, we check whether $x \in S$ by testing whether $A(h(x)) = x$. If so, we report $h(x)$ as x's *ID*, otherwise, we report that $x \notin S$. We call the string array together with the perfect hash function the *gram-indexer*. Since perfect hash function ensures no hash collision, after generating the perfect hash function, we may construct the string array concurrently over all *grams* to save construction time.

Mapping Indexes to Frequencies. we map the indexes of the target phrases to their corresponding frequencies. Here we store an integer array that stores the frequency of phrase x in position $h(x)$, defined as *gram-frequency-indexer*. This data structure can also be constructed concurrently over all grams if we use unique *ID*s generated by *gram-indexer* as the positions of frequency values.

Mapping Indexes to Phrase Contexts. we associate each target phrase with its corresponding contexts and the data structure is defined as *gram-context-indexer*. Each context consists of three components: (1) Flag indicating whether it is a *left context, right context* or *left-right context*; (2) $h(x)$ of the context interpret as a bigram (3) Frequency of this context.

According to Zipf's law, longer *n*-grams have lower frequencies, so we expect lower frequencies to occur more often. We exploit this skewed distribution of frequency values to save space by storing them using a variable-length encoding. If we sort contexts by increasing gram *ID*s rather than the *ID*s themselves. Since the differences are smaller than the *ID*s themselves, we can once again save space by storing them using a variable-length encoding.

We tried several variable-length encoding methods to perform bit packing of the context array, including Elias encoding [5] and block encoding [1, 7]. The best performing method in our experiment was achieved by the Elias ω code in the aspect of compression rate.

The construction process of *gram-context-indexer* works as follows: (1) First, we construct the context array from files. (2) Second, we sort each context array treating indexes as key information and frequencies as satellite information. (3) Next, we calculate differential values between adjacent indexes and transforming indexes into intervals. (4) Finally, we compress the context array using variable length encoding.

The overall data representation of the high-performance framework is shown graphically in Fig. 1. For two target phrases $gram_1$ and $gram_2$, (1) We query *gram-indexer* to get the index of each target phrase, defined as $index_1$ and $index_2$. (2) We retrieve the frequency

---

[1] C Minimal Perfect Hash Library: http://cmph.sourceforge.net/

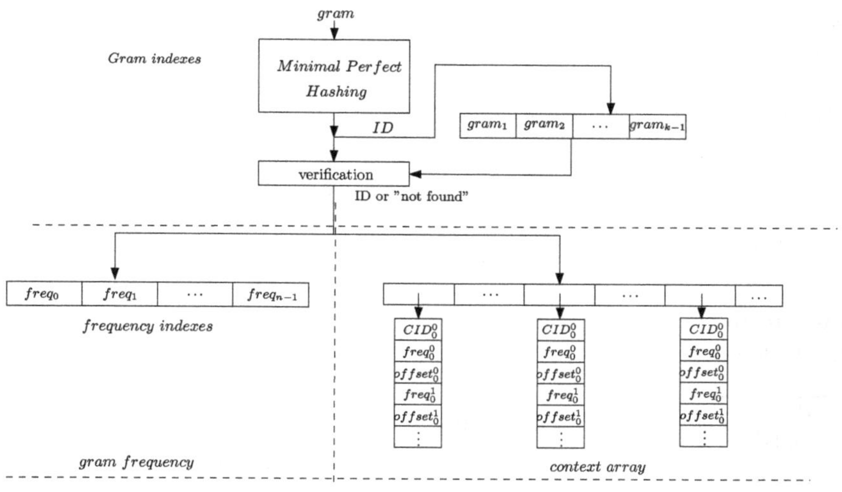

Figure 1: Data representation used by high-performance TrWP Framework, where *gram* stands for the target phrases, *index* stands for the numerical index of a gram within keyset, *freqT* stands for the frequency of target phrase, *CID* stands for the ID of first context, *offset* stands for the difference between the *ID*s of the current context and the previous contexts, *freqC* stands for the frequency of context or target phrase

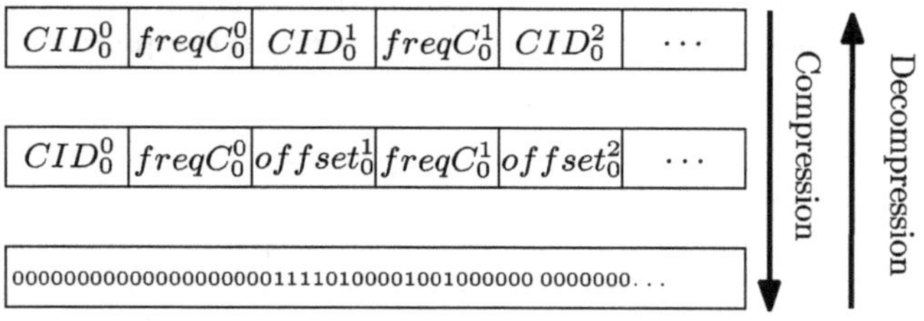

Figure 2: Compression & decompression of context array. *CID* stands for context ID, *offset* stands for the difference between consecutive *ID*s and *freqC* stands for the frequencies of the context

of each target phrase using $index_1$ and $index_2$ from *gram-frequency-indexer*. (3) We retrieve the context array in the format of bit vectors and decompress it, including the reconstruction of context *ID*s from the context *ID* differences stored in the compressed representation. (4) As the context array is already in order, it is easy to find identical context elements by performing a linear scan.

4 EVALUATION

4.1 Experiment Setup

The experiment was performed on a Linux server with 32 Intel Xeon E5-2650 @ 2.00 GHz CPUs and 256 GB of main memory. We chose Google Web 1T corpus for TrWP evaluation and calculated the similarity of 108 noun phrase pairs as done in [8]. The Google Web 1T corpus contains around 1 trillion words with n-gram length ranging from 1 to 5. The file size of unigrams to fourgrams is approximately 55 GB, There are 767,233,776 items (unigrams, bigrams and contexts) in our keyset. Due to the preprocessing done by TrWP, including transforming all n-grams into lowercase, merging

frequencies of the same lowercase n-grams and removing those instances with punctuation at the beginning or end, the size of Google n-gram corpus is shrunk, are shown in Table 2. After preprocessing, the size of the raw Google n-gram data was approximately 45G.

4.2 Speed Evaluation

First, we compare our system with the existing TrWP implementation. The existing implementation of TrWP is based on file indexing, that is, the data set of the Google Web 1T corpus was divided into hundreds of folders in a lexicographic order with unigram prefixes as folder names, when we query the system, only those n-grams which share the same prefix with the query will be loaded into memory during the target phrase frequency query and context retrieval process. Such a method is memory efficient but not optimized for fast queries because the system has frequent access to the file system during phrase similarity queries.

The implementation of our high-performance framework takes approximately five hours for the generation of perfect hash function and it takes around four hours to construct the data structures. This is a one-time overhead that would be amortized over many queries. Most of this construction time is due to disk I/O.

In our experiment, we compare the break-down of the time to compute the relatedness of 108 pairs of phrases using the file-based system and the high-performance system respectively. Since the speed improvement is large, we represent time using a log scale in Fig. 3. The high-performance system is overall faster than the file-based system by four to five orders of magnitude. We evaluated Elias γ code, Elias ω code, Elias δ code and block coding for compression.

According to Fig. 3, different compression methods have similar effects on the overall processing speed, and the decoding process of context array is expected to slow down the overall query speed by around 20%.

Table 2: Size of the files in the preprocessed Google *n*-gram dataset, with the number of *n*-grams and size in GB

Dataset	Numbers of Distinct *n*-grams	File Size [GB]
unigram	11,052,329	0.172
bigram	236,517,605	3.8
trigram	813,319,727	16
fourgram	1,086,649,416	26

Table 3: Breakdown of the time to compute the relatedness of 108 phrase pairs using 6 comparing methods

Step	Context Retrieval [s]	Calculation [s]	Overall [s]
FBS	128.206	3.456	131.662
HPS (Elias γ code)	0.134	0.469	0.604
HPS (Elias ω code)	0.119	0.460	0.579
HPS (Elias δ code)	0.111	0.516	0.627
HPS (Block code)	0.113	0.447	0.560
No compression	0	0.472	0.472

Table 4: Size of the data representation and compression rate achieved by the different compression methods

Compression	Size [GB]	Compression Rate
No compression	70	0.0 %
Elias γ code	61.380	12.3 %
Elias ω code	56.169	19.7 %
Elias δ code	58.968	15.7 %
Block (blocksize = 2) code	62.224	11.1 %

The phrase relatedness calculation mainly consists of two steps: context retrieval and calculation of phrase relatedness. A comparison of the costs of these two steps and the overall cost for the different implementations of TrWP is shown in Table 3. For the file-based system, most time is spent on context retrieval, which slows down the relatedness calculation significantly. In contrast, the high-performance system has all required information pre-loaded into memory, which guarantees significantly faster calculation speed.

4.3 Memory Evaluation

Data compression, including tokenization of unigrams, bigrams and contexts, is the key to making the space requirements of the in-memory data structures acceptable. The size of the *gram-indexer* is 40.527GB because of the string array, which is maintained to avoid false positives during index retrieval, while *gram-frequency-indexer* takes 7GB. The uncompressed size of the *gram-context-indexer* is around 70GB. Table 4 shows the memory usage of the *gram-context-indexer* using different compression methods and the compression rate compared with non-compressed *gram-context-indexer*. According to these experiments, Elias ω code achieves the highest compression rate while achieving the lowest query cost.

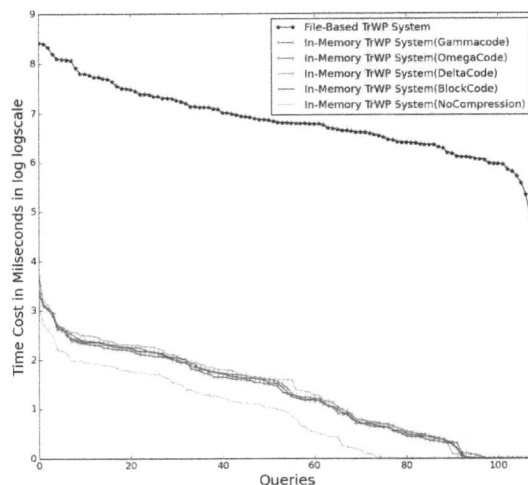

Figure 3: Speed evaluation of file-based framework and high-performance framework using log scale, x-axis indicates a specific query belongs to the 108 pairs. Target phrases with more context are expected to be slower during the query process

5 CONCLUSIONS

This paper introduced an in-memory high-performance computing framework for the phrase relatedness based on TrWP. The high-performance implementation is 4-5 orders of magnitude faster than the original file-based implementation. A substantial fraction of the speed-up was achieved by avoiding I/O when answering queries. This was made possible by carefully engineering space-efficient representations of the required data structures so that we were able to load them into memory before answering queries.

REFERENCES
[1] Paolo Boldi and Sebastiano Vigna. 2005. Codes for the World Wide Web. *Internet Math.* 2, 4 (2005), 407–429. http://projecteuclid.org/euclid.im/1150477666
[2] Fabiano C. Botelho, Rasmus Pagh, and Nivio Ziviani. 2007. Simple and Space-efficient Minimal Perfect Hash Functions. In *Proceedings of the 10th International Conference on Algorithms and Data Structures (WADS'07)*. Springer-Verlag, Berlin, Heidelberg, 139–150. http://dl.acm.org/citation.cfm?id=2394893.2394911
[3] Thorsten Brants and Alex Franz. 2006. Web 1T 5-gram Version 1. (2006).
[4] Rudi L. Cilibrasi and Paul M. B. Vitanyi. 2007. The Google Similarity Distance. *IEEE Trans. on Knowl. and Data Eng.* 19, 3 (March 2007), 370–383. DOI:https://doi.org/10.1109/TKDE.2007.48
[5] P. Elias. 2006. Universal Codeword Sets and Representations of the Integers. *IEEE Trans. Inf. Theor.* 21, 2 (Sept. 2006), 194–203. DOI:https://doi.org/10.1109/TIT.1975.1055349
[6] Aminul Islam, Evangelos Milios, and Vlado Keselj. 2012. Comparing Word Relatedness Measures Based on Google *n*-grams. In *Proceedings of COLING 2012: Posters*. The COLING 2012 Organizing Committee, Mumbai, India, 495–506. http://www.aclweb.org/anthology/C12-2049
[7] Adam Pauls and Dan Klein. 2011. Faster and Smaller N-gram Language Models. In *Proceedings of the 49th Annual Meeting of the Association for Computational Linguistics: Human Language Technologies - Volume 1 (HLT '11)*. Association for Computational Linguistics, Stroudsburg, PA, USA, 258–267. http://dl.acm.org/citation.cfm?id=2002472.2002506
[8] Md. Rashadul Hasan Rakib, Aminul Islam, and Evangelos Milios. 2016. *f: Phrase Relatedness Function Using Overlapping Bi-gram Context*. Springer International Publishing, Cham, 137–149. DOI:https://doi.org/10.1007/978-3-319-34111-8_19

Automatic Knowledge Base Construction from Scholarly Documents

Rabah A. Al-Zaidy
The Pennsylvania State University
Computer Science and Engineering
University Park, PA, USA
alzaidy@psu.edu

C. Lee Giles
The Pennsylvania State University
Information Science and Technology
University Park, PA, USA
giles@ist.psu.edu

ABSTRACT

The continuing growth of published scholarly content on the web ensures the availability of the most recent scientific findings to researchers. Scholarly documents, such as research articles, are easily accessed by using academic search engines that are built on large repositories of scholarly documents. Scientific information extraction from documents into a structured knowledge graph representation facilitates automated machine understanding of a document's content. Traditional information extraction approaches, that either require training samples or a preexisting knowledge base to assist in the extraction, can be challenging when applied to large repositories of digital documents. Labeled training examples for such large scale are difficult to obtain for such datasets. Also, most available knowledge bases are built from web data and do not have sufficient coverage to include concepts found in scientific articles. In this paper we aim to construct a knowledge graph from scholarly documents while addressing both these issues. We propose a fully automatic, unsupervised system for scientific information extraction that does not build on an existing knowledge base and avoids manually-tagged training data. We describe and evaluate a constructed taxonomy that contains over 15k entities resulting from applying our approach to 10k documents.

CCS CONCEPTS

•Information systems → Information extraction; *Document structure*;

KEYWORDS

Scholarly documents; knowledge base; taxonomy construction

1 INTRODUCTION

Typical search use for scholarly repositories such as Google Scholar, SemanticScholar, and CiteseerX, is via keyword-based queries that return ranked lists of links to scientific documents. In recent years, web search engines have introduced an entity-based approach for search. Entity-based search abilities are typically made possible by use of knowledge graphs [12]. Knowledge graphs model knowledge base information as entities and their relations. The nodes represent the entities and the set of labeled edges define the relationships between the entities. For web search engines, such as Google, a knowledge graph is built from the contents of web pages by identifying explicit entities. i.e. semantic labels provided by the website, and implicit entities that are identified by contextual analysis of the text using NLP [14]. Existing ontologies and knowledge base data are used to further enrich the extracted entities and the relations among them. For the scholarly search engine context, a similar approach can be applied since scientific documents contain meta data such as title, keywords, and bibliographic information, as well as content, which is the text of the document itself [18]. Thus, explicit entities can be easily derived from the metadata of the documents. However, if we wish to find an extraction analogous to the implicit entity identification, very few studies exist outside the biomedical domain, which mostly extract biomedical entities. In this paper we formulate the implicit entity extraction problem from scholarly documents as a knowledge base construction problem using the same definition of knowledge base as used in works such as DBpedia [3], WordNet [11], and Probase [19]. Using this formulation we focus on a single type of relation among entities: the hyponymy relation where entities, that are either nouns or noun-phrases are related via a directional *is-a* relationship. This means one of the entities is an instance of the other entity. The purpose of this formulation is to explore the possibility for a *scientific* entity-based search realm.

As web pages contain multiple forms of data, scholarly articles also contain a variety of data formats such as images, tables, algorithms, charts in addition to the text [18]. Thus, enhancing scientific search by processing queries in scholarly search engines as entity-based queries rather than keyword-based queries has merited potential. That is partly due to studies that have been able to extract and automatically analyze most forms of data found in scholarly documents [10], [1], [17], [18]. Data extraction from tables, scientific charts, and algorithms enables semantic analysis of this auxiliary content of documents for further intelligent reasoning. Recent studies provide an example of semantic analysis by representing information contained in bar charts as related entities in a semantic graph [2] .

In order for a knowledge base to be useful for scientific search purposes, it must have high accuracy of extraction and sufficient coverage of scientific concepts and entities contained in the documents. Thus, it is important to select an appropriate approach for KB construction that meets these needs. Since the content of scholarly documents is unstructured we must use an approach suitable for unstructured data sources. Additionally, the scale and diversity of content in the repositories dictate an automated approach as opposed to manually labeled seeds. In our approach we combine a

DocEng'17, September 4–7, 2017, Valletta, Malta.
© 2017 ACM 978-1-4503-4689-4/17/09...$15.00
DOI: https://doi.org/10.1145/3103010.3121043

pattern-based method, to generate a seed of relations, with an iterative learning approach that uses the seeds to harvest more entity relationships. In this paper we make the following contributions: (1) Apply an iterative algorithm to expand the space of extracted related entities. (2) Construct a domain-specific taxonomy graph that covers over 15,000 computer science-related entities. The rest of the paper is organized as follows. In Section 2 we discuss related work. Section 2 presents previous work that is most related to ours. Section 3 gives an overview of the KB construction framework. Section 4 describes our approach to extract entities and relations. Section 5 describes our taxonomy construction method. In Section 6 we show the results of our evaluation of the extracted concepts and the quality of the extracted relationships. Finally, we conclude in section 7 and describe future directions.

2 RELATED WORK

Knowledge graph construction from large scale corpora has been the focus of many studies. Examples include Google Knowledge Graph [14] , NELL [4] , YAGO [16] and DBpedia [3]. Automated approaches for extraction include the NELL [4] and KnowItAll [7] projects. These do contain many concepts that may exist in scientific texts yet they are general concepts. A more comprehensive KB that contains finer-level concepts is Probase [19]. Probase was constructed from a corpus of 1.68 billion web pages from which it harvested over 2.6 million concepts. Probase's corpus is web pages rather than research articles and scholarly content in general.

Many studies aim to extract hypernym-hyponym pairs using various approaches. One of the initial works is the one introducing the Hearst patterns [8] that have since been used by other approaches for bootstrapping. In other studies, training sets of known hypernym-hyponym pairs are used to train a model using dependency path features [15]. The model then learns new dependency paths and uses them to extract new is-a relation pairs.

Iterative approaches for knowledge base extraction such as NELL [4], and Probase [19] use a bootstrapping approach. The first two iteratively learn new syntactic patterns to improve the extraction for the next iterations. Our approach is similar to the one in NELL and Probase, in that our iterations learn more entities and relations by using knowledge extracted from previous iterations.

Automatic taxonomy construction from raw text in some cases makes use of an existing knowledge source. In the method adopted by Cimiano et al. [6], they construct a taxonomy using external knowledge such as Wordnet [11] combined with Hearst-style patterns. In other studies the approach itself does not rely on external knowledge sources to construct a taxonomy for web data but rather restricts it's corpus to a certain knowledge source, such as YAGO [16] and WikiTaxonomy [13]. Our method is similar to these in that we do not use external knowledge sources, however, they construct the taxonomies from Wikipedia articles.

3 KNOWLEDGE BASE CONSTRUCTION OVERVIEW

We propose a system to extract related entities from a set of scholarly documents. The entities are nouns and noun phrases and the type of relationship we extract is the hyponymy relation among

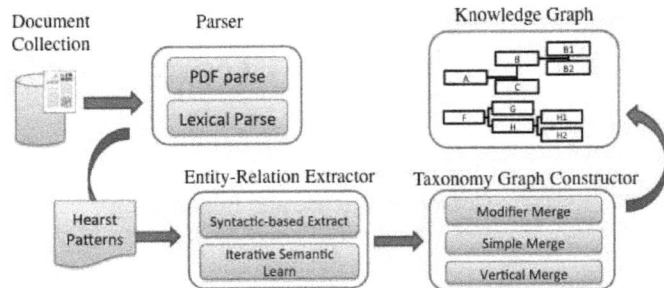

Figure 1: Knowledge base construction system

entities. A hypernym-hyponym relationship is one where one entity is an instance of the concept represented by the other entity. We follow the same formal notation common in most hyponymy extraction studies [5], [19]. For a document set D, we extract a set of sentences S that contain candidate tuples (X_i, Y_j) such that, $s = \{(X, Y_1), (X, Y_2), ..., (X, Y_k)\}$, where X is a hypernym for candidate hyponyms Y_j. Once the extraction is complete we have a set of extracted pairs, $P = \{(X_1, Y_1), (X_2, Y_2), ..., (X_N, Y_N)\}$. The knowledge base is constructed by building a taxonomy T by combining the local taxonomies identified by the tuples in the set P. We define the sets $X=\{x_1, ... ,x_m\}$ and $Y=\{y_1, ... ,y_n\}$, with $|X|$=m and $|Y|$=n, to be the sets of individual words comprising the noun phrase of a candidate hypernym and hyponym, respectively.

The pipeline of our system is shown in Figure 1. Given a set of documents in PDF format, the system generates a taxonomy represented as a graph. The system is comprised of three main modules: a parser, an entity-relation extractor, and a taxonomy graph constructor. The first module in the pipeline is the Parser. This is a syntactic parser that extracts dependency-paths to identify noun phrases. This module passes a set of parsed sentences to the next phase. The Entity-Relation Extractor and the Taxonomy Graph Constructor are described in the next two sections.

4 ITERATIVE HYPERNYM RELATION EXTRACTION

In this section we describe the two modules responsible for generating tuples of entities related with a hypernym-hyponym relation. The input to this step is a set of PDF documents D and the output is the set P of pairs (X,Y).

Since our approach does not rely on an existing knowledge base, we bootstrap our algorithm by extracting pairs using a set of hand-crafted patterns. The use of lexico-syntactic patterns for bootstrapping hyponymy extraction is a common practice since they have relatively high precision while compromising recall, which is tolerable for a bootstrapping step. We use the Hearst patterns [8] that define syntactic patterns used to denote a hyponymy relationship.

Syntactic extraction generates a set C of candidate pairs that need to be classified as acceptable pairs or ones that should be discarded. The iterative learning steps populate a set P of valid pairs that is initially empty. A first pass over the sentences will add any pair for which the hypernym phrase contains only a single word. If the hypernym phrase contains more than one word, the

Table 1: Annotator scores for extracted triple quality

Score	#NG-PL	%NG-PL	#UG-PL	%UG-PL
4	72	%54.13	27	%36.48
3	26	%19.54	19	%25.67
2	9	%6.76	7	%9.45
1	15	%11.27	14	%18.91
0	11	%8.27	7	%9.45

Table 2: Taxonomy coverage of top 3 million queries

# of top queryTerms	#of queries covered
10,000	3504
20,000	4323
30,000	4702
40,000	4915
50,000	5810

phrase must be processed by the hypernym extraction algorithm for phrase-detection. If a valid hypernym phase is detected we add the tuple to the set P. The hypernym extraction algorithm is a modified version of the probabilistic approach used by Wu et al. [19]. Given a candidate {X,Y} pair, we detect the values of $x_i \in X$ for the hypernym phrase. This may be a single value of x, or a subset, which we use as an ordered set by computing the n-grams from the set X.

5 SCIENTIFIC TAXONOMY CONSTRUCTION

The knowledge base extracted from the previous step in the set P is a set of N hypernym-hyponym pairs. In order to construct a taxonomy graph from these pairs we first represent each pair as a local taxonomy tree rooted at the hypernym with the hyponym as a child node. The construction of the taxonomy is thus reduced to a graph merging problem where initially we have N local taxonomy trees. The method first performs a ModifierNodeInsertion operation where a noun phrase that is found to be comprised of a modifier and a noun, is split into two nodes where the phrase is a child of the noun. For example, we can easily infer from the phrase *learning algorithm* that it is a subconcept of the more abstract concept *algorithm*. Next, the method performs a SimpleMerge operation, where nodes whose roots are similar and belong to the same sentence are horizontally merged into one parent node with the union of children of both nodes. In the case where the two nodes did not occur in the same sentence, the similarity between their children is used to determine whether to merge them or not. The third step used is the VerticalMerge, which aims to increase the hierarchy level in the graph. We apply this merge by observing the overlap between each child of a node and the root nodes of other local taxonomies. At the end of this step, the resulting tree contains a unique path for each entity.

6 EVALUATION

In order to evaluate our knowledge base extraction approach, we apply the method to a set of 10k papers published between 2004

and 2014 in computer science conferences. This generated over 17k candidate sentences and from that we obtained over 15k entities.

6.1 Syntactic-based Extraction

To evaluate the quality of our extracted hypernym-hyponym pairs, we randomly select pairs extracted from a subset of 400 documents. We extract the *is-a* pairs from these documents using our approach that incorporates the n-grams of the hypernym phrase and compare the results with that of applying the SuperConceptDetection algorithm described by Wu et al. [19]. We refer to our approach as NG-PL, from n-gram probabilistic learner and the baseline as UG-PL, since it considers only unigrams. From the 400 documents the number of harvested pairs is 133 and 74 when using our method and the baseline, respectively. The triples were annotated by three computer science graduate students. The annotators were asked to assign a score to each extracted tuple using an annotation scale 0-4, similar to the one proposed by Li et al. [9], defined as follows:

- **0:** The extracted relation is nonsense.
- **1:** The extracted relation is either vague or unhelpful. This covers the case where the hypernym-hyponym pair is too abstract to be useful or the phrase is not descriptive enough to substantiate a clear relationship.
- **2:** Opinion/I don't know. An example of this case the pair may contain a very specific concept that cannot be known without knowing the context of the paper it was extracted from, such as a new algorithm name that is just introduced in the paper and the annotator is not familiar with it.
- **3:** The extracted relation is somewhat true. This is used when the pair is generally correct but requires only small modification to become fully true.
- **4:** The extracted relation is correct as is.

The inter-annotator agreement was computed among the three annotations according to the average score given for each pair. The agreement result is 71% and evaluation results are shown in Table 1.

6.2 Taxonomy Evaluation

The scientific taxonomy is constructed by applying the pattern-based extraction step to the entire data set of 10k papers. This generates over 17k sentences that are candidates for containing hypernym-hyponym relationships. To evaluate the quality of the taxonomy graph we asses the coverage of the entities. To do this we perform a concept-space evaluation similar to that used by Wu et al. [19] to evaluate the coverage of the knowledge base. This measures whether the concepts extracted are ones that are frequently queried, the assumption is if a query term is found in our knowledge base, then it has good coverage. To do this, we compile a set of 3 million query logs submitted to the scholarly search engine CiteSeerX during the years 2015 and 2016. Stop-words are removed from the terms in the queries to find the top unique query terms in the entire set. The 3 million queries contained just over 500,000 unique terms. The most frequent terms were selected and looked up in the knowledge base to assess whether the knowledge base can provide more information about the concept.

Table 2 shows the number of queried topics that were found in the knowledge base. Although the knowledge base covers roughly

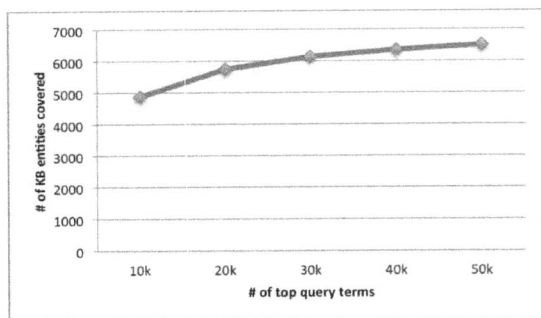

Figure 2: KB entities that are frequently queried

5% of the query terms, this percentage does increase with the increase of query terms. Several factors are to be noted here. The query logs are submitted to a search engine that contains papers on most scientific fields not only computer science. Thus, the queries we count are not selected for only computer science related queries, as our document set from which we extract the KB was. Additionally, for query terms, although stop-words were removed, they were not stemmed or lemmatized. Neither did they undergo a cleansing step to remove noisy terms.

In order to evaluate the value of the extracted entities we conduct another experiment to measure the number of entities in our knowledge base that are queried frequently by users. This is the reverse of the previous test, and implies a slightly different insight. If our entities, which are stemmed and lemmatized, are frequently queried, this suggests that they are useful extractions. Figure 2 shows the amount of entities in our knowledge base that were frequently queried. In a set of over 500,000 query terms we count the KB entities that occurred in the top 10,000-50,000 query terms. The results show that 59.76% of the KB entities are among the 0.02% most frequent queried terms, and 79.64% are among the 0.1% of queried terms. About 90% of the KB entities occur at least once in the entire set of 500,000 query terms. This small increase in entity count compared to the large increase in query terms indicates that it is possible that 10% of the KB entities are not useful terms.

7 CONCLUSIONS

Large scale knowledge graph construction from raw text is a challenging problem when the text contains domain specific concepts that are not covered by existing knowledge sources. In this paper we presented a system to extract a knowledge base from scholarly documents to harvest scientific entity-relation pairs. Our approach was tested on a set of 10,000 research articles published in computer science related conferences. The method bootstraps using a pattern-based approach to extract a seed of tuples that are used for learning new ones. A semantic learner iteratively harvests more tuples by using the knowledge gained from the previous iteration.

We also explore the effectiveness of a probabilistic scheme to identify valid hypernym phrases for extracted tuples. A taxonomy graph is then constructed using graph merging and insertion operations designed to provide as much information about entities as possible. Experimental evaluation shows that our hypernym

phrase extraction scheme is able to identify 3x more *true* hypernym/hyponym tuples than the baseline approach. From a data set of 10,000 documents and over 17,000 candidate sentences, the final taxonomy graph contains over 15,000 concepts. By sampling 400 of those documents we obtain a graph with 113 triples of which computer science annotators found over 70% of the relations to be generally true.

ACKNOWLEDGMENTS

The authors would like to thank Kunho Kim and Yuhsuan Kuo for their assistance with the evaluation of the results.

REFERENCES

[1] Rabah A Al-Zaidy and C Lee Giles. 2015. Automatic extraction of data from bar charts. In *Proceedings of the 8th International Conference on Knowledge Capture*. ACM, 30.
[2] Rabah A Al-Zaidy and C Lee Giles. 2017. A Machine Learning Approach for Semantic Structuring of Scientific Charts in Scholarly Documents. In *Twenty-Ninth IAAI Conference*.
[3] Sören Auer, Christian Bizer, Georgi Kobilarov, Jens Lehmann, Richard Cyganiak, and Zachary Ives. 2007. Dbpedia: A nucleus for a web of open data. *The semantic web* (2007), 722–735.
[4] Andrew Carlson, Justin Betteridge, Bryan Kisiel, Burr Settles, Estevam R Hruschka Jr, and Tom M Mitchell. 2010. Toward an Architecture for Never-Ending Language Learning.. In *AAAI*, Vol. 5. 3.
[5] Scott Cederberg and Dominic Widdows. 2003. Using LSA and noun coordination information to improve the precision and recall of automatic hyponymy extraction. In *Proceedings of the seventh conference on Natural language learning at HLT-NAACL 2003-Volume 4*. Association for Computational Linguistics, 111–118.
[6] Philipp Cimiano, Aleksander Pivk, Lars Schmidt-Thieme, and Steffen Staab. 2005. Learning taxonomic relations from heterogeneous sources of evidence. In *Ontology Learning from Text: Methods, evaluation and applications*.
[7] Oren Etzioni, Michael Cafarella, Doug Downey, Stanley Kok, Ana-Maria Popescu, Tal Shaked, Stephen Soderland, Daniel S Weld, and Alexander Yates. 2004. Web-scale information extraction in knowitall:(preliminary results). In *Proceedings of the 13th international conference on World Wide Web*. ACM, 100–110.
[8] Marti A Hearst. 1992. Automatic acquisition of hyponyms from large text corpora. In *Proceedings of the 14th conference on Computational linguistics-Volume 2*. Association for Computational Linguistics, 539–545.
[9] Xiang Li, Aynaz Taheri, Lifu Tu, and Kevin Gimpel. 2016. Commonsense knowledge base completion. In *Proceedings of the 54th Annual Meeting of the Association for Computational Linguistics (ACL), Berlin, Germany, August. Association for Computational Linguistics*.
[10] Xiaonan Lu, Saurabh Kataria, William J Brouwer, James Z Wang, Prasenjit Mitra, and C Lee Giles. 2009. Automated analysis of images in documents for intelligent document search. *International Journal on Document Analysis and Recognition (IJDAR)* 12, 2 (2009), 65–81.
[11] George A Miller. 1995. WordNet: a lexical database for English. *Commun. ACM* 38, 11 (1995), 39–41.
[12] Maximilian Nickel, Kevin Murphy, Volker Tresp, and Evgeniy Gabrilovich. 2016. A review of relational machine learning for knowledge graphs. *Proc. IEEE* 104, 1 (2016), 11–33.
[13] Simone Paolo Ponzetto and Michael Strube. 2007. Deriving a large scale taxonomy from Wikipedia. In *AAAI*, Vol. 7. 1440–1445.
[14] Amit Singhal. 2012. Introducing the Knowledge Graph: things, not strings. https://googleblog.blogspot.com/2012/05/introducing-knowledge-graph-things-not.html. (2012).
[15] Rion Snow, Daniel Jurafsky, Andrew Y Ng, and others. 2004. Learning syntactic patterns for automatic hypernym discovery.. In *NIPS*, Vol. 17. 1297–1304.
[16] Fabian M Suchanek, Gjergji Kasneci, and Gerhard Weikum. 2007. Yago: a core of semantic knowledge. In *Proceedings of the 16th international conference on World Wide Web*. ACM, 697–706.
[17] Suppawong Tuarob, Sumit Bhatia, Prasenjit Mitra, and C Lee Giles. 2016. AlgorithmSeer: A system for extracting and searching for algorithms in scholarly big data. *IEEE Transactions on Big Data* 2, 1 (2016), 3–17.
[18] Jian Wu, Jason Killian, Huaiyu Yang, Kyle Williams, Sagnik Ray Choudhury, Suppawong Tuarob, Cornelia Caragea, and C Lee Giles. 2015. Pdfmef: A multi-entity knowledge extraction framework for scholarly documents and semantic search. In *Proceedings of the 8th International Conference on Knowledge Capture*. ACM, 13.
[19] Wentao Wu, Hongsong Li, Haixun Wang, and Kenny Q Zhu. 2012. Probase: A probabilistic taxonomy for text understanding. In *Proceedings of the 2012 ACM SIGMOD International Conference on Management of Data*. ACM, 481–492.

Clinically Significant Information Extraction from Radiology Reports

Nidhin Nandhakumar
Faculty of Computer Science,
Dalhousie University
Halifax, NS, Canada
nidhin.nandhakumar@dal.ca

Ehsan Sherkat
Faculty of Computer Science,
Dalhousie University
Halifax, NS, Canada
ehsansherkat@dal.ca

Evangelos E. Milios
Faculty of Computer Science,
Dalhousie University
Halifax, NS, Canada
eem@cs.dal.ca

Hong Gu
Department of Mathematics and
Statistics, Dalhousie University
Halifax, NS, Canada
hgu@dal.ca

Michael Butler
Department of Medicine,
Dalhousie University
Halifax, NS, Canada
mbbutler@dal.ca

ABSTRACT

Radiology reports are one of the most important medical documents that a diagnostician looks into, especially in the emergency context. They provide the emergency physicians with critical information regarding the condition of the patient and help the physicians take immediate action on urgent conditions. However, the reports are in the form of unstructured text, which makes them time consuming for humans to interpret. We have developed a machine learning system to (a) efficiently extract the clinically significant parts and their level of importance in radiology reports, and (b) to classifies the overall report into *critical* or *non-critical* categories which help doctors to identify potential high priority reports. As a starting point, the system uses anonymized chest X-RAY reports of adults and provides three levels of importance for medical phrases. We used the Conditional Random Field (CRF) model to identify clinically significant phrases with an average f1-score of 0.75. The proposed system includes a web-based interface which highlights the medical phrases, and their level of importance to the emergency physician. The overall classification of the report is performed using the phrases extracted from the CRF model as features for the classifier. Average accuracy achieved is 85%.

CCS CONCEPTS

•**Computing methodologies** → **Machine learning approaches;** *Classification and regression trees;* •**Applied computing** → **Health care information systems;**

KEYWORDS

Information Extraction, Classification, Radiology Reports

DocEng '17, September 4-7, 2017, Valletta, Malta.
© 2017 ACM. 978-1-4503-4689-4/17/09...$15.00
DOI: http://dx.doi.org/10.1145/3103010.3103023

1 INTRODUCTION

One of the key resources of information used by doctors (especially emergency physicians) are radiology reports [13] of the patients. The radiology report comprises key medical observations dictated by the radiologist when analyzing the patient's medical imaging reports (for example, x-rays) and these are automatically transcribed to text. It is the emergency physician who makes the decision on the treatment of the medical conditions. In the case of long radiology reports, the doctor may miss some of the key observations made by the radiologist. Another complexity in the processing of radiology reports is the presence of transcription errors.

Our proposed model tries to aid the emergency physicians in automatically identifying key medical observations from the radiology report, based on the criticality level of the medical phrases, using machine learning and a web-based visual interface. The system highlights the medical phrases on the fly, based on their criticality values for the doctors. We also classify the overall report to identify if the patient is in need of urgent treatment. We have listed our main contributions as the following:

- The design of a novel system which identifies the medical phrases and their associated criticality values and presents this information in a visual interface. In terms of performance, our proposed method is able to achieve similar performance to human annotators when identifying key phrases and their criticality level.
- The design of a Web-based tagging system which can be used by doctors for annotating the radiology reports to provide training data for the machine learning model.
- We have also managed to improve the accuracy of word segmentation and spelling correction algorithms and have tuned them for use in radiology reports.
- Designing a novel binary classification system for extracting radiology reports of critical- condition patients. The proposed approach was able to achieve better performance as compared to using 'bag of words' having tf-idf weights. We have managed to use a novel list of features for better classification of the radiology reports.

We start this paper with an overview of related models, or systems, which use radiology or similar medical reports for extracting information from unstructured data. In Section 3, the overall view of our proposed model is introduced. The implementation details of each of the modules are mentioned in various subsections. We then compare and evaluate the performance of our system in Section 4. Finally, we analyze the type and cause of errors in the model and conclude the paper in Sections 5 and 6.

2 RELATED WORKS

Recently, Computational analysis of radiology reports gain a lot of attention. Most of the works focus on the identifying of specific medical conditions present in a given report and they usually deal with the classification task. Another generic area of research is the information extraction models which try to extract specific information such as medical recommendations or drug dosage from the radiology reports.

A system for identifying named entities from the radiology reports was the work done by Hassanpour [14]. The objective of this model was to identify the specific named entities from the radiology reports based on their information extraction model. They used a CRF-based model with several auxiliary features including POS tags and Radlex Lexicons [17] to identify entities of five different classes of *Anatomy, Anatomy Modifier, Observation, Observation Modifier,* and *Uncertainty*. They used 150 chest CT reports for training the system and reported an average f1-score [30] of 0.85.

Another system, Textractor [20] used the regular expressions to identify the medications and the reason for the prescription from patients' EHR (Electronic Health Record) files. The system uses the UMLS [5] concepts to identify the medication information and also uses the structure of medical reports to extract the reason for the prescriptions. Patrick and Li [24] used discharge files to identify the medication information such as Dosage, Mode, Frequency, Duration, Reason, and Context by using a hybrid machine learning and rule-based model. They used a combination of SVM [15] and CRF [31] models for identifying the entities and the rules used for final predictions.

In Information theory entropy reduction program [10] Dreyer used *Decision Trees* to extract the clinical findings and recommendations in the radiology report. However, the exact implementation details of their model is not provided by the author for replicating the results. Another work by Yetisgen [32] is a text processing pipeline for extracting recommendations from the radiology reports based on MEMM [19] model. However, the data set they used is highly unbalanced with 99% reports being negative. Another interesting model is the CTakes system [27] which identifies clinically significant phrases by the use of a combination of machine learning and rule-based models. However, the system's performance depends on the availability of up-to-date dictionaries and its performance is lowered as complexity increases.

Some of the more recent work includes the extraction of tumor information from radiology reports [33]. In this model, the authors were trying to extract tumor information for Hepatocellular carcinoma (HCC) disease. They used the CRF and MEMM models for extracting tumor's information such as tumor size, tumor count, and anatomical parts. They used a window size of 2 with a unigram model and limited the scope of the model to only 'findings' and

'impression' parts of the radiology report. The authors reported an f1-score of 0.74 in identification of tumor's information.

Our model tries to design a system that can extract clinical information without focus on any specific disease or clinical data. The information extracted can be used as key information for bigger models such as high level patient profiling systems and advanced machine learning tasks which use radiology data. We have selected a novel list of robust features in our proposed system.

3 THE PROPOSED METHOD

We implemented our system on a real-world anonymised radiology data set. The data included several spelling errors created by the automatic voice-to-text transcription, which had to be corrected before the data could be used for our machine learning model.

The overall structure of our model is shown in Figure 1. The main parts of our model include:

(1) Document Preparation
(2) Feature extraction
(3) Information Extraction
(4) Document Classification and
(5) Interface for Active Adaptive Learning

Each parts of the system is explained in detail in the following.

3.1 Document Preparation

Real world radiology reports are usually created by a voice-to-text processing system that creates text files based on the radiologist's dictation. In our model, for processing the reports effectively, we have to pre-process them before extracting the required information. The document-preparation module consists of two parts, a) the word segmentation module. b) the spelling correction module.

3.1.1 Word Segmentation. One of the most common errors in the radiology dataset is consecutive words that joined together. We implemented a word segmentation module to correct these joined-word errors. We used a probabilistic model [23] based on the Google trillion corpus [12]. This algorithm uses both unigrams and bigrams to generate the probabilistic values for each of the segmentations of the given word. The combination with a higher probabilistic value is selected as the corrected word. For example, If the word is 'isan' then, the model identifies that the words 'is' and 'an' separately produce better probability than 'isan' as a single word.

However, we cannot apply this algorithm 'out of the box', since we are dealing with medical terms. The occurrence of medical terms in the real world is much lower than common words. So the system would produce inaccurate results for most of the medical terms. For example, 'nabothian' would be segmented into 'na' + 'both' + 'ian', since these separate words are more common than 'nabothian'. For this reason we have modified the algorithm in two ways:

- We created a dictionary of unigrams and bigrams from the radiology dataset. Based on Radlex [17] and UMLS [5] ontologies, we extracted the medical and radiological terms from this dictionary. Because the occurrence of these terms are not sufficient for our task, we manipulated the word count for these terms based on their counts in the original Google n-gram corpus. We attached these terms with first

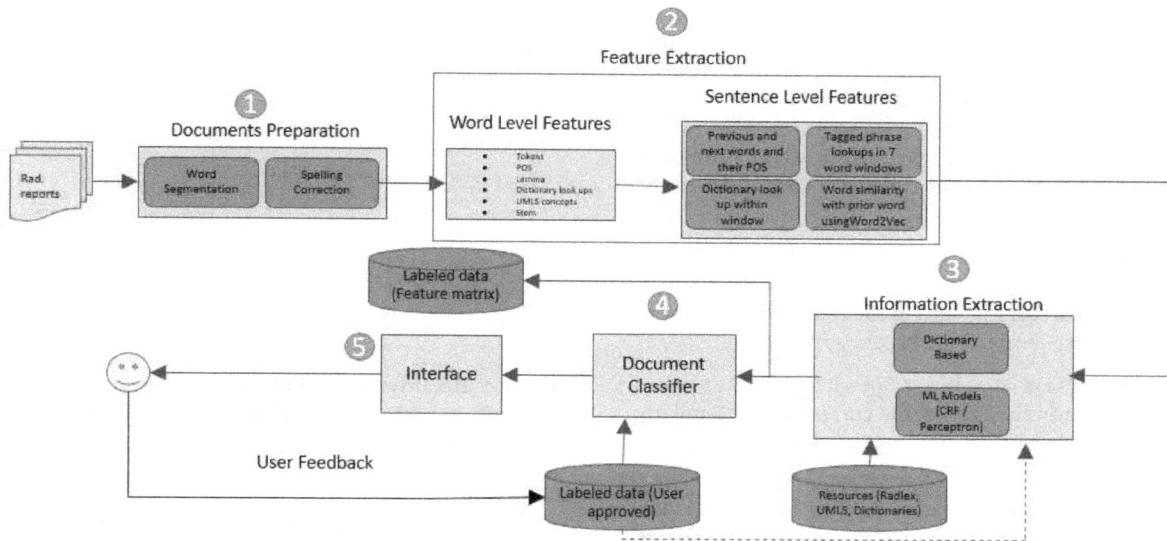

Figure 1: The overall view of the proposed system. At first all reports will be preprocessed (1) then several word and sentence level features will be extracted (2). The Information Extraction module (3) used the extracted features for identifying important phrases with their level of importance. The Document Classifier (4) classifies reports into two critical and non-critical categories based on the information exacted from the previous step. The visual interface (5) provides the user the extracted information and then tries to incorporate the user feedbacks in the system.

333,000 and 250,000 frequent unigrams and bigrams of Google trillion corpus.

- We also used Radlex [17] and UMLS [5] dictionaries which we created from the Radlex ontology and the UMLS Ontology. Each word was checked, in the UMLS and Radlex ontologies, to see if it was a valid medical term. Only terms which were not present in these dictionaries were processed for joined word error correction. This increased both the speed and accuracy of the word segmentation system.

3.1.2 Spell Correction.
The spelling correction module was used for correcting normal spell errors occurred in the system. By analyzing the radiology reports, we found that the spelling errors were comparatively less frequent than the word segmentation errors. The spelling correction system is based on a on a probabilistic model [23].

However, since we are dealing with radiology data where spelling-error occurrence is less frequent, we created the word counts from the word-segmented radiology reports from the previous step. A word will not be checked for the spelling error if it present in the Radlex or UMLS ontologies.

3.2 Feature Extraction

This section explains in detail the auxiliary features used in training the machine learning models for extracting the clinically significant medical phrases. The first set of features are the word-level features discussed in detail in Section 3.2.1 and the second ones are the sentence-level features discussed in Section 3.2.2.

3.2.1 Word-level Features.
Word-level features are auxiliary features extracted from word level syntactic and semantic analyses of reports. These features are used by the CRF model [16] for the information extraction and we explicitly defined them for enhancing the performance of the model. The various word-level features extracted are:

- Stem and lemma of the word: The *stem* is the core part of a word. For example, the stem of playing is play. The *lemma* is the canonical or dictionary form of the word.

- Part of speech: We used the MedPost/SKR part-of-speech tagger [29] to extract the POS tags for our words.

- Word length: length of the word (number of characters).

- Anatomy: This is a boolean flag value which is set if the given word is an anatomical word. The anatomy dictionary for this flag is generated from the Radlex [17] ontology.

- Suffix and prefix: We extract the first and the last two letters of a word as a two-letter prefix and suffix. We also use the first and the last three letters of the word as three-letter prefixes and suffixes, respectively.

- Critical level flags: This is a boolean flag value which is set if the given word is a high-critical, critical or non-critical word. This dictionary is created based on the tagged data set generated by the human tagger.

- Meta Label and Meta concept: This is the Meta Label and Meta Concept for a given word generated using the MetaMap [3] system.

- Filter words: The tagger automatically highlights several phrases to the human annotator, during the tagging process, based on the dictionary model. We capture explicitly the phrases which are removed by the human annotator during tagging process. These words are used to create a boolean flag feature which helps the system to eliminate some medical terms that are commonly disregarded by the emergency physicians.

3.2.2 Sentence-level features. Sentence-level features capture the context of the given word. These features focus on the previous and next words of the current word in the sentence. We defined the following sentence-level feature for our system.

- Previous and next word Part of Speech tags: These features help to identify the type of the current word. Similarly to the word-level POS, the sentence-level POS tags are generated from the MedPost [29].

- Next Negative and next positive words: This feature identifies the positive or negative sentiment words after the current word. The positive and negative sentiment word list are extracted based on the social media sentiment analysis [1]. The value of this feature is the actual positive or negative sentiment of the word.

- Previous and next negative word positions relative to the current word: This feature calculates how far the negative word is located from the current word. The negation wordlist in this feature is based on the Negex [7] trigger word list. The value of this feature is the distance of the negative word from the current word.

- Word similarity: This feature compares the similarity of current word with the previous word. We used the word2vec [21] model for extracting this feature. The word2vec model was created based on 20,000 corrected radiology reports.

- Aggressive and Anatomy descriptors: These are boolean flags set to 1 if the anatomy or aggressive descriptors (from Radlex) are present in a 7-word window size of the current word (3 previous words + current word + 3 next words).

- High-flag, crit-flag, and non-crit flags: these flags check for the high critical, critical, and non-critical word presence in the 7-word window size. These dictionaries are created based on the manual annotations.

3.3 Information Extraction Module

In the Information extraction module, we identify the three different types of phrase from the radiology reports. These phrase are *high-critical*, *critical*, and *non-critical*. We used two types of phrase extraction model: 1) Dictionary based and 2) Machine learning.

3.3.1 Dictionary based Model. The dictionary based model is used for helping the human annotator to identify the possible phrases to annotate. This system uses the Radlex ontology to identify and highlight the phrases from the radiology report to be annotated. This model is a dictionary search-based model and cannot be used to identify the type of the phrase (For example,

[1] https://github.com/jeffreybreen/twitter-sentiment-analysis-tutorial-201107

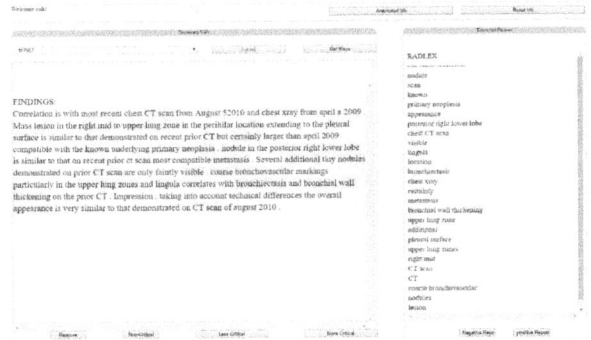

Figure 2: The interface is designed for manual tagging of the radiology reports. The highlighted text is based on dictionary model.

high-critical/critical). The interface for this model is given in Figure 2.

3.3.2 Machine learning Model. We have implemented two sequence learning models to evaluate the performance of the approach. The first is the CRF model which uses word level and sentence level features as discussed in Sections 3.2.1 and 3.2.2. This is a widely used machine learning model for identifying sequence labels. The CRF [16] model can be considered as a sequence-labeling version of logistic regression. It uses various feature functions (described in Sections 3.2.1 and 3.2.2) and learns weights to predict the sequence labels.

The model is trained to classify the phrases into three separate classes chosen after consulting with an emergency physician. Since the emergency physicians are primarily concerned with the immediate treatment of a patient's condition, it is necessary for the system to find medical phrases denoting conditions which have to be treated immediately. We use the classic BIO [6] model for labeling the training data. Prefix B-indicates the beginning part of the phrase and I-indicates the subsequent words. For example, B-Crit and I-Crit labels are used to indicate critical phrases, and the phrase 'heart is enlarged' is labeled as B-CRIT I-CRIT I-CRIT.

We also tried the structured Perceptron [8, 9] model to compare its performance with the CRF model. Structured Perceptrons is a version of Perceptron algorithms for sequence learning. Features used in this model are the same as the CRF model. The Structured Perceptron learns feature weights based on the auxiliary features extracted from each of the training samples and it uses the learned feature weights for predicting labels.

3.4 Document Classification Module

This module is used for classifying the radiology report into two classes namely critical and non-critical reports. The main purpose of classifying the report is for doctors to act quickly upon the critical reports. The document classification [15] system uses existing classification algorithms to classify the radiology reports. We have used those phrases that were extracted based on the Information Extraction module as an input to the classifiers and have compared the performance of the algorithms with 'bag of words' having tf-idf

[1] weights as features. Our purpose was to show the importance of the phrases and their extracted criticality level in classifying the reports.

3.4.1 Algorithms and their parameters. For report classification we used SGD (Stochastic Gradient descent), Random Forest and Linear SVM models. For each algorithm we compared the precision, recall and f1-score by using 'bag of words' having tf-idf [1] weights and then using critical level phrases extracted using the CRF model. The models were evaluated using 10-fold cross-validation and the average precision, recall and f1-score values of each model with the two types of features ('bag of words' having tf-idf weight and critical level phrases extracted using CRF model) were compared. For training the algorithms with extracted critical level phrases, we used a patient-level report vector, discussed in Section 3.4.2, along with some additional features such as word count and critical-level phrase count for each report.

3.4.2 Document Matrix. The Document Matrix is generated based on the output of the Machine learning model. It is essentially a vector for each of the patient reports where the columns represent the unique phrases extracted from all reports. This information can be used to quickly identify the condition of the patient from a collection of records. The level of criticality for each phrase is represented by a numeric value: a high-critical phrase is represented by +1, a critical-level phrase is represented by 0.5 and a non-critical level phrase is represented by -1.

3.5 Active Adaptive Learning Interface

Our Active Adaptive Learning Interface is the user interface which shows to the user the final phrases extracted and their criticality level. This interface can be used to edit the extracted phrases predicted by the model. The user can add/remove/change the criticality level of the phrases and the model is able to learn from the annotations of the given report in order to predict the phrases for the next report. This is achieved by including the predicted phrases and criticality levels as part of the binary level auxiliary features. This helps the system to provide higher weight to the observed word, based on corrected or previously predicted phrases. A sample screen-shot is given in Figure 3.

The interface is also able to provide the level of certainty for the phrases as well as the overall criticality level of the report. It provides a visual cue for the user, shown in a larger font-size, for those terms which are less certain. The user has the ability to edit the tag (criticality level) of the phrases. This extra information provides the user with the phrases which may have to be manually annotated. We focus only on the critical (high-critical/critical) level phrases and the OTHER type of phrases of the radiology report for providing the uncertainty levels. We omitted the uncertainty level for non-critical phrases to simplify the user's interaction and because these terms are usually not of interest of the emergency physicians. OTHER phrases are phrases which do not have any critical information (for example, medical phrases which are not tagged by the human annotator because they are not significance for judging the condition of the patient). OTHER phrases are phrases which are perceived by the system as having no information but potentially can have valuable information for the user. The system

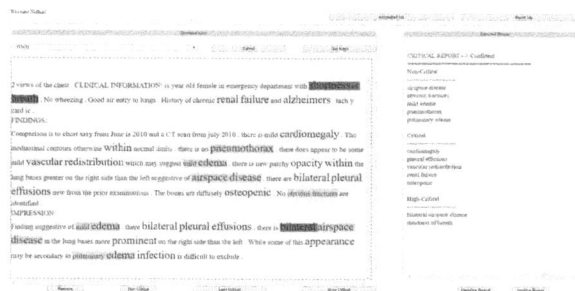

Figure 3: Final Interface which highlights the information extracted from the radiology reports along with criticality levels for the phrases extracted. The overall document class (positive/negative) is shown at the upper right corner with the confidence level.

determines a phrase as 'uncertain' based on the three cases given in the list below.

- Its high-critical prediction probability is at least 0.1 and predicted label is not high-critical.
- Critical prediction probability is at least 0.3 and predicted label is not critical.
- Predicted probability is less than 0.5 and predicted label is Other.

The system also provides the user with the overall criticality level of the report as well as the system predictions confident level. This can help doctors to identify emergency reports faster. A report is shown as a low-confidence prediction if the report class predicted distance is within one unit distance of the hyper plane. If the distance is more than one unit, it is predicted with high confidence. The distance score is negative for non-critical class and positive for the critical class.

4 RESULTS AND COMPARISON

In this section, we evaluated the proposed system performance. We divided this section into 3 parts: a) Results for the Word Segmentation module b) Results for the Machine Learning model c) Results for the Document classification.

4.1 Word Segmentation and Spell correction

The word segmentation module is used to segment the joined words present in the radiology reports. We used two methods to test our word segmentation module. Initially, we used a clean-text data set, which does not have any spelling errors, and we tested our model to check its accuracy. This provides us with an estimate of how many bogus word-segmentations are introduced, by the model, on clean text. For the second test, we created joined words (specifically radiology domain terms) and tested the system once again for the accuracy of segmentation.

For testing of the model with clean text, we used the text8 dataset [34] which contains over 3 million words. The text8 data is given to the algorithm for processing and we checked the number of words which are segmented by the model (ideally it should be 0). We obtained an accuracy of 98.9% on this data. This test was done

Table 1: Accuracy of base and implemented models for joined word error correction.

	Accuracy (Our model)	Accuracy (Base model)
Text 8 Dataset	98.90%	98.90%
Radlex random word combination 10k iterations	87.46% (bigram) 81.28% (trigram)	42.58% (bigram) 25.69% (trigram)

to make sure that the algorithm does not segment correct words present in real world documents.

For the second test, we created joined words from the words present in the Radlex ontology, chosen randomly and then combined together to create a joined word. The words chosen are medical words (not common words) in order to provide a better view of how well the system performs on uncommon words. We tested 2-word and 3-word combinations. The experiment was repeated for 10,000 iterations. We obtained an accuracy of 87.46% for 2-word combinations and 81.28% for 3-word combinations. This higher accuracy was obtained after adding the unigrams from the Google n-gram corpus for radiology terms (explained in detail on Section 3.1.1). Without adding the unigram radiology terms to the algorithm, the accuracy of 2-word combination was 42.58% and for 3-word combinations, it was 25.69%. This clearly shows that our model, with the addition of radiology terms, provides the best accuracy results. Table 1 shows the results in detail.

For evaluating the performance of the spelling correction algorithm, we used the text8 data set which has 3 million words. It was found that the algorithm produces an error rate of only 0.5%.

4.2 Machine learning Models

We used two sequence classifiers for our phrase extraction and criticality level identification. For each of the criticality levels, we used separate labels. For non-critical terms, we used B-NonCrit and I-NonCrit as the labels (Beginning word and subsequent word). Similarly, we used B-HighCrit, I-HighCrit, B-Crit, I-Crit respectively for high-critical and critical phrases. We used Conditional Random Field and Structured Perceptron as our two machine learning sequence classifiers.

4.2.1 CRF. We used the already existing fast implementation of Conditional Random Fields [16, 28] for our Model. The features used for the CRF are discussed in Section 3.2.1 and 3.2.2. We used l-bfgs [22] algorithm for the optimization. The coefficient values are dynamically calculated based on the training data.

We used 10-fold cross validation [26] on the training data. Since we do not check for inter-sentence parameters, the algorithm uses each sentence as training data. We obtained an average f1-score [30] of 0.75.

The average f1-score of non-critical, critical, and high-critical terms are 0.77, 0.70, and 0.78. The performance of critical terms is comparatively lower because of the higher uncertainty level for separating the high critical and critical terms (Figure 4). This boundary of separating critical and high-critical terms is heavily

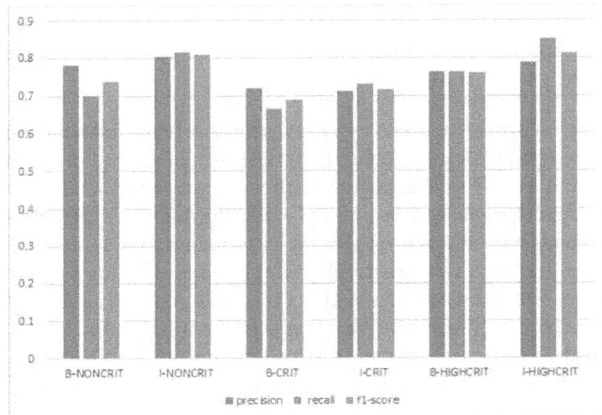

Figure 4: Precision, Recall and f1-score of the CRF model for each of the different criticality level of extracted phrases.

Table 2: Confusion matrix of CRF model with various criticality level phrases. 'O' denotes 'Other' phrases which are irrelevant or are considered of no value to the doctors. 'B' and 'I' denotes the beginning and Intermediate words of the phrase.

		Predicted labels						
		B-NONCRIT	I-NONCRIT	B-CRIT	I-CRIT	B-HIGHCRIT	I-HIGHCRIT	O
Actual Labels	**B-NONCRIT**	63	4	2	1	2	0	21
	I-NONCRIT	1	61	1	2	0	1	9
	B-CRIT	2	0	35	1	5	1	8
	I-CRIT	0	1	1	27	0	3	4
	B-HIGHCRIT	2	0	4	0	40	2	2
	I-HIGHCRIT	0	1	0	1	1	32	2
	O	12	11	5	5	3	2	1354

dependent on the type of annotator (emergency physicians in this case). The confusion matrix of the model is given as in Table 2.

4.2.2 Structured Perceptron. The Structured Perceptron [8, 9] is also an existing model which is trained based on the auxiliary features which are used to train the CRF model. The Structured Perceptrons model works similarly to other sequence classifiers such as MEMM [19] and HMMs [4, 25]. However, Structured Perceptron's performance was less than the CRF model. It was able to provide an average f1-score of 0.72. The performance for non-critical terms was much worse than CRF model (0.68). The f1-score for non-critical terms was almost the same as the CRF model (0.76). And for high-critical terms, the f1-score was lower than the CRF model (0.76). The performance of structured Perceptron for the critical labels is shown in Figure 5.

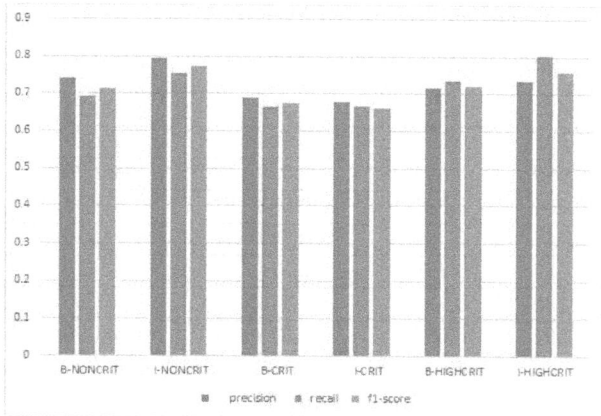

Figure 5: Precision,Recall and f1 score of the Structured Perceptron model for each of the different criticality level phrases extracted

4.2.3 Comparing CRF and Structured Perceptron. Both of these models are similar in performance. However, the CRF model performs better on average. The auxiliary features used for the training and prediction of sequence labels are the same. The CRF model is able to provide better recall than Structured Perceptron. Moreover, CRF provides the predicted probability values for the labels which can then be used for identifying the uncertainty of the predicted values. Evaluating the results for both CRF and Structured Perceptron by t-test, we obtain a p-value of 0.0549.

4.3 Feature Analysis

For our machine learning models, we have used two types of auxiliary feature:, word level, and sentence level features. In this section, we compare the models' performance based on the auxiliary features provided. For the sentence level features, we have segmented the performance graph into two parts, namely sentence level features, and flag level (or binary) features. The binary features are provided separately since the contribution of the binary features on the models' performance is significant.

As we compare the performance of the system based on the set of auxiliary features, the sentence and binary-level features provide a more significant contribution to the models' performance than do word-level features. One reason for this difference is that some of the word level features are inherently present in the sentence level features as well. For example, previous and next POS tags give similar contributions to assigning the POS tags of the current word. We assigned the current word POS tag contributes to the models' performance in special cases such as the beginning and end words of the sentence, and one-word sentences where there are no previous or next POS tags.

Binary features are part of the sentence-level feature-extraction module. These features are the main contributors to the Machine Learning model used in the active adaptive interface. These features are dynamically created based on the prior-tagged reports. For example, tagged phrases provided by humans during the training process are updated dynamically as the user uses the active/adaptive

learning interface. These features create dictionaries based on the types (high-critical, critical and non-critical) of tagged critical phrases. These features help the model to identify medical terms which are critical or high-critical on most of the reports.

The combination of the three sets of features provides the best accuracy results for our model. The sentence-level features help to increase the recall value of our model while the word-level features are used to increase the precision of our model. The f1-score comparison for various features is provided in Table 3.

4.4 Inter Annotator Score

In order to compare our model to real-world human annotation performance we asked a second annotator to annotate the radiology reports and we then examined the consistency between the two sets of annotations.

The second annotator annotated 57 random reports out of the 253 reports tagged by the first annotator. For calculating the inter-annotator score, we used two methods. First, we used a 'soft' matching algorithm that only calculates the inter-annotator agreement on phrases which were annotated by both annotators. For the second method, we calculated the Precision, Recall, and f1-score of the second annotator on annotating the reports by keeping Annotator-1 as the gold standard. In both of these methods, we used the 57 reports annotated by the second annotator (Annotator-2).

The first evaluation method involves the calculation of the soft agreement score between annotators. The formula for the soft agreement score calculation is given in Equation 1.

$$Soft\ score\ =\ AVG\left(\sum_{i=1}^{57}\frac{W_i}{N_i}\right) \qquad (1)$$

- W_i = Number of words predicted by both annotators with same criticality level in report i.
- N_i = Number of words predicted by both annotators in report i.

We obtained the soft agreement score of 71.47% on annotation. This proves that annotating a report and providing criticality levels to the phrases is a complicated task even for a human annotator who has ample domain knowledge. Moreover, reducing the annotation task to a 2-class system (critical/ non-critical) increased the inter annotation score to 85.01%. This experiment proves that the boundary of critical and high-critical can change based on the user's perception of each report. The confusion matrix for the soft score is shown in Table 4

The second evaluation method involves the training of the CRF model on the 200 reports that were not tagged by the second annotator. Once we trained the CRF model, we tested the model on the 57 reports tagged by the first annotator. We compared this result with the performance score obtained by asking the second annotator to tag the same 57 reports. The results are shown in Table 5. The CRF model gives similar performance to that of the human annotator but with higher precision. The performance dip in f1-score is due to the lower recall value, which would improved on an ongoing basis as the system acquires more data.

4.5 Document Classification

The radiology reports are classified into two classes, critical reports, and non-critical reports. The classification is based on the overall

Table 3: Precision,Recall and f1 scores for CRF model based on various features used during training process.

		B-NONCRIT	I-NONCRIT	B-CRIT	I-CRIT	B-HIGHCRIT	I-HIGHCRIT
Word Level	precision	0.656	0.676	0.647	0.577	0.569	0.625
	recall	0.625	0.797	0.584	0.546	0.501	0.613
	f1-score	0.639	0.731	0.610	0.541	0.529	0.611
Sentence Level	precision	0.756	0.768	0.601	0.531	0.653	0.681
	recall	0.683	0.739	0.483	0.395	0.511	0.579
	f1-score	0.717	0.752	0.532	0.439	0.571	0.620
Binary Level	precision	0.706	0.735	0.738	0.704	0.712	0.755
	recall	0.593	0.769	0.591	0.698	0.679	0.790
	f1-score	0.643	0.750	0.653	0.694	0.692	0.769
Combined	precision	0.781	0.804	0.720	0.712	0.762	0.788
	recall	0.702	0.816	0.666	0.731	0.762	0.850
	f1-score	0.737	0.808	0.689	0.716	0.760	0.811

Table 4: Confusion matrix for annotations done by second annotator on the radiology reports. Gold standard is based on the initial tagging done by the first annotator.

		Predicted					
		B-NONCRIT	I-NONCRIT	B-CRIT	I-CRIT	B-HIGHCRIT	I-HIGHCRIT
Actual Labels	B-NONCRIT	129	7	6	0	13	0
	I-NONCRIT	7	126	0	5	1	10
	B-CRIT	11	1	16	8	33	5
	I-CRIT	1	12	0	15	3	17
	B-HIGHCRIT	8	0	8	0	95	9
	I-HIGHCRIT	0	2	0	8	7	75

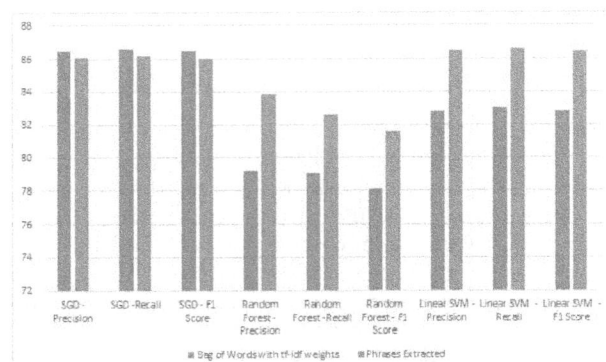

Figure 6: Report classification results comparison using 'bag of words' having tf-idf weight as features and phrases extracted by the CRF model.

report and is related to whether immediate action is required, on the patient in the emergency department. In order to analyze the relevance of the extracted phrases using the CRF model, we compared the classification accuracy of well known machine-learning algorithms using two methods. On the first trial, the reports are classified based on the 'bag of words' method having tf-idf weights assigned on those given in the report. In the second method, we used the phrases extracted using the CRF model along with the values assigned (-1 for non-critical phrases, 0.5 for critical phrases and 1 for high-critical phrases). We have used three separate machine learning algorithms (Linear Support Vector Machine, Random Forest and Stochastic Gradient Descent from the Sklearn library[2]) to compare the performance of each machine learning algorithm on these two types of feature. The comparison results are shown in Figure 6.

Comparing the results of the three algorithms on the two types of feature, we can see that the phrases extracted out-perform the 'bag of words' method having the tf-idf weights-based model on both the Random Forest [18] and Linear SVM [11]. Even on the SGD

[2]www.scikit-learn.org

(Stochastic Gradient Descent) [2] the phrases extracted have similar performance to 'bag of words' having a tf-idf weights model. Also, the phrases extracted from the reports are comparatively much fewer than 'bag of words' having a tf-idf weights model.

Using the phrases extracted we were able to achieve an average f1-score of 86.42, in comparison to the average f1-score of 86.52 for 'bag of words' having a tf-idf weights model with SGD. These results demonstrate that the phrases extracted from the radiology reports are quite powerful features in classification.

Evaluating the statistical significance using the student t-test on the results, we have obtained a p-value of 9.43E-08 and 1.1E-05, respectively, for random forest and linear SVM and for 'bag of words' having tf-idf weights model and extracted phrase features. These results show that the 'extracted phrases' method performs better on classification of the report using these algorithms.

5 ERROR ANALYSIS

We have analyzed the misclassification errors for the CRF model which used the three level criticality levels for the extracted phrases. Upon analysis, the greatest misclassification occurs on classifying

Table 5: Precision, Recall and f1-Score comparison between human annotator and CRF model.

	HUMAN ANNOTATOR			CRF MODEL		
	precision	recall	f1-score	precision	recall	f1-score
B-NONCRIT	0.6825	0.6324	0.6565	0.8140	0.5122	0.6287
I-NONCRIT	0.7241	0.6632	0.6923	0.8947	0.6041	0.7212
B-CRIT	0.2712	0.1928	0.2254	0.4583	0.4074	0.4314
I-CRIT	0.2239	0.2500	0.2362	0.4643	0.2203	0.2989
B-HIGHCRIT	0.5220	0.7308	0.6090	0.6406	0.3228	0.4293
I-HIGHCRIT	0.5682	0.7353	0.6410	0.7692	0.4000	0.5263
Average	0.5703	0.5930	0.5759	0.7359	0.4564	0.5601

the non-critical phrases, which get classified as Other. These types of error are not a big concern in emergency-room practice since the doctors are mostly concerned about critical phrases. Even on manual tagging, depending on the report, some of the medical phrases may not be tagged by the doctor as non-critical. On analyzing the results, about 22% of the total non-critical phrases were predicted as 'Other' by the system. However, less than 2% of those terms which were actually non-critical were predicted as critical by the system.

Analyzing the critical phrases, the most common misclassification was, again, the classification of a 'critical' phrase as being 'Other'. However, the misclassification rate is lower compared to the non-critical phrases. The misclassification of critical phrases as Other is about 15%. However, on further analysis, it has been identified that the same phrase is misclassified in multiple reports which adds to the misclassification percentage. For example, the phrase 'Intrathoracic' is misclassified more than once, which adds to the misclassification rate even though only one phrase is misclassified. But this problem can be solved as we increase the amount of training data. As the doctors use the active adaptive learning interface through the on-line interface, these type of errors could be reduced considerably.

Finally, for high-critical terms, the most common errors are misclassification of the criticality level. About 8% of the high critical phrases are misclassified as critical phrases by the system. However, since the doctors are able to view both critical and high-critical phrases in the interface, along with the reports, these errors would not have a significant impact on the user experience.

6 CONCLUSIONS

We propose a system that performs extraction of medical phrases and their criticality level from free-text radiology reports, and classification of the whole report as being critical or not. As radiology reports are dictated by the radiologists and transformed into text, spelling and joined-word errors appear in the text, which we automatically correct, aiming to improve the accuracy of phrase extraction and classification. Information extraction from the radiology reports, in the form of medical phrases, is complex but provides valuable data, which can be further used in populating structured data bases for data mining tasks. The complexity of our task is due to the requirement of assigning the criticality level based on the textual context of the extracted phrases. The information extraction model, based on conditional random fields, extracts medical phrases and the associated criticality level (high-critical, critical

and non-critical). The model is trained on a small corpus of reports labeled by two emergency physicians. We have demonstrated that our approach achieves performance that is comparable to the inter-annotator agreement. Using the extracted medical phrases as features, we address the report classification task that classifies entire radiology reports as critical or non-critical (i.e. whether an emergency physician needs to take immediate action on them). To allow the emergency physician user to efficiently inspect the extracted medical phrases and correct them if needed, we have built an adaptive active learning interface. Feedback provided by the user can be used for improving the performance of information extraction by on-line training.

ACKNOWLEDGMENTS

We would like to extend our gratitude to Jessie Kang from the Department of Medicine for providing us annotation for 50+ radiology reports which helped us to compare the user agreement between annotations. We would also like to thank Palomino System Innovations for their guidance and support provided in this study. This research was funded by the Natural Sciences and Engineering Research Council of Canada.

REFERENCES

[1] Akiko Aizawa. 2003. An information-theoretic perspective of tf–idf measures. *Information Processing & Management* 39, 1 (2003), 45–65.
[2] Shun-ichi Amari. 1993. Backpropagation and stochastic gradient descent method. *Neurocomputing* 5, 4-5 (1993), 185–196.
[3] Alan R Aronson. 2001. Effective mapping of biomedical text to the UMLS Metathesaurus: the MetaMap program.. In *Proceedings of the AMIA Symposium.* American Medical Informatics Association, 17.
[4] Jason Baldridge, Peter Clark, and Gokhan Tur. 2010. Human Language Technologies: The 2010 Annual Conference of the North American Chapter of the Association for Computational Linguistics. (2010).
[5] Olivier Bodenreider. 2004. The unified medical language system UMLS: integrating biomedical terminology. *Nucleic acids research* 32, suppl 1 (2004), D267–D270.
[6] Xavier Carreras, Lluís Màrquez, and Lluís Padró. 2003. A Simple Named Entity Extractor Using AdaBoost. In *Proceedings of the Seventh Conference on Natural Language Learning at HLT-NAACL 2003 - Volume 4 (CONLL '03).* Association for Computational Linguistics, Stroudsburg, PA, USA, 152–155. DOI:http://dx.doi.org/10.3115/1119176.1119197
[7] Wendy W Chapman, Will Bridewell, Paul Hanbury, Gregory F Cooper, and Bruce G Buchanan. 2001. A simple algorithm for identifying negated findings and diseases in discharge summaries. *Journal of biomedical informatics* 34, 5 (2001), 301–310.
[8] Michael Collins. 2002. Discriminative training methods for hidden markov models: Theory and experiments with perceptron algorithms. In *Proceedings of the ACL-02 conference on Empirical methods in natural language processing-Volume 10.* Association for Computational Linguistics, 1–8.
[9] Hal Daumé III and Daniel Marcu. 2005. Learning as search optimization: Approximate large margin methods for structured prediction. In *Proceedings of the 22nd international conference on Machine learning.* ACM, 169–176.

[10] Keith J Dreyer. 2014. Information theory entropy reduction program. (June 2014).

[11] Steve R Gunn and others. 1998. Support vector machines for classification and regression. *ISIS(Information Signals Images Systems) technical report* 14 (1998).

[12] Alon Halevy, Peter Norvig, and Fernando Pereira. 2009. The unreasonable effectiveness of data. *IEEE Intelligent Systems* 24, 2 (2009), 8–12.

[13] Ferris M Hall. 2000. Language of the radiology report: primer for residents and wayward radiologists. *American Journal of Roentgenology* 175, 5 (2000), 1239–1242.

[14] Saeed Hassanpour and Curtis P Langlotz. 2016. Information extraction from multi-institutional radiology reports. *Artificial intelligence in medicine* 66 (2016), 29–39.

[15] Sotiris B Kotsiantis, I Zaharakis, and P Pintelas. 2007. Supervised machine learning: A review of classification techniques. (2007).

[16] John Lafferty, Andrew McCallum, and Fernando Pereira. 2001. Conditional random fields: Probabilistic models for segmenting and labeling sequence data. In *Proceedings of the Eighteenth International Conference on Machine Learning, ICML*, Vol. 1. 282–289.

[17] Curtis P Langlotz. 2006. RadLex: a new method for indexing online educational materials 1. *Radiographics* 26, 6 (2006), 1595–1597.

[18] Andy Liaw and Matthew Wiener. 2002. Classification and regression by randomForest. *R news* 2, 3 (2002), 18–22.

[19] Andrew McCallum, Dayne Freitag, and Fernando CN Pereira. 2000. Maximum Entropy Markov Models for Information Extraction and Segmentation.. In *Icml*, Vol. 17. 591–598.

[20] Stéphane M Meystre, Julien Thibault, Shuying Shen, John F Hurdle, and Brett R South. 2010. Textractor: a hybrid system for medications and reason for their prescription extraction from clinical text documents. *Journal of the American Medical Informatics Association* 17, 5 (2010), 559–562.

[21] Tomas Mikolov, Ilya Sutskever, Kai Chen, Greg S Corrado, and Jeff Dean. 2013. Distributed representations of words and phrases and their compositionality. In *Advances in neural information processing systems*. 3111–3119.

[22] Jorge Nocedal. 1980. Updating quasi-Newton matrices with limited storage. *Mathematics of computation* 35, 151 (1980), 773–782.

[23] Peter Norvig. 2009. Natural language corpus data. *Beautiful Data* (2009), 219–242.

[24] Jon Patrick and Min Li. 2009. A cascade approach to extracting medication events. In *Australasian Language Technology Association Workshop November 28, 2009*. 99.

[25] Lawrence Rabiner and B Juang. 1986. An introduction to hidden Markov models. *ieee assp magazine* 3, 1 (1986), 4–16.

[26] Payam Refaeilzadeh, Lei Tang, and Huan Liu. 2009. Cross-validation. In *Encyclopedia of database systems*. Springer, 532–538.

[27] Guergana K Savova, James J Masanz, Philip V Ogren, Jiaping Zheng, Sunghwan Sohn, Karin C Kipper-Schuler, and Christopher G Chute. 2010. Mayo clinical Text Analysis and Knowledge Extraction System (cTAKES): architecture, component evaluation and applications. *Journal of the American Medical Informatics Association* 17, 5 (2010), 507–513.

[28] Fei Sha and Fernando Pereira. 2003. Shallow parsing with conditional random fields. In *Proceedings of the 2003 Conference of the North American Chapter of the Association for Computational Linguistics on Human Language Technology-Volume 1*. Association for Computational Linguistics, 134–141.

[29] L Smith, Thomas Rindflesch, W John Wilbur, and others. 2004. MedPost: a part-of-speech tagger for bioMedical text. *Bioinformatics* 20, 14 (2004), 2320–2321.

[30] Marina Sokolova, Nathalie Japkowicz, and Stan Szpakowicz. 2006. Beyond accuracy, F-score and ROC: a family of discriminant measures for performance evaluation. In *Australasian Joint Conference on Artificial Intelligence*. Springer, 1015–1021.

[31] Charles Sutton and Andrew McCallum. 2010. An introduction to conditional random fields. *arXiv preprint arXiv:1011.4088* (2010).

[32] Meliha Yetisgen-Yildiz, Martin L Gunn, Fei Xia, and Thomas H Payne. 2013. A text processing pipeline to extract recommendations from radiology reports. *Journal of biomedical informatics* 46, 2 (2013), 354–362.

[33] Wen-wai Yim, Tyler Denman, Sharon W Kwan, and Meliha Yetisgen. 2016. Tumor information extraction in radiology reports for hepatocellular carcinoma patients. *AMIA Summits on Translational Science Proceedings* 2016 (2016), 455.

[34] Saizheng Zhang, Yuhuai Wu, Tong Che, Zhouhan Lin, Roland Memisevic, Ruslan Salakhutdinov, and Yoshua Bengio. 2016. Architectural Complexity Measures of Recurrent Neural Networks. *arXiv preprint arXiv:1602.08210* (2016).

Towards a Transcription System of Sign Language Video Resources via Motion Trajectory Factorisation

Mark Borg
Systems and Control Engineering,
University of Malta,
Msida, Malta
mborg2005@gmail.com

Kenneth P. Camilleri
Systems and Control Engineering,
University of Malta,
Msida, Malta
kenneth.camilleri@um.edu.mt

ABSTRACT

Sign languages are visual languages used by the Deaf community for communication purposes. Whilst recent years have seen a high growth in the quantity of sign language video collections available online, much of this material is hard to access and process due to the lack of associated text-based tagging information and because 'extracting' content directly from video is currently still a very challenging problem. Also limited is the support for the representation and documentation of sign language video resources in terms of sign writing systems. In this paper, we start with a brief survey of existing sign language technologies and we assess their state of the art from the perspective of a sign language digital information processing system. We then introduce our work, focusing on vision-based sign language recognition. We apply the factorisation method to sign language videos in order to factor out the signer's motion from the structure of the hands. We then model the motion of the hands in terms of a weighted combination of linear trajectory basis and apply a set of classifiers on the basis weights for the purpose of recognising meaningful phonological elements of sign language. We demonstrate how these classification results can be used for transcribing sign videos into a written representation for annotation and documentation purposes. Results from our evaluation process indicate the validity of our proposed framework.

KEYWORDS

Sign Language Recognition; Sign Language Transcription; Annotation Tools; Factorisation Method; Computer Vision

ACM Reference format:
Mark Borg and Kenneth P. Camilleri. 2017. Towards a Transcription System of Sign Language Video Resources via Motion Trajectory Factorisation. In *Proceedings of DocEng'17, Valletta, Malta, September 4–7, 2017,* 10 pages.
https://doi.org/10.1145/3103010.3103020

1 INTRODUCTION

Sign Languages are fully-fledged natural languages used by the Deaf communities[1] as their primary method, and oftentimes the sole method, of communication. They are visual languages composed of primarily manual gestures, but also making use of other modalities (head and upper body movements, eye gaze, facial expressions, and mouthing patterns) to convey information.

The Deaf communities experience a number of difficulties when it comes to communicating with the rest of the world. First there exists a communications barrier between the hearing impaired and hearing people: few outside of the Deaf communities can understand sign languages, and only a fraction of deaf people acquire the ability to read and write spoken languages. For example, it is estimated that it takes around 9 years for a deaf child to learn the alphabet of a spoken language [29]. Secondly, as most sign languages evolved independently from each other, there can exist a communications barrier between signers themselves. It is estimated that American Sign Language (ASL) and British Sign Language (BSL) share less than 30% of their signs in common, despite the similarity of the spoken languages. While the application of assistive communication technology to this domain promises to alleviate such problems and reduce isolation of Deaf communities, this technology is still in its infancy.

A growing trend amongst Deaf communities worldwide is the use of the Internet for communication purposes. Various online video sharing sites[2] and *vlogs* (video blogs)[3] are being leveraged by the Deaf as a medium for communicating between themselves in sign language. But despite these large collections of signing video material, one can note that there is in general a lack in the amount and variety of digital information representations available for sign languages [41].

Limited is the support for the representation and documentation of sign languages in terms of writing systems, and mechanisms for creating, sharing, modifying and organising such collections of documents. From a document engineering point-of-view, while sign language content can be represented in terms of signing videos, this is not readily accessible to computational environments and information processing systems. 'Extracting' content directly from videos is currently a hard problem. Shipman et al. [49] highlights the difficulty of searching the web for sign language information

---

[1] Here we adopt the term Deaf (big D) as referring to the hearing-impaired who regard their deafness as part of their identity and culture rather than a disability. Sign Languages form an integral part of this cultural identity. In contrast, the term deaf (little d) is typically used to refer to the medical condition.

[2] Generic video sharing sites like YouTube and Vimeo, as well as specific ones like www.deafVideo.tv

[3] For example, www.deafread.com/vlogs/

due to the mostly video content, and inaccurate or little textual meta-tagging surrounding the videos.

Adding support for sign language writing systems, the creation of better sign language document representations, and improving computer vision techniques to handle the hard-to-extract video content, can help in making the "cultural memory" of the Deaf community more accessible, as well as making it more permanent.

1.1 Sign Language technologies

Figure 1 gives an overview of several sign language related technologies that are mentioned in the literature and how they do or can relate to each other via the digital information they produce/consume. The thickness of the arrows gives a rough indication of how advanced is the research performed to-date on interconnecting the technologies together.

The area of automated sign language recognition (ASLR) has received a lot of attention to date. Starting from the initial works of the likes of Tamura and Kawasaki [53], early ASLR systems opted for the use of *data gloves* for capturing hand motion [16]. Later works adopted a vision-based approach, as this is less intrusive and allows for more natural signing [12, 56, 58]. Due to the challenging nature that signing poses to the field of computer vision, the current state of ASLR research is that such systems work best within a lab setting and have had limited success on 'real-life' data. One of the best results achieved so far on 'real-life' data is that of Koller et al. [38]: on a dataset of 9 different signers and a lexicon of 1081 signs, a word error rate of 34.3% was achieved for a single signer, and 53.0% for multiple signers. Refer to the following survey papers for the latest in this area: [10, 38, 43, 59].

Sign synthesis is the opposite of ASLR: given a sign language sentence expressed in some writing system, an animation of a 3D avatar performing the sentence is generated. This area has also received its fair share of attention, and one such example is the work of Prihodko et al. [44]. A recent trend in this area is to make use of standard specifications, such as Web3D for embedding 3D content in web pages, the XML-based X3D standard file format, and the H-Anim avatar specification.

Other areas have received limited attention. Karappa et al. [35], Monteiro et al. [41] did work for identifying sign language videos amongst online video repositories based only on the motion characteristics contained within the video. Quite uniquely, Jaballah and Jemni [34] performed ASLR on synthetic videos generated by web-based 3D signing avatars.

In the area of sign language writing systems, we find a number of studies [29] that investigated the use and/or the generation of digital representations of the most commonly-used writing systems: SignWriting and HamNoSys (See Figure 2).

SignWriting, developed by Sutton [52] in 1974, is an iconic system widely used nowadays for writing down (transcribing) signs. HamNoSys (the Hamburg Notation System), released in 1989, is another notation system for describing sign language gestures [30]. It is an alphabetic system describing signs mostly on a phonetic level and thus more popular with sign linguists. The major challenge encountered when documenting sign languages using a writing system is that signing is multi-modal and the motions are concurrent (arms, body, face motions occur in parallel and on many levels) –

trying to linearise such concurrent motions can prove to be problematic [6]. Aznar [5], da Rocha Costa and Dimuro [21] have proposed a SignWriting Markup Language (SWML) for the digitisation of SignWriting, while the Signing Gesture Markup Language (SiGML) is the XML-based scripting language for representing HamNoSys [36]. do Amaral and De Martino [25] proposed an XML-based transcription system that could serve as input to a 3D avatar animation system for the purpose of sign language playback.

Another unique work is that of Stiehl et al. [51], who performed initial work on an optical glyph recognition (OGR) system for SignWriting (the equivalent of OCR for text). And Lu et al. [40] made use of a dataglove as a novel user interface for *writing* signs in SignWriting.

In the area of content-based video retrieval, Koskela et al. [39] described some early work towards querying Finnish sign language videos. Zhang and Zhang [61] employed the string edit distance for measuring the similarity of 2D hand trajectories in separate video sequences, while Aerts et al. [1], da Rocha Costa et al. [20] proposed systems for sign querying based on SignWriting.

In our literature research we did not come across any works that applied natural language processing (NLP) techniques to sign languages, although da Rocha Costa et al. [20] highlighted the need for such work.

Another area where sign language tools have made a foray is that of sign language annotation. There are several annotation tools available, the most popular being: ELAN [18], SignStream, and iLex [31]. All of these tools provide functionality to add annotations or glosses[4] to video recordings. Moreover, multiple tiers could be added, making them ideal for sign languages since a different tier could be used for each separate articulator used in signing [6].

But the process of manually annotating signs in sign language videos is highly laborious, tedious, error prone, and can depend on the expertise level of the annotator. Dreuw and Ney [26] state that the annotation real-time factor for sign languages can be as high as ×100, i.e., an hour of video takes around 100 hours to fully annotate by hand (manuals + non-manual articulation); in comparison, the same factor for spoken languages is around ×30. This is one of the reasons why at the moment richly-annotated corpora of sign languages are quite rare and available only for the major sign languages [6].

To alleviate the manual annotation process, a number of research works have investigated the use of computer vision techniques for automatic or semi-automatic annotation of sign language videos. Notable amongst these works, one can find that of Hrúz et al. [32] and Gonzalez et al. [28] – both these systems perform semi-automatic annotation, and require the human annotator to correct errors when they occur and/or propose a set of most likely sign glosses for the annotator to choose from. In Dreuw and Ney [26], early work on automatic annotation is described, achieving an annotation word error rate of 26%.

In our work we focus on vision-based ASLR using a single camera. Signing presents a number of challenges to the field of computer vision, mainly due to the fast speed of signing, motion blur, and

---

[4]Glossing is the process of transcribing a sign language to a spoken language word-for-word by finding the closest word in the spoken language to the corresponding sign. Glosses are typically denoted in all capital letters.

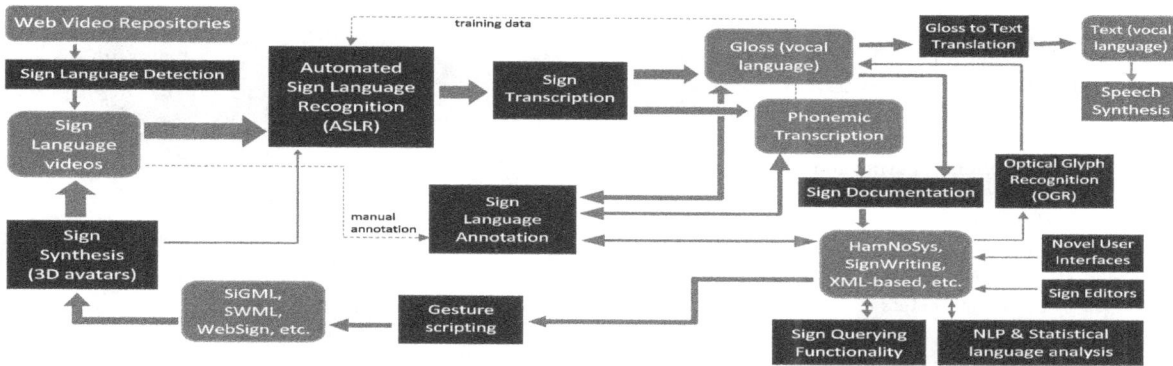

Figure 1: Sign language technologies (dark blue boxes) mentioned in the literature and how they relate to each other in terms of digital information (orange rounded boxes) transferred, produced, or consumed. Arrow thickness gives a rough indication of how advanced and/or how much research has been performed to-date on interconnecting the technologies together.

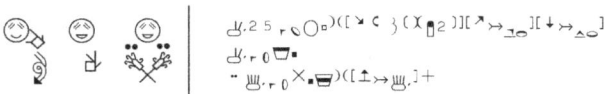

Figure 2: Different sign language writing systems: an example of transcribing the three ASL signs GOLDILOCKS THREE BEARS, using (left) SignWriting, and (right) HamNoSys (Src: adapted from http://www.signwriting.org)

the frequent and persistent occlusion and self-occlusion of the two hands and the signer's body – all these conditions contrive to make the long-term tracking of the hands very difficult.

We then explore how the output from the recognition process can be transcribed into a phonemic transcription, and in turn we will investigate how this can be documented using a sign language writing system of choice (HamNoSys). In order to be useful, here we are considering sign language information when referring to transcription and documentation. This is not *motion capture* data (the equivalent of capturing the raw audio signal in speech), but an efficient and economical representation of some of the semantically-meaningful units of signing (phonemes), that can in turn be used in information processing systems. Finally, we will look into ways of incorporating our results into a sign language annotation tool, such as ELAN.

Our main contribution lies in the use of the so-called *factorisation method* [55] for describing hand motion trajectories, and how various machine learning classifiers are applied to these trajectories in order to identify motion and hand symmetry related phonological elements. We envision two different applications for our research: (i) as accuracy improves and more phonemic elements are recognised by our system, our research could assist in the linguistic annotation of sign languages, especially for those languages that lack resources such as a lexicon (our approach can characterise motion on a phonemic level, the basic motions of the sign language, and does not require a sign lexicon per se); (ii) a partial and not-so-accurate phonemic transcription as a recognition result, can still prove useful for training an ASLR system, for example, by following in the steps of the work done by Koller et al. [37] on correcting misaligned annotated signing.

The rest of this paper is organised as follows. After covering related work in Section 2, we describe our proposed method in Section 3. Then in Section 4 we describe the experiments performed, and experimental results are evaluated in Section 5. This paper closes with a conclusion in Section 6, describing future work.

2 RELATED WORKS

The gross hand trajectories constitute a meaningful phonological element in any sign language. Thus the long-term tracking of the hands and the analysis of the hand trajectories is a critical component of any vision-based ASLR system. This is made difficult by the similarity of the two hands (easy to mistake one for the other), the closeness of the hands to each other and the body thus suffering from a lot of frequent and persistent occlusion (easy to lose track of the hands), and the highly deformable nature of the hands themselves (visual appearance varies widely).

In their work, Charles et al. [13] developed an ASLR system for estimating the human pose in long sequences of signing videos. *Random forests* are used for determining the most likely 2D positions of the shoulders, arms and hands in each video frame, and temporal information from adjacent frames is then leveraged in order to offer more robustness to hand identity switching. In the work of Koller et al. [38], tracking of the hands is performed in the 2D image plane, with *dynamic programming* used to determine the best hand trajectory over time, thus avoiding wrong local decisions.

Derpanis et al. [22] employed basic 2D hand motions in the image plane, inspired by linguistic models for sign recognition. Hand motions are represented in terms of first order kinematic features, giving rise to gesture signatures corresponding to basic ASL motions. While proving that the set of features describing the hand trajectories can help discriminate between signs, it was noted that further work is required to handle signs with large variations or significant intrinsic hand motion. The work of Hrúz et al. [32] focused on the analysis of 2D hand trajectories to characterise signs as being symmetric or not, and 1-handed or 2-handed signs. Symmetry detection is done via correlation of the trajectories of the two hands. Image region binning is used for hand location determination, and *Gaussian mixture models (GMMs)* used for recognition.

Dilsizian et al. [23] performed analysis on 3D hand trajectories captured with a depth sensor. Trajectories were normalised to handle anthropomorphic differences (people sizes) as well as differences in how far signing extends for different subjects. Sign recognition was then formulated in terms of comparing the normalised 3D trajectories. Boulares and Jemni [9] using non-linear regression to extract the major geometric structures from 3D trajectories. These are modelled in terms of conic parametric equations, thus reducing a complex trajectory into a sequential combination of different conic forms (ellipses, parabolas, hyperbolas). The motion signature values expressed as conic parameters are then fed to a *SVM* for isolated sign classification. Lu et al. [40] perform motion analysis on 3D hand trajectories captured with a data glove. Repeated hand motion is detected when the distance of a trajectory point comes close to the start position, planar motion is estimated from the angle of direction vectors, and path linearity is determined from the maximal deflection angle with respect to the straight line movement joining the endpoints. Their method is limited to isolated signing and requires that the hand starts and stops at the rest position.

Gonzalez et al. [28] apply hand trajectory analysis within a semi-automatic sign annotation system. Hand trajectories are described in terms of being straight, arc, or circular motion segments; this determination is done using the 2D image coordinates via the ratio of the distance between the start/end points and the trajectory length. While giving good results, problems are encountered in determining 1-handed versus 2-handed signs (due to extra hand motions of the non-dominant hand). Also trajectory classification is highly dependent on the ratio thresholds chosen.

In our previous work [8] we adopted a similar approach to the above works. Tracking of hand trajectories is performed in the 2D image plane, and the *multiple hypotheses tracking (MHT)* algorithm is used to offer robustness to hand identity loss by keeping multiple hypotheses about the positions of the hands over a time window. Linguistic information on the hand positions with respect to each other, such as the symmetry condition, are leveraged to help in the tracking process.

In the above works, analysis of hand motion is performed on the spatiotemporal trajectories, either directly, or else via some explicit modelling, for example via kinematic features or conic parameter equations.

In this paper we propose to tackle hand motion analysis in a different way. We formulate the problem of gross hand tracking as a *non-rigid structure from motion* problem, by applying the *factorisation method* [55] to the hand trajectories. We opt to use one of the extended versions of the standard factorisation method, mainly the *trajectory-space factorisation method* proposed by Akhter et al. [2]. This gives us a representation of the hand trajectories in terms of a weighted combination of a set of basis in trajectory space, and then we use these weight coefficients for performing motion analysis instead of using the original hand trajectories.

To our knowledge, only two previous works in ASLR have investigated the application of the factorisation method, and these focused on recovering the 3D handshapes rather than hand trajectories. Scheffler et al. [46] was one of the first to describe how the standard factorisation method can be applied to ASLR (reconstructing rigid articulated motion for the purpose of vocabulary

Figure 3: A sample video frame from the BBC Pose sequence overlaid with output of our hand tracking module. This dataset is available at: www.robots.ox.ac.uk/~vgg/data/pose/.

acquisition); though they only tested their proposed reconstruction system on synthetic data. And Ding and Martinez [24] applied the standard rigid-body factorisation under an affine camera model for recovering 3D handshapes. Due to problems in the reliable detection and tracking of fiducial features on the hands (knuckles, finger tips, wrist), they settled for manually marking the features in each and every video frame by hand. They also limited their system to isolated signing, choosing lexical signs where the handshape remains unchanged. A voting mechanism was used, over the sign's duration, to increase robustness of the 3D handshape reconstruction. While Ding and Martinez [24] observed increased robustness to occlusion, their major limitation is the manual selection of the hand features in all frames. To the best of our knowledge, no previous ASLR work has investigated the use of trajectory-based factorisation for hand motion analysis and classification.

3 OUR APPROACH

In the following subsections, we briefly explain the hand tracking system, then introduce the factorisation method, describe its application to hand trajectories, followed by our motion classification system, and finally the representation using HamNoSys.

3.1 Hand Tracking system

Our hand tracking system first starts with Haar-based face detection [57]. An adaptive skin colour model [60] is then learnt from the colour distribution of the face pixels. Candidate hand regions are generated based on the fusion of the face data, the skin likelihood map, as well as a motion likelihood map generated via weighted frame differencing. Tracking of the candidate hand regions from frame to frame is performed via the use of *Kanade-Lucas-Tomasi (KLT)* features [48]. These are sparse-sampled features that are selected based on their 'goodness' for tracking, computed from the eigenvalues of the image windows surrounding the point features and tracked across video frames via *optical flow* – the apparent motion of brightness variations in the image plane.

The challenging nature of signing gives rise to a lot of false alarms in the candidate hand regions, as well as tracking failures.

We thus embed the above hand tracking system within a *multiple hypotheses tracking* (*MHT*) framework [3]. Instead of making a 'hard' decision in each video frame of whether a candidate hand region is really a hand or not, MHT employs a deferred decision-taking mechanism by keeping multiple hypotheses, propagating these hypotheses into the future in anticipation that subsequent data will resolve the uncertainty about which of the multiple hypotheses is the correct one. Details on our hand tracking system were reported elsewhere [8]. Sample output is shown in Figure 3. The white rectangles depict face detection results, while the vertical gray line and crossmark depict the estimated midline of the signer and the torso centroid. The red open circles and arrows depict tracked KLT features that are either stationary or moving; blue open circles depict newly created KLT features to replenish lost ones. The red and green filled circles depict the positions of the detected left and right signer's hands as determined by the MHT algorithm. Thus once we have determined which set of features belongs to which hand of the signer via MHT, we then apply the factorisation method to these two sets of KLT features.

3.2 The Factorisation Method

The output from our hand tracking system is a set of KLT features for each of the signer's hands (denoted as h1, h2) tracked over a sliding time window of size $F = 15$ video frames. Let $\left(u_{f,p}, v_{f,p} \right)$ be the 2D image coordinates of the set of P_h features for hand h tracked over time window $f \in \{ f_{t-F}, \ldots, f_t \}$, where f_t is the current frame, $p \in \{ 1, \ldots, P_h \}$, and h $\in \{ h1, h2 \}$. The coordinates of the features are specified with respect to the centre of the signer's torso, estimated from the position of the face and using a pre-defined anthropometric model of an average human.

We then stack the 2D image coordinates of the P_{h1} and P_{h2} features across the full time window into a single matrix W. The factorisation method exploits the fact that this matrix W has a lot of redundancy in it, and thus uses matrix *singular value decomposition* (*SVD*) to factor W into two sub-matrices: a *motion matrix* M that contains the per-frame motion of the signer/camera, and a *shape matrix* S that contains the 3D structure of the signer's two hands.

$$W = M \, S \tag{1}$$

The motion of the hands with respect to the signer's body can be viewed as being non-rigid 'deformations' of the combined structure of the two hands with respect to the body's centre. Trajectory-space factorisation will thus factor shape matrix S into a weighted linear combination of *basis trajectories*:

$$S = \Theta \, A \tag{2}$$

where Θ is the matrix of the K trajectory basis, for some pre-defined value K, and A is the matrix with the weight coefficients. The chosen basis for our study are the *Discrete Cosine Transform (DCT) basis*. This matrix of equations is shown diagrammatically in Figure 4.

In the next subsection we will describe how we employ the coefficient matrix A as input to our classifiers for recognising some of the basic phonological elements of sign languages.

3.3 Hand Motion classification

When we investigated the results of the factorisation method on signing data, we observed that the coefficient matrix A of Eq. (2)

Table 1: Hand motion classifiers

Classifier	Class labels	Description	HamNoSys symbols
symmetry	asym	asymmetric hand motion	
	sym	mirror symmetry with respect to midline	¨
	sym	radial symmetry with respect to torso centroid	⁞
h1 stationary	moving	dominant hand (h1) is moving	
	stationary	h1 is not moving	
h2 stationary	moving	non-dominant hand (h2) is moving	
	stationary	h2 is not moving	
	at rest	h2 is not moving and is at its rest position (e.g. on signer's lap)	
motion	0	no hand motion, small hand motions, or irregular motion	
	mu	upward hand movement	↑
	mul	up-left hand movement	↗
	ml	left hand movement	↗
	mdl	downard-left hand movement	↘
	md	downward hand movement	↓
	mdr	downward-right hand movement	↙
	mr	right hand movement	←
	mur	upward-right hand movement	↖
	cm	hand follows a clockwise rotational motion	↑< ↻
	ccm	hand follows a counter-clockwise rotational motion	↑⊃ ↺

encodes useful information on the motion of the two hands. We thus leverage this observation for the development of our hand motion classification system.

Instead of working directly with the raw coefficients, we extract a number of non-parametric statistical measures from A for each of the K trajectory basis and across the point features of both hands (when considering the motion of both hands with respect to each other) and each hand individually (when considering the motion of one hand with respect to the signer's body; typically used for 1-handed signs). More specifically we use five number summary statistics [33]: median, 1st quartile $q1$, 3rd quartile $q3$, minimum and maximum of the data after removing outliers defined as values outside the range $[q1 - 1.5 \times \text{iqr} \ldots q3 + 1.5 \times \text{iqr}]$, where iqr is the interquartile range $q3 - q1$.

We define a number of classifiers for different types of hand motion that have phonological significance, and thus can serve as a basis for further work on a phonemic transcription system for sign languages. Table 1 lists the set of initial classifiers that we have selected for our proof of concept.

Here we use a binary classifier for symmetry detection and group all types of symmetrical hand motions into one class, labelled sym. The 'h1 stationary' classifier is also a binary classifier, and determines whether the dominant hand (h1) of the signer is moving or not. Unlike the previous classifier, the 'h1 stationary' classifier takes as input only the summary statistics for the feature points of the dominant hand, i.e., we compute statistics on the coefficients of matrix A that relate to hand h1. For the non-dominant hand h2, we use three classes for our stationarity classifier, in order to be able to discriminate between the case when h2 is stationary at its rest position, versus when h2 is stationary but not at its rest position. The rest position is the place where the hands stay when no arm or hand muscles are activated; this is typically on the signer's lap. In contrast, h2 can be in a stationary, but raised, position i.e., an effort is made to hold h2 stationary 'in the air'. This distinction has a linguistic value and allows for the discrimination between 1-handed and 2-handed signs.

Our final classifier focuses on detecting linear or curved motion segments. For curved motion segments, we discriminate between clockwise and counter-clockwise circular motions, as there are signs that differ in only this particular phonological element. For

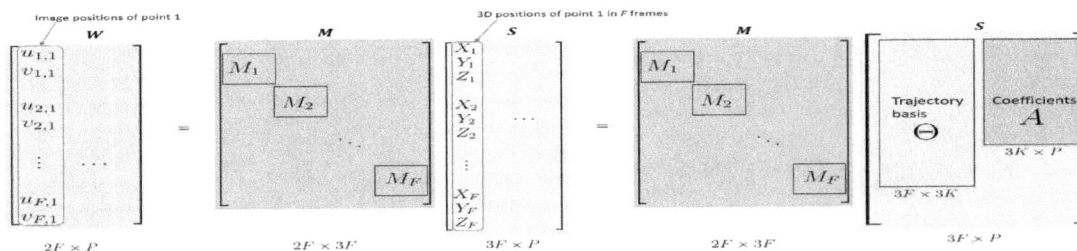

Figure 4: An illustration of the Trajectory-Space Factorisation method. Matrix W with body-centred hand image coordinates is factorised into a motion matrix M containing the signer's global motion, and a shape matrix S with the 3D structure of the signer's hands. S is in turn factorised into a set of DCT trajectory basis Θ and weighted coefficients A capturing the non-rigid trajectory changes of the hands with respect to the signer's body centroid.

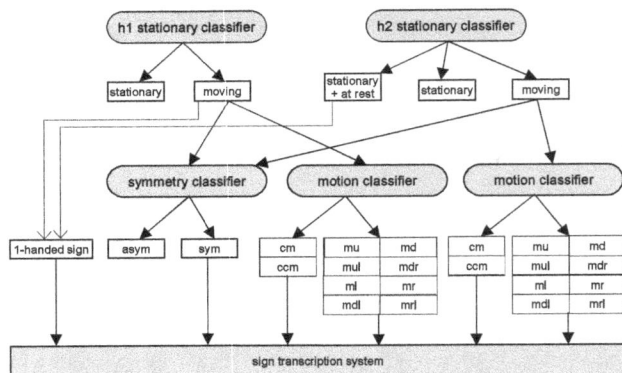

Figure 5: The classification and transcription structure

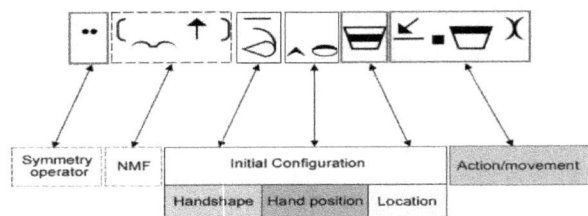

Figure 6: HamNoSys components (adapted from: Smith [50])

linear motion segments, we currently focus only on hand motion that occurs in the frontal plane, and quantise motion directions into 8 directions, 45° apart.

We then combine our set of classifiers into a graph structure, as shown in Figure 5, which in turn feeds into a sign transcription system that transcribes the classification results using a limited subset of HamNoSys symbols. The classifier grouping is done mostly for computational efficiency reasons; in the future we can investigate grouping into more complex classifier ensembles for improving machine learning.

3.4 HamNoSys transcription

We chose HamNoSys for our transcription system because of its capacity for detailed phonetic description of sign languages. The components of a HamNoSys "word" are shown in Figure 6. HamNoSys records signs in terms of hand shape, hand location, and hand movement. For 2-handed signs, the sign is preceded by a symmetry operator that defines how the description of the dominant hand copies over to the other hand. Simultaneous elements are enclosed within square brackets [30, 50]. For our initial investigation, we are going to focus on a limited subset of HamNoSys features: mainly the hand location, hand path movements, and hand symmetry for 2-handed signs (enclosed in red boxes in Figure 6).

We employ a simple transcription procedure for now: whenever a temporal change occurs in the active class label of the classifiers, we add the corresponding HamNoSys symbol to the transcription stream (refer to the last column of Table 1). To avoid the effects of classification noise and outliers, we perform temporal smoothing prior to transcription via the use of *loess* [17]. Any two changes are considered to be concurrent (enclosed within square brackets), if they happen within a certain temporal distance of each other.

Transcription output from our system is embedded within an ELAN annotation file (EAF) – this is basically an XML file format used by the ELAN annotation software [5]. We add a new tier within this file with the partial HamNoSys transcription, and we use the Unicode true type fonts available for HamNoSys for symbol representation [6]. Other formats that we can investigate in the future include the use of *SiGML* (Signing Gesture Markup Language) format, similar to the HamNoSys-to-SiGML tool developed by Kaur and Kumar [36].

4 EXPERIMENTS

We performed a number of experiments in order to evaluate our proposed system. These are described below. Here we will focus mainly on trajectory-based factorisation, our hand motion classifiers and the subsequent transcription; the implementation of our hand tracking system was reported elsewhere [8].

4.1 Datasets

As regards to video datasets, we opted for a publicly-available sign language dataset, the *ECHO Sign Language (NGT) Corpus* [19]. This

---

[5]ELAN is available at: http://tla.mpi.nl/tools/tla-tools/elan/, a general description of this annotation tool can be found in Crasborn and Sloetjes [18], and the EAF specification can be found here: http://www.mpi.nl/tools/elan/EAF_Annotation_Format.pdf.
[6]Unicode fonts for HamNoSys symbols are available here: http://vh.cmp.uea.ac.uk/index.php/SiGML_Tools.

Table 2: XGBoost hyperparameter selection

Hyperparameter	Value	Tuning approach	Range
Number of trees	1000	Fixed	
Learning rate η	0.04	Fixed → Fine-tuned	$0.02 \rightarrow [0.02, 0.04, 0.06, 0.08, 0.1]$
Row sampling	0.70	Grid Search	$[0.5, 0.7, 0.75, 0.8, 1.0]$
Column sampling	0.4	Grid Search	$[0.3, 0.4, 0.5, 0.6, 0.8, 1.0]$
Max tree depth	8	Grid Search	$[4, 6, 8, 10]$
Min leaf weight	1	Fixed → Fine-tuned	$3 \rightarrow [1, 5]$
Min split gain γ	0	Fixed	

Table 3: Accuracy results

Classifier	XGBoost	SVM	k-NN	baseline
h1 motion	89.49%	84.57%	70.74%	72.21%
h1 stationary	97.74%	96.94%	84.97%	96.54%
h2 stationary	86.97%	84.04%	63.16%	77.39%
symmetry	87.37%	76.99%	70.08%	58.51%

dataset[7] provides several video sequences of continuous signing in NGT (Dutch sign language) that are well annotated with linguistic information; these annotations are available in an EAF file, making it quite suitable for incorporating our investigations into phonemic transcription.

4.2 Trajectory-space Factorisation

As described in §3.2, we employ the trajectory space factorisation method of Akhter et al. [2] to our set of tracked KLT features of the two hands. We apply this repeatedly on our dataset using a temporal sliding window of size $F = 15$ frames, very roughly corresponding to the average time duration of sign language phonemes. As for the number of trajectory basis, we selected $K = 4$ for the full trajectory expansion, chosen empirically, while DCT is the basis of choice.

4.3 Hand motion classifiers

For the classifiers introduced in §3.3, we tried out the following supervised machine learning classifiers: *k-nearest neighbour (k-NN), support vector machines (SVMs)*, and *XGBoost*. We used *R* [45] for our experiments on classifiers.

The simplest of the three classifiers is *k*-NN, which does a simple nearest neighbour search and then takes a majority vote amongst the k closest ones. We experimented with various values of k, and found out that $k = 3$ performs the best. An SVM classifier finds the optimal hyperplane that separates the different classes by maximising the margin between them. Cost parameter C of the SVM controls the 'softness' of this margin, i.e., the degree of how many incorrectly-classified training points should be tolerated in order to improve the generalisation of the model. In addition the SVM makes use of a kernel function to map non-linearly separable data into a higher-dimensional space where the different classes then become linearly separable via a hyperplane [11]. In the case of SVMs, we used the (Gaussian) radial basis function as kernel. This kernel has a parameter γ, which controls the variance of the Gaussian and thus the influence of the training data. SVM parameters C and γ were determined via a grid search ($C = 10$ and $\gamma = 0.1$ for the h1 motion classifier).

Our third classifier is based on *gradient boosting machines (GBMs)* [42]: this is a machine learning technique which produces a strong classifier in the form of an ensemble of weak classifiers, typically *decision trees*. The model is built in an iterative way, employing *gradient boosting* method proposed by Friedman [27]: each additional weak classifier focuses on the residuals of the previous classifiers' results, using gradient descent to minimise the chosen loss function. GBMs have shown remarkable success in many areas, including that

of human gesture recognition [4]. *XGBoost* [15], short for *extreme gradient boosting*, is a particular implementation of the standard GBM that adds a number of model and algorithmic performance enhancements such as the use of a more regularized model formalization to control over-fitting, and block structure to aid algorithmic parallelisation.

GBMs have a large number of hyperparameters that need tuning. We selected decision trees as boosters, logloss as the loss function [7, p.209], and the other parameters were tuned via a grid search (See Table 2).

A challenging aspect we had is the fact that classes are unbalanced. For example, class '0' of the 'motion classifier' (standing for irregular, small, or no motions), outnumbers all of the other motions together for the non-dominant hand, accounting for over 75% of the video sequence . Many machine learning algorithms experience problems when faced with such unbalanced datasets. We thus employed the *synthetic minority over-sampling technique (SMOTE)* [14]. SMOTE is a well-known algorithm that balances the classes by generating artificial examples of minority classes based on the k nearest neighbours of these classes ($k = 5$ in our case).

5 EVALUATION

We used the first 1500 video frames of sequence NGT_AH_fab1 for our evaluation. Performance is measured in terms of the accuracy metric $Acc = (TP + TN) / (TP + TN + FP + FN)$, where TP, TN, FP, FN are determined on a frame-by-frame basis. N-fold cross-validation was used, with the number of folds N set to 10.

The accuracy results obtained are listed in Table 3. We also list the baseline classifier rate; the accuracy obtained by trivially predicting the most-frequent class. This is high for the h1 stationary classifier, because the dominant hand is rarely stationary. One can note that in most cases, *k*-NN performs worse than the baseline. For the multi-class 'hand motion' classifier applied to h1, we obtained an accuracy of 89.49% with XGBoost, against 84.57% with SVM. For the 'h1 stationary' classifier, the accuracies were: 97.74% for XGBoost, and 96.94% for SVM. And the performance obtained for the 'h2 stationary' classifier are: 86.97% for XGBoost, and 84.04% for SVM. In the case of the 'hand symmetry' classifier, we obtained accuracies of 87.37% with XGBoost and 76.99% with SVM.

From the above results, we can see that in all cases XGBoost outperforms the other two classifiers. Figures 7 and 8 illustrate the confusion matrices for the 'hand motion' classifier and for XGBoost respectively, while Figure 9 gives the ROC curve of the XGBoost version of the 'hand motion' classifier. From the confusion matrices of Figure 7, one can observe that the classifiers have a high tendency to generate false positives (the '0'-labelled column of the confusion matrices), but very little false negatives (the '0'-labelled row); this is also evident from the initial part of the ROC curve. One can further

---

[7] Available at: http://sign-lang.ruhosting.nl/echo/

169

(a) k-NN

(b) SVM

(c) XGBoost

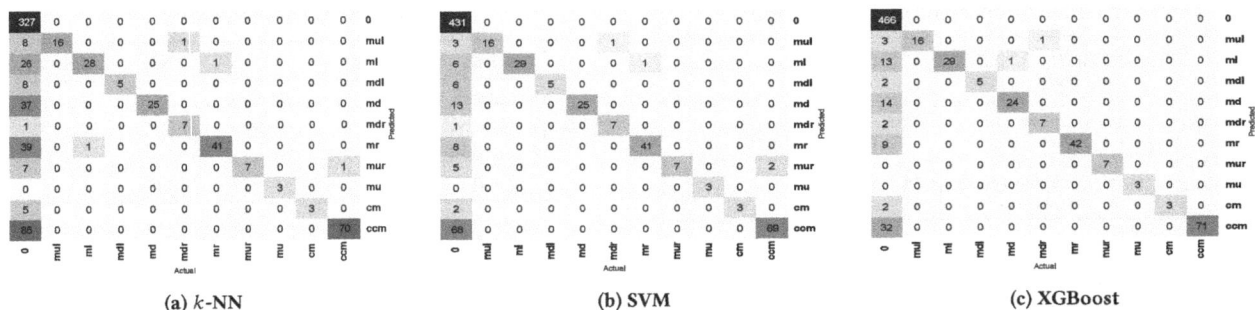

Figure 7: Confusion matrices for the k-NN, SVM, and XGBoost -based versions of the h1 hand motion classifier (Refer to Table 1 for the full class labels corresponding to the class label abbreviations used here.)

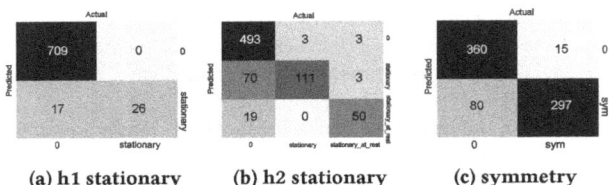

(a) h1 stationary

(b) h2 stationary

(c) symmetry

Figure 8: Confusion matrices for the XGBoost-based versions of the 'h1 stationary', 'h2 stationary', and 'hand symmetry' classifiers

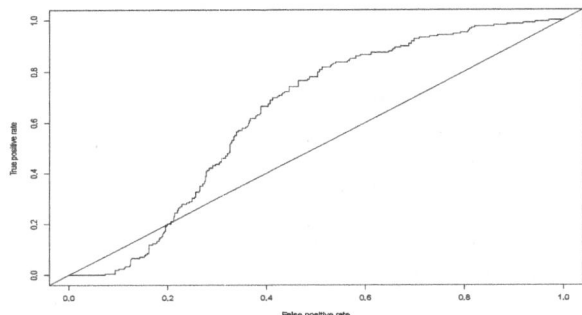

Figure 9: ROC curve for the XGBoost version of the hand motion classifier. The classifier output has been binarised (linear/circular motion vs. no motion) in this ROC plot.

note that intra-class confusion is minimal, thus we have achieved a high level of discrimination between different linear and circular motions. One possible reason for the high false-positive rate is that while the class labelled '0' covers cases where the hand h1 exhibits no motion, irregular or small motions, some of the small motions are in fact still linear in nature and interpreted as such by the classifiers. Here we have evaluated our classifiers individually; we are currently in the process of evaluating the combined classifiers via the grouping shown in Figure 5, and we expect that many of the false positives will be eliminated via the filtering effect of the early stages of this graph.

Sample output from our system are shown in Figures 10 and 11 for a symmetric sign and a sign where only hand h1 moves. Note the evident mirror-image symmetry in the coefficient matrix A in

Figure 10(d), and the lack of symmetry in Figure 11(d). In this first study, we have tested the system on this limited video sequence, mostly due to the lack of groundtruthed annotation data available.

6 CONCLUSIONS

We have shown that the application of trajectory space factorisation to gross hand movements can give rise to rich information encoded within the coefficient matrix of the DCT trajectory basis. We leveraged this structure within our classification system, employing machine learning algorithms such as XGBoost, in order to detect symmetric hand motion, detect when the hands are stationary, and to discriminate between various circular and linear hand motions. Our evaluation demonstrates the validity of our proposed system, achieving correct detection rates of 87.37% for the 'hand symmetry' binary classifier, and 89.49% accuracy for the multi-class 'hand motion' classifier in particular. Furthermore, we investigated how the results of our classifiers can be integrated into a phonemic sign language transcription system. We demonstrated this by mapping the detected motion categories to a limited subset of HamNoSys symbols, with the aim of exporting these to annotation tools, such as ELAN. The main advantage of this approach is that such a phonemic transcription does not rely on the need of a lexicon and does not require sign recognition to work.

Future work will look at incorporating classifiers for more complex motions such as zigzag motion, etc. We will also investigate the use of our method for deriving phonetically meaningful sub-units for training sign recognition, much in the spirit of the work done by Theodorakis et al. [54]. Finally, we also plan to look into integrating of our solution within ELAN. The ELAN annotation tool provides functionality for integrating various video recognisers as 'plugins' for direct operation within its framework. There are already some video recognisers available, for example, the ones based on the work of Schreer et al. [47]. We aim to follow a similar approach in order for our system to help alleviate the laborious and time-consuming sign language annotation process.

REFERENCES

[1] Steven Aerts, Bart Braem, Katrien Van Mulders, and Kristof De Weerdt. 2004. Searching SignWriting Signs. In *Proc. LREC 2004*. ELRA, 79–81.

[2] Ijaz Akhter, Yaser Sheikh, Sohaib Khan, and Takeo Kanade. 2011. Trajectory Space: A Dual Representation for Nonrigid Structure from Motion. *IEEE Trans. Pattern Anal. Mach. Intell.* 33, 7 (2011), 1442–1456.

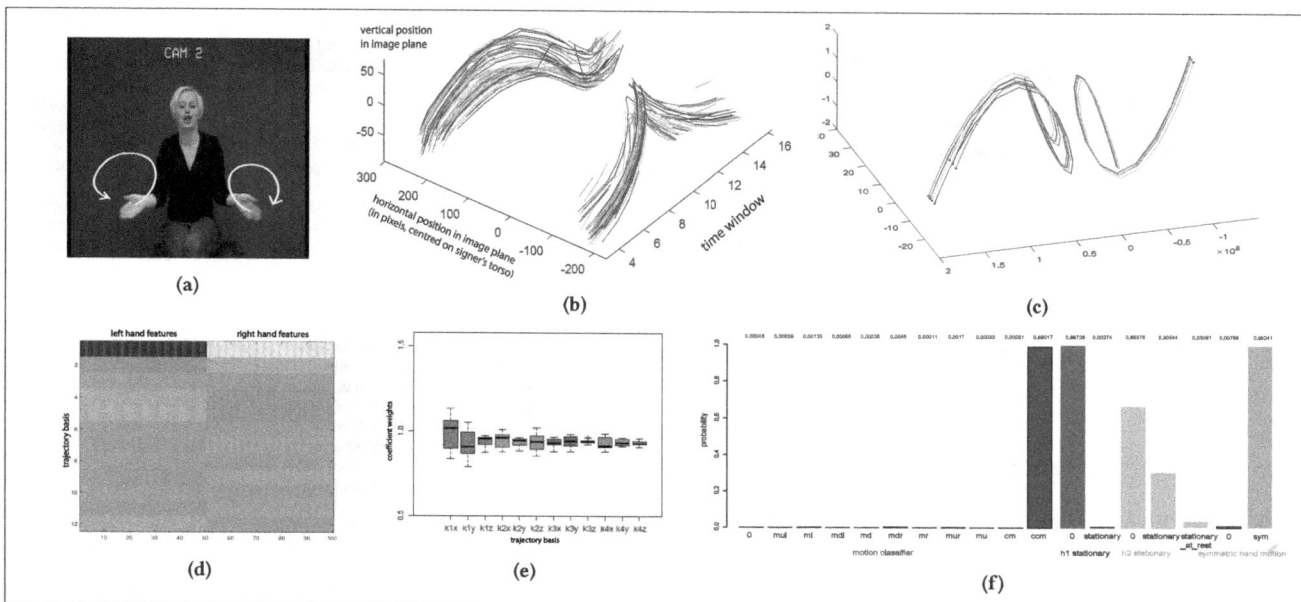

Figure 10: Output for (a) video frame #149, SHEPHERD sign. (b) The spatiotemporal trajectories of tracked features over a 15-frame window centred on frame #149, and (c) the reconstructed trajectories after performing trajectory space factorisation. (d) Coefficient matrix A of the signer's two hands – the first half (on the left) are the coefficients of the dominant hand h1; the second half are the coefficients of the non-dominant hand h2. (e) The five-number summary statistics extracted from A, where $\{KnX, KnY, KnZ\}$ are the 3D coordinates of the Nth trajectory basis. (f) Classification results correctly showing that sign SHEPHERD has circular motion (ccm for h1), none of the hands are stationary, and the sign is symmetric.

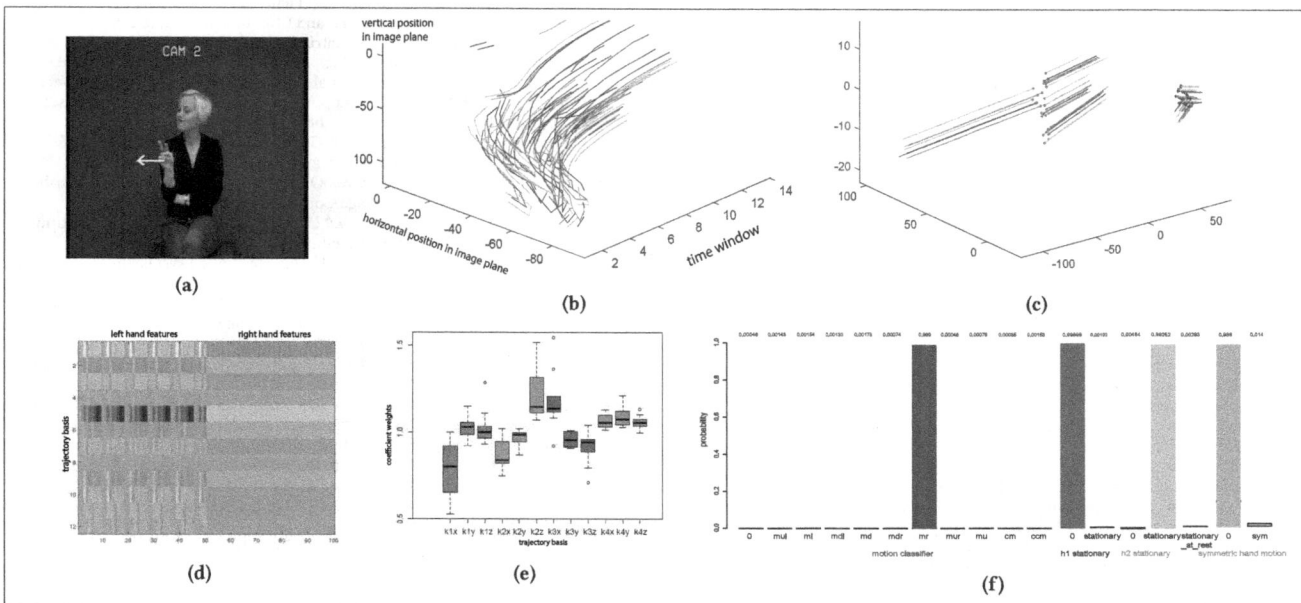

Figure 11: Output for (a) video frame #661, LOOK sign. (b) Spatiotemporal trajectories of tracked features, (c) the reconstructed trajectories after performing trajectory space factorisation, (d) coefficient matrix A of the signer's two hands, and (e) five-number summary statistics extracted from A. (f) Classification results correctly showing that in sign LOOK, the dominant hand does a linear motion to the right (mr), h2 is stationary but not at rest, and the sign is not symmetric.

171

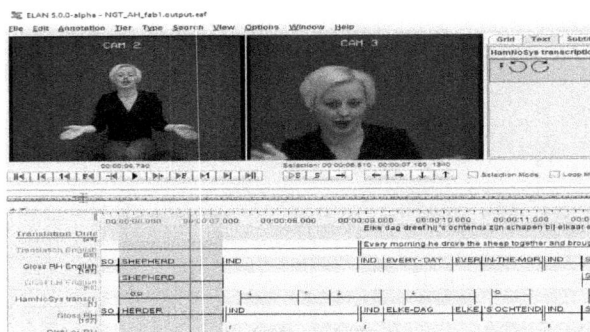

```
<TIER DEFAULT_LOCALE="en" LINGUISTIC_TYPE_REF="Default" TIER_ID="HamNoSys transcr.">
  <ANNOTATION>
    <ALIGNABLE_ANNOTATION ANNOTATION_ID="a1009" TIME_SLOT_REF1="ts113" TIME_SLOT_REF2="ts124">
      <ANNOTATION_VALUE>BB</ANNOTATION_VALUE>
    </ALIGNABLE_ANNOTATION ANNOTATION_ID="a1010" TIME_SLOT_REF1="ts119" TIME_SLOT_REF2="ts120">
      <ANNOTATION_VALUE>BB</ANNOTATION_VALUE>
    </ALIGNABLE_ANNOTATION>
  </ANNOTATION>
</TIER>
<LINGUISTIC_TYPE GRAPHIC_REFERENCES="false" LINGUISTIC_TYPE_ID="Default" TIME_ALIGNABLE="true"/>
<LINGUISTIC_TYPE CONSTRAINTS="Symbolic_Association" GRAPHIC_REFERENCES="false" LINGUISTIC_TYPE_ID="Translation" TIME_ALIGNABLE="false"/>
<LINGUISTIC_TYPE CONSTRAINTS="Symbolic_Association" GRAPHIC_REFERENCES="false" LINGUISTIC_TYPE_ID="Repetition" TIME_ALIGNABLE="false"/>
<LINGUISTIC_TYPE CONSTRAINTS="Symbolic_Association" GRAPHIC_REFERENCES="false" LINGUISTIC_TYPE_ID="Dir &amp; Loc" TIME_ALIGNABLE="false"/>
```

Figure 12: (Top) HamNoSys transcription loaded in ELAN as an additional tier. (Bottom) XML snippet from our EAF file.

[3] David Miguel Antunes et al. 2011. A Library for Implementing the Multiple Hypothesis Tracking Algorithm. *CoRR* abs/1106.2 (2011).

[4] V. Ayumi. 2016. Pose-based human action recognition with Extreme Gradient Boosting. In *IEEE Conf. SCOReD*. 1–5.

[5] Guylhem Aznar. 2005. Sign Writing Unicode Support: Using an Assisted Entry Process to Neutralize Sign and Symbol Variability. In *Interacting Bodies (ISGS)*.

[6] Katarzyna Barczewska et al. 2016. Using Components of Corpus Linguistics and Annotation Tools in Sign Language Teaching. *IJMECS* 2 (2016), 14–21.

[7] Christopher M. Bishop. 2006. *Pattern Recognition and Machine Learning*. Springer-Verlag New York, Inc.

[8] Mark Borg and Kenneth P. Camilleri. 2015. Multiple Hypothesis Tracking with Sign Language Hand Motion Constraints. In *CAIP 2015, Proc., Part II*. 207–219.

[9] Mehrez Boulares and Mohamed Jemni. 2012. 3D Motion Trajectory Analysis Approach to Improve Sign Language 3D-based Content Recognition. *Procedia Computer Science* 13 (2012), 133 – 143.

[10] Alice Caplier, Sébastien Stillittano, et al. 2008. Image and Video for Hearing Impaired People. *EURASIP Journal on Image and Video Processing* (2008), 1–14.

[11] Chih-Chung Chang and Chih-Jen Lin. 2011. LIBSVM: A Library for Support Vector Machines. *ACM Trans. Intell. Syst. Technol.* 2, 3, Article 27 (2011), 27 pages.

[12] J. Charles et al. 2013. Automatic and Efficient Human Pose Estimation for Sign Language Videos. *Int. Journal of Computer Vision* (2013).

[13] J. Charles, T. Pfister, D. Magee, D. Hogg, and A. Zisserman. 2014. Upper Body Pose Estimation with Temporal Sequential Forests. In *BMVC 2014*.

[14] Nitesh V. Chawla et al. 2002. SMOTE: Synthetic Minority Over-sampling Technique. *J. Artificial Intelligence Research* 16, 1 (June 2002), 321–357.

[15] Tianqi Chen and Carlos Guestrin. 2016. XGBoost: A Scalable Tree Boosting System. In *ACM SIGKDD Int. Conf. Knowledge Discovery and Data Mining*.

[16] Wang Chunli, Gao Wen, and Ma Jiyong. 2002. A real-time large vocabulary recognition system for Chinese Sign Language. In *Proc. GW'01*. Springer, 86–95.

[17] William S Cleveland, Eric Grosse, and William M Shyu. 1992. Local regression models. *Statistical models in S* 2 (1992), 309–376.

[18] Onno Crasborn and Han Sloetjes. 2008. Enhanced ELAN functionality for sign language corpora. In *Proc. of LREC 2008*.

[19] Onno Crasborn, E. van der Kooij, A. Nonhebel, and W. Emmerik. 2004. ECHO Data Set for Sign Language of the Netherlands (NGT). (2004).

[20] Antônio Carlos da Rocha Costa et al. 2004. A sign matching technique to support searches in sign language texts. In *LREC 2004*.

[21] Antônio Carlos da Rocha Costa and Graçaliz Pereira Dimuro. 2003. SignWriting and SWML: Paving the way to sign language processing. In *TALN'03*.

[22] Konstantinos G. Derpanis, Richard P. Wildes, and John K. Tsotsos. 2008. Definition and Recovery of Kinematic Features for Recognition of American Sign Language Movements. *Image Vision Comput.* 26, 12 (Dec. 2008), 1650–1662.

[23] Mark Dilsizian, Zhiqiang Tang, et al. 2016. The Importance of 3D Motion Trajectories for Computer-based Sign Recognition. In *Proc. LREC'16*. ELRA.

[24] Liya Ding and Aleix M. Martinez. 2009. Modelling and recognition of the linguistic components in American Sign Language. *Image Vision Comput.* (2009).

[25] Wanessa Machado do Amaral and José Mario De Martino. 2010. *Towards a Transcription System of Sign Language for 3D Virtual Agents*. Springer, 85–90.

[26] Philippe Dreuw and Hermann Ney. 2008. Towards automatic sign language annotation for the ELAN tool. In *Proc. LREC'08*. 50–53.

[27] Jerome H. Friedman. 2001. Greedy Function Approximation: A Gradient Boosting Machine. *Annals of Statistics* 29 (2001), 1189–1232.

[28] Matilde Gonzalez et al. 2012. Semi-Automatic Sign Language Corpora Annotation using Lexical Representations of Signs. In *Proc. LREC'12*.

[29] C. Guimarães, J. F. Guardezi, et al. 2014. Deaf Culture and Sign Language Writing System – A Database for a New Approach to Writing System Recognition Technology. In *47th Hawaii Int. Conf. on System Sciences*. 3368–3377.

[30] Thomas Hanke. 2004. HamNoSys - Representing Sign Language Data in Language Resources and Language Processing Contexts. In *LREC 2004*. 1–6.

[31] Thomas Hanke and Jakob Storz. 2008. iLex - A Database Tool for Integrating Sign Language Corpus Linguistics and Sign Language Lexicography. In *LREC'08*.

[32] Marek Hrúz et al. 2011. Towards Automatic Annotation of Sign Language Dictionary Corpora. *Text, Speech and Dialogue (TSD)* (2011), 331–339.

[33] Rob J. Hyndman and Yanan Fan. 1996. Sample Quantiles in Statistical Packages. *The American Statistician* 50, 4 (1996), 361–365.

[34] Kabil Jaballah and Mohamed Jemni. 2010. Toward Automatic Sign Language Recognition from Web3D Based Scenes. In *Computers Helping People with Special Needs (ICCHP 2010)*, Klaus Miesenberger et al. (Eds.). 205–212.

[35] V. Karappa et al. 2014. Detection of sign-language content in video through polar motion profiles. In *ICASSP'14*. 1290–1294.

[36] Khushdeep Kaur and Parteek Kumar. 2016. HamNoSys to SiGML Conversion System for Sign Language Automation. *Procedia Computer Science* 89 (2016).

[37] Oscar Koller, R Bowden, and H Ney. 2016. Automatic Alignment of HamNoSys Subunits for Continuous Sign Language Recognition. In *LREC 2016 Proc.*

[38] Oscar Koller, Jens Forster, and Hermann Ney. 2015. Continuous sign language recognition: Towards large vocabulary statistical recognition systems handling multiple signers. *Comput. Vision Image Understanding* 141 (2015), 108–125.

[39] Markus Koskela et al. 2008. Content-Based Video Analysis and Access for Finnish Sign Language - A Multidisciplinary Research Project. In *Proc. LREC'08*.

[40] Gan Lu et al. 2010. Hand Motion Recognition and Visualisation for Direct Sign Writing. In *Proc. Information Visualisation (IV 2010)*. IEEE, 467–472.

[41] C. D. D. Monteiro et al. 2016. Detecting and Identifying Sign Languages through Visual Features. In *2016 IEEE Int. Symposium on Multimedia (ISM)*.

[42] Alexey Natekin and Alois Knoll. 2013. Gradient boosting machines, a tutorial. *Front. Neurorobot.* (2013).

[43] Sylvie C W Ong and Surendra Ranganath. 2005. Automatic sign language analysis: a survey and the future beyond lexical meaning. *IEEE PAMI* 27, 6 (2005), 873–91.

[44] A. L. Prihodko et al. 2016. Approach to the analysis and synthesis of the sign language. In *Proc. APEIE*, Vol. 02. 502–505.

[45] R Core Team. 2017. *R: A Language and Environment for Statistical Computing*. R Foundation for Statistical Computing, Vienna, Austria. www.R-project.org

[46] Carl Scheffler, Konrad H. Scheffler, and Christian W. Omlin. 2003. Articulated Tree Structure from Motion – A Matrix Factorisation Approach. In *Proc. Annual Symposium of the Pattern Recognition Association of South Africa (PRASA)*.

[47] Oliver Schreer, Stefano Masneri, et al. 2014. Coding Hand Movement Behavior and Gesture with NEUROGES Supported by Automatic Video Analysis. In *Int. Conf. on Methods and Techniques in Behavioral Research*.

[48] Jianbo Shi and Carlo Tomasi. 1994. Good Features to Track. In *1994 IEEE Conf. on Computer Vision and Pattern Recognition (CVPR'94)*. 593–600.

[49] Frank Shipman, Ricardo Gutierrez-Osuna, et al. 2015. Towards a Distributed Digital Library for Sign Language Content. In *JCDL '15*. ACM.

[50] Robert Smith. 2013. *HamNoSys 4.0 User Guide*. Technical Report. Institute of Technology Blanchardstown Ireland.

[51] D. Stiehl et al. 2015. Towards a SignWriting recognition system. In *Proc. Int. Conf. on Document Analysis and Recognition (ICDAR)*. 26–30.

[52] Valerie Sutton. 1980. A way to analyze American Sign Language and any other Sign Language without translation into any spoken language. In *National Symposium on Sign Language Research and Teaching*.

[53] S. Tamura and S. Kawasaki. 1988. Recognition of sign language motion images. *Pattern Recognit.* 21, 4 (1988), 343–353.

[54] S. Theodorakis, V. Pitsikalis, I. Rodomagoulakis, and P. Maragos. 2012. Recognition with raw canonical phonetic movement and handshape subunits on videos of continuous Sign Language. In *IEEE Int. Conf. on Image Processing*. 1413–1416.

[55] Carlo Tomasi and Takeo Kanade. 1992. Shape and Motion from Image Streams Under Orthography: A Factorization Method. *Int. J. Comput. Vision* 9, 2 (1992).

[56] P. Vijayalakshmi and M. Aarthi. 2016. Sign language to speech conversion. In *2016 Int. Conf. on Recent Trends in Information Technology (ICRTIT)*. 1–6.

[57] Paul Viola and Michael J. Jones. 2001. Robust Real-time Object Detection. *Int. J. Comput. Vision* (2001).

[58] Ulrich von Agris et al. 2008. Rapid signer adaptation for continuous sign language recognition using a combined approach of eigenvoices, MLLR, and MAP. In *CPR 2008*. IEEE, 1–4.

[59] Ulrich von Agris, Jörg Zieren, et al. 2007. Recent developments in visual sign language recognition. *Universal Access in the Information Society* (2007).

[60] M Wimmer and B Radig. 2005. Adaptive skin color classifier. In *Proc GVIP'05*.

[61] Shilin Zhang and Bo Zhang. 2010. Trajectory based sign language video retrieval using revised string edit distance. In *Proc. MINES'10*. IEEE, 17–22.

The Intangible Nature of Drama Documents: an FRBR view

Vincenzo Lombardo
Dipartimento di Informatica e CIRMA
Università di Torino
Torino, Italy
vincenzo.lombardo@unito.it

Rossana Damiano
Dipartimento di Informatica e CIRMA
Università di Torino
Torino, Italy
rossana@di.unito.it

Antonio Pizzo
Dipartimento di Studi Umanistici e CIRMA
Università di Torino
Torino, Italy
antonio.pizzo@unito.it

Carmi Terzulli
Dipartimento di Informatica
Università di Torino
Torino, Italy
terzulli@di.unito.it

ABSTRACT

As a pervasive form of artistic expression through ages and media, drama features a twofold nature of its tangible manifestations (theatrical performances, movies, books, etc.) and its intangible abstraction (the story of Cinderella underlying Disney movie and Perrault's fable). The encoding of the intangible drama abstraction of drama documents is relevant for the preservation of cultural heritage and the didactics and research on drama documents. This paper addresses the task of encoding the notion of intangible story abstraction from the drama documents. The reference model is provided by a computational ontology that formally encodes the elements that characterize a drama, for purposes of semantic linking and inclusion in annotation schemata. By providing a formal expression posited between drama as work and its manifestations, the ontology-based representation is compliant with the model of Functional Requirements for Bibliographic Records (FRBR).

CCS CONCEPTS

• **Applied computing → Arts and humanities; Annotation;** • **Information systems →** *Ontologies*;

KEYWORDS

drama annotation, FRBR, intangible cultural heritage

ACM Reference format:
Vincenzo Lombardo, Rossana Damiano, Antonio Pizzo, and Carmi Terzulli. 2017. The Intangible Nature of Drama Documents: an FRBR view. In *Proceedings of DocEng '17, September 04–07, 2017, Valletta, Malta.*, , 10 pages.
DOI: http://dx.doi.org/10.1145/3103010.3103019

1 INTRODUCTION

Pervasive in human culture through ages, drama has increased in importance throughout the last decades, along with the widespread

availability of audiovisual media. A drama is a story conveyed through characters who perform live actions, such as Shakespeare's Hamlet, but also Tom Stoppard's Rosencrantz and Guildenstern Are Dead, David Chase's American crime TV series The Sopranos, and even reality shows, such as Keeping Up with the Kardashians, and, games, such as Ubisoft's Assassin's Creed series (cf. also Esslin's notion of 'dramatic media' [7]).

The massive availability of drama in digital form, issued from both digitalization of old media and new media productions, has transformed the traditional dialectics between text and performance into a more complex relationship between drama as an abstraction and its manifestations in multiple forms and formats. More, such a massive availability challenges the research in digital humanities, where data are typically small, structured, and enriched with metadata (see, e.g., the Text Encoding Initiative [1]). This challenge is attested by the tension between "big" and "smart" data, with the expectation that data tend to be bigger and smarter through crowdsourcing and automation [31]. The aim of building annotated data of drama heritage can be accomplished through the design of an annotation schema and the implementation of tools that can ease the task through partial automation.

Recently, there have been many approaches to the annotation of stories (a larger set than drama, including general narrative, not exclusively conveyed by characters performing actions). Annotations are going to enrich drama documents with appropriate metadata. Most of the approaches, e.g., the Story Workbench tool [9] and the DramaBank project ([6]), build upon the linguistic expression of the story, typically some natural language, and annotate story elements, such as characters and conflicts, over the linguistic layer of part-of-speech tagging and verbal frames. Other approaches are more detached from the linguistic expression: they consider the cultural object of the story and rely on conceptual models encoded in logic frameworks, e.g., the Contextus Project [2], the StorySpace ontology [34], and Drammar [13].

However, most projects work in an isolated fashion: each approach provides its own annotation schema, and do not provide the documents with a clear status. In this paper, we bridge the gap between the annotated drama documents and the widespread FRBR conceptual model. The FRBR model (Functional Requirements for

---

[1] http://www.tei-c.org/index.xml, visited on 7 July 2017.
[2] http://www.contextus.net, visited on 7 July 2017.

Bibliographical Entities) [23], designed for capturing the semantics of bibliographic information, addresses the abstract ideation (called Work, e.g., Beethoven's idea of the Ninth Symphony), the encoding in a specific language such as the text (called Expression, e.g., Berliner Philarmoniker's interpretation of the Ninth), the concrete representation (called Manifestation, e.g., some Berliner Philarmoniker's recording of the Ninth), and a single instance (called Item, e.g., some published CD of some Berliner Philarmoniker's recording of the Ninth). We employ the computational ontology Drammar to devise an annotation schema for drama documents: this supports automation through reasoning services and links the annotated documents to the FRBR conceptual model: in particular, we show that an annotated drama document is a particular Expression of the underlying drama abstraction, or Work (a form of intangible cultural heritage), encoded in the ontological format. And the drama document is the actual Manifestation of a novel, ontological linguistic Expression that is perfectly compliant with the FRBR model.

The paper is organized as follows. In the next section, we survey the related work, addressing both the annotation systems mentioned above and the inspirational works. In Section 3 we describe the intangible notion of drama abstraction and the Drammar ontology approach, with the major tenets of its representation. Then, in Section 4, we describe the annotation pipeline that relies on Drammar, the annotation tool devised to ease the task of the annotators, and the construction of the corpus of annotated drama documents. Finally, we show how the Drammar encoding can be accommodated within the framework provided by the FRBR model (Section 5). Conclusion ends the paper.

2 RELATED WORK

In recent times, the annotation of narrative documents has been prompted and influenced by two main lines of research. On the one side, the tradition of knowledge representation in AI has contributed the conceptual tools for describing the content of stories, with languages that span from scripts [30] to frames [20]. The linguistic counterpart of this line of research has resulted in resources situated at the lexico-semantic level (such as FrameNet [1] and at the interface between syntax and semantics (such as PropBank, which offers tools for representing the connection between the expression of the narrative through the text and the narrative content itself). For example, the Story Workbench tool [9] encompasses a layered annotation scheme, which uses these resources for the multi-layer annotation of narratives. On the other side, the annotation of narratives has benefited from the trend, established during the last three decades [4], of representing the content of documents in a machine-readable form. With the advent of markup languages such as Text Encoding Initiative (TEI) for encoding text in digital form and annotating their structure, the use of markup has soon become the standard in text annotation projects. In particular, projects such as Narrative Knowledge Representation Language (NKRL) [36] leveraged the use of markup languages for the representation of the narrative content of text, revamping the use of frames into the emerging scenario of media indexing and retrieval. More recently, as part of the more general effort of constructing resources for the automation of language processing and generation, Elson has proposed a template based language for describing the narrative content of text documents, with the goal of creating a corpus of annotated narrative texts, called DramaBank project [6].

The latter project focuses on the discourse relations specifically designed for modeling narrative discourse. The annotation schema is called the Story Intention Graph (SIG) and a particular annotation of a narrative is called a SIG encoding. DramaBank is a corpus of SIG encodings, collected through the work of trained annotators. A SIG encoding consists of three interconnected sections called layers: 1) the textual layer represents spans of the original discourse; 2) the timeline layer contains nodes that represent events and statives that occur in the story being narrated; 3) the interpretative layer is the layer where nodes represent goals, plans, beliefs, affectual impacts, and the underlying intentions of characters (agents). The annotation of the DramaBank project can be carried out through Scheherazade, a publicly available annotation tool. The tool provides interfaces for the three layers above. A graph shows the relationships over the nodes at the several layers. Graphic interfaces allows the inspection of nodes and arcs very easily. The SIG elaborated can be rephrased, by generating a natural language re-telling of the story, for checking the validity of the annotation produced. DramaBank consists of 110 encodings, as a methodology and the beginning of a shared corpus from which it is possible to pursue data-driven investigations of narrative structure. DramaBank addresses the narrative/story/drama features that we address in our project. A major difference is that the focus, in this case, is on the linguistic level, for its attention on fixed terminology. This task, though made easy through the graphic interface and the access to linguistic data bases, reveals to be very hard to carry out (we made a number of annotation experiments with the DramaBank tool before moving to the implementation of a novel tool). In fact, the corpus is limited to short stories, such as Aesop's fables. It would be cumbersome to annotated large dramas, where attention should be posed on conflicts on large chunks of the discourse. Our project, in fact, though grounded on a formal theory of drama, leaves a relative freedom on the annotation of terms, providing a strict annotation on intentions and conflicts, as related to the timeline incidents.

In recent years, the annotation of narrative text has evolved towards minimal schemata targeted at grasping the regularities of written and oral narratives at the discourse level [26]. However, these initiatives, rooted in narrative theories, tend to focus on the realization of narratives though a specific medium, e.g., text, neglecting the universal elements of dramatic narration that go behind the expressive characteristics of each medium.

A media-independent model of story is provided by the Onto-Media ontology, exploited across different projects (such as the Contextus Project, see footnote above) to annotate the narrative content of different media objects, ranging from written literature to comics and TV fiction. This project encompasses some concepts, such the notion of character, that are relevant for the description of drama, but, being mainly focused on the representation of events and the order in which they are exposed in media for cross-media comparison, it lacks the capability of representing the core notions of drama. In the field of cultural heritage dissemination, the StorySpace ontology [34], an ontology of story, supports museum curators in linking the content of artworks through stories, with the ultimate goal of enabling the generation of user tailored content retrieval [21]. Finally, some scholars have created representational tools for specific narrative theories, ranging from literary structuralism [25] to scriptwriting practices [33].

Drammar[3] is an ontology of drama, specifically conceived to annotate dramatic media [15]. Drammar aims at extending the use of ontologies to describe the content metadata of dramatic media in a theory-neutral, media-independent way. The use of the ontology format not only allows specifying the conceptual model of drama in a formal, unambiguous way but also makes the knowledge about drama available as a vocabulary for the interchange of annotations across different projects and readily usable for applications that encompass the manipulation of annotations by automatic reasoners and other software types. For example, [13] employ automatic reasoning techniques to compute the emotions felt by the characters on the basis of the events and the intentions manually annotated.

3 MODELING THE INTANGIBLE NATURE OF DRAMA

Throughout the multiple media, a single drama can assume several forms, fulfilling a number of its core conditions. For example, the abstraction of the oral tale Cinderella appears in, for example, Perrault's and Disney's versions. Abstracting from the media objects that exhibit a drama, we face a form of intangible cultural heritage (ICH). as shown in [17] and surveyed in section 3.1; the drama abstraction can then be encoded through the constructs of the Drammar ontology (section 3.2).

3.1 Drama as intangible cultural heritage

A number of characteristics make drama a form of ICH (cf. [32], pp. 146-148, and [17]):

(1) Drama does not reside within a specific location and can be performed in different locations and by different artists.
(2) Drama is mobile and ephemeral, since the elements of drama may be reinterpreted (Hamlet exists in many versions).
(3) Drama is limited in duration and evolving, since virtually we cannot have two manifestations of a specific drama that are totally identical; but, also, the form and function of what we call drama may change (e.g., consider the functional difference between the Greek tragedy Oedipus and the modernist play Six Characters in Search of an Author).
(4) Drama is transmitted from generation to generation, constantly evolving, skills and techniques learned by means of mimetic techniques by future generations. Young authors study drama through the experience of the manifestations of the intangible heritage that we know as drama, being such experiences as reading a text, attending a performance, watching a movie, listening to a radio drama, and so forth.
(5) Drama is often spread over large areas or dispersed (cf., e.g., the original movie The Seven Samurai and the Hollywood movie The Magnificent Seven).

(6) Drama is not safeguarded as living heritage by means of documentation, though documented in many different ways (text, score, video, audio, and so forth) through its discrete manifestations; however, drama lives and continues to develop, and such a documentation will have historical value, and help research, memory, and transmission. However, such a documentation does not contribute to the safeguarding of the drama as an ICH item; scholars foresee a collaborative environment for the creation/sharing/dissemination of the metadata that express knowledge on the essential elements of drama and theater [3].

The major assumption of our approach is that computational ontologies and semantic web technologies can fulfill the latter requirement. The digital item will be expressed in a machine-readable format, in order to limit, as far as possible, terminological ambiguities and vagueness and support accessibility and preservation. Metadata annotation for dramatic media will be carried out through the introduction of a drama ontology (major sources are [13], [15], and [17]), which encodes the major concepts and relations of the drama domain, the so-called *dramatic qualities*, which have been shared by a majority of scholars in the drama literature, and provides the terminological knowledge for the instantiating the annotation metadata for the dramatic media objects. As we will see, the digital item that preserves drama as a form of intangible cultural heritage is an expression of an abstract dramatic work in the formal language of the computational ontologies.

3.2 The Drammar ontology

In order to build a formal encoding of the dramatic elements, Drammar (see [13] and [17] for thorough descriptions) resorts to a set of theories and models that are well established in Artificial Intelligence and Computer Science . The ratio of this design strategy is twofold: on the one side, it relies on widespread, sound models, with formal properties that have been investigated in depth; on the other side, it augments the interoperability of the representation with other encodings, which can be contributed by several disciplines, such as, e.g., interactive storytelling and procedural animation.

The design of Drammar ontology relies on three representation layers (see Figure 1 for a synoptic overview). The first, the closest to the drama document to be annotated, is the observable *timeline* (middle of Figure 1), appraised through a literary text or an audiovisual medium, a succession of the incidents (or *actions*) that happen in the drama. Incidents are assembled into discrete structures, called *units*. Each succession of incidents forms a sub-timeline of the whole timeline of the drama. This level is formalized through the Situation Calculus paradigm ([19]): with sub-timelines that function as operators advancing the story world from one state to another (states aggregated in consistent state sets, ellipses in the figure), that work as preconditions and effects of some sub-timeline of incidents. The actions result from the deliberation process of the characters, named *agents* here.

The deliberation process is represented by the motivational layer (bottom of Figure 1), which centers upon the notion of the character's intention in achieving (or trying to achieve) a *goal*. The intention, or the commitment of the character, is represented by a

---

[3]https://www.di.unito.it/wikidrammar, visited on 7 July 2017.

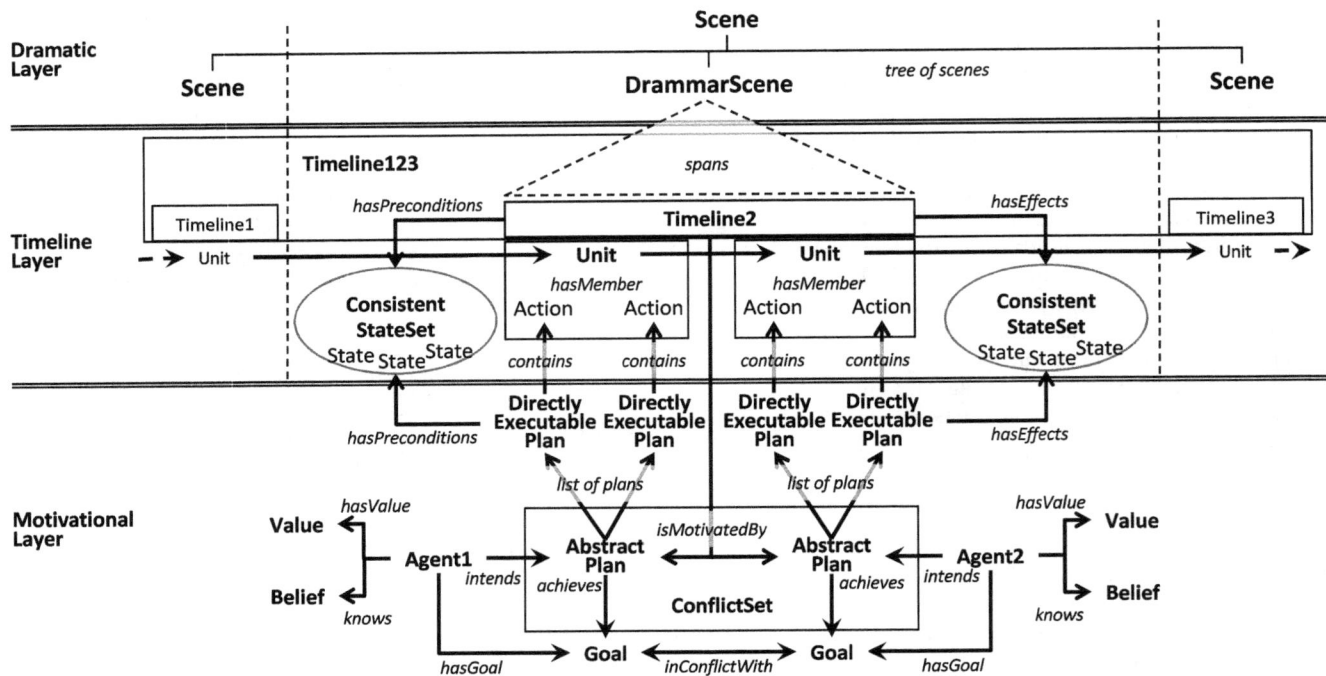

Figure 1: Layers of ontology Drammar

plan, which consists of the actions that are to be carried out in order to achieve some goal; plans are organized hierarchically, with high-level behaviors (abstract plans) formulated as lists of lower-level plans, or *subplans*, until the directly executable plans, which directly contain actions. Goals originate from the *values* of the characters that are put at stake and need to be restored, given the *beliefs* (i.e. the knowledge) of the agents. This level is formalized through the rational agent paradigm, or BDI (Belief, Desire, Intention) paradigm ([2]) (which is also applied in the computational storytelling community ([22]; [24]). This is why characters are encoded as *agents* in Drammar (bottom of Figure 1). The agent is characterized by goals, beliefs, values engaged, and plans; values can be at stake or in balance; plans can be in conflict with other plans, possibly of other agents; a conflict set aggregates all the plans, agents and goals that determine a dramatic scene (DrammarScene), through the game of alternate accomplishments. The plan is the major structure of the Motivational Layer, where all the other entities participate ([8]); plan hierarchies are trees of plans, with abstract plans that recursively dominate children subplans, until directly executable plans with actions that are actually performed by the agents in the drama; each plan hierarchy pertains to a single agent; several hierarchies (pertaining to several agents) project onto the same portion of the timeline, often with goals in conflict (actually, conflicts motivate a dramatic scene). The success/failure in achieving goals as well as in supporting own values is responsible for agents' appraisal of the drama incidents. Plans have preconditions and effects, which are consistent sets of states (where consistent means that there no two states in contradiction within the set); when some plan motivates a timeline, its preconditions and effects (the consistent state sets

mentioned above) are included in the preconditions and effect of a timeline.

The dramatic layer (top of Figure 1), which is directly inspired by the literature on drama theory, accounts for the hierachical structure of the scenes: scenes are recursively composed of daughter scenes. Scenes span timelines, that is sequences of units. Some scenes are called DrammarScenes, meaning that they are motivated by some conflict over the characters' intentions, which is the characterization of scenes according to the Drammar ontology.

The abstract ontology, expressed as a set of logical specifications of classes and properties, is expressed through a formal language to become a digital, textual artifact that can be fed to a software program (for manipulation, querying, comparison, etc.). In particular, Drammar is expressed through the ontology language, which has been designed as part of the Semantic Web project and allows conceptual models to be described in an unambiguous way, open to understanding and manipulation by both human users and software programs. The concepts and relations introduced above are encoded in the ontology Drammar, written in the Semantic Web language known as OWL (Ontology Web Language). In particular, Drammar is written in a specific sub-language, OWL2 RL (Rule Language), a syntactic and semantic restriction of OWL 2 ([13]), which provides the adequate tradeoff between expressivity and complexity with respect to the requirements of the drama domain (see ([11]) for an introduction to computational ontologies). Also, Drammar includes classes that are intended as an interface between the drama domain concepts and the linguistic and common sense types of knowledge that express the content of the drama when instantiated in media, according to the paradigm of linked data ([12]).

4 THE ANNOTATION OF DRAMA

The ontology Drammar is embedded in an annotation schema for the dramatic documents, employed with the help of specific software tools that assist the annotation process from the encoding of the metadata to their enrichment with semi-automatic tools.

4.1 Drama Annotation Workflow

The workflow of annotation in Drammar is incremental, and the consistency of the metadata can be tested at any moment through the application of reasoning techniques ([13]) and visualization tool ([18]). As the construction proceeds, more and more sophisticate structures augment the timeline of incidents extracted from the original text or video. The item can be revised subsequently, as more knowledge on the drama instance is available.

In order to clarify the description, we make reference to a running example taken from Shakespeare's *Hamlet*: the so called "nunnery" scene. In this scene, situated in the Third Act, Ophelia is sent to Hamlet by Polonius (her father) and Claudius (Hamlet's uncle, the king) to confirm the assumption that Hamlet's madness is caused by his rejected love. According to the two conspirators, Ophelia should induce him to talk about his inner feelings. At the same time, Hamlet tries to convince Ophelia that the court is corrupted and that she should go to a nunnery. In the middle of the scene, Hamlet puts Ophelia to a test to verify her honesty: guessing (correctly) that the two conspirators are hidden behind the curtain, he asks the girl to reveal where her father Polonius is. She decides to lie, by replying that he is at home. Hamlet realizes from the answer that also Ophelia is corrupted and consequently becomes very angry, realizing that there is no hope to redeem the court. The representation of the scene provided to exemplify the use of Drammar describes the excerpt in which Hamlet is testing Ophelia's honesty by asking rhetorically a question he knows the answer of, namely the current location of her father Polonius (the same room where they are, behind a curtain), and Ophelia lies by giving a false location, namely Polonius' home.

Creating Timeline and Units, Agents and Objects
The construction starts from the encoding of the total timeline of incidents (actions) as a sequence of Unit instances. Here, we identify the unit boundaries[4] and the major actions that occur in them, described through an informal sentence (e.g., "Hamlet tests Ophelia for honesty and she lies"). In this phase, we also identify the major objects and agents that participate to the incidents.

Describing Scenes and Agents
Once the sequence of units is defined, we refine the description of the agents involved by explicitly marking the conflicts that emerge from the interplay of the agents. This also leads to identifying the scenes that cluster several units together. Therefore, at this step of the workflow, the units begin to be augmented with these informal conflicts (e.g., "Hamlet wants to test Ophelia honesty") and values engaged (e.g., "Honesty at Stake" for Hamlet). Such values engaged, put at stake, underlie the formation of goals as well as the devise of plans to achieve them.

Defining the intentions

Then, we take into account the deliberative processes underlying the units and scenes. We first identify the simplest plans that motivate the incidents occurring in the units. For each agent, we build directly executable plans (e.g., the plan "Hamlet intends to ask Ophelia about Polonius' location"). This plan includes the action ("Hamlet asks Ophelia about Polonius location"), and has precondition and effect states. This plan is a subplan of the abstract plan "Hamlet intends to test Ophelia for honesty". In principle this subplan is followed by another subplan that is not deployed because Ophelia's answer is not what Hamlet was expecting (she lies about Polonius' location). Thus, the annotator can insert an underspecified plan, which is not deployed. Also, more abstract plans can be devised as annotation proceeds, intended to achieve wider spanning goals ("Hamlet intends to send Ophelia to a nunnery").

Appraising emotions with condition-action rules
Values put at stake as a result of some plan accomplishment and goals in conflict are the input to condition-action rules for the emotion appraisal ([13]). These rules compute the emotions felt by some agent given two main elements, namely the values of the same agent put at stake (or re-balanced) and the achievement of her/his own goals with respect to other agents' conflicting goals. In particular, Hamlet feels Distress about his value honesty put at stake by the achievement of Ophelia's plan that is to save Polonius' authority through lying. Hamlet also feels Reproach for Ophelia because his goals of proving Ophelia's honesty fails while Ophelia's goal to save Polonius' authority is achieved and the two goals are in conflict. Finally, the combination of Distress and Reproach, according, causes Hamlet to feel anger toward Ophelia.

4.2 The Drammar Annotated corpus

Here we illustrate the task of the annotation process and propose a pipeline for building a system that can contribute to the construction of an annotated corpus. The enterprise is called Pop-ODE (POPulating Ontology Drammar Encodes); it consists of a pipeline and a number of tools (see Figure 2).

A drama encoding annotator (on the left) works through a web-based interface to fill the tables of a data base built according to the tenets of ontology Drammar, encoded and accessible through the well-known Protégé editor [5], on behalf of the drama scholar, possibly supported by an ontology engineer. The mapper module DB2OWL, which incorporates the same tenets as the Drammar ontology, converts the data base tables into the OWL format, thus producing a Drammar instantiated ontology file (DIO file). A further software module, OWL2CHART, extracts the individuals and properties, XML Drammmar Chart file, which are then visualized by the interactive chart module ([18]). The figure does not show the emotion annotation module, separately implemented through the semantic infrastructure hosting the generated ontology (see [13] for details).

The system relies on a client server schema. The annotation is stored in a relational data base on the server; the server exposes a set of APIs, for accessing the data base tables and for validating the generated OWL file. The client is the web interface, which guides the user through the annotation of the drama, scene by scene, The web-based annotation tool allows a user to annotate drama without

---

[4]An experiment has shown the feasibility of such an approach, see ([14]), without much discrepancy over different annotators.

[5]http://protege.stanford.edu

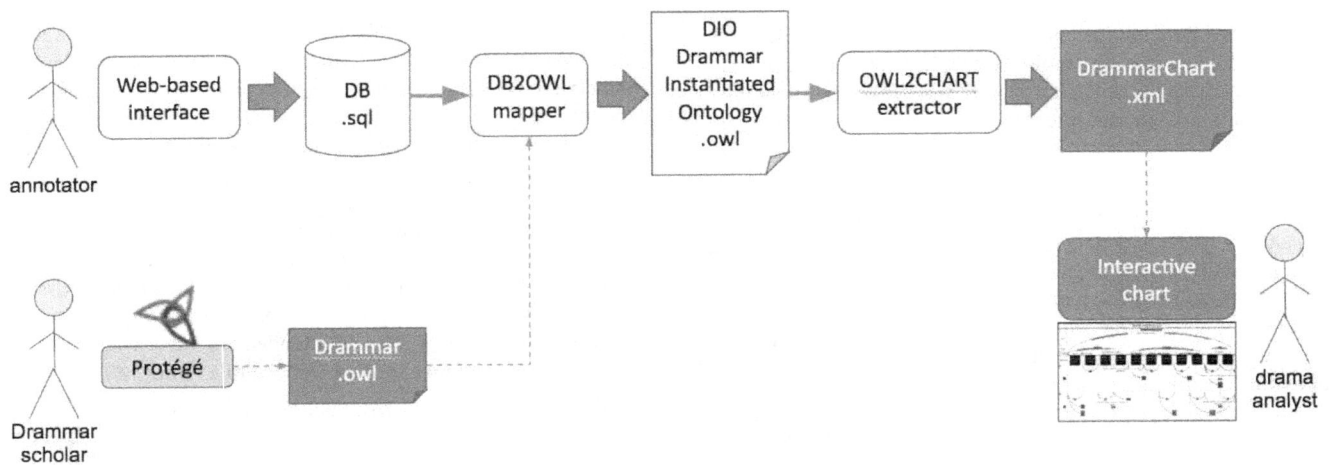

Figure 2: The Pop-ODE annotation pipeline.

knowing the details of the ontology language. The user is only required to informally know the tenets of model underlying the annotation, which are reflected in the annotation interface. Through the annotation interface, the user can create and describe a set of elements that represent the content of the drama (such as agents, plans and units) and relate them to each other (for example by binding plans to units, which equates to annotating motivations for timelines): the tags and comments inserted by the user in the annotation interface will be bound to the annotation schema automatically by the system. The tool has been designed with two main objectives in mind: the alignment of agents' intentions with respect to the incidents, and the computation of agents' emotions through the annotation of conflicts and values engaged: this choice was motivated by some earlier preliminary investigations on the visualization tool for those sections of the ontology Drammar ([16, 18]) and on the rule-based computation of emotions ([13]). In order to enable a crowdsourcing-based schema in the management of the annotation projects, the annotation tool has been developed and deployed as an online system.

The annotation tool interface implements a vertical alignment (Figure 3) between the Timeline layer and the Motivational layer, with the creation and selection of the *units* at the upper level, and the annotation of agents' *plans* – with their goals and relationships to other agents' traits – in the lower part. In yellow, the interface reports panels that pivot the two parts, respectively units (above) and plans (below). Timelines and scenes are inferred automatically by the interface. So, the user is invited (other functions are forbidden otherwise) to initially select some unit or create a new one; each unit is annotated through a formal name (identifier of the instance of the ontology class Unit) and a free textual description. By selecting the adjacent units for newly created units, the user can perceive the context of the unit along the *timeline* of incidents (these relations correspond, intuitively, to property *precedes*). The occurrence of some unit can also modify the values engaged for some agent, by putting them at stake or in balance, respectively; so, the user can

annotate on the left and the right of the current unit, respectively, the engagement of values before and after the occurrence of the unit; the annotation distinguishes between the values that are put at stake and the ones that are brought to balance.

In the lower part of the interface, the user can create the plans that motivate the actions in the unit (instance of the class Directly ExecutablePlan or AbstractPlan, respectively); each plan is described through a name, a free textual description, and possibly the description of the action (instance of the class Action) that actually implements the plan and contributes to the unit. Once a plan is selected, the user can annotate the agent that intends the plan, the goal of the plan, and the relations the plan holds with other story components. The agent that intends the plan is referenced through a formal name and a free textual description (panel of the far left of the lower part), with an annotation of pleasantness, i.e. an annotation whether the agent is perceived as pleasant or unpleasant, an annotation of whom/what the agent likes/dislikes, and finally, and most importantly, the list of values engaged for the agent. The goal of the plan (near left panel) is annotated through a formal name and a free description. The relations/attributes of the plan (panel on the right) concern its accomplishment (yes/no), the possible conflicts/supports with respect to other plans, values that are put at stake or at balance by the plan as effects of its execution or that are preconditions for its execution. Finally, this structure of the interface reflects the visualization tool that has been associated with Drammar ontology ([18]), with units and scenes on upper part of the layout, and plans and agents reported as tracks on the lower part of the layout.

The interface is implemented in Ajax, using the JQuery library, so that the annotation interface is never re-loaded during the interaction and all elements can be manipulated asynchronously by the user. An advantage of this approach is the annotation is not pipelined through a sequence of pages; rather, the user can follow the logical order she/he prefers when annotating a unit, provided

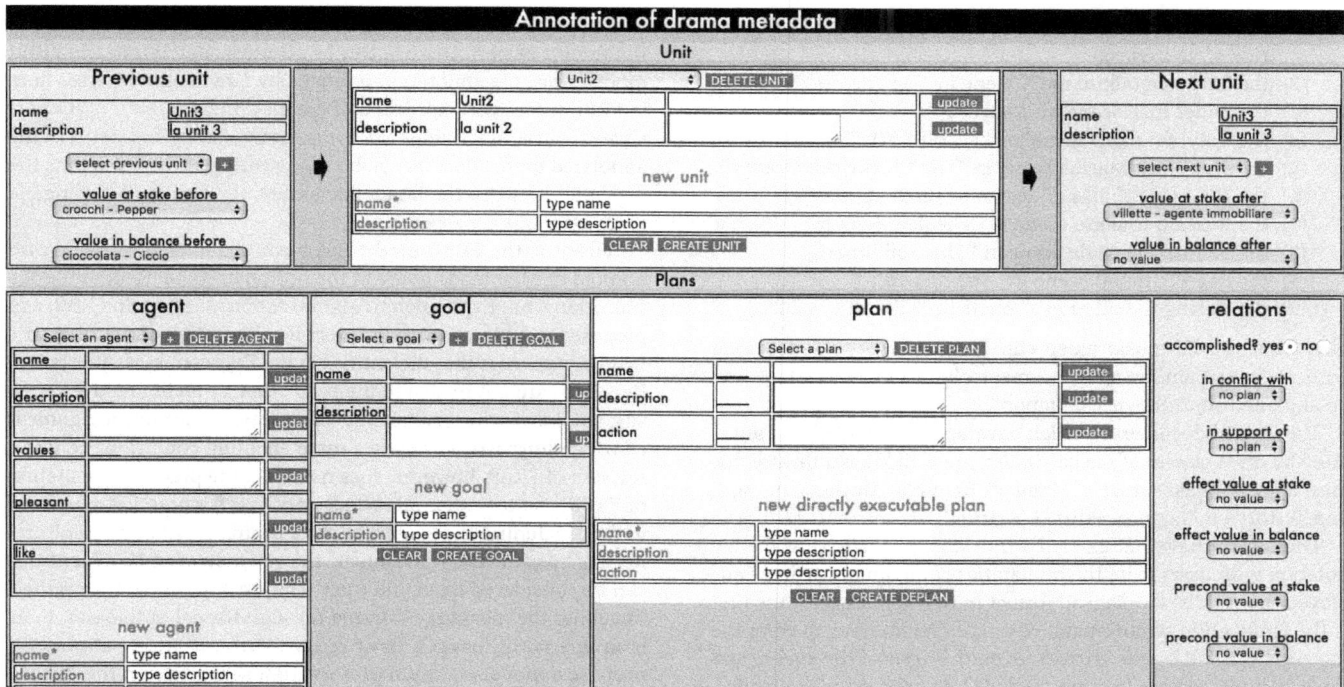

Figure 3: The annotation interface.

that the two constraints that regulate the interaction are met (first, selecting a unit, then, selecting a plan).

Any time the user creates, describes or deletes an element of the schema described above, the interface executes a call of the corresponding API, which manipulates the database via SQL queries by inserting, updating or deleting the data stored in the data base, and retrieving the updated data from it after each operation. For example, when the user creates a unit, a new row is added to the corresponding table; if the user adds a plan to it, a row is added also to the table representing the plan, with a field referencing the corresponding unit.

The data base is implemented as a mySql database. The web services are written in PHP; following a well established practice, the services return data in Json format so as to guarantee the independence of the server side implementation from the technologies employed client side. The system design allows the APIs to be called by different client side applications to update or retrieve the data. The API that support the annotation tool may be exploited, for example, by a client side application that visualizes the annotation. Or, the API it may produce the data for the translation into other formats than the relational model, such as the OWL format. For example, the Json data in Figure 4 are sent by *get_VAS_unit.php*, which retrieves from the database the values put at stake (VAS_before) and balanced (VAB_before) before and after (VAS_after and VAB_after) a given unit.

The corpus of annotated drama documents consists in two sets of drama documents, video and textual documents, respectively. The video documents are ten cult dramatic scenes from Hollywoodian movies (as selected in a course of media studies), namely

```
{
"VAS_before":
  [
    {
      "id_state":"8363",
      "id_agent":"118",
      "id_value":"65",
      "name_value":"loyalty"
    }
  ],
"VAB_before":
  [
    {
      "id_state":"8363",
      "id_agent":"118",
      "id_value":"64",
      "name_value":"honesty"
    }
  ],
"VAS_after":
  [
  ],
"VAB_after":
  [
  ]
}
```

Figure 4: Example of data extracted from the annotation database (characters' values in the preconditions and effects of a timeline).

(1) the helicopter attack scene in "Apocalypse now" (with the ride of valkyries),

(2) the "Are you talkin' me?" scene in "Taxi driver",

(3) the bullet time scene in "Matrix",

(4) the Trevi fountain scene in "La Dolce Vita",

(5) the Flat Block Marina scene in "The Clockwork Orange",

(6) the "I've seen thinks ..." scene in "Blade Runner",

(7) the Russian roulette scene in "The deer hunter",

(8) the Sollozzo omicide scene in "The Godfather",

(9) the dog VS. rabbit scene in "The Snatch",

(10) the "losing the other eye" scene in "Kill Bill - Vol. 2"

plus some drama music video clip (Taylor Swift's "You belong with me"), a dramatic advertisement clip ("Zippo" lighter), and an animated short movie ("Oktapodi").

The textual documents, which have been segmented and annotated by three classes of media studies, are well known theatre dramas, namely Shakespeare's "Hamlet", Brecht's "Mother Courage", and Testori's Italian neorealist "L'Arialda".

Though we have not carried a thorough evaluation of the annotation with users from the humanities community, we have employed the yielded ontological format in two applications: the first is the application of automatic reasoning techniques to compute the emotions felt by the characters on the basis of the events and the intentions manually annotated [13]; the second is the realization of printed charts of the characters' intentions aligned with the timeline of incidents (described in [18]), currently employed in the didactics of drama writing at the University of Torino. We are going to evaluate the appropriateness of Drammar on the adequacy of description from the point of view of research on the humanities.

5 AN FRBR VIEW OF DRAMA ANNOTATION

Since its appearance, the model known as Functional Requirements for Bibliographical Entities, or FRBR [23], has attracted the attentions of theorists in the cultural heritage domain, given its capability of dealing with the distinction between the abstract notion of work and its derived entities in a way that lends itself to generalizations to other domains than the bibliographic one. Designed with the goal of capturing "the underlying semantics of bibliographic information", FRBR acknowledges four main entities: Work, i.e., abstract ideation, Expression, i.e., the encoding of the Work in a specific language (such as text or music), Manifestation, i.e., the embodiment of the Expression in a concrete representation, and Item, a single instance of the Manifestation.

FRBR has seen several attempts at applying it to specific domains of cultural heritage, ranging from music [28] and performance [5], to intangible cultural heritage [35]. In particular, [5] resorts to FRBR to account for the problem of variation in performance, an acknowledged area of ICH: "the problem of variation is the problem of how, if a Work is defined by all the examples of it, we can determine that two examples that are not identical are nonetheless part of the same Work. This problem is especially pronounced in live performance, which, by its very nature, has the potential for each of its examples to be unique" [5] [10]. According to Doty, an ontology of drama performance should include the notion of production in order to guarantee the recognizability of a performance with respect the production it belongs to. Although Doty's claim on production

is well motivated, here we do not take any position about how the notion of performance can be accommodated into the FRBR model, since the annotation provided by Drammar addresses only, in FRBR terms, the Expression of the play. In our view, FRBR offers a valid conceptual framework for accommodating the status of the annotated drama documents, by representing at the same time the dialectics between the intangible nature of drama and its tangible manifestations across media.

Recently, the FRBR model has been challenged by [27], who pointed out the inadequacy of the notion of 'type' to describe the transition from Expression to Manifestation and Item in FRBR, and proposed to replace it with the more flexible notion of role. Renear's main argument is that the entities in the Expression-Manifestation-Item triad are not related to the each other by an immutable necessity, but only as the result of a social process of meaning assignment of which linguistic rules are a mere enabling condition. Renear's revision of FRBR, however, does not affect the practical orientation of FRBR, as the author admittedly notices: for practical purposes, in fact, including the preservation of drama as intangible cultural heritage assumed by Drammar, the properties of FRBR entities can be considered fixed and their relationships taken for granted. Encoding the meaning of drama through formal ontologies, then, is in line with Renear's most recent work on preservation: [29] propose a model of digital preservation that relies on the distinction between propositional content and symbol structure, and on the mapping between the two. The use of ontologies to represent drama documents is in line with this model, since they provide a powerful and formalized language for transmitting unambiguously a given propositional content across different encoding formats and supports.

The description of the drama abstraction provided by Drammar is itself conceptually situated at the level of Expression in FRBR, i.e. an abstract linguistic entity encoded in a Semantic Web language, the Ontology Web Language (OWL), that can be subsequently turned into a specific format among those encompassed by the specifications the version of OWL employed for Drammar (OWL2, see previous section) and finally transferred into a digital resource. So, a play and a specific production of the play can both be separately encoded in Drammar, but the representation provided by Drammar does not provide any means to describe the relation between the two, and relies on external models (such as FRBR and its derivatives, including Doty's) to account for this relationship.

In order to illustrate our claim, we resort to Fig. 5, which represents the relations of a drama, intended as intangible, abstract entity, and its realizations into tangible media, represented here by performing media. The abstract work called Hamlet (namely, Shakespeare's Hamlet, at the top of the figure) is actualized through the encoding into different expressions, each characterized by a different language: jambic English for Shakespeare's original expression of his Hamlet, filmic language for the derivative expressions devised by filmmakers (such as Lawrence Olivier and Kenneth Branagh) who adapted Shakespeare's work in the form of a movie. Each expression can be further encoded in a Drammar instantiated object (or DIO, see bottom of the figure): the obtained expressions, encoded in the ontology format, can be compared with each other, and studied in relation with the Drammar encoding of the original

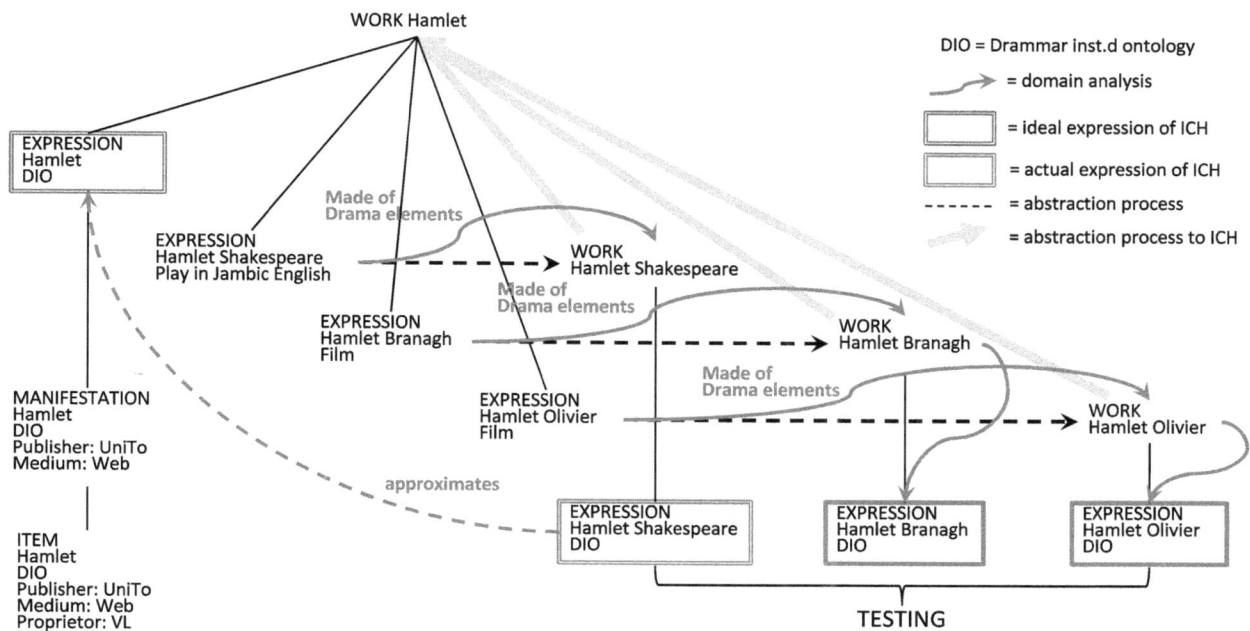

Figure 5: The expressions of drama and their annotation in FRBR, adapted from the slides presented by Barbara B. Tillett and Judith A. Kuhagen (Policy and Standards Division, Library of Congress) at Library of Congress RDA Workshop for Georgia Cataloging Summit, on 9-10 August 2011.

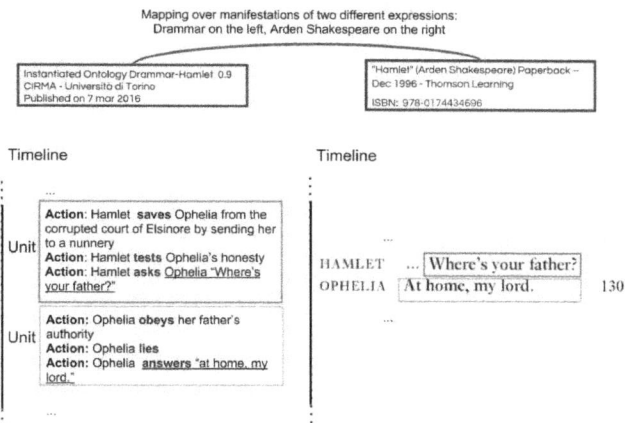

Figure 6: Detail of a Drammar Instatiated Object (DIO)

work, the expression of Intangible Cultural Heritage item named Hamlet. Each DIO concretely becomes a manifestation of its corresponding expression when encoded in a digital format that can be reproduced in several items. In particular, Figure 6 shows the parallel between the specific Drammar Instantiated Object obtained by encoding Shakespeare's expression in jambic English into the ontology language illustrated in Section 3.2 (which has been produced by using the annotation tool described in Section 4). The use of the ontology allows mediating between the ideation of the work,

which can be encoded in Drammar – being the latter independent from a specific encoding and manifestation –, and its tangible manifestations across media, in a way that can be stored, referred to, and manipulated with semantic oriented tools online and offline.

6 CONCLUSION

In this paper, we have described how the use of the Drammar ontology in drama annotation reconciles the dialectics between drama as an abstract entity, characterized by the features of intangible cultural heritage, and its multiple, diverse manifestations in media. The formal nature of the computational ontology provides both an interlinked representation, which refers to external linguistic and commonsense terminological bases for its vocabulary, and a neat status for the annotated document, namely the one of an expression for the abstract work in the OWL language. The key feature of our approach for reconciling the twofold nature of drama is given by its capability of encoding the primary elements of the drama as an intangible work in FRBR terms (namely, agent, action, conflict, unit, etc.) and delivering a tangible expression in the form of an instantiated ontology. The latter instantiated ontology can be compared with the expressions in different languages, actualized into different manifestations in old and new media.

The Drammar-based approach described here addresses the issue of interoperability of the annotation, given the formal reference to a computational ontology vocabulary and the reference to external resources for terminology. Also, it addresses the status of the annotated drama documents with respect to other cultural forms, taking the FRBR model as a reference. Being theory-neutral and language independent, the approach can be employed to annotate video and textual documents, respectively, differently from text-oriented, linguistics-based annotation schema that specifically address written drama forms.

In order to alleviate the production of the ontology annotations of dramatic media, we have also described the annotation workflow for drama documents and a web-based annotation tool. The tool implements a visual interface for the representation of the intentional motivations of the characters (agents) to act within the drama. The tool has proven to be very effective in inferring a number of classes and relations of the ontology that are syntactically important for the coherence of the representation but are cumbersome and error-prone for the task of a manual (or semi-manual) annotator. So, for example, when an annotator states that some scene is spanning from this to to that unit, the tool automatically create a timeline. We are going to make a vast and effective test of the annotation tool over several student classes, together with questionnaires and etnographic observations, to evaluate the functioning of the tool and to create a vast corpus for studies in the digital humanities.

7 ACKNOWLEDGEMENTS

The authors wish to thank the Altervista website for hosting the server of the annotation tool and several student annotation projects.

REFERENCES

[1] Collin F. Baker, Charles J. Fillmore, and John B. Lowe. 1998. The Berkeley FrameNet Project. In *Proceedings of the 36th Annual Meeting of the Association for Computational Linguistics and 17th International Conference on Computational Linguistics*, Vol. 1. Association for Computational Linguistics, 86–90.

[2] Michael E. Bratman. 1987. *Intention, Plans, and Practical Reason*. Harvard University Press, Cambridge (MA).

[3] Christie Carson. 1997. Drama and theatre studies in the multimedia age: 'Reviewing the situation'. *Literary and Linguistic Computing* 12, 4 (1997), 269–275. DOI: https://doi.org/10.1093/llc/12.4.269 arXiv:http://llc.oxfordjournals.org/content/12/4/269.full.pdf+html

[4] James H. Coombs, Allen H. Renear, and Steven J. DeRose. 1987. Markup Systems and the Future of Scholarly Text Processing. *Communication of the ACM* 30, 11 (1987).

[5] Colin Doty. 2013. The Difficulty of An Ontology of Live Performance. *InterActions: UCLA Journal of Education and Information Studies* 9, 1 (2013). http://www.escholarship.org/uc/item/3jf4g75m

[6] David K. Elson. 2012. DramaBank: Annotating Agency in Narrative Discourse. In *Proceedings of the Eighth International Conference on Language Resources and Evaluation (LREC 2012)*. Istanbul, Turkey.

[7] Martin Esslin. 1988. *The Field of Drama*. Methuen, London.

[8] Richard E. Fikes and Nils J. Nilsson. 1971. Strips: A new approach to the application of theorem proving to problem solving. *Artificial Intelligence* 2, 3–4 (1971), 189 – 208. DOI: https://doi.org/10.1016/0004-3702(71)90010-5

[9] Mark Alan Finlayson. 2011. The Story Workbench: An Extensible Semi-Automatic Text Annotation Tool. In *AAAI Publications, Workshops at the Seventh Artificial Intelligence and Interactive Digital Entertainment Conference*.

[10] Erika Fischer-Lichte. 2008. *The Transformative Power of Performance: A New Aesthetics*. Taylor & Francis. https://books.google.co.uk/books?id=Ocwq3jxiL-8C

[11] Nicola Guarino, Daniel Oberle, and Steffen Staab. 2009. What is an ontology? In *Handbook on Ontologies* (2nd edition ed.). Springer.

[12] T. Heath and C. Bizer. 2011. Linked data: Evolving the web into a global data space. *Synthesis Lectures on the Semantic Web: Theory and Technology* (2011), 1–136.

[13] Vincenzo Lombardo, Cristina Battaglino, Antonio Pizzo, Rossana Damiano, and Antonio Lieto. 2015. Coupling conceptual modeling and rules for the annotation of dramatic media. *Semantic Web Journal* 6, 5 (2015), 503–534.

[14] Vincenzo Lombardo and Rossana Damiano. 2012. Commonsense knowledge for the collection of ground truth data on semantic descriptors. In *Proceedings of the 2012 IEEE International Symposium on Multimedia (ISM 2012)*. IEEE Computer Society, 78–83.

[15] Vincenzo Lombardo and Antonio Pizzo. 2014. Multimedia tool suite for the visualization of drama heritage metadata. *Multimedia Tools and Applications* 75, 7 (2014), 3901–3932.

[16] Vincenzo Lombardo and Antonio Pizzo. 2015. The visualization of drama hierarchies. In *Proceedings of 10th International Joint Conference on Computer Vision, Imaging and Computer Graphics Theory and Applications (VISIGRAPP 2015)*. 8.

[17] Vincenzo Lombardo, Antonio Pizzo, and Rossana Damiano. 2016. Safeguarding and Accessing Drama As Intangible Cultural Heritage. *ACM Journal on Computing and Cultural Heritage* 9, 1 (2016), 1–26.

[18] Vincenzo Lombardo, Antonio Pizzo, Rossana Damiano, Carmi Terzulli, and Giacomo Albert. 2016. Interactive chart of story characters' intentions. In *Interactive Storytelling, 9th International Conference on Interactive Digital Storytelling, ICIDS 2016, Los Angeles, CA, USA, November 15–18, 2016, Proceedings*, Vol. 10045. Springer International Publishing, Cham – CHE, 415–418. DOI: https://doi.org/10.1007/978-3-319-48279-8_39

[19] John C. McCarthy. 1986. Mental Situation Calculus. In *Proceedings of the 1986 Conference on Theoretical Aspects of Reasoning About Knowledge (TARK '86)*. Morgan Kaufmann Publishers Inc., San Francisco, CA, USA, 307–307. http://dl.acm.org/citation.cfm?id=1029786.1029815

[20] Marvin Minsky. 1975. Minsky's Frame System Theory. In *Proceedings of the 1975 Workshop on Theoretical Issues in Natural Language Processing*. Association for Computational Linguistics, 104–116.

[21] P. Mulholland and T. Collins. 2002. Using digital narratives to support the collaborative learning and exploration of cultural heritage. In *Proceedings of the 13th International Workshop on Database and Expert Systems Applications*.

[22] E. Norling and L. Sonenberg. 2004. Creating Interactive Characters with BDI Agents. In *Proceedings of the Australian Workshop on Interactive Entertainment IE2004*.

[23] O' Neill, E. T. 2002. FRBR: Functional Requirements for Bibliographic Records; Application of the Entity-Relationship Model to Humphry Clinker. *Library Resources and Technical Services* 46 (2002), 150–158.

[24] F. Peinado, M. Cavazza, and D. Pizzi. 2008. Revisiting Character-based Affective Storytelling under a Narrative BDI Framework. In *Proc. of ICIDIS08*. Erfurt, Germany.

[25] Federico Peinado, Pablo Gervás, and Belén Díaz-Agudo. 2004. A description logic ontology for fairy tale generation. In *LREC Workshop on Language Resources for Linguistic Creativity*, Vol. 4. 56–61.

[26] Elahe Rahimtoroghi, Thomas Corcoran, Reid Swanson, Marilyn A. Walker, Kenji Sagae, and Andrew Gordon. 2014. Minimal Narrative Annotation Schemes and Their Applications. In *AAAI Publications, Seventh Intelligent Narrative Technologies Workshop*.

[27] Allen H Renear and David Dubin. 2007. Three of the four FRBR Group 1 entity types are roles, not types. *Proceedings of the American Society for Information Science and Technology* 44, 1 (2007), 1–19.

[28] Jenn Riley. 2008. Application of the Functional Requirements for Bibliographic Records (FRBR) to Music. *ISMIR* (2008). http://books.google.com/books?hl=en&lr=&id=OHp3sRnZD-oC&oi=fnd&pg=PA439&dq=APPLICATION+OF+THE+FUNCTIONAL+REQUIREMENTS+FOR+BIBLIOGRAPHIC+RECORDS+(+FRBR+)+TO+MUSIC&ots=oELMnIgye8&sig=8S2UtDXOI18yKcUDpFh6baLpPfs

[29] Simone Sacchi, Karen Wickett, Allen Renear, and David Dubin. 2011. A framework for applying the concept of significant properties to datasets. *Proceedings of the American Society for Information Science and Technology* 48, 1 (2011), 1–10.

[30] Roger C. Schank and Robert P. Abelson. 1975. Scripts, Plans, and Knowledge. In *Proceedings of the 4th International Joint Conference on Artificial Intelligence*, Vol. 1. Morgan Kaufmann Publishers Inc., 151–157.

[31] Christof Schöch. 2013. Big? Smart? Clean? Messy? Data in the Humanities. *Journal of Digital Humanities* 2, 3 (2013).

[32] Rieks Smeets. 2004. Intangible Cultural Heritage and Its Link to Tangible Cultural and Natural Heritage. In *Okinawa International Forum 2004 UTAKI in Okinawa and Sacred Spaces in Asia: Community Development and Cultural Heritage*, Masako Yamamoto and Mari Fujimoto (Eds.). The Japan Foundation, 137–150.

[33] Nicolas Szilas. 2016. Modeling and Representing Dramatic Situations as Paradoxical Structures. *Digital Scholarship in the Humanities* fqv071 (2016).

[34] Annika Wolff, Paul Mulholland, and Trevor Collins. 2012. Storyspace: A Story-driven Approach for Creating Museum Narratives. In *Proceedings of the 23rd ACM Conference on Hypertext and Social Media*. 89–98.

[35] Nicolas Yann. 2005. Folklore Requirements for Bibliographic Records: Oral Traditions and FRBR. In *Functional requirements for bibliographic records (FRBR) : hype or cure-all?*, Patrick. Le Boeuf (Ed.). Vol. 39. Haworth Information Press, Binghamton, NY, 179–195. https://www.researchgate.net/publication/228728033_Folklore_Requirements_for_Bibliographic_RecordsOral_Traditions_and_FRBR

[36] Gian Piero Zarri. 1997. NKRL, a knowledge representation tool for encoding the 'meaning' of complex narrative texts. *Natural Language Engineering* 3, 2 (1997).

Assessing Binarization Techniques for Document Images

Rafael Dueire Lins
UFPE/UFRPE, Recife, PE
Brazil
rdl.ufpe@gmail.com

Marcos Martins de Almeida
UFPE, Recife, PE
Brazil
mm.ufpe@gmail.com

Rodrigo Barros Bernardino
UFPE, Recife, PE
Brazil
rbbernardino@gmail.com

Darlisson Jesus
UFPE, Recife, PE
Brazil
dmj.ufpe@gmail.com

José Mário Oliveira
IFPE/UFPE, Recife, PE
Brazil
josealexandre@recife.ifpe.edu.br

ABSTRACT

Image binarization is a technique widely used for documents as monochromatic documents claim for far less space for storage and computer bandwidth for network transmission than their color or even grayscale equivalent. Paper color, texture, aging, translucidity, kind and color of ink used in handwritting, printing process, digitalization process, etc., are some of the factors that affect binarization. No algorithm is good enough to be a winner in the binarization of all kinds of documents. This paper presents a methodology to assess the performance of binarization algorithms for a wide variety of text documents, allowing a judicious quantitative choice of the best algorithms and their parameters.

CCS CONCEPTS

• **Applied computing** → **Computers in other domains** → **Publishing**

KEYWORDS

Documents; binarization; back-to-front interference; bleeding; show through; image filtering; big-data.

ACM Reference format:
R.D.Lins, M.M. de Almeida, R.B. Bernardino, D. Jesus, J.M. Oliveira. 2017. Assessing Binarization Techniques for Document Images. In *Proceedings of ACM Symposium on Document Engineering, Valetta, Malta, September 2017, (DocEng' 17),* 10 pages.
DOI: 10.1145/3103010.3103021

1 INTRODUCTION

Document image binarization is an important step in the document image analysis and recognition pipeline. Monochromatic documents claim for far less storage space and computer bandwidth for network transmission than color or grayscale documents. It is imperative to have a benchmarking dataset along with an objective evaluation methodology to capture the efficiency of current document image binarization algorithms.

The international competitions on binarization algorithms are an evidence of the relevance of this area. The most traditional of such competitions is possibly DIBCO - Document Image Binarization Competition, which was first organized at the ICDAR-International Conference on Document Analysis and Recognition in 2009 and has been repeated yearly ever since. The methodology used by DIBCO is to offer a small set of "real-world" images and their "ground-truth" binary equivalent that were "hand-generated" or "hand-retouched". Figure 1 presents the complete test set of the ten images used at DIBCO 2016, which may be obtained at http://vc.ee.duth.gr/h-dibco2016/benchmark/. As one may observe in Figure 1, the DIBCO test set is formed only by handwritten documents both in grayscale and color. Some documents present stains (1, 3, 4, 10) and aging marks (4, 9, 10). DIBCO provides an evaluation tool that yields as output the F-Measure, pseudo F-Measure, PSNR, DRD, Recall, Precision, pseudo-Recall and pseudo-Precision. Some of those measures are not usual and are explained in reference [1]. DIBCO 2017 intends to include images of typed or printed documents in its dataset, which has not been released so far (https://vc.ee.duth.gr/dibco2017/ last visited on 04th July, 2017).

As one may observe, all document images in DIBCO 2016 test set, but the first one, have the back-to-front interference, that is, whenever a document is typed or written on both sides of a sheet of paper and the opacity of the paper is such as to allow the back printing or writing to be visualized on the front side. Such image overlap phenomenon was first addressed in the literature by Lins in 1994 [2], who called it back-to-front interference. Much later, other researchers called it bleeding or

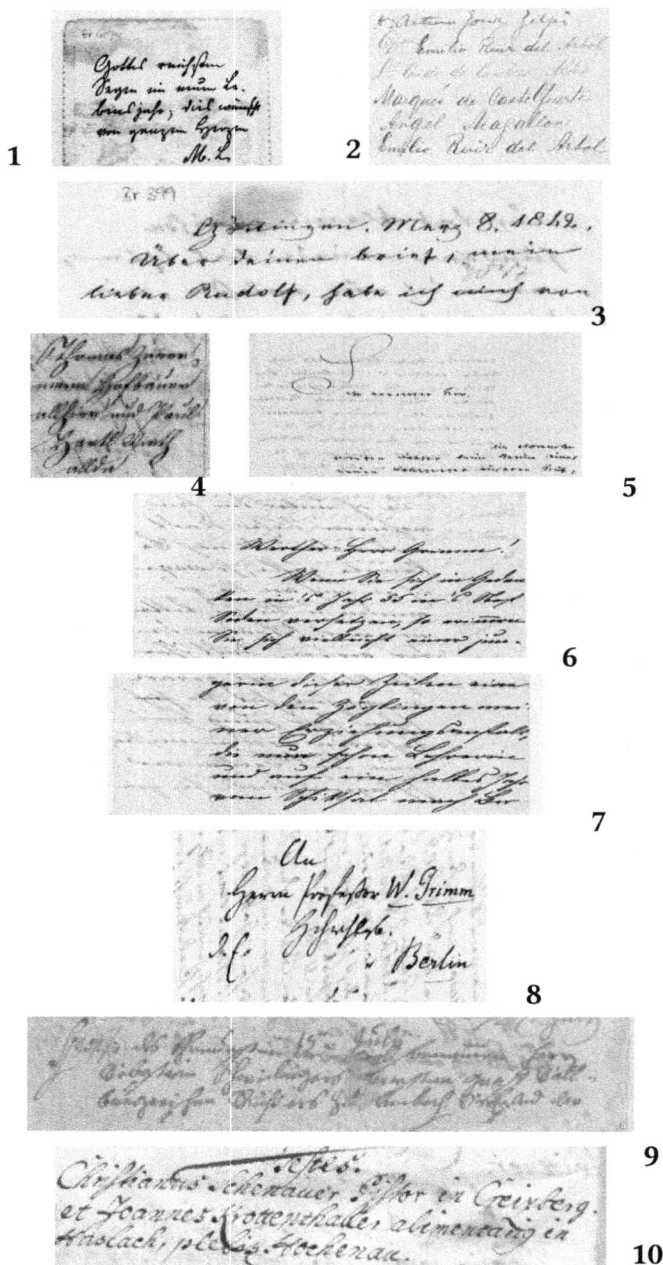

Figure 1: DIBCO 2016 Test images

show-through [3]. The human brain is able to filter out that sort of noise keeping document readability. This is not the case with automatic tools such as OCRs. The direct application of some binarization algorithms such as the one in Jasc Paint Shop Pro TM version 8 (Palette component: Gray values, Reduction component: nearest color, Palette weight: non-weighted), as many other commercial tools, yield a completely unreadable document, as the interfering ink of the backside of the paper overlaps with the binary one in the foreground. Several algorithms were developed specifically to binarize documents

with back-to-front interference [7][10][11][13], but depending on the strength of the interference present, which accounts on the opacity of the paper, its permeability, the kind and degree of fluidity of the ink used, the degree of difficulty for obtaining a good segmentation capable of filtering-out such a noise increases enormously, as new set of hues of paper and printing colors appear.

Document image binarization is extremely challenging and there is no chance of a specific algorithm to be an all case winner as many parameters may interfere in the quality of the resulting image. Besides that, a small set of test images will never be able to provide a real quality assessment of binarization algorithms. It is important to be able to have a very large test set of synthetic images representative of the universe of text documents and to know for each of them which algorithms and with which parameters, minimum space and processing time one is able to get the best binarization result. Artificial intelligence and big-data strategies now provide the resources to given a "real-world" document image to be able to decide which kind of document it better matches in such a large database. Known the best-match between the "real-world" document and the synthetic one, the set of suitable binarization algorithms and their parameters becomes known.

This paper explains the methodology used in the generation of such a large controlled database for synthetic images. A quantitative measure of quality is introduced. Some evidence of the effectiveness of the method proposed is also provided.

2 GENERATING SYNTHETIC IMAGES

Historical documents with back-to-front interference are certainly the most difficult kind of document to binarize, as paper aging introduce non-uniform textures whose color distribution may overlap with the distribution of the colors from the writing in the back of the paper. Figure 2 presents the block diagram for the generation of synthetic images.

Two images of documents of different nature (typed, handwritten with different pens, printed, etc.) are taken: F – front and V – verso (back). The verso image is offset by 10, 20 and 30 pixels to make the back image not to coincide with the front one. Then, the offset verso image is "blurred" by passing though Gaussian filters that simulate the low-pass effect of the translucidity of the verso as seen in the front part of the paper. The "blurred" verso image is now faded with a coefficient α varying between 0 and 1 in steps of 0.1. The two images are overlapped by performing a "darker" operation [20] pixel-by-pixel in the images. Paper texture is added to the image to simulate the effect of document aging. The steps in the generation of the synthetic images are explained next. It is important to remark that the two major concerns here: the first one is to have ground-truth images to be able to assess the performance of the several different binarization algorithms, the second one is to be able to have a very large set of synthetic images that will be used to train a classifier that will be able to automatically match a "real-world" image with the synthetic one.

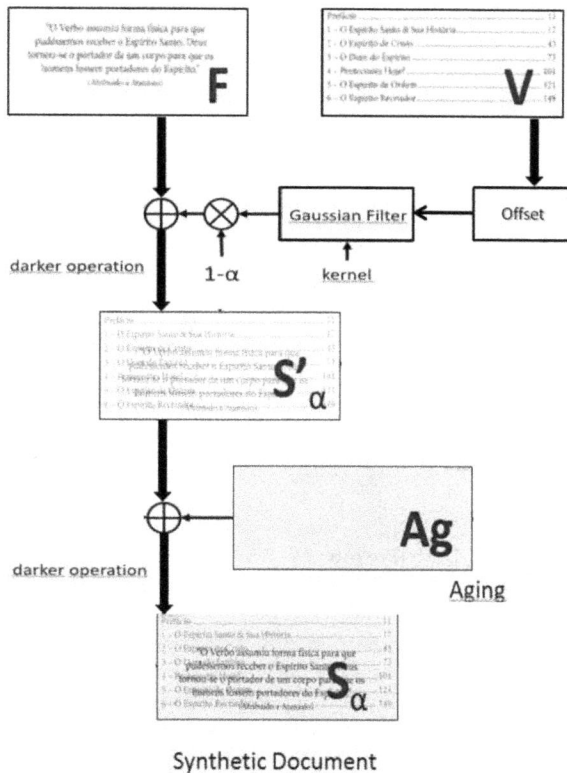

Figure 2: Block diagram of the scheme for the generation of synthetic images

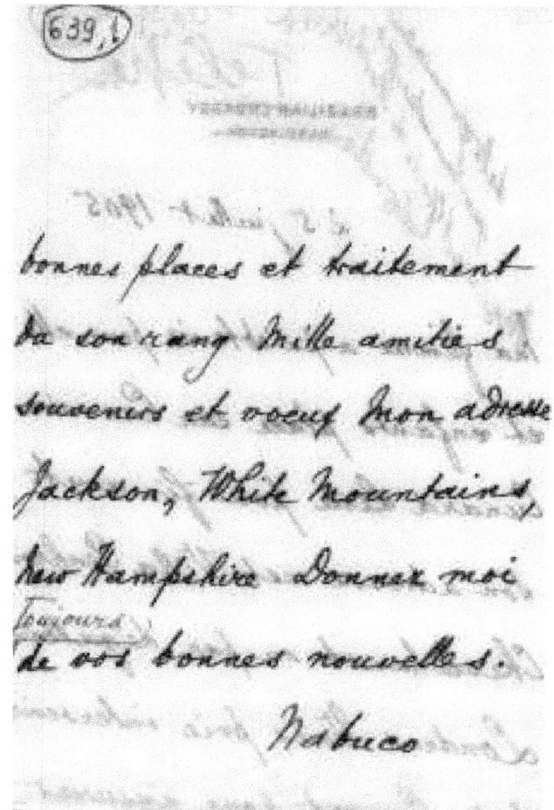

Figure 3 – Letter from Joaquim Nabuco

2.1 The Ground-truth images

The first step of the generation of synthetic images was to produce a set of images that covers all the universe of text documents: typed in mechanical typewriters, printed in inkjet, laser, offset in most usual colors (black, blue, red), handwritten with different kinds of pen (fountain, ballpen, felt pen) from different manufacturers, using black and blue ink. Such documents were typed/printed/written in good quality A4 white papers. Such images were scanned using a flatbed scanner set to a resolution of 300 dpi in true-color (24 bits RGB) yielding raster images standardized in 2,480 × 3,508 pixels. The images obtained were binarized using the standard binarization algorithm in Jasc Paint Shop Pro version 8 and are used as ground truth images and also in the generation of the synthetic images. Salt and pepper noise is removed. Such images correspond to 43 handwritten and 88 printed documents.

The set of ground truth documents of the whole DIBCO series, 61 handwritten and 25 typewritten documents, were also used here. Besides those, 14 documents electronically generated pdf documents are also used as ground-truth. Thus, currently, 231 document images compose the set of ground-truth images in total.

2.2 The Back-to-front blur

As already mentioned, documents with the back-to-front interference are much harder to binarize. Depending on the thickness of the paper, its texture, permeability, age, storage conditions (temperature, humidity, direct exposure to sun light, etc.), kind of ink, printing process or pen in case of handwritten documents, etc., the back ink is seen more or less blurred in the front side of the paper. Such effect has been modeled now as being performed by a Gaussian filter.

Two "light" Gaussian filters 3x3 and 5x5 pixel-kernels were used at the current stage of the generation of the database of synthetic images, presenting "similar" effect as the one in real documents under visual inspection. Current work is being developed to better model this effect in the different kinds of documents. For that, several samples of small windows are being used collecting parts from the foreground and back-to-front interference. The foreground window will be blurred using Gaussian filters having their parameters modified to match the one of the interference. Performing such approximation in several different kinds of documents one will be able to obtain the parameters of the different low-pass filters that better model the bleeding effect, or the back-to-front blur.

2.3 Image Fading

The origin of this project dates back to the early 1990's when the first author of this paper [4] undertook the mission of digitalizing the bequest of historic documents of Joaquim Nabuco, a Brazilian statesman, writer and diplomat, leader in the freedom of black slaves in Brazil. His active correspondence is of paramount importance for understanding the history of the Americas in the late 19th century. That bequest of about 6,500 documents encompassed over 18,000 pages. Those documents were risking of degradation due to problems in the extreme acidity of the paper. A careful analysis of the preservation staff of the Joaquim Nabuco Foundation, the social science research institute in Recife, Brazil, that keeps most of Nabuco's documents, selected about 300 documents as representative of the universe of documents. At that time, for storage restrictions and transmission of documents via FAX-simile devices, binarization was mandatory. That was exactly the first time that the back-to-front interference was reported in the technical literature [2], because about 200 of those documents were written on both sides of translucent paper, with a great variability of strength. Figure 3 presents an example of one of those letters from Nabuco bequest.

The "strength" of the back-to-front interference is modeled by the fading coefficient α. One hundred different levels of fading coefficients were chosen, thus $0<\alpha<1$ in steps of 0.01.

2.4 Adding paper texture

The texture of the paper has a strong influence the performance of binarization algorithms. Thus, it is of paramount importance to get a set of paper textures that are representative of the universe of documents intended to be modeled, from late 19th century to today, which will be used in the assessment of binarization algorithms. To do so 3,351 document images were used, of which 1,048 were from Nabuco bequest and the other 2,303 were obtained from five years of the LiveMemory Project, which generated a digital library of all the proceedings the SBrT - Brazilian Telecommunications Symposium. The images were automatically scanned looking for a window of 20x50 pixels such as the purple one shown in Figure 4.

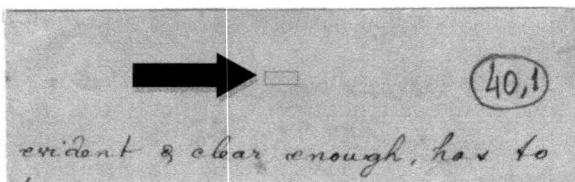

Figure 4 – Sample of the texture of paper background.

The automatic window selection was human checked to guarantee that the area has no ink or other sort of noises. For each texture sample a vector of features was built taking into account each RGB-channel of the sample, the image average filtered (R+G+B)/3, and its grayscale equivalent. For each of those 5 images the following 7 statistic measures were taken and placed in a vector: mean, standard deviation, mode, minimum value, maximum value, median, and kurtosis.

The 3,351 vectors were statistically analyzed using the hierarchical clustering method implemented in the scikit-learn library [22]. It uses a bottom up approach, where each observation starts in its own cluster, and clusters are successively merged together, providing 84 cluster distributions of paper texture as shown in Figure 5. The texture in the centroid of each of such clusters was taken as being representative of the whole cluster. The visual inspection made in the 84 clusters showed acceptable texture variation within each cluster.

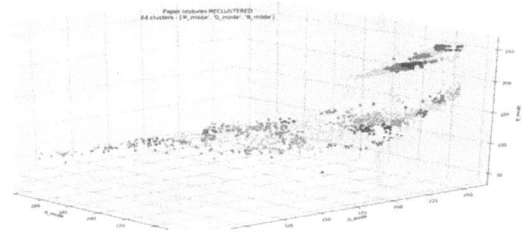

Figure 5 – Distribution of 3,351 paper textures in 84 representative clusters.

Besides those 84 centroid cluster-representative textures, 16 "isolated" textures that were left-out of the clusters were added to the texture set, totaling 100 different textures. Each of those textures is used for generating a "blank" sheet of paper to be used to colorize the synthetic image providing the "aging" effect in the scheme presented in Figure 2. For that, a RGB-image with 2,480 × 3,508 pixels (equivalent to an A4 blank sheet of paper with 300 dpi resolution) is generated. A similar technique is used to generate a 300 dpi texture for the smaller DIBCO ground-truth images. Two different texture generation strategies were adopted. In the first one, the color of each pixel is randomly chosen from the 10,000 pixels in another 100x100 pixels sample of the texture at the center of the texture cluster, providing a 300 dpi image with the same distribution as the original sample. The second technique employs image quilting [17]. Figure 6 presents an example of a texture generated using both techniques, in which the latter more closely resemble the texture of the sample document.

Each image is than added with a "darker" operation [20] generating the set of Sα synthetic images, which will be used to assess the binarization algorithms. Reference [5] proposes a parametric scheme for image compression and generation in which the paper texture is generated through a Gaussian distribution centered on the mean value of the color of the pixels. Both schemes presented here allows more "natural looking" textures that can be efficiently indexed.

The current version of the test set of synthetic images encompasses a total 2,777,000 color images (231 groud-truth x 2 blur x 100 α-fading-coefficients x 3 offsets x 100 textures-patterns x 2 texture generation schemes) and the same number of grayscale equivalent. It is probable that the analysis of the binarization of this set of 5,554,000 images will provide a better assessment of the binarization capability of algorithms than the set of only 10 images in DIBCO 2016.

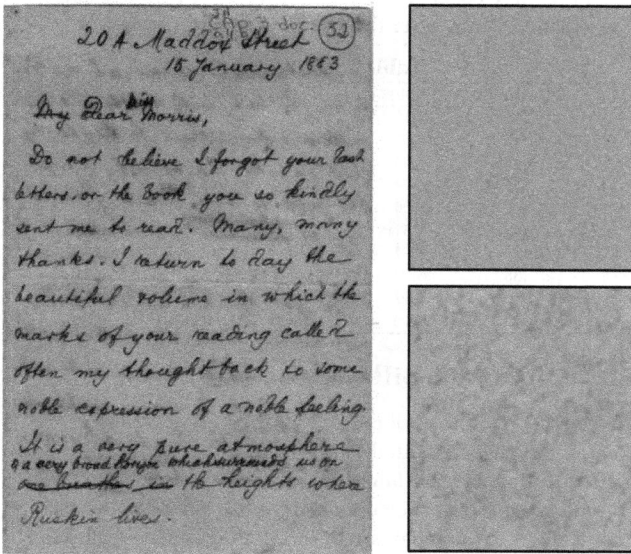

Figure 6 – (Left) Historic document. (Top-right) Texture: random distribution. (Bottom-right) Texture: image quilting.

3 ASSESSING ALGORITHMS

The enormous variety of kinds of text documents makes extremely improbable that one single algorithm is able to satisfactorily binarize all kinds of documents. Most probably, depending on the nature (or degree of complexity) of the image several or no algorithm will be able to provide good results. If binarization is part of an OCR transcription platform, the higher the correct transcription rate the better the algorithm is. It is important to remark that, according to the experiments made by the authors of this paper, OCR transcription and "visual inspection" assessment methods do not provide similar results, even in printed or typed documents. The assessment method proposed here is to provide accurate information about the binarized documents generated by the different algorithms, and the user will choose the most suitable one depending on the target application.

The assessment methodology proposed here is "image centered" instead of the traditional "algorithm centered" approach. This means that the question to be answered here is "Which are the best algorithms and their parameters to binarize image X?" instead of the traditional one "Which is the best algorithm?". Such a new approach does not provide an answer, but a set of answers. Obviously, humans are not able to handle and analyze such a large set of data, which has to be made "user-friendly" in an automated platform, currently under development by the authors.

Binarization algorithms, in general, make use of different criteria to find a threshold that splits the mapping of pixels onto white or black. Thresholding algorithms can be classified into global or local algorithms. Global algorithms define a unique threshold value for the complete image. Local algorithms first split the image into regions according to some criterion and then define threshold values for each region. In general, global algorithms are faster than local algorithms. Although local algorithms potentially provide better results as their parameters are better tuned for each small window, the kind of "tiling" effect of the small blocks tend not to yield acceptable quality results. The assessment methodology presented here works equally well with global and local binarization algorithms.

Sezgin and Sankur [6] presented a comprehensive overview and comparison of the "classical" binarization algorithms, clustering them according to their nature. From the almost forty algorithms presented there, six schemes were chosen to illustrate: Kapur-Sahoo-Wang [7], Otsu [8], Johannsen-Bille [9], Yen-Chang-Chang [10], Wu-Lu [11], and Pun [19] algorithm.

The binarization using the IsoData - Iterative Self Organizing Data Analysis Technique [18] was also tested. It is a method of unsupervised classification, and the computer runs the algorithm through several iterations until the threshold is reached.

Four algorithms specifically developed to filter-out the back-to-front interference were also assessed: Mello-Lins [13], Silva-Lins-Rocha [11], Roe-Mello [7], and Almeida-Lins-Lima [15].

The basic criterion for the choice of the algorithms assessed here was code availability. To illustrate the assessment methodology proposed here, one synthetic document was chosen with $0.1 \leq \alpha \leq$ in steps of 0.1. Samples of some of those documents are presented in Figure 7.

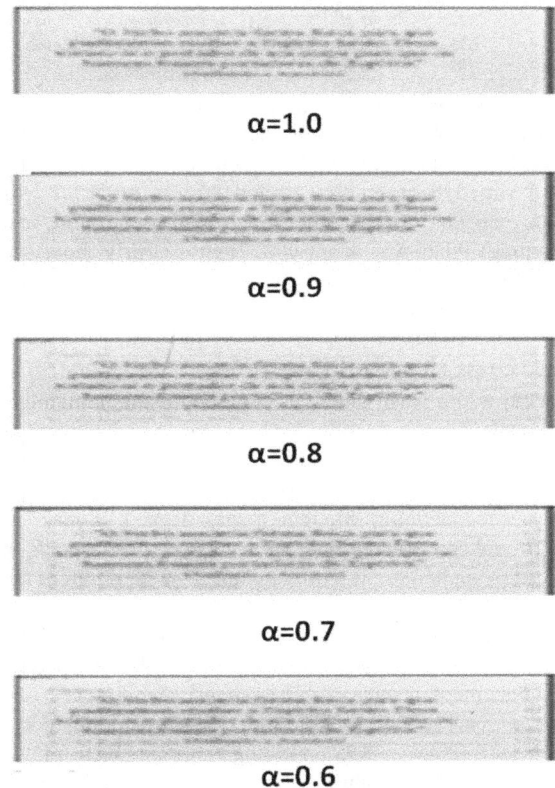

α=1.0

α=0.9

α=0.8

α=0.7

α=0.6

Figure 7 – Synthetic images with 0.6<α<1.

The tables below present: P(b|b) - the percentage of background pixels correctly mapped onto white pixels of the ground-truth image, P(f|f) – the percentage of foreground pixels correctly mapped onto black pixels of the ground-truth image, P(f|b) and P(b|f) are the percentage of mismatches. The column "Threshold" presents the value of the threshold automatically chosen by the algorithm.

The tables below present: P(b|b) - the percentage of background pixels correctly mapped onto white pixels of the ground-truth image, P(f|f) – the percentage of foreground pixels correctly mapped onto black pixels of the ground-truth image, P(f|b) and P(b|f) are the percentage of mismatches. The column "Threshold" presents the value of the threshold automatically chosen by the algorithm.

3.1 The Kapur-Sahoo-Wong Filter

The algorithm by Kapur et al. [7] considers the foreground and background images as two distinct sources, such that whenever the addition of the two entropies reach a maximum, its argument t reaches the optimal value.

Table 1: Kapur-Sahoo-Wong

α	Threshold	P(b|b)%	P(b|f)%	P(f|f)%	P(f|b)%
0.1	176	90.88	9.12	100.00	0.00
0.2	174	91.50	8.50	100.00	0.00
0.3	174	91.86	8.15	100.00	0.00
0.4	174	92.29	7.71	100.00	0.00
0.5	173	92.98	7.02	100.00	0.00
0.6	174	93.49	6.51	100.00	0.00
0.7	147	99.25	0.75	100.00	0.00
0.8	162	98.87	1.13	100.00	0.00
0.9	175	98.59	1.41	100.00	0.00
1.0	182	98.36	1.64	100.00	0.00

The analysis of the data in Table 1 reveals that there was the partial elimination of the back-to-front interference, for $0.7 \leq \alpha \leq 1.0$ as the value of background-background probability P(b|b) varied between 99.25% and 98.36%, an error less than 1.64%, considering that the foreground-foreground matching percentage P(b|b) was of 100.00%. Table 1 clearly shows that this algorithm reaches the best performance for the image with α=0.7, with a P(b|f) of 0.75%.

3.2 Otsu threshold method

Otsu [8] is the most widely used global thresholding algorithm. Otsu's algorithm is adaptive and requires no adjustment setting. It considers that there are two classes, separated by a threshold value. Otsu's algorithm makes use of Sahoo discriminator analysis for defining whether a gray level t is mapped onto foreground or background information. The result of this algorithm applied to the synthetic images with different alphas is shown in Table 2.

Although Otsu algorithm was originally developed for ultrasound images, the results above show that it performs well with document images. Table 2 shows that for $0.7 \leq \alpha \leq 1.0$, the value of background-background correct mapping percentage was $99.87\% \leq P(b|b) \leq 99.95\%$ yielding error less than 0.13%, while the foreground-foreground percentage $99.54\% \leq P(f|f) \leq 99.56\%$, an error less than 0.47%. Comparing the data presenting in Table 1

and 2 one may conclude that Otsu presented better results than Kapur-Sahoo-Wong filter for that specific set of images.

Table 2: Otsu Filter

α	Threshold	P(b|b)%	P(b|f)%	P(f|f)%	P(f|b)%
0.1	145	94.19	5.81	100.00	0.00
0.2	145	94.57	5.43	100.00	0.00
0.3	145	95.05	4.95	100.00	0.00
0.4	149	95.24	4.76	100.00	0.00
0.5	149	96.00	4.00	100.00	0.00
0.6	146	97.51	2.49	100.00	0.00
0.7	138	99.87	0.13	99.54	0.46
0.8	138	99.94	0.06	99.56	0.44
0.9	138	99.97	0.03	99.53	0.47
1.0	140	99.95	0.05	99.55	0.45

3.3 Johannsen-Bille

This method [9] uses the entropy of the gray level histogram of the digital image. Essentially, it divides the set of gray into two parts, to minimize the interdependence between them. Table 3 presents the performance obtained by this filter for the test set. The results shown demonstrate that the Johanssen-Bille filter is very unstable depending on the opacity coefficient α, as when its values were 0.3, 0.6, 0.7, and 0.8 the output was completely black images. The Johanssen-Bille algorithm presented in some of the cases (α=0.5, 0.9, 1.0) an information loss, as over 10% of the foreground pixels were mapped onto background ones.

Table 3: Johanssen-Bille

α	Threshold	P(b|b)%	P(b|f)%	P(f|f)%	P(f|b)%
0.1	142	94.49	5.51	99.52	0.48
0.2	149	94.23	5.77	100.00	0.00
0.3	210	0.00	100.00	100.00	0.00
0.4	150	95.15	4.85	100.00	0.00
0.5	100	99.97	0.03	84.63	15.37
0.6	211	0.00	100.00	100.00	0.00
0.7	211	0.00	100.00	100.00	0.00
0.8	211	0.00	100.00	100.00	0.00
0.9	112	100.00	0.00	88.39	11.61
1.0	112	100.00	0.00	88.11	11.89

3.4 Yen-Chang-Chang

The binarization algorithm by Yen-Chang-Chang [10] follows the same ideas as the one by Kapur et al. [7] in respect to the entropy distributions. The result of applying Yen-Chang-Chang Method to the test set of document images is showed in Table 4.

Table 4: Yen-Chang-Chang

α	Threshold	P(b|b)%	P(b|f)%	P(f|f)%	P(f|b)%
0.1	210	0.00	100.00	100.00	0.00
0.2	210	0.00	100.00	100.00	0.00
0.3	210	0.00	100.00	100.00	0.00
0.4	210	0.00	100.00	100.00	0.00
0.5	178	92.14	7.86	100.00	0.00
0.6	211	0.00	100.00	100.00	0.00
0.7	211	0.00	100.00	100.00	0.00
0.8	211	0.00	100.00	100.00	0.00
0.9	176	98.47	1.53	100.00	0.00
1.0	183	98.23	1.77	100.00	0.00

The results presented in Table 4 show that Yen-Chang-Chang algorithm is not suitable to binarize the test set images as seven out of ten images were mapped onto completely black images.

3.5 The Wu-Lu algorithm

The Wu-Lu binarization algorithm [11] was also originally developed for ultrasound images and seems to work particularly well in images with few contrast values. It is based on Shannon entropy and uses the lower difference between the minimum entropy of the objects and the entropy of the background as threshold value. Table 5 presents the results obtained in using Wu-Lu algorithm in the binarization of the test set images.

Analyzing the results presented in Table 5, one may see that, although the value of the percentage of background-background mapping P(b|b) did not vary much and is either 100.00% or very close to that value for all the α's, the P(f|f) value of foreground-foreground mapping varied between 36.61% and 59.72%, registering an error up to 63.39%, a strong loss of information in the text. That indicates that the Wu-Lu algorithm is possibly not suitable to binarize such set of document images.

Table 5: Wu-Lu

α	Threshold	P(b|b)%	P(b|f)%	P(f|f)%	P(f|b)%
0.1	75	99.13	0.87	62.81	37.19
0.2	75	99.00	1.00	62.45	37.55
0.3	74	99.96	0.04	61.00	39.00
0.4	73	100.00	0.00	59.72	40.28
0.5	72	100.00	0.00	57.70	42.30
0.6	71	100.00	0.00	55.86	44.14
0.7	70	100.00	0.00	54.23	45.77
0.8	68	100.00	0.00	50.21	49.79
0.9	66	100.00	0.00	45.99	54.01
1.0	62	100.00	0.00	36.61	63.39

3.6 Pun Algorithm

The algorithm proposed by Pun [19] takes as input a gray level image considered as produced by a source with an alphabet consisting of 256 statistically independent symbols. Pun considers the ratio between the *a posteriori* entropy and the total entropy as the image threshold. Table 6 presents the results of applying Pun's algorithm to the gray-level version of the synthetic images in the test set.

Table 6: Pun

α	Threshold	P(b|b)%	P(b|f)%	P(f|f)%	P(f|b)%
0.1	195	61.99	38.01	100.00	0.00
0.2	196	57.97	42.03	100.00	0.00
0.3	196	59.15	40.85	100.00	0.00
0.4	196	61.64	38.36	100.00	0.00
0.5	196	65.20	34.80	100.00	0.00
0.6	196	67.16	32.84	100.00	0.00
0.7	198	55.51	44.49	100.00	0.00
0.8	198	58.39	41.61	100.00	0.00
0.9	198	60.52	39.48	100.00	0.00
1.0	199	60.52	39.48	100.00	0.00

Pun algorithm is not suitable for the binarization of the test set of images although the P(f|f) was of 100.00% for all α's, the P(b|b) was around 60%, reaching 55.51 % for α = 0.7, meaning that are large number of background pixels were mapped onto black pixels of the monochromatic image.

3.7 The IsoData Method

Clustering is an unsupervised classification as no a priori knowledge (such as samples of known classes) is assumed to be available. The ISODATA Algorithm (Iterative Self-Organizing Data Analysis Technique Algorithm) [18] allows the number of clusters to be adjusted automatically during the iteration by merging similar clusters and splitting clusters with large standard deviations. The algorithm is highly heuristic. In the case of using the IsoData algorithm for binarizing document images the pixels in the image are iteratively sent to two clusters which will correspond to the black and white pixels. Table 7 presents the result of the binarization of the test set images using the IsoData algorithm.

Table 7: IsoData Clustering

α	Threshold	P(b|b)%	P(b|f)%	P(f|f)%	P(f|b)%
0.1	142	94.49	5.51	99.52	0.48
0.2	142	94.84	5.16	99.53	0.47
0.3	144	95.14	4.86	100.00	0.00
0.4	146	95.54	4.46	100.00	0.00
0.5	147	96.22	3.78	100.00	0.00
0.6	144	97.85	2.15	100.00	0.00
0.7	136	99.89	0.11	98.87	1.13
0.8	137	99.94	0.06	99.23	0.77
0.9	137	99.98	0.02	99.20	0.80
1.0	138	100.00	0.00	99.56	0.44

Analyzing the quality of the binarized images produced by the Isodata filter, it seems reasonable to consider important features for removing back-to-front interference: where the interference fade varied between $0.7 \leq \alpha \leq 1.0$, the value of the background-background mapping yielded an error of less than 0.11% as 99.89%<P(b|b)<100.00%. The foreground to foreground matching percentage P(f|f) had a small variation between 99.56% and 98.87%, a error less than 1.13%. It is interesting to notice that for very weak back-to-front interference (α=0.1, α=0.2) over 5% of the pixels from the paper texture were mapped onto the foreground, degrading the quality of the image. The filtering threshold varied between 136 and 147.

3.8 Mello-Lins Algorithm

The algorithm by Mello and Lins [12] is based on Shannon entropy to calculate a global threshold. It was developed with the aim of filtering out the back-to-front interference. The results obtained for the images in the test set are presented in Table 8.

Table 8: Mello-Lins

α	Threshold	P(b|b)%	P(b|f)%	P(f|f)%	P(f|b)%
0.1	174	91.19	8.81	100.00	0.00
0.2	183	89.76	10.24	100.00	0.00
0.3	181	90.58	9.42	100.00	0.00
0.4	180	91.21	8.78	100.00	0.00
0.5	178	92.14	7.86	100.00	0.00
0.6	176	93.14	6.86	100.00	0.00
0.7	174	94.47	5.53	100.00	0.00
0.8	170	97.30	2.70	100.00	0.00
0.9	165	99.19	0.81	100.00	0.00
1.0	181	98.45	1.55	100.00	0.00

All the pixels of the foreground in the test images were correctly mapped onto pixels of the foreground in the ground case images, as P(f|f)=100% for all values of α. The P(b|b) values were very high, reaching its best performance for α=0.9.

3.9 Silva-Lins-Rocha algorithm

The algorithm developed by Silva-Lins-Rocha [13] was developed to further improve the Mello-Lins algorithm. It considers the histogram distribution as the 256-symbol source (a priori source) distribution. It is assumed the hypothesis that all the symbols are statistically independent. In the case of real images one knows that this hypothesis does not hold. However, according to [13], this largely simplifies the algorithm and was supposed to yield better results than its predecessors.

The result of applying Silva-Lins-Rocha algorithm to the test images provided the results presented in Table 9.

As one may observe, considering the test set used, the Silva-Lins-Rocha actually performed better than the Mello-Lins algorithm for all values of fading coefficient but α=0.9, for some reason.

Table 9: Silva-Lins-Rocha

α	Threshold	P(b|b)%	P(b|f)%	P(f|f)%	P(f|b)%
0.1	89	97.60	2.40	78.73	21.27
0.2	95	97.77	2.23	82.80	17.20
0.3	105	97.94	2.06	86.73	13.27
0.4	115	98.17	1.83	90.60	9.40
0.5	126	98.44	1.56	94.96	5.04
0.6	137	98.80	1.20	99.22	0.74
0.7	150	98.80	1.20	100.00	0.00
0.8	161	98.98	1.02	100.00	0.00
0.9	167	99.07	0.93	100.00	0.00
1.0	165	99.26	0.74	100.00	0.00

3.10 Roe-Mello

The Roe-Mello [14] algorithm performs a local image equalization based on color constancy, and an extension to the standard difference of Gaussian edge detection operator, XDoG and Otsu binarization algorithm. The last two algorithms assessed are based on the entropy of the image, whereas the Roe-Mello one uses discriminator analysis. The threshold used by the algorithm showed very little variation, as may be observed in Table 10.

Table 10: Roe-Mello

α	Threshold	P(b|b)%	P(b|f)%	P(f|f)%	P(f|b)%
0.1	181	88.16	11.84	39.39	60.61
0.2	181	88.41	11.59	39.10	60.90
0.3	181	88.73	11.27	39.11	61.89
0.4	180	89.23	10.76	36.45	63.55
0.5	181	94.84	5.16	23.70	76.30
0.6	181	95.41	4.59	22.46	77.54
0.7	181	95.55	4.45	22.10	77.90
0.8	181	95.63	4.37	22.04	77.96
0.9	181	95.63	4.37	22.03	77.97
1.0	181	98.58	4.42	22.13	77.87

The results obtained by the Roe-Mello algorithm may be considered unsuitable for the binarization of the test set used.

3.11 The Almeida-Lins-Lima algorithm

The algorithm recently proposed by Almeida, Lins and Lima [15] is performed in four steps: filtering the image using a bilateral filter [16], splitting image into the RGB components, decision-making for each RGB channel based on an adaptive binarization method inspired by Otsu's method with a choice of the threshold level, and classification of the binarized images to decide which of the RGB components best preserved the document information in the foreground. It is far more computation intensive than its predecessors and involves training for the Decision-making block. Testing this algorithm with the same set of test images the automatically chosen threshold is equal to 126 and the channel that is chosen for providing the best results in binarizing the images is the Red channel. The results obtained are summarized in Table 11.

Table 11: Almeida-Lins-Lima

α	Threshold	P(b|b)%	P(b|f)%	P(f|f)%	P(f|b)%
0.1	126	96.49	3.51	100.00	0.00
0.2	126	96.93	3.07	100.00	0.00
0.3	126	97.66	2.34	100.00	0.00
0.4	126	99.60	0.40	100.00	0.00
0.5	126	99.87	0.13	100.00	0.00
0.6	126	99.91	0.09	100.00	0.00
0.7	126	99.94	0.06	100.00	0.00
0.8	126	99.97	0.03	100.00	0.00
0.9	126	99.99	0.01	100.00	0.00
1.0	126	100.00	0.00	100.00	0.00

The results presented for this algorithm show that for all the images in the chosen test set this algorithm performed better that its predecessors, exhibiting a steady "behavior" with the variation of the fading coefficient α. It is important to remark that this and the IsoData algorithms claim far more computational resources than the other algorithms assessed.

4 GLOBAL RESULTS

The assessment presented in the last section for the ten selected binarization algorithms presented for one test set formed by ten synthetic images obtained with ten different fading coefficients α varying from 0.1 to 1.0 in steps of 0.1 showed that the performance of the algorithms is highly dependent of the features of the document image. Further testing was made with a larger set of 1,600 synthetic images with the coefficient α varying between 0 and 1 in steps of 0.01. The average of the results of P(b|b)% and P(f|f)% were taken for each of the filters assessed for each value of α. The filters that showed both P(b|b)% and P(f|f)% average values higher than 99% and are presented in Table 12. The data presented in Table 12 corroborate the hypothesis formulated that the performance of binarization algorithms depends heavily on the "intrinsic nature" of the document image, and that a small variation in the image may yield completely different performance figures. In that sense, the data presented in this section must be read as a simple indicator of the quality of the images generated by those algorithms using a controlled test set, not being adequate to read the results as a quality classification rank for the compared algorithms.

Table 12: Overall algorithm classification for 1,600 synthetic images with 0<α<1 in steps of 0.1.

α	P(b|b)%	P(f|f)%	Filter	Threshold
1.0	100.00	100.00	Almeida-Lins-Lima	126
1.0	100.00	99.56	IsoData	138
1.0	99.95	99.56	Otsu	140
0.9	99.99	100.00	Almeida-Lins-Lima	126
0.9	99.98	99.20	IsoData	137
0.9	99.97	99.53	Otsu	138
0.9	99.07	100.00	Silva-Lins	167
0.8	99.97	100.00	Almeida-Lins-Lima	126
0.8	99.94	99.23	IsoData	137
0.8	99.94	99.56	Otsu	138
0.8	98.98	100.00	Silva-Lins	161
0.7	99.94	100.00	Almeida-Lins-Lima	126
0.7	99.25	100.00	Kapur SW	147
0.7	99.87	99.54	Otsu	138
0.6	99.91	100.00	Almeida-Lins-Lima	126
0.5	99.87	100.00	Almeida-Lins-Lima	126
0.4	99.60	100.00	Almeida-Lins-Lima	126

5 CONCLUSIONS

No binarization algorithm is an "all-kind-of-document" winner. Several factors such as paper texture, aging, thickness, tranlucidity, permability, the kind of ink, its fluidity, color, aging, etc., all may influence the performance of each algorithm. This paper presents an assessment methodology based on the controlled generation of a large set of synthetic images that allows identifying quality aspects of the binarized images.

Eleven different binarization algorithms presented in this paper were used to binarize the images in the test set database of 1,478,400 binary images that were compared with the 134,400 ground truth images, allowing to know for each of them the percentage and type of matching (P(b|b)% and P(f|f)%) and mismatched (P(b|f)% and P(f|b)%) pixels.

The authors plan to develop an image "matcher" or "classifier" that will be trained with the database developed of synthetic images. The aim of such classifier is that, given a real-world document, the platform will automatically find the closest synthetic document to it. Once that document is found, one knows the set of binarization algorithms that are more likely to provide the best results. One important point is worth remarking here is that binarization assessments tend only to consider the quality of the resulting image "for visual inspection". In the more global assessment methodology presented here, the user will be even able to choose to prioritize to minimize either the P(b|f)% or P(f|b)% errors, depending on the "sensitiveness" of the target application. For instance, if the resulting binary image will go through an OCR it may be better to have P(f|b)% < P(b|f)%.

Preliminary tests made in matching the synthetic images with "real world" documents for "visual inspection" provided very good results. The image shown in Figure 8 may witness the good quality of the binary image provided by using the Almeida-Lins-Lima algorithm in the document image presented in Figure 3. The document image in Figure 9 provides another evidence of that, using the same binarization algorithm.

The assessment strategy presented here is a generalization of the platform described in reference [20]. The current version of the assessment environment encompasses 5,554,00 images

(231 groud-truth x 2 blur x 100 α-fading-coefficients x 3 offsets x 100 textures-patterns x 2 texture generation schemes x 2 color/grayscale). The authors of this paper consider this image set representative of the universe or "real world" text documents. At present, twenty-five binarization algorithms are being assessed. Another relevant aspect that should be taken into account is that the proposed binarizarion platform accounts now for the time elapsed by each algorithm to binarize each image. This allows the user to choose the lightest algorithm that provides the best results. For instance, the computational cost of Otsu is extremely small if compared with the IsoData or the Almeida-Lins-Lima algoritms. At a later stage, space consumed will also be considered.

It is most relevant to emphasize the computational challenge involved in the task proposed here, as each of the synthetic images is over 10 MB large. If one attempts to store the 5,554,000 images, over 50 TB of storage would be needed, a volume of data unreasonable to be used. Each image is generated a time and then binarized in a pipeline with the 25 filters currently tested against the ground-truth image and the data is collected and stored. A slice of the image that corresponds to central one-fifth of it is being saved as a lossless PNG image to later be used in the training of the image matcher. A cluster with 10 machines is being used in this platform, using the technology described in the BigBatch project [21]. Priority was given to four different values of alpha (α=1 no interference, α=0.8 weak interference, α=0.6 medium interference, α=0.4 strong back-to-front interference). The partial assessment results will be made publically available as they are obtained. The authors would like to remark that even processing in a dedicated cluster with ten nodes, several months of processing are needed. The preliminary version of the DIB-Document Image Binarization platform and website is publically available at www.cin.ufpe.br/~dib.

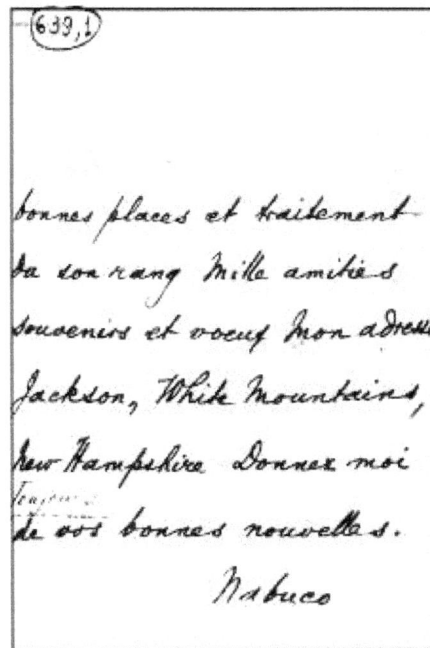

Figure 8 –Binarized version of the document shown in Figure 3 using the Almeida-Lins-Lima algorithm.

ACKNOWLEDGMENTS

The authors of this paper are grateful for those who made the code of their algorithms publically available for testing and performance analysis and to CNPq – Brazilian Government for sponsoring this research.

REFERENCES

[1] K. Ntirogiannis, B. Gatos and I. Pratikakis, Performance Evaluation Methodology for Historical Document Image Binarization, IEEE Trans. Image Proc., vol.22, no.2, pp. 595-609, Feb. 2013..

[2] R. D. Lins et al. An Environment for Processing Images of Historical Documents. Microproc. and Microprogramming, 111–121, 1995.

[3] G. Sharma. Show-trough cancellation in scans of duplex printed documents. IEEE Transaction Image Processing, v. 10, n. 5, p. 736–754, 2001.

[4] R. D. Lins. Nabuco – Two Decades of Processing Historical Documents in Latin America. Journal of Universal Computer Science. , March 2011.

[5] C. A. B. Mello and R. D. Lins. 2002. Generation of Images of Historical Documents by Composition. Symposium on Document Engineering, 127–133. 2002.

[6] M.Sezgin and B.Sankur. A Survey over Image Thresholding Techniques and Quantitative Performance Evaluation. Journal of Electronc Imaging, v. 1, n. 13, p. 146–165, 2004.

[7] J. N. Kapur, P. K. Sahoo, A. K. C. Wong. A New Method for Gray-Level Picture Thersholding Using the Entropy of the Histogram. C. Vision Graphics and Image Processing, v. 29, p. 273–285, 1985.

[8] N. Otsu. A Threshold Selection Method from Gray-Level Histograms. IEEE Transaction on Systems, Man and Cybernetics, v. SMC-9, n. 1, p. 62–66, 1979.

[9] G. Johannsen and J. A. Bille. A Threshold Selection Method Using Information Measure. ICPR'82 - Proceeding 6th International Conference on Pattern Recognition, 140–143. 1982.

[10] J. C. Yen, F. J. Chang, S. Chang. 1995. A New Criterion for Automatic Multilevel Thresholding. IEEE Transaction Image Process IP-4, 370–378.

[11] U. L. Wu, A. Songde, L. U. Haqing. 1998. An Effective Entropic Thresholding for Ultrasonic Imaging. International Conference Pattern Recognition, 1522–1524.

[12] C. A. B. Mello and R. D. Lins. Generation of Images of Historical Documents by Composition. Proceedings of the 2002 ACM symposium on Document engineering, 127–133, 2002.

[13] J. M. M. Silva, R. D. Lins, V. C. Rocha. Binarizing and Filtering Historical Documents with Back-to-Front Interference. ACM Symposium on Applied Computing, 853–858, 2006.

[14] E. Roe and C. A. B. Mello. Binarization of Color Historical Document Images Using Local Image Equalization and XDoG. 12th International Conference on Document Analysis and Recognition, August, p. 205–209, 2013.

[15] M. A. M. de Almeida, R. D. Lins, B. C. Lima, A New Binarization Algorithm for Images with Back-to-Front Interference. Submitted for publication, 2017.

[16] S. Paris, P. Kornprobst, J. Tumblin and F. Durand. Bilateral Filtering: Theory and Applications. Foundations and Trends in Computer Graphics and Vision. Vol. 4, No. 1, 1–73. 2008.

[17] A. A. Efros and W. T. Freeman. Image quilting for texture synthesis and transfer. SIGGRAPH '01 28th annual conference on Computer graphics and interactive techniques, 341-346. 2001.

[18] [N. Memarsadeghi, D. M. Mount, N. S. Netanyahu, J. Moigne. 2007. A Fast Implementation of the IsoData Clustering Algorithm. International Journal of Computational Geometry and Applications, 71–103.

[19] T. Pun. Entropic Thresholding, A New Approach. Computer Vision Graphics and Image Processing, 210–239, 1981.

[20] R. D. Lins and G. F. P e Silva. Assessing Strategies to Remove Back-to-Front Interference in Color Documents. IEEE International Telecommunications Symposium, 2010, IEEE Press, p. 1-6, 2010.

[21] G. G.Mattos, A. A. Formiga, R. D. Lins, F. M. J. Martins. BigBatch: a document processing platform for clusters and grids. ACM-SAC 2008. ACM Press, 2008. v. I. p. 434-441.

[22] Scikit-learn. http://scikit-learn.org/stable/ (visited: 31st May 2017)

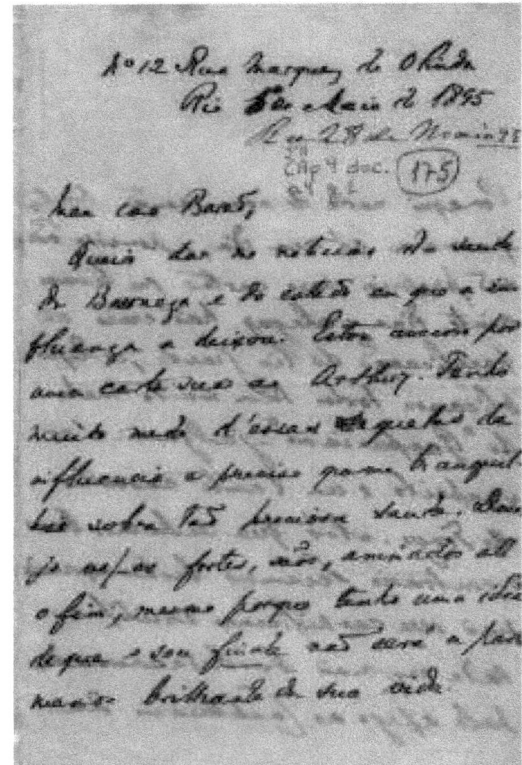

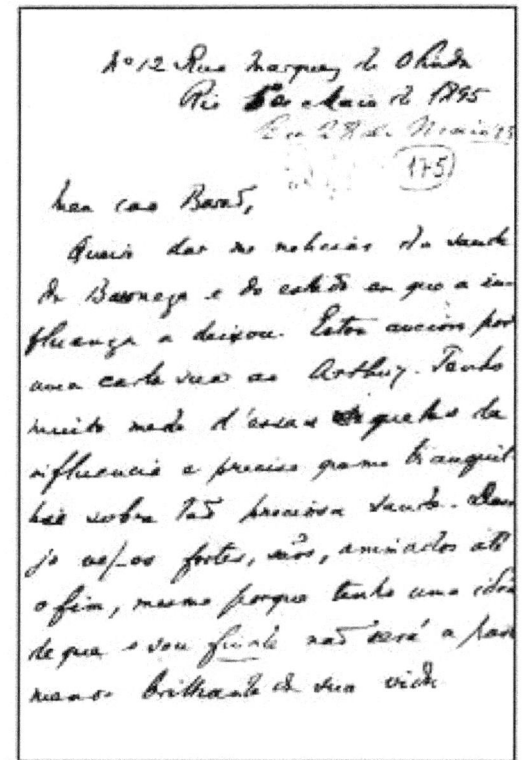

Figure 9 –Historic document and its binary version produced by Almeida-Lins-Lima algorithm.

Baseline Detection on Arabic Handwritten Documents

Ahmed Fawzi, Moisés Pastor, Carlos-D. Martínez-Hinarejos

Pattern Recognition and Human Language Technology research center - Universitat Politècnica de València

Camino de Vera, s/n

València, Spain 46022

{ahfawal,mpastorg,cmartine}@dsic.upv.es

ABSTRACT

Document processing comprises different steps depending on the nature of the documents. For text documents, specially for handwritten documents, transcription of their contents is one of the main tasks. Handwritten Text Recognition (HTR) is the process of automatically obtaining the transcription of the content of a handwritten text document. In document processing, the basic unit for the acquisition process is the page image, whilst line image is the basic form for the HTR process. This is a bottle-neck which is holding back the massive industrial document processing. Baseline detection can be used not only to segment page images into line images but also for many other document processing steps. Baseline detection problem can be formulated as a clustering problem over a set of interest points. In this work, we study the use of an automatic baseline detection technique, based on interest point clustering, in Arabic handwritten documents. The experiments reveal that this technique provides promising results for this task.

KEYWORDS

Baseline Text Detection; Handwritten Arabic Document; Extremely Randomized Trees; DBScan

1 INTRODUCTION

Document processing techniques are applied, among other tasks, to the obtention of the contents of the documents. One of the principal contents to be extracted is the underlying text of the document, sometimes with additional data that allows its interpretation. When documents contain mainly handwritten text, the recognition of these contents is a task of high interest. The solution of this problem is known as Handwritten Text Recognition (HTR) [18], which is a field that combines pattern recognition [1] and natural language processing [12] models and tools.

However, most HTR applications require the previous segmentation of the document into lines, in order to have a linear sequence to be recognised. Manual segmentation is unfeasible for large volumes of data, because of its temporal and economical cost. For this reason, automatic line detection and extraction on handwritten documents are interesting topics [20]. This problem can be attacked by using

DocEng'17, September 4–7, 2017, Valletta, Malta.
© 2017 Association for Computing Machinery.
ACM ISBN 978-1-4503-4689-4/17/09...$15.00
https://doi.org/10.1145/3103010.3121037

image processing and classification techniques. In particular, line detection and extraction are highly correlated to the obtainment of the so-called baseline for each text line [10]. A baseline is a fictitious line which follows and joints the lower part of the character bodies.

Baseline detection can be used to detect the number of lines of a page and to extract the different lines that can be used for handwritten text recognition. However, different types of scripting and alphabets may need different features for baseline detection.

In this work, we analyse how a baseline detection technique based on text contour local minimum detection, classification (using Extremely Randomised Trees [7]) and clustering (using a modified DBScan [3]) behaves for Arabic scripting [24]. Experiments show promising results for this technique and its use for this type of scripting.

The paper is organised as follows: Section 2 presents related work to baseline detection, Section 3 provides a description of the employed techniques, Section 4 describes the used dataset, Section 5 shows details on the experimental framework and the obtained results, and Section 6 summarises conclusions and future work lines.

2 RELATED WORK

The present work is devoted to baseline detection and we shall try to focus on the baseline detection state of the art, but we have to notice that, in literature, it is frequent to find the terms detection and extraction used indistinctly. According to [6], there are three types of approximations:

- Projection profiles methods [15, 24]: they are based on projections of the image density on the vertical axis, taking local minimum as separations between lines; their limitation is that they assume line horizontality and parallelism, although some corrections can be applied to allow for horizontal deviations.
- Hough transform based methods [22]: the Hough transform is used to find a line angle that fits well a set of points given an initial point; for text line segmentation, the set of points can be gravity centers [5, 11] or local minima [19] of the connected components.
- Clustering methods: the method presented in [14] has the aim to cluster connected components into sets that form the corresponding text lines; the method presented in [21] employs an Adaptive Local Connectivity Map for the same final aim.

Apart from these approximations to the problem, other approximations based on combination of techniques or heuristics have been proposed in the latest years [10].

In the specific case of Arabic text, there are proposals for single word baseline detection [16] based on image skeletons [17], on the calculation of regression lines from local minima [4], and on horizontal projections [2]. For whole lines, there are proposals which are based on slant correction, partial projection, and partial contour following [25], and based on identification of candidate baseline points and the construction of the regression curve that fits them [13].

3 TECHNICAL DETAILS

The baseline detection technique used for our experiments is based on a clustering of interest points. Thus, given a set of points pertaining to a handwritten text image, a partition of this set in disjoint clusters, each one defining a baseline. In this section we give an overview of the Top-Down Clustering Algorithm that uses Extremely Randomised Trees to obtain interest points and a modified DBScan clustering technique to build the baselines.

3.1 Extremely Randomised Trees (ERT)

Extremely Randomised Trees (ERT) [7] is a supervised classification method that combines bagging with random selection of features, which allows to get a final low variance. This classifier presents a good behaviour with few annotated training samples [8], which makes it appropriate to classification when manual annotation is costly.

3.2 Interest points

Interest points are the local minima points of the text edges pertaining to baselines; in our case, we employed a foreground contour extraction algorithm (by using blur and binarisation) for edge detection, and then a window analysis centered on each contour point for minimum detection. Not all detected minimums would pertain to the baseline (i.e., they may pertain to descendents, noise, etc.), and a selection of these points must be done.

The candidate points obtained from the previous step must be classified into interest (baseline) points and others (noise, descenders, etc.); in our case, we employed a forest of Extremely Randomised Trees (ERT) as a classifier. In the training step, candidate points that are close enough to reference baselines (those obtained as described in Section 4) are taken as positive samples, and the rest of candidate points as negative ones; the corresponding trees are trained from these labelled samples. In the test step, the trained trees are used to classify candidate points in positive (baseline) or negative points, obtaining the final set of points to be clustered.

3.3 DBScan clustering

DBScan (Density Based Spatial Clustering of Applications with Noise) [3] is a clustering algorithm based on the notion of *density-reachable*. DBScan employs a distance threshold ϵ and a minimum points population K to take points into a cluster. According to that, a point p_1 is density-reachable from another point p_2 if their distance is lower than an ϵ threshold, and in this neighbourhood there are at least K points that are density-reachable.

The clustering is performed by using a variation of the DBScan method, whose metrics were changed to use the Mahalanobis distance instead.

$$d_m(\vec{p_1}, \vec{p_2}) = \sqrt{(\vec{p_1} - \vec{p_2})^T \Sigma^{-1} (\vec{p_1} - \vec{p_2})}$$

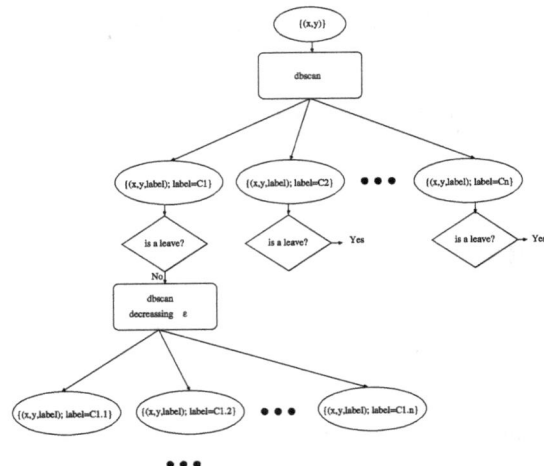

Figure 1: Top-down clustering using DBScan.

Where:

$$\Sigma = \left\{ \begin{array}{cc} \varepsilon_x & 0 \\ 0 & \varepsilon_y \end{array} \right\}$$

With $\varepsilon_x = \varepsilon$ and $\varepsilon_y = \lambda\varepsilon$.

This is done in order to take profit of the a-priori knowledge of the quasi-horizontal distribution of the local minima points of bidimensional images.

DBScan is applied to the set of interest points obtained by the ERT classification described in Section 3.2. The application follows the Top-Down Clustering process explained in Section 3.4. The obtained clusters would define the baselines for the given page.

3.4 Top-Down Clustering Algorithm

As Figure 1 shows, an initial first partition is obtained using the DBScan algorithm. Then a criteria function is used to decide if each class on the cluster is a leave or not (a baseline), in which case it will need to be split. The criteria function is based on the analysis of the slopes of the straight lines joining two consecutive points, once those points have been ordered along the x-axis. Every time a class is proposed to be split, the DBScan neighbours area, controlled by ϵ, is reduced, and the algorithm is applied to this cluster points set.

4 DATA

In this section, we refer to the data and tools which we have used in our work. We have employed a dataset of Arabic handwritten documents images that contains 123 images[1] and that was used in other works we could compare with [9]. Some page samples can be seen in Figure 2. The total number of text lines is 1955.

We have uploaded all the images of the corpus to the Transkribus annotation platform[2] in order to manually obtain the reference text baselines. The Transkribus tool was used to obtain a draft detection of text in the images and their baselines. After that, manual review and correction were done by a native Arabic writer, in order to

[1] Available in https://lampsrv02.umiacs.umd.edu/projdb/project.php?id=65
[2] https://transkribus.eu/Transkribus/

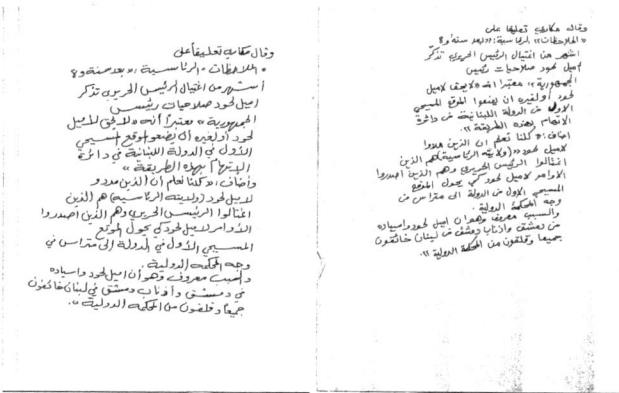

Figure 2: Sample pages from the dataset.

obtain accurate baselines to be employed in the experimental part. As a result, a set of XML files that contains, among other data, the baseline points, was obtained. Our software tools were applied on the images dataset along with their corresponding XML baseline annotations.

5 EXPERIMENTS AND RESULTS

5.1 Experimental framework

Arabic features are different from classical Latin scripting or other languages, and the corresponding optimal parameters for the method steps may be different. After some preliminary work, in our experiments a window size of 20×20 pixels was employed for the detection of candidate points. The values of the pixels in the windows were taken as features. The proximity to baseline of candidate points was calculated with a threshold of 25 pixels above and 8 pixels below. DBScan parameters were fixed to $\epsilon = 400$ and $K = 4$.

Two type of experiments were performed.

- The first experiment explores the robustness of the technique from a small number of training samples. Since manual baseline annotation is difficult and time-consuming, this approach is important because it checks if the technique is suitable for a small set of training samples. In our case, we employed one image from the dataset for training, and the rest of the images for testing, repeating it for all the available 123 images.
- The second experiment employed incremental training (more than one image) from 1 to 23 images, keeping the remaining 100 images for testing. The rationale of this experiment is to detect what is the amount of manually annotated data that is necessary to obtain the maximum performance.

In each experiment we have evaluated Precision, Recall and F-measure of detected text baseline.

5.2 First experiment: limited training data

In this experiment, each image of the dataset of 123 Arabic documents was employed for training a recognition model, while the rest of images were employed for testing. Thus, for each page image,

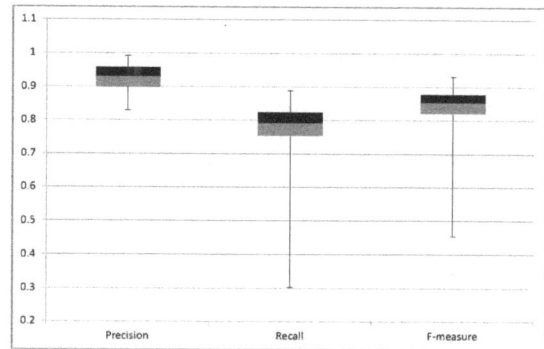

Figure 3: Box-plot whisker for results obtained from all testing sets.

Table 1: Average results obtained on all testing sets using training with one image and testing with the rest of images.

Precision	Recall	F-measure
92.7	77.9	84.4

a Random Tree was trained, and then used to detect baselines on the rest of the images (with the classification and clustering steps described above). For each training page, we calculated the average Precision, Recall and F-measure for the test set of pages. Figure 3 shows the box-plot whisker that illustrates the results obtained from the experiment. In addition, we obtained the average results for all test sets, which are shown in Table 1.

In this experiment, we wanted to test the accuracy of the method for Arabic handwritten text with a limited amount of training data. We found that most of the images obtained high accuracy results with regular distribution when measuring the results in testing experiments. There was an extreme worst result with one image of the dataset, that gave us completely different results from the rest of the images. When checking that image, we noticed that it was written with bold text size, which was different to the other images. That page presented a quite high slope as well, but this happened to other images in the dataset without affecting the baseline detection performance. As a conclusion, we can suppose that the width of the handwritten strokes has a critical effect in the classification using this technique, and that the slope is not so important.

5.3 Second experiment: incremental training

Another experiment was made based on training with more images and keeping the test set fixed. In this experiment, we have created automatically 23 trees; each tree is obtained from a different number of pages. We started with the same conditions than in the first experiment (a single page image to train the tree), and then, we increased the number of training images to get the rest of trees: from the first two images, from the first three images, and so on. The last tree was trained with 23 images. We obtained the results of using each of the 23 models for classifying the remaining 100 images of the dataset. Precision, Recall and F-measure were computed for

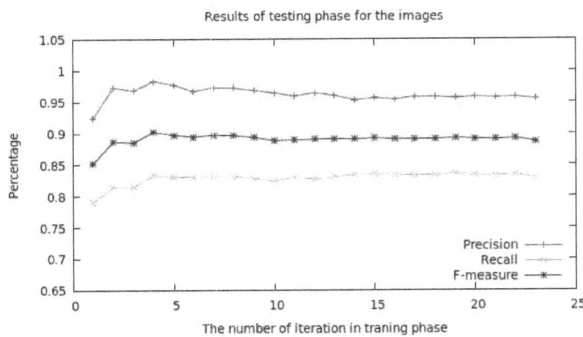

Figure 4: Results obtained for the testing over the 23 trees obtained from incremental training and 100 images of test.

each experiment. Figure 4 shows how the experiment works for the different amount of data employed for training the classifying tree.

Results show that increasing the number of images in training allows to get better results, but this improvement is limited to a reduced set of training images. In our case, we got the best results training with 4 images, that gave a Precision of 98.3%, a Recall of 83.3%, and an F-measure of 90.2%. Anyway, as plot in Figure 4 reveals, using only two pages for training provides a relevant improvement in results, and increasing the number of training data does not increase accuracy, whereas running time for training increases substantially.

6 CONCLUSION AND FUTURE WORK

In this work we have tested the behaviour of a baseline detection technique on Arabic handwriting. The automatic baseline detection technique is based on interest points (determined by ERT classifiers) clustering (performed by using DBScan). Results show that the proposed technique provides good results in Arabic handwritten text with limited training (although shows sensitivity to the width of the strokes) and that increasing the number of training data has no substantial effect after an initial accuracy improvement. Thus, this technique can be applied in a realistic framework where initially only a small amount of training data is manually annotated.

Future work will be directed to a more extensive exploration of the different parameters of the technique and how they affect to the accuracy of baseline detection. Apart from that, other techniques and classifiers, such as Conditional Random Fields [23], may be employed, as well as other datasets used as line segmentation benchmarks[3]. Finally, the main aim is to incorporate this technique in a line extraction system in order to use it for real applications.

ACKNOWLEDGEMENTS

Work partially supported by MINECO/FEDER under project CoMUN-HaT (TIN2015-70924-C2-1-R), and by Generalitat Valenciana (GVA) under reference PROMETEOII/2014/030.

[3]http://users.iit.demokritos.gr/~nstam/ICDAR2013HandSegmCont/

REFERENCES

[1] R. O. Duda, P. E. Hart, and D. G. Stork. 2000. *Pattern Classification (2nd Edition)*. Wiley-Interscience.
[2] R. El-Hajj, L. Likforman-Sulem, and C. Mokbel. 2005. Arabic handwriting recognition using baseline dependant features and hidden Markov modeling. In *Proceedings of ICDAR*. 893–897 Vol. 2. https://doi.org/10.1109/ICDAR.2005.53
[3] M. Ester, H. P. Kriegel, J. Sander, and X. Xu. 1996. A density-based algorithm for discovering clusters in large spatial databases with noise. In *Kdd*, Vol. 96. 226–231.
[4] F. Farooq, V. Govindaraju, and M. Perrone. 2005. Pre-processing methods for handwritten Arabic documents. In *Proceedings of ICDAR*. 267–271 Vol. 1. https://doi.org/10.1109/ICDAR.2005.191
[5] L. A. Fletcher and R. Kasturi. 1988. A robust algorithm for text string separation from mixed text/graphics images. *IEEE transactions on pattern analysis and machine intelligence* 10, 6 (1988), 910–918.
[6] B. Gatos, G. Louloudis, and N. Stamatopoulos. 2014. Segmentation of historical handwritten documents into text zones and text lines. In *Proceedings of ICFHR*. IEEE, 464–469.
[7] P. Geurts, D. Ernst, and L. Wehenkel. 2006. Extremely randomized trees. *Machine learning* 63, 1 (2006), 3–42.
[8] P. Geurts and G. Louppe. 2011. Learning to rank with extremely randomized trees.. In *Yahoo! Learning to Rank Challenge (JMLR Proceedings)*, O. Chapelle, Y. Chang, and T. Y. Liu (Eds.), Vol. 14. JMLR.org, 49–61.
[9] J. Kumar, W. Abd-Almageed, L. Kang, and D. Doermann. 2010. Handwritten Arabic Text Line Segmentation Using Affinity Propagation. In *Proceedings of DAS*. ACM, 135–142. https://doi.org/10.1145/1815330.1815348
[10] L. Likforman-Sulem, A. Zahour, and B. Taconet. 2007. Text line segmentation of historical documents: a survey. *International Journal of Document Analysis and Recognition (IJDAR)* 9, 2-4 (2007), 123–138.
[11] G. Louloudis, B. Gatos, I. Pratikakis, and C. Halatsis. 2008. Text line detection in handwritten documents. *Pattern Recognition* 41, 12 (2008), 3758–3772.
[12] C. D. Manning and H. Schütze. 1999. *Foundations of Statistical Natural Language Processing*. MIT Press, Cambridge, MA, USA.
[13] P. Nagabhushan and A. Alaei. 2010. Tracing and straightening the baseline in handwritten persian/arabic text-line: A new approach based on painting-technique. *International Journal on Computer Science and Engineering* 2, 4 (2010), 907–916.
[14] S. Nicolas, T. Paquet, and L. Heutte. 2004. Text line segmentation in handwritten document using a production system. In *IWFHR*, Vol. 4. 245–250.
[15] V. Papavassiliou, V. Katsouros, and G. Carayannis. 2010. A morphological approach for text-line segmentation in handwritten documents. In *Proceedings of ICFHR*. IEEE, 19–24.
[16] M. Pechwitz, S. S. Maddouri, V. Märgner, N. Ellouze, and H. Amiri. 2002. IFN/ENIT-database of handwritten Arabic words. In *Proc. of CIFED*, Vol. 2. 127–136.
[17] M. Pechwitz and V. Margner. 2002. Baseline estimation for Arabic handwritten words. In *Proceedings of IWFHR*. 479–484. https://doi.org/10.1109/IWFHR.2002.1030956
[18] T. Plötz and G. A. Fink. 2009. Markov models for offline handwriting recognition: a survey. *International Journal on Document Analysis and Recognition (IJDAR)* 12, 4 (2009), 269–298.
[19] Y. Pu and Z. Shi. 1998. A natural learning algorithm based on hough transform for text lines extraction in handwritten document. In *Proceedings of IWFHR*. 637–646.
[20] V. Romero, J. A. Sánchez, V. Bosch, K. Depuydt, and J. de Does. 2015. Influence of text line segmentation in Handwritten Text Recognition. In *Proceedings of ICDAR*. IEEE, 536–540.
[21] Z. Shi, S. Setlur, and V. Govindaraju. 2005. Text extraction from gray scale historical document images using adaptive local connectivity map. In *Proceedings of ICDAR*. IEEE, 794–798.
[22] S. N. Srihari and V. Govindaraju. 1989. Analysis of textual images using the Hough transform. *Machine vision and Applications* 2, 3 (1989), 141–153.
[23] C. Sutton and A. McCallum. 2012. An Introduction to Conditional Random Fields. *Foundations and Trends in Machine Learning* 4, 4 (2012), 267–373.
[24] A. Zahour, L. Likforman-Sulem, W. Boussellaa, and B. Taconet. 2007. Text line segmentation of historical arabic documents. In *Proceedings of ICDAR*, Vol. 1. IEEE, 138–142.
[25] A. Zahour, B. Taconet, P. Mercy, and S. Ramdane. 2001. Arabic hand-written text-line extraction. In *Proceedings of ICDAR*. 281–285. https://doi.org/10.1109/ICDAR.2001.953799

High-Performance Preprocessing of Architectural Drawings for Legend Metadata Extraction via OCR

Tamir Hassan
HP Labs
Vienna, Austria
tamir.hassan@hp.com

Jaume Verges-Llahi
HP
Barcelona, Spain
jaume.verges-llahi@hp.com

Andres Gonzalez
HP
Barcelona, Spain
andres.gonzalez@hp.com

ABSTRACT

This paper describes the results of an investigation into methods of preprocessing architectural plots to enable them to be processed very quickly via OCR, detecting the region containing the relevant metadata legend and obtaining it in machine-readable form for e.g. automated folding and filenaming applications. We show how a processing pipeline adapted to this type of content can vastly decrease processing time, maintaining acceptable accuracy. Initial results show a reduction in total processing time from 2–3 minutes to around 15 seconds for most documents encountered, with the folding orientation being correctly detected in 78% of cases and the legend region being completely detected in 60% of cases, high enough for the use-case at hand.

CCS CONCEPTS

• Applied computing → Document analysis; *Document metadata*;

KEYWORDS

Document analysis; OCR preprocessing; image processing

1 INTRODUCTION

HP's large-format printing and scanning devices are frequently employed in construction sites, where there is a need to quickly print, scan or copy architectural plots; these jobs can often amount to tens or hundreds of pages at a time. In order to increase the efficiency for the operator, we are developing intelligent systems to automatically analyse the documents to be printed or scanned. Such plots normally include a "legend" region containing important metadata about the plot (see Fig. 2 [top left] for an example).

Many printing workflows utilize machinery to automatically fold the plots after printing. In such cases, it is critical that the plot is folded in such a way that the metadata remains visible after folding. By changing the orientation of the page during printing, it is possible to ensure that a particular corner or *quadrant* will always remain face-up; our first task is therefore to detect which of the

DocEng '17, September 4–7, 2017, Valletta, Malta
© 2017 Copyright held by the owner/author(s). Publication rights licensed to Association for Computing Machinery.
ACM ISBN 978-1-4503-4689-4/17/09...$15.00
https://doi.org/10.1145/3103010.3121042

four quadrants of the page contains the metadata; if the metadata is located on more than one quadrant, we choose the one containing the most metadata elements as the "ground truth" for our problem definition. It should be noted that, in some cases, there is no unambiguous solution to this problem; for example in cases where the metadata items are distributed across the whole page edge spanning the page's height or width. Fig. 2 (top left) is an example of such an ambiguous plot for our folding application.

Our second task is to improve the operator's efficiency when scanning a large batch of physical plots. Up to now, operators have had to either name each generated file individually after feeding each plot through the scanner, or have them numbered serially. By extracting relevant metadata from the plot, we can automatically propose a meaningful filename based on a wildcard that the user has either set manually or was learned from previous scans. The operator would then only need to intervene if the respective metadata is misrecognized or the naming convention changes.

Both of the above tasks proceed under the supervision of the operator, who is given the opportunity to either accept the detected orientation and proposed filename, or make corrections if necessary. As this is an interactive process, OCR cannot proceed asynchronously, as the operator can only be expected to verify the parameters of the current file being processed; being asked about earlier files would likely lead to confusion and increased human error. Therefore, the page must be analysed very quickly, in order to avoid interrupting the workflow.

A typical A1 plot scanned (or rasterized) at 300 dpi has a dimension of over 14,000 pixels on its longest side. This limits our choice of methods for performing the page analysis; whereas off-the-shelf generic OCR solutions take over 3 minutes to process such an image, our target is to perform pre-processing and OCR within 30 seconds. Fortunately, by developing a page analysis pipeline specifically tailored to the type of content and only performing OCR on the legend region itself, we can drastically reduce processing time. Accuracy is only of secondary importance: as these workflows are operator-supervised, even an accuracy of 60% can lead to an overall improvement in efficiency, whereas processing times in the order of minutes are of no benefit at all.

2 RELATED WORK

The topic of document image analysis has been well studied over the last few decades, and most currently available commercial solutions employ a variety of techniques in the processing pipeline in order to achieve high recognition accuracy for a wide range of documents. The downside of these approaches is their processing time; given the type of content we know to expect a priori, many of these steps can be omitted or simplified. For example, in our case, we can

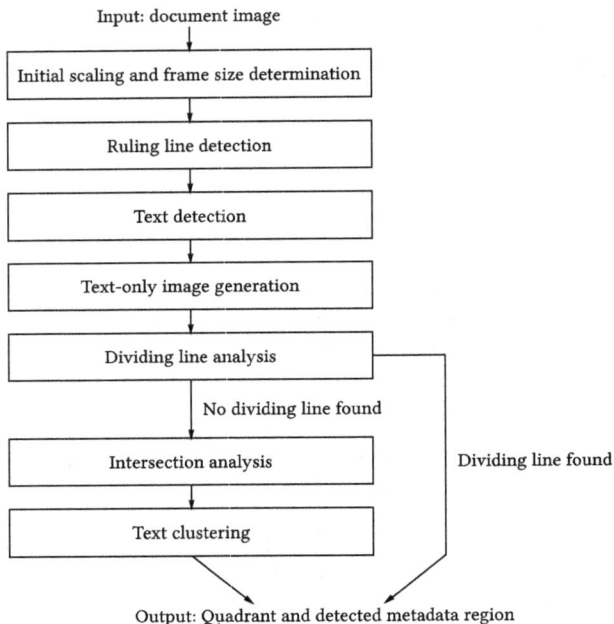

Figure 1: The processing pipeline

3 IMPLEMENTATION

This section presents our processing pipeline, which is tailored to processing documents from our domain as quickly as possible. The pipeline, which is illustrated in Figure 1, has two outputs: an integer representing one of the four quadrants of the page and an image of the detected metadata region to be fed to the OCR.

Initial scaling and frame size determination. The first step is to determine the area of the page that is occupied by the content, scale it if necessary, and perform binarization. All further processing steps work with monochrome pixels for speed. In order to estimate this area, erosion is first performed on a scaled-down (10%), binarized version of the image, in order to counteract potential noise distorting the result. The area occupied by the black pixels, when scaled back up to original coordinates, is referred to as the *frame size* in the rest of this paper. After determining the frame size, the initial image is scaled down by an integer factor using the nearest-neighbour method to achieve a resolution of approximately 200 dpi (assuming A1 size input) for OCR. Many of the following sub-steps use a smaller image of around 50 dpi to save on processing time.

Ruling line detection. A method based on RLSA is then used to detect horizontal and vertical lines, by filling in white gaps between black pixel runs if a sufficient number of black pixels in a sliding window of 5% of the frame size are encountered. To allow for minor skew, the rows of pixels above and below are also inspected. These lines, when visualized, already give a rough indication of the layout of the page (see Fig. 2 [top right]). We then subtract these ruling lines from the original binary image for text detection.

Text detection. The next stage is to detect potential text lines in the subtracted image. As we do not yet know the orientation of the page, this is performed in both horizontal and vertical directions. Classical RLSA is used, with a distance of 1% of the frame size, and connected component analysis is then performed. The components obtained from both horizontal and vertical directions are analysed, and very short lines (with a length less than two times the height) are discarded. Then, the average lengths of the remaining components are calculated; if the figure is higher for the vertical direction, the page is rotated by 90 degrees.[1] After rotation, the text heights of the horizontal lines are analysed and the average is calculated. Significantly larger or smaller lines are discarded; this "average text size" also provides a better measurement for the threshold values used in the subsequent phases of processing.

Text-only image generation. From these remaining line components, a *text mask* is created as a stencil to render only the text from the original image (see Fig. 2 [bottom left]). This is performed by painting the bounding rectangles of each connected component onto a new, white canvas, and filling them black. This image is then dilated. The pure text image is then generated by rendering only those parts of the original image for which there is a black pixel in the mask. This method helps avoid missing small parts of characters, which may not have been detected by using RLSA alone (see Fig. 2 [bottom right]).

completely forgo deskewing and can, in most cases, perform binarization using a simple global thresholding algorithm. As the ruling lines in our case are (almost) exactly horizontal or vertical, they can also be detected using simple morphological operations. Such early techniques as the Run Length Smoothing Algorithm (RLSA) and connected component analysis [7] are computationally inexpensive, and help keep runtime to a minimum.

A related topic to our problem is table recognition, of which there is a significant amount of work in the literature. A competition held at ICDAR 2013 [5] showed that commercial solutions, particularly from the OCR domain, achieved the highest performance, and that (unsurprisingly) ruled tables could in general be detected with higher accuracy than non-ruled tables using alignment and other visual cues for tabulation. However, such methods are not directly applicable to our problem, as the metadata in the legend area often has a less regular physical structure, and is not necessarily tabulated in such a way as to be recognizable as a table from its layout alone.

There have been relatively few publications in the scientific literature geared towards analysing architectural drawings as such. Systems such as [1, 2] have the much larger aim to automatically restruct a 2-D or 3-D model from the plot, and are not concerned with metadata. Furthermore, many architectural drawings featured in the literature have a significantly different layout to those in our dataset, in particular with reference to the legend area. The problem of text detection in scanned documents has also been addressed in the literature a long time ago [3], and more recently in moving images [4, 6]. Due to the fact that we also need to detect non-Latin text, we have chosen a more generic, RLSA-based approach that does not use word and/or sentence modelling.

---

[1]Note that we cannot detect rotations of 180 or 270 degrees in the preprocessing stage; this functionality is provided by Tesseract in the OCR stage.

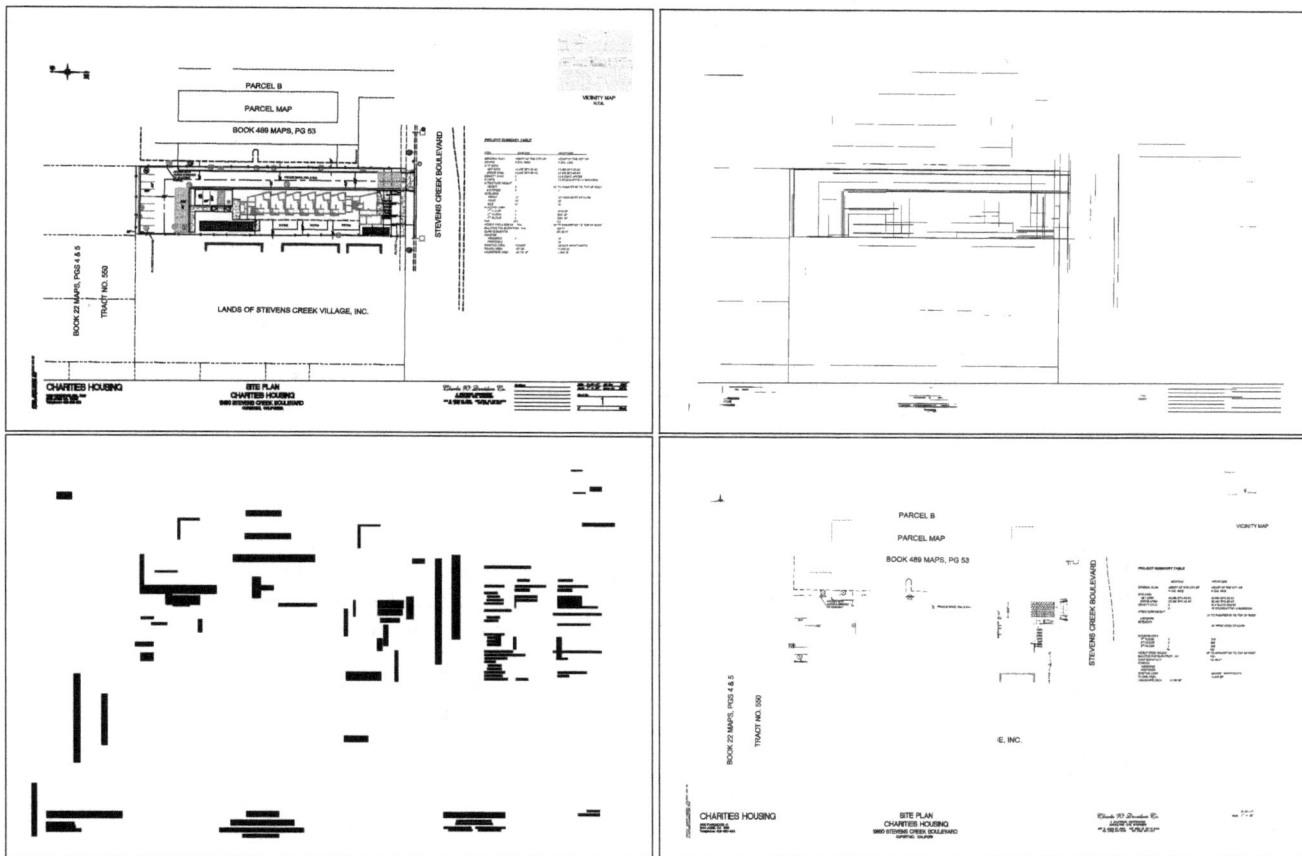

Figure 2: Sample architectural plot (top left) with the result of horizontal and vertical line-finding (top right), text mask (bottom left) and final extracted text (bottom right)

Dividing line analysis. We now proceed to determine whether the legend is separated from the remaining content by a dividing line. This is quite a common occurrence in the plots in our dataset (see Table 1). Based on the frame size, we search for a line that is sufficiently long, and close to one of the edges, but not touching it. There should also be sufficient text content between this line and the edge of the page, which we verify using the pure text image. If such a line is found, the complete area along the edge is chosen as the sub-region to be fed to the OCR. Because the edge spans two quadrants, the quadrant with the higher number of black pixels in the text-only image is chosen to be folded face-up.

Intersection analysis. If no such line is found, the system searches for structures that appear to be tabulated. We go back to the horizontal and vertical ruling lines that were detected previously. Starting with an all-black image, we mark each point at which two of these lines intersect with a grey pixel, its brightness representing the length of the longer of the two lines. The quadrant with the brightest sum of these points is then chosen as the quadrant to face up when folding.

Text clustering. Within this quadrant, we then look for the largest text region as the largest connected component in the text

mask determined above, after further dilation to merge neighbouring text lines. Given that the metadata often lies along one edge of a page, we also check to see if there is a significantly large region in a different quadrant that overlaps either horizontally or vertically. These regions are then used as input to the OCR procedure.

4 EXPERIMENTS

In order to verify the usefulness of our method, tests were performed on a dataset of 50 plots from various sources. Of these documents, 10 were scanned; the remaining 40 were born-digital PDF. For each plot, we determined whether the orientation and quadrant had been chosen correctly, and whether the complete legend metadata area had been passed to the OCR. In cases where more than one quadrant contained a roughly equal amount of metadata, either quadrant was evaluated as being correct. Cases where some metadata (even small amounts) was missing from the legend region were evaluated as being incorrect.

After investigating both ABBYY FineReader Corporate and Tesseract, we settled on version 3.04.01 of Tesseract. Its main benefit is that it is a much more lightweight application and therefore executes faster. As we perform our own layout analysis anyway, we have no need for the advanced methods employed by

	Dataset properties					Recognition results		
	Total plots	Scanned	Required rotation	Delineated legend	Ambiguous quadrant	Rotated Correctly	Quadrant det. correctly	Complete metadata region det. correctly
Number	50	10	12	39	2	43	39	30
Percentage	100%	20%	24%	78%	4%	86%	78%	60%

Table 1: Summary of dataset properties and results of recognition procedure

		Tesseract		
	Preprocessing	Rotation detection	Text recognition	Total
Minimum	0.96 s	1.05 s	0.78s	2.20 s
Mean	4.02 s	4.32 s	7.98 s	13.38 s
Median	3.26 s	3.12 s	7.05 s	11.94 s
Maximum	20.58 s	22.31 s	33.08 s	65.95 s
90% of plots below	6 s	7 s	18 s	28 s

Table 2: Timings

FineReader, not all of which can be disabled. It is, however, worth noting that FineReader is an off-the-shelf product and ABBYY offers other products that are better geared towards automated processing of larger document collections (Recognition Server and SDK).

As Tesseract normally only works with horizontal text and our preprocessing does not support rotations of 180 and 270 degrees, we first fed the OCR input to Tesseract's orientation detection mode. The results of the recognition procedure are shown in Table 1. The timings are shown in Table 2.

The results show that both rotation and quadrant detection were performed with very high accuracy. The accuracy for the metadata regions, at 60%, is also adequate for our interactive application, as it reduces the need for user interaction in scanning applications by more than half. The best results were obtained on plots with a fully delineated legend; further fine-tuning of the text clustering procedure is expected to yield an increase in accuracy for the remaining plots.

Most documents were processed within 15–20 s for the whole procedure, including OCR. These timings were obtained running on commodity hardware: an HP EliteBook 9470m with 16 GB RAM running Windows 7. This is a timeframe that is realistic for interactive, synchronous processing; further optimization of the algorithm and a move to more powerful hardware could see this figure reduced further.

A small number of plots required significantly longer — one required over a minute — to process. These were invariably all scanned documents with a high level of noise (e.g. blueprints with very low contrast), making binarization very difficult, even if more processing power and time were available. It seems that such documents trigger additional processing steps within Tesseract, resulting in a much longer processing time. Given the very limited time available, this is the one class of document that cannot realistically be processed by our system, and the user should be prompted to manually provide any required information in this case.

We are therefore planning on investigating Tesseract's layout analysis capabilities in more detail, in order to detect when such processing takes place and either bypass it or at least provide the user with a progress bar or similar feedback, allowing them to abort the process and enter the information manually if necessary. It should be noted that the layout analysis module is a recent addition to Tesseract and is actively being developed.

5 CONCLUSION/FURTHER WORK

In this paper, we have presented a system for performing document image analysis of architectural plots in order to detect their folding orientation and preprocess them so that the relevant metadata can be extracted via OCR within seconds. Our experiments have demonstrated the performance savings of our approach, and have shown that the recognition accuracy is adequate for our application. In addition to the proposed steps to further improve performance and accuracy, our next research step will deal with processing the OCR result and using it to identify the metadata in label and value pairs, delivering it in such a way that it can be integrated into our operator-controlled user interface.

A further direction of research is the use of machine learning methods instead of heuristics for performing the page analysis. Once we have a dataset of sufficient size with ground truth, this will be a direction worth pursuing.

REFERENCES

[1] Christian Ah-Soon and Karl Tombre. 1997. Variations on the Analysis of Architectural Drawings. In *ICDAR 1997: Proceedings of the Fourth International Conference on Document Analysis and Recognition*.

[2] S. Ahmed, M. Liwicki, M. Weber, and A. Dengel. 2011. Improved Automatic Analysis of Architectural Floor Plans. In *ICDAR 2011: Proceedings of the 11th International Conference on Document Analysis and Recognition*.

[3] L. A. Fletcher and R. Kasturi. 1988. A Robust Algorithm for Text String Separation from Mixed Text/Graphics Images. *IEEE Transactions on Pattern Analysis and Machine Intelligence* 10, 6 (1988).

[4] J. Gllavata, R. Ewerth, and B. Freisleben. 2004. Text Detection in Images Based on Unsupervised Classification of High-Frequency Wavelet Coefficients. In *ICPR 2004: Proceedings of the 17th International Conference on Pattern Recognition*.

[5] M. Goebel, T. Hassan, E. Oro, and G. Orsi. 2013. ICDAR 2013 Table Competition. In *ICDAR 2013: Proceedings of the 12th International Conference on Document Analysis and Recognition*.

[6] R. W. Lienhart and Frank Stuber. 1996. Automatic text recognition in digital videos. In *Image and Video Processing IV: SPIE Proceedings 2666*.

[7] G. Nagy, S. Seth, and M. Viswanathan. 1992. A prototype document image analysis system for technical journals. *Computer* 25, 7 (1992).

Preparation of Music Scores to Enable Hands-free Page Turning Based on Eye-gaze Tracking

Alexandra Bonnici
University of Malta
Malta
alexandra.bonnici@um.edu.mt

Stefania Cristina
University of Malta
Malta
stefania.cristina@um.edu.mt

Kenneth P. Camilleri
University of Malta
Malta
kenneth.camilleri@um.edu.mt

ABSTRACT

Digital copies of musical scores may be saved on tablet devices, compressing volumes of scores into a single portable device. Tablet screens are however typically smaller than printed sheet music such that the score needs to be resized for readability. This necessitates additional page turning which is made more complex when repeat instructions are used since these give rise to forward and backward page turns of the music. In this paper, we tackle this problem by first performing image analysis of the score in order to identify repeat instructions and hence flatten the score. Thus, the music player is presented the score as it should be played. We then propose the use of eye-gaze tracking to provide a hands-free page turning mechanism. Thus, the player remains in full control of when the page turn occurs. Through a preliminary study, we found that our proposed score flattening and eye-gaze page turning reduced the time spent navigating the page turns by 47% in comparison to available music score reading tools.

CCS CONCEPTS

• **Applied computing** → **Document analysis**; • **Human-centered computing** → *Pointing devices*;

KEYWORDS

Repeat detection, Flattened scores, page-turning, eye-gaze tracking

ACM Reference format:
Alexandra Bonnici, Stefania Cristina, and Kenneth P. Camilleri. 2017. Preparation of Music Scores to Enable Hands-free Page Turning Based on Eye-gaze Tracking. In *Proceedings of DocEng '17, Valletta, Malta, September 04-07, 2017*, 10 pages.
https://doi.org/10.1145/3103010.3103012

1 INTRODUCTION

Musical scores are available as digital documents through digital libraries which provide digital scans of sheet music of classical composers. Such libraries are a great asset to aspiring music players, providing immediate access to thousands of scores. The combination of digital scores and portable tablets allows music players to download sheet music directly to tablet devices and play the music off the tablet, hence compacting large volumes of works to a single, portable device [14]. This has, however, one major difficulty: music sheets are generally printed on A4 size paper whereas the digital tablet is generally smaller, causing difficulty in reading the music [2]. Music players in general expect sheet music to have stave sizes of $7.5 - 8.5$mm for reading at ease and although smaller sized scores may be read, this causes strain to the music reader [15]. To fit such a score size onto a smaller sized tablet, it would be necessary to pan the score or incur more page turns than what is usually required in a printed score.

Page turns are annoying at best, requiring the player to release one hand from the instrument to make the turn. Good quality printed scores attempt the music so that page turns coincide with a rest or pause in the music [14]. However, this is not always possible. Moreover, if the music is displayed on the reduced display space on the digital tablet device, the page turns will be more frequent and less likely to occur at convenient places on the score. Page turning is made more complex when taking into account that music may be abbreviated through the use of repeat mark symbols and written directions. Such repeats allow for smaller printed books by avoiding printing of sections of music that are the same [13]. This will require forward and backward jumps to sections of the music while playing.

Commercial software and hardware which addresses this problem does exist. For example, AirTurn[1] provides foot pedal systems which allow the music player to activate page turns by touching a foot pedal. While this is better than activating page turns with the hands, pianists, harpists and organists require the use of feet for the instrument foot pedals [14]. Automated page turning would therefore be more desirable. Tablet applications such as MobileSheets[2] and SheetMusic[3], PhonicsScore[4] and ClassicScore[5] provide such a facility by employing a scrolling score, where the rate of the scroll is determined from the tempo of a pre-recording of the music in applications such as PhonicsScore and ClassicsScore, or may be adjusted according to some preferred speed in MobileSheets and SheetMusic. Both methods are not ideal. In the first instance, the performer is restricted to perform the music at the specified speed. In the second instance, the player is restricted to a strict time for the duration of the piece which, often times, is not stylistic. Moreover, systems such as MobileSheets and SheetMusic do not cater for repeats in the music since the applications scroll through the pages sequentially without taking into account any flow information present in the score.

---

[1]http://www.airturn.com/
[2]http://www.zubersoft.com/mobilesheets/
[3]http://www.musicnotes.com/apps/
[4]http://phonicsscore.com/
[5]http://blog.naver.com/earthcores

An ideal system, would have two modes of operation; a performing mode and a browsing mode. In the performing mode, the system should present the score as it should be played rather than as it is written. This would allow the player to execute repeats in the music with little effort. In this mode, the player should be able to control the music flow without removing the hands from the instrument. In the browsing mode of operation, the player would be able to browse through the music before actually performing it. In this mode, the player should be able to quickly skim read through the score, select very short excerpts of the piece for quick study. In this mode, the player would typically be playing only short fragments of the music if at all and thus, navigation through the score using hand gestures would be more natural.

In this paper we focus on the performing mode of operation and document our investigation in digital music sheet representation, flattening the score to eliminate the need of backward navigation while playing. Moreover, we propose the use of eye-gaze tracking to give the performer full, hands-free control of the music score flow while playing. For the scope of this work, we focus on sheet music written for keyboard instruments. The rest of the paper is organised as follows: Section 2 gives an overview of related literature, Section 3 presents our proposed image preparation algorithms, Section 4 the proposed page-turning approach, Section 5 presents the evaluation methodology, Section 6 the results obtained, while Section 8 concludes the paper.

2 LITERATURE REVIEW

Since digital music is not limited to the traditional page-based structure, it is possible to take advantage of the digital device and present the music in a continuous fashion such that the next page content are made visible while the current page is still on display. For such digital sheet music systems to be successful, the player's experience must be taken into account. This will for example, restrict the size of the score such that music players may read the music with ease [2, 15]. A successful digital sheet music system must also take into account that players must remain well aware of the context of the music they are playing. This would exclude instantaneous jumps between sections of the music and would require thought on visualisations and the presentation of the music [14].

Several options for digital score visualisations have been proposed in the literature. The simplest method offers the presentation of sheet music as a continuous stream, either horizontally with the score scrolling across width of the screen, or vertically with the score scrolling across the length of the screen. Such digital layouts however are not popular with music players since it is easier to lose track of the current position on the score [2]. Alternative representations, where the score is kept static until a page turn activates overwriting old material with new have been proposed. Here, several visualisations are possible, for example, a two page system may be used with the page turn shifting the whole page to the left such that the left hand page always displays the current score page to be played while the right hand page displays the next one [5]. The screen size of a typical, portable digital tablet however does not allow for the display of two pages simultaneously without reducing the page size beyond what can be comfortably read by the music player. Alternative digital music systems which involve displaying a single page make use of the fact that the digital screen may be divided into two parts, allowing for split-page turning whereby, after some time delay, the top part of the page can display new content while the bottom part of the page retains the current content, before this too is updated. In order to indicate the change in content, visualisations such as page peeling, or highlight lines have been used [2, 5, 14].

The literature describes a variety of ways with which a page turn may be brought into effect. These include tapping on the screen [12], the use of time delays [2] as well as the use of additional hardware such as foot pedals [6], bite switches [1] and through voice-command triggers [11]. Such methods however all involve active user interaction. One approach towards automating the page turn is to use the live audio stream to trigger the page turn. This can be achieved by a priori annotating the sheet music with pre-recorded audio segments such that when a live performance matches this segment, the page turn is activated [12]. Alternatively, a spectrogram of the audio signal is matched to the score using deep neural networks, linking the score image to the music in the audio file. This allows for the display of the music image according to the current audio segment. These approach are however limited to music whose tempo is similar to that with which the system is trained [8].

To compound matters further, classical music is sometimes divided into sections and, depending on the form of the music, some of these sections may be repeated. When this occurs, for the sake of compactness of presentation in the printed score, repeat signs and instructions are used [13]. For example, music written in *ternary* form, such as the classical *minuet* consists of three sections, the third of which can be an exact repeat of the first [18]. Rather than rewriting the first section, such a repeat can be indicated in the score by a *da Capo - Fine* pair. When repeated sections are long, these would require that the music player turns pages backwards to the start of the section to be repeated. Since digital displays divide the printed scores into sub-pages for a comfortable fit on the device display space, any such repeat instructions may require going back several pages, aggravating the problem. To resolve the problem, automated page turning can be combined with a system of bookmark annotations to allow the player to go back and forth in the document with greater ease [13]. However, instantaneous jumps from page to page in the music considered distracting to music players [14]. This supports the concept of a flattened score in which all repeats of the musical score are expanded [13]. Such a flattened score may be obtained by representing the sheet music using a formal language representation, allowing the flattened score to be checked for errors in the interpretation of the repeat instructions [7, 13]. These repeat instructions are however obtained, not directly from the score, but by means of annotations which the music player must insert to the score which indicate the positions of the repeat signs and the sections which must be repeated. The localisation of repeat symbols may be automated using optical music character recognition algorithms such as that described in [17]. In this algorithm, the Hough transform is used to remove the horizontal stave lines, following which, systems are detected through connected component analysis. Bar lines are then found by observing that these consist of vertical columns along the system

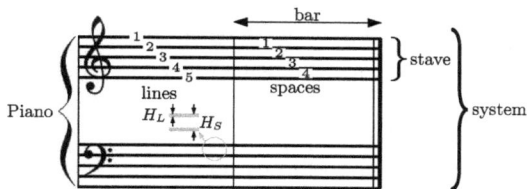

Figure 1: Music is written on a stave consisting of five equally spaced lines of thickness H_L with a separation of H_S. Thus, the stave has a height of $5H_L + 4H_S$. The single barline spanning all staves groups the staves into a system.

having at least 75% black pixels and further differentiation between bar lines and repeat symbols is made by searching for two dots adjacent to the detected bar lines [17]. In this method however, no distinction is made between the different repeat symbols nor is there any distinction made between any potential first and second endings such that while the user will not need to mark the position of the repeat symbols, the music player must still annotate the music in order to obtain the flattened score.

3 IMAGE PREPARATION OF SCORES

This section describes the image processing algorithms which prepares the scanned image of the score for eye-gaze based page turning. This includes segmenting the score first into systems, then into bars before performing symbol recognition to determine instructions related to the musical flow. Domain knowledge is then used to flatten the score.

3.1 Score segmentation into systems

Music is written on staves consisting of five equally spaced lines of line thickness H_L and line spacing H_S [10]. When music written on different staves is to be played simultaneously, the staves are grouped into systems as shown in Figure 1. The system is therefore the natural point at which the page is segmented [3]. In music notation, the system is easily identified by means of the single vertical line running across all staves as illustrated in Figure 1. This line assures that all the staves from a single connected component. However, additional performance directions such as dynamic markings, pedalling, tempo and fingering indications may appear as separate components, above, beneath or within the system [9] such that a connected component analysis would fail to pick these up as part of the system. If a horizontal projection is applied to the manuscript, the stave lines will aggregate to form columns of width equal to $4H_S + 5H_L$ [4]. Any such column may therefore be considered as a stave and tuples of such staves, depending on the number of staves per system, may be grouped to form the system. While this ensures that unconnected symbols within the system are grouped with the system, as illustrated in Figure 2, the separation between the systems is not always consistent, nor are the systems completely separable on the horizontal projection.

Thus we first find the connected components whose width is greater than $T = {}^3/_4W$, where W is the page width. This identifies those components which are most likely to be candidate systems. For each connected component whose width is smaller than T, we

Figure 2: Systems 4, 7 and 8 are taken from the same page illustrating how the separation between staves may vary across the page. In addition, systems may partially overlap.

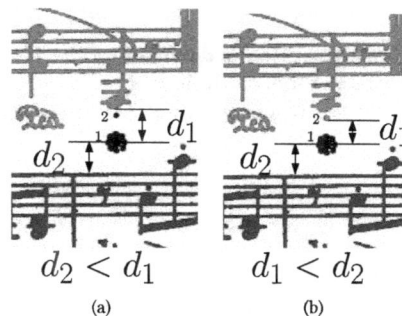

$d_2 < d_1$ (a) $d_1 < d_2$ (b)

Figure 3: Extract from a score with the pedal mark (1) and the staccato dot (2) disassociated with either system. (a) Parsing symbols in ascending order groups the pedal mark with the bottom system (blue) since $d_2 < d_1$. (b) Parsing symbols in descending will first group the staccato dot with the upper system (red) such that, at the pedal symbol, $d_1 < d_2$, grouping the pedal mark correctly. Irrespective of the order, the staccato dot will always be grouped with upper system and we consider this grouping as stable.

compute the distance to the closest identified system, grouping that component with the system. Since multiple instructions may be associated with a given note in the system, musical notation is at times cascaded vertically. When this happens, the notation may be in fact closer to the systems directly above or beneath the system which it should be associated with. The order with which the notation symbols are processed will therefore affect the association of the symbol with the system as illustrated in Figure 3.

To resolve this, we number each connected component of width smaller than T and, going through these components in ascending order, we find the system closest to that component, grouping the component with that system to create a system grouping S_a. We then repeat the process but parse the components in descending order to create a system grouping S_d. The symbol notations

Figure 4: Barlines and repeat signs used in written music (a) a barline; (b) a section break; (c) the start of a repeat section; (d) the end of a repeat section and the start of another; (e) an alternative for (d); (f) the end of a repeat section; (g) the double barline marking the end of the music

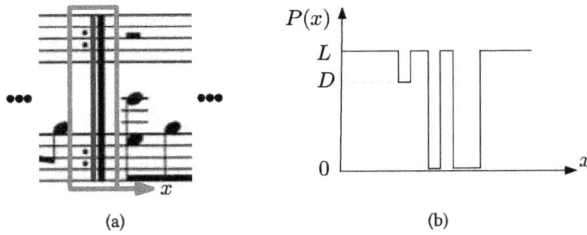

Figure 5: (a) A vertical line is detected by the Hough Transform as indicated in blue. A window of width $5H_S$ is centered on this line. (b) A vertical projection of the grey levels in this window.

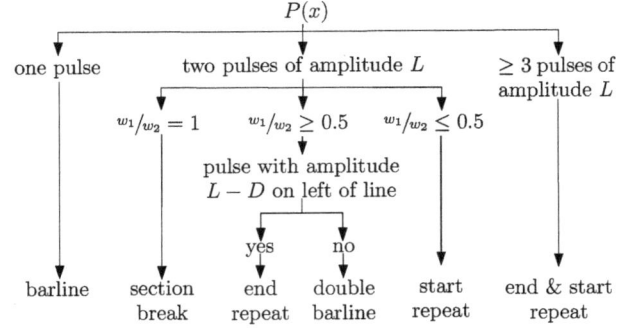

Figure 6: The classification of the detected vertical lines as barlines, section breaks, double barlines or repeats where w_1 and w_2 refers to the width of the first and second pulses with amplitude L

which are common to S_a and S_d, that is, $S_a \cap S_b$ are considered as stable and associated with their respective systems. A further nearest-neighbour association is then performed on the remaining components, using the new, stable system labels.

3.2 Barline and repeat identification

Vertical lines are used to divide the music into units. The smallest unit is the bar and this is identified by single vertical line called a *barline* (Fig. 4(a)) whose width we will denote by w. The end of the piece will be indicated with a *double barline* (Fig. 4(g)) consisting of two adjacent lines with the leftmost line having a thickness of $2w$ or greater. Section lines (Fig. 4(b)), that is two adjacent lines both of thickness w divide the longer piece into smaller parts or movements, while repeat lines (Fig. 4(c - f)) enclose those bars which the player must repeat. Here the lines are combined with repeat dots and the arrangement of thin-thick line pairs and the dots are used to indicate the start or end of the repeat sections.

To flatten the score, all of these dividing lines must be identified. We do so by applying the Hough transform, restricting the $[\rho, \theta]$ parameter space to $\theta = \pi \pm T_\theta$ where T_θ is a threshold on the line orientation to allow for some tolerance due to page deformations while scanning the document. Since note stems will also be detected by the Hough transform, we set a threshold T_P on the length of the detected lines. Since barlines span across the system, the Hough lines detected at barlines are expected to have length greater than $T_P = N_S(5H_L + 4H_S)$, where H_L is the line thickness, H_S is the spacing between the lines and N_S is the number of staves in the system with $N_S = 2$ for piano sheet music.

Once detected, the next step is to determine the type of line detected. This can be done on basis of the number of vertical lines

involved, the line thickness and the position of the repeat dots. To this extent, we a window around the detected vertical line and obtain a vertical projection $P(x) = \sum_y I(x, y)$ from this window, where $I(x, y)$ is the score image containing a single system; x spans the width of the window; and y spans the height of the window. Since the separation between pairs of lines in double barlines and repeats is typically smaller than the stave line spacing H_S, the window width is set to $5H_S$ while the height of the window is set to the height of the system. In this projection, $P(x) = 0$ when x corresponds to a column containing a vertical line. In contrast, when x corresponds to a column containing only stave lines, $P(x) = L = Y - 5H_L N_S$ where Y is the height of the window. Similarly, when repeat dots are present, $P(x) = D = L - 2dN_S$ where d is the diameter of the repeat dots. Thus, as shown in Figure 5(b), $P(x)$ will have a number of pulses whose width and amplitude are indicative of the type of line present as illustrated in Figure 6.

3.3 Written repeat instructions

Composers may include additional repeat instructions either as written instructions or as a combination of text and symbols. One such instruction is the *volta* repeats consisting of the *prima volta* and *secunda volta* and which are represented by numbered square brackets as shown in Figure 7. In this case, the player omits the whole of the *prima* section at the second playing, proceeding directly to the *secunda* section. Therefore, when a repeat symbol is detected, we check, by means of template matching, for two opposite facing right-angled corners as shown in Figure 7 to determine if this repeat is a *volta* repeat. If this is the case, we would need to locate the start of the *prima* section since the length of this section may vary. Thus, we check the previous bars for an open-facing right-angled corner until the start of the *prima* section is located.

Other written instructions typically found in classical music are the *Da Capo* and *Dal Segno* instructions which are used when music players are required to repeat sections of music. At a *Da Capo*, the player would restart playing from the beginning of the piece while a *Dal Segno* instructs the player to restart from the 𝄋 symbol. The *Da Capo* and *Dal Segno* instructions, which may be abbreviated as D. C. and D. S. respectively, may be identified by using a standard OCR

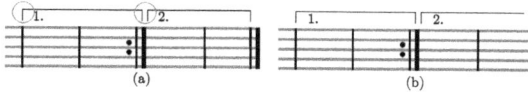

Figure 7: prima and secunda signs. The part of the brackets used as templates used for locating the prima and secunda sections are circled (a) a closed secunda sign; (b) an open-ended secunda sign

algorithm [19], limiting the search for text to the area beneath the end repeat and double bar lines, where these instructions expected to be found. In the case of *Dal Segno* instructions, template matching is performed on the score preceding the *Dal Segno* instruction to locate the *Dal Segno* symbol and hence the start of the repeated section.

Both *Da Capo* and *Dal Segno* instructions may be accompanied by either an *al Fine* or *al Coda* instructions. These instruct the music player to either terminate the repeat at the word *Fine* or to jump to a concluding *Coda* section indicated by the symbol ⊕. If the text *al Fine* is observed, the OCR is used to search for the term *Fine* at each of the preceding double bar line, section break or end repeat sign. On the other hand, if the term *al Coda* is observed, we need to search the preceding bars for the ⊕ and the start of subsequent systems for either the ⊕ symbol or the term *coda*.

A common variant to the *Da Capo* term in classical music occurs in Minuet dance form, which typically consists of a *minuet* and a *trio*, with a repeat of the *minuet* section [18]. In such cases, the *Da Capo* instruction is often altered to *Minuet Da Capo*. Thus, if a *Da Capo* term is identified, we also search for the term *Minuet* adjacent to it and if so, after the repeat, the music is terminated at the section break even if no *Fine* instruction is observed.

3.4 Flattening the Score

Once the musical flow instructions are identified, we proceed to flatten the score, writing out repeated sections in full. We start by first identifying the different movements by separating the score at the double bar lines. This allows us to treat each movement as a separate entity which is essential for flow control since the start of a new movement refreshes the reference to the start of the piece for all repeat instructions. We then find each end repeat and pair these up with the first start repeat preceding it. We do this sequentially in order to cater for the possibility of nested repeats. In doing so, we identify bars that must be repeated and insert these into the score. We note that in some instances, the first repeat of the score is an end repeat, with no matching start repeat. In such a case, the music player would repeat the music from the beginning of the score and thus, we insert an invisible start repeat sign at the beginning of the first bar. In the case of the *prima* and *secunda volta* repeats, the bars in the system that should not be played are grayed out in order to provide the music player with context within the flattened score.

Once all repeat symbols are flattened, we turn our focus on the written repeat instructions, repeating the sections according to the written terms. Note that music players would typically omit all other repeats when executing *da Capo* (and its *Minuet* variant) or *dal Segno* repeats and thus, in flattening the score we too omit these,

rewriting the section of the score as presented in the original, unflattened version. The only exception is when *prima* and *secunda volta* repeats are involved, in which case, the *prima* bars are greyed out since only the second ending is performed.

4 AUTOMATED PAGE TURNING

In order to fit the score onto the screen display size of a tablet, we opt to display the score two systems at a time which provides for readable score at the distance typically used when playing the instrument. This would require frequent page turns which we propose to automate using eye-gaze tracking techniques. Music players scan the music they are playing continuously and through the technique often referred to as looking-ahead, often times briefly fixate on notes ahead of those being executed before reverting back to the notes currently being played [16]. This looking-ahead implies that during the execution of the piece, there may be a discrepancy between the note fixated upon and that being played. This discrepancy, known as the eye-hand span, is typically of a few beats in duration and this may vary from music player to music player based on the skill level as well as with the tempo and difficulty of the piece [16]. As a cause of this discrepancy, music players often prefer to execute the page turn before the end of the page. To cater for this in our automation of the page turn, we opt for a half-page turning approach in which the system being played remains static while the other is refreshed to show the subsequent system. Since we know that the music player may look ahead, it is desirable that as the execution approaches the end of the system, the new system is already on display to allow for continuous reading. Moreover, we note that although the eye-gaze may be detected on the new system, the execution may still be of the previous system and therefore it is desirable that the change in the system does not distract the music player.

The movement of the music players gaze while reading the music therefore does not flow in a smooth scanning pattern and the recorded eye-gaze position would contain a considerable amount of impulses, where such impulses may trigger accidental page turns. Pianists in particular, shift their gaze from the score to the keyboard several times while playing in order to find keys, particularly in instances when there are large intervals between the written notes which require large leaps in the hand position on the keyboard. As a result, the eye-gaze of the pianist may exhibit strong deviations in the vertical direction. We therefore keep track only of the horizontal position of the eye-gaze, noting that there should be a change in the horizontal displacement Δx equal to the page width when the eye travels from the end of one line to the start of the next. Thus upon detecting that the music player has begun reading a new line, the page-turner waits until the eye-gaze reaches the middle of the line in order to refresh the previous line with the subsequent line. The page turning algorithm is thus given by Algorithm 1. For the purpose of this study, the eye-gaze tracking is performed using an available eye-gaze tracker system, namely the SMI RED500. The SMI RED500 samples the eye-gaze at 500Hz, by projecting infra-red illumination onto the eye region and inferring the eye movements from the position of the glint reflecting off the surface of the cornea. The user sits at a typical operating distance of 80cm-90cm from a

Figure 8: The setup used for evaluation

Algorithm 1 Page-turner algorithm

Input: Systems S, System width W
$n \leftarrow 2$
$x_0 \leftarrow$ initial eye-gaze horizontal position
PAGE TURN FLAG $\leftarrow$ FALSE
while $n < |S| - 1$ **do**
    $x_{i+1} \leftarrow$ current eye gaze horizontal position
    $\Delta x \leftarrow x_{i+1} - x_i$
    if $\Delta x > W$ **then**
        PAGE TURN FLAG $\leftarrow$ TRUE
    end if
    if $x > 0.5 * W$ and PAGE TURN FLAG is TRUE **then**
        Display System S_{n+1} instead of System S_{n-1}
        PAGE TURN FLAG $\leftarrow$ FALSE
        $n \leftarrow n + 1$
    end if
end while

17″ monitor screen, and performs head movements within a tracking head box having dimensions of 40×20cm at 70cm distance from the eye-gaze tracker, as specified by SMI. The monitor was placed on the top board of a digital piano with the gaze tracker just in front of it as shown in Figure 8. The score image was displayed in a 10″ window on the screen to emulate the smaller screen size of a tablet. The same setup was used by the violin and euphonium players.

5 EVALUATION METHODOLOGY

In order to evaluate the proposed page turning algorithms, we first evaluate the performance of the image pre-processing steps, namely the system segmentation and the repeat detection which allow us to flatten the score. Following this, we then evaluate the efficacy of the eye-gaze page turning algorithm. This section, details the evaluation methodology.

5.1 Segmentation into systems

We perform the system segmentation algorithm on eight different piano pieces containing in total 206 systems spread over 33 pages of music. The segmented systems were compared to the systems obtained after manually segmenting the pages, using the sensitivity and specificity measures [17] to determine the performance of the system segmentation algorithm. We compare the results obtained with those obtained from the horizontal projection technique described in [4].

5.2 Bar and repeat identification

To evaluate the barline and repeat detection algorithm, we manually annotate the position of the barlines, section breaks and repeats and compare these to those detected by our proposed algorithm, again using the sensitivity and specificity as performance measures. In this case, in order to compare our results with the most recent barline and repeat detection algorithm described in the literature, we use Beethoven's Piano Sonata Op 2 No 1, specifically, that available at the IMSLP[6] library since this was used for evaluation in [17]. This sonata has 493 bars, which, in this particular edition, are spread over 104 systems, covering 17 pages of music. The sonata has three double bar lines marking the end of the first, second and last movements, one section break within the last movement and eight repeat line signs, of which, two are repeat section initialisations, four are repeat section terminations and two mark the end of a repeat section and the start of another.

5.3 Score flattening

To evaluate the performance of the score flattening, algorithm was applied to 12 piano music pieces and 4 violin pieces, comparing the sequence of bars in the flattened score with that obtained by manually labelling the sequence of bar numbers which the performer is expected to play assuming that all repeats are to be observed.

5.4 Eye-gaze as a page turning mechanism

Here we would like to answer three questions namely (a) does the eye-gaze page turning modality make a difference in the flow of the music in comparison to other page-turning modalities (b) are music players receptive to the eye-gaze page turning modality and is this easy to use (c) are music players receptive to the use of flattened scores. To answer the first of these questions, we perform a preliminary quantitative study during which the 12 piano music pieces listed in Table 3 are performed to determine whether eye-gaze tracking may be used to execute page-turns seamlessly. We record the performance and manually measure the time elapsed between the execution of the last note on a page and the first note on the subsequent page, noting any pauses which interrupt the music flow. Moreover, in order to compare the performance of the eye-gaze page-turner with existing music display systems, we also performed the same 12 pieces using a manual page turning modality namely MobileSheets where the page turns required willed gestures and a timed scrolling modality, namely SheetMusic, where the music player has limited control over the page turns. We hypothesise that eye-gaze page turning will reduce the pauses incurred at page turns in comparison with page turning modalities based on hand gestures or timed scrolling.

To answer the second and third questions, we conduct a qualitative study, using the methodology reported in [17], that is, users were presented with previously unseen music sheets and asked to perform these using our eye-gaze page turning algorithm, the manual page turning and the timed scrolling page turning modalities. Music players were recruited by inviting students and teachers

---

[6]http://hz.imslp.info/files/imglnks/usimg/5/59/IMSLP05524-Btsn2_1.pdf

Table 1: Results of the system segmentation

	Sensitivity	Specificity
Horizontal Projection [4]	85.98	98.59
Proposed Method	99.97	99.99

Table 2: Results of the bar line and repeat detection. Columns 2 and 3 are reproduced from [17] (Table 1)

	Vertical Projections [17]		Proposed Method	
	Sensitivity	Specificity	Sensitivity	Specificity
Bar lines	99.8	100	99.4	100
Repeats	87.5	87.5	91.7	100

from a local arts schools and included eight pianists, a violinist and an euphonium player. In order to gauge their musicianship as well as their familiarity with music display software, participants were first asked to fill in a short survey. Through this survey, participants were asked to select from a list of 12 pieces, three pieces with which they were unfamiliar. This was done to ensure that during the study, the participants would be reading the music rather than playing from memory. Furthermore, in order to ensure that increasing familiarity with the piece of music does not affect the participant evaluation of a particular application, the order with which the applications are presented is randomised such that each different piece of music is first played with a different music application.

6 RESULTS

6.1 Segmentation into systems

Of the 33 pages of music which were segmented into systems, 202 out of the 206 (98%) systems were segmented successfully. In the four incorrectly segmented systems, one pedalling indication and one tempo direction were associated with the wrong system. In comparison, using the horizontal projection approach described in [4], there were five pages in which different systems were grouped together in their entirety. Table 1 gives the sensitivity and specificity values obtained by the proposed segmentation method, comparing these with that obtained using the horizontal projection approach. This shows that the proposed approach improves the segmentation of the sheet music into systems.

6.2 Segmentation into bars

Table 2 gives the results of our barline and repeat sign identifiers, comparing these to those using the vertical projection approach reported in [17]. We note that while there is a slight drop in the bar lines identified, having detected one less than those detected using the vertical projections, our approach fares better in the detection of repeat signs, missing just one of the nine repeat signs in the score. Moreover, the vertical projection approach described in [17] makes no distinction between single bar-lines, section breaks and double barlines or between different repeat symbols. In our approach, all detected lines were distinguished and correctly labelled.

6.3 Flattening the score

The 12 scores used in this evaluation contain 11 symbolic repeats, seven *volta* repeats, one *Minuetto Da Capo* repeat, one *Da Capo al Fine* repeat and one *Dal Segno al Coda* repeat. The flow diagram of two of these 12 scores used in this evaluation, namely *Sundial Dreams* and *Minuet*. In these scores, as with all 12 scores, the sequence of bars agreed with the manually labelled bars at all textual and symbolic repeats.

Consider the song *Sundial Dreams* as an example. This contains two *volta* repeats, one of which is nested within a *dal segno al coda* repeat. At the second bar of the music, the pianist encounters the first repeat symbol which matches the *prima volta* repeat at bar 17. The 18th bar on the flattened score will therefore correspond to the second bar on the written score. Bars 19 to 32 on the flattened score will likewise correspond to bars three to 16 of the written score, bringing back the pianist to the *volta* repeat. The pianist must then skip the *prima* at bar 17 of the written score and proceed to the *secunda* at bar 18 on the written score. Bars 35 to 66 of the flattened score will then correspond to bars 19 to 51 of the written score. Here the pianist encounters the second *volta* repeat and thus the 67th bar on the flattened score will correspond to the 36th bar of the printed score. Likewise, bars 68 to 81 on the flattened score will correspond to bars 37 to 50. As with the previous *volta* repeat, the flattened score will then skip the *prima* bar to go directly to the *secunda* bar, here encountering the *Dal Segno al Coda* instruction. Thus bar 83 on the flattened score will correspond to bar 19 of the written score, where the 𝄋 symbol was first encountered. The music proceeds until at bar 98 on the flattened score, corresponding to bar 33 on the written score the *al Coda* instruction is encountered, thereby at bar 99, the flattened score jumps to bar 53 of the written score. Thus, the 72 bars of the printed score are successfully flattened to 118 bars.

6.4 Eye-gaze as a page turning mechanism

Table 3 gives the duration of the recorded pauses for each of the three modalities evaluated. Since our proposed system presents the music player with a flattened score, for purposes of page turning, the music effectively has no repeats. In contrast, in the manual page turning and timed-scrolling modalities, the music player must navigate the repeats. We therefore distinguish between pieces which had repeats and others which did not, factoring out the pauses incurred at repeats in the pieces that contained them.

A single factor ANOVA was performed to test the hypothesis that the observed differences in the pauses is significant. The test was carried out at the 5% level of significance and was done twice: the first time excluding all pauses at repeats and the second time including all pauses. The p-values obtained are of 4×10^{-9} when the pauses include those incurred by repeats and 8×10^{-8} when these exclude the repeats. Thus, we can say that there is a significant difference between the observed pauses of the three modalities. A multiple comparison test between the three modalities using the Bonferroni correction yields the results shown in Table 4. This shows that there is a significant difference in the pauses incurred at page turns between the three different modalities. Excluding the pauses due to repeats, the eye-gaze tracking modality causes an average pause of 1.27s, the manual page turning an average pause

Table 3: Results obtained in the pilot study which compares the time delay incurred at page turns for three page-turning modalities namely the proposed eye-gaze page turning, the manual page turning based on hand gestures and the timed scrolling page turning modality. This table also shows the number of times a page turn incurred a delay.

| | | Average pause time in seconds | | | | | |
| | | including repeats | | | excluding repeats | | |
	Name	Eye-gaze	Manual	Timed	Eye-gaze	Manual	Timed
Pieces with repeats	Sundial Dreams (Kern)	1.29	2.84	5.42	1.29	1.88	3.44
	Maple Leaf Rag (Joplin)	1.64	2.38	3.63	1.64	2.19	3.15
	Columbine Sings (Martinu)	1.67	3.45	4.22	1.67	3.10	3.88
	Song for Sienna (Crain)	1.00	2.76	3.56	1.00	2.53	2.86
	Gavotte (Grieg)	1.50	2.33	5.00	1.50	2.00	2.78
	Gnosienne No. 1 (Satie)	1.20	2.67	1.58	1.20	2.50	1.50
Pieces without repeats	Papillon Noirs (Massenet)	1.50	2.46	3.00	1.50	2.46	3.00
	My Father's Favorite (Doyle)	1.00	2.44	2.90	1.00	2.44	2.90
	Prelude in C (Bach)	1.00	2.50	3.00	1.00	2.50	3.00
	Golliwog's Cakewalk (Debussy)	2.00	2.67	4.92	2.00	2.67	4.92
	Moonshadows on the Mountain (Linn)	1.50	2.56	3.57	1.50	2.56	3.57
	Nocturne in C ♯ minor (Chopin)	0	1.38	5.10	0	1.38	5.10

Table 4: Result of the Bonferroni multiple comparison test.

| | p-value | |
Comparison	incl. repeats	excl. repeats
Eye-gaze v.s. manual	1.1×10^{-3}	1.4×10^{-3}
Eye-gaze v.s. timed-scrolling	2.6×10^{-8}	4.5×10^{-8}
Manual v.s. timed-scrolling	3.3×10^{-3}	3.4×10^{-3}

Table 5: Comparison of length of the pauses incurred due to repeats and at regular page turns. Durations are in seconds.

| | Non-repeats | | At repeats | | |
Modality	mean	variance	mean	variance	p-value
Eye-gaze	1.42	0.43	n/a	n/a	n/a
Manual	2.30	1.01	5.00	5.09	2.3×10^{-5}
Timed	3.22	3.33	8.75	13.30	1.8×10^{-7}

of 2.5s and the timed-scrolling an average pause of 3.7s. Thus, we may say that the proposed eye-gaze turning modality reduces the delay at the page turns by 47% with respect to the manual page turning modality and by 61% with respect to the timed-scrolling modality.

We are also interested in identifying whether flattening the score would cause any significant effect on the pauses incurred at the page turns. This will be the case if the pauses at repeats are significantly longer than those at regular page turns. Thus, for those pieces that had repeats, we compare the pauses due to the repeat instructions with those due to regular page turns within the same piece. These are tabulated in Table 5. Note that this comparison can only be performed on the manual and timed-scrolling modalities since the eye-gaze page turning modality uses the flattened score and in effect, there is no difference between the progression of the music at repeats. A hypothesis test, performed at the 5% level of significance was carried out in order to determine whether the observed difference is significant. The probability values, given in Table 5 indicate that the observed difference in the duration of the pauses is indeed significantly different. Thus, it is expected that by flattening the score, the length of the pauses at page turns should be reduced.

6.4.1 User evaluation. Table 6 gives the instrument, musicianship level and average pause length at page turns for each participant in the user study. This demonstrates that the proposed

eye-gaze page turning may be used by music players of different levels of experience with digital scores and of different musicianship levels. Moreover, all users experienced shorter pauses with the eye-gaze page turning modality than with the other modalities as was expected after the preliminary quantitative study. The participant response to the different modalities are summarised in Table 7.

7 DISCUSSION

Although the main focus of this paper is music for keyboard instruments, the image processing algorithms used to analyse the score were kept as generic as possible in order for these to be applicable to a wider range of instruments. The system separation algorithm can be used with all classical music scores since irrespective of the number of instruments being played, all staves of all instruments will be linked together with one single barline at the start of each system. This is sufficient to identify the system as a single connected component. The identification of barlines and repeat signs is applicable to a subset of these scores, namely scores which are written for instruments of the same family such as string quartets, where the barline will span all staves and the threshold used to distinguish between barlines and note stems will still be applicable. When applied to single stave solo instruments, the barline detection algorithm may result in many false positives because it will be

Table 6: Participant demographics and the average pause length over the three pieces performed with the three different page turning modalities

Participant	Instrument	Level	Used digital scores before	Average pause length (seconds)		
				Eye-gaze	Manual	Timed-scrolling
1	Piano	Diploma	No	1.54	2.00	2.06
2	Piano	Diploma	No	1.75	3.00	4.67
3	Piano	Advanced	Yes	0.50	1.50	1.67
4	Piano	Advanced	Yes	1.34	1.67	3.73
5	Piano	Advanced	Yes	2.25	3.38	3.72
6	Piano	Intermediate	No	1.00	2.00	2.38
7	Piano	Intermediate	No	1.50	4.00	5.67
8	Piano	Intermediate	No	1.37	2.25	2.67
9	Euphonium	Intermediate	No	1.50	2.42	3.00
10	Violin	Advanced	Yes	0.00	5.20	2.75

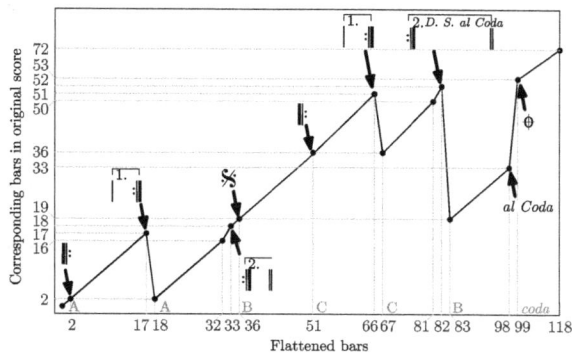

(a)

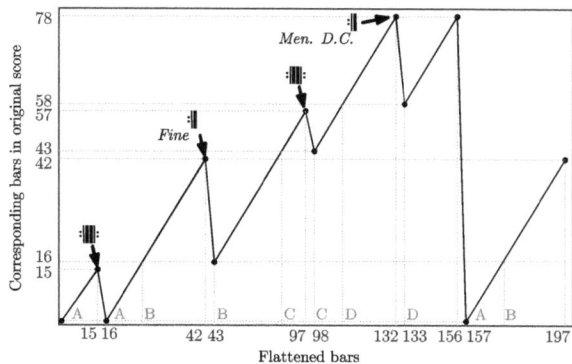

(b)

Figure 9: Flow diagram of two scores (a) *Sundial Dreams* by Michael Kern and (b) The *Minuet* from Beethoven's Piano Sonata No. 1. (Letters in red indicate the flow pattern using musical notation)

possible to find note stems which are longer than the barlines. To fully adapt the barline detection algorithm to single stave solos, the image processing algorithms must also take into consideration the note heads, a direction which we intend to explore in future work.

Table 7: User responses after evaluating performing three music pieces using the three page turning modalities.

Would you use the page-turning modality again?			
	Eye-gaze	Manual	Timed-scrolling
Yes	9	9	1
No	0	1	7
Maybe	1	0	2

Rank the modalities according to preference			
	Eye-gaze	Manual	Timed-scrolling
first	10	0	0
second	0	9	1
third	0	1	9

Did you prefer flattened scores or scores with repeats?	
flattened scores	10
scores with repeats	0

The flattened scores are being displayed using two systems at a time. While this displays keyboard music at a readable size, displayed in this manner, music for single-stave solo instruments would have too much redundant white space. This could be remedied if the user were to be allowed to select the number of systems to display on a page. The eye-gaze page turning can be easily adapted to such a scenario by adjusting the number of large right-to-left gazes required before updating the page contents.

The results obtained show that users were receptive to the use of eye-gaze as a page turning modality, with all users preferring this modality over the manual page turning and the timed-scrolling modalities. Although all three modalities incur some undesired pauses at page turns, the timed-scrolling and the manual page turning modalities required further adjustment of the score on the display, aggravating the page turning problem. In the case of the manual page turning modality this was necessary because the application split some systems over two pages and thus, the page had to be adjusted in order to read all the notes. In the case of the timed-scrolling, the users had to adjust the timing when this was not synchronised to their playing. Moreover, we note that although the timed-scrolling automates the page turns, this was the least popular modality among pianists and the common reason for this is that this modality removes the sense of control that the pianist has over the page turns, with one user stating that this modality even contributes to a sense of panic to keep up with the score. Only the violin player preferred this modality over the manual scrolling modality and the reason for this is that triggering the page turn with the bow in hand was awkward.

The pauses experienced when using our eye-gaze tracking modality are due to the limited viewpoint of the eye-gaze tracker used. When the music player moves his head beyond this viewpoint, for example, when a pianist looks down at the keyboard for a long period of time, the eye tracker will lose the eye position and there may be some delay until the eye position is located again. The user would typically be oblivious of this and would have continued playing. It would therefore be possible for the user to complete playing the system before the eye-gaze tracker regains control over the eye gaze position. Thus, the user experiences a delay between the end of the system and the page refresh. We also note that while the page turning is robust to left-right and right-left saccades of a few beats in duration, which is typical in music score reading, the page-turning mechanism may trigger accidental page turns with long and sustained leftwards gazes. This may happen when for example, a piano player has large leaps in the left hand, particularly in the lower register of the keyboard. These pauses and accidental page-turn triggers may be mitigated if the eye-gaze tracker used is replaced with a more robust tracking system. Notably one which is vision based and thus can offer a larger field of view. Such an approach could also make use of the head-pose movements of the player which would allow the system to differentiate between instances when the player is looking at the score and other times when the player is looking at the instrument or elsewhere.

Participants were also responsive to the score flattening, citing that they prefer this to going back and forth in the score when repeats occur. One user in particular had difficulties in locating where to start the repeated section and found the flattened score much easier to play from. One user suggested that at *volta* repeats, the section of music which is not to be played should be omitted rather than grayed out. Since bars vary in length according to the rhythmic complexity of the particular bar, omitting *volta* sections is not just a matter of shifting bars and the entire score would require typesetting afresh. Thus, a further research direction would be one which performs further image analysis on the score to allow for this to be re-written using MusicXML[7]. This would have the double benefit of adjusting the clarity and readability of poorly scanned scores.

8 CONCLUSION

In this paper, we present image analysis algorithms that may be used to obtain information about repeats in a music score. We also present a score flattening algorithm, allowing us to adapt a printed score document with one which is more suited for digital displays.

We then couple the flattened score with an eye-gaze page turning modality. The preliminary qualitative and quantitative studies show that the flattened score and the eye-gaze tracking provide for a more comfortable control of the musical score allowing for a smoother progression of the music. Not surprisingly, the user response indicated a strong preference to this system: the proposed adjustments to the printed score make the document more suitable for presentation on a digital device while providing full, hands-free control over the music flow. This encourages further investigation into the eye-gaze tracking to allow for more robust tracking of the eye position and hence more robust control over the document flow.

REFERENCES

[1] Bob Bell. 2012. A Better Page Turner for Organists. online blog. (July 2012). https://goingdigitalmusician.wordpress.com/2012/07/30/bob-bell-a-better-page-turner-for-organists/
[2] Timothy C Bell, Annabel Church, John McPherson, and David Bainbridge. 2005. Page turning and image size in a digital music stand. In *International Computer Music Conference*.
[3] P. Bellini, I. Bruno, and P. Nesi. 2001. Optical music sheet segmentation. In *Proceedings First International Conference on WEB Delivering of Music. WEDELMUSIC 2001*. 183–190. https://doi.org/10.1109/WDM.2001.990175
[4] Pierfrancesco Bellini, Ivan Bruno, and Paolo Nesi. 2005. *An offline Optical music Sheet Recognition*. IRM Press, Chapter 2, 40–75.
[5] Alexey Blinov. 2007. *An interaction study of a digital music stand*. Thesis. University of Canterbury, Christchurch, New Zealand.
[6] Roger B Dannenberg. 2012. Human Computer Music Performance. *Multimodal Music Processing* (2012), 121.
[7] R. B. Dannenberg, N. E. Gold, D. Liang, and G. Xia. 2014. Active Scores: Representation and Synchronization in Human Computer Performance of Popular Music. *Computer Music Journal* 38, 2 (June 2014), 51–62. https://doi.org/10.1162/COMJ_a_00239
[8] Matthias Dorfer, Andreas Arzt, and Gerhard Widmer. 2016. Towards score following in sheet music images. In *Proceedings of the International Society for Music Information Retrieval Conference (ISMIR)*.
[9] Michael Droettboom, Ichiro Fujinaga, and Karl MacMillan. 2002. Optical music interpretation. In *Joint IAPR International Workshops on Statistical Techniques in Pattern Recognition (SPR) and Structural and Syntactic Pattern Recognition (SSPR)*. Springer, 378–387.
[10] Ichiro Fujinaga. 2004. Staff detection and removal. *Visual perception of music notation: on-line and off-line recognition* (2004), 1–39.
[11] W. W. Gibbs. 2014. Hands-free sheet music [Resources-Hands On]. *IEEE Spectrum* 51, 10 (October 2014), 27–28. https://doi.org/10.1109/MSPEC.2014.6905480
[12] Christopher Graefe, Derek Wahila, Justin Maguire, and Orya Dasna. 1996. Designing the Muse: A Digital Music Stand for the Symphony Musician. In *Proceedings of the SIGCHI Conference on Human Factors in Computing Systems (CHI '96)*. ACM, New York, NY, USA, 436–ff. https://doi.org/10.1145/238386.238599
[13] Zeju Jin. 2013. *Formal Semantics for Music Notation Control Flow*. Master's thesis. Carnegie Mellon University.
[14] B. A. Laundry. 2011. *Sheet Music Unbound: A fluid approach to sheet music display and annotation on a multi-touch screen*. Master's thesis. University of Waikato.
[15] Clinton F Nieweg and Greg Vaught. 2011. Music Preparation Guidelines for Orchestral Music. *Major Orchestra Librarians' Association* (2011).
[16] Marjaana Penttinen, Erkki Huovinen, and Anna-Kaisa Ylitalo. 2015. Reading ahead: Adult music students' eye movements in temporally controlled performances of a children's song. *International Journal of Music Education* 33, 1 (2015), 36–50.
[17] Dan Ringwalt, Roger Dannenberg, and Andrew Russell. 2015. Optical Music Recognition for Interactive Score Display. In *Proceedings of the International Conference on New Interfaces for Musical Expression (NIME 2015)*. The School of Music and the Center for Computation and Technology (CCT), Louisiana State University, Baton Rouge, Louisiana, USA, 95–98. http://dl.acm.org/citation.cfm?id=2993778.2993805
[18] Charles Rosen. 1998. *The Classical Style: Haydn, Mozart, Beethoven*. W. W. Norton & Company.
[19] R. Smith. 2007. An Overview of the Tesseract OCR Engine. In *Proc. Ninth Int. Conf. Document Analysis and Recognition (ICDAR 2007)*, Vol. 2. 629–633. https://doi.org/10.1109/ICDAR.2007.4376991

---

[7]http://www.musicxml.com/

Using Abstract Anchors to Aid The Development of Multimedia Applications With Sensory Effects

Raphael Abreu
CEFET/RJ
raphael.abreu@eic.cefet-rj.br

Joel A. F. dos Santos
CEFET/RJ
jsantos@eic.cefet-rj.br

ABSTRACT

Declarative multimedia authoring languages allows authors to combine multiple media objects, generating a range of multimedia presentations. Novel multimedia applications, focusing at improving user experience, extend multimedia applications with multisensory content. The idea is to synchronize sensory effects with the audiovisual content being presented. The usual approach for specifying such synchronization is to *mark* the content of a main media object (e.g. a main video) indicating the moments when a given effect has to be executed. For example, a *mark* may represent when snow appears in the main video so that a cold wind may be synchronized with it. Declarative multimedia authoring languages provide a way to *mark* subparts of a media object through anchors. An anchor indicates its begin and end times (video frames or audio samples) in relation to its parent media object. The manual definition of anchors in the above scenario is both not efficient and error prone (i) when the main media object size increases, (ii) when a given scene component appears several times and (iii) when the application requires marking scene components.

This paper tackles this problem by providing an approach for creating abstract anchors in declarative multimedia documents. An abstract anchor represents (possibly) several media anchors, indicating the moments when a given scene component appears in a media object content. The author, therefore is able to define the application behavior through relationships among, for example, sensory effects and abstract anchors. Prior to executing, abstract anchors are automatically instantiated for each moment a given element appears and relationships are cloned so the application behavior is maintained.

This paper presents an implementation of the proposed approach using NCL (*Nested Context Language*) as the target language. The abstract anchor processor is implemented in Lua and uses available APIs for video recognition in order to identify the begin and end times for abstract anchor instances. We also present an evaluation of our approach using a real world use cases.

CCS CONCEPTS

•**Applied computing** → **Markup languages**; •**Human-centered computing** → **Hypertext / hypermedia**; •**Software and its engineering** → *Translator writing systems and compiler generators*;

KEYWORDS

Anchors; Multimedia authoring; Multisensory Content; Mulsemedia; NCL; Video Recognition

ACM Reference format:
Raphael Abreu and Joel A. F. dos Santos. 2017. Using Abstract Anchors to Aid The Development of Multimedia Applications With Sensory Effects. In *Proceedings of DocEng'17, September 4–7, 2017, Valletta, Malta.*, , 8 pages.
DOI: http://dx.doi.org/10.1145/3103010.3103014

1 INTRODUCTION

The recent advances in human-computer interactions ([4, 12, 18]) offers many opportunities to enrich multimedia experience with new features. Since the beginning of this decade there was significant commercial interest in more immersive technologies (3D displays, VR, etc). Such interest resulted in increased efforts of the multimedia community to develop new methods to enhance the user immersion in multimedia applications [21].

New kinds of immersive multimedia applications have been proposed, giving rise to the multiple sensorial media (Mulsemedia) applications [9], where traditional media content (text, image, audio, video, etc.) can be related to media objects that target other human senses (e.g. smell, haptics, etc.). To enable this applications, one can use physical sensing devices (sensors) to identify the ambient state (e.g. temperature, room size, user feedback) and actuators to generate sensory effects (e.g. wind, mist, heat) to the user.

Traditional declarative multimedia authoring languages, authoring languages for short, specify interactive multimedia applications focusing on the definition of media objects synchronization, independent of their content. Examples of authoring languages are SMIL (*Synchronized Multimedia Integration Language*) [23] and NCL (*Nested Context Language*) [11]. In the above scenario, it is interesting to take advantage of those languages abstractions for media and relationships specification in order to provide synchronization among both traditional content and also multisensory content.

An approach for synchronizing traditional and multisensory is to represent sensors and actuators as media objects and create relationships among parts of a main media object (e.g. a main video) and those media objects representing multisensory content. In order to do so, authors have to *mark* the main media object indicating when, for example, an explosion occurs so the corresponding sensory effect can be synchronized with it.

In this paper, we call a *scene component* a given element (rock, tree, dog, person, etc.) or concept (happy, crowded, dark, etc.) that appears in the main media object content.

The usual approach for *marking* when a given scene component appears in a given media object is to execute such media object and create anchors related to those components. Relationships among such anchors and the related multisensory content, therefore, define the intended synchronization.

When the application size grows, or when several scene component shall be synchronized with multisensory content, authors are required to create several anchors. The manual definition of such anchors, however, is not efficient. Moreover, such an approach can be error prone, given the size of the resulting code. This problem was presented in [22], where the authors emphasize the need for automating this process.

This paper presents an approach for automating the creation of anchors in multimedia authoring languages. Our approach is to provide a way for the author to define *abstract anchors* in multimedia documents. An abstract anchor represents (possibly) several media anchors, indicating the moments when a given scene component appears in a media object content. Relationships in the document are defined considering such abstract anchors. Prior to execution, a document with abstract anchors is processed so that, abstract anchors are automatically instantiated for each moment a given scene component appears and relationships are cloned so the application behavior is maintained.

The proposed approach was implemented using NCL as the target language. NCL is a standard for digital TV [1] and IPTV [11] services. It provides anchors for media objects, whose definition indicate their begin and end times in relation to their parent media object. In this work NCL anchors were extended so they can indicate the scene component they refer to. The Abstract Anchor Processor, *AAP* for short, uses available APIs for video recognition in order to identify when a given scene component appears in the video content. An instance of a given abstract anchor is created for each time the element appears. In sequence, document relationships are cloned for each anchor instance, maintaining the document behavior. *AAP* was implemented in Lua [10] and is available for download and use[1].

Using NCL with Abstract Anchors, *NCLAA* for short, reduces authoring effort, since anchors and document relationships are created only once, for each different scene component. In order to support our claim we present an evaluation of our approach using a real world use cases.

The remainder of the paper is organized as follows. Section 2 presents related work regarding approaches for reducing the authoring effort for multimedia and mulsemedia applications. Section 3 discusses the concept of abstract anchors, their creation in NCL and the steps for processing abstract anchors. Section 4 presents the implementation of the abstract anchor processor. Section 5 presents our approach evaluation results. Section 6 concludes the paper and presents future work.

2 RELATED WORK

A lot of attention has been devoted to reducing the authoring effort of multimedia and mulsemedia applications. Two common approaches are to provide authoring tools or template languages for those applications.

A template language allows the author to specify reusable components (placeholders) that should later be replaced by instances in the target language. More precisely, templates define generic components and express relationships between generic components that later can be duplicated to a target language by a template processor before runtime. The template processor ensures that the generic components are correctly instantiated in the target language. This section presents works focusing on templates for multimedia applications.

XTemplate [6] is a modular approach for creating templates for NCL documents. The template language proposed represents generic components and relationships among them. XTemplate specifies composite templates, which defines a spatio-temporal semantics to be reused by (possibly) several document compositions. Along with the template specification, a template processor was proposed. The processor receives as input a set of templates and a document using them and returns an NCL compliant document that can run on any standard NCL player. A similar approach is provided in [16] where authors propose the TAL template language and its associated processor.

Some template languages not only support placeholders, but also loops and conditions which often lack in declarative multimedia languages. This is the case of Luar [3]. The authors focus on authors with programming expertise, providing a way to embed Lua code in NCL documents. The Luar processor, executes the Lua code embedded in the NCL document producing an NCL compliant document.

Another approach to reduce the authoring effort is to develop visual authoring tools. These tools help the user by providing a graphical user interface (GUI) that eases or remove the need to write code. In general, such approaches target in non-expert authors, aiding the application development.

Examples of authoring tools for multimedia documents are [2, 5, 19, 20]. [2] proposes NCL Composer, an authoring tool presenting to the user a structural, a textual, and a layout view of an NCL document. It allows authors to interact with the document logical structure by representing media objects as nodes and the relationships among them as vertices.

A similar approach is presented in [19] where the NEXT tool is proposed. The difference is that NEXT is focused on templates, also providing a template view where authors may create documents using XTemplate templates.

LimSee [5] also uses templates for document authoring, in a similar approach to the one presented in [19]. Finally, xSMART [20] is used to create wizards to guide the creation of a multimedia document.

In the mulsemedia domain, much of the authoring effort is to specify scene components for synchronizing audiovisual content with sensory effects [25]. Usually, the authoring effort it to tie scene components to the sensory effects that a human should experience when they are presented [22], such as feeling cold when a snow scene is presented or feeling heat when a beach scene is presented.

In [24] the authors present an authoring tool designed for authoring mulsemedia applications, called SEVino (Sensory Effect Video Annotation Tool). SEVino provides the author an interface that presents a video timeline. Such video represents the main audiovisual content to have sensory effects synchronized with. The tool creates cells representing sensory effects (eg. fog, wind, temperature, etc.) and for a given time interval, users could select a cell

---

[1]https://github.com/raphael-abreu/NCLAAP

representing a sensory effect to be executed. After the authoring phase, the tool generates descriptions compatible with the MPEG-V standard [26], which is a standard for information exchange between digital world and real world. The MPEG-V descriptions generated by SEVino represent the sensory effects to be executed on physical devices.

Despite the advances in tools and templates for easing the authoring effort, the process of authoring a mulsemedia application is still a very expensive work in terms of effort and time. Especially when a great deal of synchronization among the audiovisual content and sensory effects is required.

Such problem gave rise to research proposing semi-automatic or automatic video description. A video description indicates for each instant of the video, the scene components that are present. Such approaches should require minimal to no author interaction at all for providing a video description, as well as to generate events based on that description.

The SEVino authors have also developed a media player capable of automatically gathering a video description and producing events on the ambient. More specifically, the proposed player can synchronize ambient lighting effects with a video presentation [24]. To achieve such synchronization, the player gather pixel color information from a video frame (usually the borders) and send the same color information to a nearby array of LED lights. This player removes the need for the user to specify the lightning effects in the multimedia document, however the approach is restricted to only one kind of effect, in this case, lightning effects.

The work presented in this paper differs from related work as follows. (i) It enables the author to describe its application abstracting the video description, using abstract anchors. (ii) It enables the author to define abstract anchors for multiple videos in a document, and not just one as the above approaches. (iii) It enables authors to synchronize any sensory effect with the application, by providing relationships among them and abstract anchors.

Although in this paper we present an approach for video description, the Abstract Anchor Processor (AAP) architecture is independent of the tool to be used for describing a media object content. Therefore, it could be used also for defining abstract anchors for audio objects.

3 ABSTRACT ANCHORS

Multimedia applications are described by multimedia documents. A document specification is described using some multimedia authoring language. Common entities for multimedia authoring languages are *nodes*, representing the document content, and *relationships*, for representing the synchronization to be performed in an application.

Different languages, such as NCL [11], provide temporal anchors for representing a subpart of a node content. *Temporal anchors* represent a subpart of a node content in the time axis. For example, a sequence of frames of a video node or a sequence of samples in an audio node. Usually, temporal anchors are defined by a begin and end, in respect to the node content.

By allowing the author to define anchors, multimedia languages enables the definition of relationships taking into account parts of a node content. Thus providing a fine-grained synchronization.

As discussed in Section 2. Template authoring languages enable the user to abstract some steps of the authoring process in favor of a more generic description. After authoring, at processing time, the template processor to "fill the blanks" with document specific content.

With that in mind, this work enables the author to make use of abstract anchors (NCLAA) to represent subparts of a node content, without explicitly describing them. It is similar to a template approach, in the sense that it enables another level of abstraction in the authoring phase.

An abstract anchor represents (possibly) several different node anchors, that are related by the node content being presented while they are active. In our approach, abstract anchors are related to scene components, such that all of its instances represent when the scene component it is associated with is being presented. Figure 1 depicts such idea, where media nodes are represented as circles and node anchors are represented as squared. Dashed lines associate an anchor to a node and solid lines represent document relationships.

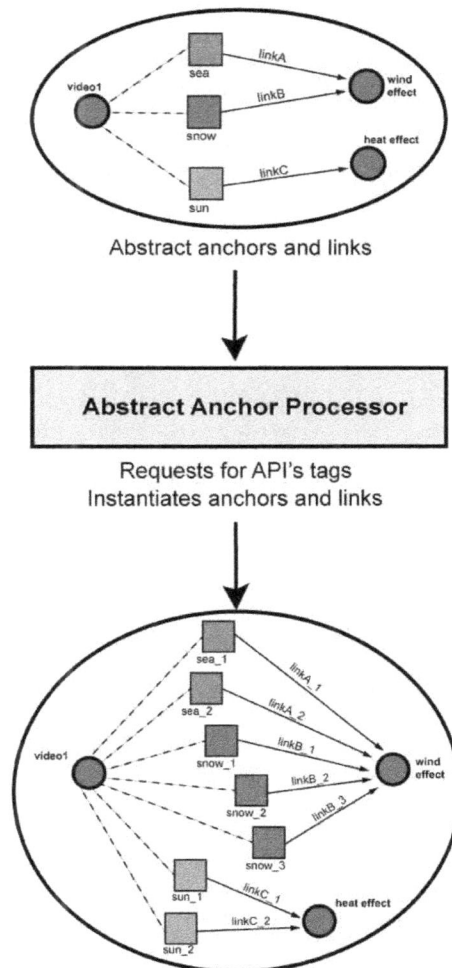

Figure 1: Abstract anchor definition and processing

The upper part of Figure 1 presents a document where media *video1* has three anchors *sea*, *snow* and *sun*. Each anchor represents a given scene component. Relationships among such anchors and medias *wind effect* and *heat effect* define when such medias shall be presented.

NCL [11], the target language used in this work, provides element media for defining nodes representing media objects. It also enables the definition of anchors using element area, child of element media. Listing 1 presents an example of media and anchor specification.

```
<media id="video1" src="video.mp4">
    <area tag="sea"/>
    <area tag="sun"/>
</media>
```

Listing 1: NCL media and anchor specification example

In order to provide the definition of abstract anchors, we extend NCL such that area elements have a new attribute tag. Such attribute indicates the scene components related to that anchor. In the example presented in Listing 1, two abstract anchors are created, one representing the instants when the sea appears in the video and the other representing the instants when the sun appears. Additionally, the author can define the tag to asterisk (*) if it should match every scene component in a document.

NCL is an event-based language such that synchronization relationships are defined based on events. NCL provides causal relationships such that when an event specified as its condition happens, one or more actions are triggered. Relationships in NCL are defined using link-connector element pairs. Connectors [15] define a general relation that is instantiated by links to a given set of participants. Listing 2 presents an example of link specification.

```
<link xconnector="onBeginStart">
    <bind role="onBegin" component="video1"
    interface="sea"/>
    <bind role="start" component="wind"/>
</link>
<link xconnector="onBeginStart">
    <bind role="onBegin" component="video1"
    interface="sun"/>
    <bind role="start" component="heat"/>
</link>
```

Listing 2: NCL link specification example

The example presented in Listing 2 defines two links. The first specifies that whenever anchor *sea* of *video1* starts, media *wind* shall be started. The second specifies that whenever anchor *sun* of *video1* starts, media *wind* shall be started. Two links are also crated to stop the wind and the head when the related anchor stops. For simplicity, they are not presented in Listing 2.

It is worth noticing that bind elements inside NCL links indicate the participants in a relationship. Attribute component indicates the participant node and an optional attribute interface restricts to a given node interface, i.e., a node anchor or property. In order to enable links to be defined over abstract anchors, we extend NCL such that attribute interface instead an anchor id may indicate its tag attribute value.

Prior to execution, a document using abstract anchors shall be processed into a final document following the NCL standard. The processing performed for abstract anchors is similar to that performed for template languages. The first step of the process is to instantiate the abstract anchors for the scene components they specify. The second step is to duplicate links for each instance of a given abstract anchors. The whole process in shown in Figure 1.

The anchor instantiation step is performed using tools for scene recognition as presented in Section 4.3. It recognizes the time instants a given scene component is presented in the video content and create anchor instances marked with temporal description. Therefore, our approach requires from authors little (or even no) prior knowledge about the media content. Anchors temporal definition is performed entirely with data acquired by recognition software.

4 ARCHITECTURE

The architecture of the Abstract Anchor Processor (*AAP*) is depicted in Figure 2.

AAP receives as input a document containing abstract anchors defined by the author. It parses the document identifying nodes that define abstract anchors and links related to them. At this step, the processor also extracts media content from those nodes. For the example in Listing 1 the processor identifies node *video1* as a node defining abstract anchors and shall extract its content (file video.mp4).

The extracted media content is sent to an external software for scene recognition. As it can be seen in Figure 2, the recognition software is decoupled from the processor. Such approach gives more freedom to the author allowing one to use different scene recognition software. The scene recognition step results in a set of tags[2] that are equivalent to ones identified in the abstract anchors defined by the author. These tags represent the scene components along with timing information about when they appear in the video.

4.1 Anchor Instantiation

According to the tags received from the scene recognition software, *AAP* instantiates the abstract anchors. The process of anchor instantiation is performed as follows. According to the scene components specified in the abstract anchor, the processor checks in the set of received tags the time instants when those components were present. It identifies adjacent instants defining intervals where scene components are present. For each resulting interval, one anchor instance is created. Listing 3 presents the result of the anchor instantiation step for the example in Listing 1.

```
<media src="video.mp4" id="video1">
    <area id="sea_1" begin="01s" end="09s"/>
    <area id="sea_2" begin="17s" end="19s"/>
    <area id="sun_1" begin="01s" end="19s"/>
    <area id="sun_2" begin="28s" end="32s"/>
</media>
```

Listing 3: Anchor instantiation step result for the example in Listing 1

---

[2]We use the same nomenclature as the scene recognition software. It shall not be confounded with XML tags.

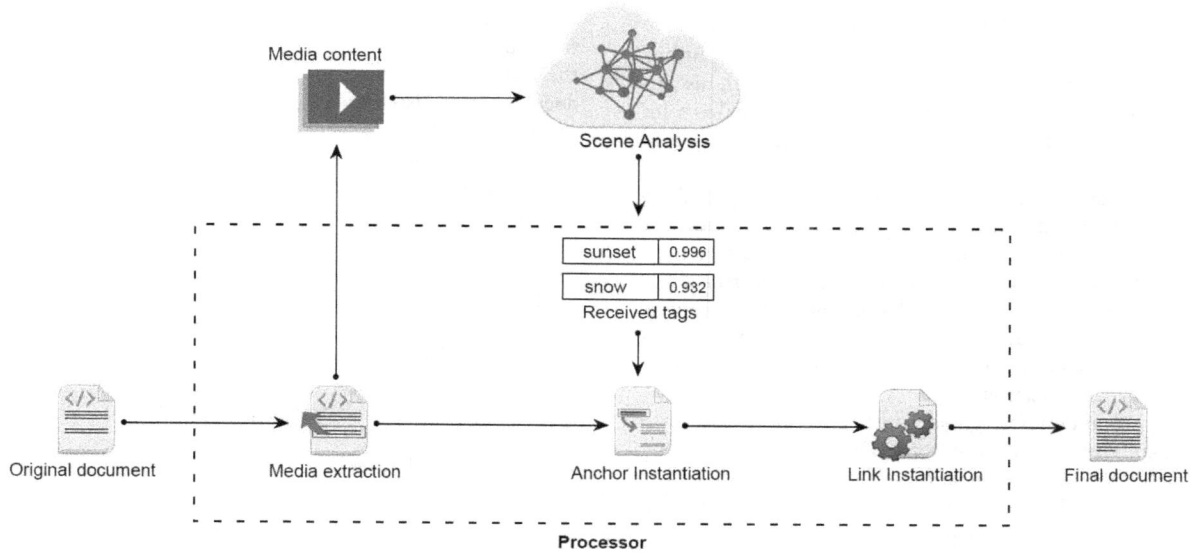

Figure 2: Abstract anchor processor architecture

In the example presented in Listing 3, the scene component sea was identified in the video in the intervals [1, 9] and [17, 19] seconds of the video. Thus two anchor instances were created, sea_1 for the first interval and sea_2 for the second one. The same is done for scene component sun, which was identified in the video inside intervals [1, 19] and [28, 32], generating anchor instances sun_1 and sun_2.

It is worth noticing that in the resulting document, the attribute tag was removed from the anchor instances. Anchor ids, which are mandatory in NCL, are created according to the tag attribute value. In order to maintain the output compatibility with the NCL standard, each anchor id is also incremented to be unique in the whole document.

4.2 Link Instantiation

After the anchor instantiation process, *AAP* is able to instantiate links that refer to abstract anchors.

For each link marked at the processing begin as using an abstract anchor, the processor examines each of its binds in order to determine its target element. Two outputs are possible.

- The bind targets a media node as a whole or a regular anchor. In that case nothing has to be done.
- The bind targets an abstract anchor of a media node. In that case the link has to be duplicated for each instance of the abstract anchor.

This process continues until no link bind targets an abstract anchor. Listing 4 presents the result of the link instantiation step for the example in Listing 2.

```
1 <link xconnector="onBeginStart">
2     <bind role="onBegin" component="video1"
       interface="sea_1"/>
3     <bind role="start" component="wind"/>
```

```
4 </link>
5 <link xconnector="onBeginStart">
6     <bind role="onBegin" component="video1"
       interface="sea_2"/>
7     <bind role="start" component="wind"/>
8 </link>
9 <link xconnector="onBeginStart">
10    <bind role="onBegin" component="video1"
       interface="sun_1"/>
11    <bind role="start" component="heat"/>
12 </link>
13 <link xconnector="onBeginStart">
14    <bind role="onBegin" component="video1"
       interface="sun_2"/>
15    <bind role="start" component="heat"/>
16 </link>
```

Listing 4: Link instantiation step result for the example in Listing 2

In the example presented in Listing 4, the first link from Listing 2 was instantiated to both instances of the abstract anchor sea. The resulting links now targets anchors sea_1 and sea_2, respectively. The same process was done for the second link from Listing 2, which was instantiated for anchors sun_1 and sun_2.

It is worth noticing that the steps of anchor instantiation and link instantiation may be executed in distinct moments. It is possible for the author to use *AAP* to first instantiate the anchors, continues to work in the document and perform the link instantiation step later.

215

4.3 Scene recognition

Given a set of abstract anchors previously defined by the author, *AAP* collects the anchors tag attribute values along with his parent element source. The resulting tags must be instantiated with temporal information that identifies where that tag appeared on the scene. Here we call this process *scene recognition*.

Scene recognition is achieved by submitting all the tag attribute values to the recognition system, which is a system that employs algorithms that can detect scene components in media content (e.g. video, audio, text analysis). These approaches return a set of tags indicating the description of a media content. Although static media can also be analysed (image and text) this work focuses on continuous media objects, which are frequently used as basis for sensory effect synchronization.

The scene recognition phase is decoupled from the processor to enable its adaptation to novel ways of recognizing features in any media format. The author can adapt the *AAP* settings for another recognition system. The only requirement is that the recognition system has to return a list of independent tags with their temporal data, according to the notation used by the processor.

In our implementation we used a video recognition API[3] based on a Convolutional Neural Networks (CNN)[14]. These neural networks have been shown as an effective method for understanding video content ([13, 28]). Figure 3 shows the result of an image recognition using such software.

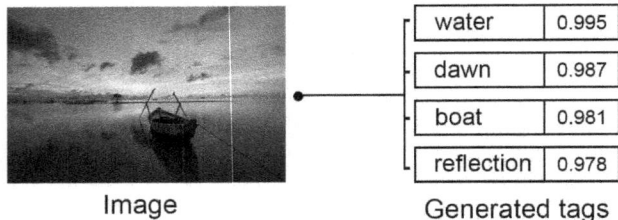

water	0.995
dawn	0.987
boat	0.981
reflection	0.978

Image   Generated tags

Figure 3: Image recognition result

The example in Figure 3 returns a set of tags indicating the scene components present in the image. Each tag is followed by the neural network prediction probability. The API can identify objects (e.g. boat), as well as individual concepts (e.g. reflection).

To recognize video content, the neural network works in a similar way of image recognition. One approach is to treat video as a series of images. However, as pointed out by [17], this approach does not account for the temporal information between frames and can lead to irrelevant concepts emerging from the scene. Nonetheless one advantage of this method is that it requires less computation time to analyse the video.

Another approach is to consider the temporal relationship between the frames and deduce the tags by analysing relationships as time passes. A advantage of this method is that it decreases the probability of returning irrelevant tags from the video and keeps only the ones that persisted though the entire time. However this approach is shown to be difficult to compute [17].

The video recognition API we used in this work, content description is performed for every second of video content. Therefore, after the instantiation phase, the events described on the multimedia document will also have a 1 second time-step.

The description of scenes by one second at a time may seem to include a great deal of delay in the specification of sensory effect synchronization with audiovisual content. However, for mulsemedia applications, works published in the literature show that user perception of a sensory effect happens in a time window of $\approx$ 1s for haptic effects [27], $\approx$ 2s for heat effects [7], $\approx$ 3s for wind effects [7, 27] and $\approx$ 25s for scent effects [8].

Given the above results, we consider that the content description of a media object with a one second step should not pose a threat to the user quality of experience. A future work is to investigate an approach to reduce such time step.

5 EVALUATION

For the purpose of evaluating of our approach we introduce a usage scenario to highlight how *AAP* supports the development of a mulsemedia application. We developed an NCL application that combines video and sensory effects to enrich the user experience. The application called "environments around the world", consists of scenes about different environments that are presented to the user.

A timeline representation of the video content and its synchronization with sensory effects is presented on Figure 4. It presents a set of key frames of the video[4] and three of the tags recognized in that part of the video. At the moment of each scene, the NCL application starts an actuator to perform a sensory effect related to that scene.

Table 1 describes the sensory effects to be synchronized when a given tag is found in the video. It varies from scent effects to wind, heat and cold effects. The effects also vary in intensity according with the scene components. One should notice, that effects can be played at the same time. It shall occurs when both tags are found in the video at the same time. Thus both area elements related to those tags will be active and, as consequence of NCL links, so shall be the sensory effects.

Table 1: Sensory effects generated by each scene component

Tag	Sensory effects
Summer	wind 50%, heat 50%
Snow	cold 100%
Forest	forest scent 100%, wind 25%
Flower	flower scent 100%, wind 25%
Storm	wind 100%, cold 50%, air humidifier 100%
Sea	wind 50%, heat 50%, air humidifier 50%
Hot	wind 50%, heat 100%

The video was described in NCL with abstract anchors indicating the scene components of interest. The cover components present in all environments. Listing 5 presents the abstract anchor specification.

---

[3]https://clarifai.com

[4]Images and videos are licensed as Creative Commons CC0 and were found at Pixabay. https://pixabay.com

Figure 4: Sensory effects generated on a video timeline

```
1  <media id="video" src="video.mp4">
2      <area tag="summer"/>
3      <area tag="snow"/>
4      <area tag="forest"/>
5      <area tag="flower"/>
6      <area tag="storm"/>
7      <area tag="sea"/>
8      <area tag="hot"/>
9  </media>
```

Listing 5: NCL abstract anchors for the application "environments around the world"

The behavior of the application is defined by a group of 7 link elements (one for each abstract anchor). Listing 6 presents an link specification for one of the abstract anchors.

```
1  <link xconnector="onBeginStartSet">
2      <bind role="onBegin" component="video"
   interface="summer"/>
3      <bind role="start" component="wind">
4          <bindParam name="intensity" value="50%
   "/>
5      </bind>
6      <bind role="start" component="heat">
7          <bindParam name="intensity" value="50%
   "/>
8      </bind>
9  </link>
```

Listing 6: NCL link specification with intensity parameters

The link presented in Listing 6 synchronizes the scene component summer to the sensory effects wind and heat. Both sensory effects are represented as media nodes in the application, and represent Lua scripts that control the actuators responsible for that effect. The scripts have an *intensity* parameter whose value is defined in NCL by parameters (lines 4 and 7). The intensity is expressed in a percentage of the maximum capable intensity the actuator can provide.

The author of this application, using *NCLAA*, has to declare 7 abstract anchors and 7 links. The application has a total of 74 lines of code to describe the behavior of the application.

After processing, according to the video content, the document has 45 anchor instances and also 45 link instances. The processed document has a total of 362 lines of code to perform the behavior described in the abstract anchors.

As can be seen in this example, using abstract anchors, the author had to declare around 15% of the resulting number of anchors and links and around 20% of the resulting lines of code. Moreover, without the use of the *AAP* the author would have to, not only, define the anchors and links, but also carefully watch the video for recognizing scene components and their timing in order to describe the anchors and their synchronization with the sensory effects. As intended, we can see a great decrease in the authoring effort with respect to manual authoring.

It is worth noting that the same code described using *NCLAA* is maintained even in case the video size changes. Given that the abstract anchors are not directly related to the video length (and timing), but only to the scene components it has, the application code does not have to change in case the video size changes. This result is also favorable to the author, as the number of anchor instances may increase with the video size.

6 CONCLUSION

This paper proposed an approach to describe multimedia application with abstract anchors. Abstract anchors represent intervals when a given scene component is presented in the media node content. Thus, a mulsemedia application author does not need have a complete knowledge of a node content for defining its synchronization with other content.

Such approach is intended to be used in a mulsemedia context, where it is common to perform sensory effect synchronization in relation to audiovisual content. The approach, however, is not restricted to it and can be used for traditional multimedia application specification.

Together with the abstract anchors, the abstract anchor processor (*AAP*) allows for the automatic generation of node anchor based on its content. It gathers information about the document and uses scene recognition software for identifying the temporal information for anchors. This approach allow automatic media synchronization to be done based on video recognition.

A positive side effect of our approach is that given that the abstract anchors are not directly related to the video length (and timing), but only to the scene components it has, the application code does not have to change in case the video size changes.

Since the *AAP* processor have broad applications with different media types. A first future work should be to integrate to it audio recognition software. The idea is to identify scene components, e.g., according to the background sound, and use such information for anchor instantiation. A use case could be the automatic synchronization of subtitles in NCL applications.

Another future work is to enhance *AAP* with the ability to infer synonyms of the words used to describe abstract anchors. The current approach for identifying scene concepts can be error prone. Sometimes it can be difficult to guess which concept the recognition software can handle. There are several recognition softwares available and they may not follow a common standard for concept naming.

Finally, one interesting future work is to improve our approach so that it can be used for live content. *AAP* has to be able to perform anchor and link instantiation at runtime. Besides some kind of caching strategy has to be used for performing the scene recognition step. The challenge to that approach is related to Quality of Experience (QoE) preservation in multimedia applications, which may be lost due to processing latency of some scene recognition software.

REFERENCES

[1] ABNT. 2011. Digital terrestrial television - Data coding and transmission specification for digital broadcasting - Part 2: Ginga-NCL for fixed and mobile receivers - XML application language for application coding. (2011). ABNT NBR 15606-2:2011 standard.

[2] Roberto Gerson A. Azevedo, Eduardo Cruz Araújo, Bruno Lima, Luiz Fernando G. Soares, and Marcelo F. Moreno. 2014. Composer: meeting non-functional aspects of hypermedia authoring environment. *Multimedia Tools and Applications* 70, 2 (2014), 1199–1228. DOI:http://dx.doi.org/10.1007/s11042-012-1216-8

[3] Diogo Henrique Duarte Bezerra, Denio Mariz Timóteo Sousa, Guido Lemos de Souza Filho, Aquiles Medeiros Filgueira Burlamaqui, and Igor Rosberg Medeiros Silva. 2012. Luar: A Language for Agile Development of NCL Templates and Documents. In *Proceedings of the 18th Brazilian Symposium on Multimedia and the Web (WebMedia '12)*. ACM, New York, NY, USA, 395–402. DOI:http://dx.doi.org/10.1145/2382636.2382718

[4] Carolina Cruz-Neira, Daniel J. Sandin, Thomas A. DeFanti, Robert V. Kenyon, and John C. Hart. 1992. The CAVE: Audio Visual Experience Automatic Virtual Environment. *Commun. ACM* 35, 6 (June 1992), 64–72. DOI:http://dx.doi.org/10.1145/129888.129892

[5] Romain Deltour and Cécile Roisin. 2006. The limsee3 multimedia authoring model. In *Proceedings of the 2006 ACM symposium on Document engineering*. ACM, 173–175.

[6] Joel André Ferreira dos Santos and Débora Christina Muchaluat Saade. 2010. XTemplate 3.0: Adding Semantics to Hypermedia Compositions and Providing Document Structure Reuse. In *Proceedings of the 2010 ACM Symposium on Applied Computing (SAC '10)*. ACM, New York, NY, USA, 1892–1897. DOI:http://dx.doi.org/10.1145/1774088.1774490

[7] H Felix, Nikita Mattar, and Julia Fr. 2014. Simulating Wind and Warmth in Virtual Reality : Conception , Realization and Evaluation for a CAVE Environment. 11, 10 (2014).

[8] Gheorghita Ghinea and Oluwakemi A. Ademoye. 2010. Perceived synchronization of olfactory multimedia. *IEEE Transactions on Systems, Man, and Cybernetics Part A:Systems and Humans* 40, 4 (2010), 657–663. DOI:http://dx.doi.org/10.1109/TSMCA.2010.2041224

[9] Gheorghita Ghinea, Christian Timmerer, Weisi Lin, and Stephen R. Gulliver. 2014. Mulsemedia : State of the Art, Perspectives, and Challenges. *ACM Transactions on Multimedia Computing, Communications, and Applications* 11, 1s (2014), 1–23.

DOI:http://dx.doi.org/10.1145/2617994

[10] Roberto Ierusalimschy. 2006. *Programming in lua* (2nd ed.). Roberto Ierusalimschy.

[11] ITU. 2009. Nested Context Language (NCL) and Ginga-NCL for IPTV services. http://www.itu.int/rec/T-REC-H.761-200904-S. (2009). ITU-T Recommendation H.761.

[12] Alejandro Jaimes and Nicu Sebe. 2007. Multimodal human–computer interaction: A survey. *Computer Vision and Image Understanding* 108, 1–2 (2007), 116 – 134. DOI:http://dx.doi.org/10.1016/j.cviu.2006.10.019 Special Issue on Vision for Human-Computer Interaction.

[13] Andrej Karpathy, George Toderici, Sanketh Shetty, Thomas Leung, Rahul Sukthankar, and Li Fei-Fei. 2014. Large-Scale Video Classification with Convolutional Neural Networks. In *Proceedings of the 2014 IEEE Conference on Computer Vision and Pattern Recognition (CVPR '14)*. IEEE Computer Society, Washington, DC, USA, 1725–1732. DOI:http://dx.doi.org/10.1109/CVPR.2014.223

[14] Y. LeCun, B. Boser, J. S. Denker, D. Henderson, R. E. Howard, W. Hubbard, and L. D. Jackel. 1989. Backpropagation Applied to Handwritten Zip Code Recognition. *Neural Comput.* 1, 4 (Dec. 1989), 541–551. DOI:http://dx.doi.org/10.1162/neco.1989.1.4.541

[15] D. C. Muchaluat-Saade and L. F. G. Soares. 2002. XConnector & XTemplate: Improving the Expressiveness and Reuse in Web Authoring Languages. *The New Review of Hypermedia and Multimedia Journal* 8, 1 (2002), 139–169.

[16] Carlos de Salles Soares Neto, Luiz Fernando Gomes Soares, and Clarisse Sieckenius de Souza. 2012. TAL-Template Authoring Language. *Journal of the Brazilian Computer Society* 18, 3 (2012), 185–199. DOI:http://dx.doi.org/10.1007/s13173-012-0073-7

[17] Joe Yue-Hei Ng, Matthew J. Hausknecht, Sudheendra Vijayanarasimhan, Oriol Vinyals, Rajat Monga, and George Toderici. 2015. Beyond Short Snippets: Deep Networks for Video Classification. *CoRR* abs/1503.08909 (2015). http://arxiv.org/abs/1503.08909

[18] Sharon Oviatt. 2003. The Human-computer Interaction Handbook. L. Erlbaum Associates Inc., Hillsdale, NJ, USA, Chapter Multimodal Interfaces, 286–304. http://dl.acm.org/citation.cfm?id=772072.772093

[19] Douglas Paulo de Mattos, Júlia Varanda da Silva, and Débora Christina Muchaluat-Saade. 2013. NEXT: graphical editor for authoring NCL documents supporting composite templates. In *Proceedings of the 11th european conference on Interactive TV and video*. ACM, 89–98.

[20] A. Scherp and S. Boll. 2005. Context-driven Smart Authoring of Multimedia Content with xSMART. In *13th ACM Multimedia*.

[21] Y. Sulema. 2016. Mulsemedia vs. Multimedia: State of the art and future trends. In *2016 International Conference on Systems, Signals and Image Processing (IWSSIP)*. 1–5. DOI:http://dx.doi.org/10.1109/IWSSIP.2016.7502696

[22] Christian Timmerer, Markus Waltl, Benjamin Rainer, and Hermann Hellwagner. 2012. Assessing the quality of sensory experience for multimedia presentations. *Signal Processing: Image Communication* 27, 8 (2012), 909–916. DOI:http://dx.doi.org/10.1016/j.image.2012.01.016

[23] W3C. 2008. Synchronized Multimedia Integration Language - SMIL 3.0 Specification. http://www.w3c.org/TR/SMIL3. (2008). World-Wide Web Consortium Recommendation.

[24] Markus Waltl, Benjamin Rainer, Christian Timmerer, and Hermann Hellwagner. 2013. An end-to-end tool chain for Sensory Experience based on MPEG-V. *Signal Processing: Image Communication* 28, 2 (2013), 136–150. DOI:http://dx.doi.org/10.1016/j.image.2012.10.009

[25] K. Yoon, B. Choi, E. S. Lee, and T. B. Lim. 2010. 4-D broadcasting with MPEG-V. In *2010 IEEE International Workshop on Multimedia Signal Processing*. 257–262. DOI:http://dx.doi.org/10.1109/MMSP.2010.5662029

[26] Kyoungro Yoon, Sang-Kyun Kim, Jae Joon Han, Seungju Han, and Marius Preda. 2015. *MPEG-V: Bridging the Virtual and Real World* (1st ed.). Academic Press.

[27] Zhenhui Yuan, Shengyang Chen, Gheorghita Ghinea, and Gabriel-Miro Muntean. 2014. User Quality of Experience of Mulsemedia Applications. *ACM Transactions on Multimedia Computing, Communications, and Applications* 11, 1s (2014), 1–19. DOI:http://dx.doi.org/10.1145/2661329

[28] Matthew D. Zeiler and Rob Fergus. 2013. Visualizing and Understanding Convolutional Networks. *CoRR* abs/1311.2901 (2013). http://arxiv.org/abs/1311.2901

Opportunistic Collaborative Mobile-Based Multimedia Authoring Based on the Capture of Live Experiences

[1]A.Omar M.Uscamayta, [1]Bruna C.R. Cunha, [2]Diogo S. Martins, [1]Maria G. Pimentel
[1]University of São Paulo - [2]Federal University of ABC - Brazil
{omar.mozo, brunaru, mgp}@icmc.usp.br[1] - santana.martins@ufabc.edu.br[2]

ABSTRACT

Despite recent results allowing collaborative video capture using mobile devices, there is a gap in promoting collaborative capture of media other than video. In this paper we report our collaborative model supporting amateur and opportunistic collaborative recording of multiple media using mobile devices. We present a case study carried out in the educational domain. We include a motivating scenario and related requirements, our proposed architecture and associated proof-of-concept prototype for supporting mobile amateur collaborative recording.

CCS CONCEPTS

• **Information systems** → **Multimedia content creation**; • **Human-centered computing** → *Ubiquitous and mobile computing systems and tools*;

KEYWORDS

Ubicomp; Annotation; Video; Ink; Audio; Photo; Bookmark; CSCW.

1 INTRODUCTION

The importance of supporting the authoring of interactive multimedia documents has motivated contributions in terms of tools for authoring [17, 20] and annotation [6, 13], as surveyed in [16]. The literature also reports efforts toward generating multimedia documents by capturing live experiences [2, 12], as reviewed in [22]. Authoring based on the capture of multiple media in collaborative live experiences has been experimented, e.g, in the context of web conferencing [23] and hospital operation theatres [9].

Despite proposals of allowing the collaborative capture of video via mobile devices [7, 8, 10], there is gap in supporting the collaborative capture of media other than video. In this paper we report our approach towards supporting amateur and opportunistic collaborative recording of multiple media using mobile devices. We focus our approach on the collaborative aspects of the authoring task. For this, we present a conceptual model which aims at supporting collaborative capture while considering the identification of the authors involved in the multimedia capture. Our collaborative model

extends previous work which modeled the multimedia authoring process based on the concepts of interaction event and annotation of existing media by anonymous users [15]. We illustrate our approach via a case study in the educational domain.

In the remainder of this paper, Section 2 highlighs related work and Section 3 presents an overview of the collaborative model we propose. Our proof-of-concept prototype is discussed in Section 4, followed by a usability evaluation in Section 5. Finally, Section 6 presents our final remarks.

2 RELATED WORK

Educational events. Researchers propose supporting the capture of live events such as work meetings, as in seminal work on ubiquitous computing [24] and in early works in the educational domain [1]. These led to generic infrastructures [19, 21] as well as systems supporting authoring multimedia via capturing live experiences as reviewed in [22], including in the educational domain [5]. Nowadays researchers offer mobile tools for individuals to capture their own experiences, as again in the educational domain [4].

Entertainment events. Proposals of collaborative recordings using mobile devices include live streaming services by simulating a professional recording [8, 10] and a non functional iOS prototype [7].

Video from communities. The fact that people are used to employ their own mobile devices to record live events has been investigated in the proposal of concerts, shows, and sport events [11, 18]. In this context, *MyVideos* is a hybrid authoring tool that integrates and synchronizes videos from an event provided by a community [3].

3 COLLABORATIVE MODEL

Previous work supports a multimedia authoring process based on the concepts of interaction event and annotation [14, 15]. The original model allows *"annotations of annotations"* to support annotations as media elements and groups concepts into four dimensions around an interaction event: Media, Interaction, Time and Space.

Figure 1 presents an extension to the original model, called *CMAIA* (Collaborative Multimedia Authoring via Interaction and Annotation). The main objective of the *CMAIA model* is to allow identification of authors involved in the collaborative capture phase of a multimedia document production. Figure 1 shows the complete *CMAIA model* along with the extensions to the original model emphasized.

- A new concept **Author** allows identifying the authors of annotations, documents and media elements;
- Three new relationships named **has author** allows associating authors with the concepts *Annotation*, *Document* and *MediaElement* from the original model.

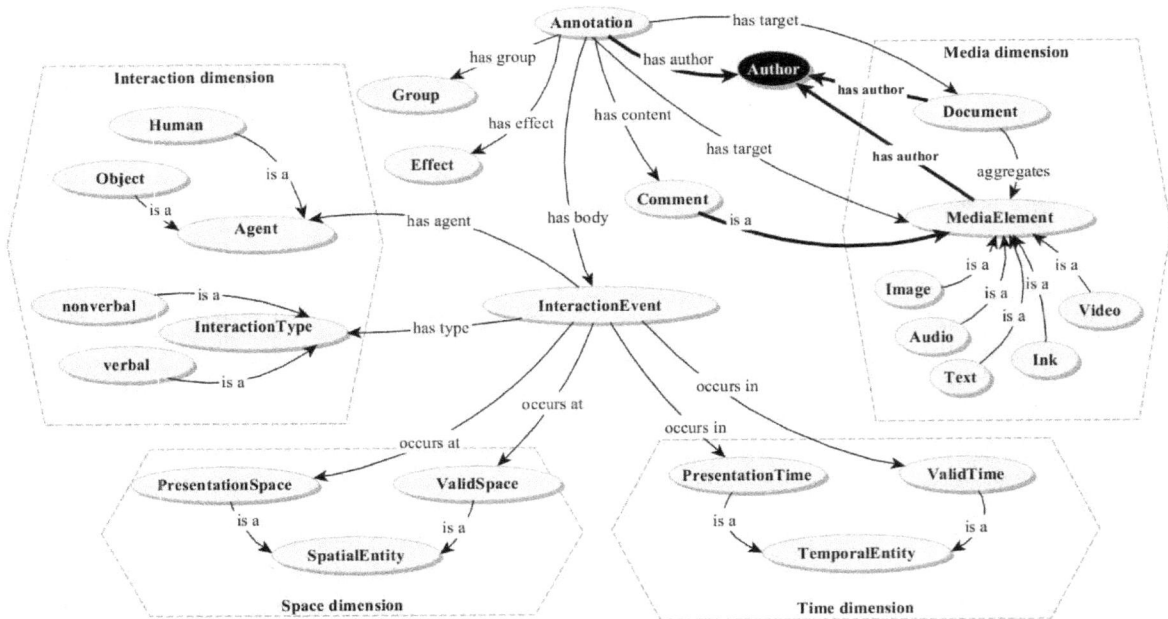

Figure 1: CMAIA conceptual model. Extensions involving novel elements are indicated in bold font.

The new concept **Author** identifies the person who originates, generates or creates a specific multimedia content. The *Author* concept is connected with the concepts *Annotation*, *Document* and *MediaElement* via relationships **"has author"**. The extension impacts the capture and access phases of the multimedia production process:

- **Capture:** The association of the *Author* concept with the *MediaElements* concept each time a participant captures media allows associating author and media. As a result, it is possible to identify not only who participated in the authoring process but also if the capture was collaborative or not;
- **Access:** In the original model, *InteractionEvent* has a relationship *has agent* with the *Agent* concept specifying the participants involved in an interaction. Since the model states that agent can be a *Human* or an *Object*, one can not assume an *Human* as the author of an annotation. In the extended model, author identification is made at capture time. Moreover, the extension allows the identification of many participants generating bookmarks independently from one another.

4 COLLABORATIVE MOVIA

Collaborative Mobile Video Annotation (*CMoViA*) is a collaborative multimedia capture tool that focuses on opportunistic *ad hoc* multimedia collaborative capture of live events by amateur users. The tool is composed of a front-end mobile application (*CMoViA app*), a back-end application (*CMoViA API*) and an application for integration with the *CMAIA* web application. The process that integrates all these tools takes advantage of a common document format and associated information integration features, as illustrated in Figure 2.

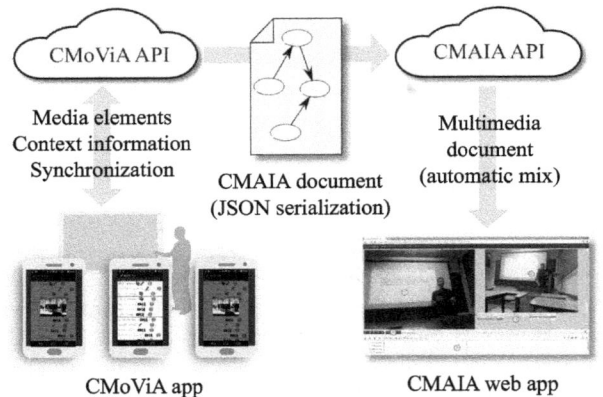

Figure 2: CMoViA and CMAIA integration

The *CMoViA app* was implemented for the Android platform. It allows features for collaborative synchronous capture and visualization of context information. Its four main features are: *1)* Synchronized capture, *2)* Multimedia selection, *3)* Context information and *4)* Mobile accessories.

As first step, users create a collaborative session or join an existing collaborative session.

Synchronized capture. In a collaborative capture context, the literature reports different ways to deal with synchronized capture. *CMoViA app* uses the support of a server (*CMoViA API*) to perform the synchronization. The media elements captured for each participant of the collaborative capture session should be synchronized with the other participants. The synchronization method allows to perform an opportunistic collaborative capture because users can join and leave the recording anytime they want.

Multimedia selection. *CMoViA app* allows capturing audio, photos, video and bookmarks. Users may choose the media type they want to capture as illustrated in Figure 3(a): video only, photo and audio, photos only, audio only, bookmarks only.

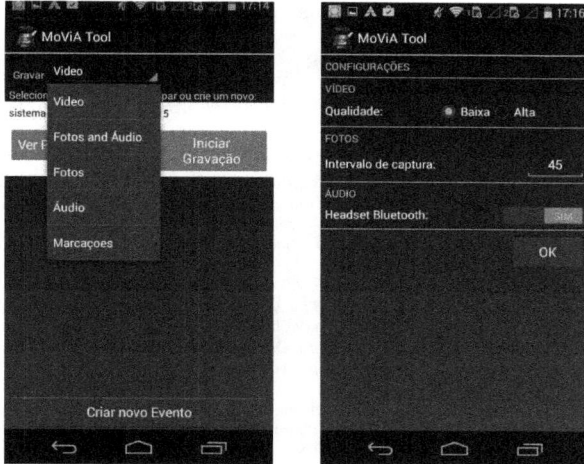

(a) Media selection (video, audio, photos and audio, audio, bookmarks)

(b) Configuration (video quality high/low, interval between photos, Bluetooth headset yes/no)

Figure 3: Configuration interfaces in *CMoViA app*

Even though many devices have high quality cameras, depending on the context users may prefer to record low quality video or, periodically, high quality pictures instead of videos. Moreover, Bluetooth headsets can be very useful to improve audio quality. *CMovia*'s configuration options include allowing to choose the video quality, the use of a Bluetooth headset, as well as the periodicity of photo capture, as shown in Figure 3(b).

We consider bookmarks a media type: they are represented as text annotations associated with time instant that was of a particular interest to the user. A bookmark can be added by touching the screen or, to avoid distraction from the main experience so as to reach the device (which may be mounted on a tripod), by using a remote shutter communicating with the device via Bluetooth.

Context information. Ubiquitous computing research highlights the importance of context information captured from users in specific actions of interest [1]. When a user joins a collaborative session, CMoVia presents an interface with context information associated with all users participating in the session (start and end time, participant's name, icons representing the media recorded, icon representing if the recording was ended or not), as illustrated in Figure 4(a). The app also provides a picture preview of the information captured by each user, for the cases in which video or photos are recorded. Figure 4(b) illustrates the preview shown upon tapping on an active participant's line in the list.

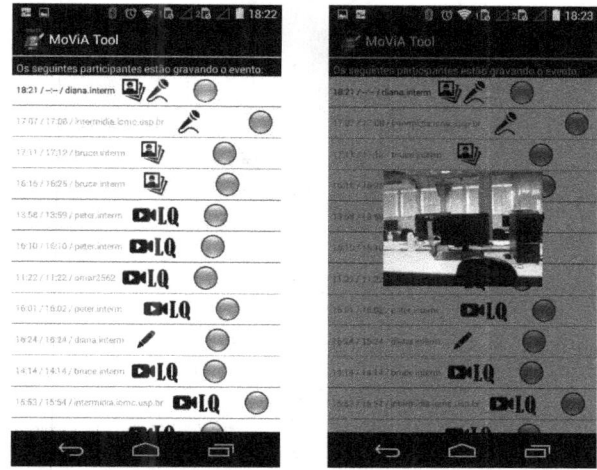

(a) List of participants in collaborative capture event (gray indicates inactive)

(b) Photo preview of user *diana.interm* who records photo and audio

Figure 4: Context information in *CMoViA app*

Visualizing the resulting multimedia document. Inspired in collaborative communities, where different users share their videos, CMoViA collaborative sessions are exported to the *CMAIA web app*, which allows to reconstruct the collaborative session as an integrated multimedia document. All captured information is represented as a JSON-serialized document that instantiates the *CMAIA model*. According to the descriptions in the document, the *CMAIA web app* automatically mixes the sessions from all authors and provides a navigation interface where users can switch between multiple media alternatives according to their needs.

Figure 5 shows the CMAIA web app interface when a collaborative multimedia document is rendered, where (1) is the part that shows photos of a specific author/user, (2) is the part that plays video of a specific user, (3) is the part with combo boxes that allow choosing the media for a specific user, (4) playback controls and (5) shows one timeline with text annotations or bookmarks of each participant in the collaborative capture.

5 USABILITY EVALUATION

We performed a usability test to collect the perception of users in a collaborative mobile capture considering a real education scenario, in two different classes. We recruited five volunteers that did not receive payment or other rewards for their participation (male graduate students, 25 to 35 years old). The participants were the same during all tests, and one person could not participate in the last test. We provided mobile devices equipped with Android for the participants. To maintain participants' anonymity, we employed fictitious user names. We used two smartphones, two tablets, one smart camera and one Bluetooth headset. We also provided tripod-like holders so participants did not have to hold the devices.

Before the experiment, we sent instructions explaining the test. To decide which media to record for the collaborative capture, we asked the participants to use as criteria: a) what other participants

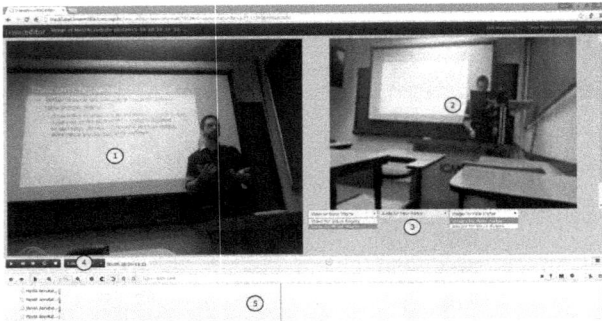

Figure 5: *CMAIA web app* reproducing a collaborative capture of 3 participants: the first captured video, the second captured photos and the third captured photos and audio using a Bluetooth headset.

were capturing, b) capture quality of other participants and c) personal choice. We observed the participants during the collaborative capture and sent questions about their experience by e-mail afterwards. After the capture, we exported the corresponding captured media to the CMAIA web app and shared the link with participants. Each participant visualized the result and answered a questionnaire about their experience during capture and their opinion about the resulting multimedia document. We used five-point Likert scale questions to ask their opinion about the capture ("I thought it was easy to perform the recording", "I thought it was easy to find out what the other participants were recording.") and about the resulting document ("I'm satisfied with the result of the collaborative recording.", "I'm able to visualize the slides with quality.", "I'm able to follow the speaker."). The questionnaire also contained open ended questions so participants could explain their answers.

The usability test revealed several issues. Participants were interested in recording these presentations because, in this specific class, they had a discussion with feedback from other students during presentations and they wanted to review this discussion. Because of that, they were also more careful while choosing which media elements to capture. In the questionnaire, responses about the capturing process were fairly positive (4.4 and 3.8), meaning that, although there were drawbacks, users thought it was easy to conduct the collaborative recording. Nonetheless, as the interface for visualization that we provided was very simple, responses were around neutral and negative (2.8, 2.6 and 3.2). Participants stated that they wanted to manipulate the zoom and need better options to control multiple audio sources. However, as we did not explore the visualization stage further, that result was expected.

6 CONCLUSIONS

Overall, our work illustrates alternatives based on the collaborative capture of live experiences that take advantage of the wide availability of mobile devices. Lessons learned from our work can be exploited by designers of collaborative systems aiming at promoting collaboration while minimizing inconvenience. Our particular design suggests that collaborative recording systems should take into consideration features that include synchronized capture, multimedia selection, context information and mobile accessories. Moreover,

designers should consider media other than video: photos and audio are broadly supported in mobile devices and, besides these media forms being less resource hungry, they can be positively used to enhance the capture experience. Last but not least, efforts should be geared towards exploiting context information that can be implicitly captured or explicitly informed by the users – the latter can be associated with the facilities offered by the application.

Future work includes providing models and templates for document exchange and investigating visualization demands.

ACKNOWLEDGMENTS
We thank the volunteers. We thank FAPESP, CNPq and CAPES.

REFERENCES
[1] G. D. Abowd and E. D. Mynatt. Charting past, present, and future research in ubiquitous computing. *ACM Trans. Comput.-Hum. Interact.*, 7(1):29–58, Mar. 2000.
[2] M. Bianchi. Automatic video production of lectures using an intelligent and aware environment. In *Mobile and Ubiquitous Multimedia*, pages 117–123, 2004.
[3] D. C. A. Bulterman, P. Cesar, and R. L. Guimarães. Socially-aware multimedia authoring: Past, present, and future. *ACM TOMCCAP*, 9(1s):35:1–35:23, Oct. 2013.
[4] E. Canessa, C. Fonda, L. Tenze, and M. Zennaro. EyApp & AndrEyA - Free apps for the automated recording of lessons by students. *IJET*, 9:31–34, 2014.
[5] E. Canessa, C. Fonda, and M. Zennaro. One year of ICTP diploma courses on-line using the automated EyA recording system. *Computers & Education*, 53(1):183–188, 2009.
[6] R. G. Cattelan, C. Teixeira, R. Goularte, and M. D. G. C. Pimentel. Watch-and-comment as a paradigm toward ubiquitous interactive video editing. *ACM TOMCCAP*, 4(4):28:1–28:24, Nov. 2008.
[7] M. de Sá, D. Shamma, and E. Churchill. Live mobile collaboration for video production: design, guidelines, and requirements. *Personal and Ubiquitous Computing*, 18(3):693–707, 2014.
[8] A. Engström, G. Zoric, O. Juhlin, and R. Toussi. The mobile vision mixer: A mobile network based live video broadcasting system in your mobile phone. In *Mobile and Ubiquitous Multimedia*, pages 18:1–18:4, 2012.
[9] T. R. Hansen and J. E. Bardram. Activetheatre—a collaborative, event-based capture and access system for the operating theatre. In *Intl. Conf. Ubiquitous Computing*, pages 375–392. Springer, 2005.
[10] A. Kaheel, M. El-Saban, M. Refaat, and M. Ezz. Mobicast: A system for collaborative event casting using mobile phones. In *Intl. Conf. Mobile and Ubiquitous Multimedia*, pages 7:1–7:8, 2009.
[11] J. Krumm, N. Davies, and C. Narayanaswami. User-generated content. *IEEE Pervasive Computing*, 7(4):10–11, Oct. 2008.
[12] R. Laiola Guimarães, P. Cesar, and D. Bulterman. Personalized presentations from community assets. In *Proc. WebMedia*, pages 257–264, 2013.
[13] R. Laiola Guimarães, P. Cesar, and D. C. Bulterman. Creating and sharing personalized time-based annotations of videos on the web. In *ACM DocEng*, pages 27–36, 2010.
[14] D. Martins and M. G. Pimentel. Activetimesheets: Extending web-based multimedia documents. In *ACM DocEng*, pages 3–12, 2014.
[15] D. S. Martins. *Models and operators for extension of active multimedia documents via annotations*. PhD thesis, ICMC-University of São Paulo, 2013.
[16] B. Meixner. Hypervideos and interactive multimedia presentations. *ACM Comput. Surv.*, 50(1):9:1–9:34, 2017.
[17] B. Meixner and H. Kosch. Interactive non-linear video: Definition and xml structure. In *ACM DocEng '12*, pages 49–58, 2012.
[18] J. Ojala, S. Mate, I. D. D. Curcio, A. Lehtiniemi, and K. Väänänen-Vainio-Mattila. Automated creation of mobile video remixes: User trial in three event contexts. In *Mobile and Ubiquitous Multimedia*, pages 170–179, 2014.
[19] M. G. Pimentel, L. A. Baldochi, Jr., and R. G. Cattelan. Prototyping applications to document human experiences. *IEEE Pervasive Computing*, 6(2):93–100, Apr. 2007.
[20] R. Spicer, Y.-R. Lin, A. Kelliher, and H. Sundaram. Nextslideplease: Authoring and delivering agile multimedia presentations. *ACM TOMM*, 8(4):53, 2012.
[21] K. N. Truong and G. D. Abowd. Inca: A software infrastructure to facilitate the construction and evolution of ubiquitous capture & access applications. In *International Conference on Pervasive Computing*, pages 140–157, 2004.
[22] K. N. Truong, G. R. Hayes, et al. Ubiquitous computing for capture and access. *Foundations and Trends® in Human–Computer Interaction*, 2(2):95–171, 2009.
[23] D. A. Vega-Oliveros, D. S. Martins, and M. d. G. C. Pimentel. "This Conversation Will Be Recorded": Automatically Generating Interactive Documents from Captured Media. In *ACM DocEng*, pages 37–40, 2010.
[24] M. Weiser. The computer for the twenty-first century. *Scientific American*, 265(3):94–104, Sept. 1991.

Personalized Ubiquitous Data Collection and Intervention as Interactive Multimedia Documents

Caio C. Viel, Kamila R. H. Rodrigues, Isabela Zaine
Bruna C. R. Cunha, Leonardo F. Scalco, Maria G. C. Pimentel
University of São Paulo, São Carlos, Brazil
{caioviel,kamila.rios,isabela.zaine,brunaru7,scalco}@gmail.com,mgp@usp.br

ABSTRACT

The Experience Sampling Method (ESM) has been proposed as a method for collecting data about people's experiences in their everyday and natural environments. ESM-based systems offer limited authoring for interactive documents designed to collect text-based responses offered as answers to text-based questions, and integrated with the non-intrusive data collection from sensors. From a document engineering perspective, ESM brings new requirements with respect to the authoring of non-trivial interaction and navigation workflow, in particular when multiple media and collaborative tasks are concerned. Tackling existing challenges, we modeled the Experience Sampling and Programmed Intervention Method (ESPIM) by combining ESM, individualized teaching procedures and ubiquitous computing toward producing interactive personalized multimedia documents applied in data collection.

CCS CONCEPTS

•Human-centered computing →Ubiquitous and mobile computing systems and tools;

KEYWORDS

Data Collection; Authoring; Multimedia; Mobile.

ACM Reference format:
Caio C. Viel, Kamila R. H. Rodrigues, Isabela Zaine
Bruna C. R. Cunha, Leonardo F. Scalco, Maria G. C. Pimentel. 2017. Personalized Ubiquitous Data Collection and Intervention as Interactive Multimedia Documents. In *Proceedings of DocEng '17, September 4–7, 2017, Valletta, Malta., , 4 pages.*
DOI: https://doi.org/10.1145/3103010.3121046

1 INTRODUCTION

The Experience Sampling Method (ESM) [3] was proposed originally in the Psychology domain as a method for collecting data about people's experiences in their everyday and natural environments. It relies on asking participants to take notes or to answer questions about their experiences at specific times. These "samples of experiences" are more accurate than answers provided at a later opportunity. Also, this process prevents important information from being forgotten by participants, which is crucial when participants with memory problems are involved [9].

From a document engineering perspective, ESM brings new requirements with respect to the authoring of non-trivial interaction workflows [8] and alternative navigation flows [11], in particular when multiple media and collaborative tasks are concerned [6, 10, 12].

Although ESM can be applied using diaries and alarms, many advantages result from using mobile devices [1, 5, 18]. Smartphones, in particular, have been shown not only to improve the application of ESM techniques [1, 5, 17] but also to be an important resource for data collection and documentation [7]. Since users have their smartphones most of the time, the devices facilitate real-time data collection in users' natural environments. In addition, data automatically collected from devices' sensors, such as GPS, complement data manually informed by participants.

Current ESM systems mainly offer support for authors to create interactive documents to collect text-based responses, offered as answers to text-based questions, integrated with the non-intrusive data collection from sensors [1, 5, 18]. Even though the collection of responses via audio and photos has been also supported [1, 5, 18], focus has been on the implicit acquisition and sharing of open standard (health) sensor data [14] and text [13]. Thus, these works do not report supporting data collection using video along with other media, neither in the questions nor in the answers, a resource already adopted by professionals using multimedia messengers [15].

More importantly, mobile devices not only allow data collection, as supported by existing solutions, but can also make it possible the application of personalized interventions planned by professionals. In other words, professionals should be able to, while planning the application of personalized questionnaires, associate tasks to be carried out by participants as a result of specific answers, behaviours or data collected. As far as we know, easy-to-use alternatives for providing the means for authoring such personalized multimedia interventions have not been reported in the literature.

In our research aiming at investigating alternatives for the two gaps above, challenges are threefold. First, questionnaires applied in data collection should be interactive multimedia personalized documents able to contain multiple media (including video, audio, images and sensor data) not only in the questions but also in the answers. Second, professionals need an intuitive and easy-to-use interface to allow authoring such documents as personalized interventions. Third, documents should also be associated with interventions provided by domain-specific tasks.

Tackling those challenges, we modeled *Experience Sampling and Programmed Intervention Method* – ESPIM [19], a method which combines ESM with procedures from Individualized Teaching [4] and Ubiquitous Computing toward producing interactive personalized multimedia documents applied in data collection.

In paper, Section 2 summarizes related work, Section 3 describes the ESPIM model and Section 4 its computational infrastructure; and Section 5 presents final remarks.

2 RELATED WORK

Early work integrating the ESM method and mobile computing was MyExperience [5]. In addition to collecting self-reported data via textual questions, the system provides an architecture that enables passive data capturing associated with context information (e.g. calendar, SMS) and sensors (e.g. GPS). The architecture also provides the configuration of contextual triggers that consider device usage information and sensors. The authoring is done via an XML-based scripts.

The PACO platform (Personal Analytics COmpanion) [1] supports conducting ESM-based experiments using smartphones by allowing researchers to set up custom experiments via web-based forms. Documents can include open questions, multiple-choice questions, and request the capture photos or audio. It is also possible to collect data from smartphone sensors. Although PACO's target audience is researchers from several areas, its interface presents programming terms and complex configurations.

The Ohmage platform [18] allows to create documents that define customized data collection based on questions and sensors which may include audio capture and device usage. Ohmage has advanced components for data analysis and visualization. However, only temporal triggers are configurable.

Important efforts have being carried out in the health domain toward defining open standardized documents facilitating the implicit acquisition, sharing, integration, analysis and visualization of text and sensor data in health domain [7], as well as in supporting building application-specific information services for use in resource-constrained environments [2]. However, works reporting the support of the data collection using video along with other media, both in questions and in responses, are not widely discussed in the literature. Moreover, most existing contributions require professionals to use complex authoring interfaces.

In such context, we aim at supporting the design and application of interventions as interactive personalized multimedia documents which model questions and corresponding answers, and allow triggering domain-specific tasks. Such document, generated using an authoring interface built via participatory design [16] involving professionals from many areas, is expected to be simple and intuitive for specialists from several domains.

3 ESPIM MODEL

Given its multidisciplinary nature, ESPIM has been modeled using a participatory approach, as cited in the previous section. Thus, different stakeholders participated in the system design and evolution process. For requirement collection, professionals from areas that include gerontology, physiotherapy, occupational therapy, psychology and education were invited to participate in semi-structured interviews.

Considering related works and requirements gathered in interviews with domain experts, the model for the data-collection and intervention system has been designed to support interactive multimedia documents containing:

Program: represents an instantiation of session for data-collection and interventions, aggregating monitoring events, participants monitored and observers involved on the monitoring;

Person: users who belong to one of two groups: participants, to whom data-collection is applied, and observers, domain experts responsible for monitoring and data-collection;

Event: situation in which data-collection or interventions occur, which are of two types: passive and active. Passive events collect data automatically from sensors during continuous time intervals. Active events collect data only when a specific situation defined by a set of triggers occurs. An event is composed of one or more interventions;

Event Trigger: situation defining moments in which an active event occur, which are of three different types: manual, temporal, and contextual;

Intervention: represents an situation in which a participant is demanded to interact with the device. I.e., it is a situation in which the user is interrupted by the device to interact with reminders, questions or task requests. An intervention can provide different stimuli: text, image, audio, video, vibration, etc.;

Sensor: object defining which data will be collect from the sensors and in which situations;

Result: responsible for the persistence of the collected data and its associated metadata. A result is always associated with a participant and an intervention.

When an observer (domain expert) specifies an active event, this expert defines a set of interventions that the participant will interact with when the event is triggered. The model offers four different types of interventions: *empty, questions, media* and *tasks.* Using these four basic constructive blocks, an expert can plan the data-collecting and remote inventions programs by authoring interactive personalized multimedia documents. The *empty intervention* is the simplest type: it does not require any input from the participant user and can be used to send simple messages or reminders. A *media intervention* is used to request a single media to the participant user, such as taking a picture or recording a video or audio. *Questions interventions* are queries that the participant user should answer. They can be open-text questions (which expects a text answer), multiple-choice questions (user selects one of several options) and multiple options questions (user selects several among multiple options). *Tasks interventions* are a special type of intervention. A task intervention allows the domain expert (observer user) to define an external application developed to collect some type of data not provided by the model. An API is exposed to externals applications to access participant data and to send results to the ESPIM server.

To promote loose coupling among the different software instances involved, and in tune with related work [13, 14], interventions are represented by a JSON Document. Using the web-based authoring interface, a domain expert, in the role of a observer, defines a document specifying how the stimuli will be presented to each participant in a smartphone application in charge of playing the interactive multimedia document with the requested content and associated interventions. The ESPIM's computational infrastructure is described in the next section.

4 ESPIM INFRASTRUCTURE

Similar to the model, ESPIM's infrastructure has been developed by an interdisciplinary team of professionals and researchers from computer science, health care and education. The high-level architecture specifies three software components – *Web Service, Authoring Interface* and *Mobile Player* – and the data exchanged between them. The RESTful *Web Service* is responsible for storing information such as the JSON document from the interventions along with its related metadata and the data collected from users on the Mobile Player. Web Service stores objects for the elements described on the model (Section 3) and is also in charge of orchestrating the storage of all media in an auxiliary Media Storage. The RIA *Authoring Interface* is used by domain experts to create documents corresponding to the data collections and interventions. The Android *Mobile Player* is used by participants to access the personalized interactive multimedia documents corresponding to the interventions. It also captures data and media, as defined by the domain specialist, and send the collected data to the Web Service.

The Authoring Interface is a RIA front-end application developed using Angular.js JavaScript framework and Bootstrap CSS framework. Using the Authoring interface, a domain expert can create customized data collection and/or intervention programs for their participants (populations of interest), who may also have observers such as relatives and caregivers, for example. The resulting multimedia document corresponds to program consisting of events that comprise a set of interventions. Currently, the Web interface allows the creation of open-ended questions, multiple-choice questions with only one selectable option or multiple option with more than one option, messages, sending and receiving media operations and tasks (in which an external application is started). These interventions are triggered on the participant's smartphone on the date and time previously defined by the expert. The authoring is done via a form that offers the functionality of associating participants to a specific program. Events are constructed using a flowchart-like dynamic form (boxes and arrows), which allows the creation of interventions and enables a flexible and visual manner of connecting them, thus creating sequential flows, as illustrated in Figure 1.

In Figure 1, document 1 specifies two options lead to the creation of two alternative flows. The flow on top (documents 2 to 3) employs different types of questions for data collection and no further alternative flows. Document 2 starts the external application indicated by the domain expert. Document 3 contains a video made available by the specialist for the user, with options for the participant to respond with another video. The flow on the bottom also defines a single flow, in this case all documents request participants to attached media as a response. Documents 3 and 4 merge to a single concluding document with concludes the interaction.

The intervention programming screen was the main discussion focus to the team members, because we sought a design solution and

interaction model that facilitated the adoption by health care and education professionals. At the same time, we sought to overcome resistance that some of these professionals may have due to previous experience with other tools and systems that were characterized by some interviewees as "boring and outdated". The drag-and-drop model with directional arrows was the solution adopted to configure the intervention flow.

Considering different needs for specialization, instead of offering a single interface or application for different users groups, ESPIM's computational infrastructure was designed to support the instantiation of different Mobile Player application to suit particular audiences.

As a case study and validation of the infrastructure, we have instantiated some Android applications for monitoring parents helping children with learning difficulties. The applications retrieve the interventions from the Web Service as a JSON Document, along with associated metadata and media uploaded by observer users. The applications generate the intervention screens dynamically by interpreting the JSON Document. In short, the applications act as presentation machines or *players*, creating a multimedia presentation based on JSON Documents and their associate media. In addition to play the interventions, the applications also dynamically create notifications based on the schedules defined in the *Event Trigger* metadata of the documents.

Figure 2 illustrates some of screens captured from the ESPIM app, which were exhibited from an interventive program planned for the parents using the Authoring Interface.

5 FINAL REMARKS

In this paper we presented the computational infrastructure developed to support ESPIM, a method to collect data of monitored participants and to promote remote interventions. ESPIM can be used by professionals and researchers from different areas and backgrounds. Instead of looking for a universal design that meets requirements from many areas, we opted to develop our computational infrastructure with loose coupled software pieces, and to use JSON documents to exchange data among them. Thus, if someone wishes to instantiate an application for a specific area, this person could use the same model and software pieces available, and then extend our mobile player to read and present the interactions specified in the JSON Document – which is tune with related work [13, 14]

In addition to the case study carried out to evaluate the Mobile Player, the authoring interface underwent a real-world usage test during a conference, a controlled usability test with psychology and education domain experts, and a heuristic evaluation. These evaluations, which are not the focus of this work, helped to find usability problems and to improve system reliability.

We are currently carrying out new evaluations with professionals from the Psychology. One real case study, which presented promising results [20], has been carried out with parents of children with learning difficulties. The aim is to monitor and improve the engagement in educational activities in participants natural environment (their home) – sample screens are illustrated in Figure 2.

We plan to integrate document engineering modeling and authoring solutions into existing efforts focusing on defining open

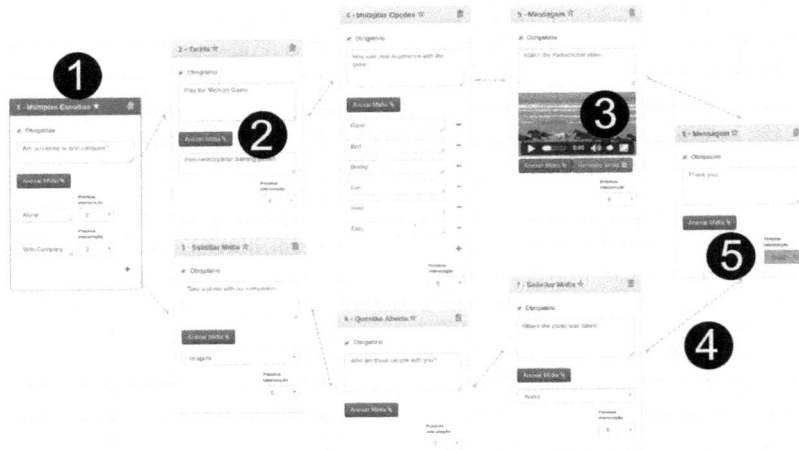

Figure 1: Program defining a personalized interactive multimedia document (fictitious).

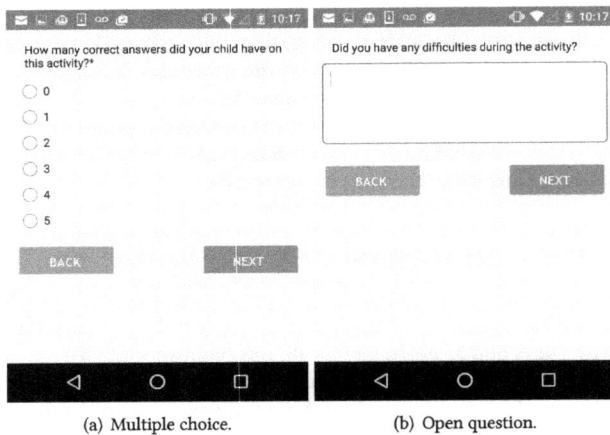

(a) Multiple choice.   (b) Open question.

Figure 2: Mobile Player presenting a portion of a genuine program for parents of children with learning difficulties.

standardized documents facilitating the implicit acquisition, sharing, integration, analysis and visualization of text and sensor data in the health domain [7]. Moreover, opportunities to supporting application-specific information services for use in resource-constrained environments [2] will also be investigated.

ACKNOWLEDGEMENTS

We thank financial grant from FAPESP (2015/18117-7; 2016/00351-6), CAPES (PROEX-7393795/D) and CNPq (312058/2015-2, 402846/2015-0, 150465/2016-5).

REFERENCES

[1] K. K. Baxter, A. Avrekh, and B. Evans. Using experience sampling methodology to collect deep data about your users. In *ACM CHI EA '15*, pages 2489–2490, 2015.

[2] W. Brunette, M. Sundt, N. Dell, R. Chaudhri, N. Breit, and G. Borriello. Open data kit 2.0: Expanding and refining information services for developing regions. HotMobile '13 Workshops, pages 10:1–10:6, 2013.

[3] M. Csikszentmihalyi, R. Larson, and S. Prescott. The ecology of adolescent activity and experience. *Journal of youth and adolescence*, 6(3):281–94, 1977.

[4] S. Epstein and B. Epstein. The first book of teaching machines. 1961.

[5] J. Froehlich, M. Y. Chen, S. Consolvo, B. Harrison, and J. A. Landay. Myexperience: A system for in situ tracing and capturing of user feedback on mobile phones. In *MobiSys '07*, pages 57–70, 2007.

[6] J. Jansen, M. Frantzis, and P. Cesar. Multimedia document structure for distributed theatre. In *ACM DocEng '15*, pages 199–202, 2015.

[7] S. Kumar, G. Abowd, W. T. Abraham, M. al'Absi, D. H. Chau, E. Ertin, and D. E. et al. Center of Excellence for Mobile Sensor Data-to-Knowledge (MD2K). *IEEE Pervasive Computing*, 16(2):18–22, 2017.

[8] Y. S. Kuo, L. Tseng, H.-C. Hu, and N. C. Shih. An XML Interaction Service for Workflow Applications. In *ACM DocEng '06*, pages 53–55, 2006.

[9] M. L. Lee and A. K. Dey. Lifelogging memory appliance for people with episodic memory impairment. In *UbiComp '08*, pages 44–53, 2008.

[10] T. N. Luong, S. Laborie, and T. Nodenot. A framework with tools for designing web-based geographic applications. In *ACM DocEng '11*, pages 33–42, 2011.

[11] C. McCormack, K. Marriott, and B. Meyer. Authoring adaptive diagrams. In *ACM DocEng '08*, pages 154–163, 2008.

[12] B. Meixner and H. Kosch. Interactive non-linear video: Definition and xml structure. In *ACM DocEng '12*, pages 49–58, 2012.

[13] ODK. Open Data Kit (ODK), 2008-. opendatakit.org.

[14] openmhealth. Open mHealth: The first and only open standard for mobile health data, 2015-. openmhealth.org.

[15] M. Petruzzi and M. Benedittis. Whatsapp: a telemedicine platform for facilitating remote oral medicine consultation and improving clinical examinations. *Oral Surgery, Oral Medicine, Oral Pathology and Oral Radiology*, 121(3):248–54, 2016.

[16] D. Schuler and A. Namioka. *Participatory design: Principles and practices*. 1993.

[17] A. Signore. Mapping and sharing agro-biodiversity using open data kit and google fusion tables. *Computers and Electronics in Agriculture*, 127:87–91, 2016.

[18] H. Tangmunarunkit, C. K. Hsieh, B. Longstaff, S. Nolen, J. Jenkins, C. Ketcham, J. Selsky, F. Alquaddoomi, D. George, J. Kang, Z. Khalapyan, J. Ooms, N. Ramanathan, and D. Estrin. Ohmage: A general and extensible end-to-end participatory sensing platform. *ACM TIST*, 6(3):38:1–38:21, 2015.

[19] I. Zaine, K. R. Rodrigues, B. C. da Cunha, C. C. Viel, A. F. Orlando, O. J. Machado Neto, Y. Magagnatto, and M. d. G. C. Pimentel. Espim: An ubiquitous data collection and programmed intervention system using esm and mobile devices. In *Webmedia '16*, pages 13–14, 2016.

[20] I. Zaine, K. R. Rodrigues, A. F. Orlando, B. C. da Cunha, C. C. Viel, O. J. Machado Neto, Y. Magagnatto, and M. d. G. C. Pimentel. Enhancing engagement in applied behavior analysis interventions for individuals with autism spectrum disorder in natural settings using mobile devices. In *Association for Behavior Analysis International - ABAI 2017*, Denver, Colorado, May. 25-29 2017.

NuSys: Towards a Document IDE for Knowledge Work

Philipp Eichmann
philipp_eichmann@brown.edu
Computer Science Department
Brown University
Providence, RI, United States

Trent Green
trent_green@brown.edu
Computer Science Department
Brown University
Providence, RI, United States

Robert Zeleznik
robert_zeleznik@brown.edu
Computer Science Department
Brown University
Providence, RI, United States

Andries van Dam
andries_van_dam@brown.edu
Computer Science Department
Brown University
Providence, RI, United States

ABSTRACT

Knowledge workers consume and annotate digital documents such as PDF files, videos, images and text notes - in some cases collaboratively - to form mental models and gain insight. An abundance of software solutions and utilities that were designed to assist users in stages of this process but not in the process as a whole, which makes knowledge work with documents unnecessarily inefficient. In this paper, we introduce ideas on how to streamline common knowledge worker tasks, such as collaboratively searching, gathering and freely arranging fragments of various media documents to gain understanding and then transforming emergent insights into interactive structured visualizations. Furthermore, we present *NuSys*, an integrated development environment (IDE) specialized for document-centric workflows, that implements the core of these ideas.

CCS CONCEPTS

•**Human-centered computing** → *User interface programming;*

KEYWORDS

User Interface; Knowledge Work; Document Handling

1 MOTIVATION

Many knowledge workers use websites, Google Docs, Office and PDF files, images, videos, and text files, etc., which we henceforth refer to as *documents*, as their primary source of information. These workers typically use multiple different software solutions and utilities to retrieve, view, consume, organize, relate, annotate, and share their documents and fragments thereof. While these applications assist users in solving specific sub-tasks of knowledge work, they do not address the requirements of a complete workflow. Instead,

DocEng '17, September 4–7, 2017, Valletta, Malta.
© 2017 Copyright held by the owner/author(s). Publication rights licensed to ACM.
978-1-4503-4689-4/17/09...$15.00
DOI: https://doi.org/10.1145/3103010.3121045

users piece together software to accomplish their tasks. For example, they may use a web browser to search for information, a notebook system to visualize and arrange clippings, a database to store structured relationships, and a screen sharing tool and email to communicate with colleagues. Managing the separate UIs, object models, data repositories and features of these multiple systems can be confusing and inefficient. As a result, users adopt inefficient strategies to cope with problems caused by context switches, lack of compatibility and incomplete functionality. Software vendors and various researchers have attempted to expand the depth of their target workflows by incorporating ever more comprehensive tool sets, but fall short of addressing the broad end-to-end needs of knowledge work. Consider the simple case where a knowledge worker wants to examine information about Nobel Laureates. In a first step, she would collect information such as their name, age, origin, portrait image etc., from different sources and informally lay out her documents on the desktop, for instance. To better organize, visualize and compute the information she is interested in, she would extract fragments from her documents and bring it into a common structure, e.g., using a spreadsheet to apply filters, calculate the average age or display the number of Laureates by country. Lastly, to externalize her findings, she would create a stylized visualization of her findings and share it with others.

Despite the existence of tools that support sub-tasks of such a use case, we know of no general purpose system that addresses the collective needs of even basic knowledge workflows such as collaboratively searching, gathering and freely arranging fragments of various media documents to gain understanding and then transforming emergent insights into interactive structured visualizations that can later be modified and re-used as intermediate work result.

2 DESIGN

With *NuSys*, we draw on the concept of software IDEs which address workflow productivity by providing a set of tools with which users can visually compose and functionally coordinate to create efficient, interactive experiences for their specific workflows. Contrary to existing solutions for knowledge work which are targeted towards specific sub-tasks, we believe that a better approach is to embody broad functionality with a small set of compatible building blocks within one uniform system. Specifically, we want to represent virtually all aspects of the workflow of knowledge workers as

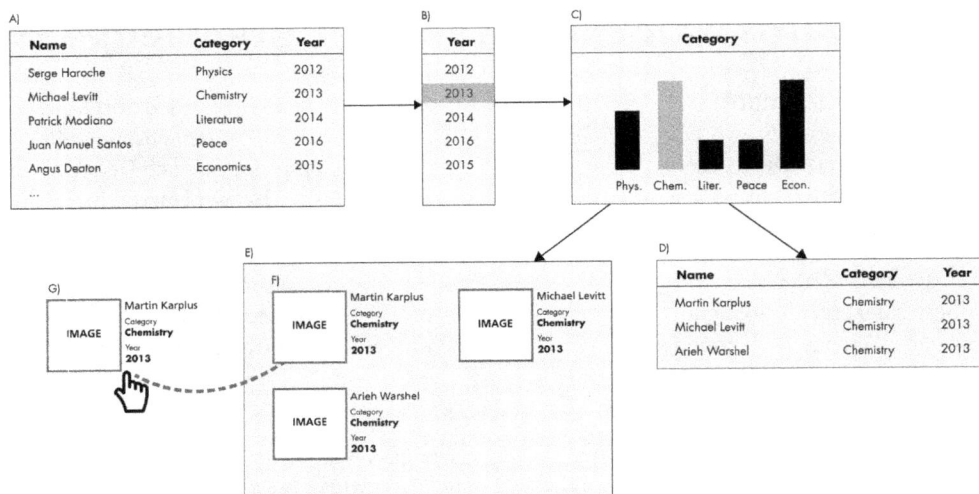

Figure 1: Illustrates how system and user-defined spatial layouts of documents can be used to create a dashboard: A) A document collection containing information about Nobel Laureates displayed in a tabular visualization. B) A document that takes all documents from collection A as input and groups (transforms) each document by their "year" attribute. C) A document that visualizes the documents matching the selection in B in a count histogram per "Category". D) Shows the resulting documents based on selection in C) in a tabular layout. E) Displays the same documents as in D) but as custom-visualizations (see Figure (2) in a grid. F,G) show how documents can be torn off a structured layout and added to the free-form canvas, for example, to collect important search results.

being operations on documents and their metadata. For example, the multiple notions of a view of a document, a search filter used to retrieve documents and a remote collaborator can all be represented in a straightforward way as documents themselves. By representing system functionality in terms of just a few basic document operations, the user experience can be driven by a small number of light-weight and fluid interactions; in turn, this can facilitate users in offloading interface reasoning to sub-conscious natural interactions. We believe further that this uniform document-centric foundation not only facilitates interaction transparency, but also generates unique opportunities for reflecting on and reusing workflows. For instance, by treating collaboration, document viewing and searching all as operations on documents, knowledge workers will implicitly, as a byproduct of their natural workflow, be creating custom "dashboards", capturing visual search histories and blending synchronous and asynchronous interactions with their colleagues. To realize these ideas, we have built *NuSys* along the following four core concepts:

Fine-Grained, Heterogeneous Working Sets (C1)

Knowledge workers should be able to assemble heterogeneous working sets of documents with no more effort than editing a text document. For instance, they may want to layout on a canvas either clippings or complete PDF, website, video, audio and image documents, or custom visualization of documents such as just the author and title. This requires an application to display a broad set of common document types inline. Creating a clipping should be as simple as making an inline selection on any media type, without any need to switch tasks to locate and apply an external tool; and,

the canvas that collects the working set of documents and fragments should itself be a document - essentially a dashboard for that working set. Collected documents should all be live, so that users can directly browse material as they collect it, without a context switch.

Externalize the Search/Find/Transform Process (C2)

Instead of treating searching as transient commands specified in a reusable search dialog, search queries can be viewed as dynamic documents that can be viewed, modified and persisted like any other document or annotation. For example, a search document can be created, alongside media documents, to represent the set of documents matching a query. However, since queries can be complex, each stage of a query can be represented as a document which is linked to the next stage, analogous to how comments in narrative thread can be linked to each other. The result of a query can then be considered a collection document with dynamic contents that update when any of its linked query documents are modified. Thus knowledge workers can externalize the thought process involved in creating a complex search/filter graph, and, in addition, traverse a found document's links to recover how the search that led to the document. Transformations and computations can similarly be viewed as dynamic documents that can be linked to any other document including search chains (Figure 1).

Flexible, User-Driven Spatial Layouts as Dashboards (C3)

Although documents and applications are often treated as being distinct things created by different types of people, typical applications can also be thought of as being documents containing content and UI elements. By exposing simple application building blocks, like search, transform, and layout elements, users can construct structured documents which in the limit behave like applications. For instance, grid and list view documents could be linked to a chain of interactive document filters to create a stylized search output that presented only relevant document details in a customized layout (Figure 1); this resulting dashboard document could then be reused in other contexts with different search parameters. In general, as workflow tasks become more repetitive or complicated, the need to create custom dashboards that transform and display data can significantly improve user efficiency. The notion is not that every task requires a dashboard, but rather that every working set of documents is a dashboard; by removing artificial barriers, nothing prevents a user from evolving an ad hoc working set of active documents into a more refined, reusable task-specific dashboard.

Collaborators as Documents (C4)

Knowledge workers often need to communicate with colleagues regarding any aspect of their work, not just the simple text passage targets afforded by common annotation tools. By treating collaborative users as documents, users can be included in any working set of documents and directed (linked) to heterogeneous selections of documents and media. For instance, an icon of a user can be dragged, like any other document to a collection of documents. Users can also be added to search or transformation chains; for example, to specify the order in which users should be given documents to review and edit.

3 NUSYS

Following the four core concepts C1-C4 outlined in the previous section, we implemented a prototype of a document IDE called *NuSys*. Our system features a collaborative workspace, which provides functionality to bring in, view, lay out, organize, annotate and share heterogeneous materials such as Office documents, multimedia files, and entire websites or fragments thereof. A workspace is an unbounded, zoomable, and pannable 2D canvas that can be shared among multiple users; changes to it are reflected among all connected clients in real-time through a cloud-based server. Following a popular "Post-It on a whiteboard" metaphor, a workspace allows users to import content as one or more documents that can be arranged, grouped and nested, annotated, linked, and tagged for subsequent retrieval. A simple text editor allows users to modify text-based documents, and provides a mechanism to open/edit formats unknown to the system in their native application (e.g., Office files). Furthermore, NuSys' user interface is optimized for, but not limited to pen/touch input. It incorporates digital ink, handwriting recognition and speech-to-text support, as well as various intuitive gestures that can be used to navigate and augment the documents and their attributes.

NuSys is capable of visualizing a variety of different formats such as images, videos, and PDF files. It also provides static views of Office Documents such as Word and Powerpoint files with navigation controls inline, and provides a means for users to create their own documents within the application, such as text, audio or video recordings **(C1)**. Each document can hold an arbitrary number of user-defined attributes that can be added or modified through an

editor. In addition, our system comes with a plugin for Google's Chrome web browser that helps users bring in content, and piece together new documents with fragments found on the Internet.

To derive more fine-grained documents from existing ones, *NuSys* supports the creation of spatial or time-based clippings for static (images, videos) or dynamic (video, audio) content respectively, by marking regions of interest. Users can define an arbitrary number of clippings on a document without affecting the original document, lay out these clippings on the workspace, and, for instance, synthesize them into a new document.

NuSys applies a default visualization to common document types and additionally provides means to let users define their own layouts of documents **(C3)**. They can modify existing layouts or create new ones by visually arranging variables of attributes associated with a document (Figure 2). The main idea is that every document or document collection can be used as an input to another document, and filters and data transformations can applied if desired (Figure 1). On one hand, this gives users great flexibility in visualizing different attributes of their content, on the other hand, it enables them to externalize search queries by building visual query graphs, similar to GraphTrails [6] **(C2)**.

NuSys comes with a set of predefined layouts for documents such as lists, grids and with a set of interactive layouts that can be used to perform search, called *tools*. Tools typically apply a transformation to the input documents, such as a grouping operation or a projection to a subset of attributes, and display the results in either one of the default layouts or visualization of aggregated values, e.g. document count per group (Figure 1).

We built our system for small workgroups with support for synchronous and asynchronous collaboration using multiple devices. *NuSys* follows a client-server model where workspaces can be accessed and manipulated in real-time by concurrent users. All changes to a workspace and documents are instantly reflected across all connected users. Connected users are represented with an icon in the lower left corner of the application. Like any other documents, users can be placed on the workspace, into collections or at specific locations on documents themselves **(C4)**. Doing so enables them to query their and other users' locations, which can, for instance, be summarized in a custom dashboard.

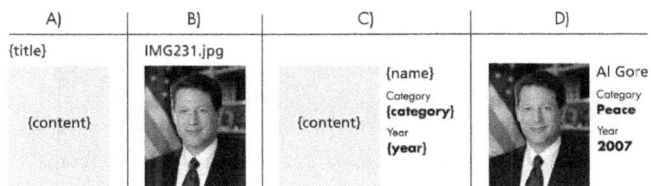

Figure 2: Illustrates the concept of custom layouts for documents: A) Shows a default layout for an image. B) Shows how an image is displayed when brought into *NuSys*; the file name becomes the title attribute, the actual image becomes "content". C) An example of a custom layout for an image document with additional, user-defined attributes "name", "category", and "year". D) Shows layout C populated with an image document

4 RELATED WORK

The idea of combining documents with user interfaces dates back to early publications such as [3, 4]. In the following, we contrast our research with more recent work in activity-based computing and spatial hypertext.

Activity-based computing attempts to encapsulate documents and applications as user activities. It tries to better reflect how knowledge workers perform their tasks by providing easy access to activity-related documents and applications. Examples include Giornata [14] and GroupBar [12]. Activities can typically either be defined manually, e.g., by explicitly creating a new activity, or automatically, where a system tries to infer an activity through currently open documents or interaction patterns [5]. There have also been efforts to provide user interfaces for collecting fragments of documents. WinCuts [13], for instance, is able to show live application clippings of selected windows. *NuSys* differs from these approaches in that it goes beyond providing easier access to documents, their views and editors. It treats documents, views on documents and searches uniformly as documents that can be flexibly laid out on a workspace. Furthermore, it provides a set of tools that operate on these documents, for example, to perform subsequent search, create clippings, and transform content.

Spatial hypertext and spatial hypermedia systems facilitate creating categories and relationships by providing means to spatially arrange information objects. Among many other benefits [11], the ease of moving an object makes spatial hypertext especially well suited for tasks where the information continually evolves [8, 10]. Many academic and commercial hypertext and hypermedia systems have emerged over the years, such as VIKI [10], or Storyspace [7] in combination with TinderBox [2]. A key aspect of insight formation is discovering and noting relationships. While *NuSys* can be seen as spatial hypertext system where relationships among documents can be encoded trough traditional (fine-grained) hyperlinks, spatial groupings and user-defined attributes, our system has less of a focus on semantics but more on the creation of flexible, user-driven spatial layouts. As such, *NuSys* can be seen as a mix of FileMaker [1], where users can create arbitrary data objects (documents), define layouts and add interactivity, and Microsoft OneNote [9], where content can be informally laid out in a free-form fashion.

5 DISCUSSION AND FUTURE WORK

Our current prototype has already proven useful in two simple cases: (1) where a scholar used *NuSys* to collect material and prepare research talks, and (2) another scholar did research on a topic that involved in-depth literature review of dozens of conference papers. Both scholars appreciated the ability to view, interact with and annotate their content on large canvas, the system's responsiveness, and the collaborative features. They also pointed out that the ability to mash up documents within the system was a great time saver. Most of all, they appreciated the smooth interplay between structured and unstructured layouts and the ability to visually formulate search queries. While this initial feedback is encouraging, there are a number of limitations that need to be addressed before we can conduct more rigorous testing.

Although we have invested a significant amount of time in developing a performant UI framework to render large corpora of documents on a single workspace, there are many details in the user interface and interactions we would like to improve. Especially designing the user interface around a visual language that allows users to populate layouts with other documents as input, and let them add custom functionality for input events is an ongoing challenge. Another area we are currently exploring is how to best present relationships between documents. In *NuSys*, relationships between documents are primarily expressed by spatial arrangements and hierarchical structures. This raises the question of how related documents, e.g., parent, child and neighboring documents within the same dashboard or elsewhere are presented to the user and which metric can be used to determine their relevance. Furthermore, the collaborative nature of knowledge work leads to an update dilemma; while real-time updates are desirable in many collaborative scenarios, altering or removing a document could confound other users. We are currently experimenting with different UIs that account for this problem. Finally, similar to the web browser plugin, we have previously experimented with plugins for Microsoft Word and Powerpoint. Our goal was to update a static visual representation of such documents in *NuSys* anytime a Word or Powerpoint file was updated. Although we successfully implemented these plugins, we have shifted our focus to the more general goal of designing a plugin architecture such that code-savvy users could help extend the interoperability of our software.

REFERENCES

[1] Apple. 2017. FileMaker. (2017). Retrieved April 1, 2017 from http://www.filemaker.com
[2] Mark Bernstein. 2007. *The Tinderbox Way*. Eastgate Systems, Inc.
[3] Eric A Bier and Ken Pier. 1991. Documents as user interfaces. In *Proceedings of the SIGCHI Conference on Human Factors in Computing Systems*. ACM, 443–444.
[4] M Cecelia Buchanan, Polle T Zellweger, and Ken Pier. 1993. Multimedia documents as user interfaces. In *Proceedings of the INTERACT'93 and CHI'93 Conference on Human Factors in Computing Systems*. ACM, 527–528.
[5] Anton N Dragunov, Thomas G Dietterich, Kevin Johnsrude, Matthew McLaughlin, Lida Li, and Jonathan L Herlocker. 2005. TaskTracer: a desktop environment to support multi-tasking knowledge workers. In *Proceedings of the 10th international conference on Intelligent user interfaces*. ACM, 75–82.
[6] Cody Dunne, Nathalie Henry Riche, Bongshin Lee, Ronald Metoyer, and George Robertson. 2012. GraphTrail: Analyzing large multivariate, heterogeneous networks while supporting exploration history. In *Proceedings of the SIGCHI conference on human factors in computing systems*. ACM, 1663–1672.
[7] Eastgate. 2017. Storyspace. (2017). Retrieved April 1, 2017 from http://www.eastgate.com/storyspace
[8] Catherine C Marshall and Frank M Shipman III. 1997. Spatial hypertext and the practice of information triage. In *Proceedings of the eighth ACM conference on Hypertext*. ACM, 124–133.
[9] Microsoft. 2017. OneNote. (2017). Retrieved April 1, 2017 from http://www.onenote.com
[10] Frank M Shipman III, Haowei Hsieh, Preetam Maloor, and J Michael Moore. 2001. The visual knowledge builder: a second generation spatial hypertext. In *Proceedings of the 12th ACM conference on Hypertext and Hypermedia*. ACM, 113–122.
[11] Frank M Shipman III and Catherine C Marshall. 1999. Spatial hypertext: an alternative to navigational and semantic links. *ACM Computing Surveys (CSUR)* 31, 4es (1999), 14.
[12] Greg Smith, Patrick Baudisch, George Robertson, Mary Czerwinski, Brian Meyers, Daniel Robbins, and Donna Andrews. 2003. Groupbar: The taskbar evolved. In *Proceedings of OZCHI*, Vol. 3. 10.
[13] Desney S Tan, Brian Meyers, and Mary Czerwinski. 2004. WinCuts: manipulating arbitrary window regions for more effective use of screen space. In *CHI'04 extended abstracts on Human factors in computing systems*. ACM, 1525–1528.
[14] Stephen Voida and Elizabeth D Mynatt. 2009. It feels better than filing: everyday work experiences in an activity-based computing system. In *Proceedings of the SIGCHI Conference on Human Factors in Computing Systems*. ACM, 259–268.

Author Index

NOTES

www.ingramcontent.com/pod-product-compliance
Lightning Source LLC
Chambersburg PA
CBHW061407210326
41598CB00035B/6131